SCOTTISH RELIGIOUS POETRY

SCOTTISH RELIGIOUS POETRY

from the sixth century to the present

AN ANTHOLOGY

Second Edition

Edited by
Linden Bicket
Emma Dymock
Alison Jack

SAINT ANDREW PRESS
Edinburgh

First published in 2024 by
Saint Andrew Press
121 George Street
Edinburgh EH2 4YN

ISBN 978-1-80083-047-9

British Library Cataloguing in Publication Data
A catalogue record for this book is available from the British Library.

It is the publisher's policy to only use papers that are natural and recyclable and that have been manufactured from timber grown in renewable, properly managed forests. All of the manufacturing processes of the papers are expected to conform to the environmental regulations of the country of origin.

Typeset by Regent Typesetting
Printed and bound in the United Kingdom by
CPI Group (UK) Ltd

Contents

Introduction xv
Acknowledgements xxv
Editors' Note xxvi

SAINT COLUMBA (*c.*521–597)
The Maker on High 1

DALLÁN FORGAILL (*fl.* 600)
from Elegy of Columba 5

ANONYMOUS (*c.*700)
The Dream of the Rood (or The Vision of the Cross) 7

SCHOOL OF COLUMBA (?8th century)
Noli Pater 11

MUGRÓN, ABBOT OF IONA (d. 981)
Christ's Cross 12

ANONYMOUS (in the mouth of Colum Cille) (*c.*1100–1150)
Delightful to Be on the Breast of an Island 14

EARL ROGNVALD KALI (ST RONALD OF ORKNEY) (d. 1158)
Mockery of Irish Monks on a Windswept Island 16

MUIREADHACH ALBANACH (*fl.* 1220)
from O great Mary, listen to me 17

ANONYMOUS (14th century)
Memorial of St Columba 19

ROBERT HENRYSON (?1424–?1506)
The Preiching of the Swallow 20

WILLIAM DUNBAR (?1456–?1513)
Rorate Celi Desuper 30
Done is a Battell on the Dragon Blak 32
Hale Sterne Superne 34
The Dregy of Dunbar 37

GAVIN DOUGLAS (*c.*1476–1522)
Conscience 41

GEORGE BUCHANAN (1506–1582)
Elegy on John Calvin 42
For Christ's Ascension 44

ATHAIRNE MAC EOGHAIN (*fl. c.*1558)
Woe to the one who takes pride in youth 45

JAMES, JOHN AND ROBERT WEDDERBURN (d. 1553, 1556, 1557)
from *The Gude and Godlie Ballates* (1567)
The Conceptioun of Christ 47
Psalm XXII 49
Musing Greitlie in my mynde 50
With huntis vp 51

WILLIAM KETHE (*c.*1530–1594)
Psalm C 53

attributed to MARY, QUEEN OF SCOTS (1542–1587)
Prayer before Execution 54

ALEXANDER HUME (*c.*1557–1609)
Of the Day Estivall 55

DONNCHADH MACRAOIRIDH (d. *c.*1630)
Ceithir rainn do rinneadh leis an là a d'eug se/
Four verses made by him the day he died 62

ELIZABETH MELVILLE OF CULROSS, LADY CUMRIE
(*fl.* 1599–1631)
from Ane Godlie Dreame
Christ speaks to the dreamer who hopes to see heaven 64

WILLIAM DRUMMOND OF HAWTHORNDEN (1585–1649)
from *Flowres of Sion*
Sonnet vi – The Booke of the World 65
Sonnet viii – The Angels for the Nativitie of Our Lord 65
Sonnet xi – For the Baptiste 66
Sonnet xii – For the Magdalene 66

SIR WILLIAM MURE OF ROWALLAN (1594–1657)
Sonnet 67

JAMES GRAHAM, MARQUIS OF MONTROSE (1612–1650)
On Himself, upon hearing what was his Sentence 68

A COMMITTEE OF THE GENERAL ASSEMBLY OF THE CHURCH OF SCOTLAND (1650)
from *The Psalms of David in Metre*
Psalm XXIII 69
Psalm CXXI 70
Psalm CXXVIII 71

SÌLEAS NA CEAPAICH/SILEAS MacDONALD (*c.*1660–*c.*1729)
Laoidh air Bàs a Fir agus a h-Ighne/
Hymn on the Deaths of her Husband and Daughter 72

ALLAN RAMSAY (1686–1758)
The Marrow Ballad 76

DONNCHADH NAM PÌOS (d. *c.*1700)
Rìgh na Cruinne ta gun Chrìch/King of the World without End 78

ROB DONN (1714–1778)
Marbhrann do chloinn Fhir Taigh Ruspainn/The Rispond Misers 80

DUGHALL BOCHANAN/DUGALD BUCHANAN (1716–1768)
bho Là a' Bhreitheanais/*from* The Day of Judgement 84

ROBERT FERGUSSON (1750–1774)
To the Tron-Kirk Bell 88
Job, Chapter III Paraphrased 90

JOHN MORISON (1750–1798)
From Hosea VI. 1–4 92

ROBERT BURNS (1759–1796)
Holy Willie's Prayer 93
Address to the Deil 96
The Cottar's Saturday Night 100

A COMMITTEE OF THE GENERAL ASSEMBLY OF THE CHURCH OF SCOTLAND (1781)
from *Translations and Paraphrases, in Verse, of Several Passages of Sacred Scripture*
IX Job xxvi.6 106
XIX. Isaiah ix. 2–8 108
LIV. 2 Timothy i.12 109

JAMES HOGG (1770–1835)
Corpus Christi Carol 110
A Cameronian Ballad 111

WALTER SCOTT (1771–1832)
Dies Irae 116

JOHN LEYDEN (1775–1811)
The Sabbath Morning 117

GEORGE GORDON, LORD BYRON (1788–1824)
from The Vision of Judgment 118

THOMAS CARLYLE (1795–1881)
Cui Bono? 123

MÀIRI NICDHÒMHNAILL/MARY MACDONALD (1789–1872)
Leanabh an Àigh/Child in the Manger 124

ANNA NIC EALAIR/ANNA MACKELLAR (*fl. c.*1800)
Luinneag Anna Nic Ealair/Anna Nic Ealair's Song 126

CHARLES, LORD NEAVES (1800–1876)
Let us all be unhappy on a Sunday: a lyric for Saturday night 128

JANE WELSH CARLYLE (1801–1866)
Nay, This is Hope 130

HORATIUS BONAR (1808–1889)
Love is of God 131

GEORGE MACDONALD (1824–1905)
The Holy Snowdrops 132
Pilate's Wife 133

JAMES MACFARLAN (1832–1862)
The Lords of Labour 134

ALEXANDER CARMICHAEL (1832–1912)
from *Carmina Gadelica*
Cuirim Fianais/I Send Witness 136
Achan Chadail/Sleep Invocation 138
Sìth/Peace 140

JAMES THOMSON ('B. V.') (1834–1882)
from The City of Dreadful Night 142

GEORGE MATHESON (1842–1906)
O Love that wilt not let me go 148

ANONYMOUS (*c.*1850)
A Disruption Rhyme 149

ROBERT LOUIS STEVENSON (1850–1894)
If this were Faith 150
Requiem 152

JOHN DAVIDSON (1857–1909)
To the Generation Knocking at the Door 153

AN T-ATHAIR AILEAN DÒMHNALLACH/FATHER ALLAN MacDONALD (1859–1905)
An Eaglais/The Church 154

JESSIE ANNIE ANDERSON (1861–1931)
At Sweet Mary's Shrine 160
The Back o' Hairst 161

VIOLET JACOB (1863–1946)
Tam i' the Kirk 162
The Deil 163

CHARLES MURRAY (1864–1941)
Gin I Was God 165

MARION ANGUS (1865–1946)
Mary's Song 166
The Mourners 167

AONGHAS MOIREASDAN/ANGUS MORRISON (1865–1942)
Madainn na Sàbaid/The Sabbath Morning 168

EDWIN MUIR (1887–1959)
One Foot in Eden 172
The Heart Could Never Speak 173
The Annunciation 174

HUGH MacDIARMID (1892–1978)
Crowdieknowe 175

NAN SHEPHERD (1893–1981)
Real Presence 176

JOE CORRIE (1894–1968)
The Image O' God 177

NAOMI MITCHISON (1897–1997)
The House of the Hare 178

ROBERT RENDALL (1898–1967)
Angle of Vision 179

WILLIAM SOUTAR (1898–1943)
Faith 180
Franciscan Episode 181

DOROTHY MARGARET PAULIN (1904–1982)
December Day 182

KATHLEEN RAINE (1908–2003)
Heirloom 183

NORMAN MacCAIG (1910–1996)
July Evening 184
A.K.'s summer hut 185

SOMHAIRLE MacGILL-EAIN/SORLEY MacLEAN (1911–1996)
Ban-Ghàidheal/A Highland Woman 186
Scotus Erigena 188

DOUGLAS YOUNG (1913–1973)
The Twenty-Third Psalm o King Dauvit 189
The Shepherd's Dochter 190

ANN SCOTT-MONCRIEFF (1914–1943)
Dirge 191
Lines Written in Autumn 1940 192

MURIEL SPARK (1918–2006)
Like Africa 193

DEÒRSA MAC IAIN DHEÒRSA/GEORGE CAMPBELL HAY (1915–1984)
Is E Crìoch Àraidh/Man's Chief End 194

W. S. GRAHAM (1918–1986)
The Found Picture 198

DÒMHNALL IAIN MACDHÒMHNAILL/DONALD JOHN MACDONALD (1919–1986)
Mi Fhìn 's a' Bheinn/The Mountain and I 200

ELMA MITCHELL (1919–2000)
The Prophet 204

EDWIN MORGAN (1920–2010)
Ring of Brodgar 205
Message Clear 206

GEORGE MACKAY BROWN (1921–1996)
Stations of the Cross: From Stone to Thorn 208
Christmas Poem 209

RUARAIDH MACTHÒMAIS/DERICK THOMSON (1921–2004)
A' Cluich Air Football Le Fàidh/Playing Football With A Prophet 210
Am Bodach-Ròcais/Scarecrow 212
Leòdhas as t-Samhradh/Lewis in Summer 214

MÀIRI M NICGHILLEATHAIN/MARY M. MACLEAN (1921–2004)
Glòir no Dórainn?/Glory or Agony? 216

ALASTAIR REID (1926–2014)
Whithorn Manse 220

IAIN CRICHTON SMITH/IAIN MAC A' GHOBHAINN (1928–1998)
When They Reached the New Land 221
Do Sheana-Bhoireannach/To an Old Woman 222

DÒMHNALL MACAMHLAIGH/DONALD MACAULAY (1930–2017)
Soisgeul 1955/Gospel 1955 226

KENNETH WHITE (1936–2023)
A High Blue Day on Scalpay 228

A. C. JACOBS (1937–1994)
Supplication 229

DIANA HENDRY (1941–)
Psalm Eighty-Eight Blues 230

JOCK STEIN (1941–)
119 Fair and Square 231

TOM LEONARD (1944–2018)
The Good Thief 232
A Humanist 233

IAN ABBOT (1947–1989)
Avoiding the Gods 234

CHRISTINE DE LUCA (1947–)
Dis life is nivver enyoch 235

JAMES McGONIGAL (1947–)
With Finnian at His Bright House in Whithorn 237

LIZ LOCHHEAD (1947–)
The Offering 238
Grace 240

CATRIONA NicGUMARAID/CATRIONA MONTGOMERY (1947–2024)
An Ceusadh/The Crucifixion 241

ALAN SPENCE (1947–)
All About the Light 242
Japanese boxes 243

MARION F. NicILLEMHOIRE/MARION F. MORRISON (1950–)
Màiri à Magdala, na h-Aonar le a Smuaintean/
Mary of Magdala by Herself 244

AONGHAS PHÀDRAIG CAIMBEUL/
ANGUS PETER CAMPBELL (1952–)
Iùdas air Cnap-deighe/Judas on an Iceberg 248

ANGUS DUNN (1953–2015)
Uist Madonna 250

IMTIAZ DHARKER (1954–)
Lapis Lazuli 251

BASHABI FRASER (1954–)
The Gurdwara in Leith 252

JOHN BURNSIDE (1955–)
Canticle 253
Nativity 254

CAROL ANNE DUFFY (1955–)
Prayer 255
Pilate's Wife 256

GERRY CAMBRIDGE (1959–)
Little Light Psalm 257

MEG BATEMAN (1959–)
Naomh/Saint 258

ROBERT CRAWFORD (1959–)
Biology 260

SANDAIDH NicDHÒMHNAILL JONES/
SANDY NicDHÒMHNAILL JONES (1960–)
XIV. Ràithean agus Rèiteachadh/XIV. Seasons and Conciliations 262

JACKIE KAY (1961–)
Baby Lazarus 268
Holy Island 269

KATHLEEN JAMIE (1962–)
The Buddleia 270
Meadowsweet 271

DON PATERSON (1963–)
Profession of Faith 272

ROB A. MACKENZIE (1964–)
Scotland 273
Blade Runner 274

A. B. JACKSON (1965–)
Isle of Arran 275

RODDY LUMSDEN (1966–2020)
The World's End 276

KENNETH STEVEN (1968–)
Columba 277

EM STRANG (1970–)
The Miracle 278

CAOIMHIN MacNÈILL/KEVIN MacNEIL (1972–)
Spring 279

TESSA BERRING (1975–)
An Intention to be Present 280

AMY JO PHILIP (1975–)
Coronach 281
Breathing is the Place to Start 282

JEN HADFIELD (1978–)
Paternoster 283

NIALL O' GALLAGHER (1981–)
An T-Eun Nach D'Rinn Sgèith/The Bird That Never Flew 284

SAMUEL TONGUE (1981–)
Theology 286

JANETTE AYACHI (1982–)
Youma and the Three Kings 287

PENNY BOXALL (1987–)
King of the Folly 288

ALYCIA PIRMOHAMED (1990–)
I Want the Kind of Permanence in a Birdwatcher's Catalogue 290

ROSEANNE WATT (1991–)
Steepel 292

About the Editors 293
Biographies 294
Acknowledgement of Sources 315
Index of Poets 319
Index of First Lines 321
Index of Poem Titles 324

Introduction

In their Introduction to the first edition of *Scottish Religious Poetry: An Anthology* the editors demonstrate they are already aware that ongoing developments in the national and religious life of Scotland would at some point necessitate a new edition. Writing in 2000 they note that they expect 'the religious insights' of Scots from a variety of ethnic backgrounds will 'appear in the poetry of this new millennium'.[1] Nearly a quarter of a century later, that new millennium seems less new and the time has certainly come to acknowledge and celebrate the range and breadth of religious insights which may be found in the poetry written in Scotland and by Scots of all faiths and none.

A recognition of the changing religious landscape of the nation was certainly an important driving force for us, the editors who have taken on the task of revising the first edition. There was also a recognition that, since 2000, Scottish Gaelic has become an even more accepted and respected presence in relation to Scotland's national identity. With The Gaelic Language (Scotland) Act 2005, much has changed regarding the language's legislative position but, on a more informal level, there have also been significant shifts in perceptions. Gaelic Medium Education is more widely available in places beyond the traditional Gaelic heartlands and there are more Gaelic speakers in urban areas, who are contributing to thriving Gaelic communities. Religion plays a part in these communities; the Church of Scotland's Gaelic Development Officer, Dr Duncan Sneddon's *Handbook of Biblical and Ecclesiastical Gaelic*, published in 2020, is indicative of the growing awareness of the need for inclusion of those worshippers who 'may have gone through Gaelic Medium Education, and have a good grasp of the language, but without a family and church background with Gaelic, feel that 'Church Gaelic' is outside their comfort zone'.[2] The time seemed right for new Gaelic poems to be gathered together in a volume such as this to address the issue and perhaps even to allow more discourse around issues of belief for 'new speakers' of the language.

But there was also, perhaps first and foremost, a frustration that the volume was out of print, and so was not available for the students we wanted to engage with the religious poetry of Scotland, or the general reader, or worship leader, who might be looking for a specific Scottish poem with a religious theme. With only one copy in the University library where we all work, one solution at least to our frustration seemed to be to offer to edit a new edition. To our

1 Meg Bateman, Robert Crawford and James McGonigal (eds), *Scottish Religious Poetry: An Anthology* (Edinburgh: St Andrew Press, 2000), p. xxvii.

2 Duncan Sneddon, *Handbook of Biblical and Ecclesiastical Gaelic*, (Edinburgh: Church of Scotland, 2020), p. 3.

delight, Christine Smith, Publishing Director at Hymns Ancient and Modern, who oversees St Andrew Press, agreed and we set about our task, daunted but enthusiastic. We were grateful too to have the support and encouragement of the three previous editors, whose work we admire so much. They made it clear they were happy for us to take this on and, as we embarked on the task, we caught a glimpse of just how much work it had been for them to lay the deep foundations on which we were building.

Our job as editors has certainly not been an easy one. Constraints of space have meant that, in order to include the new and diverse voices we want to showcase, some of the poems in the original edition have had to be sacrificed. This task has been somewhat akin to choosing between our children. Sometimes we were able to achieve this by reducing the number of poems included by a particular poet who was already well represented. We removed some of the examples of Scottish hymnody, partly because some of these examples can be found easily elsewhere. In other cases, we made the hard decision not to include a poem because it had not stood the test of time, or we felt there were other examples in the volume of a similar type. We hope we have not excised too many treasured gems as we have carried out this painful exercise.

Our desire to create space for as many new poems as possible led us to a further editorial decision which may court controversy: to remove the original version of a translated poem when it was not written in a living language. This resulted in, for example, Edwin Morgan's translation of Saint Columba's 'The Maker on High' ('Altus Prosator') appearing without its Latin version, 'Amra Choluimb Cille'/'Elegy of Columba' by Dallán Forgaill without the original old Gaelic, and Saint Ronald of Orkney's 'Mockery of Irish Monks on a Windswept Island' being included without the Old Norse. The rationale for this was that those with a keen interest in the original versions would be able to find these in the specialist scholarly editions. Keeping these poems in their original languages as well as in translation would indeed highlight the multilingual inheritance and significance of Scots writers in the past. However, this has had to be balanced against the potential to expand the range of poets we were able to include in the one volume, and we made the decision to give ourselves as much space as possible for this new work.

The need to create space for new poems was made all the more relentlessly pressing by the scholarly and popular reassessment of some of the twentieth-century poets whose work was represented in the original volume. With regard to the period before this, we added only one nineteenth-century poet, Jane Welsh Carlyle (1801–1866), whose poem 'Nay, This is Hope' worked so well as a counterpoint to her husband Thomas Carlyle's (1795–1881) 'Cui Bono?'. We made a different selection from the poetry of a small number of the other nineteenth-century writers as had been made in the original volume, choosing, for example, George MacDonald's (1824–1905) 'Holy Snowdrops' and 'Pilate's Wife' in place of his uncharacteristically rather brief and light-hearted 'Martin Elginbrodde'. However, our editorial brains were most taxed by the need to reassess the work of more recent poets. This included the already canonical, such as Norman MacCaig (1910–1996), Edwin Morgan (1920–2010), Deòrsa Mac Iain Dheòrsa/George Campbell Hay (1915–1984), Ruaraidh MacThòmais/Derick Thomson (1921–2012), and George Mackay Brown (1921–1996), whose work, from the critical distance of only a further twenty-five years, seemed to us to merit a slightly different set of examples. The Gaelic poetry of Iain Mac a' Ghobhainn/Iain Crichton Smith (1928–1998), which had not been included in the first edition, is now represented and reflects the recent work of scholars such as Moray Watson, who have ensured that Crichton Smith's Gaelic poetry has reached a wider audience with edited editions and detailed critical discussion, which had previously not been undertaken in any significant form. Also in this category is the work of female poets of a slightly earlier period, such as Violet Jacob (1863–1946) and Marion Angus (1865–1946), who were originally represented by only one poem but whose more recent reappraisal encouraged us to consider and include more of their work.

This need for reassessment was all the more pressing in the case of poets working in the latter half of the twentieth century and beyond. Many of these are represented in the original volume. However, two short and, from the perspective of today, early poems by Carol Ann Duffy (1955–) were certainly no longer sufficient or appropriate to give the former Poet Laureate her due recognition. Successive Makars for Scotland, Liz Lochhead (1947–), Jackie Kay (1961–), and Kathleen Jamie (1962–) all now have substantial bodies of work to be drawn from, and we are glad to be able to recognise their considerable importance and influence in the new edition with new selections of their poems. In the case of mid- to late-twentieth-century Gaelic poetry, the inclusion of Màiri M. NicGhillEathain/Mary M. Maclean (1921–2004), who won the Bardic Crown at the National Mod in 1951, is also a welcome addition.

All of these reappraisals had to be factored in before any additional, more contemporary poets were considered for the new volume. In this category we had poets with whose work we were already familiar, including poems we use in our teaching, but we were also greatly helped by the ideas of many of those we shared our plans with, and who passed on suggestions. In the end we had many more suggestions than we had space to cover, but we are proud to publish the work of such a diverse and strong range of contemporary poets including Christine De Luca (1947–), Imtiaz Dharker (1954–), Bashabi Fraser (1954–), Kenneth Steven (1968–), Caoimhin MacNeill/Kevin MacNeil (1972–), Alycia Pirmohamed (1990–), Sandaidh NicDhòmhnaill Jones/Sandy NicDhòmhnaill Jones (1960–), and Niall O' Gallagher (1981–).

We were convinced, as were the original editors, that Gaelic religious poetry has often been a reflection of the changing social, cultural and political position of the language, and wanted to reflect this in the new edition. Both secular and religious Gaelic poetry can be read as markers of change from the Roman Catholic symbolism inherent in Jacobite poetry, to the poetry of the Evangelical Revival, attitudes to the keeping of the Sabbath, outdoor services, and further on into the twentieth century, the biting criticism aimed at the Church in the socialist inspired poetry of Somhairle MacGill-Eain/Sorley MacLean (1911–1996) and others. Because of the fame beyond the Gaelic-speaking world of these mid-twentieth-century poets, the balance in the experience of Gaelic religious poetry tends to go in the favour of these critical pieces, but the poems in this edition also reflect the deep religious expression of both male and female poets who were often the bàrd baile ('village poets'), composing poetry and songs (and we include hymns in this category) for their communities. This edition also shows the personal connections and religious choices taken by some of these poets. For example, the broken engagement between Màiri M. NicGhillEathain/Mary M. Maclean (1921–2004) and Dòmhnall Iain MacDhòmhnaill/Donald John MacDonald (1919–1986) had a religious aspect, which reflects the wider schism between Protestant and Roman Catholic belief in the Gàidhealtachd. Mary Maclean has described her dilemma – 'although I could not have become a Roman Catholic, I know that Donald John might have become a Presbyterian … I was thinking how dismayed I would have been if he had suddenly said he would adapt to my religion. I knew that he loved me but I didn't want to force him to give up his faith.'[3] This poignant personal situation gave rise to some of the most powerful Gaelic religious poetry of the twentieth century. Maclean's poem, 'Glòir no Dórainn?'/'Glory or Agony', composed after she broke off her engagement and went into the Free Church, illustrates this commitment and sublime emotion, and is also echoed by the power of MacDonald's later writings on God. Religious and social pressures do not remove the rich personal path taken by these poets – in many ways these pressures actually go some way to enhancing the religious experience, showing how Gaelic poetry thrives under pressure. Later in the twentieth century and on into the twenty-first century, we can also glimpse a postmodern approach to religious poetry in Gaelic, with poems imagining and reimagining religious figures (e.g. Aonghas Phàdraig Caimbeul/Angus Peter Campbell's (1954–) 'Iùdas air Cnap-deighe'/'Judas on an Iceberg') as well as a reassessment of the symbolic importance of the early Church in modern religious experience (e.g. Sandy NicDhòmhnaill Jones' (1960-) 'XIV. Ràithean agus Rèiteachadh Quartus Decimus Cantus'/'Seasons and Conciliations Quartus Decimus Cantus', which is part of a celebration of key events in Columba's life and aspects of his legacy, marking 1500 years since St Columba's birth).

For us as editors there was also, of course, the significant body of important and relevant poetry written by the three original editors to be considered, who in a very self-effacing manner agreed they would not include any of their own work in the first volume. We are pleased to include examples of poems by Meg Bateman, Robert Crawford and James McGonigal, and have a keen sense that the new volume is greatly enhanced by these contributions. It is poetic justice, if there is such a thing. Let it be noted that if there is ever a third edi-

3 Timothy Neat with John MacInnes, *The Voice of the Bard: Living Poets and Ancient Tradition in the Highlands and Islands* (Edinburgh: Birlinn, 1999), p. 43.

tion of this volume, its editors may be reassured they do not have to address this issue with regard to any of the present editors, who (thus far) generously leave the writing of poetry to others.

The Introduction to the first edition offers an elegant and erudite reflection on the history of religious poetry in Scotland and remains recommended reading for anyone wanting to understand better the sweep of this history from the time before 'Scotland' as we understand it existed to the end of the twentieth century. It also sets out some of the criteria for selection the editors followed. Although not explicitly stated, they seem to have included the work of poets who were born, were raised or lived in Scotland while they were active as poets, a set of overlapping and permeable boundaries which we have also followed. We have also sought to maintain something of the diversity of the previous editorial team, with one of us a minister in the Church of Scotland, another an Elder in the Kirk and another a practising Roman Catholic. All of us are academics with feet in literary, theological and/or biblical studies fields, with a variety of interdisciplinary expertises. We hope these are reflected in a positive way in our selection, just as a similar diversity pro-actively enriched the first volume.

The editorial team's scholar of Scottish Catholic fiction, who also has keen interests in Orcadian literature and in Scottish women's poetry, was especially eager to find a place in the anthology for the Catholic convert and Orcadian poet Ann Scott-Moncrieff (1914–1943). And the addition of works by other mid-century poets has highlighted the wide spread of denominational perspectives to be found in twentieth-century Scottish poetry – something that has not always been appreciated within Scottish literary criticism. 'Angle of Vision' by Scott-Moncrieff's polymathic Orcadian contemporary Robert Rendall (1898–1967), a member of the Open Brethren, finds its way into this new edition of the anthology for the first time, its reflections on the 'cosmic tide' connecting the (Orcadian) particular to the universal. Similarly, under Dorothy Margaret Paulin's (1904–1982) Episcopalian perspective, reflections on the Solway Firth lead to a much broader appreciation of 'earth's ageless peace'.

The Gaelic scholar in the editorial team was aware of the position of the university educated Gaelic poets of the mid-twentieth century who were often scathing in their opinion of the Church, particularly when their own beliefs leaned towards socialism and communism. However, the situation has always been more nuanced than that – even Sorley MacLean, whose sympathy for the Highland Woman in 'Ban-Ghàidheal' leads to his accusatory tone with Christ, still shows how ingrained religion is within his own poetry with his high register, sermon-like Gaelic. While MacLean and Iain Crichton Smith look to the symbolic woman in their exploration of religion within their community and their own selves (for example, Crichton Smith's 'Do Sheana Bhoireannach'/'To An Old Woman'), the Gaelic editor was keen for the anthology to also highlight the other side of the modern Gaelic experience of religion and belief, with the women's voice being represented by the likes of Catriona NicGumaraid/Catriona Montgomery (1947–2024) and Meg Bateman (1959–), as well as earlier poets such as Anna Nic Ealair/Anna MacKellar (*fl.* 1800) and Màiri NicDhòmhnaill/Mary MacDonald (1789–1872), showing the richness and beauty inherent in their relationship to Christ.

The biblical scholar in the editorial team always warmed to the biblical phrase, or image, or character, but particularly the reimagining of the biblical story in any poem under discussion. So the case was made to keep Tom Leonard's (1944–2018) 'The Good Thief', although its inclusion was never in serious doubt. A recognition of the importance of the Psalms in Scottish church life through the ages meant that an example of the sixteenth-century translations by the Wedderburns and William Kethe (d.1594), the metrical Psalms of the seventeenth century and Douglas Young's (1913–1973) translation of the Twenty-Third Psalm from the twentieth century all kept their place. Diana Hendry's (1941–) 'Psalm Eighty-Eight Blues', Gerry Cambridge's (1959–) 'Little Light Psalm' and Jock Stein's (1941–) reworking of Psalm 119, 'Fair and Square' were added as new responses to these polyvalent texts and their heart-felt responses to the divine. Also added was Carol Ann Duffy's 'Pilate's Wife', a fleshing out of that biblical character's very minor role, as significant as Duffy's much better known 'Prayer', in which the biblical references are more implied than central.

That final choice raises the question of the trickiest of the three categories we were working with, having defined 'Scottish' and accepting 'Poetry' as reasonably self-evident. Duffy's 'Pilate's Wife' might be rooted in a biblical character, but is it appropriately identified as 'religious', in the way that her poem 'Prayer' might more obviously be categorised?

Certainly the poem engages with the nature of both humanity and divinity through the lens of the narrator's real and imagined interaction with Jesus, and we are drawn to Pilate's wife's interpretation of these encounters precisely because she has a role to play in the wider biblical drama. We have access to the messy, unfathomable story of the crucifixion and what led to it only through half-remembered witness accounts and the thought-processes of key players in the decades afterwards, as reflected in the Gospel accounts. Duffy's poem adds to our impression of that pivotal moment in the Christian story and offers us a new version of the truth which the character of Pilate in the Gospels at least also sought. The poem is not scripture, of course, but it is scriptural exegesis of a sort that leads us to argue this poem is religious to its very core. A similar case could be made for Marion F. NicIllemhoire/Marion F. Morrison's (1950–) poem 'Mairi a Magdala, na h-Aonar le a Smuaintaen' ('Mary of Magdala by Herself'), which is another very particular and striking exegesis of the biblical text.

Like the editors of the first volume, we continued to grapple with the question of what makes a poem 'religious'. The question is certainly more complicated today than it was in 1940 when Lord David Cecil was editing The *Oxford Book of Christian Verse*, and confined himself to poems which expressed 'Christian feeling' which was 'consistent with the doctrines of orthodox Christianity'.[4] For Helen Gardner in 1972, editing *The Faber Book of Religious Verse*, a sense of obligation and commitment within a poem, as response to revelation of a higher power, was what distinguished a religious poem from one which indulged in 'metaphysical speculation, religious musing or … incidental apprehension of the divine'.[5] – and which was not included. That response might include 'strong doubt', perhaps echoing at least the much more open perspective of R.S. Thomas, who in *The Penguin Book of Religious Verse* in 1963 indicated that he had 'attempted to broaden the meaning of the term 'religious' to accommodate twentieth-century sensibility'.[6] For Thomas, unsurprisingly for anyone who is aware of his own brittle, honest poetic work, conventional religious language no longer conveys what is true religious experience for many contemporary writers or readers. And so sections of his anthology focus on poems of the self, of negation and of the 'impersonal or un-nameable' alongside sections on consciousness of God and of completion. Religious poems for Thomas involve 'brooding' on self, destiny and mystery 'without any irritable reaching after fact or reason', to paraphrase Keats.[7] In a comparison of the three editorial positions, Gardner is more accepting of a critical and inclusive stance in her choice of religious poems than Cecil had been prepared to be, while reining in Thomas's predilection for 'brooding' as a religious category.

In the first volume of *Scottish Religious Poetry: An Anthology*, it seems that the editors are closer to Gardner's position than Thomas's. In their Introduction they suggest that religious poetry presents itself as 'working within something already given or handed on' rather than the newly created.[8] The religious poem is a response, and invites a response, to a 'revelation of the power and mystery of the divine'.[9] This response need not be one of positive acceptance, and may include rejection of such revelation, or doubt about its validity, or a satirical reaction to its outworking in the world. Poems may express any of these and still be categorised as 'religious'. The editors go on that their chief editorial concern was to select poems for their 'power rather than their piety'.[10] Impact within specific Scottish historical and religious contexts was a determining factor in the selection process of the original editors.

The present editors continued to reflect on whether or not evidence of a response to divine revelation within the poem and impact on the reader individually, or nationally and historically, remained the key indicators of a poem's religious suitability for the volume. In this regard, the recently published *The Poet's Quest for God: 21st Century Poems of Faith, Doubt and Wonder*,

---

4 Lord David Cecil (ed.), *The Oxford Book of Christian Verse* (Oxford: OUP, 1940), p. v.

5 Helen Gardner (ed.), *The Faber Book of Religious Verse* (London: Faber, 1972), p. 7.

6 R.S. Thomas (ed.), *The Penguin Book of Religious Verse* (Harmondsworth: Penguin, 1963), p. 9.

7 Thomas (ed.), *The Penguin Book of Religious Verse*, p. 11.

8 Bateman, Crawford and McGonigal (eds), *Scottish Religious Poetry*, p. xix.

9 Bateman, Crawford and McGonigal (eds), *Scottish Religious Poetry*, p. xix.

10 Bateman, Crawford and McGonigal (eds), *Scottish Religious Poetry*, p. xviii.

edited by Fr. Oliver Brennan and Todd Swift offered a rather different starting point.[11] This book came into being when the editors put out a call for suggestions of poems written in the twenty-first century which offered comfort or support to readers who were spiritual seekers from a variety of religious backgrounds. As a result, over two thousand poems were suggested, with a broad range of responses to the notion of the existence of God, from the positive to the negative, the accepting to the angry. The volume offers 445 of these poems, claiming they are

> great poems jostling together to reinvent and shape the way we think about, read, imagine and consider both poetry, and the search for spiritual truths beyond (or almost beyond) mortal ken, human desire.[12]

The range of these poems is impressive but the idea that 'faith, doubt and wonder', or the 'search for spiritual truths' might be the only criteria for selection feels uncomfortably close to Thomas's 'brooding'. The current editors sought to interrogate 'wonder' and 'search' as sufficient conditions for a poem to be classed as 'religious' for the new volume of *Scottish Religious Poetry*. Perhaps the original editors resonated with the Scottish psyche wisely when they held on to the idea of a religious poem responding to something already given or handed on, a response to a pre-existing understanding of divine revelation from whatever tradition. The distinction is a fine one but important. In his poem 'A.K.'s Summer Hut' Norman MacCaig may imagine the place as sacred in direct opposition to those Christian beliefs and places of worship which by implication involve 'tortures' and 'savage crucifixions' in the terms of the poem. But the poem is a reaction to a recognised religious impulse rather than an expression of a vague 'wonder'. It celebrates 'An exhilaration of peace,/a sounding Grace with trinities galore'. MacCaig is offering his own excoriating perspective, but it relates to a recognised theological tradition and this poem has its place in the Anthology.

For many readers, Malcolm Guite's thesis that all poems engage in the creative impulse which finds its source in God and all embody something of the Spirit of the incarnation is a step too far,[13] although some will find this a powerfully generative idea, echoing the perspective of George Mackay Brown for whom there could 'never be art without religion'.[14] For Guite, writing from a similarly Christian perspective, poets are particularly attuned to the trans-

11 Fr. Oliver Brennan and Todd Swift (eds), with Kelly Davio and Cate Myddleton-Evans, *The Poet's Quest for God: 21st Century Poems of Faith, Doubt and Wonder* (London: Eyewear Publishing Ltd, 2016).

12 Brennan and Swift (eds), *The Poet's Quest for God*, p. 18.

13 As argued most fully in Guite's *Faith, Hope and Poetry: Theology and the Poetic Imagination* (Abingdon: Routledge, 2016).

14 George Mackay Brown, 'Tablet Essay' (1996), OLA D124/2/3/11, held in Orkney Archive, quoted in Linden Bicket, *George Mackay Brown and the Scottish Catholic Imagination* (Edinburgh: Edinburgh University Press, 2017), p. 179.

figuration of language so that the meaning and mystery of life itself might glimmer through their words. He argues this immanence of meaning and significance within a poem may lead to a new understanding of transcendence through the mediating work of the imagination. Perhaps Guite appeals to a wider range of readers, however, when he suggests a poem can 'renew and deepen our vision of the world' at the same time as it may 'enrich our understanding of theology'.[15] A transfiguration of vision occurs when a poem is read with this intention and expectation and 'the mirror a poem holds up becomes a window onto the Divine'.[16] At least some of the poets represented in the Anthology, from St Columba onwards, might well hope that their work has this effect, writing from a position of faith themselves. However, the religious commitment, or otherwise, of any of the poets included here, was not presumed or a factor in our selection.

To this point, Malcolm Guite again offers an approach which allows for a distance to be maintained between a poet's religious convictions at any given moment in their life (in so far as this might be accessible in the first place) and reading their poems as 'religious', if we are so inclined. Referring to Geoffrey Hill and Seamus Heaney specifically, although the point is surely valid for all poets, Guite notes:

> When I refer to their 'faith and doubt', or to their imaginative apprehension of transcendent truths as I find it in their writings, I am always speaking of 'the poet in the poem': the imaginative insight is in that arrangement of words, expressed by the poet in the first person … I do not pretend to any knowledge of their own spiritual life, but only wish to observe the ways in which their writings might nurture and illuminate ours.[17]

Difficult as it may be in the classroom or lecture hall in practice, holding to this general principal keeps poetry commentators honest, and highlights *their* own role in the process of making meaning, religious or otherwise, out of a poem. For the current editors, it has also allowed us to categorise a poem as religious whether or not the actual poet would use the same term of themselves.

In summing up, we seek to acknowledge that the category 'religious poem' is not fixed and while we as editors of the new volume are standing on the shoulders of giants such as Helen Gardner and R. S. Thomas and Robert Crawford, Meg Bateman and James McGonigal, our volume will reflect this moment and our perspectives. For us that involves a generosity of spirit in finding the religious in a poem but it also involves a sensitivity, even a bias towards, those poems which respond to the revealed, given, handed-down aspects of theological thinking and belief, rather than simply a sense of wonder

15 Guite, *Faith, Hope and Poetry*, p. 15.
16 Guite, *Faith, Hope and Poetry*, p. 15.
17 Guite, *Faith, Hope and Poetry*, p. vii.

at the possibilities of what might loosely be termed the 'spiritual'. That places the new volume absolutely within the tradition of the first, but also loosens it slightly it from the first editors' focus on the impact in personal or national or historical terms of the poems selected. The poetic response need not be positive or orthodox, and it need not come from a place of conviction on the part of the poet. But it should engage the reader in something recognisably religious, rather than turn the reader in another direction entirely.

There is a poem by Robert Crawford, one of the editors of the first volume, which we have come to regard as a sort of metaphor for our endeavour. While its reference point is presumably that of religious faith, it has also served as an encouragement in our own work as editors: to accept our limitations and to get on with it. In recognition of and thanks to the three original editors, it is a fitting end to this Introduction:

My faith
Hangs by a thread.
It always has.
No point
Spending long
Going over it,
Worrying,
Will it snap?
Will it go?
Is it the wrong
Kind of faith?
Better just to take it
And sew.[18]

18 Robert Crawford, *Testament* (London: Jonathan Cape, 2014), p. 55.

Acknowledgements

The editors owe a debt of gratitude to the many people and organisers who contributed in different ways to the publication of the volume. The Royal Society of Edinburgh, the Drummond Trust and the Scottish Network for Religion and Literature were generous in their funding, which enabled us to pay for editorial assistance and the necessary permissions for the poems we have included. James Thieke did sterling editorial work in the early days of the project. Beth Dufour of ClearPermissions patiently, cheerfully and thoroughly sorted out the labyrinthine process of obtaining permissions for us. We would like to thank Ronnie Renton for invaluable advice on Gaelic poems and translations, and Jessica Barbier-Marsden, Kathleen Lambie, Ian MacDonald, and Niall O'Gallagher for assistance with copyright permissions. The National Library of Scotland and the Edinburgh University Library were places of respite and inspiration. We would particularly like to thank Samuel Tongue and the Scottish Poetry Library for offering us space to work, volumes of poetry to consult and advice whenever we asked for it. Rob A. Mackenzie, poet and minister, pointed us in the right direction. Christine Smith, Publishing Director at Hymns Ancient and Modern, and Mary Matthews, Editorial Manager, were supportive and full of words of wisdom throughout. Finally, we offer our thanks to Meg Bateman, Robert Crawford and James McGonigal for establishing the extensive foundations on which we have had the pleasure to build, and the warm encouragement they gave us to do so.

Editors' Note

Following the lead of the editors of the first edition, we have made no attempt to standardise Scots or Gaelic orthography. Where they seemed helpful, line-by-line glosses of Scots words have been supplied, including those added by the first editors and by Dr Nicola Royan, whose glossing we acknowledge with gratitude. Christine De Luca supplied her own glosses for her poem 'Dis life is nivver enyoch'.

We have provided the poets' own translations, and translations by others when a poem has previously been untranslated by the poet. We have attempted to offer the most up-to-date versions of original Gaelic poems wherever possible.

In order to allow readers to engage with the poems with as little prose interference as possible, we have gathered almost all biographical and other notes at the back of the book, where they are arranged alphabetically according to the name of the poet.

ST COLUMBA

c.521–597

THE MAKER ON HIGH

Ancient exalted seed-scatterer whom time gave no progenitor:
he knew no moment of creation in his primordial foundation
he is and will be all places in all time and all ages
with Christ his first-born only-born and the holy spirit co-borne
throughout the high eternity of glorious divinity:
three gods we do not promulgate one God we state and intimate
salvific faith victorious: three persons very glorious.

Benevolence created angels and all the orders of archangels
thrones and principalities powers virtues qualities
denying otiosity to the excellence and majesty
of the not-inactive trinity in all labours of bounty
when it mustered heavenly creatures whose well devised natures
received its lavish proffer through power-word for ever.

Came down from heaven summit down from angelic limit
dazzling in his brilliance beauty's very likeness
Lucifer downfalling (once woke at heaven's calling)
apostate angels sharing the deadly downfaring
of the author of high arrogance and indurated enviousness
the rest still continuing safe in their dominions.

Dauntingly huge and horrible the dragon ancient and terrible
known as the lubric serpent subtler in his element
than all the beasts and every fierce thing living earthly
dragged a third – so many – stars to his gehenna
down to infernal regions not devoid of dungeons
benighted ones hell's own parasite hurled headlong.

Excellent promethean armoury structuring world harmony
had created earth and heaven and wet acres of ocean
also sprouting vegetation shrubs groves plantations
sun moon stars to ferry fire and all things necessary
birds fish and cattle and every animal imaginable
but lastly the second promethean the protoplast human being.

Fast upon the starry finishing the lights high shimmering
the angels convened and celebrated for the wonders just created
the Lord the only artificer of that enormous vault of matter
with loud and well judged voices unwavering in their praises
an unexampled symphony of gratitude and sympathy
sung not by force of nature but freely lovingly grateful.

Guilty of assault and seduction of our parents in the garden
the devil has a second falling together with his followers
whose faces set in horror and wingbeats whistling hollow
would petrify frail creatures into stricken fearers
but what men perceive bodily must preclude luckily
those now bound and bundled in dungeons of the underworld.

He Zabulus was driven by the Lord from mid heaven
and with him the airy spaces were choked like drains with faeces
as the turgid rump of rebels fell but fell invisible
in case the grossest villains become willy-nilly
with neither walls nor fences preventing curious glances
tempters to sin greatly openly emulatingly.

Irrigating clouds showering wet winter from sea-fountains
from floods of the abysses three-fourths down through fishes
up to the skyey purlieus in deep blue whirlpools
good rain then for cornfields vineyard-bloom and grain-yields
driven by blasts emerging from their airy treasuring
desiccating not the land-marches but the facing sea-marshes.

Kings of the world we live in: their glories are uneven
brittle tyrannies disembodied by a frown from God's forehead:
giants too underwater groaning in great horror
forced to burn like torches cut by painful tortures
pounded in the millstones of underworld maelstroms
roughed rubbed out buried in a frenzy of flints and billows.

Letting the waters be sifted from where the clouds are lifted
the Lord often prevented the flood he once attempted
leaving the conduits utterly full and rich as udders
slowly trickling and panning through the tracts of this planet
freezing if cold was called for warm in the cells of summer
keeping our rivers everywhere running forward for ever.

Magisterial are his powers as the great God poises
the earth ball encircled by the great deep so firmly
supported by an almighty robust nieve so tightly
that you would think pillar and column held it strong and solemn
the capes and cliffs stationed on solidest foundations
fixed uniquely in their place as if on immovable bases.

No one needs to shows us: a hell lies deep below us
where there is said to be darkness worms beasts carnage
where there are fires of sulphur burning to make us suffer
where men are gnashing roaring weeping wailing deploring
where groans mount from gehennas terrible never-ending
where parched and fiery horror feeds thirst and hunger.

Often on their knees at prayer are many said to be there
under the earth books tell us they do not repel us
though they found it unavailling the scroll not unrolling
whose fixed seals were seven when Christ warning from heaven
unsealed it with the gesture of a resurrected victor
fulfilling the prophets' foreseeing of his coming and his decreeing.

Paradise was planted primally as God wanted
we read in sublime verses entering into Genesis
its fountain's rich waters feed four flowing rivers
its heart abounds with flowers where the tree of life towers
with foliage never fading for the healing of the nations
and delights indescribable abundantly fruitful.

Quiz sacred Sinai: who is it has climbed so high?
Who has heard the thunder cracks vast in the sky-tracts?
Who has heard the enormous bullroaring of the war-horns?
Who has seen the lightning flashing round the night-ring?
Who has seen javelins flambeaus a rock-face in shambles?
Only to Moses is this real only to the judge of Israel.

Rue God's day arriving righteous high king's assizing
dies irae day of the vindex day of cloud and day of cinders
day of the dumbfoundering day of great thundering
day of lamentation of anguish of confusion
with all the love and yearning of women unreturning
as all men's striving and lust for worldly living.

Standing in fear and trembling with divine judgement assembling
we shall stammer what we expended before our life was ended
faced by rolling videos of our crimes however hideous
forced to read the pages of the conscience book of ages
we shall burst out into weeping sobbing bitter and unceasing
now that all means of action have tholed the last retraction.

The archangelic trumpet-blast is loud and great at every fastness
the hardest vaults spring open the catacombs are broken
the dead of the world are thawing their cold rigor withdrawing
the bones are running and flying to the joints of the undying
their souls hurry to meet them and celestially to greet them
returning both together to be one not one another.

Vagrant Orion driven from the crucial hinge of heaven
leaves the Pleiades receding most splendidly beneath him
tests the ocean boundaries the oriental quandaries
as Vesper circling steadily returns home readily
the rising Lucifer of the morning after two years mourning:
these things are to be taken as type and trope and token.

X spikes and flashes like the Lord's cross marching
down with him from heaven as the last sign is given
moonlight and sunlight are finally murdered
stars fall from dignity like fruits from a fig-tree
the world's whole surface burns like a furnace
armies are crouching in caves in the mountains.

You know then the singing of hymns finely ringing
thousands of angels advancing spring up in sacred dances
quartet of beasts gaze from numberless eyes in praise
two dozen elders as happiness compels them
throw all their crowns down to the Lamb who surmounts them
'Holy holy holy' binds the eternal trinity.

Zabulus burns to ashes all those adversaries
who deny that the Saviour was Son to the Father
but we shall fly to meet him and immediately greet him
and be with him in the dignity of all such diversity
as our deeds make deserved and we without swerve
shall live beyond history in the state of glory.

translated from the Latin by Edwin Morgan

DALLÁN FORGAILL

fl. 600

from ELEGY OF COLUMBA

I

Not newsless is Níall's land.
No slight sigh from one plain,
but great woe, great outcry.
Unbearable the tale this verse tells:
Colum, lifeless, churchless.
How will a fool tell him – even Neire –
the prophet has settled at God's right hand in Sion.
Now he is not, nothing is left to us,
  no relief for a soul, our sage.
For he has died to us, the leader of nations who guarded the living,
he has died to us, who was our chief of the needy,
he has died to us, who was our messenger of the Lord;
for we do not have the seer who used to keep fears from us,
for he does not return to us, he who would explain the true Word,
for we do not have the teacher who would teach the tribes of the Tay.
The whole world, it was his:
It is a harp without a key,
it is a church without an abbot.

II

By the grace of God Colum rose to exalted companionship;
awaiting bright signs, he kept watch while he lived.
His lifetime was short,
scant portions filled him.
He was learning's pillar in every stronghold,
he was foremost at the book of complex Law.
The northern land shone,
the western people blazed,
he lit up the east
with chaste clerics.
Good the legacy of God's angel
when he glorified him.

V

He ran the course which runs past hatred to right action.
The teacher wove the word.
By his wisdom he made glosses clear.
He fixed the Psalms,
he made known the books of Law,
those books Cassian loved.
He won battles with gluttony.
The books of Solomon, he followed them.
Seasons and calculations he set in motion.
He separated the elements according to figures among the books of the Law.
He read mysteries and distributed the Scriptures among the schools,
and he put together the harmony concerning the course of the moon,
the course which it ran with the rayed sun,
and the course of the sea.
He could number the stars of heaven, the one who could tell all the rest
which we have heard from Colum Cille.

X

This is the elegy of the king who rules me.
He will protect us in Sion.
He will urge me past torments.
May it be easily dark defects go from me.
He will come to me without delay,
the descendant of Cathair's offspring, Coirpre, with dignity.
Vast the variations of the poem, vast the splendid sun of heaven,
I have no time.

translated from the Old Gaelic by Thomas Owen Clancy

ANONYMOUS

c.700

THE DREAM OF THE ROOD
(or THE VISION OF THE CROSS)

Listen! Hear how I dreamed a great dream
After midnight while most men slept.
It seemed I saw the tree of glory
Held high in heaven, haloed with light,
Blazing as a beacon. Every bough was
Brilliantly golden; gleaming jewels
Girdled earth's surface – five shone also
Ranged at right-angles – and crowds of angels
All through the universe viewed it with awe,
No gangsters' gallows. High, holy spirits
Marvelled with men and all of mighty creation.
　That symbol was sacred, and I was stained
With sinful scars. I saw glory's tree
Shawled with light, joyfully shining;
Gems had clothed those forest branches,
Yet through gold's glint I still could glimpse
Tokens of torture, of that first time
Blood ran from its right side. Writhing,
I dreaded my dream. The shifting symbol
Changed colours and coating; once, wet with blood,
It stood in gore; once, again, it glittered with treasure.
　I lay a long time, anxiously looking
At the Saviour's tree, till that best of branches
Suddenly started to speak:
　'Years, years ago, I remember it yet,
They cut me down at the edge of a copse,
Wrenched, uprooted me. Devils removed me,
Put me on show as their jailbirds' gibbet.
Men shouldered me, shifted me, set me up
Fixed on a hill where foes enough fastened me.

I looked on the Lord then, Man of mankind,
In his hero's hurry to climb high upon me.
I dared not go against God's word,
Bow down or break, although I saw
Earth's surface shaking. I could have flattened
All of those fiends; instead, I stood still.
Then the young hero who was King of Heaven,
Strong and steadfast, stripped for battle,
Climbed the high gallows, his constant courage
Clear in his mission to redeem mankind.
I flinched when he touched me, but dared not fall
Or stoop to the soil. I had to stand.
Created a cross, I carried the King,
The stars' strong Lord. I dared not bow.
They drove in dark nails, deep, cruel wounds
Are in me still, I could not stop them.
They cursed us both. I was black with blood
Sprung from His side once he sent His Soul on its way.
On that hill I held out in horror,
Saw Heaven's Ruler ceaselessly racked;
Low clouds lessened the Light of Lights,
God's corpse; darkness cut in
Black under cumulus, creation wept,
Crying for the King's death, Christ on his wooden cross.
Yet keen men came from far up-country,
Walking to the King. I kept watch.
Though scarred with sorrow, I stooped to their hands,
Totally humble. There they held God,
Hefted him from his hard trials, left me
Shot through with arrows, standing streaming with blood.
They laid him down, weary, stood at his head
Just looking at God; tired out after his torments,
He took time to rest. They started to hew
Out of bright stone in sight of his slayers
The strong Saviour's tomb. They sang,
Sobbed, and sang in that sorry gloaming,
Saddened to go again, leaving behind
The lonely Lord laid there. Then we three crosses
Witnessed and wept; a wail went up

From warrior comrades; the corpse,
Seat of the soul, grew cold.
Suddenly someone started to axe us
Flat to the field. The three crosses crashed.
God's friends, His servants, found me buried,
Dumped in a deep pit. They decorated me
With silver and gold.
                    Hear now, friend,
How I tholed the work of the wicked,
Tearings and torments. The time has come
When worshippers honour me far and wide
Across all countries, throughout creation
Men pray to this sign. On me God's Son
Suffered; for that I am set up high
Shining in heaven, and I can heal
Any person who fears me in faith.
Once I was taken for toughest torture,
Monstrous to men, before I opened
The right road for people on earth.
God in His glory, the sky's Guard, gave me
To tower above trees, as He made in grace
His mother also, Mary herself,
Much more marvellous in all men's minds
Than the rest of the race of women.
    My friend, you must obey your vision.
Work out in words, tell people this dream
Of the tree of glory against which God
Suffered for mankind's many sins
And the ancient evil of Adam.
He dined on death there, but rose up Lord,
Hero and helper, he climbed into heaven
From where He'll descend on the Day of Judgement,
Almighty God, the Lord with good angels,
The mighty Maker, to search out mankind,
Judging each as each on earth
Deserved in this life unlasting.
None on that day can hear without dread

God's voice. In front of great crowds
He will ask for the man who might be willing
To brave bitter death as Christ did on those beams.
People will fear Him, few have considered
What to begin to say to the Saviour.
He who on earth has carried the crucifix
Bright in his breast, the best of symbols,
Need not cower then; God shall greet
All who come through the cross to their homes in heaven,
Every soul from the earth.'
  My heart grew happy when I heard that cross.
I lay alone, my spirit longing,
Urging my soul on its journey.
Now, more than all, I live my life
Hoping to see that tree of glory
And worship it well. My will
Spurs my spirit; yon cross protects me.
My strong friends are few. They have gone away
From the wealth of this world in search of God,
Living now with the high Lord of heaven.
Every day I expect that moment
When the cross of the King I caught sight of on earth
Will fetch me far from this fleeting state
To bring me where true glory blossoms
Joyfully in heaven, where the host of God
Banquets in bliss forever;
Then he shall set me to stay in splendour,
Housed with the holy in the hall of my Lord.
Hero, who here in the past knew horror
On earth on the criminal's cross,
Be my friend, God, who gave us our lives,
Redeemer who gave us homes in heaven.
New hope came with bountiful blessings
For those who before knew nothing but burning.
Mighty and masterful, coming with massed
Hosts of the holy to the house of God,
The one almighty Son was sure
Of victory then, elating with angels
And all of those who had in heaven
Places in glory when their Prince was coming,
The Lord God almighty, home.

translated from the Old English by Robert Crawford

SCHOOL OF COLUMBA

?8TH CENTURY

NOLI PATER

Father, do not allow thunder and lightning,
lest we be shattered by its fear and its fire.

We fear you, the terrible one, believing there is none like you.
All songs praise you throughout the host of angels.

Let the summits of heaven, too, praise you with roaming lightning.
O most loving Jesus, O righteous King of Kings.

Blessed for ever, ruling in right government,
is John before the Lord, till now in his mother's womb,
filled with the grace of God in place of wine or strong drink.

Elizabeth of Zechariah begot a great man:
John the Baptist, the forerunner of the Lord.

The flame of God's love dwells in my heart
as a jewel of gold is placed in a silver dish.

translated from the Latin by Gilbert Márkus

MUGRÓN, ABBOT OF IONA

D. 981

CHRIST'S CROSS

Christ's cross across this face,
across the ear like this,
Christ's cross across this eye,
Christ's cross across this nose.

Christ's cross across this mouth.
Christ's cross across this throat.
Christ's cross across this back.
Christ's cross across this side.

Christ's cross cross this stomach,
(like this it is just fine).
Christ's cross across this gut,
Christ's cross across this spine.

Christ's cross across my arms
from my shoulders to my hands.
Christ's cross across my thighs.
Christ's cross across my legs.

Christ's cross with me before.
Christ's cross with me behind.
Christ's cross against each trouble
both on hillock and in glen.

Christ's cross east towards my face,
Christ's cross west towards sunset.
South and north, ceaselessly,
Christ's cross without delay.

Christ's cross across my teeth
lest to me come harm or hurt.
Christ's cross cross my stomach.
Christ's cross across my heart.

Christ's cross up to heaven's span.
Christ's cross down to earth.
Let no evil or harm
come to my body or soul.

Christ's cross cross my sitting,
Christ's cross cross my lying.
Christ's cross, my whole power
till we reach heaven's King.

Christ's cross across my church,
across my community.
Christ's cross in the next world.
Christ's cross in the present-day.

From the tip of my head
to the nail of my foot,
Christ, against each peril
the shelter of your cross.

Till the day of my death,
before going in this clay,
joyfully I will make
Christ's cross across my face.

translated from the Gaelic by Thomas Owen Clancy

ANONYMOUS (in the mouth of Colum Cille)

c.1100–1150

DELIGHTFUL TO BE ON THE BREAST OF AN ISLAND

Delightful it would be on the breast of an island
  on a rocky clifftop,
from there I could often ponder
  the calm of the ocean.

I'd see her heavy billows
  on glittering surface,
as they sang thus to their Father
  in eternal surging.

I'd see her smooth clean bays and beaches
  (no mournful meeting);
I'd hear the call of wondrous seabirds,
  a cry of gladness.

I'd hear the thunder of the breakers
  against the headlands,
I'd hear a clamour beside the graveyard,
  the sound of the ocean.

I'd see her noble birdflocks
  on the teeming ocean;
I'd see her whales,
  the greatest of all wonders.

I'd see her ebbing and flooding
  in their order;
may my name be – I tell a secret –
  'Back towards Ireland'.

My heart would be succoured
    by gazing at it,
I'd lament my every evil –
    hard to broadcast.

I would bless the Lord Almighty
    who maintains all:
heaven with its pure, loving orders,
    land, shore and water.

On some book I would ponder,
    for the soul beneficial;
a while beseeching beloved heaven,
    a while psalm-singing.

A while plucking dulse from the skerries,
    a while fishing,
a while giving food to the needy,
    a while in a rock-cell.

A while contemplating the prince of Heaven,
    holy the purchase;
a while toiling, nothing too taxing;
    it would be delightful.

translated from the Gaelic by Meg Bateman

EARL ROGNVALD KALI (ST RONALD OF ORKNEY)

D.1158

MOCKERY OF IRISH MONKS ON A WINDSWEPT ISLAND

I've seen sixteen women
at once with forelock on forehead,
stripped of the old age of the earth
of the serpent-field, walk together.
We bear that witness
that most girls here—
this isle lies against the storms
out west—are bald.

women with forelock on forehead: monks with Celtic tonsure, wearing habits which seem feminine in Norse dress; *old age of the earth of the serpent-field*: *serpent-field* 'gold, on which dragons lie'; its *earth* 'gold-adorned woman'; her *old age* 'facial hair' (i.e. the monks are clean-shaven); *bald* 'tonsured'.

translated from the Old Norse by Paul Bibire

MUIREADHACH ALBANACH

fl. 1220

from O GREAT MARY, LISTEN TO ME

O great Mary, listen to me,
    praying to you should be my zeal;
on your brother turn not your back,
    Mother of the King of all.

*

You, Mary, Mother of God,
    no-one ever knew your joy,
a royal tree divided in three,
    heaven's King was in your womb.

May I be guided by you both
    into your good house and your fort,
O great Mary, O my soul,
    O golden apple, apple-tree new-grown.

O food, O clothing to dispose,
    O tresses rippling as in a field,
O Mother, O Sister, O Love,
    your poor brother rightly steer.

*

Mother of God, let's make peace,
    O great Mary, calm your rage,
whose tresses are most rich in hue,
    red gold ingot in a vessel of clay.

*

O Trinity, O Mary mild,
    base is every glory but yours,
O Four in One, hear my lay,
    not from you a gift of gold.

O Virgin Mary, O dark brow,
    O great nurse, O garden gay,
of all women the most beloved,
    give me heaven despite my shame.

*

A miraculous child for your breast,
    for your pure fair fresh hair,
your Son and Father both
    on your knee, O noble bright branch.

Your belly rises up full
    like the belly of the trout;
without ever lying with you
    the Lord made Mary's Son.

*

No woman but you in my house –
    over it may you be host;
to false women may I not cleave,
    nor to what is mine to own.

With no regard for hounds or herds
    or studs of horses, O white swan,
or others' drinking-horns and stock,
    without their women and their dogs.

Raise to me your dark brow
    and your face like calf's blood,
raise, so that I might see
    the noble bright combed locks.

Raise to me your foot and palm
    and the rich heavy glossy head
and the young round sharp blue eye
    so with your soft tresses I may feast.

translated from the Classical Gaelic by Meg Bateman

ANONYMOUS

14TH CENTURY

from THE INCHCOLM ANTIPHONER

MEMORIAL OF ST COLUMBA

Mouth of the dumb,
light of the blind,
foot of the lame,
to the fallen stretch out your hand.
Strengthen the senseless,
restore the mad.
O Columba, hope of Scots,
by your merits' mediation
make us companions
of the blessed angels.
Alleluia.

translated from the Latin by Gilbert Márkus

ROBERT HENRYSON

?1424–?1506

THE PREICHING OF THE SWALLOW

The hie prudence and wirking mervelous,
The profound wit off God omnipotent,
Is sa perfyte and sa ingenious, so
Excellent far all mannis jugement:
Forquhy to Him all thing is ay present, Because
Rycht as it is or ony tyme sall be,
Befoir the sicht off His Divinite.

Thairfoir our saull with sensualitie
So fetterit is in presoun corporall, prison
We may not cleirlie understand nor se
God as He is nor thingis celestiall;
Our mirk and deidlie corps naturall
Blindis the spirituall operatioun –
Lyke as ane man wer bundin in presoun.

In Metaphisik Aristotell sayis
That mannis saull is lyke ane bakkis ee soul; bat's eye
Quhilk lurkis still als lang as licht off day is, which; as
And in the gloming cummis furth to fle; fly
Hir ene ar waik, the sone scho may not se: eyes; weak; sun; she; see
Sa is our saull with fantasie opprest illusion
To knaw the thingis in nature manifest.

For God is in His power infinite,
And mannis saull is febill and over-small,
Off understanding waik and unperfite, imperfect
To comprehend Him That contenis all:
Nane suld presume be ressoun naturall
To seirche the secreitis off the Trinitie,
Bot trow fermelie and lat all ressoun be. believe; leave; by

Yit nevertheless we may haif knawlegeing
Off God Almychtie be His creatouris
That he is gude, fair, wyis and bening: — benign
Exempill tak be thir jolie flouris
Rycht sweit off smell and plesant off colouris,
Sum grene, sum blew, sum purpour, quhyte and reid, — purple
Thus distribute be gift off His Godheid.

The firmament payntit with sternis cleir, — stars
From eist to west rolland in cirkill round, — rolling
And everilk planet in his proper spheir,
In moving makand harmonie and sound;
The fyre, the air, the watter and the ground –
Till understand it is aneuch, iwis, — enough, indeed
That God in all His werkis wittie is. — wise

Luke weill the fische that swimmis in the se;
Luke weill in eirth all kynd off bestiall; — of beasts
The foulis fair sa forcelie thay fle, — so strongly
Scheddand the air with pennis grit and small; — sweeping through; wings
Syne luke to man, that He maid last off all,
Lyke to His image and His similitude:
Be thir we knaw that God is fair and gude.

All creature He maid for the behufe — needs
Off man and to his supportatioun
Into this eirth, baith under and abufe,
In number, wecht and dew proportioun;
The difference off tyme and ilk seasoun
Concorddand till our opurtunitie,
As daylie be experience we may se. — by

The somer with his jolie mantill off grene,
With flouris fair furrit on everilk fent, — trimmed on every garment
Quhilk Flora Goddes, off the flouris quene,
Hes to that lord as for his seasoun lent,
And Phebus with his goldin bemis gent — beautiful
Hes purfellit and payntit plesandly — adorned
With heit and moysture stilland from the sky. — falling

Syne harvest hait, quhen Ceres that goddes	
Hir barnis benit hes with abundance;	filled
And Bachus, god off wyne, renewit hes	
The tume pyipis in Italie and France	empty casks
With wynis wicht and liquour off plesance;	strong; delight
And Copia Temporis to fill hir horne,	the Season of Plenty
That never wes full of quheit nor uther corne.	pale
Syne wynter wan, quhen austerne Eolus,	stern Aeolus
God off the wynd, with blastis boreall	northern
The grene garment off somer glorious	
Hes all to-rent and revin in pecis small;	
Than flouris fair faidit with froist man fall,	Then, must
And birdis blyith changit thair noitis sweit	
In styll murning, neir slane with snaw and sleit.	nearly
Thir dalis deip with dubbis drounit is,	pools
Baith hill and holt heillit with frostis hair;	forest hidden
And bewis bene laifit bair off blis	boughs are left bare
Be wicket windis off the winter wair;	wild
All wyld beistis than from the bentis bair	heaths
Drawis for dreid unto thair dennis deip,	fear
Coucheand for cauld in coifis thame to keip.	Cowering; hollows
Syne cummis ver, quhen winter is away,	Then; spring
The secretar off somer with his sell,	seal of office
Quhen columbie up-keikis throw the clay,	columbine peeks out
Quhilk fleit wes befoir with froistes fell;	frightened; cruel frosts
The mavis and the merle beginnis to mell;	blackbird; mate
The lark onloft with uther birdis haill	aloft
Than drawis furth fra derne over doun and daill.	concealment
That samin seasoun, into ane soft morning,	
Rycht blyth that bitter blastis wer ago,	
Unto the wod, to se the flouris spring	
And heir the mavis sing and birdis mo,	other birds
I passit furth, syne lukit to and fro	
To se the soill that wes richt sessonabill,	
Sappie and to resave all seidis abill.	receive

Moving thus-gait grit myrth I tuke in mynd — this way
Off lauboraris to se the besines – — labourers
Sum makand dyke and sum the pleuch can wynd,
Sum sawand seidis fast frome place to place, — sowing seeds
The harrowis hoppand in the saweris trace: — jerking; sower's track
It wes grit joy to him that luifit corne — loved
To se thame laubour baith at evin and morne.

And as I baid under ane bank full bene, — lingered, fair
In hart gritlie rejosit off that sicht,
Unto ane hedge, under ane hawthorne grene,
Off small birdis thair come ane ferlie flicht, — remarkable flock
And doun belyif can on the leifis licht — straightaway; did
On everilk syde about me quhair I stude –
Rycht mervellous – ane mekill multitude.

Amang the quhilks ane swallow loud couth cry, — did
On that hawthorne hie in the croip sittand:
'O ye birdis on bewis heir me by,
Ye sall weill knaw and wyislie understand
Quhair danger is or perrell appeirand;
It is grit wisedome to provyde befoir,
It to devoyd – for dreid it hurt yow moir.' — avoid; fear

'Schir Swallow,' quod the lark agane and leuch, — said; laughed
'Quhat have ye sene that causis yow to dreid?'
'Se ye yone churll,' quod scho, 'beyond yone pleuch — labourer
Fast sawand hemp and gude linget seid? — sowing; linseed
Yone lint will grow in lytill tyme indeid, — flax
And thairoff will yone churll his nettis mak, — nets
Under the quhilk he thinkis us to tak.

'Thairfoir I reid we pas quhen he is gone — advise
At evin, and with our naillis scharp and small
Out off the eirth scraip we yone seid anone
And eit it up; for giff it growis, we sall
Have cause to weip heirefter ane and all:
Se we remeid thairfoir furth with instante –
Name leuius laedit quicquid praeuidimus ante. — Forewarned is forearmed

'For clerkis sayis it is nocht sufficient	scholars
To considder that is befoir thyne ee;	eye
Bot prudence is ane inwart argument	
That garris ane man provyde and foirse	causes; foresee
Quhat gude, quhat evill is liklie for to be,	
Off everilk thing behald the fynall end	
And swa fra perrell the better him defend.'	
The lark lauchand the swallow thus couth scorne,	laughing; did
And said scho fischit lang befoir the net –	
The barne is eith to busk that is unborne –	child; easy; dress
All growis nocht that in the ground is set –	
The nek to stoup quhen it the straik sall get	blow
Is sone aneuch – deith on the fayest fall:	those utterly fated
Thus scornit thay the swallow ane and all.	
Despysing thus hir helthsum document,	warning
The foulis ferlie tuke thair flicht anone;	suddenly
Sum with ane bir thay braidit over the bent	a whirr; darted; heath
And sum agane ar to the grene wod gone:	
Upon the land quhair I wes left allone	
I tuke my club and hamewart couth I carie,	
Swa ferliand as I had sene ane farie.	As amazed
Thus passit furth quhill June, that jolie tyde,	season
And seidis that wer sawin off beforne	
Wer growin hie, that hairis mycht thame hyde,	hares
And als the quailye craikand in the corne;	croaking
I movit furth, betuix midday and morne,	
Unto the hedge under the hawthorne grene	
Quhair I befoir the said birdis had sene.	
And as I stude, be aventure and cace,	by chance
The samin biridis as I haif said yow air –	same; earlier
I hoip because it wes thair hanting-place,	suppose; habitat
Mair off succour or yit mair solitair –	offering safety and seclusion
Thay lychtit doun: and quhen thay lychtit wair,	alighted
The swallow swyth put furth ane pietuous pyme,	immediately; cry
Said: 'Wo is him can not bewar in tyme!	

'O blind birdis and full off negligence,
Unmyndfull of your awin prosperitie,
Lift up your sicht and tak gude advertence! heed
Luke to the lint that growis on yone le! flax; lea
Yone is the thing I bad forsuith that we, indeed
Quhill it wes seid, suld rute furth off the eird: earth
Now is it lint; now is it hie on breird. sprung up high

'Go yit quhill it is tender and small
And pull it up – let it na mair incres:
My flesche growis, my bodie quaikis all; wrinkles in terror
Thinkand on it I may not sleip in peis.'
Thay cryit all and bad the swallow ceis,
And said: 'Yone lint heirefter will do gude,
For linget is to lytill birdis fude. linseed

'We think, quhen that yone lint-bollis ar ryip, flax-pods
To mak us feist and fill us off the seid
Magre yone churll, and on it sing and pyip.' In spite of; twitter
'Weill,' quod the swallow, 'freindes, hardilie beid: so be it
Do as ye will, bot certane sair I dreid;
Heirefter ye sall find als sour as sweit
Quhen ye ar speldit on yone carlis speit. spreadeagled; man's spit

'The awner off yone lint ane fouler is, owner
Richt cautelous and full off subteltie; sly
His pray full sendill-tymis will he mis seldom
Bot giff we birdis all the warrer be; if; more careful
Full mony off our kin he hes gart de, caused to die
And thocht it bot ane sport to spill thair blude:
God keip me fra him, and the Halie Rude!'

Thir small birdis haveand bot lytill thocht These
Off perrell that mycht fall be aventure,
The counsell off the swallow set at nocht,
Bot tuke thair flicht and furth togidder fure; went
Sum to the wode, sum markit to the mure. went
I tuke my staff quhen this wes said and done,
And walkit hame, for it drew neir the none.

The lynt ryipit, the carll pullit the lyne,	ripened, flax-stalks
Rippillit the bollis and in beitis set,	removed; seeds; small bundles
It steipit in the burne and dryit syne,	
And with ane bittill knokkit it and bet,	bettle (tool); beat
Syne swingillit it weill and hekkillit in the flet;	scutched; dressed it indoors
His wyfe it span and twynit it into threid,	
Off quhilk the fowlar nettis maid indeid.	

The wynter come, the wickit wind can blaw;	
The woddis grene wer wallowit with the weit;	
Baith firth and fell with froistys wer maid faw,	uneven
Slonkis and slaik maid slidderie with the sleit:	Hollows and dells
The foulis fair for falt thay fell off feit;	went in fear of falling
On bewis bair it wes nar bute to byde,	no help
Bot hyit unto housis thame to hyde.	hurried

Sum in the barn, sum in the stak off corne	
Thair lugeing tuke and maid thair residence;	lodging
The fowlar saw, and grit aithis hes sworne	oaths
Thay suld be tane trewlie for thair expence:	
His nettis hes he set with diligence,	
And in the snaw he schulit hes ane plane,	cleared; space
And heillit it all over with calf agane.	covered; chaff

Thir small birdis seand the calff wes glaid;	seeing
Trowand it had bene corne they lychtit doun;	Believing
Bot of the nettis na presume they had,	suspicion
Nor of the fowlaris fals intentioun;	
To scraip and seik thair meit thay maide thame boun:	got ready
The swallow on ane lytill branche neir by,	
Dreiddand for gyle, thus loud on thame couth cry:	Fearing a trick

'Into that calf scraip quhill your naillis bleid;	
Thair is na corne – ye laubour all in vane;	
Trow ye yone churll for pietie will yow feid?	
Na, na! He hes it heir layit for ane trane;	
Remove I reid, or ellis ye will be slane;	Get out
His nettis he hes set full prively,	
Reddie to draw; in tyme be war forthy.'	beware therefore

Grit fule is he that puttis in dangeir
His lyfe, his honour, for ane thing off nocht;
Grit fule is he that will not glaidle heir
Counsall in tyme, quhill it availl him nocht;
Grit fule is he that hes na thing in thocht
Bot thing present – and efter quhat may fall
Nor off the end hes na memoriall.

Thir small birdis for hunger famischit neir,
Full besie scraipand for to seik thair fude, — busy scraping
The counsall off the swallow wald not heir –
Suppois thair laubour dyd thame lytill gude.
Quhen scho thair fulische hartis understude
Sa indurate, up in ane tre scho flew; — obdurate
With that this churll over thame his nettis drew.

Allace, it wes grit hartsair for to se — heartache
That bludie bowcheour beit thay birdis doun, — butcher
And for till heir, quhen thay wist weill to de, — realised they would die
Thair cairfull sang and lamentatioun! — pained
Sum with ane staf he straik to eirth on swoun,
Off sum the heid he straik, off sum he brak the crag, — neck
Sum half on lyfe he stoppit in his bag. — half alive

And quhen the swallow saw that thay wer deid,
'Lo,' quod scho, 'thus it happinnis mony syis — many a time
On thame that will not tak counsall nor reid — advice
Off prudent men or clerkis that ar wyis;
This grit perrell I tauld thame mair than thryis;
Now ar thay deid and wo is me thairfoir!'
Scho tuke hir flicht, bot I hir saw no moir.

Moralitas

Lo, worthie folk, Esope that nobill clerk, — Aesop
Ane poet worthie to be lawreate,
Quhen that he waikit from mair autentik werk, — was free from; important
With uther ma this foirsaid fabill wrate, — others too
Quhilk at this tyme may well be applicate — applicable
To gude morall edificatioun,

Haifand ane sentence according to ressoun.   Having a valid signification
This carll and bond of gentrice spoliate,   husbandman bereft of kindness
Sawand this calf thir small birdis to sla,
It is the feind, quhilk fra the angelike state
Exylit is as fals apostata;   apostate
Quhilk day and nycht weryis not for to ga
Sawand poysoun in mony wickit thocht
In mannis saull, quhilk Christ full deir hes bocht.

And quhen the saull as seid into the eird
Gevis consent unto delectioun,   to indulging
The wickit thocht beginnis for to breird   sprout
In deidlie sin – quhilk is dampnatioun;
Ressoun is blindit with affectioun,
And carnall lust gouis full grene and gay,
Throw conseutude hantit from day to day.   custom practised

Proceding furth be use and consuetude,   by custom
The sin ryipis, and schame is set onsyde;   ripens
The feynd plettis his nettis scharp and rude,   weaves
And under plesance previlie dois hyde;   secretly
Syne on the feild he sawis calf full wyde –
Quhilk is bot tume and verray vanitie   empty; actual
Of fleschlie lust and vaine prosperitie.

Thir hungrie birdis wretchis we may call,   These
Ay scraipand in this warldis vane plesance,
Greddie to gadder gudis temporall,   Greedy
Quhilk as the calf ar tume without substance,
Lytill of availl and full of variance,
Lyke to the mow befoir the face of wind   dust
Quhiskis away and makis wretchis blind.

This swallow quhilk eschaipit is the snair
The halie preichour weill may signifie,
Exhortand folk to walk and ay be wair
Fra nettis of our wickit enemie –
Quha sleipis not, bot ever is reddie,
Quhen wretchis in this warld calf dois scraip,

To draw his net than thay may not eschaip.
Allace, quhat cair, quhat weiping is and wo
Quhen saull and bodie departit ar in twane!
The bodie to the wormis keitching go,   abode
The saull to fyre, to everlestand pane.
Quhat helpis than this calf, thir gudis vane,   these possessions
Quhen thow art put in Luceferis bag
And brocht to hell and hangit be the crag?   neck

Thir hid nettis for to persave and se,   perceive
This sarie calf wyislie to undestand,
Best is bewar in maist propseritie;
For in this warld thair is na thing lestand;   lasting
Is na man wait how lang his stait will stand,   No man knows
His lyfe will lest, nor how that he sall end
Efter his deith, nor quhidder he sall wend.   go

Pray we thairfoir quhill we ar in this lyfe
For four thingis: the first, fra sin remufe;
The secund is fra all weir and stryfe;   war
The third is perfite cheritie and lufe;
The feird thing is – and maist for oure behufe –   fourth; needs
That is in blis with angellis to be fallow.   companion
And thus endis the preiching of the swallow.

WILLIAM DUNBAR

?1456–?1513

RORATE CELI DESUPER

Rorate, celi desuper! — Pour down, heavens, dew from above
Hevins, distill your balmy schouris,
For now is rissin the brycht day ster
Fro the ros, Mary, flour of flouris. — rose
The cleir sone quhome no clud devouris,
Surminting Phebus in the est,
Is cumin of his hevinly touris — Has come from; towers
Et nobis puer natus est. — And unto us a child is born

Archangellis, angellis and dompnationis, — dominations
Tronis, potestatis and marteiris seir, — Thrones; powers; many
And all ye hevinly operationis,
Ster, planeit, firmament and speir, — sphere
Fyre, erd, air and watter cleir,
To him gife loving, most and lest,
That come into so meik maneir — in so humble a
Et nobis puer natus est.

Synarris, be glaid and pennance do
And thank your makar hairtfully,
For he that ye mycht nocht cum to
To yow is cumin full humly, — in full humility
Your saulis with his blud to by
And lous yow of the feindis arrest, — free you from
And only of his awin mercy, — own
Pro nobis puer natus est. — For us

All clergy, do to him inclyne
And bow unto that barne benyng, — child of grace
And do your observance devyne
To him that is of kingis king.
Ensence his altar, reid and sing — Burn incense at
In haly kirk with mynd degest, — solemn
Him honouring attour all thing, — beyond
Qui nobis puer natus est. — who

Celestiall fowlis in the are,
Sing with your nottis upoun hicht, — notes on high
In firthis and in forrestis fair
By myrthfull now at all your mycht,
For passit is your dully nycht;
Aurora hes the cluddis perst, — Dawn; pierced
The son is rissin with glaidsum lycht
Et nobis puer natus est. — And

Now spring up, flouris, fra the rute,
Revert yow upwart naturaly, — spring up once more
In honour of the blissit frute
That rais up fro the rose, Mary:
Lay out your levis lustely,
Fro deid tak lyfe now at the lest,
In wirschip of that prince wirthy,
Qui nobis puer natus est.

Syng, hevin imperiall, most of hicht, — highest
Regions of air mak armony.
All fishe in flud and foull of flicht
Be myrthfull and mak melody.
All *Gloria in excelsis* cry, — Glory in the highest
Hevin, erd, se, man, bird and best:
He that is crownit abone the sky — above
Pro nobis puer natus est!

DONE IS A BATTELL ON THE DRAGON BLAK

Done is a battell on the dragon blak;	against
Our campioun Chryst confoundit hes his force;	champion; has overthrown his power
The yettis of hell ar brokin with a crak,	gates
The signe triumphall rasit of the croce.	standard; raised; cross
The divillis trymmillis with hiddous voce,	devils tremble; voice
The saulis ar borrowit and to the bliss can go,	souls; redeemed
Chryst with his blud our ransonis dois indoce:	ransoms; endorse
Surrexit Dominus de sepulchro.	The Lord is risen from the tomb
Dungin is the deidly dragon Lucifer,	beaten
The crewall serpent with the mortall stang,	cruel; sting
The auld kene tegir with his teith on char	fierce tiger; teeth bared
Quhilk in a wait hes lyne for us so lang,	which; ambush; lain
Thinking to grip us in his clowis strang.	claws
The mercifuil lord waid nocht that it wer so;	did not wish
He maid him for to felye of that fang:	lose that prey
Surrexit Dominus de sepulchro.	
He for our saik that sufferit to be slane	
And lyk a lamb in sacrifice wes dicht	made ready
Is lyk a lyone rissin up agane	
And as gyane raxit him on hicht.	giant stretched himself on high
Sprungin is Aurora radius and bricht;	risen is Dawn, radiant
On loft is gone the glorious Appollo;	into the heavens; the sun
The blisfull day depairtit fro the nycht:	separated from
Surrexit Dominus de sepulchro.	
The grit victour agane is rissin on hicht	great
That for our querrell to the deth wes woundit.	cause
The sone that wox all paill now schynis bricht,	sun, grew
And, dirknes clerit, our fayth is now refoundit.	
The knell of mercy fra the hevin is soundit,	
The Cristin ar deliverit of thair wo;	Christians
The Jowis and thair errour ar confoundit:	Jews
Surrexit Dominus de sepulchro.	

The fo is chasit, the batteil is done ceis; — ended
The presone brokin, the jevellouris fleit and flemit; — gaolers frightened away
The weir is gon, confermit is the peis, — war; ended
The fetteris lowsit and the dungeoun temit; — fetters unbound; emptied
The ransoun maid, the presoneris redemit; — prisoners redeemed
The feild is win, ourcumin is the fo, — field is won
Dispulit of the tresur that he yemit: — guarded
Surrexit Dominus de sepulchro.

HALE, STERNE SUPERNE

Hale, sterne superne, hale, in eterne, — star on high; eternity
In Godis sicht to schyne:
Lucerne in derne for to discerne, — lantern; darkness by which to see
Be glory and grace devyne! — By
Hodiern, modern, sempitern, — for this day and this age and forever
Angelicall regyne, — queen of angels
Our tern inferne for to dispern, — darkness; hellish; disperse
Helpe, rialest roysne — most royal rose
Ave Maria, gracia plena: — *Hail Mary, full of grace*
Haile, fresche floure femynyne; — fresh flower womanly
Yerne us guberne, virgin matern, — diligently; govern; mother
Of reuth baith rute and ryne. — pity; root and bush

Haile, yhyng benyng fresche flurising, — young; gentle; blossoming
Haile, Alphais habitakle! — of Alpha; dwelling place
Thy dyng ofspring maid us to syng — worthy
Befor his tabernakle.
All thing maling we doune thring — malign; thrust down
Be sicht of his signakle, — sign
Quhilk king us bring unto his ryng — which; kingdom
Fro dethis dirk umbrakle. — from death's dark shadow
Ave Maria, gracia plena:
Haile, moder and maide but makle; — mother; without stain
Bricht syng, gladyng our languissing — sign bringing joy to our sorrow
Be micht of thi mirakle. — power

Haile, bricht be sicht in hevyn on hicht, — bright to look upon; heaven on high
Haile, day-sterne orientale! — day-star of the east
Our licht most richt in clud of nycht, — light; true; cloud; night
Our dirknes for to scale. — darkness to disperse
Hale, wicht in ficht, puttar to flicht — valiant in fight
Of fendis in battale! — fiends
Haile, plicht but sicht, hale, mekle of mycht, — unclear; unseen; great in power
Haile, glorious virgin, hale!
Ave Maria, gracia plena:
Haile, gentill nychttingale, — gracious nightingale

Way stricht, cler dicht, to wilsome wicht	straight; clearly marked
That irke bene in travale.	are weary in journeying

Hale, qwene serene, hale, most amene,	kindly
Haile, hevinlie hie empyrs!	high empress
Haile, schene, unseyne with carnale eyne,	beautiful one; unseen; eyes
Haile, ros of paradys!	
Haile, clene bedene ay till conteyne,	wholly pure; ever to continue
Haile, fair fresche floure-de-lyce,	lily
Haile, grene daseyne, haile fro the splene,	fresh daisy; from the heart
Of Jesu genitrice!	begetter
Ave Maria, gracia plena:	
Thow baire the prince of prys,	bore; glory
Our teyne to meyne and ga betweyne,	affliction; mediate
As humile oratrice.	humble intercessor

Haile, more decore than of before	beautiful
And swetar be sic sevyne!	sweeter by seven such
Our glore forlore for to restore	glory gone
Sen thow art quene of hevyn.	since
Memore of sore, stern in aurore,	mindful of our grief; star at dawn
Lovit with angellis stevyne,	praised by angels' voices
Implore, adore, thow indeflore,	virgin
To mak our oddis evyne!	forgive our sins
Ave Maria, gracia plena:	
With lovingis lowde ellevyn	praises; eleven
Quhill store and hore my youth devore,	adversity; old age; devour
Thy name I sall ay nevyne.	shall; name

Empryce of prys, imperatrice,	empress
Bricht polist precious stane,	polished
Victrice of vyce, hie genitrice	conqueror
Of Jesu lord soverayne,	
Our wys pavys fro enemys	wise; shield
Agane the feyndis trayne,	against the fiend's deception
Oratrice, mediatrice, salvatrice,	mediator, saviour
To God gret suffragane!	great assistant
Ave Maria, gracia plena;	
Haile, sterne meridiane,	star of midday
Spyce, flour-de-lice of paradys,	spice
That baire the gloryus grayne.	seed

Imperiall wall, place palestrall — magnificent palace
    Of peirles pulcritud, — peerless beauty
Tryumphale hall, hie trone regall — royal throne
    Of Godis celsitud! — God's majesty
Hospitall riall, the lord of all — royal refuge
    Thy closet did include, — chamber; enclose
Bricht ball cristall, ros virginall, — globe; crystal
    Fulfillit of angell fude, — filled with the food of angels
        Ave Maria, gracia plena:
    Thy birth has with his blude — child; blood
Fra fall mortall originall — from the first fall which brought death
    Us raunsound on the rude. — ransomed; cross

THE DREGY OF DUNBAR

We that ar heir in hevins glory,
To yow that ar in purgatory,
Commendis us on our hairtly wyis;
I mene we folk in parradyis,
In Edinburch with all mirrines,
To yow of Strivilling in distres, Stirling
Quhair nowdir plesance nor delyt is, neither
For pety this epistell wrytis.
O ! ye heremeitis and hankersaidilis, anchorites
That takis your pennance at your tablis,
And eitis nocht meit restorative,
Nor drynkis no wyn confortative,
Nor aill bot that is thyn and small,
With few coursis into your hall,
But cumpany of lordis and knychtis, without
Or ony uder gudly wichtis,
Solitar walkand your allone, walking alone
Seing no thing bot stok and stone; lifeless things
Out of your panefull purgatory,
To bring yow to the blis and glory
Off Edinburgh, the mirry toun,
We sall begyn ane cairfull soun,
Ane dergy devoit and meik, dirge
The Lord of blis doing beseik
Yow to delyver out of your noy, annoyance
And bring yow sone to Edinburgh joy,
For to be mirry amang us;
And sa the dergy begynis thus.

Lectio prima.
The Fader, the Sone, and Haly Gaist,
The mirthfull Mary virgene chaist,
Of angellis all the ordouris nyne,
And all the hevinly court devyne,
Sone bring yow fra the pyne and wo pain
Of Strivilling, every court manis fo,
Agane to Edinburghis joy and blis,

Quhair wirschep, welth, and weilfar is,
Pley, plesance, and eik honesty: — also
Say ye amen for cheritie.

Responsio, Tu autem Domine.
Tak consolatioun In your pane,
In tribulatioun Tak consolatioun,
Out of vexatioun Cum hame agane,
Tak consolatioun In your pane.

Iube Domine benedicere.
Oute of distress of Strivilling toun
To Edinburch blis, God mak yow boun. — ready

Lectio secunda.
Patriarchis, profeitis, and appostillis deir,
Confessouris, virgynis, and marteris cleir,
And all the saitt celestiall, — assembly
Devotely we upoun thame call,
That sone out of your panis fell, — awful pains
Ye may in hevin heir with us dwell,
To eit swan, cran, pertrik, and plever, — crane, partridge
And every fische that swymis in rever;
To drynk with us the new fresche wyne,
That grew upoun the rever of Ryne,
Fresche fragrant clairettis out of France,
Of Angers and of Orliance,
With mony ane cours of grit dyntie: — gourmet's delight
Say ye amen for cheritie.

Responsorium, Tu autem Domine.
God and Sanct Jeill Heir yow convoy — St Giles; convey
Baith sone and weill, God and Sanct Jeill
To sonce and seill, Solace and joy, — plenty and prosperity
God and sanct Geill Heir yow convoy.

Iube Domine benedicere.
Out of Strivilling panis fell, — pains; cruel
In Edinburch ioy sone mot ye dwell. — may

Lectio tertia
We pray to all the Sanctis of hevin,
That ar aboif the sterris sevin,
Yow to deliver out of your pennance,
That ye may sone play, sing, and dance
Heir in to Edinburch and mak gude cheir,
Quhair welth and weilfair is but weir; without war
And I that dois your panis discryve describe
Thinkis for to vissy yow belyve; visit; soon
Nocht in desert with yow to dwell,
Bot as the angell Sanct Gabriell
Dois go betwene fra hevinis glory
To thame that ar in purgatory,
And in thair tribulatioun
To gif thame consolatioun,
And schaw thame quhen thair panis ar past
They sall till hevin cum at last;
And how nane servis to haif sweitnes
That nevir taistit bittirnes,
And thairfoir how suld ye considdir
Of Edinburch bliss, quhen ye cum hiddir,
Bot gif ye taistit had befoir
Of Strivilling toun the panis soir;
And thairfoir tak in patience
Your pennance and your abstinence,
And ye sall cum, or Yule begyn, before
Into the bliss that we ar in;
Quhilk grant the glorious Trinitie!
Say ye amen for cheritie.

Responsorium.
Cum hame and dwell No moir in Strivilling;
Frome hiddous hell Cum hame and dwell,
Quhair fische to sell Is non bot spirling; spratlike
Cum hame and dwell No moir in Strivilling.

Et ne nos inducas in temptationem de Strivilling:
Sed libera nos a malo illius.
Requiem Edinburgi dona eiis, Domine,
Et lux ipsius luceat eiis.
A porta tristitie de Strivilling,
Erue, Domine, animas et corpora eorum.
Credo gustare statim vinum Edinburgi,
In villa viventium.
Requiescant Edinburgi. Amen.

Deus qui iustos et corde humiles
Ex omni eorum tribulatione liberare dignatus es,
Libera famulos tuos apud villam de Stirling versantes
A penis et tristitiis eiusdem,
Et ad Edinburgi gaudia eos perducas,
Ut requiescat Strivilling. Amen.

Note on 'The Dregy of Dunbar'

The *dregy* or *dirige* was named after the opening antiphon of the Office of the Dead, read at burial or memorial services: *Dirige, Deus meus, in conspectu tuo viam meam* (Direct my path, O God, in Thy sight). Dunbar partly follows its division into three lessons and their responses in shortened form: *Tu autem, domine* for 'And may you also, Lord, have mercy on us' and *Iube, domine* for 'Send us your blessing, Lord.'

The Latin in the final section opens with a parody of The Lord's Prayer, and proceeds to an ironic version of the conclusion of Lauds, sung after the Matins of the Dead:

> 'And lead us not into the temptation of Stirling, but deliver us from its evil. The peace of Edinburgh grant unto them, O Lord, and let its light shine upon them. Out of the gates of sadness in Stirling bring forth, O Lord, their bodies and their souls. I know that I shall taste the wine of Edinburgh in the habitation of the living. May they shortly rest in peace in Edinburgh. Amen.
>
> 'O God, who art pleased to set free the just and humble of heart from their sufferings, liberate now thy servants who dwell in the town of Stirling from the pain and sorrows of that place, and lead them happily to the joys of Edinburgh. Amen.'

GAVIN DOUGLAS

c.1476–1522

CONSCIENCE

Quhen halie kirk first flurist in youthheid, — the time of youth
Prelatis wer chosin of all perfectioun;
Off conscience than the brydill had to leid, — bridle
And conscience maid the hale electioun. — choice
Syn eftir that come schrewit correctioun, — cursed
And thocht that conscience had our large ane weid, — too big a coat
And of his habite out cuttit thay ane skreid. — shred

And fra conscience the *con* thay clip away,
And maid of conscience *science* and a na mair; — learning
Bot yit the kirk stude weill full mony day,
For it wes rewlit be mene of wit and layre. — knowledge
Sayn eftir that *sciens* began to payr, — grow worse
And thocht at *sciens* was our lang ane iaip. — too long a joke
The *sci* away fast can thay rub and scraip. — did

And fra *scie* of *science* wes adew, — parted
Than left thai nocht bot this sillab *ens*,
Quhilk in our language singnifies that schrew, — evil creature
Riches and geir, that gart all grace go hens; — made
For *sciens* both and faythfull conscience
So corruptit ar with this warldis gude
That falset ioukis in everie clerkis hude. — falsehood lodges

O hungerie *ens*, cursit with caris calde! — cold
All kynd of folk constrenis thow to wirk:
For the that theif Iudas his maister sald, — thee; sold
For the Symon infectit halie kirk.
To poysoun Iustis thow dois never irk.
Thow fals *ens*, go hens, thow monsture peralous!
God send defens with conscience in till ws. — unto us

GEORGE BUCHANAN

1506–1582

ELEGY ON JEAN CALVIN

Some may think life goes out like snuff: finis.
Other imagine spirits surviving but to hell
With that: literally: they scorn the pains to come,
They live with the roaring Styx on their shoulder.
Both would have a case for fears and tears,
Both ought to shudder and make others shudder.
But to us, Calvin, although you have been filched
In your mid-fifties from your helpless friends,
As if death had seen enough of your achievements,
Weeping and breast-beating are totally inappropriate,
All the oppression of a second burial,
Lachrymose lying verbal *pompes funèbres*.
For the dead weight of your body with its apprehensions
Has left you, you are beyond the stars, you nudge
God, you enjoy the one your mind adored,
You see pure light within pure light, you drink
Divinity poured brimming into you,
Your life has become an everlasting thing
Unanxious, impervious to empty-headed joys
Or devastating fears or the hammer of grief
Or the cancer of disease creeping from body to soul.
As for me, I call that morning which released you
From bitterest cares a very birthday: snatched
To the stars, you re-entered your old homeland,
You left a repellent exile behind, your mind
Scoffs at any second death, rules the supposed
Rule of fate, steps into the vista
Of an immeasurable life. Consider:
As the soul slides through the limbs of the body
At its awakening, impatient with the deadweight flesh,
Jetting its invigoration from head to heel,
So when it leaves, it leaves a stiffening shell
Without breath, leaves nothing but the crumbling
Of a foul mound of clay: and is that all, all?
But God is the soul of the soul. God absent,
The soul is wrapped in deepest darkness, prey
To mocks and fleers and prestidigitations,

Thinking shadows bright and evil good.
But give it its one great draught of godhead
And the dark dissolves and flickering phantoms go
And the naked face of truth lunges forward
In its eternal light, eternal day,
Resisting every twilight, every shadow
Cruel muffling night might try to bring.
You, Calvin, have earned and reached your haven
Where you rest in peace and calm, but grudging death
Could not but leave some part of you on the earth.
That part is the monuments, untarnishable,
Of your genius, and once the crackle and flash
Of mean-spirited envy has gone dark and dead,
Your fame will ripple out to every shore
Where the true faith shines.
                                        Where it does not,
Grey superstition will shiver at the mention
Of your ghostly name, at the gleam of the mask
Of your genius, just as in recent times
You struck fear into a wretched brace of mitres:
Clement the Seventh, total stranger to clemency,
Paul the Third, that famous pederast,
Paul the Fourth, more straightforward in viciousness,
Julius the Third, driven raging mad,
Pius the Fourth, from a brotherhood of impiety.
The usurper of the seat of good old Romulus,
The tyrant threatening stake and sword, the assumptor
Of the crown of hell, would-be Pluto of power,
Harpy of godly theft, Fury of heretic flames,
Charon ferrying indulgences, Carberus barking
Under his triple tiara, will be dazzled blind
By the light of invading truth and overthrown
By the thunder and terror of your tongue, and in the end
Will guarantee his own infernal punishments:
Parched with thirst as waters welter round him,
Pushing back the stone that will not stay there,
Pierced by beaks of liver-riving vultures,
Pouring liquids into sievelike pitchers,
Prostrated on a turning wheel of eternal fire.

translated from the Latin by Edwin Morgan

FOR CHRIST'S ASCENSION

Heads back and cheer, you crowds of faithful souls!
The enemy's defeated and your hero
Climbs high up to the bailey gates of Heaven,
Like any warrior badged with dust and blood
Straight from the fight, to let his Father hear
What the good wounds on head and torso say.
Clouds like a drawbridge drop to take his stride,
Heaven's gates swing open wide for him and all
His army to pass through, with songs of angels
Heralding their entry. Heaven shines; Hell pales.
The world, drymouthed, watches Death's tears fall.
Now veterans reckon up their just rewards:
Prince, with your Heavenly Father's strength and Spirit,
Help us footsoldiers find room at your feast.

translated from the Latin by James McGonigal

ATHAIRNE MAC EOGHAIN

*fl. c.*1558

WOE TO THE ONE WHO TAKES PRIDE IN YOUTH

Woe to the one who takes pride in youth,
in a borrowed form, in a grey eye,
in a graceful figure, in comely face,
in shining, soft, yellow, curling locks.

If God should have given to *you*, oh man,
– only deluded people do they deceive –
teeth like foam and a slender waist,
to you alone they are a dream.

The petals of life are false blossom,
it is dangerous for the body to aim to buy them,
do not take pride on account of the world,
all too soon will you be stripped of its leaves.

If even so you gain – no cause for pride –
the petals of life that do not last,
always keep in mind the state of man
that makes the world a foe to every one.

Remember the hoarding of hedgehogs,
dangerous for your garnering to be as they,
it will only entail your soul in pain,
from it do not expect the fruit of the earth.

With an apple on the tip of every spine
they carry them to a special place,
leaving the soft-turfed smooth-grassed wood
they leave them buried in a hole.

Thus will the fox of the world find you
oh body, resist spending your desires,
the soul at the mouth of the cave,
the most wretched of stories, oh body of clay.

All you have acquired of gold and wealth,
of horses and cows, though it were a wicked deed,
you will not be allowed any of them with you
but a linen shroud of this world, O man.

The body's ignorance is part of its pride,
our fear to go on up,
pride of youth is an ignoble thing to be despised
to be concerned with happiness is all the greater woe.

translated from the Classical Gaelic by Meg Bateman

JAMES, JOHN AND ROBERT WEDDERBURN

D.1553, 1556, 1557

from *THE GUDE AND GODLIE BALLATES* (1567)

THE CONCEPTIOUN OF CHRIST

Let vs reioce and sing,
And praise that michtie King,
  Quhilk send his Sone of a Virgine bricht. sent
    La. Lay. La.
And on him tuke our vyle nature,
Our deidlie woundis to cure,
  Mankynde to hald in richt.
    La. Lay. La.
Sanct Luk wrytis in his Gospell,
God fend his Angell Gabriell,
  Unto that Virgine but defame. without stain
    La. Lay. La.
For to fulfill the Prophesie,
Was spousit with Josaph fre,
  Mary scho had to name: she
    La. Lay. La.
Thir wordis to hir he did reheirs. These; rehearse
Haill Mary! full of grace,
  The Lord God is with thé.
    La. Lay. La.
Thow blyssit Virgine mylde,
Thow sall consaue ane Chylde
  The pepill redeme sall he:
    La. Lay. La.
Quhais power and greit micht,
Sall be in Goddis sicht,
  Quhilk from the Father of micht is send,
    La. Lay. La.

Jesus his name ye call,
Quhilk salbe Prince ouir all
    His Kingdome sall haue nane end.
        La.   Lay.   La.
Than spak that Virgin fre,
Behald, how sall this be,
    Seeing I knaw na man?
        La.   Lay.   La.
Than said the Angell chaist,
Be the power of the Haly Gaist,
    Quhilk all thing wirk he can.
        La.   Lay.   La.
Elizabeth thy cousing also,
Sex monethis with chylde can go,
    At quhais birth greit joy sall be:
        La.   Lay.   La.
Call him Johne, sayis the Angell bricht,
Quihilk is send be Goddis micht,
    The Lordis way prepair sall he.
        La.   Lay.   La.

VSQUE QUO DOMINE. PSAL. XXII, WITH THE TUNE OF EXAUDI, DEUS, ORATIONEM MEAM

O Lord, how lang for euer wil thow forget,
And hyde thy face fra me, or yit how lang
Sall I reheirs thy counsell in my hart?
Quhen sall my hart ceis of this sorie sang?
O Lord, behald, help me, and licht my eine,
That suddand sleip of deid do me na teine. does not vex me

Or ellis quhen my enemies seis my fall,
We did preuaill, sone will thay say on me:
And gif thay se me be thame brocht in thrall,
Thay will reioyce into thair tyrannie
Bot I in God hes hope, and traist to se
His godly help, than sall I loue the Lord
Quhilk did me saue fra them that had me schord. menaced

MUSING GREITLIE IN MY MYNDE

Mvsing greitlie in my mynde,
The folie that is in mankynde,
Quhilk is sa brukill and sa blind, brittle
　　And downe sall cum, downe ay, downe ay.

Leuand maist part in all vice, Living
Nouther sa gracious, nor sa wyse,
As out of wretchitnes to ryse,
　　Bot downe to cum, downe ay, downe ay.

And all this warld to weild thow had,
Thy body perfit and properlie maid,
Yit man, as floure, thow sall said,
　　And downe thow sall cum, downe ay.

Thocht thow war euer eternall,
As man that neuer fuld haue ane fall,
Yit doutles die thow sall,
　　And downe sall cum, downe ay, downe ay.

Thocht thow war man neuer sa thrall powerful
Remember yit that die thow sall;
Quha hiest clymmis gettis greitest sall,
　　And downe sall cum, downe ay, downe ay.

Thocht thow war neuer of sa greit degre,
In riches nor in dignitie,
Remember, man, that thow mon die, must
　　And downe sall cum, downe ay, downe ay.

Thair is na King, nor Empreour,
Duke, nor Lord of greit valure,
Bot he sall faid as lely floure,
　　And downe sall cum, downe ay, downe ay.

Quhair is Adam, and Eve his wyfe,
And Hercules, with his lang stryfe,
And Matussalem, with his lang lyfe? Methuselah
　　Thay all ar cum downe ay, downe ay.

WITH HUNTIS VP

With huntis vp, with huntis vp,
  It is now perfite day,
Jesus, our King, is gane in hunting,
  Quha lykis to speid thay may.

Ane cursit fox lay hid in rox
  This lang and mony ane day,
Deuouring scheip, quhill he micht creip, frighten
  Nane micht him schaip away.

It did him gude to laip the blude lap
  Of young and tender lammis,
Nane culd he mis, for all was his,
  The young anis with thair dammis.

The hunter is Christ, that huntis in haist,
  The hundis ar Peter and Paull,
The Paip is the foxe, Rome is the rox,
  The rubbis vs on the gall.

That cruell beist, he neuer ceist,
  Be his vsurpit power,
Under dispens to get our penneis, pennies
  Our saulis to deuoir.

Quha culd deuyse sic merchandise
  As he had thair to sell,
Onles it war proud Lucifer,
  The greit maister of Hell.

He had to sell the Tantonie bell, St Anthony's bell
  And pardonis thairin was;
Remissioun of sinnis in auld scheip skinnis,
  Our saulis to bring from grace.

With bullis of leid, quhyte wax and reid, papal Bulls
  And vther quhylis with grene,
Closit in ane box, this vsit the fox,
  Sic peltrie was neuer sene. rubbish

With dispensatiounis and obligatiounis,
  According to his law,
He wald dispens, for money from hence,
  With thame he neuer saw.

To curs and ban the sempill pure man,
  That had nocht to flé the paine;
Bot quhen he had payit all to ane myte, to his last mite
  He mon be obsoluit than. must be absolved then

To sum, God wot, he gaue tot quot, as directed
  And vther sum pluralitie; openly
Bot first with pennies he mon dispens,
  Or ellis it will nocht be.

Kingis to marie, and sum to tarie, marry
  Sic is his power and micht,
Quha that hes gold, with him will he hold,
  Thocht it be contrair all richt. against

O blissit Peter, the foxe is ane lier,
  Thow knawis weill it is nocht sa,
Quhill at the last, he salbe downe cast
  His peltrie, pardonis, and all. rubbish

WILLIAM KETHE

c.1530–1594

PSALM C

All people that on earth do dwell,
Sing to the Lord with cheerful voice.
Him serve with mirth, his praise forth tell,
Come ye before him and rejoice.

Know that the Lord is God indeed;
Without our aid he did us make:
We are his flock, he doth us feed,
And for his sheep he doth us take.

O enter then his gates with praise,
Approach with joy his courts unto:
Praise, laud, and bless his name always,
For it is seemly so to do.

For why? the Lord our God is good,
His mercy is for ever sure;
His truth at all times firmly stood,
And shall from age to age endure.

ATTRIBUTED TO MARY, QUEEN OF SCOTS

1542–1587

PRAYER BEFORE EXECUTION

O merciful Father, my hope is in thee!
O Gracious Redeemer, deliver thou me!
My bondage bemoaning, with sorrowful groaning,
  I long to be free;
Lamenting, relenting and humbly repenting,
O Jesu, my Saviour, I languish for thee!

translated from the Latin anonymously

ALEXANDER HUME

c.1557–1609

OF THE DAY ESTIVALL — midsummer

O perfite light, quhilk schaid away — divided
The darkenes from the light,
And set a ruler ou'r the day,
Ane uther ou'r the night;

Thy glorie when the day foorth flies
Mair vively dois appeare — vividly
Nor at midday unto our eyes — than
The shining sun is cleare.

The shaddow of the earth anon
Remooves and drawes by,
Sine in the east, when it is gon, — then
Appeares a clearer sky;

Quhilk sunne perceaves the little larks, — which; soon
The lapwing and the snyp, — snipe
And tunes their sangs like Natures clarks,
Ou'r midow, mure and stryp. — meadow; stream

Bot everie bais'd nocturnall beast — frightened
Na langer may abide;
They hy away, baith maist and least, — hurry
Them selves in house to hide.

They dread the day, fra thay it see, — when
And from the sight of men
To saits and covars fast they flee, — dens and coverts
And lyons to their den.

Oure hemisphere is poleist clein, — polished
And lightened more and more,
While everie thing be clearely sein, — until
Quhilk seemed dim before;

Except the glistering astres bright,   stars
Which all the night were cleere,
Offusked with a greater light   obscured
Na langer dois appeare.

The golden globe incontinent   immediately
Sets up his shining head,
And ou'r the earth and firmament
Displays his beims abread.   abroad

For joy the birds with boulden throts,   swollen
Agains his visage shein,   against; bright
Takes up their kindelie musicke nots   natural notes
In woods and gardens grein.

Up braids the carefull husbandman,   rises; farmer
His cornes and vines to see,
And everie tymous artisan,   early
In buith worke busilie.   covered stall

The pastor quits the slouthfull sleepe   shepherd
And passis forth with speede,
His little camow-nosed sheepe   snub
And rowtting kie to feede.   lowing cattle

The passenger from perrels sure   traveller
Gangs gladly foorth the way:
Breife, everie living creature   in brief
Takes comfort of the day.

The subtile, mottie rayons light   containing motes; beams of light
At rifts thay are in wonne,   entered
The glansing thains and vitre bright   sparkling vanes; glass
Resplends against the sunne.   shines

The dew upon the tender crops,
Lyke pearles white and round
Or like to melted silver drops,
Refreshes all the ground.

The mystie rocke, the clouds of raine,   vapour
From tops of mountaines skails,   evaporates
Cleare are the highest hils and plaine,
The vapors takes the vails.

Begaried is the saphire pend ornamented; vault
With spraings of skarlet hew, streaks
And preciously from end till end
Damasked white and blew. patterned

The ample heaven of fabrik sure workmanship
In cleannes dois surpas
The chrystall and the silver pure,
Or clearest poleist glas.

The time sa tranquill is and still,
That nawhere sall ye find.
Saife on ane high and barren hill, except
Ane aire of peeping wind. piping

All trees and simples, great and small, herbs
That balmie leife do beir,
Nor thay were painted on a wall, than if
Na mair they move or steir. stir

Calme is the deepe and purpour se,
Yee, smuther nor the sand; Indeed, smoother than
The wals that woltring wont to be waves; tossing
Are stable like the land.

Sa silent is the cessile air, yielding
That every cry and call,
The hils and dails and forrest fair
Againe repeates them all.

The rivers fresh, the callor streames. cool
Ou'r rockes can softlie rin,
The water cleare like chrystall seames,
And makes a pleasant din.

The fields and earthly superfice surface
With verdure greene is spread,
And naturallie, bur artifice, without
In partie coulors cled.

The flurishes and fragrant flowres, blossoms
Throw Phoebus fostring heit, god of the sun
Refresht with dew and silver showres,
Casts up ane odor sweit.

The clogged, busie, bumming beis,   laden
That never thinks to drowne,
On flowers and flourishes of treis
Collects their liquor browne.

The sunne maist like a speedie post   messenger
With ardent course ascends,
The beautie of the heavenly host
Up to our zenith tends;

Nocht guided be na Phaeton
Nor trained in a chyre   drawn; by; chariot
Bot be the high and haly On,
Quhilk dois allwhere impire.   govern

The burning beims downe from his face
Sa fervently can beat,
That man and beast now seekes a place
To save them fra the heat.

The brethles flocks drawes to the shade
And frechure of their fald,   freshness
The startling nolt, as they were made,   stampeding cattle; mad
Runnes to the rivers cald.

The heards beneath some leaffie trie,   shepherds
Amids the flowers they lie,
The stabill ships upon the sey   still
Tends up their sails to drie.   stretch

The hart, the hynd, and fallow deare
Are tapisht at their rest,   are crouching
The foules and birdes that made the beare   noise
Prepares their prettie nest.

The rayons dures descending downe   harsh rays
All kindlis in a gleid,   low coal
In cittie nor in borroughstowne   burgh
May nane set foorth their heid.

Back from the blew paymented whun   whinstone pavement
And from ilk plaister wall
The hote reflexing of the sun
Inflams the aire and all.

The labowrers that timellie raise,	early
All weerie, faint and weake,	
For heate downe to their houses gaise,	
Noone meate and sleepe to take.	midday meal
The callowr wine in cave is sought,	cool; cellar
Mens brothing breists to cule;	sweating, cool
The water cald and cleare is brought,	
And sallets steipt in ule.	salads; oil
Some plucks the honie plowm and peare,	plum
The cherrie and the pesche,	peach
Sume likes the reymand London beare,	foaming
The bodie to refresh.	
Forth of their skepps some raging bees	hives
Lyes out and will not cast,	settle outside; swarm
Some uther swarmes hyves on the trees,	make hives
In knots togidder fast.	clusters
The corbeis and the kekling kais	crows; cackling jackdaws
May scarce the heate abide,	
Halks prunyeis on the sunnie brais	hawks preen
And wedders back and side.	sun bathes
With gilted eyes and open wings	gilded
The cock his courage shawes,	
With claps of joy his breast he dings,	strikes
And twentie times he crawes.	
The dow with whisling wings sa blew	dove
The winds can fast collect,	
Hir pourpour pennes turnes mony hew,	purple feathers
Against the sunne direct.	
Now noone is went, gaine is mid-day,	gone
The heat dois slake at last,	
The sunne descends downe west away,	
Fra three of clock be past.	
A little cule of braithing wind	gentle
Now softly can arise,	
The warks throw heate that lay behind	
Now men may enterprise.	

Furth fairis the flocks to seeke their fude
On everie hill and plaine,
Ilk labourer, as he thinks gude,
Steppes to his turne againe.

The rayons of the sunne, we see,
Diminish in their strength,
The schad of everie towre and tree   shadow
Extended is in length.

Great is the calme, for everiequhair
The wind is sitten downe,   settled
The reik thrawes right up in the air   smoke curls
From everie towre and towne.

Their firdoning the bony birds   warbling
In banks they do begin,
With pipes of reides the jolie hirds   shepherds
Halds up the mirrie din.

The maveis and the philomeen,   thrush; nightingale
The stirling whissilles lowd,   starling
The cuschetts on the branches green   pigeons
Full quietly they crowd.   coo

The gloming comes, the day is spent,   dusk
The sun goes out of sight,
And painted is the occident   west
With pourpour sanguine bright.   blood-red

The skarlet nor the golden threid,   scarlet cloth
Who would their beawtie trie,
Are nathing like the colour reid
And beautie of the sky.

Our west horizon circuler,
Fra time the sunne be set,
Is all with rubies (as it wer)
Or rosis reid ou'rfret.   embroidered

What pleasour were to walke and see,
Endlang a river cleare,   along
The perfite forme of everie tree
Within the deepe appeare!

The salmon out of cruifs and creils   wickwork traps; basket traps
Up hailed into skowts,   pulled; flat-bottomed boats
The bels and circles on the weills,   bubbles; pools
Throw lowpping of the trouts.   leaping

O, then it were a seemely thing,
While all is still calme,
The praise of God to play and sing,
With cornet and with shalme.   woodwind instrument

Bot now the hirds with mony schout
Cals uther be their name:
'Ga, Billie, turne our gude about,   beasts
Now time is to go hame.'

With bellie fow the beastes belive   full; quickly
Are turned fra the corne,
Quhilk soberly they hameward drive,
With pipe and lilting horne.

Throw all the land great is the gild   clamour
Of rustik folk that crie,
Of bleiting sheepe fra they be fild,
Of calves and rowting ky.   lowing cattle

All labourers drawes hame at even,
And can till uther say,
Thankes to the gracious God of heaven,
Quhilk send this summer day.   sent

DONNCHADH MacRAOIRIDH

D. *c*. 1630

CEITHIR RAINN DO RINNEADH LEIS AN LÀ A D'EUG SE

Beir mise leat, a Mhic Dè,
  Agad fèin a b'ait leam tàmh;
Cum air do shlighe gu dlùth
  Mo chridhe is mo rùn 's mo ghràdh.

M'ùrnaigh agus m'aithrigh bhuan
  Bhith agad gach uair 's gach tràth;
Nar peacaidh uile leig linn –
  Tuilleadh cha dèan sinn gu bràth.

Achain eile dh'iarrmaid ort,
  Feudaidh do thoil-s' thobhairt dùinn:
An t-anam bhith agad fèin
  'S a' cholann chrè dhol san ùir.

Gu bhith air cathair nan àgh
  Cuide ri càch far a bheil,
Bho is tu as fiosraich mar a tàim
  Beir mise leat tràth is beir.

FOUR VERSES MADE BY HIM THE DAY HE DIED

Take me with You, Son of God,
  with You I'd gladly live;
and keep these three close to Your path:
  my heart, my wish, my love.

May all my prayers be with You now,
  my tears forever flow;
forgive my every sin –
  I can commit no more.

One other gift I ask of You,
  – and grant it soon, I trust:
that You will catch hold of the soul
  when my clay meets earth's dust.

To be standing soon at the throne of joy,
  part of the happy crowd;
since You can see the truth in me,
  Christ, take me with You – now.

translated from the Gaelic by Meg Bateman and James McGonigal

ELIZABETH MELVILLE OF CULROSS, LADY CUMRIE

fl. 1599–1631

from ANE GODLIE DREAME

CHRIST SPEAKS TO THE DREAMER WHO HOPES TO SEE HEAVEN

I am the way, I am the treuth and lyfe,
I am thy spous that brings thee store of grace:
I am thy luif, quohom thou wald faine imbrace,
I am thy joy, I am thy rest and peace.
Ryse up anone and follow efter mee,
I sall the leid into thy dwelling place:
The Land of rest thou langs sa sair to sie
I am thy Lord that sone sall end thy race.

With joyfull heart I thankit him againe,
Reddie am I (said I) and weill content
To follow thee, for heir I leive in paine,
O wretch unworth, my dayes ar vainlie spent.
Nocht ane is just bot all ar fearcelie bent,
To rin to vyce, I have na force to stand:
My sinnes increase quhilk maks me sair lament,
Mak haist, O Lord, I lang to sie that Land.

WILLIAM DRUMMOND OF HAWTHORNDEN

1585–1649

from FLOWRES OF SION

[*Sonnet vi*]

THE BOOKE OF THE WORLD

Of this faire Volumne which wee World doe name,
If wee the sheetes and leaues could turne with care,
Of Him who it correctes, and did it frame,
Wee cleare might read the Art and Wisedome rare?
Finde out his Power which wildest Pow'rs doth tame,
His Prouidence extending euerie-where,
His Iustice which proud Rebels doeth not spare,
In euerie Page, no, Period of the same:
But sillie wee (like foolish Children) rest
Well pleas'd with colour'd Velame, Leaues of Gold,
Faire dangling Ribbones, leauing what is best,
On the great Writers sense nee'r taking hold;
Or if by chance our Mindes doe muse on ought,
It is some Picture on the Margine wrought.

[*Sonnet viii*]

THE ANGELS FOR THE NATIVITIE OF OUR LORD

Runne (Sheepheards) run where *Bethleme* blest appeares,
Wee bring the best of newes, bee not dismay'd,
A Saviour there is borne, more olde than yeares,
Amidst Heavens rolling hights this Earth who stay'd;
In a poore Cotage Inn'd, a Virgine Maide
A weakling did him beare, who all upbeares,
There is hee poorelie swadl'd, in Manger lai'd,
To whom too narrow Swadlings are our Spheares:
Runne (Sheepheards) runne, and solemnize his Birth,
This is that Night, no, Day growne great with Blisse,

In which the power of *Sathan* broken is,
In Heaven bee glorie, Peace unto the Earth.
  Thus singing through the Aire the Angels swame,
  And Cope of Starres re-echoed the same.

[*Sonnet xi*]

FOR THE BAPTISTE

The last and greatest Herauld of Heauens King,
Girt with rough Skinnes, hyes to the Desarts wilde,
Among that sauage brood the Woods foorth bring,
Which hee than Man more harmlesse found and milde:
His food was Blossomes, and what young doth spring,
With Honey that from virgine Hiues distil'd;
Parcht Bodie, hollow Eyes, some vncouth thing
Made him appeare, long since from Earth exilde.
There burst hee foorth; All yee, whose Hopes relye
On God, with mee amidst these Desarts mourne,
Repent, repent, and from olde errours turne.
Who listned to his voyce, obey'd his crye?
  Onelie the Ecchoes which hee made relent,
  Rung from their Marble Caues, repent, repent.

[*Sonnet xii*]

FOR THE MAGDALENE

These Eyes (deare Lord) once Brandons of Desire,
Fraile Scoutes betraying what they had to keepe,
Which their owne heart, then others set on fire,
Their traitrous blacke before thee heere out-weepe:
These Lockes, of blushing deedes the faire attire,
Smooth-frizled Waues, sad Shelfes which shadow deepe,
Soule-stinging Serpents in gilt curles which creepe,
To touch thy sacred Feete doe now aspire.
In Seas of Care behold a sinking Barke,
By windes of sharpe Remorse vnto thee driuen,
O let mee not expos'd be Ruines marke,
My faults confest (Lord) say they are forgiuen.
  Thus sigh'd to Iesvs the Bethanian faire,
  His teare-wet Feete still drying with her Haire.

SIR WILLIAM MURE OF ROWALLAN

1594–1657

SONNET

O three times happie, if the day of grace
In my darke soule did (though but dimly) dawne,
If to my struggling thoughts proclamd were peace,
If from mine eyes the vaile of darknesse drawne,
If once the seed of true repentance sawne
Made gushing streames leave furrowes on my face;
Sinnes menstruous rags in pure transparent laune
Were chang't, O then how happie were my cace!
So darknesse paths no more my feete should trace,
So ever on a quyet conscience feast
Repentance planted so should vice displace,
So clenst from sinne, sinne's filth I should detest!
Grace, light, repentance, inward peace I crave,
Grant these, good Lord, for mee thy selfe who gave.

JAMES GRAHAM, MARQUIS OF MONTROSE

1612–1650

ON HIMSELF, UPON HEARING WHAT WAS HIS SENTENCE

Let them bestow on ev'ry Airth a Limb;
Open all my Veins, that I may swim
To Thee my Saviour, in that Crimson Lake;
Then place my purboil'd Head upon a Stake;
Scatter my Ashes, throw them in the Air:
Lord (since Thou know'st where all these Atoms are)
I'm hopeful, once Thou'lt recollect my Dust,
And confident Thou'lt raise me with the Just.

A COMMITTEE OF THE GENERAL ASSEMBLY OF THE CHURCH OF SCOTLAND

1650

from THE PSALMS OF DAVID IN METRE

PSALM XXIII

The Lord's my shepherd, I'll not want.
  He makes me down to lie
In pastures green: he leadeth me
  the quiet waters by.

My soul he doth restore again;
  and me to walk doth make
Within the paths of righteousness,
  ev'n for his own name's sake.

Yea, though I walk in death's dark vale,
  yet will I fear none ill:
For thou art with me; and thy rod
  and staff me comfort still.

My table thou hast furnished
  in presence of my foes;
My head thou dost with oil anoint,
  and my cup overflows.

Goodness and mercy all my life
  shall surely follow me:
And in God's house for evermore
  my dwelling-place shall be.

PSALM CXXI

I to the hills will lift mine eyes,
    from whence doth come mine aid.
My safety cometh from the Lord,
    who heav'n and earth hath made.
Thy foot he'll not let slide, nor will
    he slumber that thee keeps.
Behold, he that keeps Israel,
    he slumbers not, nor sleeps.

The Lord thee keeps, the Lord thy shade
    on thy right hand doth stay:
The moon by night thee shall not smite,
    nor yet the sun by day.
The Lord shall keep thy soul; he shall
    preserve thee from all ill.
Henceforth thy going out and in
    God keep for ever will.

PSALM CXXVIII

Bless'd is each one that fears the Lord,
    and walketh in his ways;
For of thy labour thou shalt eat,
    and happy be always.
Thy wife shall as a fruitful vine
    by thy house' sides be found:
Thy children like to olive-plants
    about thy table round.

Behold, the man that fears the Lord,
    thus blessed shall he be,
The Lord shall out of Sion give
    his blessing unto thee:
Thou shalt Jerus'lem's good behold
    whilst thou on earth dost dwell.
Thou shalt thy children's children see,
    and peace on Israel.

SÌLEAS NA CEAPAICH/ SILEAS MacDONALD

c.1660–c.1729

LAOIDH AIR BÀS A FIR AGUS A H-IGHNE

'S mór mo mhulad 's mi 'm ònar,
  'S mi 'm shuidhe ann an seòmar gun luaidh,
Is nach faic mi tighinn dachaigh
  Fear cumail mo chleachdaidh a suas,
Fear a dh'fhadadh mo theine
  Is a dh'éigheadh gach deireas a nuas:
Ona chaidh sibh an taisgeadh
  'S goirt a chaochail mo chraiceann a shnuadh.

'S tric mo shùilean ri dòrtadh
  Ona thug iad thu Mhòr-chlaich a suas,
'S nach faic mise 'n t-àite
  'S an do chuir iad mo ghràdh-sa 's an uaigh;
Dh'fhàg sibh Anna aig a' bhaile
  'S bidh mise 'ga ghearan gu cruaidh,
A' sìor-amharc a' bhalla
  Aig na chuir iad i 'm falach gu buan.

'S mór mo mhulad 's mo chùram
  'Nuair a shileas mo shùilean gu làr,
Nach eil spiorad na h-ùmhlachd
  Ann am thaic 'ga mo ghiùlan na's fheàrr;
Gu dol air mo ghlùinibh
  'S 'gam liùbhairt do Phrionnsa nan Gràs,
On tha sgeula ro-chinnteach
  Gu bheil sinn uile fo chìs aig a' Bhàs.

Chan ann gu tighinn a rithisd
  Chaidh cuideachd mo chridhe-sa uam;
Gus an ruig mise iad-san
  Chan fhaicear leam iad gu Là Luain:
On nach tilleadh air ur n-ais duibh,
  Ach ur cnàimhean air seacadh 's an uaigh,
Righ dèan iochd ri ur n-anam
  'N comh-chomunn nan Aingeal tha shuas.

A HYMN ON THE DEATHS OF HER HUSBAND AND DAUGHTER

Great my sorrow and lonesomeness
as I sit in a room without talk,
with no sign of the man returning
who kept me the way I was wont,
a man who kindled my embers,
and sent out orders for anything we lacked,
since you were laid in the graveyard
the appearance of my skin has changed.

Since they took you up to Mortlach,
my eyes have often shed tears,
as I cannot see the resting place
where they laid my love in the grave;
I lament it sorely
that you all left Anna behind
as I stare at the wall
in which they have hidden her forever.

Great my sorrow and my worry
when my tears fall to the ground
that I do not have the spirit of humility
to give me better support
to go down on my knees
and yield myself to the Prince of Grace,
since it is certain knowledge
that we must all pay tribute to Death.

It is with no intention of returning
that I have been deserted by the ones that I love;
not until Doomsday
will I reach them and see them again;
since all that would return of you
were your bones withered in the grave,
Lord, have mercy on your souls
in communion with the angels above.

’S beag mo ghnothach ri féilltibh
    No dh’ amharc na réise ri m’ bheò,
No m’ aighear ri daoine:
    Chaidh mo chuid-sa dhiùbh cuide fo ’n fhòd;
Ona dh’fhalbh iad le chéile,
    An dithis nach tréigeadh mi beò,
Rìgh thoir dhomh-sa bhith leughadh
    Air an aithreachas gheur a bh’ aig Iòb.

’Nuair thig latha a’ bhràtha
    ’S bhios na trompaidean àghmhor ’gan seinn,
’S thig Crìosd anns a’ chathair
    Ghabhail cunntais is taca de chloinn,
Bidh na gobhair ’s na caoirich
    An sin air gach taobh dhe ’gan roinn:
’S mairg a théid anns an teine
    Nach teirig ’s nach deilich ri ’n druim.

Gheibh na caoirich an deas-làmh,
    ’S na gobhair am feasd an làmh chlì,
’S an uair bhios Crìosd a’ toirt breith:
    ‘Thigibh dhachaigh, a chlann a rinn sìth,
Gu rìoghachd ur n-Athar
    Far nach cluinn sibh ach aighear gun strì:
Sgriosar sìos a’ chuid eile
    Do ’n teine nach teirig a chaoidh.’

Glòir thoir do Mhac Muire
    Thug ’e ghibht domh gun d’fhuiling mi leòn,
Thug de bhròn ’s de leann-dubh dhomh
    Gus na theirig de m’ fhuil agus m’ fheòil,
Gus an tigeadh mo Shlànair
    A rithisd ’gam shàbhaladh beò;
Rìgh, glac m’ anam an latha ud
    ’S thoir suas e gu Cathair a’ Cheòil.

Little my interest in markets
or watching the race anymore
or making merry with others –
my own ones have gone below the sod,
since those two left together
who would never desert me in life,
God, make me start reading
of the bitter penance of Job.

On the day of Judgement
when the glorious trumpets sound,
when Christ takes account of His children
collecting their rents on His throne,
then the sheep and the goats will be parted,
shed off on His either side,
and woe to the ones for the furnace,
whose undying fire will never leave their backs.

The sheep will take the right-hand
and the goats the left
when Christ passes judgement:
'You children who made peace,
come home to your Father's Kingdom
where you will hear joy without strife;
let the others be cast asunder,
down to the eternal fire.'

Glory to the Son of Mary
who gifted me with suffering pain,
with so much grief and dejection
that my blood and my flesh have gone,
until the coming of my Saviour
restores me to life again;
on that day to the City of Music
take up my soul, O King.

translated from the Gaelic by Meg Bateman

ALLAN RAMSAY

1686–1758

THE MARROW BALLAD

On seeing a stroling congregation going to a field meeting, May 9th, 1738.

To the tune of: *Fy let us a' to the bridal.*

O fy, let us a' to the meeting,
  For there will be canting there, — tale-telling
Where some will be laughing, some greeting,
  At the preaching of Erskine and Mair.
Then rouze ye up, Robie and Willy!
  The lasies are raiking awa, — running
In petty-coats white as the lilly,
  And biggonets prind on fou braw. — linen caps; pinned; attractively

And there will be blinkan eyed Bessy,
  Blyth Baby, and sweet lipet Megg,
And mony a rosie cheek'd lassie
  With coats kiltet to their mid-legg.
To gar them gang clever and lightly,
  We'll carry their hose and their shoon; — stockings; shoes
Syne kiss them and clap them fou tightly, — fondle; very
  As soon as the sermon is done.

The sun will be sunk in the west
  Before they have finished the wark:
Then behind a whin bush we can rest,
  Ther's mekle good done in the dark. — much
There Tammy to Tibby may creep,
  Slee Sandy may mool in with Kate; — make love
While other dowf sauls are asleep, — unenergetic
  We'll handle deep matters of state.

And shou'd we deserve the black stools, penance stools
For geting a gamphrell with wean, fool
We'll answer we're no siccan fools
To obey them that have the oaths tane. taken
When the lave's to the parish kirk gawn, rest's
On Sundays – we'll rest us at hame,
An' runing to hills now and than
Makes it nowther a sin nor a shame. neither

Then up with the brethren true blew,
Wha lead us to siccan delight, such
And can prove it, altho they be few,
That ther is naebody else wha is right,
And doun with all government laws,
That are made by the Bishops of Baal,
And the thieves wha climb o'er the kirk waws walls
And come not in by a right call.

DONNCHADH NAM PÌOS

D.C.1700

RÌGH NA CRUINNE TA GUN CHRÌCH

Rìgh na cruinne ta gun chrìch,
 Dèan mi cuimhneach ort gach tràth;
Na leig air sheachran mi
 Air slighe ta baoith bàth.

Seòl mise san t-slighe cheart,
 Rìgh nam feart ta fos ar cionn;
An leth aon-Iosa, do Mhac,
 Math gach peacadh rinneadh liom.

Math dhom gach peacadh gu lèir
 Do rinneadh liom fèin a ghnàth,
Agus saor-sa mi bho lochd
 Bho is fiosrach thu nochd mar tàim.

Tàim-se nochd gu truagh,
 Tàim-se truaillidh amo chorp;
Ta mo chridhe-sa fo leòn,
 Ta peacadh bàis air mo lot.

Ach Fhir dh'fhuiling bàs ri crann
 Le pianta teann is cam bhreith,
Dìon-sa mise, a Mhic mo Dhè,
 Cuir-sa gu treun as mo leth.

Cruthaich unnam-s' cridhe nuadh,
 Fhir a chaidh san uaigh gun lochd,
Bho is fiosrach thu mar a tà
 An cridhe cnàmh namo chorp.

Deònaich dhom aithrigh gu tràth –
 Na leig-se mu làr mo dhìth,
Bho is tusa tobar gach gràis
 Bhuaineadh as gach càs mi, a Rìgh.

KING OF THE WORLD WITHOUT END

King of the world without end,
    make me mindful of you always;
do not suffer me to go astray
    on a path that is wicked and vain.

Guide me in the path that is right,
    King of all virtues in Heaven above;
forgive every sin committed by me,
    for the sake of Jesus, Your only Son.

Forgive utterly my every sin
    that I through habit have incurred,
and as You know how I am tonight
    deliver me from harm.

Tonight I am in deep despair,
    in my body I am corrupt;
my heart is wounded sore,
    mortal sin has me undone.

But Man who suffered death on the Cross
    with false judgement and agonising pains,
protect me, O Son of my God,
    do fierce battle for my sake.

Create in me a new heart,
    Man who went without sin to the grave,
since you know how the heart
    lies rotting in my frame.

Do not abandon me in my need,
    grant me penitence in time;
for You are the well of each grace
    that could pluck me from all danger, King.

translated from the Gaelic by Meg Bateman

ROB DONN

1714–1778

MARBHRANN DO CHLOINN FHIR TAIGH RUSPAINN

'Nan luighe seo gu h-ìosal
Far na thìodhlaic sinn an triùir
Bha fallain, làidir, inntinneach
Nuair dh' inntrig a' bhliadhn' ùr;
Cha deachaidh seachad fathast
Ach deich latha dhith o thùs;
Ciod fhios nach tig an teachdair-s' oirnn
Nas braise na ar dùil?

Am bliadhna thìm bha dithis diubh
Air tighinn on aon bhroinn,
Bha iad 'nan dà chomrad
O choinnich iad 'nan cloinn,
Cha d' bhris an t-aog an comann ud
Ged bu chomasach dha 'n roinn,
Ach gheàrr e snàth'nn na beath'-s' aca
Gun dàil ach latha 's oidhch'.

Aon duine 's bean on tàinig iad,
Na bràithrean seo a chuaidh,
Bha an aon bheatha thìmeil ac'
'S bha 'n aodach d 'an aon chluaimh,
Mun aon uair a bhàsaich iad
'S bha 'n nàdar d' an aon bhuaidh,
Chaidh 'n aon siubhal dhaoine leo
'S chaidh 'n sìneadh san aon uaigh.

Daoine nach d' rinn briseadh iad
'S e fiosrachail do chàch,
'S cha mhò a rinn iad aon dad
Ris an can an saoghal gràs,
Ach ghineadh iad, is rugadh iad,
Is thogadh iad, is dh' fhàs,
Chaidh stràchd d 'an t-saoghal theiris orr',
'S mu dheireadh fhuair iad bàs.

THE RISPOND MISERS

Lying in their lowly state
are three we buried here,
though they were strong and healthy,
and lively at New Year;
ten days only have gone by
since then – who can be sure
that our dread Summoner is not,
unknown to us, as near?

Within one year a pair of them
had come from the one womb,
and they had been close comrades
since their childhood in one room;
their fellowship is still intact,
unsevered by the tomb –
within two days Eternity
has plucked them from Time's loom.

These brothers now departed
came from one man and wife,
their clothes were made from the one fleece,
each lived the self-same life;
their deaths came close together,
their natures were alike,
the one procession bore their dust
and laid it out of sight.

These men broke no commandments,
as far as we can trace,
nor did their deeds show anything
of what the world calls grace;
they were conceived and brought to birth,
were nursed, and grew apace,
a swatch of life passed by them
and Death put them in their place.

Nach eil an guth seo labhrach
Ris gach aon neach againn beò,
Gu h-àraidh ris na seann daoinibh
Nach d' ionnsaich an staid phòsd',
Nach gabh na tha 'na dhleasdanas
A dheasachadh no lòn,
Ach caomhnadh nì gu falair dhoibh
'S a' falach an cuid òir?

Cha chaith iad fèin na rinn iad,
Agus oighreachan cha dèan,
Ach ulaidhnean air shliabh ac'
Bhios a' biathadh chon is eun.
Tha iad fon aon dìteadh,
Fo nach robh 's nach bi mi fhèin,
Gur duirche, taisgte 'n t-òr ac'
Na 'n uair bha e 'n tòs sa' mhèinn.

Barail ghlic an Aird Rìgh:
Dh' fhàg e pàirt de bhuidheann gann
Gu feuchainn iochd is oileanachd
D 'an dream d 'an tug e meall.
Carson nach tugteadh pòrsan
Dhe 'n cuid stòrais aig gach àm
Do bhochdaibh 'n Aoin a dheònaicheadh
An còrr a chur 'na cheann?

An dèidh na rinn mi rùsgadh dhuibh –
Tha dùil agam gun lochd –
'S a liuthad focal fìrinneach
A dhìrich mi nur n-uchd,
Tha eagal orm nach èisd sibh
Gu bhith feumail don a' bhochd
Nas mò na rinn na fleasgaich ud
A sheachdain gus a-nochd.

Surely this sounds a warning
to each one of us alive,
especially old bachelors,
unlearned in married love:
men who will not spend on food
the cash to which they cleave,
saving for a funeral feast
the gold that they must leave.

They'll never spend what they have made,
and make no heirs besides;
their treasures on the hillsides
are food for dogs and birds;
they stand condemned – though I can plead
'not guilty' in assize –
of hoarding darklier their gold
than ever did the mines.

The High King in His providence
wisely left some men short,
to test the sense of charity
of those who have a lot;
these should surely give a part
of all the wealth they've got
to His poor folk; He's ready
to increase their meagre stock.

In spite of this straight talking –
and I feel it's only right –
and all the words of truth I've put
directly in your sight,
I fear you will not listen,
or give the poor a bite,
any more than these did
a week ago tonight.

translated from the Gaelic by Derick Thomson

DUGHALL BOCHANAN/ DUGALD BUCHANAN

1716–1768

Bho LÀ A' BHREITHEANAIS

'N sin fàsaidh rudhadh anns an speur,
   Mar fhàir' na maidne 'g èirigh dearg,
Ag innse gu bheil Iosa fèin
   A' teachd 'na dhèidh le latha garbh.

Grad fhosglaidh às a chèil' na neòil,
   Mar dhoras seòmair an Ard-Rìgh,
Is foillsichear am Breitheamh mòr
   Le glòir is greadhnachas gun chrìoch.

Tha 'm bogha-frois mun cuairt d 'a cheann,
   'S mar thuil nan gleann tha fuaim a ghuth,
'S mar dhealanach tha sealladh 'shùl
   A' spùtadh às na neulaibh tiugh.

A' ghrian, àrd-lòcharan nan speur,
   Do ghlòir a phearsa gèillidh grad:
An deàlradh drillseach thig o 'ghnùis,
   A solas mùchaidh e air fad.

Cuiridh si uimpe culaidh bhròin,
   'S bidh 'ghealach mar gun dòirt' oirr' fuil;
Is crathar cumhachdan nan speur
   A' tilgeadh nan reult' às am bun.

Bidh iad air uideal anns an speur
   Mar mheas air gèig ri ànradh garbh,
Tuiteam mar bhraona dh' uisge dlùth,
   'S an glòir mar shùilean duine marbh.

Air carbad-teine suidhidh e,
   'S mun cuairt da beucaidh 'n tàirneanach,
A' dol le 'ghairm gu crìoch nan nèamh
   'S a' reub' nan neul gu doineannach.

from THE DAY OF JUDGEMENT

The heavens have a ruddy glow,
like morning dawn red in the sky,
telling us that Christ himself
comes in its wake with a rough day.

The clouds come suddenly apart,
an opening to the High King's room,
and the great Judge is then revealed,
in endless joy and glory come.

A rainbow placed around his head,
his voice's sound like glens in flood;
like lightning, glances from his eyes
come spouting from each darkling cloud.

The sun, high lantern of the skies,
bows down before the glorious sight;
his countenance's radiant sheen
entirely smothers the sun's light.

It puts the clothes of sorrow on;
the moon seems to be bathed in blood;
and heaven's powers are shaken sore,
wrenching each star out from its root.

Like fruit on branches tossed by storm
they waver weakly in the skies,
falling like drops of water fast,
their glory that of dead men's eyes.

On fiery chariot he sits
as thunder makes its roaring sounds,
ripping the clouds tempestuously
with calls that reach Heaven's outmost bounds.

O chuibhlibh 'charbaid thig a-mach
　Sruth mòr de theine laist' le feirg,
'S sgaoilidh 'n tuil ud air gach taobh
　A' cur an t-saoghail 'na lasair dheirg.

Leaghaidh na dùile nuas le teas,
　Ceart mar a leaghas teine cèir;
Na cnuic 's na sléibhtean lasaidh suas,
　'S bidh teas-ghoil air a' chuan gu lèir.

Na beannta iargalt' nach tug seach
　An stòras riamh do neach d' an deòin,
Ta iad gu fialaidh 'taosgadh mach
　An ionmhais leaght' mar abhainn mhòir.

Gach neach bha sgrìobadh cruinn an òir
　Le sannt, le dò-bheart no le fuil,
Làn chaisgibh nis bhur n-ìota mòr
　'S an asgaidh òlaibh dheth on tuil.

O sibhse rinn ur bun den t-saoghal,
　Nach tig sibh 's caoinibh e gu geur,
Nuair tha e gleacadh ris a' bhàs
　Mar dhuine làidir dol don eug.

A' chuisle chleachd bhith fallain fuar
　Ri mireag uaibhreach feadh nan gleann,
Tha teas a chlèibh ga smùidreadh suas
　Le goilibh buaireis feadh nam beann.

Nach faic sibh 'chrith tha air mun cuairt,
　'S gach creag a' fuasgladh anns gach sliabh!
Nach cluinn sibh osnaich throm a bhàis
　'S a chridhe sgàineadh staigh 'na chliabh!

An cùrtain gorm tha nunn on ghrèin,
　'S mun cuairt don chruinne-chè mar chleòc,
Crupaidh an lasair e r 'a chèil'
　Mar bheilleig air na h-èibhlibh beò.

Out from beneath his chariot's wheels
fire lit with wrath comes in a stream,
and that flood spreads on every side
till the whole world is a red flame.

The elements all melt with heat
as fire melts wax with its hot breath;
the hills and moors are all aflame
and all the oceans boil and seethe.

The fearsome mountains that by choice
never gave anyone their stores
now let their molten treasure out
as a great river freely pours.

All you who scraped with ploughs for gold,
greed-driven, prone to vice and blood,
now you can slake your desperate thirst
and drink your fill from out the flood.

O you who set on world your store,
come and lament with every breath,
as now it wrestles with its end
like a strong man approaching death.

The rill that once was hale and cold,
and bubbled proudly through the glens,
now has its hot and smoky breath
and fiercely boils among the bens.

Can you not see it trembling there
as the rocks gape on the high ground?
As its heart splits within its chest
can you not hear death's doleful sound?

The blue drape spread out from the sun,
cloaking the universe entire,
is wrinkled up by that red flame
like birch-tree bark in living fire.

translated from the Gaelic by Derick Thomson

ROBERT FERGUSSON

1750–1774

TO THE TRON-KIRK BELL

Wanwordy, crazy, dinsome thing, — Worthless; noisy
As e'er was fram'd to jow or ring, — toll
What gar'd them sic in steeple hing — made
  They ken themsel',
But weel wat I they coudna bring
  War sounds frae hell. — Worse

What de'il are ye? that I shud ban, — curse
Your neither kin to pat nor pan; — pot
Not uly pig, nor master-cann, — oil-vessel; piss-vessel
  But weel may gie
Mair pleasure to the ear o' man
  Than stroak o' thee.

Fleece merchants may look bald, I trow, — confident
Sin a' Auld Reikie's childer now — Edinburgh's children
Maun stap their lugs wi' teats o' woo, — wool
  Thy sound to bang, — overcome
And keep it frae gawn thro' and thro'
  Wi' jarrin' twang.

Your noisy tongue, there's nae abideint, — abiding
Like scaulding wife's, there is nae guideint; — guiding
Whan I'm 'bout ony bus'ness eident, — eager
  It's sair to thole;
To deave me, than, ye tak' a pride in't — stun
  Wi' senseless knoll.

O! war I provost o' the town,
I swear by a' the pow'rs aboon, — above
I'd bring ye wi' a reesle down; — clatter
  Nor shud you think
(Sae sair I'd crack and clour your crown) — batter
  Again to clink.

For whan I've toom'd the muckle cap, — emptied; cup
An' fain wud fa' owr in a nap, — eagerly
Troth I cud doze as sound's a tap, — top
  Wer't na for thee,
That gies the tither weary chap — the other
  To waukin me.

I dreamt ae night I saw Auld Nick;
Quo he, 'this bell o' mine's a trick,
A wylie piece o' politic,
  A cunnin snare
To trap fock in a cloven stick, — folk
  'Ere they're aware.

As lang's my dautit bell hings there, — fondled
A' body at the kirk will skair; — take fright
Quo they, 'gif he that preaches there
  Like it can wound,
We douna care a single hair
  For joyfu' sound.'

If magistrates wi' me wud 'gree,
For ay tongue-tackit shud you be, — with a speech impediment
Nor fleg wi' antimelody — frighten
  Sic honest fock,
Whase lugs were never made to dree — suffer
  Thy doolfu' shock.

But far frae thee the bailies dwell,
Or they wud scunner at your knell,
Gie the foul thief his riven bell,
  And than, I trow,
The by-word hads, 'the de'il himsel' — proverb holds
  Has got his due.'

JOB, CHAPTER III PARAPHRASED

Perish the fatal Day when I was born,
The Night with dreary darkness be forlorn;
The loathed, hateful, and lamented night
When Job, 'twas told, had first perceiv'd the light;
Let it be dark, nor let the God on high
Regard it with the favour of his eye;
Let blackest darkness and death's awful shade
Stain it, and make the trembling earth afraid;
Be it not join'd unto the varying year,
Nor to the fleeting months in swift career.
Lo! Let the night in solitude's dismay
Be dumb to joy, and waste in gloom away;
On it may twilight stars be never known;
Light let it wish for, Lord! but give it none;
Curse it let them who curse the passing day,
And to the voice of mourning raise the lay;
Nor ever be the face of dawning seen
To ope its lustre on th' enamel'd green;
Because it seal'd not up my *mother's womb*,
Nor hid from me the Sorrows doom'd to come.
Why have I not from *mother's womb* expir'd?
My life resign'd when life was first requir'd?
Why did supporting knees prevent my death,
Or suckling breasts sustain my infant breath?
For now my soul with quiet had been blest,
With kings and counsellors of earth at rest,
Who bade the house of desolation rise,
And awful ruin strike tyrannic eyes,
Or with the princes unto whom were told
Rich store of silver and corrupting gold;
Or, as untimely birth, I had not been,
Like infant who the light hath never seen;
For there the wicked from their trouble cease,

And there the weary find their lasting peace;
There the poor prisoners together rest,
Nor by the hand of injury opprest;
The small and great together mingl'd are,
And free the servant from his master there;
Say, Wherefore has an over-bounteous heaven
Light to the comfortless and wretched given?
Why should the troubl'd and oppress'd in soul
Fret over restless life's unsettled bowl,
Who long for death, who lists not to their pray'r,
And dig as for the treasures hid afar;
Who with excess of joy are blest and glad,
Rejoic'd when in the tomb of silence laid?
Why then is grateful light bestow'd on man,
Whose life is darkness, all his days a span?
For 'ere the morn return'd my sighing came,
My mourning pour'd out as the mountain stream;
Wild visag'd fear, with sorrow-mingled eye,
And wan destruction piteous star'd me nigh;
For though nor rest nor safety blest my soul,
New trouble came, new darkness, new controul.

JOHN MORISON

1750–1798

FROM HOSEA VI. 1–4

Come, let us to the Lord our God
With contrite hearts return:
Our God is gracious, nor will leave
The desolate to mourn.

His voice commands the tempest forth,
And stills the stormy wave;
And though His arm be strong to smite,
'Tis also strong to save.

Long hath the night of sorrow reigned,
The dawn shall bring us light:
God shall appear, and we shall rise
With gladness in His sight.

Our hearts, if God we seek to know,
Shall know Him, and rejoice;
His coming like the morn shall be,
Like morning songs His voice.

As dew upon the tender herb,
Diffusing fragrance round;
As showers that usher in the spring,
And cheer the thirsty ground:

So shall His presence bless our souls,
And shed a joyful light;
That hallowed morn shall chase away
The sorrows of the night.

ROBERT BURNS

1759–1796

HOLY WILLIE'S PRAYER

O Thou, wha in the heavens dost dwell,
Wha, as it pleases best thysel',
Sends ane to heaven and ten to hell,
A' for thy glory,
And no for ony guid or ill
They've done afore thee!

I bless and praise thy matchless might,
Whan thousands thou hast left in night,
That I am here afore thy sight,
For gifts an' grace
A burnin' an' a shinin' light
To a' this place.

What was I, or my generation,
That I should get such exaltation,
I wha deserve sic just damnation,
For broken laws,
Five thousand years 'fore my creation,
Thro' Adam's cause.

When frae my mither's womb I fell,
Thou might hae plunged me in hell,
To gnash my gums, to weep and wail,
In burnin' lake,
Whar damned devils roar and yell
Chain'd to a stake.

Yet I am here a chosen sample,
To show thy grace is great an' ample;
I'm here a pillar in thy temple,
Strong as a rock,
A guide, a buckler an' example
To a' thy flock.

But yet, O L—d! confess I must,
At times I'm fash'd wi' fleshly lust; troubled
An' sometimes too, wi' warldly trust
Vile self gets in;
But thou remembers we are dust,
Defil'd in sin.

O L—d! yestreen, thou kens, wi' Meg, yesterday; knows
Thy pardon I sincerely beg,
O! may it ne'er be a livin' plague
To my dishonour,
An' I'll ne'er lift a lawless l–g
Again upon her.

Besides, I farther maun avow, must
Wi' Lizie's lass, three times I trow;
But, L—d, that Friday I was fow, drunk
When I came near her,
Or else, thou kens, thy *servant true*
Wad ne'er hae steer'd her.

Maybe thou lets this *fleshy thorn*
Beset thy servant e'en and morn,
Lest he o'er high and proud shou'd turn,
'Cause he's sae *gifted*;
If sae, thy han' maun e'en be borne,
Until thou lift it.

L—d bless thy chosen in this place,
For *here* thou hast a *chosen race*;
But G–d confound their stubborn face,
And blast their name,
Wha bring thy rulers to disgrace
An' public shame.

L—d mind G–n H—n's deserts,
He drinks, an' swears, an' plays at cartes, cards
Yet has sae mony takin' arts
Wi' grit an' sma',
Frae G–d's ain priest the people's hearts
He steals awa'.

An' whan we chasten'd him therefore,
Thou kens how he bred sic a splore, commotion
As set the warld in a roar
O' laughin' at us;
Curse thou his basket and his store,
Kail an' potatoes. cabbage

L—d hear my earnest cry an' pray'r,
Against that presbyt'ry o' Ayr;
Thy strong right hand, L—d make it bare,
Upo' their heads,
L—d weigh it down, and dinna spare,
For their misdeeds.

O L—d my G–d, that glib-tongu'd A——n,
My very heart an' saul are quakin',
To think how we stood sweatin', shakin',
An' p—d wi' dread,
While he wi' hingin' lips and snakin'
Held up his head.

L—d in the day of vengeance try him,
L—d visit them wha did employ him,
An' pass not in thy mercy by 'em,
Nor hear their pray'r;
But for thy people's sake destroy 'em,
And dinna spare.

But, L—d remember me and mine
Wi' mercies temp'ral and divine,
That I for gear and grace may shine,
Excell'd by nane,
An' a' the glory shall be thine,
Amen, Amen!

ADDRESS TO THE DEIL

O Prince, O chief of many throned pow'rs,
That led th' embattl'd Seraphim to war —
MILTON

O Thou, whatever title suit thee!
Auld Hornie, Satan, Nick, or Clootie!
Wha in yon cavern grim an' sootie,
Clos'd under hatches,
Spairges about the brunstane cootie, — scatters; brimstone tub
To scaud poor wretches! — scald

Hear me, *auld Hangie*, for a wee,
An' let poor, *damned bodies* bee;
I'm sure sma' pleasure it can gie,
Ev'n to a *deil*,
To skelp an' scaud poor dogs like me, — strike
An' hear us squeel!

Great is thy pow'r, an' great thy fame;
Far kend an' noted is thy name;
An' tho' yon *lowan heugh's* thy hame, — blazing pit
Thou travels far;
An' faith! thou's neither lag nor lame, — tardy
Nor blate nor scaur. — shy; timid

Whyles, ranging like a roaran lion, — sometimes
For prey, a' holes an' corners tryin;
Whyles, on the strong-wing'd tempest flyin,
Tirlan the *kirks*; — rattling
Whyles, in the human bosom pryin,
Unseen thou lurks.

I've heard my rev'rend *Graunie* say,
In lanely glens ye like to stray;

Or where auld, ruin'd castles, gray,
Nod to the moon,
Ye fright the nightly wand'rer's way,
Wi' eldritch croon. eerie

When twilight did my *Graunie* summon,
To say her pray'rs, douse, honest woman! genteel
Aft 'yont the dyke she's heard you bumman, humming
Wi' eerie drone;
Or, rustling, thro' the boortries coman, elder trees
Wi' heavy groan.

Ae dreary, windy, winter night,
The stars shot down wi' sklentan light, slanting
Wi' you, *mysel*, I gat a fright,
Ayont the lough; loch
Ye, like a *rass-buss*, stood in sight, clump of rushes
Wi' waving sugh. murmur

The cudgel in my nieve did shake, fist
Each bristl'd hair stood like a stake,
When wi' an eldritch, stoor *quaick*, *quaick*, harsh
Amang the springs,
Awa ye squatter'd like a *drake*, fluttered in water
On whistling wings.

Let *Warlocks* grim, an' wither'd *Hags*,
Tell how wi' you on ragweed nags, ragwort
They skim the muirs an' dizzy crags,
Wi' wicked speed;
And in kirk-yards renew their leagues,
Owre howcket dead. exhumed

Thence, countra wives, wi' toil an' pain, country
May plunge an' plunge the *kirn* in vain; churn
For Oh! the yellow treasure's taen
By witching skill;
An' dawtet, twal-pint *Hawkie's* gane petted; giving 12 pints at a milking
As yell's the Bill. dry; bull

Thence, mystic knots mak great abuse,
On *Young-Guidmen*, fond, keen an' croose; bold
When the best *wark-lume* i' the house, penis
By cantraip wit, magic
Is instant made no worth a louse,
Just at the bit.

When thowes dissolve the snawy hoord, thaws
An' float the jinglan icy boord,
Then *Water-kelpies* haunt the foord,
By your direction,
An' nighted Trav'llers are allur'd
To their destruction.

An' aft your moss-traversing *Spunkies* spirits
Decoy the wight that late an' drunk is: man
The bleezan, curst, mischievous monkies blazing
Delude his eyes,
Till in some miry slough he slunk is,
Ne'er mair to rise.

When MASONS' mystic *word* an' *grip*,
In storms an' tempests raise you up,
Some cock or cat, your rage maun stop,
Or, strange to tell!
The *youngest Brother* ye wad whip
Aff straught to *H–ll.*

Lang syne in EDEN'S bonie yard,
When youthfu' lovers first were pair'd,
An' all the Soul of Love they shar'd,
The raptur'd hour,
Sweet on the fragrant, flow'ry swaird,
In shady bow'r.

Then you, ye auld, snick-drawing dog!
Ye cam to Paradise incog,
An' play'd on man a cursed brogue, trick
(Black be your fa'!)
An' gied the infant warld a shog, shake
'Maist ruin'd a'.

D'ye mind that day, when in a bizz, state of commotion
Wi' reeket duds, an' reestet gizz, smoking clothes; cured wig
Ye did present your smoutie phiz, smutty face
'Mang better folk,
An' sklented on the *man of Uzz*, aimed
Your spitefu' joke?

An how ye gat him i' your thrall,
An' brak him out o' house an' hal',
While scabs an' botches did him gall,
Wi' bitter claw,
An' lows'd his ill-tongu'd, wicked *Scawl*
Was warst ava?

But a' your doings to rehearse,
Your wily snares an' fechtin fierce,
Sin' that day MICHAEL did you pierce,
Down to this time,
Wad ding a *Lallan* tongue, or *Erse*,
In Prose or Rhyme.

An' now, auld *Cloots*, I ken ye're thinkan,
A certain *Bardie's* rantin, drinkin,
Some luckless hour will send him linkan, walking quickly
To your black pit;
But faith! he'll turn a corner jinkan,
An' cheat you yet.

But fare-you-weel, auld *Nickie-ben!*
O wad ye tak a thought an' men'!
Ye aiblins might—I dinna ken— perhaps
Still hae a *stake*—
I'm wae to think upo' yon den,
Ev'n for your sake!

THE COTTAR'S SATURDAY NIGHT

*INSCRIBED TO R. A****, ESQ;*

Let not Ambition mock their useful toil,
Their homely joys, and destiny obscure;
Nor Grandeur hear, with a disdainful smile,
The short and simple annals of the Poor.
(Gray, 'Elegy Written in a Country Churchyard')

I

My lov'd, my honor'd, much respected friend,
No mercenary Bard his homage pays;
With honest pride, I scorn each selfish end,
My dearest meed, a friend's esteem and praise:
To you I sing, in simple Scottish lays,
The *lowly train* in life's sequester'd scene;
The native feelings strong, the guileless ways,
What A**** in a *Cottage* would have been;
Ah! tho' his worth unknown, far happier there I ween!

II

November chill blaws loud wi' angry sugh;
The short'ning winter-day is near a close;
The miry beasts retreating frae the pleugh;
The black'ning trains o' craws to their repose:
The toil-worn COTTER frae his labor goes,
This night his weekly moil is at an end,
Collects his *spades*, his *mattocks* and his *hoes*,
Hoping the *morn* in ease and rest to spend,
And weary, o'er the moor, his course does hameward bend.

III

At length his lonely *Cot* appears in view,
Beneath the shelter of an aged tree;
Th' expectant *wee-things*, toddlan, stacher through
To meet their *Dad*, wi' flichterin noise and glee.
His wee-bit ingle, blinkan bonilie,
His clean hearth-stane, his thrifty *Wifie's* smile,

The *lisping infant*, prattling on his knee,
  Does a' his weary *kiaugh* and care beguile, carking anxiety [Burn's note]
And makes him quite forget his labor and his toil.

IV

Belyve, the *elder bairns* come drapping in, soon
  At *Service* out, amang the Farmers roun';
Some ca' the pleugh, some herd, some tentie rin watchful
  A cannie errand to a neebor town:
Their eldest hope, their *Jenny*, woman-grown,
  In youthfu' bloom, Love sparkling in her e'e,
Comes hame, perhaps to shew a braw new gown,
  Or deposite her sair-won penny-fee,
To help her *Parents* dear, if they in hardship be.

V

With joy unfeign'd, *brothers* and *sisters* meet,
  And each for other's weelfare kindly spiers:
The social hours, swift-wing'd, unnotic'd fleet;
  Each tells the uncos that he sees or hears. news
The Parents partial eye their hopeful years;
  Anticipation forward points the view;
The *Mother*, wi' her needle and her sheers,
  Gars auld claes look amaist as weel's the new; makes
The *Father* mixes a' wi' admonition due.

VI

Their Master's and their Mistress's command,
  The *youngkers* a' are warned to obey; young folk
And mind their labors wi' an eydent hand, diligent
  And ne'er, tho' out o' sight, to jauk or play: trifle
'And O! be sure to fear the LORD alway!
  'And mind your *duty*, duely, morn and night!
'Lest in temptation's path ye gang astray,
  'Implore his *counsel* and assisting *might*:
'They never sought in vain that sought the LORD aright.'

VII

But hark! a rap comes gently to the door;
  Jenny, wha kens the meaning o' the same,
Tells how a neebor lad came o'er the moor,
  To do some errands, and convoy her hame.
The wily Mother sees the *conscious flame*
  Sparkle in *Jenny's* e'e, and flush her cheek,

With heart-struck, anxious care enquires his name,
  While *Jenny* hafflins is afraid to speak; nearly
Weel-pleas'd the Mother hears, it's nae wild, worthless *Rake*.

VIII

With kindly welcome, *Jenny* brings him ben;
  A *strappan youth*, he takes the Mother's eye;
Blythe *Jenny* sees the *visit's* no ill taen;
  The Father cracks of horses, pleughs and kye.
The *Youngster's* artless heart o'erflows wi' joy,
  But blate an' laithfu', scarce can weel behave; diffident; bashful
The Mother, wi' a woman's wiles, can spy
  What makes the *youth* sae bashfu' and sae grave;
Weel-pleas'd to think her *bairn's* respected like the lave. rest

IX

O happy love! where love like this is found!
  O heart-felt raptures! bliss beyond compare!
I've paced much this weary, *mortal round*,
  And sage EXPERIENCE bids me this declare—
'If Heaven a draught of heavenly pleasure spare
  'One *cordial* in this melancholy *Vale*,
''Tis when a youthful, loving, *modest* Pair
  'In other's arms, breathe out the tender tale,
'Beneath the milk-white thorn that scents the ev'ning gale.'

X

Is there, in human form, that bears a heart—
  A Wretch! a Villain! lost to love and truth!
That can, with studied, sly, ensnaring art,
  Betray sweet Jenny's unsuspecting youth?
Curse on his perjur'd arts! dissembling smooth!
  Are *Honor*, *Virtue*, *Conscience*, all exil'd?
Is there no Pity, no relenting Ruth,
  Points to the Parents fondling o'er their Child?
Then paints the *ruin'd Maid*, and *their* distraction wild!

XI

But now the Supper crowns their simple board,
  The healsome *Porritch*, chief of SCOTIA'S food:
The soupe their *only Hawkie* does afford, cow
  That 'yont the hallan snugly chows her cood: partition
The *Dame* brings forth, in complimental mood,
  To grace the lad, her weel-hain'd kebbuck, fell, hoarded cheese, strong

And aft he's prest, and aft he ca's it guid;
   The frugal *Wifie*, garrulous, will tell,
How 'twas a towmond auld, sin' Lint was i' the bell. year, flax

XII

The cheerfu' Supper done, wi' serious face,
   They, round the ingle, form a circle wide;
The Sire turns o'er, with patriarchal grace,
   The big *ha'-Bible*, ance his *Father's* pride:
His bonnet rev'rently is laid aside,
   His *lyart haffets* wearing thin and bare; grey temples
Those strains that once did sweet in ZION glide,
   He wales a portion with judicious care; chooses
'And let us worship GOD!' he says with solemn air.

XIII

They chant their artless notes in simple guise;
   They tune their *hearts*, by far the noblest aim:
Perhaps *Dundee*'s wild-warbling measures rise,
   Or plaintive *Martyrs*, worthy of the name;
Or noble *Elgin* beets the heaven-ward flame, kindles
   The sweetest far of SCOTIA'S holy lays:
Compar'd with these, *Italian trills* are tame;
   The tickl'd ears no heart-felt raptures raise;
Nae unison hae they, with our CREATOR'S praise.

XIV

The priest-like Father reads the sacred page,
   How *Abram* was the Friend of GOD on high;
Or, *Moses* bade eternal warfare wage,
   With *Amalek's* ungracious progeny;
Or how the *royal Bard* did groaning lye,
   Beneath the stroke of Heaven's avenging ire;
Or *Job's* pathetic plaint, and wailing cry;
   Or rapt *Isaiah's* wild, seraphic fire;
Or other *Holy Seers* that tune the *sacred lyre*.

XV

Perhaps the *Christian Volume* is the theme,
   How *guiltless blood* for *guilty man* was shed;
How HE, who bore in heaven the second name,
   Had not on Earth whereon to lay His head:
How His first *followers* and *servants* sped;
   The *Precepts sage* they wrote to many a land:

How *he*, who lone in *Patmos* banished,
Saw in the sun a mighty angel stand;
And heard great *Bab'lon's* doom pronounc'd by Heaven's command.

XVI

Then, kneeling down to HEAVEN'S ETERNAL KING,
The *Saint*, the *Father*, and the *Husband* prays:
Hope 'springs exulting on triumphant wing,' Pope's *Windsor Forest*
That *thus* they all shall meet in future days: [Burns's note]
There, ever bask in *uncreated rays*,
No more to sigh, or shed the bitter tear,
Together hymning their CREATOR'S praise,
In *such society*, yet still more dear;
While circling Time moves round in an eternal sphere

XVII

Compar'd with *this*, how poor Religion's pride,
In all the pomp of *method*, and of *art*;
When men display to congregations wide,
Devotion's ev'ry grace, except the *heart!*
The POWER, incens'd, the Pageant will desert,
The pompous strain, the sacerdotal stole;
But haply, in some *Cottage* far apart,
May hear, well-pleas'd, the language of the *Soul*;
And in His *Book of Life* the Inmates poor enrol.

XVIII

Then homeward all take off their sev'ral way;
The youngling *Cottagers* retire to rest:
The Parent-pair their *secret homage* pay,
And proffer up to Heaven the warm request,
That HE who stills the *raven's* clam'rous nest,
And decks the *lily* fair in flow'ry pride,
Would, in the way *His Wisdom* sees the best,
For *them* and for their *little ones* provide;
But chiefly, in their hearts, with *Grace divine* preside.

XIX

From scenes like these, old SCOTIA'S grandeur springs,
That makes her lov'd at home, rever'd abroad:
Princes and lords are but the breath of kings,
'An honest man's the noblest work of GOD:'
And *certes*, in fair Virtue's heavenly road, certainly
The *Cottage* leaves the *Palace* far behind:

What is a lordling's pomp? a cumbrous load,
   Disguising oft the *wretch* of human kind,
Studied in arts of Hell, in wickedness refin'd!

XX

O SCOTIA! my dear, my native soil!
   For whom my warmest wish to heaven is sent,
Long may thy hardy sons of *rustic toil*,
   Be blest with health, and peace, and sweet content!
And O may Heaven their simple lives prevent
   From *Luxury's* contagion, weak and vile!
Then howe'er *crowns* and *coronets* be rent,
   A *virtuous Populace* may rise the while,
And stand a wall of fire around their much-lov'd ISLE.

XXI

O THOU! who pour'd the *patriotic tide*,
   That stream'd thro' great, unhappy WALLACE' heart;
Who dar'd to, nobly, stem tyrannic pride,
   Or *nobly die*, the second glorious part:
(The Patriot's GOD, peculiarly thou art,
   His *friend*, *inspirer*, *guardian*, and *reward!*)
O never, never SCOTIA'S realm desert,
   But still the *Patriot*, and the *Patriot-Bard*,
In bright succession raise, her *Ornament* and *Guard!*

A COMMITTEE OF THE GENERAL ASSEMBLY OF THE CHURCH OF SCOTLAND

1781

from TRANSLATIONS AND PARAPHRASES, IN VERSE, OF SEVERAL PASSAGES OF SACRED SCRIPTURE

IX. JOB XXVI. 6, TO THE END

Who can resist th' Almighty arm
  that made the starry sky?
Or who elude the certain glance
  of God's all-seeing eye?
From him no cov'ring vails our crimes;
  hell opens to his sight;
And all Destruction's secret snares
  lie full disclos'd in light.

Firm on the boundless void of space
  he pois'd the steady pole,
And in the circle of his clouds
  bade secret waters roll.
While nature's universal frame
  its Maker's pow'r reveals,
His throne, remote from mortal eyes,
  an awful cloud conceals.

From where the rising day ascends,
  to where it sets in night,
He compasses the floods with bounds,
  and checks their threat'ning might.
The pillars that support the sky
  tremble at his rebuke;
Through all its caverns quakes the earth,
  as though its centre shook.

He brings the waters from their beds,
    although no tempest blows,
And smites the kingdom of the proud
    without the hand of foes.
With bright inhabitants above
    he fills the heav'nly land,
And all the crooked serpent's breed
    dismay'd before him stand.

Few of his works can we survey;
    these few our skill transcend:
But the full thunder of his pow'r
    what heart can comprehend?

XIX. ISAIAH IX. 2–8

The race that long in darkness pin'd
  have seen a glorious light;
The people dwell in day, who dwelt
  in death's surrounding night.
To hail thy rise, thou better Sun!
  the gath'ring nations come,
Joyous, as when the reapers bear
  the harvest treasures home.

For thou our burden hast remov'd,
  and quell'd th' oppressor's sway,
Quick as the slaughter'd squadrons fell
  in Midian's evil day.
To us a Child of hope is born;
  to us a Son is giv'n;
Him shall the tribes of earth obey,
  him all the hosts of heav'n.

His name shall be the Prince of Peace,
  for evermore ador'd,
The Wonderful, the Counsellor,
  the great and mighty Lord.
His pow'r increasing still shall spread,
  his reign no end shall know:
Justice shall guard his throne above,
  and peace abound below.

LIV. 2 TIMOTHY I.12

I'm not asham'd to own my Lord,
  or to defend his cause,
Maintain the glory of his cross,
  and honour all his laws.
Jesus, my Lord! I know his name,
  his name is all my boast;
Nor will he put my soul to shame,
  nor let my hope be lost.

I know that safe with him remains,
  protected by his pow'r,
What I've committed to his trust,
  till the decisive hour.
Then will he own his servant's name
  before his Father's face,
And in the new Jerusalem
  appoint my soul a place.

JAMES HOGG

1770–1835

CORPUS CHRISTI CAROL

The heron flew east, the heron flew west,
The heron flew to the fair forest;
She flew o'er streams and meadows green
And a' to see what could be seen:
And when she saw the faithful pair,
Her breast grew sick, her head grew sair;
For there she saw a lovely bower,
Was a' clad o'er wi' lilly-flower;
And in the bower there was a bed
With silken sheets, and weel down spread
And in the bed there lay a knight,
Whose wounds did bleed both day and night,
And by the bed there stood a stane,
And there was a set a leal maiden,
With silver needle and silken thread,
Stemming the wounds when they did bleed.

(from the recitation of his mother, Margaret Laidlaw)

A CAMERONIAN BALLAD

'O what is become o' your leel goodman,
  That now you are a' your lane?
If he has joined wi' the rebel gang,
  You will never see him again.'

'O say nae 'the rebel gang,' ladye,
  It's a term nae heart can thole,
For they wha rebel against their God,
  It is justice to control.

When rank oppression rends the heart,
  'An' rules wi' stroke o' death,
Wha wadna spend their dear heart's blood
  For the tenets o' their faith?

Then say nae 'the rebel gang,' ladye,
  For it gi'es me muckle pain;
My John went away with Earlston,
  And I'll never see either again.'

'O wae is my heart for thee, Janet,
  O sair is my heart for thee!
These covenant men were ill advised,
  They are fools, you may credit me.

Where's a' their boastfu' preaching now,
  Against their king and law,
When mony a head in death lies low,
  An' mony mae maun fa'?'

more

'Ay, but death lasts no for aye, ladye,
  For the grave maun yield its prey;
And when we meet on the verge of heaven,
  We'll see wha are fools that day:

We'll see wha looks in their Saviour's face
    With holiest joy and pride,
Whether they who shed his servants' blood,
    Or those that for him died.

I wadna be the highest dame
    That ever this country knew,
And take my chance to share the doom
    Of that persecuting crew.

Then ca' us nae rebel gang, ladye,
    Nor take us fools to be,
For there is nae ane of a' that gang,
    Wad change his state wi' thee.'

'O weel may you be, my poor Janet,
    May blessings on you combine!
The better you are in either state,
    The less shall I repine.

But wi' your fightings an' your faith,
    Your ravings an' your rage,
There you have lost a leel helpmate, loyal
    In the blossom of his age.

An' what's to come o' ye, my poor Janet,
    Wi' these twa babies sweet?
Ye hae naebody now to work for them,
    Or bring you a meal o' meat;

It is that which makes my heart sae wae,
    An' gars me, while scarce aware,
Whiles say the things I wadna say,
    Of them that can err nae mair.'

Poor Janet kissed her youngest babe,
    And the tears fell on his cheek,
And they fell upon his swaddling bands,
    For her heart was like to break.

'O little do I ken, my dear, dear babes,
    What misery's to be thine!
But for the cause we hae espoused,
    I will yield thy life and mine.

O had I a friend, as I hae nane,
For nane dare own me now,
That I might send to Bothwell brigg,
If the killers wad but allow,

To lift the corpse of my brave John,
I ken where they will him find,
He wad meet his God's foes face to face,
And he'll hae nae wound behind.'

'But I went to Bothwell brigg, Janet,
There was nane durst hinder me,
For I wantit to hear a' I could hear,
An' to see what I could see;

And there I found your brave husband,
As viewing the dead my lane, by myself
He was lying in the very foremost rank,
In the midst of a heap o' slain.'

Then Janet help up her hands to heaven,
An' she grat, an' she tore her hair,
'O sweet ladye, O dear ladye,
Dinna tell me ony mair!

There is a hope will linger within
When earthly hope is vain,
But when ane kens the very worst,
It turns the heart to stane!'

'O wae is my heart, John Carr; said I,
That I this sight should see!
And when I said these waefu' words,
He liftit his een to me.

"O art thou there, my kind ladye,
The best o' this warld's breed,
And are you gangin' your liefu lane, quite alone
Amang the hapless dead?"

I hae servants within my ca', John Carr,
And a chariot in the dell,
An' if there is ony hope o' life,
I will carry you hame mysel'.

"O lady, there is nae hope o' life –
   And what were life to me!
Wad ye save me frae the death of a man,
   To hang on a gallows tree?

I hae nae hame to fly to now,
   Nae country an' nae kin,
There is not a door in fair Scotland
   Durst open to let me in.

But I hae a loving wife at hame,
   An' twa babies dear to me;
They have naebody now that dares favour them,
   An' of hunger they a' maun dee. must

Oh, for the sake of thy Saviour dear,
   Whose mercy thou hopest to share,
Dear lady take the sackless things blameless
   A wee beneath thy care!

A long fareweel, my kind ladye,
   O'er weel I ken thy worth;
Gae send me a drink o' the water o' Clyde,
   For my last drink on earth."'

'O dinna tell ony mair, ladye,
   For my heart is cauld as clay;
There is a spear that pierces here,
   Frae every word ye say.'

'He was nae feared to dee, Janet,
   For he gloried in his death,
And wished to be laid with those who had bled
   For the same enduring faith.

There were three wounds in his boardly breast,
   And his limb was broke in twain.
An' the sweat ran down wi' his red heart's blood,
   Wrung out by the deadly pain.

I rowed my apron round his head, rolled
   For fear my men should tell,
And I hid him in my lord's castle,
   An' I nursed him there mysel' –

An' the best leeches in a' the land doctors
    Have tended him as he lay,
And he never has lacked my helping hand,
    By night nor yet by day.

I durstna tell you before, Janet,
    For I feared his life was gane,
But now he's sae well, ye may visit him,
    An' ye's meet by yoursels alane.'

Then Janet she fell at her lady's feet,
    And she claspit them ferventlye,
And she steepit them a' wi' the tears o' joy,
    Till the good lady wept to see.

'Oh, ye are an angel sent frae heaven,
    To lighten calamitye!
For in distress, a friend or foe
    Is a' the same to thee.

If good deeds count in heaven, ladye,
    Eternal bliss to share,
Ye hae done a deed will save your soul,
    Though ye should never do mair.'

'Get up, get up, my kind Janet,
    But never trow tongue or pen, believe
That a' the warld are lost to good,
    Except the covenant men.'

Wha wadna hae shared that lady's joy,
    When watching the wounded hind,
Rather than those of the feast and the dance,
    Which her kind heart resigned?

Wha wadna rather share that lady's fate,
    When the stars melt away,
Than that of the sternest anchorite,
    That can naething but graen an' pray?

WALTER SCOTT

1771–1832

DIES IRAE

That day of wrath, that dreadul day,
When heaven and earth shall pass away,
What power shall be the sinner's stay?
How shall he meet that dreadful day?

When, shrivelling like a parchèd scroll,
The flaming heavens together roll;
When, louder yet, and yet more dread,
Swells the high trump that wakes the dead;

O, on that day, that wrathful day,
When man to judgment wakes from clay,
Be Thou the trembling sinner's stay,
Though heaven and earth shall pass away!

JOHN LEYDEN

1775–1811

THE SABBATH MORNING

With silent awe I hail the sacred morn,
That slowly wakes while all the fields are still.
A soothing calm on every breeze is borne.
A graver murmer gurgles from the rill;
And echo answers softer from the hill;
And sweeter sings the linnet from the thorn.
The skylark warbles in a tone less shrill:
Hail, light serene! hail, sacred Sabbath morn!
The rooks float silent by in airy drove.
The sun a placid yellow lustre throws.
The gales that lately sighed along the grove
Have hushed their downy wings in dead repose.
The hovering rack of clouds forgets to move –
So smiled the day when the first morn arose.

GEORGE GORDON, LORD BYRON

1788–1824

from THE VISION OF JUDGMENT

Saint Peter sat by the celestial gate,
   And nodded o'er his keys: when, lo! there came
A wondrous noise he had not heard of late –
   A rushing sound of wind, and stream, and flame;
In short, a roar of things extremely great,
   Which would have made aught save a Saint exclaim;
But he, with first a start and then a wink,
Said, 'There's another star gone out, I think!'

But ere he could return to his repose,
   A Cherub flapped his right wing o'er his eyes –
At which Saint Peter yawned, and rubbed his nose:
   'Saint porter,' said the angel, 'prithee rise!'
Waving a goodly wing, which glowed, as flows
   An earthly peacock's tail, with heavenly dyes:
To which the saint replied, 'Well, what's the matter?
'Is Lucifer come back with all this clatter?'

'No,' quoth the Cherub: 'George the Third is dead.'
   'And who *is* George the Third?' replied the apostle:
'*What George? what Third?*' 'The King of England,' said
   The angel. 'Well! he won't find kings to jostle
Him on his way; but does he wear his head?
   Because the last, we saw here had a tustle, [Louis XVI (beheaded)]
And ne'er would have got into Heaven's good graces,
Had he not flung his head in all our faces.

'He was – if I remember – King of France;
   That head of his, which could not keep a crown
On earth, yet ventured in my face to advance
   A claim to those of martyrs – like my own:
If I had had my sword, as I had once
   When I cut ears off, I had cut him down;
But having but my *keys*, and not my brand,
I only knocked his head from out his hand.

'And then he set up a headless howl,
That all the Saints came out and took him in;
And there he sits by Saint Paul, cheek by jowl;
That fellow Paul – the parvenu! The skin
Of Saint Bartholomew, which makes his cowl
In heaven, and upon earth redeemed his sin,
So as to make a martyr, never sped
Better than did this weak and wooden head.

'But had it come up here upon its shoulders,
There would have been a different tale to tell:
The fellow-feeling in the Saint's beholders
Seems to have acted on them like a spell;
And so this very foolish head Heaven solders
Back on its trunk: it may be very well,
And seems the custom here to overthrow
Whatever has been wisely done below.'

The Angel answered, 'Peter! do not pout:
The King who comes has head and all entire,
And never knew much what is was about –
He did as doth the puppet – by its wire,
And will be judged like all the rest, no doubt:
My business and your own is not to inquire
Into such matters, but to mind our cue –
Which is to act as we are bid to do.'

While thus they spake, the angelic caravan,
Arriving like a rush of mighty wind,
Cleaving the fields of space, as doth the swan
Some silver stream (say Ganges, Nile, or Inde,
Or Thames, or Tweed), and midst them an old man
With an old soul, and both extremely blind,
Halted before the gate, and, in his shroud,
Seated their fellow-traveller on a cloud

But bringing up the rear of this bright host
A Spirit of a different aspect waved
His wings, like thunder-clouds above some coast
Whose barren beach with frequent wrecks is paved;
His brow was like the deep when tempest-tossed;
Fierce and unfathomable thoughts engraved
Eternal wrath on his immortal face,
And *where* he gazed a gloom pervaded space.

As he drew near, he gazed upon the gate
Ne'er to be entered more by him or Sin,
With such a glance of supernatural hate,
As made Saint Peter wish himself within;
He pottered with his keys at a great rate,
And sweated through his Apostolic skin:
Of course his perspiration was but ichor,
Or some such other spiritual liquor.

The very Cherubs huddled all together,
Like birds when soars the falcon; and they felt
A tingling to the tip of every feather,
And formed a circle like Orion's belt
Around their poor old charge; who scarce knew whither
His guards had led him, though they gently dealt
With royal Manes (for by many stories,
And true, we learn the Angels all are Tories).

As things were in this posture, the gate flew
Asunder, and the flashing of its hinges
Flung over space an universal hue
Of many-coloured flame, until its tinges
Reached even our speck of earth, and made a new
Aurora borealis spread its fringes
O'er the North Pole; the same seen, when ice-bound,
By Captain Parry's crew, in 'Melville's Sound.'

And from the gate thrown open issued beaming
A beautiful and mighty Thing of Light,
Radiant with glory, like a banner streaming
Victorious from some world-o'erthrowing fight:
My poor comparisons must needs be teeming
With earthly likenesses, for here the night
Of clay obscures our best conceptions, saving
Johanna Southcote, or Bob Southey raving. [a religious fanatic; a poet]

'Twas the Archangel Michael: all men know
The make of Angels and Archangels, since
There's scarce a scribbler has not one to show,
From the fiends' leader to the Angels' Prince.
There also are some altar-pieces, though
I really can't say that they much evince
One's inner notions of immortal spirits;
But let the connoisseurs explain *their* merits.

Michael flew forth in glory and in good;
   A goodly work of him from whom all Glory
And Good arise; the portal past – he stood;
   Before him the young Cherubs and Saints hoary –
(I say *young*, begging to be understood
   By looks, not years; and should be very sorry
To state, they were not older than St. Peter,
But merely that they seemed a little sweeter).

The Cherubs and the Saints bowed down before
   That arch-angelic Hierarch, the first
Of Essences angelical who wore
   The aspect of a god; but this ne'er nursed
Pride in his heavenly bosom, in whose core
   No thought, save for his Maker's service, durst
Intrude, however glorified and high;
He knew him but the Viceroy of the sky.

He and the sombre, silent Spirit met –
   They knew each other both for good and ill;
Such was their power, that neither could forget
   His former friend and future foe; but still
There was a high, immortal, proud regret
   In either's eye, as if 'twere less their will
Than destiny to make the eternal years
Their date of war, and their 'Champ Clos' the spheres. [Tournament ground]

But here they were in neutral space: we know
   From Job, that Satan hath the power to pay
A heavenly visit thrice a-year or so;
   And that the 'Sons of God,' like those of clay,
Must keep him company; and we might show
   From the same book, in how polite a way
The dialogue is held between the Powers
Of Good and Evil – but t'would take up hours.

And this is not a theologic tract,
   To prove with Hebrew and with Arabic,
If Job be allegory or a fact,
   But a true narrative; and thus I pick
From out the whole but such and such an act
   As sets aside the slightest thought of trick.
'Tis every tittle true, beyond suspicion,
And accurate as any other vision.

The spirits were in neutral space, before
   The gate of Heaven: like eastern thresholds is
The place where Death's grand cause is argued o'er,
   And souls despatched to that world or to this;
And therefore Michael and the other wore
   A civil aspect: though they did not kiss,
Yet still between his Darkness and his Brightness
There passed a mutual glance of great politeness.

THOMAS CARLYLE

1795–1881

CUI BONO?

What is hope? A smiling rainbow
   Children follow through the wet;
'Tis not here, still yonder, yonder:
   Never urchin found it yet.

What is life? A thawing iceboard
   On a sea with sunny shore: –
Gay we sail; it melts beneath us;
   We are sunk, and seen no more.

What is man? A foolish baby,
   Vainly strives, and fights, and frets;
Demanding all, deserving nothing; –
   One small grave is what he gets.

MÀIRI NicDHÒMHNAILL/ MARY MacDONALD

1789–1872

LEANABH AN ÀIGH

Leanabh an àigh, an leanabh aig Màiri,
Rugadh san stàball, Rìgh nan Dùl;
Thàinig don fhàsach, dh'fhuiling nar n-àite –
Son' iad an àireamh bhitheas dhà dlùth!

Ged a bhios leanabain aig rìghrean na talmhainn
An greadhnachas garbh is anabarr mùirn,
'S geàrr gus am falbh iad, 's fàsaidh iad anfhann,
An àilleachd 's an dealbh a' searg san ùir.

Cha b 'ionann 's an t-Uan thàinig gur fuasgladh –
Iriosal, stuama ghluais e'n tùs;
E naomh gun truailleachd, Cruithfhear an t-sluaigh,
Dh'èirich e suas le buaidh on ùir.

Leanabh an àigh, mar dh'aithris na fàidhean;
'S na h-àinglean àrd', b'e miann an sùl;
'S E 's airidh air gràdh 's air urram thoirt dhà –
Sona an àireamh bhitheas dhà dlùth.

CHILD IN THE MANGER

Child in the manger,
   Infant of Mary;
Outcast and stranger,
   Lord of all!
Child who inherits
   All our transgressions,
All our demerits
   On Him fall.

Once the most holy
   Child of salvation
Gently and lowly
   Lived below;
Now, as our glorious
   Mighty Redeemer,
See Him victorious
   O'er each foe.

Prophets foretold Him,
   Infant of wonder;
Angels behold Him
   On His throne;
Worthy our Saviour
   Of all their praises;
Happy for ever.
   Are His own.

translated from the Gaelic by Lachlan MacBean

ANNA NIC EALAIR/ANNA MACKELLAR
*fl. c.*1800

LUINNEAG ANNA NIC EALAIR

Is ann am bothan bochd a' bhròin
  A chuir mi eòlas ort an toiseach;
As thug mi thu gu tigh mo mhàth'r
  'S an d' rinn mi d' àrach car tamuill.

'S e do ghaol-sa, a ghaoil,
  'S e do ghaol-sa rinn mo tharruing;
'S e do ghràdh-sa, a rùin,
  Rinn mo dhùsgadh 's a' mhadainn.

Tha thu mar dhubhar carraig mhòir
  Am fearann sgìth is mi làn airsneil;
'N uair a thionndaidh riut mo shùil
  'S ann bha thu an rùn mo ghlacadh.

'S ann a thug thu dhomh do ghaol
  Fo dhubhar craobh an aiteil;
As comh-chomunn do rùin
  Ann an gàradh nan ubhall.

Is mìllse leam do ghaol na'm fion,
  Seadh am fion, 'nuair is treis' e,
'S 'n uair a thug thu dhomh do ghràdh
  'S ann a dh' fhàilnich mo phearsa.

'S ann a thug thu dhomh do d' ghràdh
  Gus an d'fhàilnich mo phearsa;
'S gus am b' éigin domh a ràdh
  'Cùm air do làmh a charaid.'

'S ann a dh' éirich thu le buaidh
  As an uaigh suas le cabhaig,
Amhluidh dhùisgeas do shluagh
  Suas le buaidh anns a' mhadainn.

'S chaidh thu suas air ionad àrd
  Dh' ullach' àite do m' anam;
'S tha thu 'g ràdh gu 'n tig thu rìs
  A choimh-lìonadh do gheallaidh.

ANNA NIC EALAIR'S SONG

It was in the wretched poor stall
that I first came to know you;
and I took you to my mother's house
where for a while I nursed you.

It was your love, my love,
it was your love that drew me,
it was your love, my dear,
that awoke me in the morning.

You're like the shade of a great rock
in a troubled land where I walk in sadness;
when I looked to you for help
you desired my encapture.

You gave me your love
in the juniper's shadow,
and the company of your regard
in the garden of apples.

Sweeter to me your love than wine,
even wine at its strongest;
when you showed me your esteem
it made my body falter.

You gave me of your love
until it overwhelmed me
and I had to call out
'Friend, stop your caresses.'

You have risen up with haste
from the grave, victorious;
likewise will your host awake,
triumphant in the morning.

And you went up to a place on high
to prepare my soul a lodging,
and you say you'll come back again
to bring about your promise.

translated from the Gaelic by Meg Bateman

CHARLES, LORD NEAVES

1800–1876

LET US ALL BE UNHAPPY ON SUNDAY: A LYRIC FOR SATURDAY NIGHT

We zealots, made up of stiff clay,
  The sour-looking children of sorrow,
While not over-jolly today,
  Resolve to be wretched tomorrow.
We can't for a certainty tell
  What mirth may molest us on Monday;
But, at least, to begin the week well,
  Let us all be unhappy on Sunday.

That day, the calm season of rest,
  Shall come to us freezing and frigid;
A gloom all our thoughts shall invest,
  Such as Calvin would call over-rigid,
With sermons from morning to night,
  We'll strive to be decent and dreary:
To preachers a praise and delight,
  Who ne'er think that sermons can weary.

All tradesmen cry up their own wares;
  In this they agree well together:
The Mason by stone and lime swears;
  The Tanner is always for leather;
The Smith still for iron would go;
  The Schoolmaster stands up for teaching;
And the Parson would have you to know,
  There's nothing on earth like his preaching.

The face of kind Nature is fair;
  But our system obscures its effulgence:
How sweet is a breath of fresh air!
  But our rules don't allow the indulgence.
These gardens, their walks and green bowers,
  Might be free to the poor man for one day;
But no, the glad plants and gay flowers
  Mustn't bloom or smell sweetly on Sunday.

What though a good precept we strain
    Till hateful and hurtful we make it!
What though, in thus pulling the rein,
    We may draw it as tight as to break it!
Abroad we forbid folks to roam,
    For fear they get social or frisky;
But of course they can sit still at home,
    And get dismally drunk upon whisky.

Then, though we can't certainly tell
    How mirth may molest us on Monday;
At least, to begin the week well,
    Let us all be unhappy on Sunday.

JANE WELSH CARLYLE

1801–1866

NAY, THIS IS HOPE

Nay, this is Hope: a gentle dove,
   That nestles in the gentle breast,
Bringing glad tidings from above
   Of joys to come and heavenly rest.

And this is Life: ethereal fire
   Striving aloft through smothering clay;
Mounting, flaming, higher, higher!
   Till lost in immortality.

And Man – oh! hate not nor despise
   The fairest, lordliest work of God!
Think not He made the good and wise
   Only to sleep beneath the sod!

HORATIUS BONAR

1808–1889

LOVE IS OF GOD

Beloved, let us love: love is of God;
In God alone hath love its true abode.

Beloved, let us love: for they who love,
They only, are His sons, born from above.

Beloved, let us love: for love is rest,
And he who loveth not abides unblest.

Beloved, let us love: for love is light,
And he who loveth not dwelleth in night.

Beloved, let us love: for only thus
Shall we behold that God Who loveth us.

GEORGE MacDONALD

1824–1905

THE HOLY SNOWDROPS

Of old, with goodwill from the skies,
  The holy angels came;
They walked the earth with human eyes,
  And passed away in flame.

But now the angels are withdrawn,
  Because the flowers can speak;
With Christ, we see the dayspring dawn
  In every snowdrop meek.

God sends them forth; to God they tend;
  Not less with love they burn,
That to the earth they lowly bend,
  And unto dust return.

No miracle in them hath place,
  For this world is their home;
An utterance of essential grace
  The angel-snowdrops come.

PILATE'S WIFE

Strangely thy whispered message ran,
  Almost in form behest!
Why came in dreams the low-born man
  To part thee from thy rest?

It may be that some spirit fair,
  Who knew not what must be,
Fled in the anguish of his care
  For help for him from thee.

For rather would I think thee great;
  That rumours upward went,
And pierced the palisades of state
  In which thy rank was pent;

And that a Roman matron thou,
  Too noble for thy spouse,
The far-heard grandeur must allow,
  And sit with pondering brows.

And so thy maidens' gathered tale
  For thee with wonder teems;
Thou sleepest, and the prisoner pale
  Returneth in thy dreams.

And thou hast suffered for his sake
  Sad visions all the night:
One day thou wilt, then first awake,
  Rejoice in his dear light.

JAMES MacFARLAN

1832–1862

THE LORDS OF LABOUR

They come, they come, in a glorious march,
   You can hear their steam-steeds neigh,
As they dash through Skill's triumphal arch,
   Or plunge 'mid the dancing spray.
Their bale-fires blaze in the mighty forge,
   Their life-pulse throbs in the mill,
Their lightnings shiver the gaping gorge,
   And their thunders shake the hill.
      Ho! these are the Titans of toil and trade,
         The heroes who wield no sabre;
      But mightier conquests reapeth the blade
         That is borne by the lords of labour.

Brave hearts like jewels light the sod,
   Through the mists of commerce shine,
And souls flash out, like stars of God,
   From the midnight of the mine.
No palace is theirs, no castle great,
   No princely pillar'd hall,
But they well may laugh at the roofs of state,
   'Neath the heaven which is over all.
      Ho! these are the Titans of toil and trade,
         The heroes who wield no sabre;
      But mightier conquests reapeth the blade
         Which is borne by the lords of labour.

Each bares his arm for the ringing strife
   That marshals the sons of the soil,
And the sweat-drops shed in their battle of life
   Are gems in the crown of Toil.
And better their well-won wreaths, I trow,
   Than laurels with life-blood wet;

And nobler the arch of a bare bold brow,
Than the clasp of a coronet.
  Then hurrah for each hero, although his deed
    Be unblown by the trump or tabor.
  For holier, happier far is the meed
    That crowneth the lords of labour.

ALEXANDER CARMICHAEL

1832–1912

from CARMINA GADELICA

(collected and edited by Carmichael)

CUIRIM FIANAIS

(fuidheall)

Cuirim fianais gu Moire,
  Màthair chobhair an t-sluaigh;
Cuirim fianais gu Brìghde,
  Muime mhìn-ghil an Uain;

Cuirim fianais gu Peadail,
  Ostal eagail is suain;
Cuirim fianais gu Calum,
  Ostal airin is cuain;

Cuirim fianais gu Flathas,
  Dh'fhios na Cathair tha shuas;
Cuirim fianais gu Mìcheil,
  Ard-mhìlidh nam buadh;

Cuirim fianais gu Athair,
  A dh'altaich gach cré;
Cuirim fianais gu Crìosda,
  Fhuair mìostath is péin;

Cuirim fianais gu Spiorad,
  A ligheas mo chreuchd,
'S a dh'fhàgas mi gile
  Mar chanach an t-sléibh.

I SEND WITNESS

(a fragment)

I send witness to Mary,
Mother who aids men;
I send witness to Brigit,
Pure tender Nurse of the Lamb;

I send witness to Peter,
Apostle of fear and of sleep;
I send witness to Columba,
Apostle of shore and sea;

I send witness to Heaven,
To the City on high;
I send witness to Michael,
Noble warrior triumphant;

I send witness to Father,
Who formed all flesh;
I send witness to Christ,
Who suffered scorn and pain;

I send witness to Spirit,
Who will heal my wound,
Who will make me as white
As the cotton-grass of the moor.

translated from the Gaelic by Alexander Carmichael

ACHAN CHADAIL

Laighim sìos a nochd
  Le Brìghde nam brot,
Le Muire nan sìth,
  Le Iosa nam bochd.

Laighim sìos a nochd
  Le Brìghde na ciùin,
Le Muire na toirt,
  Le Mìchael mo rùin.

Laighim sìos a nochd
  Am fochair Rìgh nan dùl,
Am fochair Crìosd nan nochd,
  Am fochair Spioraid Nùmh.

Laighim sìos a nochd
  Le na naoi croisean fionn,
O bharra mo chinn
  Gu traighean mo bhonn;
    O bharra mo chinn
      Gu traighean mo bhonn.

SLEEP INVOCATION

I lie down this night
With Brigit of the mantles,
With Mary of peace,
With Jesus of the poor.

I lie down this night
With Brigit of calmness,
With Mary revered,
With Michael of my love.

I lie down this night
Near the King of life,
Near Christ of the destitute,
Near the Holy Spirit.

I lie down this night
With the nine angels,
From the crown of my head
To the soles of my feet;
    From the crown of my head
    To the soles of my feet.

translated from the Gaelic by Alexander Carmichael

SÌTH

Sìth Dhé dhomh, sìth dhaoine,
Sìth Chaluim Chille chaomha,
Sìth Mhoire mhìn na gaoldachd,
Sìth Chrìosda Rìgh na daondachd,
  Sìth Chrìosda Rìgh na daondachd,

Air gach uinneig, air gach doras,
Air gach toll a leigeas solas,
Air ceithir oiseannan mo thaighe,
Air ceithir oiseannan mo leaba,
  Air ceithir oiseannan mo leaba;

Air gach nì a chì mo shùil,
Air gach sìon a tha dha m' bhrù,
Air mo chorp a tha dh'an ùir
Is air m'anam thàin os cionn,
  Air mo chorp a tha dh'an ùir
  Is air m'anam thàin os cionn.

PEACE

The peace of God, the peace of men,
The peace of Columba kindly,
The peace of Mary mild, the loving,
The peace of Christ, King of tenderness,
    The peace of Christ, King of tenderness,

Be upon each window, upon each door,
Upon each hole that lets in light,
Upon the four corners of my house,
Upon the four corners of my bed,
    Upon the four corners of my bed;

Upon each thing my eye takes in,
Upon each thing my mouth takes in,
Upon my body that is of earth
And upon my soul that came from on high,
    Upon my body that is of earth
    And upon my soul that came from on high.

translated from the Gaelic by Alexander Carmichael

JAMES THOMSON ('B. V.')
1834–1882

from THE CITY OF DREADFUL NIGHT

'Per me si va nella città dolente.' – Dante

'Poi di tanto adoprar, di tanti moti
D'ogni celeste, ogni terrena cosa,
Girando senza posa,
Per tornar sempre là donde son mosse;
Uso alcuno, alcun frutto
Indovinar non so.'

'Sola nel mondo eterna, a cui si volve
Ogni creata cosa,
In te, morte, si posa
Nostra ignuda natura;
Lieta no, ma sicura
Dell' antico dolor …
Però ch' esser beato
Nega ai mortali e nega a' morti il fato.' – Leopardi

PROEM

Lo, thus, as prostrate, 'In the dust I write
 My heart's deep languor and my soul's sad tears.'
Yet why evoke the spectres of black night
 To blot the sunshine of exultant years?
Why disinter dead faith from mouldering hidden?
Why break the seals of mute despair unbidden,
 And wail life's discards into careless ears?

Because a cold rage seizes one at whiles
 To show the bitter old and wrinkled truth
Stripped naked of all vesture that beguiles,
 False dreams, false hopes, false masks and modes of youth;
Because it gives some sense of power and passion
In helpless impotence to try to fashion
 Our woe in living words howe'er uncouth.

Surely I write not for the hopeful young,
  Or those who deem their happiness of worth,
Or such as pasture and grow fat among
  The shows of life and feel nor doubt nor dearth,
Or pious spirits with a God above them
To sanctify and glorify and love them,
  Or sages who foresee a heaven on earth.

For none of these I write, and none of these
  Could read the writing if they deigned to try:
So may they flourish, in their due degrees,
  On our sweet earth and in their unplaced sky.
If any cares for the weak words here written,
It must be some one desolate, Fate-smitten,
  Whose faith and hope are dead, and who would die.

Yes, here and there some weary wanderer
  In that same city of tremendous night,
Will understand the speech, and feel a stir
  Of fellowship in all-disastrous fight;
'I suffer mute and lonely, yet another
Uplifts his voice to let me know a brother
  Travels the same wild paths though out of sight.'

O sad Fraternity, do I unfold
  Your dolorous mysteries shrouded from of yore?
Nay, be assured; no secret can be told
  To any who divined it not before:
None uninitiate by many a presage
Will comprehend the language of the message,
  Although proclaimed aloud for evermore.

I

The City is of Night; perchance of Death,
  But certainly of Night; for never there
Can come the lucid morning's fragrant breath
  After the dewy dawning's cold grey air;
The moon and stars may shine with scorn or pity;
The sun has never visited that city,
  For it dissolveth in the daylight fair.

Dissolveth like a dream of night away;
    Though present in distempered gloom of thought
And deadly weariness of heart all day.
    But when a dream night after night is brought
Throughout a week, and such weeks few or many
Recur each year for several years, can any
    Discern that dream from real life in aught?

For life is but a dream whose shapes return,
    Some frequently, some seldom, some by night
And some by day, some night and day: we learn,
    The while all change and many vanish quite,
In their recurrence with recurrent changes
A certain seeming order; where this ranges
    We count things real; such is memory's might.

A river girds the city west and south,
    The main north channel of a broad lagoon,
Regurging with the salt tides from the mouth;
    Waste marshes shine and glister to the moon
For leagues, then moorland black, then stony ridges;
Great piers and causeways, many noble bridges,
    Connect the town and islet suburbs strewn.

Upon an easy slope it lies at large,
    And scarcely overlaps the long curved crest
Which swells out two leagues from the river marge.
    A trackless wilderness rolls north and west,
Savannahs, savage woods, enormous mountains,
Bleak uplands, black ravines with torrent fountains;
    And eastward rolls the shipless sea's unrest.

The city is not ruinous, although
    Great ruins of an unremembered past,
With others of a few short years ago
    More sad, are found within its precincts vast.
The street-lamps always burn; but scarce a casement
In house or palace front from roof to basement
    Doth glow or gleam athwart the mirk air cast.

The street-lamps burn amidst the baleful glooms,
  Amidst the soundless solitudes immense
Of rangèd mansions dark and still as tombs.
  The silence which benumbs or strains the sense
Fulfils with awe the soul's despair unweeping:
Myriads of habitants are ever sleeping,
  Or dead, or fled from nameless pestilence!

Yet as in some necropolis you find
  Perchance one mourner to a thousand dead,
So there; worn faces that look deaf and blind
  Like tragic masks of stone. With weary tread,
Each wrapt in his own doom, they wander, wander,
Or sit foredone and desolately ponder
  Through sleepless hours with heavy drooping head.

Mature men chiefly, few in age or youth,
  A woman rarely, now and then a child:
A child! If here the heart turns sick with ruth
  To see a little one from birth defiled,
Or lame or blind, as preordained to languish
Through youthless life, think how it bleeds with anguish
  To meet one erring in that homeless wild.

They often murmur to themselves, they speak
  To one another seldom, for their woe
Broods maddening inwardly and scorns to wreak
  Itself abroad; and if at whiles it grow
To frenzy which must rave, none heeds the clamour,
Unless there waits some victim of like glamour,
  To rave in turn, who lends attentive show.

The City is of Night, but not of Sleep;
  There sweet sleep is not for the weary brain;
The pitiless hours like years and ages creep,
  A night seems termless hell. This dreadful strain
Of thought and consciousness which never ceases,
Of which some moments' stupor but increases,
  This, worse than woe, makes wretches there insane.

They leave all hope behind who enter there:
    One certitude while sane they cannot leave,
One anodyne for torture and despair;
    The certitude of Death, which no reprieve
Can put off long; and which, divinely tender,
But waits the outstretched hand to promptly render
    That draught whose slumber nothing can bereave.*

II

Because he seemed to walk with an intent
    I followed him; who, shadowlike and frail,
Unswervingly though slowly onward went,
    Regardless, wrapt in thought as in a veil:
Thus step for step with lonely sounding feet
We travelled many a long dim silent street.

At length he paused: a black mass in the gloom,
    A tower that merged into the heavy sky;
Around, the huddled stones of grave and tomb:
    Some old God's-acre now corruption's sty:
He murmured to himself with dull despair,
Here Faith died, poisoned by this charnel air.

Then turning to the right went on once more,
    And travelled weary roads without suspense;
And reached at last a low wall's open door,
    Whose villa gleamed beyond the foliage dense:
He gazed, and muttered with a hard despair,
Here Love died, stabbed by its own worshipped pair.

Then turning to the right resumed his march,
    And travelled streets and lanes with wondrous strength,
Until on stooping through a narrow arch
    We stood before a squalid house at length:
He gazed, and whispered with a cold despair,
Here Hope died, starved out in its utmost lair.

**Though the Garden of thy Life be wholly waste, the sweet flowers withered, the fruit-trees, barren, over its wall hang ever the rich dark clusters of the Vine of Death, within easy reach of thy hand, which may pluck of them when it will* [J.T.'s note.]

When he had spoken thus, before he stirred,
I spoke, perplexed by something in the signs
Of desolation I had seen and heard
In this drear pilgrimage to ruined shrines:
When Faith and Love and Hope are dead indeed,
Can Life still live? By what doth it proceed?

As whom his one intense thought overpowers,
He answered coldly, Take a watch, erase
The signs and figures of the circling hours,
Detach the hands, remove the dial-face;
The works proceed until run down; although
Bereft of purpose, void of use, still go.

Then turning to the right paced on again,
And transversed squares and travelled streets whose glooms
Seemed more and more familiar to my ken;
And reached that sullen temple of the tombs;
And paused to murmur with the old despair,
Here Faith died, poisoned by this charnel air.

I ceased to follow, for the knot of doubt
Was severed sharply with a cruel knife:
He circled thus for ever tracing out
The series of the fraction left of Life;
Perpetual recurrence in the scope
Of but three terms, dead Faith, dead Love, dead Hope.*

* Life divided by that persistent three $\frac{LXX}{333} = .\dot{2}1\dot{0}$. [J.T.'s note]

GEORGE MATHESON

1842–1906

O LOVE THAT WILT NOT LET ME GO

O Love that wilt not let me go,
 I rest my weary soul in Thee:
I give Thee back the life I owe,
That in Thine ocean depths its flow
 May richer fuller be.

O Light that followest all my way,
 I yield my flickering torch to Thee:
My heart restores its borrowed ray,
That in Thy sunshine's blaze its day
 May brighter, fairer be.

O Joy that seekest me through pain,
 I cannot close my heart to Thee:
I trace the rainbow through the rain,
And feel the promise is not vain,
 That morn shall tearless be.

O Cross that liftest up my head,
 I dare not ask to fly from Thee:
I lay in dust life's glory dead,
And from the ground there blossoms red
 Life that shall endless be.

ANONYMOUS

*c.*1850

A DISRUPTION RHYME

The Wee Kirk,
The Free Kirk,
The Kirk withoot the steeple;
The Auld Kirk,
The cauld Kirk,
The Kirk withoot the people.

ROBERT LOUIS STEVENSON

1850–1894

IF THIS WERE FAITH

God, if this were enough,
That I see things bare to the buff
And up to the buttocks in mire;
That I ask nor hope nor hire,
Nut in the husk,
Nor dawn beyond the dusk,
Nor life beyond death:
God, if this were faith?

Having felt thy wind in my face
Spit sorrow and disgrace,
Having seen thine evil doom
In Golgotha and Khartoum,
And the brutes, the work of thine hands,
Fill with injustice lands
And stain with blood the sea:
If still in my veins the glee
Of the black night and the sun
And the lost battle, run:
If, an adept,
The iniquitous lists I still accept
With joy, and joy to endure and be withstood,
And still to battle and perish for a dream of good:
God, if that were enough?

If to feel, in the ink of the slough,
And the sink of the mire,
Veins of glory and fire
Run through and transpierce and transpire,
And a secret purpose of glory in every part,
And the answering glory of battle fill my heart;
To thrill with the joy of girded men

To go on forever and fail and go on again,
And be mauled to the earth and arise,
And contend for the shade of a word and a thing not seen with the eyes:
With the half of a broken hope for a pillow at night
That somehow the right is the right
And the smooth shall bloom from the rough:
Lord, if that were enough?

REQUIEM

Under the wide and starry sky,
Dig the grave and let me lie.
Glad did I live and gladly die,
    And I laid me down with a will.

This be the verse you grave for me:
Here he lies where he longed to be;
Home is the sailor, home from sea,
    And the hunter home from the hill.

JOHN DAVIDSON

1857–1909

TO THE GENERATION KNOCKING AT THE DOOR

Break – break it open; let the knocker rust:
Consider no 'shalt not', and no man's 'must':
And, being entered, promptly take the lead,
Setting aside tradition, custom, creed;
Nor watch the balance of the huckster's beam;
Declare your hardiest thought, your proudest dream:
Await no summons; laugh at all rebuff;
High hearts and youth are destiny enough.
The mystery and the power enshrined in you
Are old as time and as the moment new:
And none but you can tell what part you play,
Nor can you tell until you make assay,
For this alone, this always, will succeed,
The miracle and magic of the deed.

AN T-ATHAIR AILEAN DÒMHNALLACH/FATHER ALLAN MACDONALD

1859–1905

AN EAGLAIS

Innseam sgeul mun aona bhàrca,
An aon té s tréine chaidh air sàile,
Nach fhaca sùil té riamh a b' àille,
Dalta an t-saoir a rinn a càradh,
Eadar druim is cliathaich is clàraidh –
Chuir e h-uile bòrd an tàthadh dhi
'S cha robh cearb air saothair a làimh'-sa.

Thug e fichead bliadhna 'n sàs innt'
Is trì diag mun tug e a thàl dith,
'S dh'fhàg e i gu daingeann, làidir –
Cha tig i ás a chèil' gu bràch air.

A farrdhruim, cha ghiubhas bàn i,
A thollte le giùrain 's a chnàmhadh,
No darach ruighinn, chan e b' fheàrr leis,
Ach am fiodh sa choill' bu tàireil,
Irisleachd a bhios ag ràdh ris.

Thòisich e a shaothair an stàball,
Far nach faighte reudan *àrdain*,
Chuir an gaise anns gach bàta
Thog ri crannaibh na siùil bhàna,
'N dùil gun ruigeadh àit' an Àirdrigh,
Gus na chìosnaicheadh an dànachd,
Mar a dh'éirich do na h-ainglean
A chaidh fodha an loch nach tàmh ann.

THE CHURCH

I'll tell a tale of a single ship,
The strongest that was ever launched,
Than which no eye has spied more splendid:
Adopted child of the wright who repaired her,
All of her keel and hull and flooring –
He fixed together her every plank
And faultless was the work of His hand.

He worked on her for twenty years
And thirteen until He took away his adze,
Leaving her watertight and strong –
She won't ever come apart on Him.

Her slip-keel, no white pine is it
That barnacles could pierce and wear away,
Or tough oak, that is not what He liked,
But the timber most scorned in the wood –
Humility is what they call it.

He began his labours in a stable
Where the rot of *pride* was absent
Which has blemished every boat
That has hoisted white sails to her masts,
Imagining she'd reach the High King's place
Until their importunity was crushed,
Exactly as happened to the angels
Who sank in a lake where none survive.

Tonnan dearga, lasraich gharga,
Dìol a chorruich-sa gu feargach,
Fhuair an tàmailt bho a luchd fharmaid
Bha cho lìonmhor dha ri'n àireamh,
Is cho loinnearach 'nan àilleachd
Ris na rionnagan tha deàrrsadh
Ré na h-oidhche anns na h-àrdaibh:
Gun chuimhn' no taing air son na thàrladh
Orra a bhuadhannan 's a ghràsan;
Sann a dh'aontaich iad le Sàtan –
'S air a chomhairle chaidh gu blàr leis,
'S gun ruaigte an Tighearna bho àros,

'S mar a thàrladh dhan a' chàraid
A shuidhicheadh an sòlas Phàrais,
A chuairticheadh le h-uile tàlann
Gus na dh'éist iad ris an Nàmhaid
Bha gan spreòdadh le smaoin dhàna,
Choisinn dhaibh an ruaig on ghàrradh,
Is am fuadachadh bho chàirdeas
Bhith fo riasladh gach mèinn sgràthail;
Is fad' an saoghal a bhith fo ànradh,
Gu 'n sgaradh o'm beatha am bàs iad,

Shiubhail e air feadh an fhàsaich,
'S anns an Éipheit fad' o chàirdean
Thug e aon seachd bliadhn' gun tàmh ann,
Air tòir gach fiodh a b' fheàrr dhan bhàta;
'S air tilleadh dha gu baile Nàsret
Ghabh e locair, tuagh is tàl rith'
'S chuir e snas is neart 's gach pàirt dith.

H-uile bliadhna ach trì roimh bhàs dha
Cha robh fois a dh'oidhch' no là dha,
Ach ga togail suas nas àirde
Gus na dh'fhàgadh i cho stàtail
Nach seallte Àrca Noë làmh rith' –
Bu mhaireannaich' na 'n t-òr a tàirnean
Bha fuaigheal 's a càradh cho làidir,
Nach bu bheud dhi cuan, dh'a ghàbhachd.

Red waves, turbulent flames,
Expressing His anger forcefully,
He was insulted by His rivals,
Who were too many for Him to count,
And as brilliant in their beauty
As the stars that coruscate
All the night long around the skies:
With no memory or gratefulness
For the powers and grace that were given them,
They had made a pact with the Devil –
Agreeing to take his side in the battle
To drive the Lord away from His palace.

And as had happened to the couple
Who had been placed in Heaven's bliss
Surrounded by every luxury
Until they listened to the Devil
Tempting them with impertinent thoughts
Which earned their expulsion from the garden,
And their banishment from friendship
To be wracked by every ghastly desire;
And for all their days to be distressed
Till death deprived them of their lives,

He travelled all around the desert
And in Egypt, far from his kinsfolk,
He spent full seven restless years
In search of each timber best for the boat,
And when He got back to Nazareth's town
He took a plane, an axe and an adze to it
And made each part of it neat and strong.

Each year but three before He died
There was no rest for Him night or day,
Nothing but building her higher and higher
Till she was looking so majestic
That she put Noah's Ark in the shade –
Her nails were more permanent than gold,
Her sutures and fittings so strong that no sea
Could damage her, dangerous though it be.

Thogadh suas innt' trì chroinn àrda,
Creideamh, dòchas, agus gràdh iad.
Bha i deas gu dol air sàile,
'S thriall Mac Dé air feadh gach àite
Thional sgioba ghlic gun dànachd
Ris an earbadh anns gach gàbhadh i.
Thug e trì bliadhna le ànradh
Gan ionnsachadh sa h-uile sàrchleas –
Cha robh fios a sheasadh càs daibh,
Cha robh cleas, no car, no tàbhachd
Dh'fheumte chleachdadh leò ri ànsid'
Nach do chuir gu domhain annta;
'S chuireadh air an luing mar cheannard
Gaisgeach treun air liathadh a sheann-duin',
B' eòlach riamh o òig' bhith 'n gàbhadh,
'S dh'ionnsaich dha an ailm a làimhseach':
Peadar a ainm, bha mheas cho àraid.

Three high masts were hoisted in her,
They were faith and hope and love.
She was ready to go to sea
And God's Son travelled everywhere
To gather a wise and phlegmatic crew
Who could be trusted with her in a crisis.
He spent three tempestuous years
Instructing them in each special skill –
There was no way of withstanding danger,
No method, turn, or trick of the trade
That they must practise in foul weather
That He didn't put deep inside them.
And on the ship was placed a skipper
A brave hero who'd greyed into a veteran,
Accustomed to danger from his youth,
And he was trained to take the helm:
Peter his name, his faith outstanding.

translated from the Gaelic by Ronald Black

JESSIE ANNIE ANDERSON

1861–1931

AT SWEET MARY'S SHRINE

I'll sleep me soun' the nicht while sigh
  The saughs an' tender Ythan: willows
They're singin' tae the sairest he'rt
  That e'er Luve aince was blythe in.

Luve broke my he'rt, an' got within –
  He only tried tae pain it: –
How could Luve brak' sae saft a he'rt? –
  I never socht tae hain it. protect

I tak' the simple, ae-fauld thing honest
  That's been sae sairly siftit, sieved
An' lay it on sweet Mary's shrine,
  An' leave her grace tae lift it.

THE BACK O' HAIRST

It's the Back o' Hairst upon Ythanside,
   An' the leme o' the rowan's deid
That mindit me i' the mids o' my hairst
   Upon hairt-wrung draps o' bluid.

'Twas a' but a puir, scant hairst that I shore,
   But I gaithered it wi' a will;
Now I rest my hands on his cross, and pray
   Saint Andrew to sain the mill.

May never a mealoch o' bitterness fa'
   Frae the mill whaur I grind my corn;
An' may I hain naething o'care or kann
   As I bake my breid the morn.

An' I'll licht a can'le the morn's nicht
   When I gang to sweet Mary's Shrine,
For, although the leme o' the rowan's deid,
   She's lichtit this hairt o' mine.

An' I'll licht anither to God Whase Grace
   Ga'e strength to win throu' wi' it a';
Though 'twas hungry lan' that I seedit in,
   An' kepit owre miekle snaw.

VIOLET JACOB

1863–1946

TAM I' THE KIRK

O Jean, my Jean, when the bell ca's the congregation
O'er valley and hill wi' the ding frae its iron mou',
When a'body's thochts is set on their ain salvation,
   Mine's set on you.

There's a reid rose lies on the Buik o' the Word afore ye
That was growin' braw on its bush at the keek o' day, dawn
But the lad that pu'd yon flower i' the mornin's glory
   He canna pray.

He canna pray, but there's nane i' the kirk will heed him
Whaur he sits sae still his lane at the side o' the wa', by himself
For nane but the reid rose kens what my lassie gied him –
   It and us twa.

He canna sing for the sang that his ain he'rt raises,
He canna see for the mist that's afore his een, eyes
And a voice droons the hale o' the psalms and the paraphrases
   Crying 'Jean! Jean! Jean!'

THE DEIL

Beside the birks I met the Deil,
   A wheen o' words I niffered wi' him
And, clear and lang, the wuds amang
   The merle sang whaur ye couldna see him;
The pale spring licht was late when he
   Was whustling tae the Deil and me.

I didna think it was himsel',
   I thocht he had been auld an' crookit,
Sae thrawn an' grim in ilka limb
   Ye'd ken him by the way he lookit;
Wha'd think the Deil wad linger on
   Tae listen till a bird like yon?

They tell't me that the Deil was black
   And blacker nor the corbie's feather,
But, loopin' doon, a-lowe wi' noon,
   Nae burn broun frae the peat an' heather,
Had e'er the shine ye wad hae seen
   Laid sleepin' i' the Deevil's een.

'The polestar kens ma bed,' says he,
   'I hae the rovin' gled for brither,
The hill crest is ma hoose o' rest,
   An' it's far west that I'd seek anither;
Alang the edge o' simmer nicht
   The wildfire is ma ingle-licht.'

The wuds were still, the merle was hame,
   The mist abune the strath was hangin',
Yet I could see him smile tae me
   When syne he turned him tae be gangin',
And ne'er a faur-ye-weel he spak'
   As he gaed frae me, lookin' back.

Ma feyther's hoose is puir an' cauld,
The winter winds blaw lang and sairly,
The muircocks ca' and hoodie craw,
It's nichtfa' sune, we're workin' airly;
Oot i' the wuds, the lee lang year
Nae treid amang the birks ye'll hear.

Fu' mony a man has speir'd at me
And thocht a wife he micht be findin',
But na—there's nane I could hae ta'en
But just ane that I'll aye be mindin';
Him that ma mither kens richt weel
Had been nae ither nor the Deil!

CHARLES MURRAY

1864–1941

GIN I WAS GOD

Gin I was God, sittin' up there abeen, If; above
Weariet nae doot noo a' my darg was deen, slog; over
Deaved wi' the harps an' hymns oonendin' ringin', deafened
Tired o' the flockin' angels hairse wi' singin',
To some clood-edge I'd daunder furth an', feth, stroll
Look ower an' watch hoo things were gyaun aneth. going below
Syne, gin I saw hoo men I'd made mysel' Then
Had startit in to pooshan, sheet an' fell, poison; shoot; slaughter
To reive an' rape, an' fairly mak' a hell steal
O' my braw birlin' Earth, – a hale week's wark –
I'd cast my coat again, rowe up my sark, roll; shirt
An', or they'd time to lench a second ark, before; launch
Tak' back my word an' sen' anither spate, flood
Droon oot the hale hypothec, dicht the sklate, concern; wipe the slate
Own my mistak', an', aince I'd cleared the brod, board
Start a'thing ower again, gin I was God.

MARION ANGUS

1865–1946

MARY'S SONG

I wad ha'e gi'en him my lips tae kiss,
Had I been his, had I been his;
Barley breid and elder wine,
Had I been his as he is mine.

The wanderin' bee it seeks the rose;
Tae the lochan's bosom the burnie goes;
The grey bird cries at evenin's fa',
'My luve, my fair one, come awa'.'

My beloved sall ha'e this he'rt tae break,
Reid, reid wine and the barley cake,
A he'rt tae break, and a mou' tae kiss,
Tho' he be nae mine, as I am his.

THE MOURNERS

They carried her to the little kirk
Through the autumn day—
The little kirk among the trees.
Sombre, sad and ill at ease
I heard the mourners say:
'She was once a fine lass;
All flesh is as grass.
We go down, every one,
In sorrow when our day is done.'

When they came to the little kirk
Very old and grey,
Fair shone the elder-trees,
Elm and oak and mulberries,
In beauty magical
Robed for the festival
Of this their dying day.
And still I heard them say:
'We go down, every one,
In sorrow when our day is done.'

AONGHAS MOIREASDAN/ ANGUS MORRISON

1865–1942

MADAINN NA SÀBAID

Cia bòidheach sèimh madainn na Sàbaid,
gu sònraichte air an dùthaich,
co-ainm an là air an d'éirich
ar Slànaigheir bho uaigh a bhàis,
's 'na dhéidh sin an ùine gheàrr
chaidh e suas 'na ghlòir
gu deas-làmh na Cathrach.
Gu ruig an là sin,
là deireannach na seachdain
bho chruthachadh an t-saoghail,
's mar chuimhneachan air aiseirigh
goirear dheth a' chiad là den t-seachdain
gu ruig deireadh na cruinne.
Ar leam gu bheil na diasan arbhair
cromadh an ceann le beic spéiseil,
a' toirt urraim don mhadainn
mhaiseach chiùin-bhog ghrinn,
a' ghrian mhór-gheal bheannaichte
ag òradh mullach nan cruach
is binnean nam beann
air dhòigh barraichte 's an t-alltan
ri m' thaobh le crònan nas mìlse
na 'n àbhaist air a shlighe
troimhn àilean gus an sluigear e
am beul a' chuain bhith-bhuan.
Tha an t-ainmhidh fhéin
a' mealtainn na fois bheannaichte,
's an t-each gu sicir seasgair
san stàball 'na laigh gun charachadh,
'S e cho mothachail, mo thruaigh,
ri cuid den chinne-daoine
air sochairean spéiseil an là seo.
Tha 'n duine air fois fhaotainn bho obair lathail,
's gu dleasail ma tha e air sligh' a dhleasnais
a' triall don eaglais gu ìota a riarachadh

THE SABBATH MORNING

How lovely and quiet is the Sabbath morning,
especially in the country,
named for the day when our Saviour
arose from the grave of his death,
and a short time after that
he went up in his glory
to the right hand of the Throne.
Until that day
the last day of the week
since the creation of the world,
and in memory of resurrection
it will be called the first day of the week
until the end of the globe.
It seems to me that the ears of corn
are bending their heads in respectful bow,
honouring the morning
that's lovely, calmly-soft and elegant,
the brilliant blessed sun
gilding the tops of the hills
and the mountain peaks
in a splendid way while the burn
beside me croons more sweetly
than usual on its way
through the meadow till it's swallowed
in the mouth of the eternal sea.
Even the animal
enjoys the blessed rest,
with the horse sensible and snug
in the stable lying motionless,
he being as aware, sad to say,
as some of mankind
of the treasured benefits of this day.
Man has got rest from his daily toil,
and dutifully if he is on the path of duty
he goes to church to satisfy his thirst

le deoch ùrail á tobar prìseil na slàinte
gheibh e bhon aoghair chràbhach,
's e gu deas uidheamaichte,
ma tha e san spiorad togarrach
gu sin a thoirt dha.
Tha dleasaileachd is dleasaileachd ann.
Iain còir 's am fuar-chràbhadh
air ruigheachd thar bhàrr do smige
cha d'fhàiltich mi air madainn na Sàbaid,
ged bha thu coibhneil gu leòir
nuair thachair mi ort air madainn Di-Luain,
's do choimhearsnach a choisicheas
na mìltean don eaglais
's nach gabh sochair 'carbad-coise' –
iad seo 'nan eisimpleir air beachdan cuid
mar as còir an t-Sàbaid a naomhachadh,
lagh nan deas-ghnàth air faotainn
barrachd àite 'nan cridhe na feartan
an spioraid a dh'ath-bheothaicheas.
Sealladh eile.
Na mìltean cur là na Sàbaid
fo'n casan gu dàna ladarna,
's an là chaidh ullachadh air an son
gu fois a ghabhail cho tàireil 'nan sùil
ris a' mheanbhchuileig.
Beachdan ceàrr air tighinn am follais
is sgoilean mì-Chrìostail air an là naomh
air togail cinn an-siud 's an-seo
anns a bheil cuspairean air an càramh
ri cridheachan na h-òigridh
tha calg-dhìreach an aghaidh teagasg a' Bhìobaill,
cluiche dibhearsan spòrs feala-dhà
air fàs cho cumanta, 's a dh'fhaodas a bhith
ceadaichte 's iomchaidh air làithean eile,
mar gum b'e crìoch àraidh an duine
ith òl 's bi subhach.
Dìomhanas nan dìomhanas.
Ciamar ma-tà a their thu
as còir don t-Sàbaid
bhith air a cumail?
Mar èarlas air an fhois shìorraidh
chaidh ullachadh dhaibhsan
aig a bheil gràdh do Dhia.

with a refreshing drink from the precious well of salvation
which he gets from the pious shepherd,
he being ready and prepared,
if he is in spirit liberated
to give him that.
There's duty and there's duty.
Honest John whose hypocrisy
has stretched past the tip of your chin
greeted me not on the Sabbath morning,
though you were decent enough
when I met you on Monday morning,
and your neighbour who walks
miles to church
and won't make use of a tramway car –
these are examples of some folk's opinions
of how the Sabbath should be kept holy,
the ceremonial law having found
more room in their hearts than the virtues
of the spirit which brings back to life.
Another view.
The thousands trampling the Sabbath
underfoot with brazen impudence,
the day prepared for them
to take their rest as contemptible in their eyes
as the midge.
Wrong opinions have come to light
with un-Christian schools on the holy day
appearing here and there
in which subjects are drummed
into young people's hearts
which are totally opposed to the teaching of Scripture,
games entertainment sports amusement
have become so common, and which may be
permissible and proper on other days,
as if man's chief end were
eat drink and be merry.
Vanity of vanities.
How then do you say
the Sabbath ought
to be kept?
As a pledge of the eternal rest
that has been prepared for those
who have love for God.

translated from the Gaelic by Ronald Black

EDWIN MUIR

1887–1959

ONE FOOT IN EDEN

One foot in Eden still, I stand
And look across the other land.
The world's great day is growing late,
Yet strange these fields that we have planted
So long with crops of love and hate.
Time's handiworks by time are haunted,
And nothing now can separate
The corn and tares compactly grown.
The armorial weed in stillness bound
About the stalk; these are our own.
Evil and good stand thick around
In the fields of charity and sin
Where we shall lead our harvest in.

Yet still from Eden springs the root
As clean as on the starting day.
Time takes the foliage and the fruit
And burns the archetypal leaf
To shapes of terror and of grief
Scattered along the winter way.
But famished field and blackened tree
Bear flowers in Eden never known.
Blossoms of grief and charity
Bloom in these darkened fields alone.
What had Eden ever to say
Of hope and faith and pity and love
Until was buried all its day
And memory found its treasure trove?
Strange blessings never in Paradise
Fall from these beclouded skies.

THE HEART COULD NEVER SPEAK

The heart could never speak
But that the Word was spoken.
We hear the heart break
Here with hearts unbroken.
Time, teach us the art
That breaks and heals the heart.

Heart, you would be dumb
But that your word was said
In time, and the echoes come
Thronging from the dead.
Time, teach us the art
That resurrects the heart.

Tongue, you can only say
Syllables, joy and pain,
Till time, having its way,
Makes the word live again.
Time, merciful lord,
Grant us to learn your word.

THE ANNUNCIATION

The angel and the girl are met.
Earth was the only meeting place.
For the embodied never yet
Travelled beyond the shore of space.
The eternal spirits in freedom go.

See, they have come together, see,
While the destroying minutes flow,
Each reflects the other's face
Till heaven in hers and earth in his
Shine steady there. He's come to her
From far beyond the farthest star,
Feathered through time. Immediacy
Of strangest strangeness is the bliss
That from their limbs all movement takes.
Yet the increasing rapture brings
So great a wonder that it makes
Each feather tremble on his wings.

Outside the window footsteps fall
Into the ordinary day
And with the sun along the wall
Pursue their unreturning way.
Sound's perpetual roundabout
Rolls its numbered octaves out
And hoarsely grinds its battered tune.

But through the endless afternoon
These neither speak nor movement make,
But stare into their deepening trance
As if their gaze would never break.

HUGH MacDIARMID
1892–1978

CROWDIEKNOWE

Oh to be at Crowdieknowe
When the last trumpet blaws,
An' see the deid come loupin' owre — leaping
The auld grey wa's.

Muckle men wi' tousled beards,
I grat at as a bairn — wept, child
'll scramble frae the croodit clay
Wi' feck o' swearin'. — plenty

An' glower at God an' a' his gang
O' angels i' the lift — sky
– Thae trashy bleezin' French-like folk — those, blazing
Wha gar'd them shift! — made

Fain the weemun-folk'll seek
To mak' them haud their row
– *Fegs, God's no blate gin he stirs up* — faith (an exclamation), backward, if
The men o' Crowdieknowe!

NAN SHEPHERD

1893–1981

REAL PRESENCE

Clear as the endless ecstasy of stars
  That mount for ever on an intense air;
  Or running pools, of water cold and rare,
In chiselled gorges deep amid the scaurs,
So still, the bright dawn were their best device,
  Yet like a thought that has no end they flow;
  Or Venus, when her white unearthly glow
Sharpens like awe on skies as green as ice:

To such a clearness love is come at last,
  Not disembodied, transubstantiate,
    But substance and its essence now are one;
  And love informs, yet is the form create.
No false gods now, the images o'ercast,
  We are love's body, or we are undone.

JOE CORRIE

1894–1968

THE IMAGE O' GOD

Crawlin' aboot like a snail in the mud,
    Covered wi' clammy blae, — blue muck
Me, made after the image o' God –
    Jings! but it's laughable, tae.

Howkin' awa' 'neath a mountain o' stane, — Digging
    Gaspin' for want o' air,
The sweat makin' streams doon my bare back-bane
    And my knees a' hauckit and sair. — hacked

Strainin' and cursin' the hale shift through,
    Half-starved, half-blin', half-mad;
And the gaffer he says, 'Less dirt in that coal
    Or ye go up the pit, my lad!'

So I gi'e my life to the Nimmo squad
    For eicht and fower a day;
Me! made after the image o' God –
    Jings! but it's laughable, tae.

NAOMI MITCHISON

1897–1997

THE HOUSE OF THE HARE

At the time I was four years old
I went to glean with the women,
Working the way they told;
My eyes were blue like blue-bells,
Lighter than oats my hair;
I came from the house of the Haldanes
Of work and thinking and prayer
To the God who is crowned with thorn,
The friend of the Boar and the Bear,
But oh when I went from there,
In the corn, in the corn, in the corn,
I was married young to a hare!

We went to kirk on the Sunday
And the Haldanes did not see
That a Haldane had been born
To run from the Boar and the Bear,
And the thing had happened to me
The day that I went with the gleaners,
The day that I built the corn-house,
That is not built with prayer.
For oh I was clean set free,
In the corn, in the corn, in the corn,
I had lived three days with the hare!

ROBERT RENDALL

1898–1967

ANGLE OF VISION

But, John, have you seen the world, said he,
Trains and tramcars and sixty-seaters,
Cities in lands across the sea—
Giotto's tower and the dome of St. Peters?

No, but I've seen the arc of the earth,
From the Birsay shore, like the edge of a planet,
And the lifeboat plunge through the Pentland Firth
To a cosmic tide with the men that man it.

WILLIAM SOUTAR

1898–1943

FAITH

Look up; and yonder on the brae,
Like a sang in silence born,
Wi' the dayspring o' the day
Walks the snaw-white unicorn.

Sae far awa he leams in licht; gleams
And yet his glitter burns atween
The darkness hung ahint the hicht
And hidden in the lifted e'en. eyes

Look doun and doun; frae ilka airt
The flutherin worlds through darkness fa':
But yon bricht beast walks, in the hert,
Sae far awa; sae far awa.

FRANCISCAN EPISODE

Francis, wha thocht the gospel-words
Guid-news for ilka body,
Aince preach'd a sermon to the birds
And catechis'd a cuddie — horse

He was the haliest saint o' a'
Be grace and be affliction;
And kent God's craturs, great or sma',
Were ane in their election.

But ae day, when he was fell thrang — very busy
Confabbin wi' a gander,
A course gleg stug him sic a stang — cleg; sting
As fair rous'd up his dander.

'Be aff!' yapp't Francis wi' a yowt, — roar
'To Beelzebub your maister:'
And gied the gutsy beast a clowt
To gar it gang the faster.

DOROTHY MARGARET PAULIN

1904–1982

DECEMBER DAY

I ask no lovelier thing
Than this December silver:
See how the light flakes off the new-turned plough
Under the slow great swing
Of branches, silver-boled;
Not all the silken, tender ways of spring
Can over-pass this cold
And windy beauty; see
Where thin-blown ripples spreading
Pattern the water with a mesh of gold.
Not war, nor present misery,
Can rout earth's ageless peace
Or check the steady rhythm of her soil
To yield and year's increase.
Yet sun in earth, yet love in man works on,
And shall not cease.

KATHLEEN RAINE

1908–2003

HEIRLOOM

She gave me childhood's flowers,
Heather and wild thyme,
Eyebright and tormentil,
Lichen's mealy cup
Dry on wind-scored stone,
The corbies on the rock,
The rowan by the burn.

Sea-marvels a child beheld
Out in the fisherman's boat,
Fringed pulsing violet
Medusa, sea gooseberries,
Starfish on the sea-floor,
Cowries and rainbow-shells
From pools on a rocky shore,

Gave me her memories,
But kept her last treasure:
'When I was a lass,' she said,
'Sitting among the heather,
'Suddenly I saw
'That all the moor was alive!
'I have told no one before.'

That was my mother's tale.
Seventy years had gone
Since she saw the living skein
Of which the world is woven,
And having seen, knew all;
Through long indifferent years
Treasuring the priceless pearl.

NORMAN MacCAIG

1910–1996

JULY EVENING

A bird's voice chinks and tinkles
Alone in the gaunt reedbed –
   Tiny silversmith
Working late in the evening.

I sit and listen. The rooftop
With a quill of smoke stuck in it
   Wavers against the sky
In the dreamy heat of summer.

Flowers' closing time: bee lurches
Across the hayfield, singing
   And feeling its drunken way
Round the air's invisible corners.

And grass is grace. And charlock
Is gold of its own bounty.
   The broken chair by the wall
Is one with immortal landscapes.

Something has been completed
That everything is part of,
   Something that will go on
Being completed forever.

A. K.'S SUMMER HUT

It clamps itself to a rock, like a limpet,
And creeps up and down in a tide of people,
Hardly ever stranded in a tideless sabbath:
A pilgrimage place where all hymns are jubilant.

The starry revolutions around it,
The deer circling in new foundations
Of old worlds, the immortal noise
Of the river ghosted with salmon – these

Are a bloodstream it's a blood-drop in.
Such sharing. Such giving. See, at the window,
That silly chaffinch, practically talking Gaelic,
And the eiders domestic as farmyard ducks

And the lady gull yacking for her breakfast.
If I were a bethlehemish star I'd stand fixed
Over that roof, knowing there'd be born there
No wars, no tortures, no savage crucifixions.

But a rare, an extraordinary thing –
An exhilaration of peace, a sounding
Grace with trinities galore – if only
Those three collared doves in the rowan tree.

SOMHAIRLE MACGILL-EAIN/ SORLEY MACLEAN

1911–1996

BAN-GHÀIDHEAL

Am faca Tu i, Iùdhaich mhòir,
rin abrar Aon Mhac Dhè?
Am fac' thu 'coltas air Do thriall
ri strì an fhìon-lios chèin?

An cuallach mheasan air a druim,
fallas searbh air mala is gruaidh;
's a' mhias chreadha trom air cùl
a cinn chrùbte bhochd thruaigh.

Chan fhaca Tu i, Mhic an t-saoir,
rin abrar Rìgh na Glòir,
am measg nan cladach carrach siar,
fo fhallas cliabh a lòin.

An t-earrach seo agus seo chaidh
's gach fichead earrach bhon an tùs
tharraing ise 'n fheamainn fhuar
chum biadh a cloinne 's duais an tùir.

'S gach fichead foghar tha air triall
chaill i samhradh buidh nam blàth;
is threabh an dubh-chosnadh an clais
tarsainn mìnead ghil a clàir.

Agus labhair T' eaglais chaomh
mu staid chaillte a h-anama thruaigh;
agus leag an cosnadh dian
a corp gu sàmhchair dhuibh an uaigh.

Is thriall a tìm mar shnighe dubh
a' drùdhadh tughaidh fàrdaich bochd;
mheal ise an dubh-chosnadh cruaidh;
is glas a cadal suain a-nochd.

A HIGHLAND WOMAN

Hast Thou seen her, great Jew,
who art called the One Son of God?
Hast Thou seen on Thy way the like of her
labouring in the distant vineyard?

The load of fruits on her back,
a bitter sweat on brow and cheek,
and the clay basin heavy on the back
of her bent poor wretched head.

Thou hast not seen her, Son of the carpenter,
who art called the King of Glory,
among the rugged western shores
in the sweat of her food's creel.

This Spring and last Spring
and every twenty Springs from the beginning,
she has carried the cold seaweed
for her children's food and the castle's reward.

And every twenty Autumns gone
she has lost the golden summer of her bloom,
and the Black Labour has ploughed the furrow
across the white smoothness of her forehead.

And Thy gentle church has spoken
about the lost state of her miserable soul,
and the unremitting toil has lowered
her body to a black peace in a grave.

And her time has gone like a black sludge
seeping through the thatch of a poor dwelling:
the hard Black Labour was her inheritance;
grey is her sleep tonight.

translated from the Gaelic by the author

SCOTUS ERIGENA

An cuala sibh an sgeulachd
mun Scotach Erigena
a labhair an aghaidh an Taghaidh
dà latha, gun sgìths air;
's a chuir às do Ifrinn cuideachd
's don Pheacadh aig dìorras
is eagnaidheachd a labhairt
mun deach a stad chum sìthe?
Nach bochd nach cualas a leithid
am badaibh nan Sisìdear.

SCOTUS ERIGENA

Did you hear the tale
about Scotus Erigena
who spoke out against the Election
for two days, without tiring;
and who also abolished Hell
and Sin with the unfailing vehemence
and subtlety of his argument
before he was forced to fall silent?
Pity a voice like his was not heard
among the flock of Seceders.

translated from the Gaelic by Emma Dymock

DOUGLAS YOUNG

1913–1973

THE TWENTY-THIRD PSALM O KING DAUVIT

Composed on St Andrews Day, 1942, in Edinburgh Prison

The Lord's my herd, I sall nocht want.
  Whaur green the gresses grow
sall be my fauld. He caas me aye
  whaur fresh sweet burnies rowe. roll

He gars my saul be blyth aince mair
  that wandert was frae hame,
and leads me on the straucht smaa gait
  for sake o His ain name.

Tho I suld gang the glen o mirk
  I'ld grue for nae mischance,
Thou bydes wi me, Thy kent and cruik staff
  maks aye my sustenance.

Thou spreids ane brod and gies me meat board
  whaur aa my faes may view,
Thou sains my heid wi ulyie owre You bless; oil
  and pours my cogie fou. bowl

Nou seil and kindliness sall gae blessing
  throu aa my days wi me,
and I sall wone in God's ain hous dwell
  at hame eternallie.

THE SHEPHERD'S DOCHTER

Written on the occasion described in Fife in 1949

Lay her and lea her here i the gantan grund,
  the blithest, bonniest lass o the countryside,
  crined in a timber sark, hapt wi the pride
o hothouse flouers, the dearest that could be fund.

Her faither and brithers stand, as suddentlie stunned
  wi the wecht o dule; douce neebours side by side
  wriest and fidge, sclent-luikan, sweirt tae bide
while the Minister's duin and his threep gane wi the wind.

The murners skail, thankful tae lea thon place
  whar the blithest, bonniest lass liggs i the mouls,
  Lent lilies lowp and cypresses stand stieve,
Time tae gae back tae the darg, machines and tools
  and beasts and seeds, the things men uis tae live,
and lea the puir lass there in her state o Grace.

gantan: yawning *crined*: shrunk *timber sark*: wooden shirt, coffin *hapt*: wrapped
wecht: weight *dule*: grief *douce*: sober, sedate *wreist*: strain *fidge*: fidget
sclent-luikan: looking sideways *sweirt*: reluctant *while*: until *duin*: finished
threep: harangue *skail*: scatter *liggs*: lies *mouls*: clods *lowp*: leap *stieve*: stiff
darg: day's work

ANN SCOTT-MONCRIEFF

1914–1943

DIRGE

Now words are a' tae smoosh
And argument's in bruck,
The way you kent was best
To raise us oot o' muck.

By is the spirting tears:
The ree-raa cries instead,
Waaly feet walk the street,
'Plane dirls for the dead.

Now for a while sib
To your daithless flesh we haud,
The biding bairn, the high-sky loon,
And man made like to God.

A' slidders: owrehaillet we
Catch inklan o' the word and see
The upstair room, the famyous supper spread,
By Christ Jesus wi' wine and bread.

LINES WRITTEN IN AUTUMN 1940

Split, heart, split, like the gowk chestnut,
Cast off the nylded spottered shell,
Those spongey barbs that you know well
Were never yet received, but
Grow interiorly from vanity.
Green, splumed-out, surface-deep,
Sad stucco growths! You yet must threep
Real agony to reach reality.
The shelter of those splaying leaves
Won't last you long
Though now they seem so strong
Streaked by the wind, a giant's neaves.
So leap, heart, leap, split and bound,
Splairge on this new autumn stoney frosted ground.
Break, heart, break… for skinkling store
Of pebble-truth within, for seed,
The brown bright bairnie's bead,
The smooth infinity of core.

MURIEL SPARK

1918–2006

LIKE AFRICA

He is like Africa in whose
White flame the brilliant acres lie,
And all his nature's latitude
Gives measure of the simile.

His light, his stars, his hemisphere
Blaze like a tropic, and immense
The moon and leopard stride his blood
And mark in him their opulence.

In him the muffled drums of forests
Inform like dreams, and manifold
Lynx, eagle, thorn, effect about him
Their very night and emerald.

And like a river his Zambesi
Gathers the swell of seasons' rains,
The islands rocking on his breast,
The orchid open in his loins.

He is like Africa and even
The dangerous chances of his mind
Resemble the precipice whereover
Perpetual waterfalls descend.

DEÒRSA MAC IAIN DHEÒRSA/ GEORGE CAMPBELL HAY

1915–1984

IS E CRÌOCH ÀRAIDH

Chan eil do shàsachadh a-bhos;
  'ſs e doras taigh do ghràidh an uaigh.
Chan eil an saoghal truagh nam beò
  ach fàsach fògraidh 's iomraill chruaidh.

Is e tha 'n sgeul ar là gu lèir
  roimh-ràdh bu chòir a leum ri luaths;
chan fhoillsichear do shùil fon ghrèin
  smior is meud an Leabhair Bhuain.

Is deuchainn gheàrr ar beatha bhochd,
  laimrig an aiseig null gar tìr.
A-bhos tha 'n t-olc 's na sìontan borb,
  ach thall tha foirfeachd agus sìth.

A mholadh sin don Uile ghlic,
  don Dia tha biothbhuan, math is treun,
a las a' ghrian 's na reultan òir
  os cionn gleann a' bhròin 's nan deur.

A mholadh do Aoghaire nan neul,
  a their ris a' Chèitein 'Gabh mu thuath';
Buachaill an t-samhraidh measg nan crann,
  foghair is geamhraidh d'A chloinn truaigh.

A thulgas an seòl mara mall
  bhos is thall air oir an fhuinn;
is Dorsair tùr nan gaoth, 's dan rèir
  bheir leum is laighe air na tuinn.

A sgeadaicheas a' choille lom,
  's a bheir a trusgan donn don ùir;
a roinneas gàire oirnn is deòir,
  breith, bàs, breòiteachd, slàint' is lùths.

MAN'S CHIEF END

Your satisfaction is not to be had in this life;
the door to the house that you love is the grave.
The wretched love of the living
is but a wilderness of exile and hard wandering.

The tale of all our days
is but a foreword to be quickly passed over;
the pith and bulk of the Eternal Book
is revealed to no eye under the sun.

Our poor life is but a short trial,
the jetty of the ferry across to our land.
On this side are evil and the savage storms,
beyond are perfection and peace.

Praise be for it to the All-wise,
to the God who is eternal, good and powerful,
who lit the sun and the golden stars
above the glen of grief and tears.

Praise for it to the Shepherd of the clouds,
who says to the Maytime: 'Go northwards';
to the Herdsman of the summer among the trees,
of autumn and winter for his wretched children.

Who rocks the slow tide
hither and thither on the lip of the land;
who is Doorkeeper of the tower of the winds, and by them
makes the waves leap and lie down.

Who clothes the bare woodland,
and gives its brown raiment to the soil;
who shares out laughter and tears to us,
birth, death, sickliness, health and vigour.

A thùr dhuinn òige, fàs is aois,
  a shnaidh an saoghal is a sgiamh,
a dh'fhosgail romhainn muir is tìr,
  am magh 's cruth mìorbhailteach nan sliabh.

A thùr ar Bith dhuinn iomadh-fhillt',
  inntinn is colainn, ceann is làmh,
's a thug e dhuinn gu 'mholadh leis,
  's chan ann 'na oidhch' a' meath roimhn là.

Gabh gu deònach ri 'lagh glic,
  siubhail A shlighe ceum air cheum;
lean cumadh sìorraidh a' Phuirt Mhòir
  a rinn E dhuinn mar cheòl ar gnè.

Cluich an t-ùrlar mall air tùs,
  's gach roinn 'na dhèidh le lùths nad chuir,
air Crùnluath bras do là cuir ceann,
  till air an ùrlar mhall is sguir.

An Dia sin as Athair leat,
  'na sheirc a chruthaich sinn gu lèir,
nach binn am moladh Dha o 'chloinn,
  a dìmeas mu na rinn E fhèin?

Is e A smuain an t-anam maoth,
  's e 'anail chaomh a' bheatha bhlàth.
Dèan Da moladh sona fìor.
  Meal is mol sàr ghnìomh A làmh.

Who devised youth, and growth and age for us,
who carved the world and its beauty,
who opened sea and land before us,
the plain and the wondrous shapes of the hills.

Who devised our being for us so manifold,
mind and body, heart and hand,
and gave it to us to praise Him with it,
and not as a night waning before the day.

Accept His wise law willingly,
travel His path step by step;
follow the eternal composition of the Pibroch
He made for us as the music of our nature.

Play first the slow Urlar,
and after it each part with vigour in your cadences,
complete the headlong Crunluath of your days,
return to the slow Urlar and cease.

That God whom you esteem Father,
who created us all in His affection,
is it not sweet praise for Him from His children,
their contempt for what He Himself fashioned?

The delicate soul is His thought;
warm life is His dear breath.
Make a true and happy praise for Him.
Enjoy and praise the excellent work of His hands.

translated from the Gaelic by the author

W. S. GRAHAM

1918–1986

THE FOUND PICTURE

1

Flame and the garden we are together
In it using our secret time up.
We are together in this picture.

It is of the Early Italian School
And not great, a landscape
Maybe illustrating a fable.

We are those two figures barely
Discernible in the pool under
The umbra of the foreground tree.

Or that is how I see it. Nothing
Will move. This is a holy picture
Under its varnish darkening.

2

The Tree of Life unwraps its leaves
And makes its fruit like lightning.
Beyond the river the olive groves.

Beyond the olives musical sounds
Are heard. It is the old, authentic
Angels weeping out of bounds.

3

Observe how the two creatures turn
Slowly toward each other each
In the bare buff and yearning in

Their wordless place. The light years
Have over-varnished them to keep
Them still in their classic secrets.

I slant the canvas. Now look in
To where under the cracking black,
A third creature hides by the spring.

The painted face is faded with light
And the couple are aware of him.
They turn their tufts out of his sight

In this picture's language not
Wanting to be discovered. He
Is not a bad man or a caught

Tom peeping out of his true time.
He is a god making a funny
Face across the world's garden.

See they are fixed they cannot move
Within the landscape of our eyes.
What shall we say out of love

Turning toward each other to hide
In somewhere the breaking garden?
What shall we say to the hiding god?

DÒMHNALL IAIN MACDHÒMHNAILL/ DONALD JOHN MACDONALD

1919–1986

MI FHÌN 'S A' BHEINN

Mun chladhaich tuil nan àrd na claisean eagach
Tha 'n-diugh a' drùdhadh leotha fallas d' aodainn,
Bha thus' air freiceadan a' cumail faire
Air gnè gach beatha bha fod chomhair sgaoilte.

Am fac' thu cruth ar beatha gabhail àite
Mun tugadh binn a' bhàis air iarmad Eubha?
'S bhon sheachain thu bàs-bhinn a' chinne-daonna,
Bheil thusa fhathast ann a' saoghal Eden?

'N do dh'fhiosraich thu tro ruith gach millean bliadhna
An tuigse dhìomhair air nach cuimsich m' eòlas –
Gach linn thar linn mar thig mar leabhar ùr dhut,
Mar ionnan rionnag-iùil do dh'fhear an t-seòlaidh?

Tha mise tomhas dìomhaireachd na cruinne,
A' cladhach ann am meinn nach liubhair òr dhomh,
A' rannsachadh tro dhuibhre dhall na h-aineoil:
Carson is Ciamar? Càite, Cuin? Cion m' eòlais!

A bheil an dìomhaireachd tha dhòmhsa falaicht' –
An tuigs' a cheileadh bhuam tro mheas a' ghàrraidh –
So-lèirsinneach is soilleir dhuts' bhod thùsadh?
An e mo shùilean-sa tha dùint' a-mhàin dhomh?

A bheil mo bhith an suidheachadh nach lèir dhomh?
'N e d' aghaidh charrach fhèin tha fìor dom shùilean?
'N e cirb den chùirtean a tha togail suas dhomh
Nuair thilleas taibhs' à uaigh a chaidh a dhùnadh?

A bheil thu fhèin den t-saoghal cruinne-cè seo
'S mar ionnan do dh'fhear cèin dom lèirsinn dhaonnda?
'S a bheil na dh'eug bho chaidh gu bàs ar dìteadh
Mum thimcheall nuair a dhìreas mi rid aodann?

THE MOUNTAIN AND I

Before heaven's floods carved those winding furrows
That drain today the sweat of your brow
You were a guardian watching over
All forms of life spread before you.

Did you see our life take shape
Before the sentence of death on Eve's descent –
And as you avoided that sentence on mankind,
Are you still in the world of Eden?

Did you learn with the passing of each million years
Understanding of mysteries my mind cannot grasp –
Each century coming as a new book to you,
As the guiding star is to the sailor?

I can but guess at the secrets of the universe,
Clawing in a mine that grants me no gold,
Searching through blind darkness of my ignorance:
Why and How? Where? When? Oh, how little I know!

Is the mystery which is hidden from me –
That understanding lost through the fruit of Eden –
Clear and obvious to you since the beginning?
Is it only my eyes that are closed?

Do I live in a state I cannot perceive?
Is your own rugged face real to my eyes?
Is a corner of the curtain lifted for me
When there returns a vision from the grave?

Are you yourself of this worldly universe
But as an alien to my human sight?
Are all those dead since we were condemned to mortality
Around me as I ascend your face?

Nan sealbhaichinn an tuigse dhomh a dh'innseadh
Ciod e is cionnas beath' is brìgh nan ròsan,
An tigeadh taisbeanadh tro dhuibhre m' aineoil
A mhìnicheadh bith-mhaireannachd na glòrach?

Mas ann le sùilean dùint' a' bhàis a chì mi
Na ceistean air am mìneachadh nan lànachd,
'S e faoineis mhòr dom inntinn a bhith rùrach
Is m' aineolas a' drùdhadh tro mo bhàrdachd.

If I were granted that sense which could tell me
What is the meaning of life and the essence of roses,
Would there emerge through the darkness of my ignorance
A revelation of the eternity of glory?

If it is only with the closed eyes of death
That I will have these questions answered fully,
Then it is folly for my mind to search
And ignorance pervades my poetry.

translated from the Gaelic by Bill Innes

ELMA MITCHELL

1919–2000

THE PROPHET

I take the measure of the pyramids
And dodge the trams.
Iam the stone the builders have neglected
Under Hungerford Bridge.
With time and Thames I flow
Beside the unhurried Liffey and the Mersey,
My voice is heard in Liverpool and London
And Birmingham beheld my massive silence.

I am Daniel, in the den of Lyon's,
I shall arise, out of the public library,
The first of them that sleep.

EDWIN MORGAN

1920–2010

RING OF BRODGAR

'If those stones could speak –' Do not wish too loud.
They can, they do, they will. No voice is lost.
Your meanest guilts are bonded in like frost.
Your fearsome sweat will rise and leave its shroud.
I well recall the timeprint of the Ring
of Brodgar we discovered, white with dust
in twenty-second-century distrust
of truth, but dustable, with truths to bring
into the freer ages, as it did.
A thin groan fought the wind that tugged the stones.
It filled an auditorium with pain.
Long was the sacrifice. Pity ran, hid.
Once they heard the splintering of the bones
they switched the playback off, in vain, in vain.

MESSAGE CLEAR

 am   i
                                if
i am   he
      he r   o
      h   ur   t
     the re   and
      he   re   and
      he re
 a   n   d
     the r   e
i am   r   ife
                   i n
            s   ion and
i   d   i e
 am e res   ect
 am e res   ection
                    o   f
     the   life
                    o   f
  m   e   n
           sur e
     the   d   i e
i   s
            s   e t   and
i am the   sur   d
 a   t   res   t
                    o   life
i am he r   e
i a   ct
i   r u   n
i m   e e   t
i   t   i e

i   s   t   and
i am th   o   th
i am   r   a
i am the su   n
i am the s   on
i am the e rect on   e if
i am   re   n   t
i am   s   a   fe
i am   s   e   n   t
i   he e   d
i   t e   s   t
i   re   a d
a   th re   a d
a   s   t on   e
a   t   re   a d
a   th r   on   e
i   resurrect
a   life
i am   i n   life
i am   resurrection
i am the resurrection and
i am
i am the resurrection and the life

GEORGE MACKAY BROWN

1921–1996

STATIONS OF THE CROSS

From Stone to Thorn

Condemnation
The winter jar of honey and grain
Is a Lenten urn.

Cross
Lord, it is time. Take our yoke
And sunwards turn.

First Fall
To drudge in furrows till you drop
Is to be born.

Mother of God
Out of the mild mothering hill
And the chaste burn.

Simon
God-begun, the barley rack
By man is borne.

Veronica
Foldings of women. Your harrow sweat
Darkens her yarn.

Second Fall
Sower-and-Seed, one flesh, you fling
From stone to thorn.

Women of Jerusalem
You are bound for the Kingdom of Death. The enfolded
Women mourn.

Third Fall
Scythes are sharpened to bring you down,
King Barleycorn.

The Stripping
Flails creak. Golden coat
From kernel is torn.

Crucifixion
The fruitful stones thunder around,
Quern on quern.

Death
The last black hunger rages through you
With hoof and horn.

Pietà
Mother, fold him from those furrows,
Your broken bairn.

Sepulchre
Shepherd, angel, king are kneeling, look,
In the door of the barn.

CHRISTMAS POEM

We are folded all
In a green fable
And we fare
From early
Plough-and-daffodil sun
Through a revel
Of wind-tossed oats and barley
Past sickle and flail
To harvest home,
The circles of bread and ale
At the long table.
It is told, the story –
We and earth and sun and corn are one.

Now kings and shepherds have come.
A wintered hovel
Hides a glory
Whiter than snowflake or silver or star.

RUARAIDH MacTHÒMAIS/ DERICK THOMSON

1921–2004

A' CLUICH AIR FOOTBALL LE FÀIDH

Ma bha thu riamh a' cluich air football le fàidh
leanaidh a' chuimhne sin riut,
cha tèid i fodha ann an cop phàipearan-naidheachd,
ann a sprùilleach chairtean bingo;
turchairt spioradail.
'Sann air fàidhean an Aonaidh a b' eòlaich mi,
ach thuig mi, gu math tràth,
gu robh fàidhean anns an Eaglais Shaoir cuideachd,
fàidhean ann am Barraigh
agus eadhon anns an Eilean Sgitheanach,
agus beag air bheag thuig mi
nach robh tròcair an Tighearna air a cuingealachadh
ri creud no ceàrnaidh
no eadhon cànan.
'Se 'm peacadh as motha
a bhith càrnadh a' ghràis gu lèir 'na do chliabh fhèin.

PLAYING FOOTBALL WITH A PROPHET

If you ever played football with a prophet
you will remember it,
the memory is not submerged in the froth of newspapers,
in the strewn bingo cards:
a spiritual jetsam.
I was better acquainted with Church of Scotland prophets,
but understood, quite young,
that there were prophets in the Free Church too,
prophets in Barra,
and even in Skye,
and bit by bit I came to know
that the Lord's mercy is not confined
by creed or region,
or even language.
The greatest sin
is to pile all of the Grace in your own creel.

translated from the Gaelic by the author

AM BODACH-RÒCAIS

An oidhch' ud
thàinig am bodach-ròcais dhan taigh-chèilidh:
fear caol àrd dubh
is aodach dubh air.
Shuidh e air an t-sèis
is thuit na cairtean ás ar làmhan.
Bha fear a siud
ag innse sgeulachd air Conall Gulban
is reodh na faclan air a bhilean.
Bha boireannach 'na suidh' air stòl
ag òran, 's thug e 'n toradh ás a' cheòl.
Ach cha do dh'fhàg e falamh sinn:
thug e òran nuadh dhuinn,
is sgeulachdan na h-àird an Ear,
is sprùilleach de dh'fheallsanachd Geneva,
is sguab e 'n teine á meadhon an làir
's chuir e 'n tùrlach loisgeach nar broillichean.

SCARECROW

That night
the scarecrow came into the cèilidh-house:
a tall, thin black-haired man
wearing black clothes.
He sat on the bench
and the cards fell from our hands.
One man
was telling a folktale about Conall Gulban
and the words froze on his lips.
A woman was sitting on a stool,
singing songs, and he took the goodness out of the music.
But he did not leave us empty-handed:
he gave us a new song,
and tales from the Middle East,
and fragments of the philosophy of Geneva,
and he swept the fire from the centre of the floor
and set a searing bonfire in our breasts.

translated from the Gaelic by the author

LEODHAS AS T-SAMHRADH

An iarmailt cho soilleir tana
mar gum biodh am brat-sgàile air a reubadh
's an Cruthaidhear 'na shuidhe am fianuis a shluaigh
aig a' bhuntàt 's a sgadan,
gun duine ris an dèan E altachadh.
'S iongantach gu bheil iarmailt air an t-saoghal
tha cur cho beag a bhacadh air daoine
sealltainn a-steach dha'n an t-sìorruidheachd;
chan eil feum air feallsanachd
far an dèan thu chùis le do phrosbaig.

LEWIS IN SUMMER

The atmosphere clear and transparent
as though the veil had been rent
and the Creator were sitting in full view of His people
eating potatoes and herring,
with no man to whom He can say grace.
Probably there's no other sky in the world
that makes it so easy for people
to look in on eternity;
you don't need philosophy
where you can make do with binoculars.

translated from the Gaelic by the author

MÀIRI M NicGHILLEATHAIN/ MARY M. MACLEAN

1921–2004

GLÒIR NO DÓRAINN?

Ged as greadhnach an saoghal
'S ged as dripeil clann-daoine
'Sireadh mire is maoin agus eòlas,
Is faoin-bhreaghas gun fheum iad,
Siùbhlaidh seachad gu léir iad –
Seadh, cha mhair an cruinn-cé, ged as mòr e
Oir nuair lìbhrigear 'n àithne
Théid gach bìdeag dheth smàladh,
Ged bu diongmhalta tàitht' e, gach òirleach;
Bidh gach nì dol ás àite
'S bidh na mìltean fo sgànradh
Ri aghaidh rìoghalachd gàirdein Iehòbha

Bidh na reubalaich bhrùideil
A mheudaich euceart an t-saoghail
Leis gach eucoir bha ùdlaidh is deòmhnaidh
Air an àithneadh don chùirt ud:
Siud a' bhàirlinn nach diùlt iad –
Siud an t-àit' 'n téid an rùsgadh gun tròcair;
Bidh na gadaichean cùilteach
Bha tric a' seachnadh na sùla
Agus misgeirean mùigeach an òst-thaigh
'S luchd mionnain, bhreug agus cùl-chain
Le'm briathran neo-chùbhraidh
Uil' am fianais fo sgrùdadh na Mòrachd.

Ach se cheist dh'fheumar fhuasgladh
Mus tig breisleach na h-uair seo:
Bheil ar teisteanas shuas ann an òrdugh?
'S nuair bhios am feasgar a' ciaradh
'S a théid gach freastal ás fianais
Ca' 'm bi seasmhachd na sìorraidheachd mhòir dhuinn?
'N ann a' seinn le Fear Saoraidh
Ann an aoibhneas a lùchairt
Gu saoghal nan saoghal ri sòlas?

GLORY OR AGONY?

Though the world is exuberant
And humankind intent
On seeking pleasure and riches and knowledge,
They're of no consequence or use,
They all disappear –
Indeed, the universe won't last, for all its size,
For when commandment is given
Every scrap will be destroyed of it,
Though firmly cemented, each inch of it;
All the bits will be exploding
And thousands will be terrified
Facing the regal arms of Jehovah.

All the barbarous rebels
Who've stoked social injustice
With each crime that's been sinister and evil
Will be summoned to that court:
It's the writ they can't refuse
That's the place where they'll be flayed without mercy;
The surreptitious thieves
Who'd not look you in the eye
And all the snarling drunkards of the bar-room
And blasphemers, liars and defamers
With all their foul-smelling words
Will all assemble for inspection by the Lord.

But here's the question to be answered
Before the trauma of this time:
Is our testament on high all in order?
And when the night is approaching
And all help is disappearing
Where will we stand in all eternity?
Joining in song with the Redeemer
In the pleasures of His palace
To world without end in contentment?

No a' plosgail san truaighe
Bhios a' losgadh 's nach fuaraich
'S fadadh-spuinge an uabhais ga theòdhadh?

Ann an eachdraidh na Fìrinn,
Air an deachdadh gu cinnteach,
Se seo faclan an dìtidh gu sònraicht':
"Cha b' aithne dhomh riamh sibh –
Dèanaibh imeachd ás m' fhianais
Do bhras-theine sìorraidh na dòrainn."
Bidh an sloc tha gun ìochdar
An-sin a' fosgladh le mianan
Chum an glacadh le giallaibh gun tròcair;
Pronnasg lasrach ga bhiathadh,
Cha tig laigs' air a chìocras
Ach ataidh le dian-theas an còmhnaidh.

A' chuid tha 'n taice ri Crìosta,
Ged as lapach gu fìor iad,
Cha bhris nàmhaid no diabhal na còrdan
A tha gu sàbhailt' gan aonadh
Ris an t-Slànaighear chaomh ud
Le a bhàs a dh'ionnlaid an dò-bheart;
Tha iad sàraichte sgìtheil,
Tha peacadh-nàdair a' strì riu,
Tha trioblaidean millteach san fheòil ac',
Ach tha 'n gealladh gràsmhor ag inns' dhaibh
Á lànachd na Fìrinn
Gur h-oighreachan cinnteach air Glòir iad.

Siud an dachaigh bhios éibhneach,
Cha bhi gearain no éigheach,
Caismeachd-bàis cha séidear gu brònach,
Cha bhi cridhe fo phéin ann,
Cha bhi snighe air léirsinn,
Bidh na rìghrean gu léir toirt an glòir ann;
Geatan fosgailt' gun seul orr',
Cha bhi oidhch' ann no reultan,
Solas-coinnle chan fheumar sna seòmair,
'S gathan aoibhneach na gréine
Cha bhi boillsgeadh dhiubh fhéin ann,
Oir bidh soillse Uan Dhé ann mar lòchran.

Or palpitating in the ghastliness
Which burns and never cools
With the tinder of horror inflaming it?

In the text of the Scriptures,
Truthfully written,
Are the following words of damnation:
'I've never known you at all –
Go now from my presence
To the swift lasting flames of perdition."
The bottomless pit
Will then open with a yawn
To seize them with merciless jaws;
With burning brimstone to feed it,
Its hunger won't slacken
But will keep swelling with ferocious heat.

Those who depend upon Christ,
Even if utterly weak,
No enemy or devil can break
The cords that safely unite them
To that compassionate Saviour
Through his death which cleansed their iniquities;
They're tormented and wearied,
With original sin tempting them
And troubles belabouring their flesh,
But the gracious promise is telling them
From the fullness of Scripture
That they are definite heirs of Glory.

That's the home that is blissful,
Without cry or complaint,
No death-march is mournfully blown,
No heart will be anguished,
No eye will shed tears there,
All the kings will invest it with glory;
Open gates without seal on them,
Neither night there nor stars,
No candlelight's needed in its rooms,
And joyful beams of the sun –
Even they will not gleam there,
For the Lamb of God will shine forth as its lantern.

translated from the Gaelic by Ronald Black

ALASTAIR REID

1926–2014

WHITHORN MANSE

I knew it as Eden,
that lost walled garden,
past the green edge
of priory and village;
and, beyond it, the house,
withdrawn, white,
one window alight.

Returning, I wonder,
idly, uneasily,
what eyes from inside
look out now, not in,
as once mine did,
and what might grant me,
a right of entry?

Is it never dead, then,
that need of an Eden?

Even this evening,
estranged by age,
I ogle that light
with a child's greed,
wistfully claiming
lost prerogatives
of homecoming.

IAIN CRICHTON SMITH/ IAIN MAC A' GHOBHAINN

1928–1998

WHEN THEY REACHED THE NEW LAND

When they reached the new land they rebuilt the old one,
they called the new mountains by old names,

they carved a Presbyterian church on the hill.
Nevertheless there was a sort of slantness,

a curious odd feeling in the twilight
that the mountain had shifted, had cast off its name

and even the Christ in the window seemed different
as if he had survived deserts and was not

a shepherd whom they imagined with his sheep
and his long staff high on the rainy hills.

It was much later before they made it all fit
and by then it was a new land.

They could have changed the names of the mountains
and could have walked in the familiar streets

built by their own strivings. It was then
that their old land was swallowed by the new;

and Christ a haunter of their own deserts,
the birds the colourful haunters of their own

trees and gardens. And they were at peace
among their settled, naturalised names.

DO SHEANA-BHOIREANNACH

Tha thu san eaglais ag èisteachd
air being mhì-chofhurtail ri briathran
fear nach eil ach leth do bhliadhnan.

'S tha mise nam shuidhe 'n seo a' sgrìobhadh
nam facal cearbach s': gun fhios 'n e 'n fhìrinn
no bhreug bhòidheach tha nam inntinn.

Ach, aon tè tha tighinn air m' inntinn,
thusa nad shuidhe air beulaibh cùbainn
nad aid dhuibh shìmplidh: na do chòta
(dubh cuideachd) 's na do bhrògan
a choisich iomadh sràid mhòr leat.

Cha b' e sgoilear thu na do latha.
('S iomadh madainn a sgoilt thu sgadan
's a bha do làmhan goirt le salainn,
's a' ghaoth gheur air oir do sgine,
's d' òrdagan reòtht' le teine.)

Cha chuala tusa mu dheidhinn Dharwin
no Fhreud no Mharx no 'n Iùdhaich eile,
Einstein leis an inntinn ealant':
no ciall a' bhruadair a bhruadraich thu
's tu raoir nad rùm nad theann-chadal.
Cha chuala tu mar a theicheas na reultan
mar bhan-righinnean ciùin tro na speuran,
's cha chuala tu mar a shuidheas an leòmhann
le ceann borb aig a' bhòrd leinn.

Ach suidhidh tu 'n sin air beulaibh cùbainn
's nì thu nad aonranachd iomadh ùrnaigh
's ma bheireas am ministear air làimh ort
bidh toileachas a' lìonadh d' inntinn.

TO AN OLD WOMAN

You are in the church listening,
sitting on an uncomfortable bench to the words
of one who is only half your age.

And I am sitting here writing
these corrupted words, and not knowing whether it is the truth
or the beautiful lie that is in my mind.

But there is one person who comes into my mind,
you sitting in front of a pulpit
in your simple black hat, and in your coat
(black as well) and in your shoes
that have walked many a long street with you.

You were not a scholar in your day.
(Many a morning did you gut herring, and
your hands were sore with salt,
and the keen wind on the edge of your knife,
and your fingers frozen with fire.)

You have never heard of Darwin
or Freud or Marx or that other Jew,
Einstein, with the brilliant mind:
nor do you know the meaning of the dream you dreamed
last night in your room in heavy sleep.
You haven't heard how the stars move away from us
like calm queens through the sky.
And you haven't heard how the lion
with his fierce head sits at the table with us.

But you sit there in front of the pulpit
and in your loneliness you say many a prayer
and if the minister shakes you by the hand
your mind is filled with happiness.

Cuimhnichidh tu air làithean eile,
searmon cho dìreach ris a' pheilear,
samhradh a' dòrtadh timcheall eaglais,
fàinne òir is teisteanas
ròsan a' fosgladh samhraidh
mar ùr-Bhìoball na do chuimhne.

'S cuimhnichidh tu air iomadh bàs
is iomadh latha a chaidh fàs,
uaireadair anns na ballachan
a' diogadh do shaoghail gu a cheann.

Gu soirbhich do shaoghal gu math leat
's tu nise air do shlighe dhachaigh
tro shràidean geal mar inntinn duine
fosgailt' le oir na sgine,
's balaich nan seasamh nan cuid aimhreit
a' sgrùdadh neonitheachd: 's geur a sheall iad
riuts' a' falbh, gun armachd, tarsainn
sràid a' losgadh mu do chasan,
gun armachd ach do spiorad còrdail
nach do chuir saoghal riamh an òrdugh
ach a chumas tu, tha mi 'n dòchas,
slàn nad neoichiontas mar chòta.

You remember other days,
a sermon direct as a bullet,
a summer pouring around a church,
a gold ring and the testimony
of roses opening summer
like a new Bible in your memory.

And you will remember many a death
and many days which went waste,
a clock in the wall
ticking your world to its end.

May your world prosper
and you on your way home
over the white streets like a man's mind,
open with the edge of the knife,
and boys standing in their quarrelsomeness
studying nothingness: keenly they looked
at you going without armour across
a street burning at your feet,
without armour but your harmonious spirit
that never put a world in order
but which will keep you, I hope,
whole in your innocence like a coat.

translated from the Gaelic by the author

DÒMHNALL MACAMHLAIGH/ DONALD MACAULAY

1930–2017

SOISGEUL 1955

Bha mi a raoir anns a' choinneamh;
bha an taigh làn chun an dorais,
cha robh àite suidhe ann
ach geimhil chumhang air an staighre.

Dh' éisd mi ris an t-sailm: am fonn
a' falbh leinn air seòl mara
cho dìomhair ri Maol Dùn:
dh'éisd mi ris an ùrnaigh
seirm shaorsinneil, shruthach –
iuchair-dàin mo dhaoine.

An uair sin thàinig an searmon
– teintean ifrinn a th' anns an fhasan –
bagairt neimheil, fhuadan
a lìon an taigh le uamhann is coimeasg.

Is thàinig an cadal-deilgneach na mo chasan …

GOSPEL 1955

I was at the meeting last night;
the house was full, packed to the door,
there was no place for me to sit
but a cramped nook on the stairs.

I listened to the psalm: the tune
transporting us on a tide
as mysterious as Maol Duin's; [A miraculous navigator in early Gaelic literature]
I listened to the prayer
a liberating, cascading melody –
my people's access to poetry.

Then we got the sermon
– the fires of hell are in fashion –
vicious, alien threats
that filled the house with confusion and terror.

And I got pins-and-needles in my feet …

translated from the Gaelic by the author

KENNETH WHITE

1936–2023

A HIGH BLUE DAY ON SCALPAY

This is the summit of contemplation, and
    no art can touch it
blue, so blue, the far-out archipelago
    and the sea shimmering, shimmering
no art can touch it, the mind can only
    try to become attuned to it
to become quiet, and space itself out, to
    become open and still, unworlded
knowing itself in the diamond country, in
    the ultimate unlettered light

A. C. JACOBS

1937–1994

SUPPLICATION

Lord, from this city I was born in
I cry unto you whom I do not believe in:
(Spinoza and Freud among others saw to that)
Show me in this place in which I started
Where I have gone wrong.

Descend neither in Kirk nor synagogue
Nor university nor pub.

But on a handy summit like Ben Lomond
Make me a new Sinai, and please God
Can we have less of the thou-shalt-not?

DIANA HENDRY

1941–

PSALM EIGHTY-EIGHT BLUES

Lord, when I'm speechless
when something – not just sorrow
but under that – a dull, numb, nameless dreich
about the heart I hardly seem to have,
when this afflicts me,
when hope's been cancelled,
when the pilot light of me's put out,
when every reflex and response
has been extinguished,

send word, snowdrop, child, light.

JOCK STEIN

1941–

119 FAIR AND SQUARE

No tapestry complete without a square
jaw somewhere, to remind tame images
that words do more than chatter,
show how *torah* draws a frame for life
to challenge slipshod needlework,
set out certain things that matter.

No book complete without some ordering
of chapters, sequences of numbers, letters
sailing A to Z, the blacks, the whites,
all shades of tighter petit point let loose
upon a canvas sea, like decorated buoys
which mark each passage with eight riding lights.

No symphony complete without a switch
from law to liberty, a swatch of tones,
an itch unwrapped so strings rehearse
its secret. Bless you, ancient makar, shrewd
composer, artist, stitcher: you have left
your needle prints so clear in every verse.

No life complete without God's art and music
hidden in our sober prose, artless, silent,
waiting for the word to waken, say hello,
and introduce a new dimension, dancing
intimacy to the edge of long horizons,
splashing colour on a great allegro.

TOM LEONARD

1944–2018

THE GOOD THIEF

heh jimmy
yawright ih
stull wayiz urryi
ih

heh jimmy
ma right insane yirra pape
ma right insane yirwanny us jimmy
see it nyir eyes
wanny uz

heh

heh jimmy
lookslik wirgonny miss thi gemm
gonny miss thi GEMM jimmy
nearly three a cloke thinoo

dork init
good jobe theyve gote thi lights

A HUMANIST

The son of an immigrant, he had eschewed the culture of his father as also that of the land into which he was born.

The religion of his father was once the religion of the indigenous natives, but they had rejected and overthrown it.

And the son was yet seen as of that tribe which corroded the native culture and language.

An outsider, he felt at home with the art and culture of other outsiders, for many years he found companionship across space and time.

But from within he came to realise himself as instance of the universal human. The universal human is inclusive and absolute, there is no individual outside it.

This sense of the universal human is the home of all those who have won through to become themselves.

And much trouble in the world is caused by those who remain self-sequestered in their perceived province of the exclusive.

IAN ABBOT

1947–1989

AVOIDING THE GODS

They have come
to scald our blood, to call us out
from our bright houses to the twisted shadows under trees.
Let us not listen to them. Do not let them in.

There beyond the darkened garden, in the obscure forest,
the night expends itself in numberless small deaths.
That is the way of them, the way of predators. A kind
of innocent destruction
but destruction nonetheless.

Let us abandon them
to moulder on their crosses,
beat their iron wings; to redeploy their armies and invent
new forms of sinning and guilt.

Let us remain here, calmly
taking bread, and wine, and speech.
And in the morning
take our limbs to work, and walk behind
the swaying, fuming breath of cattle.

And let us look for our salvation
in the language we have come to teach ourselves.

CHRISTINE DE LUCA

1947–

DIS LIFE IS NIVVER ENYOCH — enough

1
'Kuml' – Pagan burial site
(Iceland National Museum)

Shö lies, foetal, in a shell-saand grave
apön her richt side, maybe facin da sun;
twa steyns abön her skull
een at her fit. — one, foot

Her left hench-bane lies across her richt — haunch-bone
da knap-bane below da tidder een — knee-bone, other
left airm curled inta her richt airm.
Shaklebanes, fingers, cöts, taes — wrists, ankles
der aa dere, young an unwörn. — they are

Her grave-goods: twa shalls,
a pebble, whit micht a bön a blade.
Naethin ta busk her fur her journey — bedeck
nedder beads nor redder; — neither, comb
an nae sign o a lover.
Best no tink o her final ooers
fur der a peerie grave aside her — small
wi a rikkel o mintie banes. — emaciated, tiny
Twa steyns at da head, een at da fit.

***

I lie i mi bed on mi richt side, foetal,
facin aest. Mi left knee rests jöst below
da tidder, left airm across mi bosie. — bosom
A'm said mi göd wirds, an tanks — prayers
fur tree score year an ten.
But I still draem lik a pagan.

2

Christian burial (1916–1918)
(Hólavallagarður Cemetery, Reykjavik)

Fowr fine sons lie here:
tree deed young, barely twa year
apairt. Wha kens what ailed dem?
Did da Great Frost Winter tak hits toll?

Der böried tagidder, sidey-fur-sidey, — side by side
da grave aest-wast. Laid oot straicht,
apö der backs, haands likkly crossed.
Only Stefán med hit ta fifty, maybe
outlived da midder an faider. — mother, father
Murnin claes wis nivver affa da back, — mourning
blinnds barely liftit.

But noo hit's a gairden, a Eden,
wi whitebeam an rowan
an birds i der thoosands
brakkin da silence.

***

Whin I win haem I email mi son, — reach, home
tell him da birds wis a chorus,
dey jöst aboot daeved me; — deafened
an da bunches o berries on rowans
wis redder as bluid.

3

Eftir hearin Etgar Keret, Israeli writer, spaekin
at da Reykjavik International Literary Festival

Da peerie bairn akses da faider
    Foo lang do fock live fur? — how
Da faider says
    Twa hunder year if you dunna smok
Da bairn says
    Dat's no lang enoych
Da faider cöllies aboot him: — comforts
    Ya, dat hit is; hit's plenty lang
Da bairn gowls — cries loudly
    Na, hit's no nearly lang enoych
Da faider greets wi him — weeps
    Du's richt, mi jewel. — you, my dear little one
    Hit's no nearly lang enoych.

JAMES McGONIGAL

1947–

WITH FINNIAN AT HIS BRIGHT HOUSE IN WHITHORN

Bewildering as light is off the firth, but I could
say his name at least. Come from the west,
he honoured our world with wonders.

There were riddles in a far-travelled face,
snow cloud of hair, a brow like the sea,
hands that spoke different languages.

I am lost for words when I listen again.
At other times forget even to notice that he is
no longer here. How did I lose sight of that

white head in the crowd? I was busy
with other business. One by one we flew
from his fingers like grain –

in dribs and drabs trudged back to life again,
woke with no hand touching the shoulder
to starlight or daylight. Good morning, whatever.

He told us faith is always vanishing, behind
the craig, beyond those rowan trees – pursue, pursue
like hunters do.

With him the memory of everything's a river.
We gathered on its shingle banks to hear
old words dipped clean.

LIZ LOCHHEAD

1947–

THE OFFERING

Never in a month of them
would you go back.
Sunday,
the late smell of bacon
then the hard small feeling
of the offering in the mitten.
Remember how the hat-elastic cut.
Oh the boredom,
and how a lick of spittle got purple dye or pink
from the hymn-book you worried.

Maybe your neighbour would
have technicoloured pictures of
Jesus curing lepers
between the frail tissue pages of her bible
or she'd stroke you with the velvet
of a pressed rosepetal
till someone sucking peppermint
and smelling of mothball
poked you and hissed that you weren't to fidget.
Remember the singing
(with words and actions)
and how you never quite
understood the one about Nic-
odemus Coming to the Lord by Night.

Sunday,
perhaps an auntie
would visit with a cousin. Every Sunday
everyone would eat ice cream
and your mothers would compare you,
they'd stand you by the doorstop
and measure you up.

Sunday, maybe later in the evening
There'd be a Brethren Meeting.
Plain women wearing hats to cover
uncut hair. And
singing, under lamp-posts, out in our street.
And the leader
shouted the odds on Armageddon, he
tried to sell Salvation.
Everybody turned their televisions up.

Never in a month of them
should you go back.
Fond hope.
You'll still find you do not measure up.
The evangelist still mouths behind glass unheard.
You'll still not understand
the singing, the action or the word.
Ice cream will cloy, too sweet, too bland.
And the offering
still hard and knotted in your hand.

GRACE

Written for the Royal Incorporation of Architects in Scotland
on the occasion of the Annual Fellows Dinner, 2012

Once in Moab
before *the land of milk and honey*
it was written in Deuteronomy
that before breaking bread together, friends, we should
take pause, and then say grace.
Which was to say we were to bless
what blessed us with everything that was good.
God – or the
land of the wheat and the barley, the
source of all our food,
the land of the vine and the fig and the pomegranate,
the land of the oil-olive and the syrup-date.

This is Scotland, this
Our one small country in this great wide world, which is
our one, wondrous, spinning, dear green place.
What shall we build of it, together
in this our one small time and space?

We are far from Deuteronomy,
far from long forgotten
Moab, far from any *land of milk and honey* –
we are where *nothing is written*

Yet tonight
together
For good food and even better fellowship,
whether we have a God or not
our gratitude cannot be denied.

And we shall eat, and we shall be satisfied.

CATRIONA NicGUMARAID/ CATRIONA MONTGOMERY

1947–2024

AN CEUSADH

Air dealbh fhaicinn de 'An Ceusadh' le Mìcheal Angelo:
do mo mhàthair fhèin

Thusa 'n-sin a' deuradh na fala,
mis' an-seo a' sileadh nan deur…
a' mhàthair a' caoidh a cuid cloinne
a tha fhathast 'na cuideachd 's a dh'fhalbh.

THE CRUCIFIXION

On seeing 'The Crucifixion' by Michelangelo: for my own mother

You there dripping the blood,
I here pouring the tears …
the mother lamenting her children
who are both in her company and gone.

translated from the Gaelic by the author

ALAN SPENCE

1947–

ALL ABOUT THE LIGHT.

(For Victoria Crowe)

Ultimately it's all about the light –
catching the light, celebrating the light,
the light of consciousness by which we see,
the light that comes at last to know itself,
the self-revealing light in everything,
within, without. It's all about the light.
Circumspice – look and the world's made new.
It's all about, it shines in the clear light.
Behold and be beholden. Look and see
the sheer particularity of things.
Snow moment. Winter fence. Numinous tree.
Considered silence. Hidden moon. Blue thaw.
Dark dog and hillside. Shape of the shadow.
Reflected contemplation. Lying snow.
Praise the everyday, the vision, the dream.
Ultimately it's all about the light.

JAPANESE BOXES

(Daibutsu, Great Buddha, Kamakura)

I sit inside
the compassionate Buddha
who sits inside
this world of things
which sits inside
the universe
which sits inside
the great void
which sits inside
my heart

MARION F. NicILLEMHOIRE/ MARION F. MORRISON

1950–

MÀIRI À MAGDALA, NA H-AONAR LE A SMUAINTEAN

Bha dròbhan dhiubh air cladaichean Ghalile
Gràisg nan sgothan iasgaich,
'S an cuid sìol a' fannachadh leis an acras
Beòil fosgailte
Sùilean dall.

Is tusa led threud
Ag èaladh gu tìr
Falamh.
Na beathaichean acrach, air an clisgeadh,
Na marsantan a' gearan 's a' caitheamh smugaidean
'S gam sgrùdadh gu drùiseach.

Air dhut do ghàirdeanan fhosgladh,
Bhiathadh iad agus dh'fhàs iad socair.
Am measg an t-sluaigh
Sheas thu
Fada os cionn chàich.
Fada nad bharail fhèin – a rèir choltais.
Bha brunndail a' dol
Is fathannan a' dol mun cuairt
A dh'aindeoin do shùilean bàidheil
A' glaodhaich,

'Bi timcheall orm
Bheir urram dhomh
Thoir gaol dhomh.'

Cho luath 's a mhothaich thu dhòmhsa
Bha thu aig mo dhoras;
Cha b' e ruith ach leum
Agus bha iad mionnaichte
Gun robh sinn còmhla
Ann an gaol.
(Leig mi leotha.)

MARY OF MAGDALA BY HERSELF

The shores of Galilee awash with them.
All starved, those foul fisher folk
With their spawn. Mouths agape.
Eyes blank.

And you with your raggedy band sliding ashore
Empty to the gunnels.
The merchants
With their beasts hungry and nervous
Muttered and spat,
Rolling their eyes over me in leering speculation.

In the spreading of your arms, somehow they were fed and quietened.
Your height alone quelled them as you stood head and shoulders
On the hillside
Above the rest.
Above yourself – some said.
There was already muttering
Despite your eloquent eyes
Pleading,

'Know me,
Praise me,
Love me.'

One penetrating look
And you were soon at my door;
And famously they said we 'shared a love'.
(I let it stick.)

Thadhal thu orm gun teagamh,
Ach cha b' ann 'son pòg sgreamhail
A' bhàis bhig.
Dh'ung mi thu le ola
Ach cha deach ar cridheachan thairis.

Ann am priobadh na sùla
Bha thu mar uirsgeul
Cha do dh'amhairc mi air do chràdh neo air na dh'fhuiling thu.
Do bhàs.
Na boireannaich a' sgiamhail,
Dhubh mi às iad
Làn pròis gun robh mo chridhe fhèin
A' cumail a-mach às.

Ach – gun fhiosta – thill thu thugamsa
Dìreach aon turas
Mar chomharradh air an deireadh ùr.

Ach bho àm gu àm
Air cladaichean Tabgha
Bidh thu tighinn fa-near dhomh
Aig dol fodha na grèine
Am measg nan reultan aognaidh
A' chraobh bhàn-dhearg almon
'S a blàthan cùbhraidh
A' cur na fìrinne eagalaich mu sgaoil.

And yes, you did call on me,
But not for us the reechy kiss
The little death.
I anointed you with oil
But our hearts
Did not run over.

Before I knew it
You were past tense.
I did not watch the death throes.
I shut out the *ululantes*
Quite proud of my own heart
Beating a retreat.

And then you were back – just once to me
Like a consummation of a new ending.

Sometimes on the shore at Tabgha
I catch you in the sun setting
Just to a pinpoint
Among the bleak stars
And gaze upon the pink almond tree
Scenting the cruel truth.

translated from the Gaelic by the author

AONGHAS PHÀDRAIG CAIMBEUL/ ANGUS PETER CAMPBELL

1952–

IÙDAS AIR CNAP-DEIGHE

Air fhaicinn le Naomh Brianan air a thuras

Chan fhaca sinn e an toiseach
anns an t-sìorraidheachd gheal.

Bha sinn air a bhith seòladh
siar cho fada. Èirinn fhèin

cho uaine
nuair a dh'fhàg sinn, 's ceò

fad an rathaid gu tuath
fo stiùir nan reultan-iùil,

's nuair a shaoil sinn uile caillte
mhothaich sinn dha, na laighe

shìos air cnap-deighe, a' gabhail fois
fhionnar an là. Latha

mach dha, duais fhuar
airson aon choibhneas uaireigin

an t-saoghail, mus do dh'fhag na buinn
trichead e an seo, na chrith.

JUDAS ON AN ICEBERG

As seen by St Brendan on his voyage

We didn't notice him at first
in the eternal whiteness.

We'd been sailing west
for such a long time. Ireland

was of course green
when we left it, then

the fog all the way north
guided by the polar stars,

and when all seemed lost
there we saw him, lying

down on an iceberg, basking
in the cool of the day. His

single day out, a chilling reward
for a solitary kindness done once

upon a time, before the thirty pieces
of silver left him here, shivering.

translated from the Gaelic by the author

ANGUS DUNN

1953–2015

UIST MADONNA

There is nothing here,
in all the wide ocean
to stop the wind
that frays the edge of the land.
On the foredune,
dry from the long sunlight and the sea breeze,
sand slips.
In the slack behind the dunes,
the brown bird lies low
in her nest among the grasses:
even here, sand moves, held in nets of buttercup roots.
When the storm comes,
sand flows like water, stings like hail –
air eating the earth.
Small white houses
grip the soil of the machair,
One window gleaming all night long
to light the way home –
though some will not return.
Up on the hillside,
thin sheep graze on rocks,
and there the Lady stands
looking past the ocean
out to the furthest West
from where no one of us returns.

IMTIAZ DHARKER

1954–

LAPIS LAZULI

If you thirst for blue beyond ultramarine,
here is the blue that stains the artist's hand,
lifted out of the most precious seam
in the generous heart of Badakshan

to place an azure light in the Pharaoh's eyes
after he is gone, lap at the Virgin's cloak,
seep into the masjid walls. A prize
to protect the wearer, allow the hope

that a simple ore could save the prey
and shield the savaged heart from harm;
that in a broken land it could find a way
to wrap the child in sacred blue, a charm

or talisman to still the approaching drone,
if you could only mine the prayer inside the stone.

BASHABI FRASER

1954–

THE GURDWARA IN LEITH

Where the city stops at an ocean's brink
Once ships set sail or docked to rest
They paused to ponder on the kingdom
Looming through the morning mists.

Bhai, Landa, Kasbia, Potwal
Ronde, Rathour, Sheber, Digpal
Names repeated like a mantra
From the cradle of their yatra — journey

Unified in prayer, they had sought
Tenement flats to pray and meet
Till St Thomas opened doors to greet
A community from a divided state.

The khalsa symbol of balance, power and continuity
Now meditates on the pinnacle of a dockside city.

JOHN BURNSIDE

1955–

CANTICLE

When it rains
and the garden is cool

and blackbirds return to the wet
borders of our land,

we think ourselves the tenants
of a borrowed house,

with nothing to protect, nothing to claim,
only the moment when singing is resumed

amongst the trees,
and evening fills the grey and green

reflections of the people we reveal
in darkened glass:

the people in a psalm,
firstborn and true,

arriving here by chance,
just passing through.

NATIVITY

A spill of yew
like Christ's blood
in the snow;
and somewhere in the hedge,
just yards away,
a fleck of presence
waiting to be born.

No angel at the gate.
No guiding star.
We make this world
from gravity and light
and we alone, God's grace
by other means:

a flock of redwings
flitting through the fog,
woodrush
and fescue,
wintergreen,
Rose of Sharon.

CAROL ANNE DUFFY

1955–

PRAYER

Some days, although we cannot pray, a prayer
utters itself. So, a woman will lift
her head from the sieve of her hands and stare
at the minims sung by a tree, a sudden gift.

Some nights, although we are faithless, the truth
enters our hearts, that small familiar pain;
then a man will stand stock-still, hearing his youth
in the distant Latin chanting of a train.

Pray for us now. Grade 1 piano scales
console the lodger looking out across
a Midlands town. Then dusk, and someone calls
a child's name as though they named their loss.

Darkness outside. Inside, the radio's prayer –
Rockall. Malin. Dogger. Finisterre.

PILATE'S WIFE

Firstly, his hands – a woman's. Softer than mine,
with pearly nails, like shells from Galilee.
Indolent hands. Camp hands that clapped for grapes.
Their pale, mothy touch made me flinch. Pontius.

I longed for Rome, home, someone else. When the Nazarene
entered Jerusalem, my maid and I crept out,
bored stiff, disguised, and joined the frenzied crowd.
I tripped, clutched the bridle of an ass, looked up

and there he was. His face? Ugly. Talented.
He looked at me. I mean he looked at *me*. My God.
His eyes were eyes to die for. Then he was gone,
his rough men shouldering a pathway to the gates.

The night before his trial, I dreamt of him.
His brown hands touched me. Then it hurt.
Then blood. I saw that each tough palm was skewered
by a nail. I woke up, sweating, sexual, terrified.

Leave him alone. I sent a warning note, then quickly dressed.
When I arrived, the Nazarene was crowned with thorns.
The crowd was baying for Barabbas. Pilate saw me,
looked away, then carefully turned up his sleeves

and slowly washed his useless, perfumed hands.
They seized the prophet then and dragged him out,
up to the Place of Skulls. My maid knows all the rest.
Was he God? Of course not. Pilate believed he was.

GERRY CAMBRIDGE

1959–

LITTLE LIGHT PSALM

21st December

Glaurlight.
   Dankpuddlelight; light
poor as a dosser's pocket.
   Duskalldaylight
too drab to praise as grey.
   Light the diamond
lost in the mine;
   light divine
in the older way.

Spacelight.
   Light of celandine;
pollenlight
   sudden in faces.
Jaywinglight—its turquoise
   flash. Light
of the May. Keylight turning
   in the ash of dawn,
loosening seizedlight
   on this mirk day.

MEG BATEMAN

1959–

NAOMH

Le taing do Tim Robinson

Sheall an duine Tobar Chaluim Chille
dhan eòlaiche shìos air a' chladach,
is dh'fhaighnich e gu dè,
na bharail-san, am ball-acfhainn
a bha an Naomh air a chleachdadh
gus a chladhach cho domhainn is cho rèidh
san aol-chloich chruaidh.

Mhìnich an t-eòlaiche
mar a b' e dòirneag bu choireach,
a bha glacte san t-sloc iomadh bliadhna,
is mar a shnaidheadh i an toll
le gach làn-mara
's i a' bleith na creige
ann an sluaisreadh an t-sàil.

Cha bu dad nas lugha
urram an duine dhan Naomh
oir bha fianais aige a-nis
air fhoighidinn is air ro-fhios,
is air meud a chuid tròcair
leis an do cheannsaich e an cuan
gus uisge-leighis a ghleidheadh dha threud.

SAINT

With thanks to Tim Robinson

The man showed the geologist
St Columba's Well on the shore,
and asked him his opinion
of the sort of tool
the saint might have used
to have bored the hole
so deep and smooth.

The geologist explained
it was made by a pebble
trapped in a hollow through the ages;
how it had rounded the basin
at every high-water,
grinding the rock down
in the swirling brine.

No less then the devotion
of the man to the saint,
for now he had evidence
of his patience and prescience,
and of the magnitude of his mercy
by which he had constrained the ocean
to safeguard healing water for his flock.

translated from the Gaelic by the author

ROBERT CRAWFORD

1959–

BIOLOGY

For Lewis

Our days and ways, our chromosomes are numbered,
Lettered, making up a long, tagged story,

A still unfolding Book of Genesis,
But one, like poetry, lost in translation,

So most of us, to find the original sense,
Must call to mind some song our mother sang,

One taken in with nursery rhymes and milk,
Then dream we come to love strange dialects –

From *zymogens* to *Avogadro's number* –
Whose folktales speak in strands of narrative,

Dense, trailing clauses scribbled by pipettes,
Enzyme legends, each a secret pathway

Through tiny mitochondric organelles,
Where carnitine, the label proteins read,

Acts out unseen, wee recognition scenes,
Atom-fine get-togethers, microbondings,

Pos and neg held in a cyclic shape,
And there, in trees, in cats' or human kidneys,

Articulates a sort of Word made flesh,
Goes recognised, unspoken, joins together

Mice, people, choughs, so colourlessly proving
Gut feelings true, that all are held in one

Genetic myth, one Loch Ness-deep, compelling.
Deft, intermolecular embrace.

SANDAIDH NicDHÒMHNAILL JONES/ SANDY NicDHÒMHNAILL JONES

1960–

XIV. RÀITHEAN AGUS RÈITEACHADH

Quartus Decimus Cantus

Thig na ràithean mun cuairt
seòlaidh bliadhna eile seachad
sèididh a' ghaoth
is cluinnear torrann a' chuain.
Èighidh a' chorra-mhonaidh,
ceileiridh an uiseag
's an smeòrach,
is cluinnear ràc nan traon,
trùman eàrr-ite an naoisg,
is ospag-taibhs'
na caillich-oidhche.

Thig na ràithean mun cuairt
is buainidh na manaich
lusan an earraich 's an t-samhraidh,
na machrach, na mòintich 's na tràghad
mar bhiadh – is mar ìocshlaint.
Meas an tuirc allta, lus na machraidh
curran talmhainn, dail-chuach
iubhar beinne, lus na feannaig.

Cuairt-beatha na manachainn
is a ruithim làitheil.
Obair sgrìobhaidh, leughaidh,
ionnsachaidh is ùrnaigh.

Agus sibhse, a Chaluim:
ur làithean fhèin a' fàs
nas gainne is nas daoire
feasgar ur beò is sibhs'
aig aois a' gheallaidh
an aba air abaich, 's a' fàs ullamh.

XIV. SEASONS AND CONCILIATIONS

Quartus Decimus Cantus

The seasons come full circle
another year passes
the wind blows, carrying
the ocean's roaring sound.
The crane cries,
the lark warbles and
the thrush sings;
hear the corncrake's rasp,
the snipe's tail-whirring,
the barn-owl's
ghostly sigh.

The seasons come full circle
and the monks gather
spring and summer herbs,
plants of machair, moor and shore.
for food, for medicinal remedy.
St John's wort, wild thyme,
wild carrot, dog-violet,
juniper, crowberry.

The monastery's cycle of life
and daily rhythm.
The work of writing, reading,
Learning, prayer.

And you, Columba:
your days growing
scarcer and more precious
in the evening of your life,
at the age of promise
an abbot of mature years,
his span near accomplished.

Nur suidhe nis air tràigh ear Ì;
fàileadh sàillte na mara
a' sèideadh air a' ghaoith;
sibhs' a' coimhead air caolas Mhuile
is fada thall thairis air;
's a' toirt sùil is smuain air ais.

Cuimhne leanabachd an Èirinn
meas air na manaich a dh'àraich
's a dh'ollamhnaich sibh.
Àireamhan nan oileanach
agaibh fhèin a' sìor-dhìreadh;
cuid dhiubh san Eòrpa
is feadh an t-saoghail
a' sgaoileadh sgrioptair,
soisgeul, litearrachd.
Feadhainn eile a' neartachadh
Paruchia Ì na h-Alba 's na h-Èireann
buaidh is cliù Manachainn Ì
a' sìor-fhàs.

Agus sibhs' air triall iomadh turas
feadh Alba, cuairt do Bhridei
agus grunn cheannardan Cruithneach eile.
Is taisteal air ais do Èirinn:
ur soirbheas aig còmhdhail Druim Ceat
a' toirt rèiteachadh do chàch,
eadar cinnidhean
is a' gabhail suaimhneas
an ath-rèiteachaidh dhachaigh,
an tìr-dhàimh;
a bha cho fada na fhadal
dhuibh fèin.

'S sibhse a' meòrachadh
air a' bhreith is a' chunntas
dlighe do Dhia leinn uile
air stairsneach ceann-crìche.
's E a' measadh slighe beatha
mac an duine:

Sitting now on Iona's east-facing beach,
with the sea's salty fragrance
carried on the breeze;
gazing over the sound to Mull
and far beyond;
casting your mind back in time.

Memories of boyhood in Ireland,
regard for the monks who raised
and schooled you.
Your own students,
their number ever increasing;
some of them in Europe
and the wider world
spreading the scriptures,
gospel, literacy.
Others cultivating
Iona's Paruchia in Scotland and Ireland
the monastery's influence and reputation
steadily growing.

And you have travelled frequently
through Scotland, visiting Bridei
and several other Pictish leaders.
And a return to Ireland:
your success at the Convention of Druim Ceat
where you reconciled
the clans' differences,
negotiating a settled peace
back home in the land
of your kinship,
sorely missed
and for so long.

Reflecting
on the judgment and accounting
due, on the threshold of life's end,
from us all to God.
He who will assess the
human path in life:

slighe sleamhainn caol
le leathad cas air gach taobh,
's sinne le ceuman critheanach
a' sgogadh air an druim:
eadar deuchainn is feuchainn,
eadar doirbh is soirbh, daor is saor
doilleir is soilleir, dorch is sorch:
eadar dòlas is sòlas,
eadar Donas is sonas,
eadar dubhailc is subhailc.

a slippery narrow path
a precipitous slope on either side,
and we, with faltering steps,
teetering on the ridge:
between testing and proving,
easy or hard, costing dear or nought
murky and clear, dark and light:
grief and solace,
harm and joy,
vice and virtue.

JACKIE KAY

1961–

BABY LAZARUS

When I got home
I went out into the garden –
the frost bit my old brown boots –
and dug a hole the size of my baby
and buried the clothes I'd bought anyway.
A week later I stood at my window
and saw the ground move and swell
the promise of a crop,
that's when she started crying.
I gave her a service then, sang
Ye banks and braes, planted
a bush of roses, read the Book of Job,
cursed myself digging a pit for my baby
sprinkling ash from the grate.
Late that same night
she came in by the window,
my baby Lazarus
and suckled at my breast.

HOLY ISLAND

All winter I was waiting
for something to give
and today I felt it,
a small crack,
the sun on the sandy dunes
by the Causeway,
the feel of the land
so close to the sea.
Nick and me and the dog
striding along
by the old Benedictine monastery
till we walked into
a new vocabulary –
hope, benevolence, benediction –
after the long wintering
of false starts,
the same day over and over,
the spring at last here –
I said a small prayer,
the wind on my hair.

KATHLEEN JAMIE

1962–

THE BUDDLEIA

When I pause to consider
a god, or creation unfolding
in front of my eyes –
is this my lot? Always
brought back to the same
grove of statues in ill-
fitting clothes: my suddenly
elderly parents, their broken-down
Hoover; or my quarrelling kids?

Come evening, it's almost too late
to walk in the garden, and try,
Once again, to retire the masculine
God of my youth
by evoking instead the divine
in the lupins, or foxgloves, or self-
seeded buddleia,
whose heavy horns flush as they
open to flower, and draw
These bumbling, well-meaning bees
which remind me again,
of my father . . . whom, Christ,
I've forgotten to call.

MEADOWSWEET

Tradition suggests that certain of the Gaelic
women poets were buried face down.

So they buried her, and turned home,
a drab psalm
hanging about them like haar,

not knowing the liquid
trickling from her lips
would seek its way down,

and that caught in her slowly
unravelling plait of grey hair
were summer seeds:

meadowsweet, bastard balm,
tokens of honesty, already
beginning their crawl

toward light, so showing her,
when the time came,
how to dig herself out –

to surface and greet them,
mouth young, and full again
of dirt, and spit, and poetry.

DON PATERSON

1963–

PROFESSION OF FAITH

God is not the sea, but of its nature:
He scatters like the moonlight on the water
or appears on the horizon like a sail.
The sea is where He wakes, or sinks to dreams.
He made the sea, and like the clouds and storms
is born of it, over and over. Thus the Creator
finds himself revived by his own creature:
he thrives on the same spirit he exhales.

I'll make you, Lord, as you made me, restore
the soul you gifted me; in time, uncover
your name in my own. Let that pure source
that pours its empty heart out to us pour
through my heart too; and let the turbid river
of every heartless faith dry up for ever.

after Antonio Machado

ROB A. MACKENZIE

1964–

SCOTLAND

After Alastair Reid

It was a day common in this corner of the planet,
when daffodils bent double in sleet and wind,
and black umbrellas shattered in the hand.
Spring lay buried in dirt. Greyness entered
the skin. I pressed through empty Sabbath streets—
the nation was shopping in the malls, or choosing
Swedish furniture to compensate for the woodchip
on its walls. I found a Starbucks and a woman
of uncommon beauty behind the counter.
'What a morning!' I cried. 'Why not try an extra shot
of espresso?' she replied. 'It's just the day for it.'
Her smile brightened the hour and meant
Now pay for it, and pay for it, and pay for it.

BLADE RUNNER

Tell me once more of your conversion,
your decluttered ambition to mine
a pure theology by candlestub.
take me to the back street barber
to chop my priestly beard, and then let's
split up. It's too late for me to bugger
off to the Episcopalians and become
a bishop, which is all you ever wanted
through the jumble sale years,
when asking 'What would Descartes do?'
was your answer to everything.
I will save my chin hair in this leather
wallet labelled, *Relics of a Sinner*,
ready made for the bells and smells
of futuristic Edinburgh – cat-calling
choirs rattling pails after closing time
among winged taxis and unfinished
tramlines, like a cut of *Blade Runner*
directed only by CCTV cameras –
a confusing place to be religious.

A. B. JACKSON

1965–

ISLE OF ARRAN

Prehensile Lord, between you and me
there is always some god almighty
animal playing gooseberry,

its breathing
laboured, deep-sea, its head
laced with injuries.

And I remember —
that holiday trek, a boy
too high on his first horse,

fear-dazzled and saddle-sore,
pulling up short before a
half-ton black

bull which guarded the gate ahead.
Back in Brodick, fried cod with vinegar,
crazy putting while midges bit.

Between you and me
the Minotaur —

RODDY LUMSDEN

1966–2020

THE WORLD'S END

Supposing you were wrong and I was right,
I was lying through there thinking
of a place where we and the land must part,

of where a child swings on a wire fence
watching, and where might be found
a paperback whodunnit, blown brown,

where a river stalls and seeps into the grass,
where all the footprints lead one way
and no one, on a late shift, stamps your pass,

where a clisp of light in the willow-herb
is what was dropped from the swag
in the chase, or a shred of a Sixties hothouse;

a place some call a border, some an edge,
as if the many missing or a saviour
will rise in welcome when we step over.

KENNETH STEVEN

1968–

COLUMBA

A film lies across the water meadows
like a muslin shawl. Birds lament
among rushes, their low voices trailing
like beads of glass. The sun has not been born yet,
remains under woods and hills.
Columba goes down, his ankles buried by soft water,
bygreen fronds, slippery, making no more sound
than a deer. The swans drift over the water,
so white they hurt the eyes. He stops,
forgetting everything as he watches the stoop and silver
of their grace, the sudden rippling of their backs
cast by wind, the furling of the huge wings
like shards of ice. They too are prayers,
personified, awakenings of God
in the morning water land.
He goes on, to the strange stone head
carved and lying dormant in the grass;
those wide eyes that never blinked,
the ringlets of stone hair curling
about the enigma of a half-buried face.
He comes here, even though the smiths who cut this
have known only gods of wood and loam,
have chanted under the wheels of stars,
made strange offerings of wheat and fire and gold.
Here at the water meadow's end he finds the Christ
ripe in his heart, his lips brim with words
that soar like larks into the sky,
almost as if some spring of light and joy
wells from the ground beneath.
He kneels in the wet softness of the earth
and smells the springtime yellow in his veins –
becomes the place he prays in.

EM STRANG

1970–

THE MIRACLE

We cross the western boundary,
carrying the body to the horses.
The flies test us all,
land on our eyelids like tiny black kisses.

The hearse horse is calm – God bless him –
as we harness and double-knot
in what little daylight's left.

It's a short ride but the stench is strong
and if the birds had been to eat
we could've saved ourselves the ritual,
could've let her lie.

It's at the low copse we notice it:
a strange light where the burials are.
It's blue like an ice-hole
or how we might imagine
the inside of the moon.

The horses snort.

Before we realise,
we've dismounted into the dust.

Someone takes off their hat
and we stand like birds.

The body is up and walking to the light,
arms and legs intact.

If we could speak,
words would climb out of our mouths
and doubt all over the night.

CAOIMHIN MACNÈILL/ KEVIN MACNEIL

1972–

SPRING

Spring does not belong to the ordinary
senses. Watch how shadows deepen
and revive in the swooning sun.
(Their black glow is the quease and seethe
of jealousies I have known.)

Flowers settle, bees bubble with life,
miniatures of colourful lust.
(So, too, the dawn I arose by
my impossible love's side.)

Winter's bone-and-ice trees breathe light.
(They are buddhists rooted
in the warm flesh of fact.)

And how this universe, the dharma wheel, turns
to a woman's most intimate gesture!

(And how afterwards summer appeared
to astound us with its ordinariness.)

TESSA BERRING

1975–

AN INTENTION TO BE PRESENT

I bought a bathmat
on Sunday morning

the equivalent

of not worshipping God
at exactly the same time

I needed to soap myself

to peel things off
and not slip over

I love the way Veronica
puts on lip salve

in the movie
about her double life

and I certainly know
what dew is

and how wetness
slides around a hand

The bathmat is off white
almost grey

a bit like something
to feel sad about

something to kneel down on
perhaps pray

AMY JO PHILIP

1975–

CORONACH

The deid breakfast quait-like at wir table.
They tak their saits afore we're waukent,
waitin sounless on a taste o warmth.

They cleek us by wir airms tae talk aboot
the afairs o daith, strauchlin tae fin
a caller vyce. We hae nocht tae say

tae the deid — nocht or ower muckle:
mair nor a bodie can bear tae speak oot
mair nor a word or a life can haud —

syne we sit an listen day efter day
ettlin for the wee bit word that'll gar
the stounin in wir herts devaul,

an the deid bide anent us in wir kitchen,
their whisperin vyces a souch o pain,
a seasonless smirr on the gless.

BREATHING IS THE PLACE TO START

Let everything
    have breath.

        Let there be
    no limit but
  the next lungful.

Let silence
    be the only thing
    to fall silent,

        even the grave
    become glad
with laughter

as God the mother
    lifts to her face
    chaos

        for that first
    fond kiss.

JEN HADFIELD

1978–

PATERNOSTER

(For A. B. J.)

Paternoster. Paternoster.
Hallowed be dy mane.
Dy kingdom come.
Dy draftwork be done.
Still plough the day
And give out daily bray
Though heart stiffen in the harness.
Then sleep hang harness with bearbells
And trot on bravely into sleep
Where the black and the bay
The sorrel and the grey
And foals and bearded wheat
Are waiting.
It is on earth as it is in heaven.
Drought, wildfire,
Wild asparagus, yellow flowers
On the flowering cactus.
Give our daily wheat, wet
Whiskers in the sonorous bucket.
Knead my heart, hardened daily.
Heal the hoofprint in my heart.
Give us our oats at bedtime
And in the night half-sleeping.
Paternoster. Paternoster.
Hallowed be dy hot mash.

NIALL O' GALLAGHER

1981–

AN T-EUN NACH D'RINN SGÈITH

Laigh an t-eun gun ghluasad air an làr.
Thàinig iad nan gràisg: 'Is ann a dh' eug
brù-dhearg, mharbh *esan* e', 'n gille sèimh
a rinn iad a thrèigsinn mar bu ghnàth.
Cha tug e an aire ach, le gràdh,
rinn e nead le làmhan agus shèid
anail shocair, thlàth air a dà sgèith
sgaoileadh beatha feadh gach ite 's cnàmh'.

Dh'fhan i tiotan air a bhois
a' ceilearadh air leth-chois
mus do thog i oirre tron an sgleò.

Theich a threud ach cha do chlisg
an gille le làmhan brisg',
cluas sa lios ri bualadh sgèith an eòin.

THE BIRD THAT NEVER FLEW

The bird lies stock-still on the ground.
The gang moves in: "the robin's deid –
he kilt him". The quiet boy is betrayed,
as happens when stuff goes down,
but he pays no heed and lovingly
makes a nest with his hands and blows
soft, warm breath into her bones,
her feathers, and fills her wings with life.

She hovers an instant on his palms
on one leg, singing,
then takes off into the dark.

Everyone else long gone, the boy still cups his hands
and, unflinching,
listens for a wingbeat in the yard.

translated by Peter Mackay

SAMUEL TONGUE

1981–

THEOLOGY

Before I leave the cottage,
I wait for the fire to die
and rake the embers into ash.
I am the responsible one —
this means I fear the worst.
Outside, the winding night
suggests snow. The stars are
bright pinholes, old games
of 'pin-the-tail' on the gods.
I turn up my collar and pray
that God won't find me;
hope that I'm not lost.

JANETTE AYACHI

1982–

YOUMA AND THE THREE KINGS

The imam, a witch doctor and the local visionary
arrive like three kings hovering with offerings,
they fold and stretch in silhouette, light incense
shrouded in spells and prayers, swinging amulets,
clinking sacks of ruin stones, spitting into potions.
Their healing hands cupping mist and the half-dark.

They all knew each other like a secret
bowing into houses with their curious whispers
to save the living or wave away the dead
with royal blood, holy water, dirges and second sights.

Youma surrendered her weight to their presence
she watched the beaded curtain dance in the doorway
where a weave of light eclipsed the cement floor
to settle like a gauze draped over her skin.

I was bound to the vortices of voodoo, kismet, curse,
this premonition of how she would look two days later
after my flight back home, when the undertaker would offer
her last gift wrapping her in a silk-thread muslin before burial.
The three kings hovering in the background
absolutely still in silhouette.

PENNY BOXALL

1987–

KING OF THE FOLLY

I scoured the *Globe*, the *List* and the *Gazette*
for situations vacant these last months.
The search near fruitless, I had almost quit
before unwontedly I scored this plum,
this golden possibility, this peach.
The masters like the hours I keep (quite none)
and stipulate the levels of decay
to propagate. They like the look – the thought –
of me, the wildman in the foliage,
a visitor unvisiting, unkempt.

They built this wilderness: forced gunpowder
to blast from wordless ground a fitting art,
and summoned springs where nothing welled before.
My home will be decrepit, dank, just so.
They scooped a rock out for me, sunk the grass,
erected statues to the living dead;
then brought in chicken bones to rake the mud,
commissioned shells from coasts I've never seen
to foster sounds, like small abandoned caves.
I barely look at them, my mind's eye full
with truths which I'd do better to forget.
Thus set, I'll live in visions; I'll invent
more proper observations to report.

I know my place and peer out from the tomb
as Jesus must have done, though I've the gift
of time. They come here full of faith and I
can't disappoint. They're certain, for their coin,
to spot sublime reflections in the dark.
Memento mori realised in flesh:
they carve initialled hearts and then vacate.
I'm served my daily porridge from a skull.
How do I live for loneliness? Just think.
I'm less a fellow than belief; a piece
of theatre scenery, a prop.

Am I the gardener? No, madame – he's waged:
a young man from the village I once knew
but now ignore. For sure, I sneak at dusk
sometimes, kill time among the hops, scoff pork
(the which my contract certainly forbids);
but I'm a careful occupant of night,
make sure I'm back by dawn, my garments creased
in places my superiors approve,
my whiskers freshly dirtied, eyes set wild.

The mornings are my best times. I awake
to birdsong and the sound of air.
The rain I relish, too; a physical
exertion of God's immanence, a hint.
It alters all, releases that strange smell
– though 'smell' is not the word – and pricks the earth
with loveliness: an inward pulse like nothing
in the world. It makes my hair stand up. I live
in these huge moments of capacity –
my plot, my furtherment, my little will.

ALYCIA PIRMOHAMED

1990–

I WANT THE KIND OF PERMANENCE IN A BIRDWATCHER'S CATALOGUE

At Lochend Park, swans tendril together
the shape of my longing,

a languid rippling trail of water.
I lean over the edge of the pond, see petals of my face

glinting in the water, a Tuesday morning vase
of unhurried thoughts and magenta

lipstick –

Any birdwatcher will tell you
that winged boats

do not howl through their sharp, pyramid beaks.

That sound clicking through
waterlogged bodies

must be the prosody of my own desires.
I shower in the summer solstice light

and read my morning prayers off the cracked
screen of my phone

– Forgi/ve me

as if a corner of my yearning refracts into an alternate
universe,

a parallel world, a symmetrical ruffled wing.

I reorient myself on the path, into a body turned
away from its doubling,

sick of my own gaze staring back.

There is departure in every window, in every
wind-rustled seed.

– Forgi/ve me
for desiring the permanence of a birdwatcher's catalogue

each line of pigment an absolute, a trail of ink
never slipping beyond its typeset world.

ROSEANNE WATT

1991–

STEEPEL

It doubtless was / a holy thing / to see them there,
the ling, lying open / on the stones, / unfolded
from the thick / books of their bodies, / pining for
that hallowed / bloom of salt; / the haafmen still
there, too, / on the ayre, / stacking, unstacking
and restacking them / into a structure built / not
for reaching heaven / but as a tome / to keep their
summer in; / its sacred texts / of sun, sea and wind

About the Editors

Linden Bicket is Lecturer in Literature and Religion in the School of Divinity at the University of Edinburgh. She is the author of *George Mackay Brown and the Scottish Catholic Imagination* (Edinburgh University Press: 2017). She is also co-editor (with the late Douglas Gifford) of *The Fiction of Robin Jenkins: Some Kind of Grace* (Brill: 2017) and (with Kirsteen McCue) a centenary edition of George Mackay Brown's *An Orkney Tapestry* (Birlinn: 2021). She has published articles and book chapters on patterns of faith and scepticism in literature, and particularly on modern Catholic fiction and poetry.

Emma Dymock teaches classes in Celtic and Scottish Studies at the University of Edinburgh. Her PhD focussed on Sorley MacLean and the symbolism of landscape in his poetry, and since then she has published books and articles on Gaelic poetry, prose and drama with a particular focus on Modernism and the Scottish Renaissance. She is co-editor (with Christopher Whyte) of *Caoir Gheal Leumraich/White Leaping Flame: Sorley MacLean Collected Poems* (Polygon: 2011), and editor of *Naething Dauntit: the Collected Poems of Douglas Young* (Humming Earth: 2016).

Alison Jack is Professor of Bible and Literature in the School of Divinity at the University of Edinburgh, and Principal of New College. Her most recent monograph is *The Prodigal Son in English and American Literature: Five Hundred Years of Literary Homecomings* (Oxford University Press: 2019). Her current research interests include the contrasting influences of the Bible in twentieth century Irish, American and Scottish poetry.

Biographies

IAN ABBOT (1947–1989) was born in Perth and was based for much of his adult life in Whitebridge, south of Inverness. He held numerous jobs while attempting to establish himself as a poet, and his first collection, *Avoiding the Gods*, was published in 1988. His poetry often dramatized the struggle for inspiration in a world full of obstacles. He died in a car crash in 1989 and a new edition, *Finishing the Picture*, which included his unpublished work, was published by Kennedy and Boyd in 2015.

JESSIE ANNIE ANDERSON (1861–1931) was born in Ellon, Aberdeenshire. After a childhood accident left her paralysed, she was educated at home by her mother. Thirteen volumes of her poetry were published in the early years of the twentieth century, and many more appeared in the periodical press. Scottish ecclesiastical history was an abiding feature of her work, as were nature, the seasons, and childhood. Although she was raised in the Church of Scotland, Anderson was later received into the Roman Catholic Church.

MARION ANGUS (1865–1946) grew up as a daughter of the manse in Arbroath. On the death of her father she moved to Aberdeenshire to care for her sister and invalid mother. Her poetic voice, which did not develop until after the First World War, was distinctive in the Scots revival movement, often catching the terseness of the ballads which influenced her work. Recent editions of her writing include *The Singin Lass: selected work of Marion Angus* edited by Aimée Chalmers (2006).

ANON (*c.*700) 'The Dream of the Rood'. This is one of the greatest surviving Old English poems. The earliest known version forms some textual fragments carved on the Ruthwell Cross in what is now Dumfries-shire. The poem is written in a distinctively northern form of Old English, which would have been spoken in Northumbria when that kingdom extended on both sides of what is now the Scottish-English border.

ANON, from the Incholm Antiphoner (14th century). This short piece comes from the Latin manuscript known as the Incholm Antiphoner, which takes its name from the island in the Firth of Forth on which a monastery dedicated to Columba was founded. In antiphonal singing, verses are sung alternately as responses.

JANETTE AYACHI (1982–) is a Scottish-Algerian poet who was born in London, was educated at the Universities of Stirling and Edinburgh, and is now based in Edinburgh. Her first full poetry collection *Hand Over Mouth Music* (2019) won the Saltire Poetry Book of the Year Literary Award (2019). Her poetry (as well as her essays and other prose writing) have been translated into numerous languages. Her second poetry collection, *QuickFire, Slow Burning*, will be published in 2024.

MEG BATEMAN (1959–) was born in Edinburgh. She studied Gaelic at the University of Aberdeen and achieved a doctorate in Scottish Gaelic religious poetry. She is a poet, academic and short story writer. She taught Gaelic at the University of Edinburgh and the University of Aberdeen and is now Professor in Gaelic Language and culture at Sabhal Mòr Ostaig, Skye. Her poetry collections include *Òrain Ghaoil/Love Songs* (1990), *Aotromachd agus dàin eile/Lightness and other poems* (1997), *Soirbheas/Fair Wind* (2007) and *Transparencies* (2013).

TESSA BERRING (1975–) was raised in West Yorkshire, has lived in Aberdeen and was a student of sculpture and drawing at Edinburgh College of Art. She is now based in Edinburgh, and is one twelfth of '12', a women's Scottish poetry collective. Her most recent collection of poetry is *Folded Purse* (2022).

DUGHALL BOCHANAN/DUGALD BUCHANAN (1716–1768) was born in Strathyre, Perthshire. He composed poems in Scots and Scottish Gaelic and he helped the Rev. James Stuart of Killin to translate the New Testament into Scottish Gaelic. He was influenced by English Puritan writings and his spiritual verse was deeply religious, appealing to Highlanders to forsake the secular at a time when Jacobite and Hanoverian differences had greatly impacted his world.

HORATIUS BONAR (1808–1889) served as a minster in Kelso from 1837 to 1866, before joining the Free Church and becoming minister of Chalmers Memorial Church in Edinburgh. His hymns were collected in three volumes as *Hymns of Faith and Hope.*

PENNY BOXALL (1987–) is a poet and writer of children's fiction who has also worked extensively in museums, including the Ashmolean in Oxford. She grew up in Aberdeenshire and Yorkshire and has an MA in Poetry from the University of East Anglia. She has published three collections of poems, *Ship of the Line* (2014), *Who Goes There?* (2018) and, with woodblock artist Naoko Matsubara, *In Praise of Hands* (2020). In 2016 she won the Edwin Morgan Poetry Award.

GEORGE MACKAY BROWN (1921–1996) came from Stromness in Orkney and, with the exception of studies with Edwin Muir at Newbattle Abbey College and then at the University of Edinburgh, he remained there all his life. His novels, short stories and poems (notably *Fishermen with Ploughs*, 1971) explore characters and places from Orkney's past and present within the perspective of his Catholic faith.

GEORGE BUCHANAN (1506–1582) was born at Moss, near Killearn, in Stirlingshire, and educated at the universities of Paris and St Andrews. Exiled for a satirical attack on Cardinal Beaton, he taught at the university of Coimbra in Portugal, but was condemned as a heretic and imprisoned by the Inquisition. Despite Protestant sympathies, he became tutor to Mary, Queen of Scots, and later to King James VI. He was regarded as one of the finest European Latinists of his day, and became Moderator of the newly founded Church of Scotland in 1567.

ROBERT BURNS (1759–1796) was born near Alloway and worked on his father's farm at Mossgiel, near Mauchline, Ayrshire. He achieved fame with the publication of *Poems, Chiefly in the Scottish Dialect* in Kilmarnock in 1786; soon a volume of his verse was published in Edinburgh where he was received as a 'Heaven-taught ploughman'. A great song collector as well as an original poet, Burns wrote in English and in Scots. In later life he worked as an exciseman in Dumfries; rheumatic heart disease killed him.

JOHN BURNSIDE (1955–) was born in Dunfermline, and brought up there and in Northamptonshire. In several remarkable collections (including *Common Knowledge* (1991), *Gift Songs* (2010) and *Apostasy* (2023) he has explored nature, the numinous and their intersections, and while declining to be categorised as a religious poet, he remains intensely interested in ideas of the soul, incarnation and resurrection.

AONGHAS PHÀDRAIG CAIMBEUL/ANGUS PETER CAMPBELL (1952–) was born in Lochboisdale, South Uist. He graduated in Politics and History from the University of Edinburgh. He is an award-winning poet, journalist, broadcaster, novelist, and actor. His poetry draws on Gaelic folklore and magical realism. His novel, *The Girl On the Ferry Boat,* was the first to be published simultaneously in Gaelic and English. His poetry collections include *The Greatest Gift* (1992), *One Road* (1994), *Meas air Chrannaibh/Fruit on Brainches/Fruit on Branches* (2007), *Aibisidh/ABC* (2011) and *Stèisean* (2018).

GERRY CAMBRIDGE (1959–) is a poet, critic, essayist and editor with substantial interests in print design and typography as well as a background in natural-history photography. His publications include: *Notes for Lighting a Fire* (HappenStance Press, 2012), which was shortlisted for the Scottish Mortgage Investment Trust's book of the year award 2013; *Aves* (Essence Press, 2007), prose poems about wild birds; *Madame Fi Fi's Farewell and*

Other Poems (Luath Press, 2003); and *'Nothing But Heather!': Scottish nature in poems, photographs and prose* (Luath Press, 1999). He founded the transatlantic magazine *The Dark Horse*, still Scotland's leading poetry journal, in 1995.

JANE WELSH CARLYLE (1801–1866) was born in Haddington. After her marriage to Thomas Carlyle she lived in Edinburgh and Craigenputtock before moving to London in 1834. Although she did not publish anything in her lifetime, she was a prodigious and famous writer of letters to her many friends and acquaintances in the literary and social world of the time. Much of this correspondence was edited and published by Thomas after her death.

THOMAS CARLYLE (1795–1881) was born in Ecclefechan in Dumfriesshire and entered Edinburgh University at the age of 15. He became a teacher, then an essayist specialising in German literature and political history. His best known work is *Sartor Resartus* (1833–34). Among contemporaries, his ideas were deeply influential in their close focus on the private virtues of work and duty and the public strengths of heroic leaders.

ALEXANDER CARMICHAEL (1932–1912) was born on Lismore. He was educated at Greenock Academy. He was an exciseman in the Hebrides and is best known for the field research, which he conducted on Gaelic culture, much of which was published in *Carmina Gadelica* (1900), a collection of prayers, hymns, charms, incantations, blessings, poems, songs, and proverbs.

SAINT COLUMBA (*c.*521–597) Born in Donegal, Columba studied in Ireland and founded the monastery at Derry before being exiled to Scotland for his part in the Battle of Cúl Dreimhne in 563. Landing on the island of Iona, he founded a monastery there which was, and is today, one of the great centres of Christianity in Scotland.

SCHOOL OF COLUMBA (?eighth century) The hymn, 'Noli Pater', which appears in the Irish *Liber Hymnorum*, is one of a number of hymns traditionally associated with Columba and Iona. It appears to be a lyrical amalgam of several elements.

A COMMITTEE OF THE GENERAL ASSEMBLY OF THE CHURCH OF SCOTLAND in 1650 oversaw the adoption of psalm translations drawn up by the Westminster Assembly. These often incorporated earlier work by Scottish poets. The first line of the 23rd Psalm, for instance, comes from a version by Zachary Boyd (1584–1654), while much of the rest draws on a 1639 version by Sir William Mure of Rowallan (see below). These metrical psalms came to be associated with Scotland because of their widespread use throughout the country. A further Committee was appointed in 1741 to extend the available metrical psalmody. Their immediate suggestions were considered too evangelical by the Moderates in the General Assembly, but in 1781 there appeared Translations and Paraphrases, in verse, of several Passages of Sacred Scripture, later supplemented in the early nineteenth century and generally known as The Paraphrases.

JOE CORRIE (1894–1968) worked as a miner in Fife before becoming a full-time writer, and is best known for his early plays, particularly *In Time o' Strife* (1926), which portrayed working-class life and language with a frankness and humour sometimes likened to those of Sean O'Casey's plays in Ireland.

ROBERT CRAWFORD (1959–) was born in Belshill, Lanarkshire and studied at the Universities of Glasgow and Oxford. He was Bishop Wardlaw Professor of Poetry at the University of St Andrews until his retirement in 2020. He has published widely as a biographer, literary critic, translator, editor and historian, as well as his own collections of poetry including *Selected Poems* (2005), *Testament* (2014) and *The Scottish Ambassador* (2018).

JOHN DAVIDSON (1857–1909) was born in Barrhead, where his father was a minister of the Evangelical Union. He taught briefly in Scotland before working as a writer and journalist in London. His 'Fleet Street Eclogues' made new poetic use of the modern city scene, and the materialistic *Testaments*, proclaiming the need for social reform and a scientific outlook, influenced Hugh MacDiarmid.

CHRISTINE DE LUCA (1947–) was born and raised in Shetland and now lives in Edinburgh. She has worked in education and was Edinburgh's Makar from 2014 to 2017. She writes in Shetland Dialect and English and is one of the founders of the Hansel Co-operative Press which promotes literary and artistic work in Shetland and Orkney. She is a novelist as well as a poet, and often collaborates with artists and musicians in her work. Her collections include *Plain Song* (2002), *Edinburgh: Singing the City* (2017) and *Veeve* (2021).

IMTIAZ DHARKER (1954–) was born in Lahore, Pakistan, and grew up in Glasgow. She was educated at the University of Glasgow, and is currently Chancellor of Newcastle University. A self-described 'Scottish Muslim Calvinist', Dharker's work reflects on themes of place, home, journeys, gender, conflict and displacement. In 2014, Dharker was awarded the Queen's Gold Medal for Poetry. She withdrew from consideration for the position of Poet Laureate in 2019, noting the need for privacy in order to write. She is also an artist and documentary film-maker. Her most recent collection is *Luck is the Hook* (2018).

MÀIRI NICDHÒMHNAILL/MARY MACDONALD (1789–1872) was born at Ardtun, northeast of Bunessan on the Ross of Mull. She was the daughter of a Baptist cleric, Duncan MacDougal. MacDonald was a Gaelic poet and a crofter's wife. A devout Baptist, she composed many of her own song and poems while sitting at her spinning wheel.

AN T-ATHAIR AILEAN DÒMHNALLACH/FATHER ALLAN MACDONALD (1859–1905) was born in Fort William. He was a Roman Catholic priest, folklorist, and activist for Crofter's rights, and free elections. As a Gaelic poet, his work was radically innovative. In his poem, 'An Eaglais'/'The Church', Father Allan draws on the ancient metaphor of the Catholic Church as the Barque of St. Peter, reimagining Christ as a Hebridean shipwright, with the poem being in the style of a waulking song.

ROB DONN (1714–1778) was born at Allt na Caillich in Strathmore, Sutherland. His poetry was greatly influenced by the Jacobite Rebellion and its aftermath with impassioned responses to events such as the Dress Act 1746. His poetry was often centred on social commentary. Unable to read or write, Donn dictated his poetry from memory towards the end of his life.

DONNCHADH NAM PÌOS (d. *c.*1700) was also known as Donnchadh MacRath. He was the compiler of the Fernaig MS – a number of the poems included in this compilation were composed by Donnchadh and his work is often characterised by its Jacobite and episcopalian sympathies. He was the son and heir of Alexander Macrae of Inverinate, who served as Chamberlain of Kintail to the third Earl of Seaforth.

GAVIN DOUGLAS (*c.*1476–1522) was born in Tantallon Castle, East Lothian, son of the fifth Earl of Angus. Educated at the University of St Andrews, in 1503 he became Provost of St Giles, and in 1515 Bishop of Dunkeld. With his *Eneados* (a Scots version of Virgil's *Aeneid*) he became the first person to translate an entire classical epic into a modern vernacular language. Exiled in the wake of Flodden, he died of plague in England.

WILLIAM DRUMMOND OF HAWTHORNDEN (1585–1649) studied at the University of Edinburgh and inherited the family estate of Hawthornden, near Edinburgh, on his father's death in 1610. He lived there in retirement, writing much verse in the Petrarchan tradition, including the religious sonnets, songs and madrigals of *Flowres of Sion* (1623). Ben Johnson visited him in 1618, and wrote an account of their conversation. Drummond donated over 600 volumes (including two quartos by Shakespeare) from his magnificent private library to the University of Edinburgh from the mid-1620s.

CAROL ANN DUFFY (1955–) was born in Glasgow but has worked mainly in England where she was brought up. Her poetry, including such collections as *Selling Manhattan* (1987), *Mean Time* (1993), *Feminine Gospels* (2002) and *Sincerity* (2018), has made a powerful impact with its confidence and range, and she is also a playwright of renown. She was the UK's

Poet Laureate from 2009–2019, the first female and the first Scottish holder of that role, and has sought to bring poetry more openly into national life. She is Creative Director of the Manchester Metropolitan University Writing School.

WILLIAM DUNBAR (?1456–?1513) studied at the University of St Andrews and, from 1500, became court poet to King James IV, who perished with many of his nobility at the Battle of Flodden in 1513. Dunbar's work includes bawdily secular as well as religious poems and is remarkable for its energetic versatility. He delights in the elaborate language of 'aureate diction'.

ANGUS DUNN (1953–2015) was born in Clydebank but brought up and based in the Highlands and he was a prizewinning novelist and short story writer as well as a poet. His poetry was published in a wide range of magazines and anthologies, although there is only one full collection of his poetic works, *High Country*, published in 2015. He was editor of *Northwords* magazine and a tutor at the creative writing centre Moniack Mhor.

ROBERT FERGUSSON (1750–1774) was born in Edinburgh and educated at St Andrews University. He became a clerk in Edinburgh and a member of the town's Cape Club before falling ill with severe depression. He died suddenly in Darien House, a hospital for the mentally ill, at the age of twenty-four. Fergusson was a sophisticated writer in English and Scots. His memory was venerated by Burns, who paid for Fergusson's tombstone in Edinburgh's Canongate Kirkyard.

DALLÁN FORGAILL (*fl.* 600) 'The Little Blind One of Testimony'/Eochu mac Colla was probably a professional poet based in Ireland. He had experience of monastic life and was venerated as a saint. 'Amra Choluimb Chille' is thought to have been composed shortly after Columba's death in 597 and may have been commissioned by Áed, King of Cenel Conaill, St Columba's cousin. It became a sacred text studied by students in Irish monasteries. On composing this panegyric to Columba, the poet is said to have regained his sight. Four of its ten principal sections are given here.

BASHABI FRASER (1954–) is a poet, playwright, academic, translator and editor who was born and grew up in India. She lives in Edinburgh and has a PhD from the University of Edinburgh. She is Professor Emerita of English and Creative Writing at Edinburgh Napier University and her publications span poetry, children's fiction and academic research. All reflect in different ways her interest in Scotland and India and the relationship between the two lands, cultures and people. Her poetry collections include *Tartan and Turban* (2004), *Letters to my Mother and Other Mothers* (2015) and *Patient Dignity* (2021).

GEORGE GORDON, LORD BYRON (1788–1824) was born in London and educated in his mother's city, Aberdeen, then at Harrow and Cambridge. Byron was intimately acquainted with Calvinism from his childhood. The success of his longer narrative poems, finest of which is *Don Juan*, made him an international celebrity, scandalizing and delighting readers with his ironic accounts of erotic and other matters. He died at Missolonghi, supporting the Greek struggle against the Turks.

JAMES GRAHAM, MARQUIS OF MONTROSE (1612–1650) was educated at the University of St Andrews, and signed the National Covenant against the Anglican policy of King Charles I, though he later fought on the King's side in the Civil War. Eventually, after exile in Europe, he was executed in Edinburgh for attempting to lead a Highland rebellion in favour of King Charles II.

W. S. GRAHAM (1918–1986) was born in Greenock but lived most of his life in poverty in Cornwall. His poetry offers oblique but powerful and often moving exploration of the mysteries of language and being, where oddness of syntax and imagery mirrors the complexities of communication itself.

JEN HADFIELD (1978–) grew up in Cheshire, the daughter of a Canadian mother and a British father. She was educated at the Universities of Edinburgh and Glasgow, and, after travel in Shetland and the Western Isles for her first collection *Almanacs* (2005), now makes Shetland her home. *Almanacs* won the Eric Gregory Award (2003). Hadfield was also the winner of the T. S. Eliot Prize (2008) for her second collection, *Nigh-No-Place* (2008), making her the youngest ever writer to win the prize. Her incantatory work reflects on place, belonging, and wildness. She writes in both English and Shetland dialect.

DIANA HENDRY (1941–) was born in the Wirral and now lives and works in Edinburgh. She has worked as an English teacher, journalist and tutor in creative writing for the Open University, the University of Bristol, and the Arvon Foundation. She has published six full collections of poetry, beginning with *Making Blue* (1995). As well as writing poetry, Hendry is the author of short stories and over forty books for children, of which *Harvey Angell* won a Whitbread Award in 1991.

ROBERT HENRYSON (?1424–?1506) worked as a schoolteacher in Dunfermline, and may have studied at Glasgow University. Regarded as one of the greatest Scottish poets, he is best remembered for his Aesopian *Moral Fables* and for his *Testament of Cresseid*, which takes up the story of the heroine of Chaucer's *Troilus and Criseyde*.

JAMES HOGG (1770–1832) was born on an Ettrick farm and spent years as a shepherd before coming to Edinburgh in 1810 and working as an editor and poet. A friend of Walter Scott, he had a rich knowledge of Border oral culture. His great novel *The Private Memoirs and Confessions of a Justified Sinner* (1824) examines extreme Calvinist belief.

ALEXANDER HUME (*c.*1557–1609) was son of the fifth Lord Polwarth and studied at the University of St Andrews. After spending time at the court of King James VI, where he wrote his beautiful, clear poem about midsummer's day, 'Of the Day Estivall', he became a minister of the Church of Scotland.

A. B. JACKSON (1965–) is a Glasgow-born poet, who was raised in Cheshire and educated at the University of Edinburgh and at Sheffield Hallam University. His first collection, *Fire Stations* (2003), won the Forward Prize for Best First Collection (2003). In August 2010 his poem 'Treasure Island' won first prize in the Edwin Morgan International Poetry Competition. He now lives in Pitlochry.

VIOLET JACOB (1863–1946) was born near Montrose into a landed family. She married an army officer and spent time in India, then returned to the North-East. She wrote short stories and novels but was primarily a poet, and her confident local voice was one of the earliest in the twentieth century revival of writing in Scots.

A. C. JACOBS (1937–1994) was born in Glasgow where he grew up in a traditional Jewish family, which moved to London in 1951. He later lived in Israel, Scotland, London, Italy and Spain, where he died. He once wrote 'My real language is probably Scots-Yiddish', and he became a translator of Hebrew poetry. His *Collected Poems* and *Selected Translations* were published in 1996.

KATHLEEN JAMIE (1962–) was raised in Currie near Edinburgh, studied philosophy at the University of Edinburgh, and now lives in Fife. The strength and independence of her poetic voice was recognised early, in *Black Spiders* (1982) and *The Way We Live* (1987). The natural world has increasingly been the focus of her work in poetry and in non-fiction prose, with the poetry collections *The Treehouse* (2004) and *The Overhaul* (2012) and the essay collections *Findings* (2005), *Sightlines* (2012) and *Surfacing* (2019) all reflecting on landscape and the environment. In 2021, Jamie was appointed Scots Makar.

JACKIE KAY (1961–) was born in Edinburgh and brought up in Glasgow. She studied at Stirling University and has written extensively about her experience of being black, adopted, lesbian and Scottish in her work, which includes plays, novels, biography and autobiography as well as poetry for adults and children. Collections of her poetry include *The Adoption Papers* (1991), *Life Mask* (2005), *Fiere* (2011) and *Bantam* (2017). She was Scotland's Makar from 2016–2021, and is Professor of Creative Writing at the University of Newcastle.

WILLIAM KETHE (*c.*1530–1594), a Scot, spent time in Frankfurt and Geneva, where he helped to translate the Bible into English and to compile a book of metrical psalms. 'All people that on earth do dwell' was originally published in Geneva in 1561, then in the first Scottish Psalter in 1564. In the Scottish Psalter Kethe's 'Him serve with fear' in line three became 'Him serve with mirth'. Kethe went on to become rector of Childe Okeford in Dorset.

TOM LEONARD (1944–2018) was an influential Glasgow poet and critic whose experimentation with the rhythms and tones of colloquial language combines humour with a committed sense of social justice for the disenfranchised. His anthology *Radical Renfrew* reveals the richness of working-class writing in nineteenth-century newspapers and journals. From 2001 until 2009 he was joint Professor in Creative Writing at the University of Glasgow.

JOHN LEYDEN (1775–1811) was educated at Edinburgh University and tutored in St Andrews. A tenant farmer's son from Denholm, Roxburghshire, he taught himself thirty languages. In 1799 he published *Discoveries and Settlements of Europeans in Northern and Western Africa*. He helped Walter Scott collect Border Ballads, then emigrated to the Far East, dying in Java shortly after publishing a book on Burmese, Malay and Thai languages.

LIZ LOCHHEAD (1947–) was born near Motherwell, studied at the Glasgow School of Art and worked as a teacher before becoming a full-time writer of poetry and drama. Her poetry draws vividly on orality, musicality and performance. The revision and interrogation of myth and fairy tale, and sharp social observations are evident from her earliest works. Like Edwin Morgan, Lochhead was made Poet Laureate of Glasgow (2005–11) and then Scots Makar (2011–16). She was awarded the Queen's Gold Medal for Poetry in 2015.

RODDY LUMSDEN (1966–2020) was born in St Andrews and educated at the University of Edinburgh. His first collection *Yeah, Yeah, Yeah* (1997) explored the chaotic nature of contemporary Scottish urban life in a style which blended aplomb with formal elegance, while *The Book of Love* (2000), was shortlisted for the T. S. Eliot Prize, and *So Glad I'm Me* (2017) was shortlisted for the T. S. Eliot Prize (2017) and the Saltire Society Scottish Poetry Book of the Year Award (2018). Lumsden was the author of nine collections of poetry, and was also editor of *Identity Parade: New British and Irish Poets* (2010) and *The Best British Poetry 2011* (2011).

IAIN MAC A' GHOBHAINN/IAIN CRICHTON SMITH (1928–1998) was born in Glasgow and was brought up in Lewis. He was educated at the University of Aberdeen and trained as a teacher at Jordanhill College, Glasgow. He taught English at Clydebank High School and Oban High School and retired from teaching in 1977 to become a full-time writer. He is known as a writer of both English and Gaelic short stories, novels and poems. His poetry collections include *Bùrn is Aran* (1960), *Bìobuill is Sanasan-Reice* (1965), *Rabhdan is Rudan* (1973), *Eadar Feall-Dhà is Glaschu* (1974), and *Na h-Eilthirich* (1983).

DÒMHNALL MACAMHLAIGH/DONALD MACAULAY (1930–2017) was born in Bernera, off Lewis. He was a poet and editor of Gaelic poetry. He taught at the University of Edinburgh, Trinity College Dublin and the University of Aberdeen, and from 1991–1996, he was Chair of Celtic at the University of Glasgow. His published poetry appeared in *Seòbhrach às a' Chloich* (1967) and in *Deilbh is Faileasan /Images and Reflections* (Acair, 2008), and he edited the anthology *Nua-bhàrdachd Ghàidhlig/Modern Scottish Gaelic Poems* (1976).

NORMAN MACCAIG (1910–1996) was a classicist by education, a primary headteacher (and latterly university lecturer) by profession, and a much-loved poet and reader of his own poetry. He explored the natural world of his Gaelic ancestors, and the cityscape of his native Edinburgh, in lyrics which are sharp, surprising, wry, metaphysical and, sometimes, bleak. His poetry collections include *A Common Grace* (1960), *The White Bird* (1973) and *The Equal Skies* (1980).

DÒMHNALL IAIN MACDHÒMHNAILL/DONALD JOHN MACDONALD (1919–1986) was born in Peninerine, South Uist. He came from a family of tradition-bearers, which greatly influenced his ability to compose Gaelic poems of his own. In World War II, he served in the 51st (Highland) Division and was taken prisoner at St Valéry and spent the rest of the war in prison camps. After the war, he returned to crofting, and he won the Bardic Crown at the National Mod in 1948 with his poem 'Moladh Uibhist'. As well as a poet, he was an active folklore collector. His collected poetry was published posthumously in *Chì Mi/I See* (1998), edited by Bill Innes.

HUGH MACDIARMID (1892–1978) was born in Langholm, Dumfriesshire, and its landscape shaped him as much as Orkney's did Muir. As journalist and polemicist for a variety of literary and political causes, as well as by his formidable poetic range, he made a major impact on twentieth-century Scottish literature. His *A Drunk Man Looks at the Thistle* (1926) combines metaphysical speculation with satirical or intimate reflections on Scottish life.

GEORGE MACDONALD (1824–1905) was a weaver's son and Congregationalist minister who became an original writer of such fairy tales as *The Princess and the Goblin* (1872) and *The Princess and the Curdie* (1883), often coloured by Christian and mystical symbolism or shaped by powerful allegories of good and evil. His vividly imagined adult fiction influenced C. S. Lewis and J. R. R. Tolkien.

ATHAIRNE MAC EOGHAIN (*fl. c.*1558) belonged to the hereditary family of MacEwans, who were poets to the Campbells of Glenorchy. The 1631 Gaelic translation of Calvin's Catechism, *Adtimchioll an Chreidimh* contains this poem as well as another which is also attributed to him.

JAMES MACFARLAN (1832–1862) lived a short, self-destructive life, mostly in poverty, in Glasgow. His poems caught the sense of alienation in the nineteenth century city, as well as the attention of Dickens (who published some in his journal *All the Year Round*) and Thackeray, who admired the poem printed here.

SOMHAIRLE MACGILL-EAIN/SORLEY MACLEAN (1911–1996) was born at Oscaig, Raasay. He is one of the most influential Gaelic poets of the twentieth century. His *Dàin do Eimhir* (*Poems to Eimhir*), published in 1943, showed how modernism could be melded with Gaelic tradition. He was educated at the University of Edinburgh, and he taught English at Boroughmuir Secondary School, Edinburgh, and Plockton Secondary School, where he was Headmaster until his retirement in 1972. He was an influential figure of both the Gaelic Renaissance and the Scottish Literary Renaissance, forming friendships with the likes of Hugh MacDiarmid and Douglas Young. *Reothairt is Contraigh (Spring Tide and Neap Tide): Selected Poems 1932–72* was published in 1977 and *O Choille gu Bearradh/ From Wood to Ridge* in 1989.

DEÒRSA MAC IAIN DHEÒRSA/GEORGE CAMPBELL HAY (1915–1984) was born in Elderslie, Renfrewshire and he was raised in Tarbert, where he acquired the Gaelic language from his mother and the older generation of the village. Hay was educated in Edinburgh at John Watson's and Fettes, before studying at Corpus Christi College, Oxford. He was an excellent linguist and could speak and read a number of languages including Gaelic, Danish, Swedish, Icelandic, Irish and modern Greek. He was a committed Scottish Nationalist and resisted subscription in World War II before joining the Royal Army Ordnance Corp, serving in Algeria, Tunisia, Italy and Greece. A number of his poems deal with the injustice and horror of war including *Mochtàr is Dùghall* (1982). He composed poems in Gaelic, English and Scots and his publications included *Fuaran Sléibh* (1947), *Wind on Loch Fyne* (1948) and *O na Ceithir Àirdean* (1952).

ROB A. MACKENZIE (1964–) was born in Glasgow and has lived in Seoul, Lanarkshire, and Turin. He is currently a Church of Scotland minister in Leith. He was the reviews editor for *Magma* poetry magazine and now runs the Blue Diode Press. His poetry is sharp, sometimes playful and often satirical. Volumes of his poetry include *The Opposite of Cabbage* (2009), *The Good News* (2013) and *The Book of Revelation* (2020).

CAOIMHIN MACNÈILL/KEVIN MACNEIL (1972–) was born and raised on the Isle of Lewis. As well as writing poetry, novels and plays, he has also written for radio, television, and film. His collection *Love and Zen in the Outer Hebrides* (1998), won the Tivoli Europa Giovani International Prize in 2000. He is a Lecturer in Creative Writing at the University of Stirling, and a practising Buddhist, researching areas of congruence between Buddhist tenets and creative writing practice.

DONNCHADH MACRAOIRIDH (d. *c.*1630) was a bard to the MacDonalds of Sleat, Skye. He also had clan loyalties to the MacKenzies of Wester Ross. Four of his poems can be found in the Fernaig MS. Three of these poems are religious in theme and exhibit a complete acceptance of God's will.

RUARAIDH MACTHÒMAIS/DERICK THOMSON (1921–2012) was born in Stornoway, Isle of Lewis. He was a poet, academic and is known as the father of modern Gaelic publishing. He lectured in Celtic at the Universities of Edinburgh and Aberdeen, and he was Professor of Celtic at the University of Glasgow from 1963 to 1991. He co-founded the quarterly Gaelic magazine *Gairm* in 1952, and he founded the Gaelic Books Council in 1968. As well as writing and editing books on Gaelic literature and culture, his own verse has been published in numerous collections, beginning with *An Dealbh Briste/The Broken Picture* in 1951. *Meall Garbh/The Rugged Mountain* appeared in 1995. His poetry covers a number of themes, including homeland, education, and politics in the form of Scottish Nationalism.

MARY, QUEEN OF SCOTS (1542–1587), daughter of King James V and Mary of Guise-Lorraine, came to Scotland in 1561, having succeeded to the Scottish throne when she was six days old. As a Catholic monarch at the time of the Scottish Reformation, she attempted a policy of religious reconciliation, but was overthrown in 1567 after her marriage to the Earl of Bothwell following the murder of her second husband, her cousin Darnley. She abdicated in favour of her son, James VI, but was eventually executed in England, accused of plotting against Queen Elizabeth I.

GEORGE MATHESON (1842–1906) is remembered as a hymn writer. He was born in Glasgow, and, although blind from the age of 18, pursued a brilliant academic career at the University there. He became minister at Innellan, and then in Edinburgh, writing many works of devotion.

JAMES MCGONIGAL (1947–) was born in Dumfries, was raised there and in Glasgow, and was a schoolteacher and then teacher educator at the University of Glasgow, where he was Professor of English in Education until his retirement in 2009. He has published widely as an editor and critic, is Literary Executor of Edwin Morgan, and his biography *Beyond the Last Dragon: A Life of Edwin Morgan*, was published by Sandstone Press in 2010. His own collections of poetry include the tri-lingual poem in English, Scots and Irish Gaelic, *Passage/An Pasaíste*, (2004) and *Cloud Pibroch* (2010), which received the Michael Marks Poetry Award.

ELIZABETH MELVILLE, LADY CULROSS (*fl.* 1599–1631) was daughter of Sir James Melville of Halhill and Christian Boswell. She married John Colville, son of Alexander Colville, Commendator of Culross. Her major allegory, *Ane Godlie Dreame*, expressed her Calvinism but also reflected earlier medieval and Renaissance literary conventions. It was published by Robert Charteris in 1603, making Elizabeth Melville the first Scotswoman to see her work in print. In 2002, almost 3500 lines of verse attributed to Elizabeth Melville were discovered in the 'Bruce Manuscript', a volume of sermons which is held within the New College Library Special Collections at the University of Edinburgh.

ELMA MITCHELL (1919–2000) was born in Airdrie. A librarian, she worked in broadcasting and in journalism in London before settling in Somerset. Her compassionate and energetic poetry was published as *The Human Cage* (1979).

NAOMI MITCHISON (1897–1997) published over 70 books in her long career, and is best known for her novels and stories which evoke the world of classical Greek and Rome, although her thematic range is wide. She had a long association with Carradale in Kintyre, forcefully expressed in two long narrative poems 'The Alban Goes Out' (1939) and 'The Cleansing of the Knife' (1947).

AONGHAS MOIREASDAN/ANGUS MORRISON (1865–1942) was born in Ullapool. He was a collector of Gaelic songs and pipe tunes, as well as being a Gaelic poet himself. As a tea and coffee merchant he was widely travelled and many of his poems are set in various locations around the Highlands. He was Secretary and Treasurer of the Gaelic Society of Inverness from 1904 to 1907. His *Òrain nam Beann* was published in 1913 and *Dàin agus Òrain Ghàidhlig* was published in 1929.

EDWIN MORGAN (1920–2010) was born in Glasgow and combined an academic career in English Literature (latterly as Professor at the University of Glasgow) with an energetic creative life involving translation, experimental sound and visual poetry, opera and verse drama, as well as many collections notable for their lyricism, sharp social observation and modernity. *Collected Poems* (1990) and *Collected Translations* (1996) reveal this remarkable range. He was appointed OBE in 1992, received the Queen's Gold Medal for Poetry in 2000, and was announced as the first Poet Laureate of Glasgow in 1999. In 2004 he was named the first Scots Makar of modern times.

JOHN MORISON (1750–1798) was educated at King's College in Aberdeen where he took his MA in 1771. A distinguished Scottish divine and poet, he became minister at Canisbay in 1780 and was a notable contributor to the volume of *Translations and Paraphrases, in Verse, of Several Passages of Sacred Scripture* issued by the Church of Scotland in 1781.

MUGRÓN, ABBOT OF IONA (d. 981) was Abbot of Iona and head of the Columban family of monasteries in both Scotland and Ireland from 965. The poem here follows the form of the *lorica* (breastplate), a formulaic poem chanted to gain both the physical and spiritual protection of the Godhead, of a particular saint or divine object.

EDWIN MUIR (1887–1959) was born in Deerness, Orkney. A traumatic early move to industrial Glasgow continued to shape the archetypal terrain of his poetry. He worked in London as a writer and critic, as well as in Rome and in Prague, where he and his wife, the novelist Willa Anderson, made notable translations of Franz Kafka. His best-known poetry volumes include *The Labyrinth* (1949) and *One Foot in Eden* (1956).

MUIREADHACH ALBANACH (*fl.* 1220) belonged to an Irish family of hereditary poets, the Uí Dálaigh. He lived in Lissadell (Co. Sligo). In 1213, after killing his chief's steward, he escaped to Scotland where he made his name as bard to the Mormaer of Lennox. It was during this time that he established the MacMhuirichs, the longest serving family of hereditary poets in Scotland. He was a Crusader and travelled to Acre, Damietta and Rome. He was given a pardon from his crime and was allowed to return to Ireland in 1228. The poem included here, which addresses the Virgin Mary as the Queen of Heaven is found in the Book of the Dean of Lismore.

SIR WILLIAM MURE OF ROWALLAN (1594–1657) was born at Rowallan, Ayrshire, the family estate. A good deal of the poetry of this 'pios and learned' man was written in support of the Covenanters. He became a member of the Scottish Parliament in 1645, having fought in the Scottish army at the Battle of Marston Moor in the preceding year.

CHARLES MURRAY (1864–1941) was born in Alford, Aberdeenshire, and for most of his life worked as a civil engineer in South Africa. He retired to the North-East, where his collection *Hamewith* (1900) had already made him well-known through its supple and authentic use of Aberdeenshire Scots.

CHARLES, LORD NEAVES (1800–1876) was born into a legal family in Edinburgh and became a judge in the court of session in 1854. He contributed regularly to *Blackwood's Magazine*, and his *Songs and Verses, Social and Scientific* (4th edition, 1875) are lively expressions of his wide ranging interests.

SANDAIDH NicDHÒMHNAILL JONES/SANDY NicDHÒMHNAILL JONES (1960–) is a Gaelic poet, translator, composer, and songwriter. She was the Gaelic Crowned Bàrd for 2019–2021, and has won the Wigtown Gaelic Poetry Prize and the Córn Úi Néill trophy, among other literary awards. Her collection of Gaelic poetry and songs *Crotal Ruadh – Red Lichen* was published in 2016, with her second collection, *An Seachdamh*

Tonn – The Seventh Wave following in 2021, both published by Acair Books. *An Naomhsgeul as Buaine: Sgàthan Cinne-Daonna is Aiteal Dhè – The Most Enduring Saint's Fable: Mirror of Humanity and Glimpse of God,* also published in 2021, by Sallan Ltd, was commissioned by the Royal Irish Academy to mark 1500 years since the birth of St Columba in 521.

ANNA NIC EALAIR/ANNA MACKELLAR (*fl.* 1800) belonged to Argyll or Perthshire. The poem featured in this anthology is her own surviving work and is of the tradition of the Highland Evangelical Revivals of the late 18th and 19th centuries.

MÀIRI M. NICGHILLEATHAIN/MARY M. MACLEAN (1921–2004) was born at Knockqueen, North Uist. She is known for her Gaelic poetry, short stories and articles, many of which appeared in publications such as *An Gaidheal, The Stornoway Gazette, The Free Church Monthly Record,* and *Am Pàipear.* She won the Bardic Crown at the National Mod in 1951 for her poem 'Do Bheinn Eubhal'. Many of her poems are deeply religious in theme. Her collection of short stories, *Lus-Chrùn á Griomsaidh* appeared in 1970 and her novel. *Gainmheach an Fhàsaich* was published in 1971.

CATRÌONA NICGUMARAID/CATRIONA MONTGOMERY (1947–2024) was born in Roag, near Dunvegan in Skye. She graduated with a degree in Celtic and Scottish History at Glasgow University, and she trained to be a teacher at Jordanhill College. As well as teaching Gaelic and modern studies at schools in Glasgow and Dundee, she worked as an actress and writer for the BBC and other companies. Montgomery was the first writer in residence at Sabhal Mòr Ostaig. She was given the hundredth Bardic Crown of An Comunn Gàidhealach in 2003. Montgomery's poetry has been published in *Gairm*, *Akros*, *Chapman*, and *Lines Review.* Her publications include *A' Choille Chiar* (with Mòrag NicGumaraid) (1974), *Rè na h-Oidhche* (1994), and *Àilleagan am Measg nam Flùr* (2018).

MARION F. NICILLEMHOIRE/MARION F. MORRISON (1950–) is a Gaelic poet and writer, who was born in Barra and raised in Glasgow. She is now based on South Uist. She studied at Glasgow University, gaining an MA and an MLitt, and was a teacher in Glasgow, Daliburgh, South Uist and Benbecula. She was the winner of the Scottish Book Trust New Writers Award in 2017 for Gaelic poetry. Her first collection of poems in Gaelic and English, *Adhbhar ar Sòlais/Cause of our Joy*, was published in 2018.

NIALL O' GALLAGHER (1981–) was born in Edinburgh. He studied and taught at the University of Glasgow before becoming a journalist, translator and poet. His poetry often describes an urban Gaelic experience, and his use of Classical Gaelic forms has been highly praised. In 2019 he was named Bàrd Baile Ghlaschu, the City of Glasgow's first Gaelic Poet Laureate. *Beatha Ùr* was published in 2013, followed by *Suain nan Trì*

Latha (2016), *Fo Bhlàth* (2020) and *The Sounds of Love/Fuaimean Gràidh: Selected Poems* (2023).

DON PATERSON (1963–) is from Dundee and combines work as a poet, playwright, jazz musician, poetry editor and Professor in the School of English at the University of St Andrews. His poetry is distinctive in its use of formal and technical elements and a strict adherence to rhyme and metre, although its subject matter, narrative voice and use of humour and allusion may be thoroughly jarring and unexpected. His poetry collections include *Nil Nil* (1993), *Rain* (2009) and *Zonal* (2020).

DOROTHY MARGARET PAULIN (1904–1982) was born in Dumfries and educated at the University of Edinburgh. She was editor of the *Gallovidian Annual*, *Scottish Home and Country*, and the *Soil Association Magazine*. She was Liaison Officer for the Department of Agriculture for Scotland during the Second World War, and indeed much of her poetry reflects her passion for environmental and agricultural matters. Her collections of poetry include *Country Gold and other poems* (1936) and *Solway Tide* (1955).

AMY JO PHILIP (1975–) is the first out transgender priest in the Scottish Episcopal Church. Before transitioning, she published two collections with Salt – *The North End of the Possible* (2013) and *The Ambulance Box* (2009) as well as two pamphlets with HappenStance Press. A further publication is forthcoming with Blue Diode Press. She currently serves as non-stipendiary clergy in Bo'ness, where she lives.

ALYCIA PIRMOHAMED (1990–) was born in Canada and was educated at the Universities of Oregon and Edinburgh. She is the author of *Faces that Fled the Wind* (2018), *Hinge* (2020), and *Another Way to Split Water* (2022). She is co-founder of the Scottish BPOC Writers Network, and a co-organiser of the Ledbury Poetry Critics. In 2020, she was the winner of the Edwin Morgan Poetry Prize. Pirmohamed is the curator and editor of *Ceremony* (2019), a BAME anthology of new Scottish Writing. She is also co-editor of *They Rise Like A Wave: An Anthology of Asian American Women Poets* (2022), and *Re·creation: An Anthology of Queer Poetry* (2022).

KATHLEEN RAINE (1908–2003) was born in Ilford, Essex, the child of the English teacher and Methodist lay preacher George Raine, and his wife, Jessie, née Wilkie, a Scotswoman whose language and lore made a considerable impact on her daughter's imagination. Raine's contemplative and lyrical poetry was also influenced by the writings of William Blake, W. B. Yeats, and Edwin Muir, in its focus on inner spiritual quest and the relationship between dream and reality, and between the human and natural worlds. Raine was received into the Roman Catholic Church in the 1940s but became disillusioned with Catholicism and was later interested in Eastern religious traditions, spiritual symbols and mysticism.

ALLAN RAMSAY (1686–1758), born in Leadhills, Lanarkshire, became a wig-maker, then a bookseller, founding a circulating library in Edinburgh. A poet and anthologist, he was active in reviving interest in poetry in Scots collected in such anthologies as *The Ever Green* (1724). His pastoral verse-drama *The Gentle Shepherd* won much praise, and Burns admired his work.

ALASTAIR REID (1926–2014) was born in Whithorn and was a son of the manse. He spent much of his life abroad, working in Spain, the United States, Latin America and the Caribbean as a cultural journalist, translator and poet. *Whereabouts: Notes on Being a Foreigner* (1987) reflects on this experience.

ROBERT RENDALL (1898–1967) was born in Glasgow to Westray parents, but, as he was a sickly child, his mother brought him back to Kirkwall in Orkney in 1905. A draper, member of the Open Brethren, and noted natural historian, Rendall was central to the newly founded Orkney Antiquarian Society (1922) and produced his study of conchology, *Mollusca Orcadensia*, in 1955–56. A close friend of other Orcadian writers, artists and historians, including Ernest W. Marwick, Edwin Muir, Stanley Cursiter and George Mackay Brown, his collections of poetry include *Country Sonnets* (1946), *Orkney Variants* (1951), and *Shore Poems* (1957).

EARL ROGNVALD KALI (ST RONALD OF ORKNEY) (d. 1158) was nephew of St Magnus of Orkney, in whose honour he built Kirkwall Cathedral in the Viking style, after conquering the Northern Isles in 1136. A poet and friend of poets, he was murdered in Caithness in 1158.

WALTER SCOTT (1771–1832) studied at Edinburgh University and became Sheriff Depute of Selkirkshire in 1799. He made his literary reputation as a ballad collector and as poet of such best-selling works as *The Lay of the Last Minstrel* (1805). Later he authored a series of globally successful historical novels, beginning with *Waverley* (1814). An Episcopalian, Scott's portrayal of Scotland was complex and massively influential.

ANN SCOTT-MONCRIEFF (1914–1943) was a poet, short story writer, journalist, and popular children's author. She grew up in Orkney and began her traineeship as a journalist on *The Orcadian* before moving to Fleet Street to continue her career. She began, but did not complete, a course in archaeology at the University of Edinburgh, leaving after a term to marry the writer George Scott-Moncrieff. Both converted to Roman Catholicism in 1940. Scott-Moncrieff's best-known work is her children's tale *Auntie Robbo* (1941).

NAN SHEPHERD (1893–1981) studied at Aberdeen University, and from 1919 worked as a lecturer in English Literature at the Aberdeen Training Centre for Teachers (later the College of Education). In 1928 Shepherd's first novel, *The Quarry Wood*, was published. This was followed by *The*

Weatherhouse (1930) and *A Pass in the Grampians* (1933). Eventually, in 1934, Shepherd published her only volume of poems, *In the Cairngorms*. It is full of visionary and intense reflections on the natural world and is characterised by the exploration of geographical as well as spiritual terrain. Shepherd's last book, *The Living Mountain*, written in the 1940s and initially rejected for publication, was finally published in 1977. She is now seen as an important forerunner of the new nature writing.

SÌLEAS NA CEAPAICH/SILEAS MACDONALD (*c.*1660–*c.*1729) grew up in Lochaber. She was the daughter of Gilleasbuig, chief of the Catholic MacDonalds of Kepoch. She moved to Tomintoul on her marriage to Gordon of Camdell. Her poetry is varied and includes political Jacobite verse, traditional praise and poems about her family and her faith. See Colm O Baoill's *Bardachd Shìlis na Ceapaich* (1972).

WILLIAM SOUTAR (1898–1943) was born in Perth and was raised in the tradition of the United Original Secession Church (the 'Auld Lichts'). He joined the Royal Navy in 1916. After two years with the North Atlantic Fleet, Soutar was demobilised and matriculated at the University of Edinburgh, where he studied medicine, before changing his degree to English Literature. A diagnosis of ankylosing spondylitis left him increasingly bedridden, yet he continued to record his vivid response to life in poems, journals, and dreambooks. An important poet of the Scottish Literary Renaissance, he produced poetry for children and adults in Scots and English.

MURIEL SPARK (1918–2006) is better known as a novelist and short story writer than as a poet, although she edited *Poetry Review* in the 1940s and published her *Collected Poems* in 1967. Though her childhood and education in Edinburgh provided material for *The Prime of Miss Jean Brodie* (1961), she lived in international locations throughout her life, including in New York, Rome, and Tuscany. In 1937, she made her way, aged nineteen, to Southern Rhodesia (now Zimbabwe) to marry Sydney Oswald Spark. This experience fed into the poem 'Like Africa'. From a Jewish family, Spark became a Catholic in 1954. Her tombstone in Tuscany is inscribed with the words: 'MURIEL SPARK/POETA'.

ALAN SPENCE (1947–) was born in Glasgow and educated at the University of Glasgow, where he started a degree in Law before switching to English and Philosophy. He has lived in London, Milan, and New York, and now lives in Edinburgh where, with his wife, he runs the Sri Chinmoy Meditation Centre. As well as a poet, Spence is a novelist and short story writer. He is Professor Emeritus in Creative Writing at University of Aberdeen, and was appointed Edinburgh Makar in 2017. He received the Japanese honour, the Order of the Rising Sun, in 2018. His most recent poetry collections, *Edinburgh Come All Ye* and *Thirteen Ways of Looking at Tulips*, were published in 2022.

JOCK STEIN (1941–) is a Church of Scotland minister who has had a wide-ranging influence on the spiritual life of the nation through his parish ministry in Dundee, his wardenship of Carberry Tower and his role as Editor of the Handsel Press. He has recently graduated with a Creative Research PhD from Glasgow University. His thesis was published as *Temple and Tartan: Psalms, Poetry and Scotland* (2022) and includes poetry written in response to the Psalms.

KENNETH STEVEN (1968–) was born in Glasgow, grew up in Perthshire and is now based in Argyll. He studied at the University of Glasgow and has lived and studied in Norway. He is a painter as well as a writer of poetry, novels, short stories and features for adults and children. His inspiration comes from the landscape around him and many of the features of Celtic Christianity, including the history of Iona and the Celtic saints. Publications include *Splinters* (1997), *Salt and Light* (2007) and *Letting in the Light* (2016).

ROBERT LOUIS STEVENSON (1850–1894) wrote novels, essays, travel books, plays and poetry for children and adults. Born in Edinburgh, he studied first engineering and then law before travelling for the sake of his health through Europe, the United States and ultimately the Pacific, where he became a powerful critic of European exploitation.

EM STRANG (1970–) is a poet and novelist, whose first full collection *Bird-Woman* (2016) was the winner of the Saltire Award for the Best Scottish Poetry Book of the Year as well as shortlisted for the Seamus Heaney Poetry Centre's Prize for the Best First Collection (2017). Strang is also a mentor and workshop leader. Strang's second collection, *Horse-Man* (2019), was shortlisted for the 2021 Ledbury Munthe Best Second Collection Prize.

JAMES THOMSON ('B. V.') (1834–1882) was born in Port Glasgow and educated at an army school in Chelsea, before becoming an army schoolmaster. Rationalist and atheistic ideas attracted him. His isolation and alcoholism in London contributed to the dark themes of life's futility in 'The City of Dreadful Night' (1874), a powerful pessimistic vision of late Victorian urban existence.

SAMUEL TONGUE (1981–) came to Glasgow to study for a PhD in Literature, Theology and the Arts and has not yet left Scotland. Having completed his degree and having taught at Glasgow University, he is now Project Co-ordinator at the Scottish Poetry Library. His first full poetry collection, *Sacrifice Zones* was published in 2020 and his pamphlet collections include *Stitch* (2018) and *The Nakedness of the Fathers* (2022).

ROSEANNE WATT (1991–) is a poet, musician, and film-maker from Shetland. Educated at the University of Stirling, she writes in both English and Shetland Dialect. In 2018, she won the Edwin Morgan Poetry Award for Scottish poets under 30. Her first collection *Moder Dy* (2019) was a New

Statesman Book of the Year (2019). It was also joint-winner of the Highland Book Prize (2019), and received a Saltire Literary Award for Poetry Book of the Year (2019), as well as The Society of Authors Eric Gregory Award (2020), and the Somerset Maugham Award (2020). Watt is current poetry editor for the online literary journal *The Island Review*.

JAMES, JOHN and ROBERT WEDDERBURN (d. 1553, 1556, 1557) were the sons of a Dundee merchant, educated at the University of St Andrews, and eventually banished from Scotland for their Protestant beliefs. Enthusiasts for reformation, they compiled the *Gude and Godlie Ballatis*, a collection of ballads and sacred as well as secular songs.

KENNETH WHITE (1936–2023) was born in Glasgow and studied there and at the Universities of Munich and Paris, where he became professor of twentieth century poetics at the Sorbonne in 1983. Travel and real or imagined pilgrimage are his characteristic themes, as in *Travels in the Drifting Dawn* and *The Bird Path: Collected Longer Poems* (both 1989).

DOUGLAS YOUNG (1913–1973) was a linguist, translator and scholar. He was born in Tayport, Fife, and studied Classics at St Andrews and Oxford, later teaching the subject at universities in Scotland and North America. He was Chairman of the Scottish National Party from 1942 to 1945.

Acknowledgement of Sources

IAN ABBOT, 'Avoiding the Gods', from *Finishing the Picture* (Kennedy & Boyd, 2015), p. 23, reproduced with permission from R. Abbot. ANONYMOUS, 'The Dream of the Rood', © Robert Crawford, with thanks to Robert Crawford for permission to reprint his translation of 'The Dream of the Rood' which appears in *The Penguin Book of Scottish Verse*, eds Robert Crawford and Mick Imlah (2000; reprint, Penguin Classics, 2006), reprinted with permission from Robert Crawford. ANONYMOUS (in the mouth of Colum Cille), 'Delightful to Be on the Breast of an Island', translated by Meg Bateman from *Duanaire na Sracaire: Anthology of Medieval Gaelic Poetry* (Birlinn, 2007), pp. 14–17, reprinted with permission from M. Bateman and the publisher. ANONYMOUS, 'Memorial of St Columba', translated by Gilbert Márkus, from *The Triumph Tree: Scotland's Earliest Poetry AD 550–1350*, edited by T. O. Clancy (Canongate, 1998), reprinted by permission of the translator. JANETTE AYACHI, 'Youma and the Three Kings', from *Hand Over Mouth Music* (Liverpool University Press, 2019), p. 33, reprinted with permission of the publisher. MEG BATEMAN, 'Naomh'/'Saint', from *Soirbheas/Fair Wind* (Edinburgh: Polygon, 2007), pp. 28–29, with permission from M. Bateman. TESSA BERRING, 'Intention to be Present', from *Bitten Hair* (Leith: Diode Press, 2019), pp. 32–33, reprinted with permission from the publisher. DUGALD BUCHANAN, from 'La a'Bhreitheanais'/'The Day of Judgement' from *Gaelic Poetry in the Eighteenth Century: A Bilingual Anthology*, edited and translated by Derick Thomson (Association for Scottish Literary Studies, 1993), permission applied for. PENNY BOXALL, 'King of the Folly', from *Who Goes There?* (Scarborough: Valley Press, 2018), pp. 16–17, Reproduced with permission from P. Boxall. GEORGE MACKAY BROWN, 'Stations of the Cross: From Stone to Thorn', 'Christmas Poem', from *The Collected Poems of George Mackay Brown* (John Murray, 2005), reprinted by permission of the publisher. GEORGE BUCHANAN, 'Elegy for John Calvin', translated by Edwin Morgan, © Edwin Morgan, reprinted by permission of the publisher; 'For Christ's Ascension', translated by James McGonigal, © James McGonigal, reprinted by permission of the translator. ROBERT BURNS, 'Holy Willie's Prayer', 'Address to the Deil', 'The Cottar's Saturday Night', from Selected Poems and Songs (Oxford University Press, 2014), ed. by Robert P. Irvine; reprinted by permission of the editor. JOHN BURNSIDE, 'Canticle' from *Feast Days* (Seeker & Warburg, 1992); 'Nativity' from Apostasy (Brighton, 2022), reproduced with permission from John Burnside. AONGHAS PHADRAIG CAIMBEUL/ ANGUS PETER CAMPBELL, 'Iudas air cnap-deighe'/'Judas on an Iceberg', from *Aibisidh* (Edinburgh: Polygon, 2011), pp. 92–93, reprinted with permission of the publisher. GERRY CAMBRIDGE, 'Little Light Psalm', from *Notes for Lighting a Fire* (Fife: Happenstance Press, 2013), p. 13, reprinted with permission from the author. ST COLUMBA, 'Altus Prosator'/'The Maker on High' from *Collected Translations* by Edwin Morgan (Carcanet Press, 1996), reprinted by permission of the publisher. SCHOOL OF COLUMBA, 'No Pater', translated by Gilbert Márkus, from *Iona: The Earliest Poetry of a Celtic Monastery*, ed. T. O. Clancy and Gilbert Markus (Edinburgh University Press 1995), reprinted with permission of the translator and the publisher. JOE CORRIE, 'The Image o' God', from *The Image o' God* (Porpoise Press, 1937), permission applied for. ROBERT CRAWFORD, 'Biology', from *Full Volume* (London: Cape Poetry, 2008), p. 36; 'Thread' from *Testament* (London: Cape Poetry, 2014), p. 55, reprinted with permission from the publisher. CHRISTINE DE LUCA, 'Dis life is nivver enyoch', from *Northern Alchemy* (Patrician Press, 2020), reprinted with permission of C. De Luca. IMTIAZ DHARKER, 'Lapis Lazuli', from *Luck is the Hook* (Hexham, Bloodaxe Books, 2018), p. 61, reproduced with permission of Bloodaxe Books, www.bloodaxebooks.com. AN T-ATHAIR AILEAN DÒMHNALLACH/FATHER ALLAN MACDONALD, 'An Eaglais'/'The Church', translated by Ronald Black, from *Eilein na h-òige: the poems of Fr Allan McDonald*, ed. by Ronald Black (Mungo, 2002), pp. 242–247, Gaelic transcript by John Lorne Campbell. English translation reproduced with permission from Ronald Black. ROB DONN, 'Marbhrann do chloinn Fhir Taigh Ruspainn'/'The Rispond Misers', translated by Derick Thomson, from *Gaelic Poetry in the Eighteenth Century: A Bilingual Anthology*, edited by Derick Thomson (Association for Scottish Literary Studies, 1993), permission applied for. DONNCHADH NAM PIOS, 'Righ na Cruinne ta gun Chrich'/'King of the World Without End', translated by Meg Bateman, from *Gair nan clarsaich: An Anthology of 17th century Gaelic Poetry* (Birlinn, 1994), pp. 182–185, Reprinted with permission from M. Bateman and publisher. CAROL ANN DUFFY, 'Prayer', 'Pilate's Wife', from *Collected Poems* (Picador, 2015), reprinted with permission from the publisher. ANGUS DUNN, 'Uist Madonna', from *High Country* (Sandstone Press, 2015), reprinted with permission of Vertebrate Publishing. DALLAN FORGAILL, from 'Amra Choluimb Cille'/'Elegy of Columba', translated by T. O. Clancy, from *Iona: The Earliest Poetry of a Celtic Monastery*, edited by T. O. Clancy and Gilbert Márkus (Edinburgh University Press, 1995), reprinted by permission of the publisher. BASHABI FRASER, 'The Gudwara in Leith', from *Ragas and Reels: Visual and Poetic Stories of Migration and Diaspora* (Edinburgh: Luath Press, 2012), p. 95, reproduced with permission of the publisher and courtesy of Dr. Bashabi Fraser. W. S. GRAHAM, 'The Found Picture', reprinted with permission from The Estate of W. S. Graham. JEN HADFIELD, 'Paternoster' from *Nigh-No-Place* (Bloodaxe Books, 2008), reproduced with permission of Bloodaxe Books, www.bloodaxebooks.com. DIANA HENDRY, 'Psalm Eighty-Eight Blues', reprinted with permission of D. Hendry. A. B. JACKSON, 'Isle of Arran', from *Fire Stations* (London: Anvil Press Poetry Ltd., 2003), p. 33, reprinted with permission of the publisher. A. C. JACOBS, 'Supplication' from *Collected Poems and Selected Translations*, edited by John Rety and Anthony Rudolf (The Menard Press/Hearing Eye, 1996), © Estate of A. C. Jacobs c/o Menard Press, reprinted by permission of the publisher. JACKIE KAY, 'Baby Lazarus' from *Darling: New & Selected Poems* (Bloodaxe Books, 2007), used by permission of the publisher; 'Holy Island', Copyright © 2011, Jackie Kay, used by permission of The Wylie Agency (UK) Limited. TOM LEONARD, 'The Good Thief', 'A Humanist', reprinted with permission of the Estate of Tom Leonard. LIZ LOCHHEAD, 'The Offering', from *Dreaming Frankenstein & Collected Poems* (Polygon, 1984), 'Grace' from *Fugitive Colours* (Edinburgh: Polygon, 2016), reprinted with permission from the publisher. RODDY LUMSDEN, 'The World's End' from *Mischief Night: New & Selected Poems* (Bloodaxe Books, 2004), reproduced with permission of Bloodaxe Books, www.bloodaxebooks.com. IAIN MAC A'GHOBHAINN/IAIN CRICHTON SMITH, 'When They Reached the New Land' from *The Exiles* (Carcanet Press, 1984), reprinted by permission of the publisher; 'Do Sheana-Bhoireannach', original Gaelic Source: *Iain Mac a' Ghobhainn: A' Bhàrdachd Ghàidhlig* (Acair, 2013), pp. 61–62; poems © Donalda Henderson. DONALD MACAULAY, 'Soisgeul 1955'/'Gospel 1955' from *Nua-Bhardachd Ghaidlig* (Southside, 1976), reproduced with permission from the family of Domhnall MacAmhlaigh. NORMAN MACCAIG, 'July Evening', 'A.K.'s Summer Hut' from *The Poems of Norman MacCaig* (Birlinn, 2010), reprinted by permission of Birlinn. DÒMHNALL IAIN MACDHÒMHNAILL/DONALD JOHN MACDONALD, 'Mi Fhìn 's a' Bheinn'/'The Mountain and I', by © the Estate of Donald John Macdonald, The English translation © Bill Innes: Source: *Chì Mi: The Gaelic Poetry of Donald John MacDonald* (Acair, 2021). Reproduced with permission. Original Gaelic reproduced with permission from Margaret Campbell. HUGH MACDIARMID, 'Crowdieknowe', from *Complete Poems, 1920–1976* (Martin Brian & O'Keefe, 1978), reprinted by permission of Carcanet Press. ATHAIRNE MACEOGHAIN, 'Woe the one who takes pride in youth', translated by Meg Bateman, from *Duanaire Na Sracaire* (Birlinn, 2007), p. 58, reprinted by permission of the translator and publisher. SOMHAIRLE MACGILL-EAIN/SORLEY MACLEAN, 'Ban-Ghàidheal'/'A Highland Woman', from *From Wood to Ridge: Collected Poems* (Carcanet, 1989), reprinted by permission of the publisher; 'Scotus Erigena', translated by Emma Dymock, from *Caoir Gheal Leumraich/White Leaping Flame: Sorley MacLean Collected Poems* (Polygon, 2011), pp. 54–55, reprinted by permission of the publisher. DEÒRSA MAC IAIN DHEÒRSA/GEORGE CAMPBELL HAY, 'Is E Crioch Araidh'/'Man's Chief End', from *Collected Poems and Songs of George Campbell Hay* (Edinburgh University Press, 2003), permission applied for. ROB A. MACKENZIE, 'Scotland' from *The Opposite of Cabbage* (Salt Publishing 2009), p. 20; 'Blade Runner' from *The Good News* (Salt Publishing, 2013), p. 6, reprinted with permission of the publisher. CAOIMHIN MACNÈILL/KEVIN MACNEIL, 'Spring', from *Love and Zen in the Outer Hebrides* (Edinburgh: Canongate, 1998), p. 26, reprinted with permission from publisher and K. MacNeil. DONNCHADH MACRAOIRIDH, 'Ceithir rainn do rinneadh leis an la a d'eug se'/'Four verses made by him the day he died', translated by Meg Bateman and James McGonigal, permission applied for. RUARAIDH MACTHOMAIS/DERICK THOMSON, 'Leodhas as t-Samhradh'/'Lewis in Summer', 'A' Cluich Air Football Le Faidh'/'Playing Football with A Prophet' and 'Am Bodach-Ròcais'/'Scarecrow', from *Plundering the Harp: Collected Poems 1940-1980* (Macdonald, 1982), permission applied for. JAMES MCGONIGAL, 'With Finnian at his Bright House in Whithorn', *The Leaves of the Years: Poems, Essays and Memories in William Neill's Centenary Year*, ed. Hugh McMillan and Stuart A. Paterson, pp. 144–145, reproduced with permission from J. McGonigal. NAOMI MITCHISON, 'The House of the Hare' from *The Cleansing of the Knife and Other Poems* by Naomi Mitchison (Canongate Press), reproduced by permission of David Higham Associates. ELMA MITCHELL, 'The Prophet', from *The Poor Man in the Flesh* (Harry Chambers/Peterloo Poets, 1976), permission applied for. AONGHAS MOIREASDAN/ANGUS MORRISON, 'Madainn na Sabaid'/'The Sabbath Morning', translated by Ronald Black, from *An Tuil: Anthology of 20th Century Scottish Gaelic Verse* (Polygon, 1999), pp. 38–41, reproduced with permission from Ronald Black. EDWIN MORGAN, 'Message Clear', 'Ring of Brodgar', from *Collected Poems* (Carcanet, 1990), reprinted by permission of the publisher. MUGRON, 'Christ's Cross', translated by T. O. Clancy, from *The Triumph Tree: Scotland's Earliest Poetry, AD 550–1350* (Canongate, 1998), reprinted by permission of the translator. EDWIN MUIR, 'One Foot in Eden', 'The Heart Could Never Speak', 'The Annunciation', from *The Complete Poems of Edwin Muir*, edited by P. H. Butter (ASLS, 1991), reprinted by permission of Faber & Faber. MUIREADHACH ALBANACH, from 'O great Mary, listen to me', translated by Meg Bateman, © Meg Bateman, reprinted by permission of the translator. SANDAIDH NICDHOMHNAILL JONES/SANDY NICDHOMHNAILL JONES, 'XIV Raithean agus Reiteachadh'/'XIV Seasons and Conciliations', from *An Naomhsgeul as Buaine: Sgathan Cinne-daonna is Aiteal-Dhe* (Sallan Ltd, 2021), pp. 54–57, reproduced with permission of S. Jones. ANNA NIC EALAIR, 'Luinneag Anna Nic Ealair'/'Anna Nic Ealair's Song', translated by Meg Bateman, reprinted with permission from M. Bateman. MÀIRI M NICGHILLEATHAIN/MARY MACLEAN, 'Glòir no Dórainn?'/'Glory or Agony', translated by Ronald Black from *An Tuil: Anthology of 20th Century Scottish Gaelic Verse*, ed. by Ronald Black (Polygon, 1999), pp. 442–445, reprinted with permission from the Estate of Mary Maclean. CATRIONA NICGUMARAID/CATRIONA MONTGOMERY, 'An Ceusadh'/'The Crucifixion', from *Iain Mac a' Ghobhainn: A' Bhàrdachd Ghàidhlig* (Acair, 2013), pp. 132–134. Poems © Donalda Henderson. Translated for this edition with permission. MARION F. NICILLEMHOIRE/

MARION F. MORRISON, 'Mairi a Magdala, na h-Aonar le a Smuaintaen'/'Mary of Magdala by Herself', from *Adhbhar Ar Solais* (Halifax: Bradan Press, 2018), pp. 14–17, reprinted with permission of the publisher. NIALL O'GALLAGHER, 'An T-eun Nach D'Rinn'/'The Bird That Never Flew' from *Fo Bhlàth* (CLÀR, 2020), translated in *Fuaimean Graidh/The Sounds of Love: Selected Poems* (Francis Boutle, 2023), by Peter Mackay, reprinted with permission of Peter Mackay and CLÀR. DON PATERSON, 'Profession of Faith' from *The Eyes* (Faber & Faber, 1999), reprinted with permission of the publisher. DOROTHY MARGARET PAULIN, 'December Day', reproduced with permission from M. Kaye. AMY JO PHILIP, 'Coronach', from *The Ambulance Box* (Salt Publishing, 2009), p. 41; 'Breathing is the Place to Start' from *The North End of the Possible* (Salt Publishing, 2013), p. 45, reprinted with permission from Amy Jo Philip. ALYCIA PIRMOHAMED, 'I Want the Kind of Permanence in a Birdwatcher's Catalogue', from *Another Way to Split Water* (Polygon Birlinn, 2022), p. 10, reprinted with permission of the publisher. KATHLEEN RAINE, Heirloom' from *Collected Poems 1935–1980* (Allen & Unwin, 1981), reprinted by permission of Faber & Faber. ALASTAIR REID, 'Whithorn Manse', reprinted with permission of the Estate of Alastair Reid. ROBERT RENDALL, 'Angle of Vision', from *Shore Poems and Other Verse* (The Kirkwall Press, 1957), permission applied for. EARL ROGNVALD KALI, 'Mockery of Irish monks on a windswept island', translated by Paul Bibire, reprinted by permission of the translator. ANN SCOTT-MONCRIEFF, 'Dirge' and 'Lines Written in Autumn 1940', reproduced with permission from L.J. Findlay. NAN SHEPHERD, 'Real Presence', from *In the Cairngorms* (Galileo Publishers, 2014 (first published 1934)), reproduced with permission from Galileo Publishers. SILEAS NA CEAPAICH/SILEAS MACDONALD, 'Laoidh air Bas a Fir agus a h-Ighne'/'Hymn on the Deaths of her Husband and Daughter', transcribed by Colm Ó Baoill from *Bàrdachd Shìlis na Ceapaich* (Edinburgh: Scottish Gaelic Texts Society, 1972), translated by Meg Bateman, © 1972 Colm Ó Baoill, reprinted with permission. Translation reprinted with permission from M. Bateman. MURIEL SPARK, 'Like Africa' from *All the Poems by Muriel Spark* (Carcanet Press), © Copyright Administration Limited, reproduced by permission of David Higham Associates. ALAN SPENCE, 'All About The Light', from *Edinburgh Come All Ye* (Edinburgh: Scotland Street Press, 2022), p. 45, 'Japanese Boxes', from *Glasgow Zen* (Edinburgh: Canongate, 2002), p. 21, reprinted with permission of A. Spence. JOCK STEIN, '119 Fair and Square', from *Temple and Tartan: Psalms, Poetry and Scotland* (Haddington: Handsel Press, 2022), p. 240, reprinted with permission of J. Stein. KENNETH STEVEN, 'Columba', from *Island: Collected Poems* (Edinburgh: Saint Andrew Press, 2009), pp. 31–32, reprinted with permission from Kenneth Steven. EM STRANG, 'The Miracle', *Bird-Woman* (Bristol: Shearsman Books, 2016), pp. 19–20, reprinted with permission from E. Strang. SAMUEL TONGUE, 'Theology', from *Sacrifice Zones* (Red Squirrel Press, 2020), p. 11, reprinted with permission of the publisher. ROSEANNE WATT, 'Steepel' from *Moder Dy* (Birlinn, 2019), p. 23, reprinted with permission of the publisher. KENNETH WHITE, 'A High Blue Day on Scalpay' from *Handbook for the Diamond Country: Collected Shorter Poems, 1960–1990* (Mainstream Publishing, 1990), reprinted by permission of the publisher. DOUGLAS YOUNG, 'The Shepherd's Dochter' from *Naething Dauntit: The Collected Poems of Douglas Young* (Humming Earth, 2016), edited by Emma Dymock; 'The Twenty-Third Psalm o King Dauvit' from *A Clear Voice: Douglas Young, Poet and Polymath* (Macdonald, 1976), © Clara Young, reprinted by permission of Clara Young.

Every effort has been made to trace or contact all copyright holders. The Publishers would be pleased to rectify any omissions brought to their notice at the earliest opportunity.

Index of Poets

Index of First Lines

Index of Poem Titles

Land Speed Record

OSPREY

Land Speed Record

A complete history of the record-breaking cars from 39·24 to 600+m.p.h.

Cyril Posthumus and David Tremayne

Colour illustrations by Michael Roffe

Published in 1985 by
Osprey Publishing Limited,
12–14 Long Acre, London WC2E 9LP
Member company of the George Philip Group
A first edition was published in 1971

British Library Cataloguing in Publication Data
Posthumus, Cyril
Land speed record: a complete history of record-breaking cars from 39.24 to 600+MPH.——2nd ed.
1. Automobiles, Racing——Speed records——History
I. Title II. Tremayne, David
796.7′2 GV1030

ISBN 0-85045-641-x

Dedicated to Mowbray Garden whose original idea this book was and whose enthusiasm has seen it through to reality – C.P.

For Richard Noble in respect for his determination and for helping me fulfil an ambition.
And for Tom Palm for his considerable help and support, and because young guys shooting for the moon need all the encouragement they can get – D.T.

Design Behram Kapadia
Editor this edition Tim Parker

Filmset and printed in England by
BAS Printers Limited, Over Wallop, Hampshire

Contents

Source of illustrations

The authors and publishers wish to thank the following people who have kindly supplied photographs and/or drawings which appear in this book:
Associated Press Ltd; Barratt's Photo Press Ltd; Griff Borgeson; BP Oil Ltd; Jack Brady; Craig Breedlove; Ken Davies; Dunlop Company Ltd; *L'Equipe*, Paris; Firestone Tire & Rubber Company, Ohio; Fox Photos Ltd; General Motors, New York; Goodyear Tire & Rubber Company, Ohio; Anthony S. Heal; *Hot Rod Magazine*; Radio Times Hulton Picture Library; Ferdinand C. W. Kasmann; Keystone Press Agency Ltd; Ludvigsen Associates; Charles Lytle; T. A. S. O. Mathieson; Mercedes-Benz (G.B.) Ltd; Mobil Oil Company Ltd; Dean Moon; William A. Moore; *Motor*; *Motoring News*; *Motor Trend*; National Motor Museum; the Owen Organisation; Tom Palm; Petersen Publishing; *Quattroruote*, Milan; Reaction Dynamics Inc; *Road & Track*; Ian Robinson; Rolls-Royce Ltd; Shell Oil Company; Sport & General Press Agency Ltd; Thrust Cars Ltd/Charles Noble; Mick Walsh; Robert W. Young.

List of Colour Plates

Foreword

On the face of it, the World Land Speed Record might seem simple: obtain the most powerful engine available to you, assemble a team of specialists prepared to take career risks, build the smallest practical car-ferry to take the whole outfit to a remote desert track 6,000 miles from home . . . and have a go. But then the problems really start. Is the weather going to hold? Is the track viable? Is the money going to last? Has the car the transonic aerodynamics, stability, performance and reliability to do the job? Is the driver the right man? Do we have the right team?

A cynic might define an *LSR* attempt as a group of fanatical motor racing addicts gambling vast sums of sane sponsors' money against the weather, with a few days of highly dangerous transonic driving thrown in. In fact, to be successful the car ends up being as complex as a jet fighter and you find yourselves undertaking what any aerospace contractor would never in their right mind attempt – developing a high-performance vehicle in unhospitable conditions with limited finance, miles from home and in front of the world's media.

But, to me, the *LSR* is the greatest of all motor sports: the risk is the greatest, the thrill of driving an *LSR* car is unbeatable – that car has to be able to out-accelerate any front-line jet fighter to your target speed, if you are going to be in with a chance. The cost is huge – and the reward? Well, that's simply a paper certificate and the opportunity to take part – that's all. . . .

The *LSR* rules are very straightforward – the car must make two passes over the measured mile or kilometre within 60 minutes, must have four or more wheels and be steered by two or more of them. This is the world of unlimited racing and no more rules governing the car or the course are necessary; other than to ensure that essential timing is carried out by impartial, recognized and competent authorities.

In essence, of course, the *LSR* is about people; start with a highly motivated and hard-working team and gradually all the essential hardware, money and equipment will come together – but it will only happen if the sponsors see that the quality is of the highest, the programme achievable and, consequently, the risk to their money, reputation and careers is definable.

But the *LSR* has its other side. Gordy Flux, Thrust's chief mechanic, voiced it in November 1983: 'It's stupid – no sooner do we become the best *LSR* team in the world than we find that we can no longer practise our skills.' I know that all the Thrust team will echo those words, but to raise our record we will need a new car, a lot more money and – the catalyst which will release the goodies – somebody to *take* our record. Till then, we are stuck. . . .

Man has to make progress, measured by breaking records; it would be a terrible shame if our record stood like Gary Gabelich's for 13 years. With international communication, interest and motivation, the Land Speed Record could become one of the world's great sporting events – it has all the essential ingredients of risk, speed, danger, the unknown, popular appeal and high technology, whilst costs are still within corporate sponsorship budgets. So, let's have a challenge. . . .

Within the Thrust team, Cyril Posthumus' first edition of this book was known as The Bible – we learned a great deal from the text, and my copy has seldom left my briefcase for nine years, being hauled around as the reference for lectures, meetings with sponsors, and the many, many meetings with would-be sponsors who were not able to join us in the challenge we offered them. The book is tremendous, but, since events in the late seventies and eighties, has needed updating.

David Tremayne had been an avid follower of the *LSR* long before we first met, right at the start of the Thrust 2 programme. His tremendous zest for impartial accuracy and detail establishes his work as the standard that few achieve. His enthusiasm for Project Thrust and his understanding of our many difficulties endeared him to the team, so that he became a team member in 1983 responsible for our public relations.

I simply cannot think of two better *LSR* enthusiasts to produce this book – and it is a great privilege for me to write the foreword to this outstanding work on our sport.

Richard Noble, 1984

Introduction

$\text{SPEED} = \frac{\text{Distance}}{\text{Time}}$. Put like that it may not sound very exciting, but make the object at speed a car, the distance a mile and the time 5·683 sec. To cover a mile in 5·683 sec. means a speed of 633·468 m.p.h. – the current world record for that distance – and if that leaves you cold, this is no book for you. How quickly can *you* cover a mile in *your* car? If you do it in 40 sec. you're breaking the law in most countries nowadays, yet Richard Noble did the distance in well under 6 sec!

Despite the law, you probably have a good idea of your car's all-out maximum speed. Most people manage to find it out somehow, somewhere. 'What'll she do?' has been one of the most popular lay questions since the dawn of motoring. Never mind how she runs in traffic, or climbs hills, or takes turns; the crowning question always concerns top speed. Owners of fast-looking cars in the 'thirties, weary of the question, joked about the 'What'll Club' of earnest inquirers, and the same curiosity prevails today, even though flat-out speed on the road can only be reached in chancy defiance of the law.

One-hundred-and-fifty years ago the term 'miles per hour' had little meaning, but as steam trains and coaches came in, it proved a handy gauge for assessing speed. The man who took five hours to walk 20 miles into the nearest town could best appreciate the new locomotion on being told that a train covered the same distance in one hour; one-fifth of his walking time, and 20 miles per hour. Such a rate was giddy progress in 1845. Fifty years later, 25 miles per hour was something achieved with much noise and smell by 'they noo motors'; 60 miles per hour was 'a mile a minute' and Jules Verne stuff, quite impossible.

As motor vehicles multiplied, speed became the criterion of their performance. Its fascination was not exclusive to the onlooker; the begoggled driver of a new 'motor' and his dust-jacketed passengers were just as keen to know what it would 'do', even though as far as horse-conscious Britain was concerned they were dogged by police should they venture beyond 12 m.p.h. But if they couldn't find out first hand, then it was thrilling to read about other people motoring at maximum.

What *was* maximum? Could a horseless carriage really travel at 30 m.p.h.? The early road races were a guide: Levassor won the 1895 Paris–Bordeaux–Paris at an average speed including all stops of 15 m.p.h. over 732 miles; the comte de Dion won the 1897 Paris–Dieppe at 24·6 m.p.h.; Charron won the 1898 Paris–Amsterdam at 26·9 m.p.h. If such super-drivers set such averages, including stops, what kind of maximum speeds did they attain?

The drivers were as curious about this as the public, and many an illicit match was fought along the poplar-lined roads of France to resolve who was fastest, until someone had the idea of a special meeting, with timekeepers and stopwatches, to see just how fast cars *could* go. Thus was born the Land Speed Record, *LSR* for short; the fastest an automobile has travelled on land. They found it was 39·24 m.p.h.

That was in 1898, and intrepid people have been breaking that figure ever since. Today it stands at 633·468 m.p.h., and has been broken 62 times. The subject is too fascinating for this to be the first book on the *LSR*, and certainly not the last. It differs from the others in bringing the subject up to date, and in containing numerous colour plates of the record-breaking cars, but it does follow the example of the others in stressing, or reiterating, that technically the absolute land speed record does not exist. Officially it is the flying kilometre or flying mile, since one or other of these distances invariably produces the highest speed a man-driven vehicle can achieve.

Until 1965 that vehicle had to have at least two driven wheels, but the advent of jet propulsion caused the F.I.A. (Féderation Internationale de l'Automobile) to introduce a class for 'Specials' which rely on sheer 'squirt' for their speed. They and their younger rocket-powered brothers are now so fast that they have outpaced the more conventional 'automobiles' by over 200 m.p.h. Things happen terribly quickly when you motor a mile in under 6 sec., and their drivers are as much pioneers as were the older heroes who first topped 100, 200, 300 and 400 m.p.h.

The fascination of the subject increases the deeper one delves, but discrepancies in speeds and times in different accounts of record achievements bring confusion too. We have tried to achieve accuracy throughout, but the passage of time has left some mild inconsistencies resulting, one suspects, from happy-go-lucky conversions from k.p.h. to m.p.h. or vice versa. For these and any other variations in the number of decimal places in given speeds, we ask the indulgence of readers.

Finally, it will perhaps be helpful to make an important point. The current land speed record procedure is not to calculate the average of a driver's speed over two passes through a measured distance, but to average the elapsed *times*, converting the result from seconds into miles per hour.

1

The beginnings

'Fie, sir – twenty miles in one hour upon a coach? No man could rush so fast through the air and continue to draw breath!'

Dr Johnson to James Boswell

Johnson's belief in the suffocating effects of speed upon man was widely held until the advent of steam locomotion in the nineteenth century. As the railways established themselves and the engines found reliability, it is certain that on long, straight, downhill sections the bolder drivers 'hit it up' and reached speeds of 35 and 40 m.p.h. As early as 1829 Goldsworthy Gurney claimed 'an extreme rate' of between 20 and 30 m.p.h. for his steam road coach, while Nathaniel Ogle spoke of '32 to 35 m.p.h.' for his vehicle before 1831. A British train was claimed to have attained a speed of 81·8 m.p.h. at Wellington Bank, Somerset, as early as 1854, while a French locomotive reached 89·48 m.p.h. at Champigny Pont sur Yonne in 1890, although one wonders how accurate the timing was.

Thus we may be sure that by 1898, the year of the first land speed record, rates of 55 to 60 m.p.h. on favourable stretches of line were attained by steam trains in Britain and abroad – and equally sure that bold passengers put their heads out of the carriage windows to sample the sensation of the air (and smoke) rushing by, killing – not themselves – but the worthy Dr Johnson's medieval theory. As for horseless carriages, we find that in the Bordeaux–Biarritz road race of 1898, the winner

The Belgian, Camille Jenatzy, in his winning Jenatzy electric car on the starting line at the Chanteloup hill-climb of November 1898. His success, and the failure of his opponent, comte Gaston de Chasseloup-Laubat in his rival electric car, the Jeantaud, sparked off their famous series of duels at Achères for the speed record.

averaged 26·7 m.p.h. on his Bollée, stops included, while speeds *en route* of 35 and 40 m.p.h. were attained – and windscreens had yet to be invented.

We can but assume, then, that the comte de Chasseloup-Laubat's new land speed record of 62·233 kilometres per hour (39·24 m.p.h.), created at Achères in December 1898 in an electric car, was a dull spectacle. No smoke or steam, no thunder of exhausts, the car 'emitting no visible vapour nor effluvium' – merely a whine changing to a purposeful hum and it was gone. It was highly significant, none the less.

By then the automobile, whether petrol, steam or electric powered, had been in existence for a dozen years, and inevitably prodigious claims were made for its remarkable velocity, not only by hostile minions of the law (particularly in horse-bound Britain) but by proud owners of the new locomotion, and ignorant, easily-impressed onlookers. Now at least they all had a yardstick – the fastest motor-car in the world could do less than 40 m.p.h.; and if that seemed a bit tame when compared with a steam train in full cry, doubtless someone would come along soon and have a go at beating it. . . .

The seeds of rivalry

The inception of the motor-car speed record on 18 December 1898 was owed entirely to the introduction of motor-car speed hill-climbing to the Paris area less than a month earlier. The connection is important. M. Paul Meyan, one of the founders of France's national motor club, the Automobile Club de France (A.C.F.) and director of the pioneer motoring journal *La France Automobile*, persuaded his co-proprietors to sponsor a timed hill-climb at Chanteloup, about twenty miles from Paris, up a $1\frac{1}{8}$-mile, 1 in 12 gradient on 27 November 1898. No less than fifty-four cars turned up for the competition and forty-seven made the climb, an electric car built in Paris but designed and driven by a Bruxellois named Camille Jenatzy making the fastest ascent of all at about 18 m.p.h.

Second fastest was a Bollée petrol car, and third a Panhard-Levassor. Amongst the also-rans was another electric car, a Paris-built Jeantaud driven by the comte Gaston de Chasseloup-Laubat, another co-founder of the A.C.F. and a pioneer racing driver. His hopes of success at Chanteloup were foiled by sidechains which persistently jumped their sprockets on get-away.

A week later *La France Automobile* published a special announcement, to the effect that they were replacing a projected Concours Commercial on 18th December with a *course de vitesse* for cars of all kinds, 'at the request of one of our friends'. It would be held over a carefully marked-out 2,000-metre stretch of smooth, level, open road in Achères park, near St Germain, north of Paris. This venue was, in fact, familiar ground to pioneer *automobilistes* anxious to try out their cars for speed, and it seemed the perfect chance for Chasseloup-Laubat and Jenatzy to match their electrics. Certainly the comte (the 'friend' of *La France Automobile*, perhaps?) was the first entrant, and it was unfortunate that this time Jenatzy had to

go to Belgium and could not be present, and the Jeantaud had only petrol-engined vehicles as rivals. Despite the very short notice of the event, entries poured in, and so, on the day, did some 300 to 400 members of the public.

The streamlined Jeantaud electric car with 'windcutting' nose with which the comte de Chasseloup-Laubat set a new land speed record at Achères on 4 March 1899, at a speed of 57·6 m.p.h.

The two-kilometre stretch of road was divided into two for timing purposes, the first kilometre for standing start speeds, the second for flying start figures. Two timekeepers with stopwatches were posted at the start, two at the first kilometre, and two at the second; they included M. Louis Mors of the famous Mors electrical concern, whose brother Émile was the constructor of the then up-and-coming Mors car.

Drizzle rather spoiled the meeting for the public, but the macadamized surface was little affected when the business of the day began. Chasseloup-Laubat's Jeantaud appeared in sober 'touring' form with box-like front, no attempt at streamlining, and the driver seated high on the right in one of two basket seats. It had a single 36 h.p. electric motor coupled to the rear wheels by chains, and driven by Fulmen non-rechargeable batteries which contributed materially to the car's formidable weight of 1,400 kg. (3,204·5 lb.).

However, they also contributed to its speed, for a series-wound electric motor animated by ample current is ideal for a quick get-away, giving maximum torque at low r.p.m., tapering off at higher speeds, and the Jeantaud easily beat its petrol rivals. While they snorted and stammered on the line, then went off to staccato, ear-abusing barks of noise and a reek of fumes, the comte's motor merely whined,

Left: Camille Jenatzy; *right:* the comte Gaston de Chasseloup-Laubat

then rose to a frantic ringing hum as the starter, M. Paul Meyan himself, gave the signal, and the Jeantaud departed, trailing a few blue sparks and a slight tang of ozone.

His time was 1 min. 12·6 sec. through the standing kilometre, and 57 sec. through the flying kilometre, a speed of 63·157 k.p.h. or 39·245 m.p.h. – the world's first official land speed record. Second fastest was Loysel's 3-litre Bollée *Torpille*, a formidable racing machine of its day at 35·5 m.p.h., and third Giraud's Bollée at 33·6 m.p.h. It was a little deflating to learn that the Jeantaud's new record was 1 sec. slower than the *cycling* record through the flying kilometre of 56 sec.!

A challenge is flung

Camille Jenatzy the Belgian, later famous as the 'Red Devil' and a far 'hairier' driver than his trim red goatee beard suggested, reacted splendidly to the news. In a letter to *La France Automobile* expressing his regret at not being at Achères on 18th December, he issued a *défi* – a challenge – to Chasseloup-Laubat, declaring his confidence in beating the Jeantaud under the same course conditions within one month, concluding with the customary cordial salutations – which the comte returned, together with acceptance of the challenge.

On 17 January 1899 the pair met in combat at Achères, and Jenatzy, the challenger, had first run. With none of the drama and spectacle surrounding later record-breakers, his boxy machine, the Chanteloup winner, sped away to clock 1 min. 8 sec. for the first kilometre and 54 sec. for the second, a speed of 41·42 m.p.h., which beat Chasseloup–Laubat's time by 3 sec. For the first time, the land speed record had been broken.

Ten minutes later the comte took his place on the line, shooting off at flag-fall to lower Jenatzy's nice new record with 51·2 sec. through the flying kilometre or

43·69 m.p.h. – which could have been faster still had his motor not burned out in the last 200 metres owing to so quick and violent a discharge of current. Two new records in a day, and a challenger defeated! M. Meyan's journal fairly bubbled with the news. A very determined Jenatzy returned to Achères ten days later for another attempt; it was very cold but the January wind had dried the course, then obligingly dropped, and the Belgian lowered the flying kilometre time to 44·8 sec. – a speed of 49·92 m.p.h. – and the fourth *LSR* had been created.

Almost a month later Chasseloup-Laubat tried to retrieve the honours for the marque Jeantaud, which had a strong grip on the Paris electric taxi market. First, however, the motor burned out as he was moving up to the line, and when he returned a day later the course was in a bad condition through frost, with many stones displaced and the ground too hard to roll. But on 4th March he was back, the Jeantaud looking notably different from the previous December, now with equal-sized wheels and new bodywork made at the Jeantaud carriage works in Paris, wearing a 'windcutting' nose, streamlined undertray and a pointed tail. In a wonderful run Chasseloup knocked no less than 6 sec. off Jenatzy's flying kilometre, covering it in 38·8 sec., a speed of 57·6 m.p.h. Thus early did aerodynamics win a speed record, precipitating the birth of the world's first *LSR* 'Special'.

Over 100 k.p.h.

Jenatzy's reply was sensational. Ever since his much publicized challenge had been defeated he had had the Compagnie Internationale des Transports Automobiles Électriques Jenatzy busy building a new car – the first of the long line of fascinating record-breaking 'freaks' which still continue today. On a semi-elliptically sprung chassis (duplicated at the rear) with the smallest wood-spoked wheels and the thickest-section Michelin tyres ever seen at that time, was mounted a special cigar-shaped body formed of *partinium* – a kind of aluminium alloy invented by the Frenchman, Henri Partin. This body was designed by Léon Auscher of Carrosserie Rothschild of Paris, the Company which built it.

Two big electric motors, boxed in, were mounted on the rear axle; they turned at 900 r.p.m. and drove direct to the wheels, while the Fulmen batteries were stowed inside that striking streamlined shell. The streamlining effect was rather spoiled by the driver himself, who with his tiller, rheostat and other controls sprouted out of the body into the airflow; it was only 1899, however, and aerodynamics were in their infancy. The car weighed 1,450 kg., or approximately 29 cwt., of which some 6 cwt. were batteries; its name was *La Jamais Contente* – 'The Never Satisfied', aptly summing up Camille Jenatzy's attitude.

La Jamais Contente
Location of motors

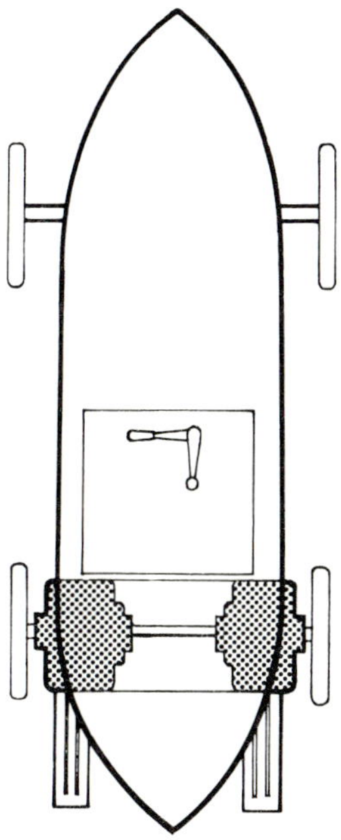

Jenatzy chose 1st April for his attempt with the new car. To take advantage of a new stretch of road, the starting point was moved 200 metres, and the *commissaires* and *chronométreurs* were still marking off the new second kilometre point when the over-eager Jenatzy 'lanced' his new *engin de vitesse* up the course. The time-keepers, unprepared for him, missed his flying kilometre time and the disappointed

Belgian, convinced he had broken the record substantially, had to call it a day, having exhausted his accumulators.

But he was back at Achères twenty-eight days later, and this time there were no mistakes. Jenatzy's blue *bolide* did the standing kilometre in a remarkable 47·8 sec., and brought the flying figure down from 38·8 to 34·0 sec., a speed of 65·79 m.p.h. or 105·904 k.p.h. The 100 k.p.h. barrier had been broken, while in less than five months the *LSR* had been improved five times, rising from 39·24 to 65·79 m.p.h. – well above the speed at which man would suffocate. . . .

The world's first land speed record 'Special' – Jenatzy's electric car, *La Jamais Contente* with bullet-like, streamlined body of *partinium* alloy, in which, on 29 April 1899, the Belgian became the first to exceed 60 m.p.h. and 100 k.p.h. His speed of 65·79 m.p.h. stood as the record for three years.

Jenatzy and *Jamais Contente* surrounded by admirers after their success at Achères

2

Road racers v. steam

'Of the grandstand, of the public, and of the people lining the course, I saw nothing. I felt, on approaching the measured kilometre as I opened my auxiliary pump, a frightening thing thrusting me forward as if I were a projectile from a gun. . . .'

Léon Serpollet

Camille Jenatzy was well satisfied in the end. *La Jamais Contente* had avenged the earlier humiliation of a challenger's defeat, and his 65·79 m.p.h. record was to stay unbroken for three years. By then petrol and steam-powered road cars had caught up and passed the electrics with their unavoidable handicaps of heavy batteries and limited range.

The third aspirant for *LSR* honours was an Englishman, the Hon. Charles S. Rolls, whose name, coupled with that of Royce, was soon to epitomize British quality motoring at its highest peak. His mount in April 1902 was French, however, one of the formidable new 60 h.p., 9·2-litre, 4-cylinder Mors racing cars designed by *ingenieurs* Brasier and Terrasse. This was the new, thrusting Parisian marque which was intruding on long-established Panhard territory in the great town-to-town races of the time; it was immensely fast, and its direct drive on top gear, and the first shock absorbers aimed to check spring rebound on bumps, were novel features of the time on large racing cars.

Rolls went to the same Achères road where Chasseloup-Laubat and Jenatzy had fought out their duel, but he could not better a speed of 63·10 m.p.h., and retired

determined to try again. Swiftly another petrol contender came forward, the American millionaire amateur William K. Vanderbilt Jr., whose great hobby was motor-cars, and whose wealth enabled him to obtain the finest equipment of the time. In 1902 he purchased examples both of the new Mors '60' and the latest Mercedes-Simplex '40'; this was the 1902 development of the sensational 35 h.p. Mercedes which introduced the world to pressed steel chassis, honeycomb radiator, mechanically operated inlet valves and gate-type gearchange, and it set new standards of refinement and performance. At Achères, Vanderbilt exactly equalled

Léon Serpollet with the streamlined steam car managed 76·6 m.p.h. on the Promenade des Anglais in Nice in 1903, insufficient to wrest back his 1902 75·06 record set in his older *Oeuf de Pâques* machine.

Jenatzy's speed of 65·79 m.p.h. through the kilometre with the Mercedes, a performance which caused a stir. To equal was not to beat, however, and the next land speed record-holder, as it transpired, was neither electric- nor petrol-driven, but powered by steam.

Steam is an obliging form of motive power in that, unlike electricity or petrol, it produces more power the greater the load, and possesses such flexibility that a gearbox and its consequent friction-loss is unnecessary. Léon Serpollet was one of the world's most talented steam car exponents. He invented the flash boiler which produced instant superheated steam by passing water through a heated coiled tube, and through the years he perfected his steam vehicles, adopting paraffin heating, automatic fuel and water feeds, and a condensing plant to use up waste exhaust.

One of the highlights of early racing days was the Nice 'Speed Week' staged early in the season from 1899 to 1909. It generally included a road race taking in neighbouring resorts, a hill-climb up La Turbie and culminated in speed trials on Nice's famous Promenade des Anglais, with diverse class divisions and the Henri de Rothschild Cup for the best overall performer through the flying kilometre. This *Semaine de Vitesse* was a popular and important shop window for manufacturers showing off their latest products, and Mercedes in particular always shone there.

Their trendsetting 35 h.p. car scored wins in the 1901 road race, the hill-climb and in the class speed trials, but when it came to the ultimate honour, the Rothschild Cup, six of their new cars and two Panhards were bested by Serpollet's steam car. Nor was it a narrow defeat, for Werner in the quickest of the Mercedes was a humble 6 sec. slower than the steamer! Serpollet's speed was 62·76 m.p.h., 3 m.p.h. slower than Jenatzy's *LSR* of 1899. Now he determined to do better.

The car he brought out on to the Promenade des Anglais on 13 April 1902 had a 2·95 × 3·54 in., 4-cylinder, single-acting steam unit turning at 1,220 r.p.m. There is some doubt about the exact identity of the car, for Serpollet built three special sprint steamers between 1901 and 1903, at least two being called *Œuf de Páques* or 'Easter Egg' for their rounded profiles, and for the fact that Nice week centred around Easter and Serpollet supplied the surprises. The third car had a lower, more modern, wedge-shaped body, and in Serpollet's own 1902 publicity proclaiming his new record this car is illustrated.

Whichever the exact form of body, 13 April 1902 was Serpollet's great day. He whistled through the flying kilometre in 29·8 sec., a speed of 75·06 m.p.h., beating four of the latest Mercedes-Simplex '40's, gaining his third Rothschild Cup in a row, and breaking Jenatzy's land speed record by over 9 m.p.h. Once through the timing trap it took him almost another kilometre to bring his car to a stop – the engine, shut off sharply, providing the only braking power from 75 m.p.h.

Internal combustion moves in

Although defeated by steam at Nice, the petrol-engined cars were now moving in fast. The great road races were developing more powerful, more efficient engines.

The 60 h.p. road-racing Mors car was a strong land speed record contender during 1902. In July, baron de Caters, seen here, exactly equalled Serpollet's record of 75·06 m.p.h., and in the next few months Vanderbilt, Fournier and Augières improved it to 76·08, 76·60 and 77·13 m.p.h. respectively.

The electrics were now woefully limited in contrast, and Léon Serpollet, sated by success, relaxed his efforts and concentrated on the production side of the Gardner-Serpollet car business. Activity in quest of the *LSR* now intensified elsewhere, with Mercedes and Mors the warring marques.

In late April, William K. Vanderbilt tried twice to match Serpollet's record, first on the Chartres-Bonneval road where he clocked 67·78 m.p.h. during a match with Henri de Rothschild, both of them driving Mercedes-Simplex '40's. The two millionaires then moved on to a stretch of road between Ablis and St Arnoult, where they were joined by yet another millionaire, the American Wolf Bishop, with a third '40'. Again Vanderbilt was quickest at 69·04 m.p.h., recorded by official A.C.F. timekeepers as the fastest speed ever by a petrol-engined car, though not fast enough to beat Serpollet.

The next one to try was the Belgian baron Pierre de Caters. His mount was one of the 60 h.p., Paris–Vienna road-race Mors, which he drove in a speed trial outside Bruges in July 1902, and was timed through the flying kilometre at 29·8 sec. – exactly equalling the speed of Serpollet. Petrol had at last matched the performance of steam, but not surpassed it, though this was not long in coming. A month later Vanderbilt settled the issue, switching from his Mercedes '40' to the more powerful 60 h.p. Mors he had driven in the Paris–Vienna race, and going to

Henri Fournier, famous as winner of both the Paris–Bordeaux and Paris–Berlin road races in a Mors in 1901, held the land speed record for a fortnight during 1902 at 76·60 m.p.h., driving a 60 h.p. Mors.

the same Ablis–St Arnoult road where he had sported with the other millionaires. Making quite the noisiest attempt on the land speed record so far, the roaring Mors was through the flying kilometre in 29·4 sec., a speed of 76·08 m.p.h. For the seventh time the *LSR* had been broken, and a petrol-powered car held it at last.

What an American amateur could do with a French Mors, a French professional could do better; so reasoned the great Henri Fournier, famed winner of Paris–Bordeaux and Paris–Berlin in 1901, and on 5th November, with very few fireworks, he deposed Vanderbilt as 'king of speed' by $\frac{1}{5}$ sec., making a run at 76·60 m.p.h. on a newly-found course at Dourdan. This was a venue which the A.C.F. now sought to establish as the 'official' course for record attempts, setting up electrical timing apparatus which relied no longer on human reaction and human error as did stopwatches.

Much to his disgust, the professional Fournier's tenure of the *LSR* was a mere fortnight, when a presumptive but prosperous Paris merchant and amateur driver named Augières borrowed the same car from the Mors factory and drove it through the same measured kilometre at 29 sec. dead, setting a new record at 77·13 m.p.h. Slowly, too slowly, the figure was creeping towards 80 m.p.h., but the game of chipping miserable fifths of a second off the record ended the following July with the coming of a new challenger who carved off a full 6 m.p.h.

Horsepower tells

Gobron-Brillié was yet another Paris-based motor manufacturer, who built strong, reliable cars with an unusual but dependable kind of engine. The record-breaker which they fielded in 1903 was of a similar type, but larger and very powerful. It had a 4-cylinder 110 h.p. engine of opposed piston type; i.e. with two pistons to each cylinder, the lower one linked directly through a connecting rod to the crankshaft in the normal way, the upper one to a cross-head which transmitted the thrust to the crankshaft down below via external tubular connecting rods and crankpins at 180 degrees.

The bores measured 140 mm. and the combined strokes 220 mm., giving an overall capacity of 13·547 c.c. The engine was naturally massive, about 4 ft. long and 3 ft. 6 in. high, and the main benefits claimed for its design complications were increased piston area at reduced piston speed, and freedom from vibration. Certainly the Gobron-Brillié was far less frenzied than the average racing car of its time, being tractable and quiet at low speeds, but that it was also effective at high speeds the Belgian Arthur Duray demonstrated very convincingly at a speed trial meeting held outside Ostend in July 1903.

He took the high, ungainly Gobron-Brillié, its radiator and scuttle cowled in, through the flying kilometre in only 26·8 sec., a speed of 83·47 m.p.h., while to drive the lesson home, a second, similar car driven by Louis Rigolly was runner-up. The cars went on to score similar double victories in the Laffrey, Chateau-Thièrry and Gaillon hill-climbs, emphasizing their versatility.

The big $13\frac{1}{2}$-litre Gobron-Brillié with opposed-piston engine, in which the Belgian, Arthur Duray, set a new record of 83·47 m.p.h. at Ostend in 1903. Later that year he raised it to 84·73 m.p.h. at Dourdan, France.

Mors drivers strove to depose Gobron-Brillié from their new role of 'fastest on earth'. The Hon. Charles Rolls took his latest car, one of the illustrious 70 h.p. 'Dauphin' type Mors which outshone all others in the 1903 Paris–Madrid race, to a private course on the Duke of Portland's estate at Clipstone, near Welbeck in Nottinghamshire, England. There he was timed by officials of the Automobile Club of Great Britain and Ireland (the A.C.G.B.I., forerunners of the R.A.C.) to cover the kilometre in 26·4 sec. – a speed of 84·73 m.p.h.

This would have been the first *LSR* established on British soil, but alas, the A.C.F. declined to recognize Rolls's new figures on the grounds that they did not approve the system of timing employed. True, the Clipstone course was distinctly downhill, but this was a disappointing decision for Rolls. The same snag of 'approved timing' had also denied another Mors exponent, baron de Forest, a place in the list when he had reduced Duray's time by $\frac{1}{5}$ sec. (26·6 sec., 84·09 m.p.h.) during the Irish Speed Fortnight in Phoenix Park, Dublin.

It was not the last time that the French authorities would reject a record claim; such autocracy, though irritating, served to maintain fair standards in record attempts so far as single runs in the most favourable direction *could* be fair. Only the Americans were openly to defy A.C.F. attempts to control speed records internationally, to the detriment of the *LSR* as a tidy, straightforward record.

Whether officially recognized or not, Duray obviously felt uneasy about the Dauphin Mors's performances, and resolved to put the record beyond their reach. He took the big Gobron-Brillié to the A.C.F.'s 'official' course at Dourdan this time, but there, try as he might, he could not better Rolls's time of 26·4 sec. He equalled it, however, and as the British attempt was not accepted, Duray and Gobron had the record for a second time; their speed was 84·73 m.p.h. or 136·363 k.p.h. Duray would have liked to break the 140 k.p.h. barrier, but by then it was November, so he rested content in having put Mors in their place and awaited the next challenger.

3

America takes an interest

'Winning a race or making a record was then the best kind of advertising. So I fixed up the *Arrow*. . . .'

Henry Ford

Apart from Arthur Duray's effort at Ostend in July 1903, every successful attempt on the *LSR* so far had taken place on French soil. Henry Ford, founder of one of the world's largest motor manufacturing concerns, was the first to attack it on American territory. Strictly 'territory' means land, but Ford did it on water: frozen water. Ideal in one way, for an ice-locked lake is unquestionably dead level; but it posed problems such as adhesion on get-away and at speed, and 12 January 1904 was the one and only occasion on which a land speed record attempt was made on ice.

Ford chose so unlikely a month as January because it was a week before the New York Automobile Show, where he was launching a new Model B, and he wanted to publicize the name Ford in every manner possible. Lake St Clair, Michigan, not far from Detroit, is a smaller stretch of water amidst the Great Lakes, connecting Lake Huron with Lake Erie, and upon its frozen surface a mile was measured out, with a good run-in and run-out beyond. No kilometre was marked in; the Americans were not bothered with a 'Froggy' thing like that. Hot cinders were spread around, particularly at the start, to give some grip to the *Arrow's* spindly tyres.

Henry Ford waiting in the driver's seat of the *Arrow* with a very meagre metal shield for protection against the icy blast he would be subjected to at over 90 m.p.h., while his mechanic 'Spider' Huff attends to the engine before the record attempt.

Little more than a chassis, engine, and four wheels, the Ford *Arrow* set a new figure of 91·37 m.p.h. driven by Henry Ford himself over the frozen surface of Lake St Clair, near Detroit, in January 1904. This first achievement by an American-built car, driven by an American in America, was recognized by the A.A.A. but not the European authorities.

Arrow was the twin to the more famous Ford *999* car raced by Barney Oldfield, and named after a famous New York Central express train reputed to have travelled at 112 m.p.h. as far back as 1893, near Grimesville, New York. Both cars had been built in 1902, and were of crude and massive concept, with enormous 7 in. × 7 in., 4-cylinder engines totalling over 16·7 litres and driving direct by shaft and open bevel gears to the rear axle. There was no gearbox, no differential, and no rear springs, while the clutch was a wooden block expanding against the inner flange of the immense flywheel, which measured 2 ft. in diameter, was 6 in. thick and weighed 230 lb.

Arrow had been wrecked in a crash at Milwaukee in 1903 (and its driver killed), so Henry Ford rebuilt it with cold weather record-breaking specifically in mind. The chassis was of steel-armoured ash, and carried no body except for a pair of bucket seats, but he fitted a rudimentary metal shield ahead of the handlebar steering to ward off some of the icy blast, and removed the deep, ugly, flat radiator normally used, replacing it with a small, brass header tank and a cold water tank above the engine. On a frozen lake in January, *Arrow* would more likely need warming than cooling, and he heavily lagged the intake pipes and gave the engine a good, long warming up. Then he signalled 'O.K.' to the timekeepers and moved out to the start.

The savage bellow of that monster engine heralded the start of Ford's attempt on the mile record. It must have been a blenching experience, for as soon as he picked up speed he found that the apparently smooth surface of the ice was marred by fissures where it had partly thawed, then frozen again. His passage across these at over 90 m.p.h. was a desperate series of leaps and bounds. In his own words: 'I never knew how it was coming down. When I wasn't in the air I was skidding, but somehow I stayed topside up and on the course, making a record that went all over the world.'

But it was worth it. His time through the flying mile was 39·4 sec., and his speed 91·37 m.p.h., a handsome 7 m.p.h. increase on Duray's figure, the first over 140 k.p.h. and over 90 m.p.h. records, and an extremely brave performance by one who never claimed any high speed driving talent for himself. The ironic part of it all was that, in fact, the record did not go 'all over the world' as Ford had written. The American Automobile Association (known as 'the three A's') supervized the timing and accepted the figures, but the A.C.F., the only body who could officially ratify the record, declined to do so as they did not recognize the A.A.A. as the American national authority.

There is little question that Ford's figures were, in fact, accurate, and most authorities include the record in their *LSR* lists. One feels in any case that the Americans, when informed of the French attitude, did not accord to the A.C.F. the respect that august body felt it was entitled to, and like Craig Breedlove many years later, said words to the effect that if they didn't like it, they could go jump in a lake, frozen or otherwise. . .

From ice to sand

Like Fournier in 1902, Ford kept his record – official or not – for under a fortnight, when the millionaire Vanderbilt thoughtlessly deprived him of it. Ford was probably less annoyed than Fournier; his record had served its publicity purpose admirably. But even so, it was galling that, in order to break it, Vanderbilt should resort both to a warm Florida beach instead of an uncharitably frozen Michigan lake, and a German Mercedes instead of an American car. As it happened the course chosen by Vanderbilt, the Ormond–Daytona beach, was to figure vitally in *LSR* attempts for the next thirty years.

Ormond–Daytona, more often abbreviated simply to Daytona, is a vast, straight and level stretch of sand on the East Florida coast. In all it measures 23 miles, but a river and a pier interrupt its length and the maximum distance available to cars was about 15 miles. It is formed mainly from countless wet-packed fragments of white coquina clamshells, and at low tide becomes as firm as concrete when all conditions are favourable. There were no roads, fences, trees or banks to impede a driver's progress, and Ormond–Daytona, first used in 1902 by Alexander Winton to set a national record, was deemed a 'natural' for ultra-high speed motoring.

The Florida Speed Week was inaugurated there in 1903, with numerous class races and sprints, culminating in attempts on the flying mile record, and it was during the 1904 Week that William K. Vanderbilt Jr. was successful in breaking Henry Ford's flying mile record by $\frac{2}{5}$ sec., raising it to 92·30 m.p.h. His car was a big white Mercedes '90', a superbly proportioned racing car with an 11·9-litre, 165 × 140 mm., 4-cylinder engine having overhead inlet valves and side exhaust valves. Five of these '90's had been destroyed in the great fire at Mercedes' Canstatt factory in 1903, but more were built, and Vanderbilt's was the very car shown at the Paris Salon.

The next 'Speed Week' on the calendar brought the next record. Two months after the Florida meeting came the Nice *Semaine de Vitesse* on the Promenade des Anglais, and there Gobron-Brillié returned to the fray with an improved 130 h.p. car of 15·1 litres. Louis Rigolly of the Gobron works drove it, minus bonnet and any attempt at streamlining, over a course now decidedly bumpy and getting beyond record-making status as the magic 100 m.p.h. mark drew nearer. His speed in such conditions was astonishing. Said one motoring journal's reporter: 'Rigolly's car, marvellously controlled, was upon us with a low rumble, seeming scarce to touch the ground but rather as if balanced above it. The meteor crossed the finishing line, we were drowned in dust. . . . And there was an explosion of surprise and joy when the timekeepers announced an unbelievable 152·542 k.p.h. for the flying kilometre. . . .'

France had the record back at 94·78 m.p.h. – but not for long.

On to 100 m.p.h. and over

Two months elapsed and Mercedes retorted through the popular Belgian sportsman, baron Pierre de Caters and a Gordon Bennett road racing '90' on the Nieuport road outside Ostend. 'Just to annoy Panhard, Mors and Gobron-Brillié a little', as he said, he chopped $\frac{3}{5}$ sec. off the Gobron's time, setting the target figure at 156·25 k.p.h. or 97·25 m.p.h. 100 m.p.h. was now less than 3 m.p.h. away; two more months passed and then Rigolly took the big, ugly Gobron-Brillié to Belgium for the July speed trials on the Ostend–Nieuport road.

There he met new opponents in Paul Baras and a 100 h.p. Gordon Bennett-type Darracq, a marque then forcing its way into prominence with several sprint and

The 90 h.p. Gordon Bennett-type, road-racing Mercedes with which the Belgian baron de Caters set the record at 97·25 m.p.h. in May 1904. In the group lined up behind are Camille Jenatzy (*second from left*) and Caters (*fourth from left*).

hill-climb wins, though failing dismally in full-distance road races. Baras's car was one of those built for the 1904 Gordon Bennett Cup race but which failed to qualify; a bold design, none the less, with mechanically-operated overhead inlet valves in an over-square 160 × 140 mm., 11·3-litre, 4-cylinder engine. It had three speeds, shaft drive at a time when chains were thought essential for high-powered cars, advanced bodywork with enclosed sides, a neat rear as a change from the usual crude bolster tank, and – remarkably – steering column gear-change.

At Ostend horsepower told once again, and the bigger-engined Gobron beat the interloper by $\frac{2}{5}$ sec. Rigolly's time was 21·6 sec. and his speed a resounding 103·55 m.p.h. – a crushing retort to Mercedes's 97·25 m.p.h. This breaking of the 100 m.p.h. barrier had a particular impact in non-metric Britain. Four days later Rigolly further demonstrated the versatile performance of the ungainly Gobron by placing fourth with it in the Circuit des Ardennes race, whereas Baras had to retire his Darracq from the same event.

But Darracq's day was to come sooner than some expected. In November 1904, four months after Baras's defeat at Ostend, a convoy of cars left the Suresnes factory of the Société A. Darracq and headed for Belgium and the Nieuport road outside Ostend. The course was closed, official time-keepers took up their posts, and three Darracqs – a voiturette driven by Villemain, a light car driven by Héméry, and the 100 h.p. Gordon Bennett car driven by Baras – went out in turn to attack records. Each was successful, the climax of the day being Baras's flying kilometre in 21·4 sec., a speed of 104·52 m.p.h. and a new land speed record.

France regained the record in July 1904, when Louis Rigolly clocked 103·55 m.p.h. in the 130 h.p. Gobron-Brillié during the Ostend speed trials.

Louis Rigolly, official driver for Gobron-Brillié, who twice took the land speed record with the unconventional opposed-piston engined cars.
Right : a glimpse of the massive engine.

That the car which couldn't attain 100 m.p.h. in July should exceed 104 m.p.h. in November could be put down to design progress, save that the Gordon Bennett car was obsolete anyway and due for replacement. A subsequent account had it that before Baras's attempt one vital kilometre stone was moved a little closer to its neighbour, but we will never know the truth now. . . .

Enter Britain

Darracq was the fifth marque to contest the *LSR* with a road-racing car. The sixth, and last, was the famous British firm of Napier, who sent Arthur E. Macdonald out to the 1905 Florida Speed Week at Daytona with the big 90 h.p. car known as L48. Like the Mercedes, this had overhead inlet and side exhaust valves, but was unique in racing in having six cylinders, each measuring 159 × 127 mm., giving the healthy overall capacity of 15 litres. The power passed through a two-speed gearbox and a propeller shaft to the rear axle, and tubular radiators ran each side along the bonnet instead of ahead of it, giving a useful low-drag nose and a pleasanter, less perpendicular shape than was usual at that time. Overall weight was modest at 19·6 cwt., and the resultant power-to-weight ratio made the big green Napier a strong contender on the Ormond–Daytona beach. Macdonald won three trophies and broke seven records during the meeting, the most important one being the flying mile in 24·4 sec. – a speed of 104·65 m.p.h., which bettered Baras's Darracq figure by $\frac{1}{5}$ sec., just enough to encourage the British into thinking that a Briton in a British car now held the land speed record for the first time.

Its tenure was an uneasy one. According to whose rules one accepted, it either didn't hold the record at all, it held it for less than an hour, or it held it for almost twelve months. It happened like this. Before the Napier's six cylinders had scarcely cooled, a new challenger came out onto the Daytona beach – a very special kind of

(*Opposite, above*) Paul Baras in the 11·3-litre Gordon Bennett-type road-racing Darracq was clocked through a flying kilometre at Ostend in 21·4 sec., $\frac{1}{5}$ sec. faster than Rigolly, and a record speed of 104·52 m.p.h., in November 1904.

(*Opposite, below*) Arthur Macdonald chipped another $\frac{1}{5}$ sec. off the flying mile in the 15-litre, 6-cylinder Napier, raising the record to 104·65 m.p.h. at Ormond Beach, Daytona, Florida in January 1905. The French refused to recognize the Napier's figures.

25

5

Mercedes, called the *Flying Dutchman*. This was built by Herbert Bowden of Boston, using two Mercedes '60' engines, installed one behind the other in an extended Mercedes chassis (see Chapter 18 for further details). Despite bumps and a side breeze this early records 'Special' eclipsed Macdonald's 104·65 m.p.h. with a devastating run at 109·75 m.p.h., but remarkably the Florida authorities disqualified the 'double Mercedes' on the grounds that it weighed well over the 1,000 kg. (2,204 lb.) maximum limit set for Speed Week events.

Even if ineligible for a sprint victory, the car's timing was the same as that for the Napier, and but for obstructive regulations Bowden's figure should have been acceptable as a land speed record, and the Bostonian's name inscribed in the list of record-holders. As it was, the French continued to ignore *any* records made on American soil, either Macdonald's or Bowden's, and still regarded Baras's 104·52 m.p.h. as fastest ever. Thus it was that in 1905 the ridiculous situation prevailed whereby America, Britain and France all felt that they, and nobody else, held the world's land speed record! It would almost be a relief when the next record-breaker came along and settled the issue.

Two Mercedes '60' engines mounted in tandem drove Herbert Bowden's special *Flying Dutchman* through the Daytona flying mile at 109·75 m.p.h. on the same day that Arthur Macdonald set his record.

Bowden, Mechanic and the '*Dutchman*' on the beach at Daytona.

4

From road racers to 'Specials'

'Considerations of transmission, control, silent and easy running are, however, of minor importance, the supreme effort being to render directly available as vast a power as possible, upon a framework in which lightness and strength are combined in such a way that the whole mechanism may be hurled through the air in one overmastering rush. . . .'

R. T. Sloss in THE BOOK OF THE MOTOR CAR, 1905

In 1905 the land speed record car at last emerged from its road-racing car phase. The latter was no longer fast enough, and first bigger engines, then streamlining became essentials. Alexandre Darracq, whose road-racing Gordon Bennett car just scraped in as an *LSR* holder, quickly realized this and set his engineer, Louis Ribeyrolles, to designing a special car.

Taking two of their 'over-square' 160 × 140 mm. 4-cylinder blocks, he converted the heads to full overhead valves, then mounted them at 90 degrees on a special crank-case to produce a 22·5-litre 200 b.h.p. V8 which turned at 1,200 r.p.m. Forked connecting rods were used, and a single central camshaft above the crankshaft worked all the valves by pushrods and rockers. There were twin carburettors, and the air intake pipes passed close to the exhaust pipes – an early form of 'hot spot' to heat the air on its way into the engine.

This unit, the ancestor of the modern production type V8, was fitted into a small, wire-wheeled chassis of only 8 ft. 6 in. wheelbase (the average road racer measured around 9 ft. 4 in.) and drove through a two-speed gearbox and shaft final drive. A neat 'V' radiator wrapped around the engine, with a cylindrical fuel tank, pointed at

(*Opposite*) Victor Héméry and his mechanic wait while the engine of the 200 h.p., V8 Darracq warms up. Héméry raised the record to 109·65 m.p.h. on the Arles-Salon road in late December 1905.

The 200 h.p. Darracq *en route* to its new land speed record. It subsequently enjoyed a successful European sprint and hill-climbing career.

Although not the first V8 engine in motor racing, the 200 h.p., $22\frac{1}{2}$-litre Darracq unit designed by Ribeyrolles paved the way to the modern V8, so popular for its compactness and flexibility. It combined two Gordon Bennett-type, 4-cylinder blocks set at 90 degrees on a common crankcase.

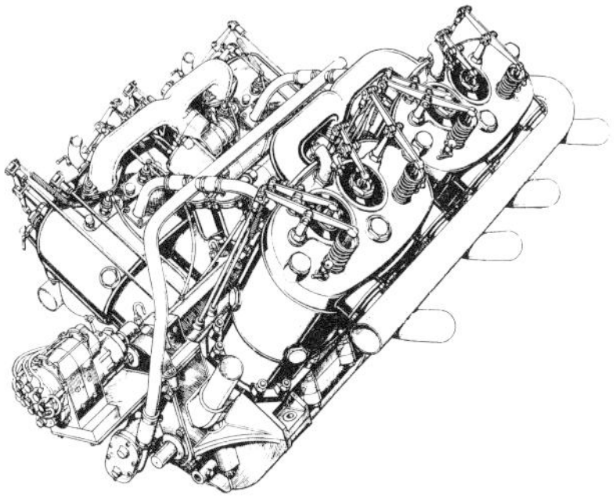

the front, located just above the 'V' of the engine. The bodywork was non-existent – just two bucket seats on the skimpy-looking chassis; and with an overall weight of $19\frac{1}{4}$ cwt. and that 200 b.h.p. engine, the potential of this new Darracq was formidable.

The car was rushed straight from the works in Paris just after Christmas 1905, and taken to a long straight stretch of road between Arles and Salon in the Carmargue district of France just north of Marseilles. There, after several experimental runs, Victor Héméry showed what the new car could do by adding nearly 4 m.p.h. to Macdonald's 104·65 m.p.h. figure, thus restoring the *LSR* to France without question – save in American eyes!

Héméry's new record put an end to much of the controversy, as well as the claim of Swiss Frederic Dufaux. Six weeks earlier, on November 15, the racing driver had passed through the kilometre in 23 seconds in the four-cylinder, 26-litre Dufaux constructed by his brother Charles. Thus the 150 b.h.p. machine equalled de Caters' 1904 97·25 m.p.h. figure, although it failed to improve it. If, as some did, you accepted that the records of de Caters, Baras (101·679 and 104·530), Rigolly (103·561), MacDonald *and* Bowden were unofficial, then Dufaux officially held the record for some six weeks.

A come-back for steam

But if France still didn't want to know about Bowden's 109·75 m.p.h., another American certainly did, and was ready to have a stab at beating it with a very special car indeed. The Stanley Steamer was a respected performer in touring car form on American and European roads, and after some successful forays at Ormond–Daytona and in hill-climbs, the brothers Francis E. and Freeland O. Stanley of Newton, Massachusetts, decided to further the good name of their products on the international record front. Léon Serpollet had already shown what steam could do when it came to sheer velocity, but since 1902 the petrol exponents had had things all their own way and were inclined to dismiss the external combustion engine as *passé*. They had a shock coming.

In 1905 the Stanley Company began work on a record car, using convenient stock parts such as a standard boiler and horizontal twin-cylinder, double-acting engine, fully elliptic front and rear suspension, and a tubular steel frame giving an 8 ft. 4 in. wheelbase, but uniting them to produce one of the most visionary 'freaks' in *LSR* history. The engine, which had ball bearing mains and big ends, only fifteen moving parts and a weight of only 185 lb., was installed at the extreme rear of the chassis, its two cranks driving forward direct to the rear wheels through spur gears and a differential.

The boiler was reinforced to withstand a pressure of 900–1,000 lb. p.s.i., and was mounted ahead of the rear axle; and the driver sat low amidships, ahead of the power department, just as on a modern Grand Prix car. The only difference was that in the Stanley he sat on the floor and worked two steering bars instead of a steering wheel. The body, inevitably, was likened to an upturned boat, and the structure was, in fact, designed by a boat-building firm, the J. R. Robertson Co. Inc. of Auburndale, Boston. It was made of thin cedar strips covered with canvas and the underside was completely filled in by a flat, full-length underpan.

The wheels were slender wire-type, to which clincher tyres were security-bolted, and the whole carefully balanced; while the only brakes, at the rear, were mounted inboard close to the differential to reduce unsprung weight, anticipating this 'modern' feature on racing cars by almost fifty years. Heating of the boiler was by a gasoline burner, and a brass funnel discharging fumes from this behind the driver was the only protuberance in the clean, streamlined shape of the car which completely covered the suspension. Weight was a very modest $14\frac{1}{2}$ cwt., and estimated horsepower at full boost an approximate 120 b.h.p. at 800 r.p.m.

The Stanley record car was called the *Rocket*, an appropriate title considering the mode of take-off for this pyrotechnic device. With no clutch or gear-changing to worry about, the driver's drill was to hold the car stationary on the brake, let the boiler pressure build up to its maximum of 1,000 lb., then release everything and 'fire', when the car would rocket away to a fierce hiss of unleashed steam power. A run-in of five to six miles along the dead straight beach at Daytona was taken in order to work up to maximum speed before entering the measured distance, and in practice runs for the highly eventful 1906 Florida Speed Week, the Stanley had already given an inkling of its potential by clocking 30·6 sec. through the mile, 1·8 sec. faster than Bowden's controversial 109·75 m.p.h. record.

With its concentration of weight on the back wheels, the front end tended to lift, but the front spring location was modified and in the Speed Week the maroon-coloured *Rocket* was a star performer. Driver Fred Marriott set five new records, won three trophies, and defeated strong petrol-powered opposition, much to their dissatisfaction. The 200 h.p. V8 Darracq, official *LSR* holder, was the Stanley's most formidable rival, and although it enjoyed brief success in the flying kilometre

runs, when Louis Chevrolet set a new record of 19·4 sec., the Stanley swiftly demolished this with 18·4 sec. – 121·57 m.p.h.!

127·6 m.p.h. in 1906!

In the subsequent flying mile trials, Chevrolet clocked 30·6 sec., to which Marriott retorted with 28·2 sec., an electrifying 127·6 m.p.h., an improvement of no less than 18 m.p.h. on the 'official' *LSR*. Incredibly, the Paris authorities would not recognize Marriott's speed through the mile, but accepted the kilometre figure of 121·57 m.p.h. as the new land speed record, and the petrol-powered exponents retired disgruntled, for even that speed was beyond their capabilities. From 109 to 121 m.p.h. in one bite was a tremendous increase, and it looked as if Marriott's figure would stay unchallenged for some time.

But the Stanley brothers knew they had not exploited the full potential of the *Rocket* yet. For the fifth Florida Speed Week in 1907 they fitted a new boiler able to take 1,300 lb. p.s.i. of steam pressure, and modified the engine and gearing. Then out went Marriott on to a beach that was in as poor a shape as the Speed Week itself that year. After their 1906 beating no foreign competitors came over, while instead of proclaiming the Stanley *Rocket* as an outstanding upholder of American prestige, a large proportion of the local press chastized it as a freak.

Practice revealed two troublesome gullies running across the course, one each side of the measured mile, which sent the car darting seawards for desperate seconds before Marriott righted it, still managing to clock 29 sec. through the distance. During the actual event, taking almost nine miles for his run-up, he entered the mile at speeds variously estimated at 132 m.p.h., 190 m.p.h., 'over 190 m.p.h.' and between '196 and 198 m.p.h.' (the latter gauged by professors of the Massachusetts Institute of Technology). Whatever Marriott's real speed, it was disastrous when he hit one of the gulleys.

The front of the *Rocket* lifted, it rose some 15 to 18 feet in the air, turning sideways as it flew, then smashed back on to the beach about 100 feet further on. The boiler burst, the car broke up, and bits of debris were flung far around. Fearing the worst for the driver in such a crash, rescuers were amazed to find him unconscious but alive, with four cracked ribs, a broken breastbone, facial injuries, and his right eye out of its socket. A doctor who happened to be holidaying close by took him to a hotel for attention, there pressing the eyeball back into place with a spoon! 'Now it's the best eye I've got' later quipped a fully recovered Marriott, who lived to 83.

But it was death for the enterprising *Rocket* and for the Stanleys' record-breaking ambitions. In Europe the news of this first serious accident in pursuit of the *LSR*, and of the destruction of the car, was received with frank relief, though it took almost four years to reinstate internal combustion as the dominant power.

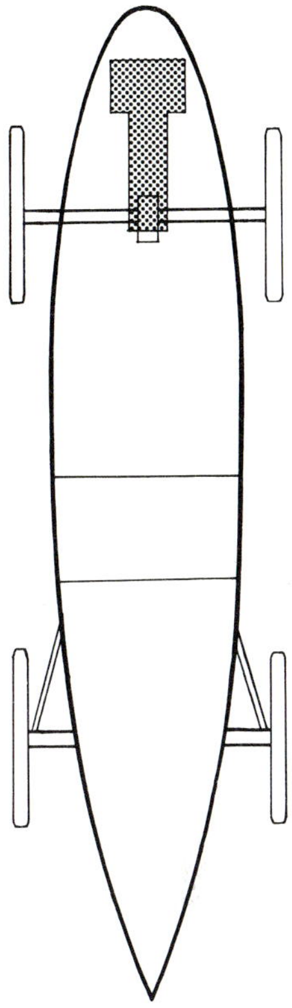

The Stanley Steamer
Rear location of engine and transmission

(*Opposite, above*) The Stanley brothers of Newton, Massachusetts, startled the records world in 1906 with their remarkably advanced-looking machine with rear-mounted steam power unit. Called the *Rocket*, it raised the land speed record from 109·75 m.p.h. to 121·57 m.p.h., driven by Fred Marriott at Ormond-Daytona. His flying mile at 127·6 m.p.h. was not recognized by the European authorities.

(*Opposite, below*) The horizontal twin-cylinder, double-acting steam power unit of the Stanley *Rocket* followed standard Stanley touring design but was larger. It was fed by a boiler 30 in. in diameter and 18 in. deep, and withstood a steam pressure of over 1,000 lb. p.s.i.

The splendid-looking *Blitzen* Benz won the record back for petrol-engined cars after the Stanley Steamer's remarkable achievement had stood for three years. Héméry clocked 125·95 m.p.h. at Brooklands in November 1909.

The vast 21½-litre engine of the *Blitzen* Benz, with four great cylinders and exposed, pushrod-operated overhead valves.

Germany joins in

By 1909 the V8 Darracq was well past its prime, though it had garnered a rich harvest in hill-climb and sprint wins and local records in lieu of the coveted 'fastest ever' title. The demise of the French Grand Prix after 1908, and economic uncertainties, left most manufacturers reluctant to undertake costly ventures such as record-breaking now that special cars were essential, and it looked as if the Stanley Steamer's accepted 121·57 m.p.h. figure, let alone its fantastic 127·66 m.p.h., would stand for ever.

Then out of Germany came a new challenger bearing the oldest name in the business, Benz, who after savouring road racing successes in 1908 now emulated Darracq and developed a special 200 h.p. machine for record-breaking and hill-climbing. Power, as ever, was the great prerequisite of success, and power the new Benz certainly had. The engine had four monstrous cylinders in two blocks of two, with a bore and stroke for each of 185 × 200 mm., giving a capacity of 21.5 litres. The valves, larger than many modern pistons, were overhead, operated by exposed pushrods and rockers, and there was dual ignition by two Bosch magnetos and two Bosch plugs per cylinder.

Maximum power was attained at 1,600 r.p.m., and transmitted through a cone clutch, four-speed separate gearbox, and sidechains on huge sprockets. There was little technically unusual about the vast new Benz, which mechanically resembled an enlarged 1908 Grand Prix racer, though endowed with a beautifully streamlined body produced by chief designer Georg Diehl. The riding mechanic's seat was staggered behind the driver's to keep cockpit width down; there was a pointed tail; a distinctive beaked brass radiator; four stub exhausts and, initially, wood-spoked wheels as on the Grand Prix car.

The wheelbase was only 112 in., and dry weight just over 26·6 cwt. Few cars so large managed to look so clean and beautifully proportioned, and only the chain drive dated it as pre-Great War. Its name was as exciting as its looks, for they called it the *Blitzen* ('Lightning') Benz.

After preliminary wins at Frankfurt, Semmering and Tervueren in Belgium, the Benz was sent in 1909 to Britain, of all places, to the new Brooklands track opened at Weybridge in 1907. There Benz's number one driver, Victor Hémery, ex-Darracq, warmed the car up, setting some standing start records, then went out for Marriott's kilometre record of 121·57 m.p.h., running the reverse, or clockwise, way of the track. The deep bass rhythm of the big white car thrown back from the still clean, unweathered banking, was awe-inspiring, and Hémery was clocked at 125·95 m.p.h. This figure was duly ratified as the new land speed record by the A.I.A.C.R. (Association International des Automobile Clubs Reconnus), successors to the A.C.F. as the world authority for motor racing and record control.

Hémery went on to try for the mile record, but could not work up sufficient speed on the Brooklands banking and returned only 115·923 m.p.h., although clocked at 127·877 m.p.h. through a half-mile.

At Brooklands on this occasion the new Holden electrical timing apparatus was being used, which gave record figures to three places of decimals for the first time. The various record distances on the track were marked out by the Director-General of Ordnance Surveys himself.

Lightning at Daytona

Having taken the French version of the land speed record, the big white Benz was sent down to Southampton, on to the liner *Majestic*, and across the Atlantic to New York, where it went on display in the Benz Company's showrooms. There the famous Barney Oldfield, barnstorming race-driver who toured the U.S.A. each year with a circus of cars, bought the *Blitzen* for an alleged $10,000, and lost little time in railing it down to Ormond–Daytona beach for an attempt at the flying mile.

Unleashed on a smooth, straight, flat course in March 1910 the magnificent-looking Benz boomed through the mile traps in 27·33 sec. – an average of 131·275 m.p.h. The Stanley Steamer had been deposed at last and petrol was king again – except that the A.I.A.C.R., like its forerunner the A.C.F., refused to recognize Oldfield's new record, created on American soil! Warned that 'them Froggies' would probably be awkward 'as usual', Oldfield shrugged and lost no time in adding 'Holder of the World's Speed Record' to the list of achievements painted on his special train.

Four months after Hémery's Benz record, the American Barney Oldfield raised the record to 131·275 m.p.h. at Daytona beach, driving the same car.

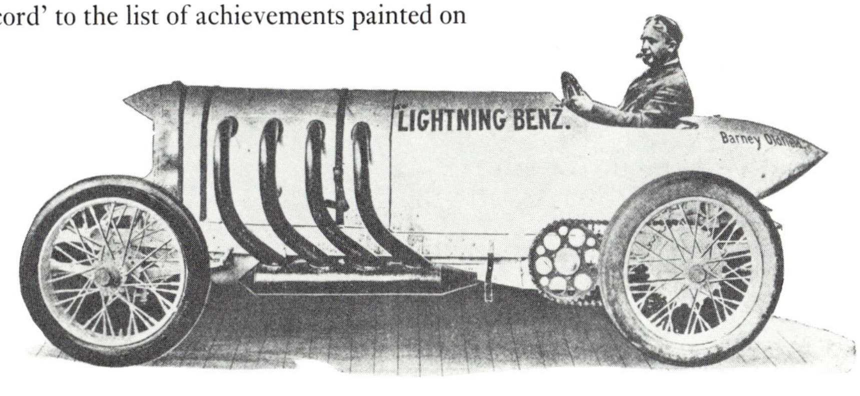

19

5

The endless quest for power

'Off we started for Brooklands, and I soon found that on wood paving the engine [of the 200 h.p. Benz] has so much power that the rear wheels just spun if you even looked at the accelerator too sharply. I went from one side of the road to the other, and never have I heard so much said to me before or since by bus-drivers and others. . . .'

Major L. G. Hornsted in THE AUTOCAR

During 1910 there was a significant development concerning the land speed record. Largely at the instigation of Britain's Royal Automobile Club, the A.I.A.C.R. ruled that, from the beginning of 1911, two record runs, one in each direction, must be made on the same course, the deciding figure being a mean of the two times. This was, of course, to ensure that advantage was not taken of a strong wind in one direction or a favourable gradient. It was a fair and sensible arrangement, but the Americans, whose A.A.A. was still not recognized by the A.I.A.C.R. as the official adjudicatory body in the United States, decided to ignore it, continuing to recognize one-way records even though this isolated their achievements from those of Europe. This 'to hell with Europe' attitude, largely bred by irritation at repeated French rejection of American speed claims in the past, was to confuse the records issue for some years yet to come.

Meantime the gallant *Blitzen* Benz, after performing so nobly for its new master at Daytona, was subjected to the rough and tumble of a season of dirt and grass track racing all over the U.S.A., as 'No. 1' car in the Oldfield travelling circus. Fortunately its vast reserve of power meant that it was little stressed; it kept its

Barney Oldfield's *Blitzen* Benz stoically endured a season of grass and dirt-track racing all over the United States after setting the flying mile record at 131·275 m.p.h. at Daytona in 1910. Then Bob Burman raised the U.S. record with the same Benz to an unofficial 141·37 m.p.h. in 1911, and subjected it to a further season's 'barnstorming'.

tune with minimal maintenance, performed spectacularly wherever it went, broke countless local records, and emerged battered but unbowed from these indignities.

In 1911, however, Barney Oldfield lost his national racing permit for competing in a non-A.A.A.-sanctioned meeting, so he sold up his racing equipment, including the Benz. It was acquired by one Ed Moross for another spectacular barnstorming American, 'Wild Bob' Burman, to race, and apart from subjecting it to another season's roughing it in fields and on cinders, he emulated Barney Oldfield in taking it to Daytona to see what could be done about *the* record.

That was in April 1911, by which time the A.I.A.C.R.'s two-way ruling was in force. When, therefore, Bob Burman claimed to have broken Oldfield's flying mile with a one-way run in 25·40 sec. or 141·37 m.p.h. (over 10 m.p.h. faster), the Americans accepted it, whereas the French rejected it. Things stayed that way for three years: Hémery recognized as 'the world's fastest' at 125·95 m.p.h. in Europe, Burman 'the world's fastest' to the U.S.A. at 141·37 m.p.h. Benz of Mannheim, at least, were content – both sides had used the *Blitzen* to secure the honours.

On 24 June 1914 at Brooklands track, the British driver L. G. Hornsted took out a dark blue Benz with 200 h.p. *Blitzen*-type engine fitted, and made the first attempt on the *LSR* under the new rulings. He clocked 128·16 m.p.h. one way, and 120·23 m.p.h. the other, indicating very clearly how favourable conditions could enhance the speed. His mean speed of 124·10 m.p.h. was accepted by the A.I.A.C.R. as the

The first two-way holder of the land speed record was the British driver L.G. Hornsted with a 200 h.p. *Blitzen*-engined Benz; he attained a mean speed of 124·10 m.p.h. at Brooklands track in June 1914, being clocked at 128·16 m.p.h. in one direction and 120·23 m.p.h. in the other.

Swinging the 200 h.p., 21½-litre engine of Hornsted's big blue Benz over compression required two strong, brave men.

new two-way land speed record despite the fact that Héméry's 1909 figure with the *Blitzen* Benz was 125·95 m.p.h., though set up before the two-way rule applied.

It was all very puzzling, but Benz themselves didn't hesitate to advertise that one of their cars had beaten the World's Mile Record – at 128·16 m.p.h.! (Hornsted's best speed). This generous interpretation of fact also, significantly, suggested that even Benz themselves did not accept Burman's 1911 claim of 141·37 m.p.h. Perhaps this was not so surprising. When Bob Burman came to Europe and discussed his Daytona record with Hornsted, the latter asked sceptically how he'd managed to get as much as 140 m.p.h. out of a *Blitzen*. 'Nothing to it' replied 'Wild Bob'. 'We just marked out a mile on the beach before high tide, and when the sea went down again – Boy, that mile had shrunk!'

The first monsters

The Great War came and went, and with its going men's thoughts could be turned to happier, more inconsequential things such as motor-racing and record-breaking. The Americans, never so deeply involved in the war as Europe, were quickly at it, Ralph de Palma turning out with a fine-looking V12 Packard (see Chapter 18 for more details) four months after the Armistice to record 149·875 m.p.h. one way at Daytona.

But though the United States was only too willing to accept this as *the* record, the A.I.A.C.R. was not, nor were they when Tommy Milton bettered the Packard's speed in 1920 with a shattering 156·03 m.p.h. in an ingenious twin-engined Duesenberg (see Chapter 18), again at Daytona, but again one way only. Thus Hornsted's official two-way figure of 124·10 m.p.h. stood for a long eight years, looking rather foolish, in eyes other than British, before a legitimate challenger came forward again.

This was the famous 350 h.p. Sunbeam, which ushered in the era of aero-engined *LSR* vehicles. Unlike later ones, it was so versatile that it also figured in track racing and hill-climbing; excelled, indeed, at such activities before being turned loose on the record. Sunbeam of Wolverhampton built many aircraft engines during the War; they were never outstanding performers, but they were reliable, and the nominal 350 b.h.p. (actually 355 was attained on the bench) at a gentlemanly 2,100 r.p.m. of a somewhat modified 'Manitou' 60 degree V12 unit as used in coastal defence seaplanes was ample when fitted into a narrow, semi-elliptically sprung car chassis to propel it very fast indeed.

As an aero-engine where every ounce counted, light alloy figured strongly in the 'Manitou'; the engine had single overhead camshafts to each bank, and three valves – one inlet and two exhaust – per cylinder. One block was said to measure 110 × 135 mm. in bore and stroke, and the other 110 × 142 mm., presumably a case of using up what was available at the works, for Sunbeam designer Louis H. Coatalen was a master improviser, while the Company shareholders approved any measure of economy in those early post-war days of doubtful stability.

The pistons were of aluminium; twin B.T.H. magnetos nourished twenty-four plugs, two per cylinder, and there were two Claudel Hobson twin-choke carburettors and dry sump lubrication. The crankshaft ran in seven plain main bearings, and the flywheel of this large, impressive 18·3 litre power unit measured 22 in. in diameter. The clutch was of dry plate type, transmitting to a separate four-speed gearbox (without reverse, incidentally), open propeller shaft and bevel rear axle. To counter excess front end weight the chassis side members at the rear were filled with lead, but despite this the running weight of the car, carrying a sleek single seater body, was under 32 cwt.

Sunbeam designer and racing team manager Louis Coatalen, and driver Kenelm Lee Guinness congratulate each other on the 350 h.p. Sunbeam's new record.

This Sunbeam was built in 1920, and had the experience of several Brooklands races and a Continental hill-climb win behind it when, on 17 May 1922, Kenelm Lee Guinness (founder of the famous K.L.G. sparking plug company) took it out on to the famous Weybridge concrete to attack speed records. Sunbeams weren't chancing any French obstruction in this foray; through Col. Lindsay-Lloyd, Brooklands Clerk of the Course who had charge of the time-keeping, they saw to it that the timing equipment employed was officially approved by the A.I.A.C.R. in advance, and arranged to send it sealed to their Paris headquarters for checking afterwards.

The timing gear was set up along the flat Railway Straight between the Members' and Byfleet bankings, and 'K.L.G.' used the full Outer Circuit lap to build up speed for each record. The Brooklands bankings were never as helpful to a car in attaining its maximum speed as theory had it; nevertheless, on quite a windy day,

Kenelm Lee Guinness in the big 350 h.p. Sunbeam with which he established a new land speed record at a mean of 133·75 m.p.h. at Brooklands in May 1922. The car had a Sunbeam Manitou 60 degree, V12-cylinder aero-engine measuring 18·3 litres.

Guinness succeeded in breaking several short distance records, the relevant one being the flying kilometre at 130·35 m.p.h. going into the wind, and at 137·15 m.p.h. with its help. That meant a mean speed of 133·75 m.p.h. and a new 'official' land speed record, 9·7 m.p.h. faster than Hornsted's 1914 figure with the Benz. It was the third and last time that historic Brooklands proved adequate for the creation of an absolute *LSR*.

Guinness's record lasted for over two years, but not without counterclaim. One particularly spectacular one came from America, where in 1922 Sigmund ('Sig') Haugdahl laid claim to having attained a speed of 180 m.p.h. at Daytona in a Wisconsin-engined car (see Chapter 19). This was never recognized, even in the U.S.A., but around the same time a determined new aspirant came on the scene, an ex-Royal Flying Corps captain of Scottish descent. His name was Malcolm Campbell, and he was destined to have very great influence indeed on the land speed record.

A man named Campbell

Having seen what the 350 h.p. Sunbeam could do, Malcolm Campbell persuaded Sunbeam team chief and engineer Coatalen to let him try the big car on Saltburn sands, a month after Guinness has set the new *LSR*. Campbell was an accomplished racing driver, having raced at Brooklands before the war, and he handled the Sunbeam deftly. By stop-watch he exceeded 134 m.p.h. one way on the sands, but no official timing had been arranged, and the run merely served to whet Campbell's appetite for record-breaking.

There ensued what must have been an entertaining battle of wits during the next few months between the shrewd and crafty Coatalen and the ambitious Campbell, as the latter sought to persuade the former to sell him the 350 h.p. Sunbeam. By April 1923 Coatalen softened and Campbell had his way, paying a large but unspecified sum for the car, which he promptly entered for the international speed trial meeting to be held at Fanoe, Denmark. This was a holiday island off the coast of Jutland, and the trials were held on an eight-mile-long beach before thousands of vacationists.

Despite soft patches of sand, bumps and resultant wheelspin, the car performed superbly, clocking a mean speed of 136·31 m.p.h. through the kilometre, and 137·72 m.p.h. through the mile. Campbell was delighted – until he learned that the electrical timing system used by the Danes was of a type not approved by the A.I.A.C.R., and the new record was disallowed. The Danish Motor Club even sent the apparatus to Paris for checking, but although A.I.A.C.R. officials admitted its accuracy they would not recognize Campbell's figures.

Disappointed but even more determined, Campbell consulted the Boulton and Paul aircraft concern about modifications to the Sunbeam to improve its performance. They recommended a new, long tail with head fairing, covered-in rear suspension and a radiator cowling. The body revisions were subsequently carried

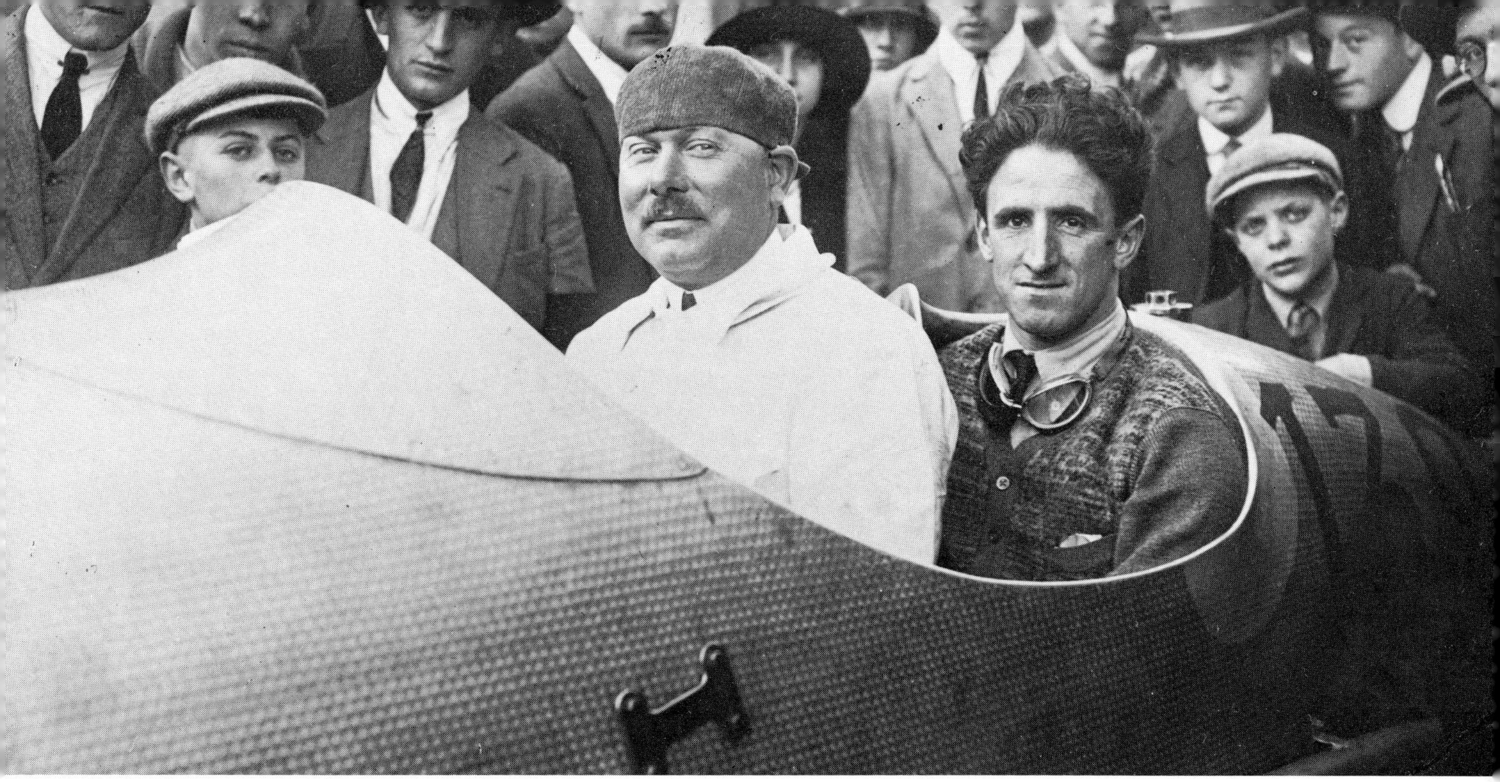

René Thomas broke the record at 143·31 m.p.h. during the 1924 Arpajon sprint meeting in the V12, 10·6-litre Delage. Note the engine-turned aluminium body finish.

out by Jarvises of Wimbledon during the first half of 1924. The car emerged resplendent in Campbell's own favourite shade of blue, and bore the name *Bluebird* as had several of his racing cars since 1912. Once again he entered for the Fanoe speed trials, with a new *LSR* as his most important target; but meanwhile new challengers intervened to make that objective yet more difficult to achieve.

France had not held the *LSR* since 1905, nineteen long years before, but now, somewhat unexpectedly, a French car capable of breaking the record appeared. The Delage company, first of Levallois, then of Courbevoie, had been famous since 1908, when one of their cars won the Grand Prix des Voiturettes at Dieppe. Since then their greatest triumph had been in the 1914 Indianapolis 500 Miles Race, when works driver René Thomas took a 1913 Grand Prix Delage into first place. After the war Delage had Grand Prix aspirations again, but these took time to resolve, so in the meantime they constructed two big 6-cylinder overhead valve cars, one a 5·1 litre, the other a 5·9; both were called *La Torpille* (the Torpedo).

They were used extensively in hill-climbs and sprints but lacked the extreme performance to tackle the 133·75 m.p.h. speed record. At that time Delage were working on a V12 Grand Prix car, and this gave the engineers Plancton and Lory the idea of producing a larger V12 by uniting two of the *Torpille*-type cylinder blocks. These were of modified touring pattern, measuring 90 × 140 mm., and the pair, angled at 60 degrees with the vertical overhead valves operated by pushrods inside the 'V', totalled a healthy 10·6 litres. Aided by four Zenith carburettors and two Scintilla magnetos, the result was 280 b.h.p. at 3,200 r.p.m., taken through a four-speed gearbox and propeller shaft to the rear wheels.

As the car was intended for hill-climbs as well as sprint work, four-wheel brakes were fitted, with assistance from a gearbox-driven servo. The chassis was

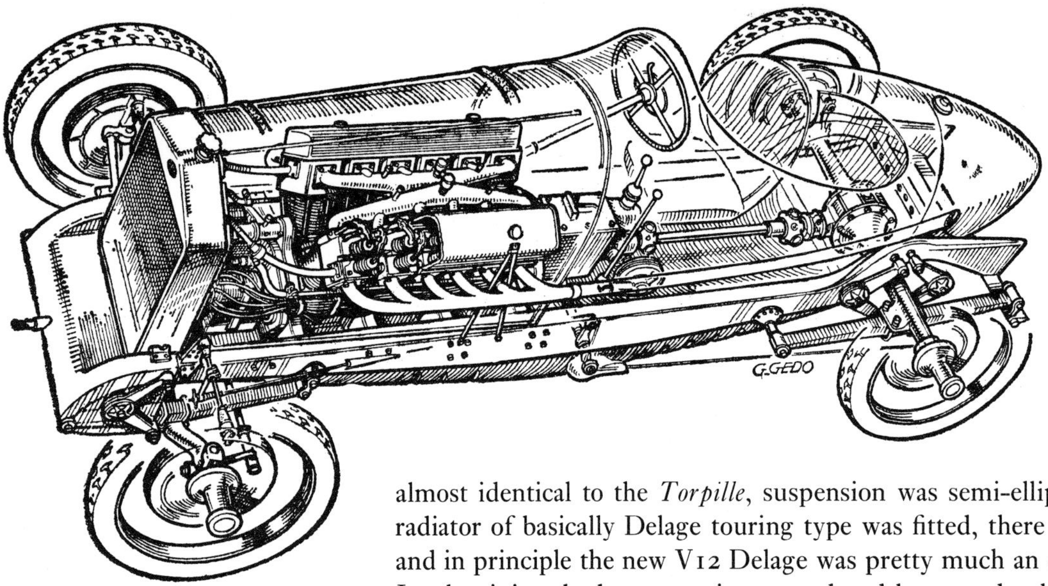

A cutaway drawing of Thomas's 10·6-litre, 12-cylinder Delage.

almost identical to the *Torpille*, suspension was semi-elliptic all round, a vertical radiator of basically Delage touring type was fitted, there was a long undershield, and in principle the new V12 Delage was pretty much an oversize Grand Prix car. Its aluminium body was engine-turned and lacquered pale blue, giving the car an unusual and attractive appearance.

The big Delage appeared in 1923 when René Thomas won the Gaillon hill-climb outside Paris, then went to the Geneva speed trials where he attained 129·3 m.p.h. for the kilometre – within 4 m.p.h. of the record despite a short run-up. Obviously the car had the potential, and when, in 1924, the Moto Club de France (M.C.F.) decided to hold a records meeting at Arpajon, on the main N20 from Paris to Orléans, Louis Delage decided that Thomas should take part with the big *Douze Cylindrées*.

The duel at Arpajon

The Arpajon road was 4¼ miles long, smooth and straight, but narrow and dangerous with a ditch and a long row of plane trees on each side. It was one of the most hazardous of all courses used for land speed record attempts. It was there that René Thomas met a redoubtable opponent in the Englishman Ernest Eldridge with his monstrous Fiat Special, and the duel they fought recalled the struggle between Chasseloup-Laubat and Jenatzy on another stretch of French road outside Paris a quarter-century before.

Eldridge's Fiat had none of the design sophistication of the V12 Delage. Taking the old chassis of lengthened 1907 Grand Prix pattern used in *Mephistopheles*– the huge Fiat which Nazzaro brought to Brooklands in 1908 – Eldridge had lengthened it a further 18 in. by riveting and welding in an extra length of channel (reputedly from a London bus) each side. Into the result he then inserted an immense 6-cylinder, 24-valve, 300 h.p. Fiat type A-12 aviation engine of World War I pattern, measuring 160 × 180 mm. – giving the formidable capacity of 21,714 cc.

This power plant drove the rear wheels through a four-speed gearbox and side chains; the whole device was crudely made, with an ugly special radiator and sombre finish, yet its rakish lines with radiator set far back, the huge bonnet, the cockpit almost over the rear axle, short stubby tail and huge exhaust pipe sweeping back, gave it a savage attractiveness; it looked the epitome of the ultra-high speed car of the 'twenties.

When all the motor-cycles and smaller sports and racing cars had had their runs at Arpajon, the 'over 5-litre' racing class turned out – Thomas's Delage and Eldridge's Fiat. The Frenchman took the first run, the Delage travelling smoothly, quietly, but very, very fast to clock a two-way mean of 143·26 m.p.h. for the kilometre and 143·31 m.p.h. for the mile. The crowds, excited at his speed, closed dangerously on the road, and at the end of his return run one tyre threw a tread; it didn't check his pace, and Thomas emerged the new land speed record-holder *pour la France*. 'At 200 k.p.h. the road is like a narrow passage' he declared.

Then out came the intrepid Eldridge in the desperate-looking Fiat; a bestial roar from its engine, spinning rear wheels, and he was away, the car slewing from side to side in dangerous fashion and sending the crowds rushing back from the verges as it thundered through the measured distances. A brief lull while it turned, a rising roar, and Eldridge was through again; 146·8 m.p.h. his kilometre time, 145·2 his mile! Thomas had lost his brand new *LSR*. . . . Or had he?

Whether he did it of his own accord, or was encouraged to do so by other Frenchmen interested in the honour of being 'fastest on land' is not known, but René Thomas entered a protest against the Fiat, declaring that it had no reverse gear fitted, as was required by regulations drafted in the vain hope of keeping *LSR* vehicles within the bounds of ordinary automobile design. The organizers had no choice but to disqualify Eldridge, and Thomas and the Delage were reinstated as winners at Arpajon and holders of the land speed record.

Ernest Eldridge beat René Thomas's new record speed at Arpajon in his massive 21·7-litre aero-engined Fiat, clocking 146·8 m.p.h. through the flying kilometre. Thomas's protest at the lack of a reverse gear disqualified the Fiat, however, and the record was disallowed. Note the spinning rear wheels in this start shot.

BP
BP

6

Sunbeams shine again

'No matter how formidable a difficulty may appear, there must always be some way to overcome it.'

Sir Malcolm Campbell

(*Opposite*) Major Henry Segrave in the Sunbeam at Southport in 1926, when he raised the record to 152·33 m.p.h. on 4 litres only.

The man brave enough to drive that vast, unwieldy 21-litre Fiat on the narrow Arpajon road at over 140 m.p.h. was not going to take disqualification on some piffling technical grounds lying down. Ernest Eldridge took the car away to his hired workshop in Paris, and there he and his helpers devised a reverse gear after forty-eight hours of day and night work. He was sportingly granted permission by the Département des Ponts et Chaussées to use the Arpajon road for a repeat attempt at the record, as soon as he was ready, and in due course he booked it from dawn to 7.00 a.m. on Saturday, 12 July 1924. Meantime Parry Thomas, the great Brooklands driver, wrote an anxious letter to the press, stressing that *he* was not the Thomas who had so unsportingly protested against the Fiat's lack of a reverse.

At 4.00 a.m. on 12th July a light mist hung over Arpajon. Some fifty gendarmes had arrived and moved out to police the course; the Chevalier René de Knyff, President of the Sporting Commission of the A.C.F. and his entourage were present, as were Robert Sénéchal, acting president of the M.C.F., several racing drivers including Divo, Morel, Moriceau and Scales, but not René Thomas, and about 500 members of the public. By request of the police, they all spread out along

A cutaway drawing of the huge Eldridge Fiat with which, in 1924, Ernest Eldridge took his revenge on René Thomas and Delage by beating their record six days after their protest had nullified his earlier success at Arpajon. He averaged 146·01 m.p.h. through the flying kilometre.

one side of the road, leaving the other clear. By then Eldridge had arrived with the Fiat; officials gathered round it to verify that it now had a working reverse gear, were duly satisfied, and Knyff bade the record attempt begin.

The Fiat rumbled away, spitting and banging in the cold morning air, to the far end, then the ground throbbed to the beat of that mighty engine and Eldridge and riding mechanic Gedge tore through the measured stretches with a thrilling roar. Just before crossing the kilometre strip on the return run, a tread snaked off the Fiat's right rear tyre into the air and landed in the grass; Eldridge pressed on although the tyre disintegrated before the end, turned and limped slowly back. A pause, then M. Collin on the *porte-voix* announced the times – 229·008 k.p.h. (142·3 m.p.h.) for the kilometre and 229·129 k.p.h. (142·38 m.p.h.) for the mile. Not fast enough.

Eldridge was not surprised; the Fiat had given some gargantuan coughs and splutters *en route*, but it was thoroughly warm now. He slightly adjusted the carburation while the tyre was changed, then set off, giving the enthralled crowd a repeat of his thunderous progress down the course and back. The silence as the car disappeared to the far end was suddenly broken by Collin's voice over the loudspeaker – 'Les records sont battus!' – 146·01 m.p.h. for the kilometre, 145·89 m.p.h. for the mile. Eldridge had taken his revenge over Thomas and Delage, and an Englishman in a very mixed 'Special' of Italian origin was the new *LSR* holder – and a highly popular one despite his having defeated a French car on French soil.

The A.C.F. and M.C.F. fêted him at the Hotel Lafontaine in Arpajon, and over lunch René de Knyff toasted Eldridge's great victory and his sporting spirit. Before his success the Fiat Company of Turin had shown no interest in Eldridge's activities; perhaps his primitive monster *was* a little *infra dig* for the proud Italian

firm. But when news came of his new record they were naturally glad to advertise the feat.

Malcolm Campbell's 350 h.p. Sunbeam *Bluebird* after shedding the front tyre which killed a boy spectator at Fanöe beach during the 1924 speed trials there.

Campbell on the hunt

Thwarted in his attempts on the *LSR* at Saltburn in 1922 and Fanöe in 1923, Malcolm Campbell was now faced with Eldridge's 146·01 m.p.h. of July 1924 instead of Guinness's 133.75 m.p.h. of two years before. It simply increased his determination. In late August the modified *Bluebird* went to Denmark for its second round at the Fanöe speed trials. This time the beach was in bad condition after severe gales, and another worry was poor control of the crowds, held back only by rope 'barriers', who tended to move into the centre at the finish to see the cars speeding towards them.

Campbell warned the organizers of the danger to the public should a car go out of control, and was further disturbed when, on his first run through the mile, *Bluebird* skidded and shed both its rear tyres. These were of beaded edge type, held on the wheel by security bolts, but the skid dislodged them and one inner tube wound itself around the brake mechanism, throwing the car into a worse skid.

For his actual record attempt, Campbell had his mechanic Leo Villa fit wired-edge tyres to the rear wheels, which took most of the thrust, and left beaded-edge tyres on the front. He was travelling at about 150 m.p.h. near the end of the mile when the offside front cover flew off; he wrestled the car to a stop, but the tyre shot off course, struck a boy spectator, ripped through the timing box containing officials including Col. Lindsay-Lloyd, who was overseeing the timing on Campbell's behalf, bounced over more spectators, and finished up in the sea.

Land speed record cars were more versatile over forty years ago. This is the René Thomas 10·6-litre Delage, being raced by John Cobb at Brooklands in 1931.

The meeting was abandoned; the unfortunate boy, rushed to hospital, died there, and at the subsequent inquest Campbell, who naturally emphasized his earlier warning to the organizers, was exonerated from blame. He returned to England after as unsatisfactory an 'I told you so' session as anyone could experience, still minus the record he so desired.

Fanöe beach never figured again in *LSR* history; certainly Campbell didn't rush to go there again, and instead he found a beach near Carmarthen in South Wales, known as Pendine Sands. Seven miles long, it looked ideal for record work, so after a preliminary recce he arranged for Col. Lindsay-Lloyd and official R.A.C. time-keepers with approved apparatus to be present during the last weekend of September 1924, and prepared *Bluebird* for another bid.

The car was fitted with new camshafts which sharpened its performance. Ace discs were fitted to the rear wheels, while Dunlop, spurred on by the tyre troubles affecting all *LSR* contenders at that time, had developed a new straight-sided cover and well-based rims which eliminated the serious danger of errant tyres.

Nearing 150 m.p.h.

On his first trial run Campbell encountered a new trouble – the sands were patchy with hard and soft areas, the soggier areas slowing the car as if it were suddenly braked, and he could only manage 145·24 m.p.h. Next day things weren't much better; a strong cross wind blew and the sand was still very wet. None the less an impatient, determined Campbell got a kilometre two-way run at an average of 15·305 sec. or 146·16 m.p.h., which meant that at last the record was his – by a mere 0·15 m.p.h.

It was success, but only just, and that would not satisfy the Campbell temperament for long. 150 m.p.h. – 2½ miles a minute – was a mere 4 m.p.h. away, and Campbell knew that *Bluebird* was easily capable of topping that figure. Even so, he was already nursing ambitious plans to build an all-new car, and put up the Sunbeam for sale in November 1924 at a price of '£1,500 (or near offer), capable of easily breaking its own record in better weather . . . .' He listed the speeds in gears as 61 m.p.h. in first, 120 m.p.h. in second, 142 m.p.h. in third and 168 m.p.h. in top, but despite this, and the *cachet* of owning the fastest car in the world, there were, surprisingly, no takers. One wonders what its value is today, preserved as a unique historic car at the Montagu Motor Museum down in Hampshire.

A.I.A.C.R. record rules

At the end of 1924 the A.I.A.C.R. issued a series of clear, water-tight regulations covering all record-breaking from absolute land speed figures to international class records from Class A (over 8 litres) to Class J (350 c.c.). These regulations did not depart in principle from those laid down in 1914 requiring two-way runs, but they clarified various points, and were thus important to all would-be record-breakers.

First of a long series of land speed record successes fell to Malcolm Campbell in September 1924 at Pendine Sands, South Wales, where he averaged 146·16 m.p.h. in the big Sunbeam despite the wet beach.

It was laid down that the measured distance over which a car is timed must not have an average gradient of more than 1 per cent; that the distance must be covered in both directions; that the two runs must take place within half an hour of each other; and that the record speed would be the mean average of the two runs. The distance had to be surveyed in two directions by an authorized surveyor, and his certificate of its correctness, together with another certificate testifying him to be a fit and proper person to make the survey, had to accompany the certificate of the timing of the record, provided by a recognized automobile club of the country wherein the record was set up.

The actual timing had to be by an automatic device which was accurate to within 1/100 sec., and a certificate of its accuracy, provided by a responsible body (in Britain the Kew Observatory) had to accompany the claim.

At that time many manufacturers of car components and accessories, fuels and oils, were paying *primes* or bonuses to successful record-breakers who used their products; such *primes* were naturally substantial for the land speed record and this fact, plus the clarification of the rules, let alone the *réclame* of being 'the world's fastest', meant an ever-increasing interest in the *LSR*.

J.G.Parry Thomas, an inveterate class record-breaker at Brooklands, was one who was attracted to what was loosely known as 'the World's Record'. After the death of Count Louis Zborowsky during the 1924 Italian Grand Prix at Monza, Thomas acquired his huge Liberty aero-engined Higham Special, and was rebuilding it very much with the *LSR* in mind. It was known, also, that Sunbeam were taking a fresh interest, their speed image having somewhat faded since their 1923 Grand Prix victory.

There was news, too, of a sophisticated French-built machine, the 10-litre *Djelmo* (see Chapter 19) and when it became obvious to Malcolm Campbell by 1925 that his new record car would be a long time coming yet, he must have been glad that he still had the old 350 h.p. *Bluebird*. A tidy-minded, fussy man, he was set on 'cleaning up' his record by taking it over a neat 150 m.p.h., besides making it more difficult for rivals. So once again, in July 1925, the Campbell *équipe* wended its way to Wales. This time the sands of Pendine were ideal, and with very little drama *Bluebird*, now wearing long exhaust pipes instead of stubs, blasted through the flying kilometre at a mean of 150·869 and the mile at 150·766 m.p.h.

(*Opposite, above*) Major Segrave and his wife before the record-breaking run with the 4-litre Sunbeam at Southport in 1926.

(*Opposite, below*) The ever-versatile 4-litre Sunbeam in a Spanish road race in 1926.

An engineering tonic

For the third time the gallant old aero-engined Sunbeam had taken the record. The Sunbeam Company themselves must have been obliged to Malcolm Campbell for the prestige he gained them as the fastest marque in the world. As pioneers in the use of vast, unstressed aero-engines in record cars, it was surprising that their second challenger should have been a far smaller, more scientific and technically more efficient design. The 4-litre, 12-cylinder Sunbeam was indeed a tonic to fastidious engineers who winced at the crudeness of the monsters. It was to prove one of the world's most versatile speed machines, racing on Grand Prix circuits and high-speed tracks, in hill-climbs and in sprints – and it bid for *LSR* honours.

Its modest engine capacity of 4 litres, at a time when it took 18·3 for success, seemed ridiculous, but Coatalen the opportunist had taken two blocks from the obsolete 2-litre, twin overhead camshaft, 6-cylinder Grand Prix Sunbeam engines, and mounted them in a 75 degree 'V' on a specially made crankcase housing a roller bearing crankshaft. Supercharging in Grands Prix was by then a *sine qua non* to performance, and the V-12, too, was supercharged, using a big Roots-type blower and single Solex carburettor which helped it to produce about 306 b.h.p. at 5,300 r.p.m. This, in a larger version of the Grand Prix chassis and two-seater bodywork, weighing in all about 18 cwt. (over 13 cwt. less than *Bluebird*) commanded an impressive power-to-weight ratio, and the car's theoretical speed on a 3·5:1 final drive was 160 m.p.h.

The driver of this fascinating new Sunbeam was Major Henry Segrave, winner for Sunbeam of the famous 1923 French Grand Prix and other road races. He took the newly completed, still unpainted car to Brooklands for tests late in 1925 and, despite running on eleven cylinders only and suffering considerable wheelspin, he

was clocked at 145 m.p.h. through the half-mile. Segrave and the car, now painted red, then adjourned to Southport in March 1926 for the attempt on the record. A neat radiator cowling and fairings to the suspension were fitted, but the Sunbeam retained its road-racing aero-screen, front brakes and Grand Prix-style tail without head fairing.

Southport was picked in preference to Pendine for its better accessibility from the Wolverhampton factory, and though shorter than the Welsh beach it was long enough for a car with the fierce accelerative power of the 4-litre Sunbeam. Choosing a time in mid-March when the tides were suitable, Sunbeams arranged with the R.A.C. for official time-keepers to be present, and without more ado Segrave got down to it. The beach was bumpy, sending the Sunbeam leaping in the air, and practice runs revealed an alarming weakness in supercharger casings which kept distorting under pressure and breaking.

In all, six casings were damaged without the record coming any nearer, and Irving the designer was all for returning to Wolverhampton with the car and adapting two smaller blowers in preference to the troublesome larger one. Segrave prevailed upon him to modify one supercharger at a local workshop to give it at least three minutes' life – all Segrave declared he'd need for an attack on the kilometre and mile. To save running the engine needlessly the car was towed to the time-keepers' box for verification, then hot water was poured into the radiator, Segrave was push-started, and motored slowly down to the southern end.

He made his first run on scarcely more than three-quarter throttle, then opened out fully for the return. He was moving very fast and was well into the timed kilometre when he hit a gully formed by water draining off the beach; the Sunbeam leapt into the air (subsequent measuring showed a gap of 49 ft. between its tyre marks!), and with the rear wheels free the engine raced and the supercharger failed again. But Segrave got his record just the same, for his average through the kilometre turned out at 152·33 m.p.h., and Campbell's *Bluebird* was dethroned by a car with an engine less than a quarter the size.

(*Opposite, above*) Tyre changing on Campbell's *Bluebird* between his two successful runs at Pendine in September 1924; the car is resting on boards to prevent it sinking in the soft sand. Note the stub exhaust system and neat formed windscreen.

(*Opposite, below*) Campbell in the gallant old 350 h.p. Sunbeam broke his own record on a much drier Pendine in July 1925, clocking 150·869 m.p.h. through the flying kilometre.

The heart of Segrave's 4-litre Sunbeam was the 12-cylinder supercharged engine comprising two 2-litre Grand Prix blocks and heads mounted at 75 degrees on a special crankcase with roller bearing crankshaft.

Colour Plates

Jeantaud, March 1899
La Jamais Contente, December 1899
Serpollet, April 1902
Paris-Vienna type 60 h.p. Mors, 1902
Gobron-Brillié, 1903
Ford *Arrow*, January 1904
Mercedes, January 1904
Gobron-Brillié, 1904
Mercedes, May 1904
Darracq, November 1904
Napier, January 1905
Darracq V8, December 1905
Stanley *Rocket*, January 1906
Blitzen Benz, November 1909
Blitzen Benz, March 1910
Benz, June 1914

JEANTAUD

March 1899, 57·6 m.p.h. (93·724 k.p.h.)

Driven by Comte Gaston de Chasseloup-Laubat

One electric motor driven by Fulmen batteries through side chains to rear wheels.

La Jamais Contente

December 1899, 65·79 m.p.h. (105·904 k.p.h.)

Driven by Camille Jenatzy

Two electric motors driven by Fulmen batteries with direct drive to rear wheels. Streamlined body of 'Partinium' light alloy.

SERPOLLET

April 1902, 75·06 m.p.h. (120·771 k.p.h.)

Driven by Léon Serpollet

4-cylinder, single-acting steam power unit driving rear wheels direct through connecting rods.

PARIS–VIENNA TYPE 60 H.P. MORS

1902, 76·08 m.p.h. (122·431 k.p.h.), 76·60 m.p.h. (123·249 k.p.h.), 77·13 m.p.h. (124·102 k.p.h.)

Driven respectively by William K. Vanderbilt Jr., Henri Fournier, and amateur driver Augières

4-cylinder, 9·2-litre, 60 b.h.p. petrol engine; four-speed gearbox; chain final drive.

GOBRON–BRILLIÉ

1903, 83·47 m.p.h. (134·325 k.p.h.), 84·73 m.p.h. (136·353 k.p.h.)

Driven by Arthur Duray

4-cylinder, 13·5-litre, 110 b.h.p. opposed-piston petrol engine; four-speed gearbox; chain final drive. Chassis of brazed steel tubing.

FORD *Arrow*

January 1904, 91·37 m.p.h. (147·014 k.p.h.)

Driven by Henry Ford

4-cylinder, 16·7-litre, 72 b.h.p. engine; no gearbox or differential; shaft final drive. No rear springs.

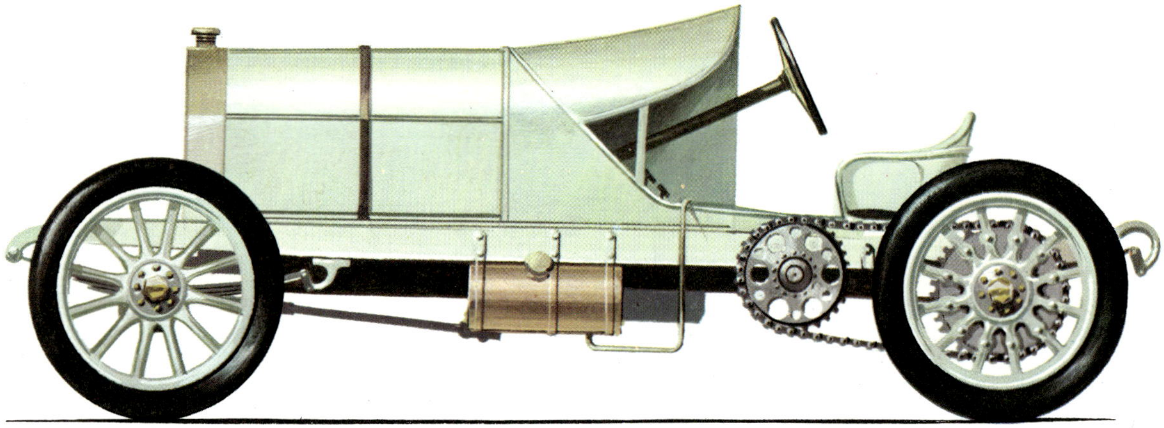

MERCEDES

January 1904, 92·30 m.p.h. (148·510 k.p.h.)

Driven by William K. Vanderbilt Jr.

4-cylinder, 11·9-litre, 90 b.h.p. engine; four-speed gearbox; chain final drive.

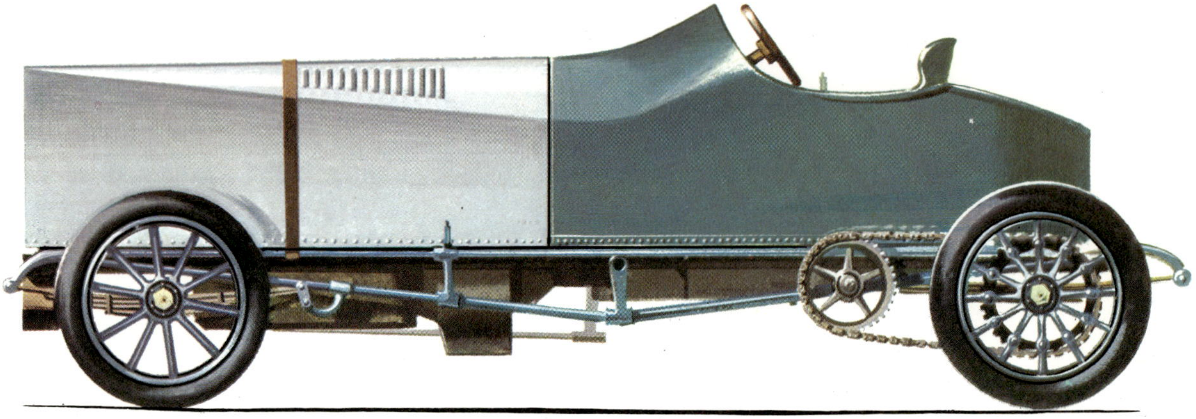

GOBRON-BRILLIÉ

1904, 94·78 m.p.h. (152·542 k.p.h.), 103·55 m.p.h. (166·628 k.p.h.)

Driven by Louis Rigolly

4-cylinder, 13·6-litre, 130 b.h.p., opposed-piston engine, four-speed gearbox; chain final drive. Chassis of brazed steel tubing.

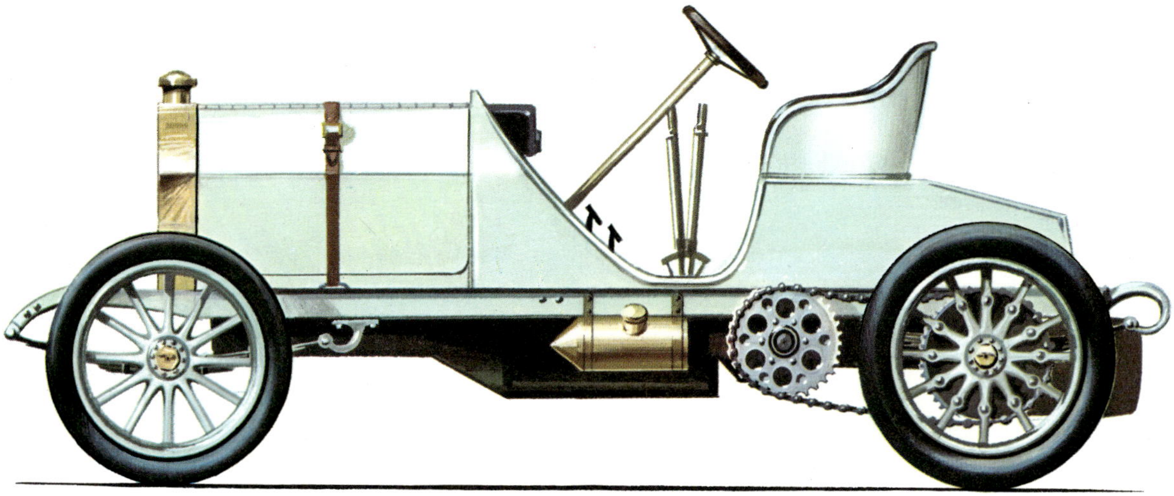

MERCEDES
May 1904, 97·25 m.p.h. (156·941 k.p.h.)
Driven by Baron Pierre de Caters
4-cylinder, 11·9-litre, 90 b.h.p. engine; four-speed gearbox; chain final drive.

DARRACQ
November 1904, 104·52 m.p.h. (168·188 k.p.h.)
Driven by Paul Baras
4-cylinder, 11·3-litre, 100 b.h.p. engine; four-speed gearbox; shaft final drive.

NAPIER

January 1905, 104·65 m.p.h. (168·381 k.p.h.)

Driven by Arthur E. Macdonald

6-cylinder, 15-litre, 90 b.h.p. engine; two-speed gearbox; shaft final drive.

DARRACQ V8

December 1905, 109·65 m.p.h. (175·422 k.p.h.)

Driven by Victor Hémery

V8 o.h.v., 22·5-litre, 200 b.h.p. engine; two-speed gearbox; shaft final drive.

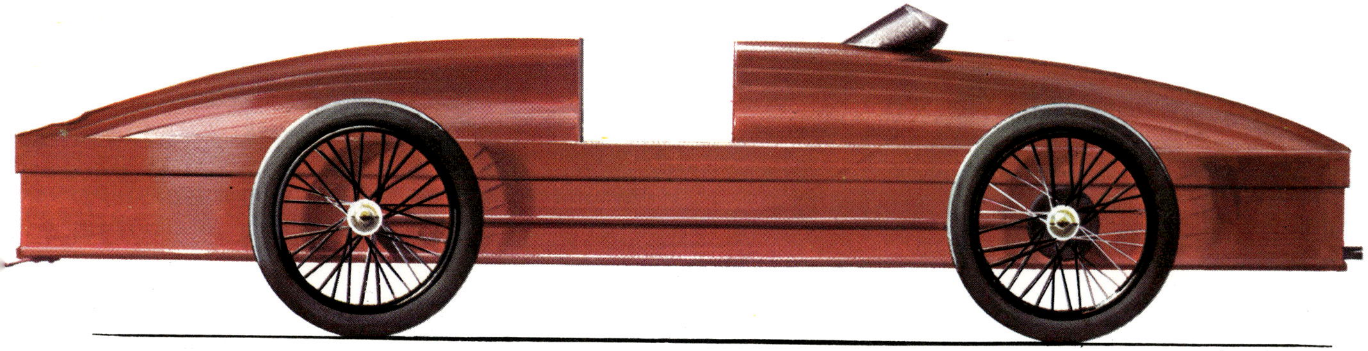

STANLEY *Rocket*

January 1906, 121·57 m.p.h. (195·638 k.p.h.)

Driven by Fred Marriott

Twin-cylinder horizontal, rear-mounted steam power unit driving rear wheels direct through connecting rods. No gearbox. Streamlined body of canvas-covered cedar, with full-length underpan.

Blitzen BENZ

November 1909, 125·95 m.p.h. (202·655 k.p.h.)

Driven by Victor Heméry

4-cylinder, o.h.v., 21·5-litre, 200 b.h.p. engine; four-speed gearbox; chain final drive.

Blitzen BENZ

March 1910, 131·275 m.p.h. (211·256 k.p.h.)

Driven by Barney Oldfield

4-cylinder, o.h.v., 21·5-litre, 200 b.h.p. engine; four-speed gearbox; chain final drive.

BENZ

June 1914, 124·10 m.p.h. (199·171 k.p.h.) [under the new two-way ruling]

Driven by L. G. Hornsted

4-cylinder, o.h.v., 21·5-litre, 200 b.h.p. engine; four-speed gearbox; chain final drive.

7

Parry Thomas and *Babs*

'I am not of the opinion of those people who are going to condemn record-breaking. We all know that the history of England has been made up by pioneers, and these attempts by brave men only show that, in 1927, the manhood of the British Empire is not dead.'

Dr. R.L. Thomas, Coroner at the inquest on John Godfrey Parry Thomas, killed at Pendine, March 1927

The next gladiator to enter the arena was John Godfrey Parry Thomas, a heavily built Welshman of forbidding mien which concealed a kindly nature. Besides being a superb and fearless driver, as an engineer he was a genius who was responsible for the very advanced Leyland Eight luxury private car, one of which he modified into the highly successful Leyland-Thomas with which he set the Brooklands lap record in 1925 at 129·36 m.p.h.

The Higham Special which he purchased for £125 after Zborowsky's death had an enormous 400 h.p., 26·9-litre, 45 degree V12 American Liberty aero-engine, fitted into a long, slender chassis made by Rubery Owen and equipped with those longitudinal bracing stays designed to impart extra beam strength, which were popular wear on Brooklands track cars of the 'twenties. Transmission was through a scroll clutch and pre-war four-speed Benz gearbox and sidechains, and as a discriminating engineer Parry Thomas must undoubtedly have viewed this antediluvian creation with mixed enthusiasm.

He could not afford to build a record car of more modern specification, however, and in that great Liberty motor and the Higham's chassis he could see the makings

Parry Thomas and his mechanic strive to eliminate persistent misfiring in the huge 26·9-litre, V12 Liberty aero-engined *Babs*, before attacking Segrave's record at Pendine in April 1926. Parry Thomas broke it twice in two days, first at 169·30 m.p.h., then at 171·09 m.p.h.

Thundering over the sands of Pendine, *Babs* with her chain drive and streamlined bodywork was a mixture of ancient and modern.

of a potential record-breaker. He set to work, fitting a new sloping radiator of Leyland pattern with header tank mounted further back over the scuttle to keep height down, and a new Leyland front axle and steering column. He gave the engine new Miralite pistons and a revised carburation system with four Zenith instruments, replaced the ancient scroll clutch with a most effective multi-plate design of his own, and clothed the whole in a respectable offset single-seater body of pleasing shape, with a big front cowl enclosing the radiator and the chassis dumb-irons, and a long tapering tail with head-fairing. The entire car was painted white with light blue chassis members. Stub exhausts, six per side, projected rearward adding to the purposeful appearance of this new *LSR* car, which Thomas called *Babs*.

He took it to Pendine late in 1925 to try it out, but the beach was far too wet for anything like record speeds, so he returned to Brooklands, worked on the car over the winter, spent a whole day in April 1926 testing and tuning it on the track, then loaded *Babs* on to a six-wheeled Scammell lorry provided by Shell-Mex Ltd, and took it back to Pendine. On 27th April Thomas made his attack, and *Babs* with its thunderous engine, threshing chains and thick black smoke belching from the exhaust stubs was certainly an exciting spectacle as it charged across the sands.

The engine never ran perfectly, misfiring persistently, while the course was soft in patches, causing the car to snake considerably. Nevertheless, Thomas broke the

Crowds swarm around *Babs* and Parry Thomas after their 1926 success at Pendine.

LSR very handsomely, adding virtually 17 m.p.h. to Segrave's six-week-old figure, with a mean speed through the flying kilometre of 169·30 m.p.h. Knowing that *Babs* could do better, Thomas was not satisfied. He worked away at the carburation in an effort to cure that maddening misfiring, and took the car out again the following day for another attempt.

Though the misfiring was not completely exorcised the car was in better fettle, and this time Thomas raised the record to 171·02 m.p.h. for the kilometre and 170·624 m.p.h. for the mile, after which, having given Messrs Segrave, Campbell and any other potential challengers something substantial to think about, *Babs* was reloaded on to the Scammell and the party went home.

Campbell replies

After two full years' work, Malcolm Campbell's new *Bluebird* was completed by November 1926 and shown to the press. It was a most impressive car; no crude 'Special' with ex-World War I aero-engine squeezed into a convenient chassis, but a land speed record machine built absolutely from scratch regardless of cost. Only the engine was an adaptation: a massive 450 b.h.p., 23·9-litre Napier Lion with twelve cylinders in three rows of four, arranged like an inverted broad arrow. This was a post-war aero design used in a variety of R.A.F. Fleet Air Arm and civil

"BP"
BRITISH "BP" PE
PETROL

aircraft, and the loan to Campbell of one from the Napier factory by permission of the Air Ministry was testimony to his persuasiveness.

The chassis, an extremely sturdy affair with gracefully tapered side members, big machined cross-members and underslung axles, was designed by Amherst Villiers, a talented engineer and tuner, and built by Vickers Ltd. Assembly of the car was by the Robin Hood Engineering Works, an offshoot of Kenelm Lee Guinness's K.L.G. sparking plug factory at Putney Vale, and an Italian engineer named Joseph Maina, a friend of Campbell's head mechanic Leo Villa, was responsible for the general layout, the two-piece front axle, the duplicated steering gear using two Marles units, and the special three-speed epicyclic gearbox, called the F.B.M. (Foster-Brown-Maina) and built by Beard & Fitch Ltd.

Originally there was a startling proposal to use solid tyres on this *Bluebird* to obviate the tyre troubles still prevalent then, but eventually Dunlop developed special covers for Campbell, all this being part of the incredible service this company has provided to land speed record contenders for over forty years, building up a unique fund of knowledge on ultra-high-speed tyres.

The springs were the usual semi-elliptics all round with restricted 'give'; Clayton-Dewande servo-assisted four-wheel brakes were employed, and the radiator header tank, echoing Parry Thomas's idea on *Babs*, was mounted on the scuttle behind the engine to keep the bonnet low. Rudge-Whitworth wire wheels were fitted, and the body, built by Jarvis and Sons of Wimbledon, was a superbly shaped single-seater. With its oval-shaped radiator cowl set well back and its elegant profile fitting over the engine like a glove, the new *Bluebird* had something of the balanced comeliness of the rare 1,100 c.c. single-seater Bugatti which Malcom Campbell happened to own and race at that time. Yet with its big fairings over the rocker boxes, its 12 ft. 1½ in. wheelbase, and long tail, the Napier-Campbell, to give it its proper title, was almost twice the size of any Bugatti.

Painted in Campbell's favourite blue, this was a very beautiful record car, superbly engineered, but also a very expensive one, with practically every component specially made. Campbell was reckoned to have spent over £9,500 on the car, whereas record-holder Parry Thomas paid £125 for *his* car and spent perhaps another £800 rebuilding it. Campbell's aim when *Bluebird* was first laid down was three miles a minute – 180 m.p.h. – but here was Thomas already within 9 m.p.h. of that target *and* working to improve it. There were reports, moreover, that Sunbeam were building a very special twin-engined car with 200 m.p.h. as their goal! Never a patient man, Campbell positively itched to get the *LSR* honours back before his expensive new car was out of date.

Without waiting for good weather and tides, he took the car to Pendine on New Year's Day of 1927, and on 2nd January made his first foray. The sands were soaking and the car had to stand on broad metal sheets to prevent the wheels sinking until ready to move off. With the engine running, Campbell drove off the sheets in bottom gear – and as he tried to change up the engine stalled. *Bluebird* began to sink into the soggy sands, and was down to the chassis before a rush of helpers

(*Opposite*) Malcolm Campbell's handsome and extremely expensive 22·3-litre Lion-engined Napier-Campbell *Bluebird* with which he broke Thomas's record at Pendine in February 1927, averaging 174·883 m.p.h. in two wet, hectic runs. Here the car is on duck-boards prior to setting off on its record run.

heaved it out and rolled it back on to the metal sheets. He managed to get moving the next day, but the epicyclic gearbox was very troublesome, and additional problems with braking and the body made it essential to return to Campbell's workshops at Povey Cross, Surrey, for modifications.

Returning to Wales a fortnight later, he got in several exploratory runs before returning yet again to Povey Cross for more changes, and was back at Pendine for the third time at the beginning of February. The beach was still very wet and very bumpy, but Campbell hit on the idea of ploughing a furrow on the seaward side along the entire six-mile course to drain the water away. A lorry and local ploughman were quickly procured, but a strong wind from the sea and a turning tide rather qualified its success.

Campbell would not wait. He shot off and was through the flying kilometre at a

Campbell trying out his new car on the streaming-wet Pendine Sands.

spanking 179·158 m.p.h. – just $\frac{3}{5}$ sec. short of the 180 m.p.h. mark he sought. On the run back he set off even faster, only to hit a severe bump which threw him up from his seat into the airstream; his goggles were whipped back by the blast of wind, and while he struggled with one hand to replace them he lost speed, and his kilometre speed dropped to 170·608 m.p.h. Yet his mean for the two runs, 174·883 m.p.h. still gave him the record, over 3 m.p.h. faster than *Babs* earlier, while he also broke the mile record at 174·223 m.p.h.

Success at last, after all the effort, must have been a big relief to Campbell, but once again he was only partly satisfied. But for that bump on the sand he could have broken the 180 m.p.h. barrier; as it was, he'd have to wait and see what Thomas could do, and hope that Segrave's fantastic new Sunbeam wasn't ready yet.

The Pendine tragedy

On Tuesday, 1 March 1927, Parry Thomas arrived at Pendine with his improved *Babs.* A new Delaney-Gallay radiator enabled the bonnet to be appreciably lowered, and it now fitted so closely over the Liberty engine that two big bulges were necessary to accommodate the protruding valve covers. The radiator intake was now smaller, the drive chains and the fore-end of the rear wheels were now shrouded by long, curved aluminium fairings, and wheel discs were fitted all round. That this was the old, agricultural-looking Higham Special now seemed inconceivable. Thomas had also improved engine performance, and made a simple rearward adjustment of the weight distribution by fitting two lead-filled tubes across the chassis at the rear, and installing a box of lead shot alongside the driver's seat.

As so often seemed the case at Pendine, the weather was bad and the course in poor condition on Tuesday and Wednesday. Like Campbell, Thomas felt an urgent need to attack the record without delay and on Thursday, though the

A cutaway drawing of Parry Thomas's Liberty-engined *Babs.*

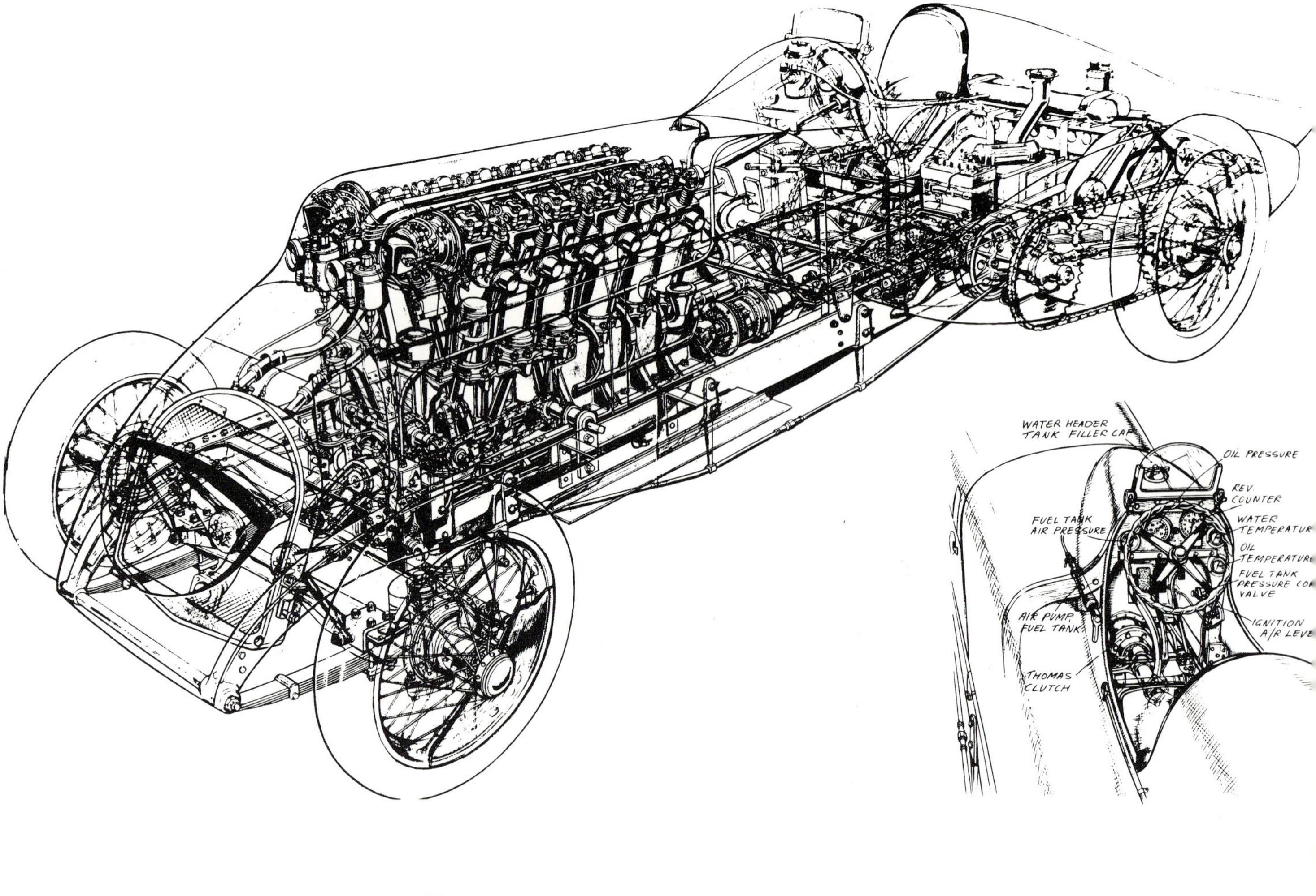

Babs, her streamlining further improved, seen at 170 m.p.h. on the Pendine beach as Parry Thomas strives to regain his record from Campbell's *Bluebird*.

weather was still disagreeable and he still felt miserable after a severe bout of influenza, he decided to make his bid. After two preliminary runs to warm the car up he set off at speed, but neither *Babs* nor the timing apparatus was in a good mood and the runs were abortive. He worked a while on the carburation, made two more runs with the engine still misfiring, then got in a faster run at over 170 m.p.h.

Thomas had just completed the measured mile on his return run when *Babs* was seen to slew. It went suddenly out of control, rolled, righted itself, then swathed a gigantic arc in the sand, ending up with the engine on fire. Nobody was close enough to the accident to state exactly what happened. Horrified onlookers led by mechanic Jock Pullen rushed to rescue the driver, but poor Thomas was beyond help; he had been virtually decapitated.

At the inquest it was generally assumed that the offside driving chain had broken, or had come off its sprockets, smashing upwards through the flat steel guard and the aluminium fairing, and striking the unfortunate Thomas's head. The chain, the radius arm, or the wheel could have broken; perhaps one or more spokes had caught in the final drive sprocket and dislodged the chain. Racing driver and engineer Leslie G. Callingham of Shell-Mex thought a stone or some other object must have caused the chain to be diverted from the sprocket; the theories regarding this grisly tragedy were numerous, but as the years passed, it became generally accepted that the chain, somehow displaced or broken and flying upwards, was responsible for Thomas's death. As to his speed in that final, fatal run, it was never known, for the timing wire too had been broken by the savage contortions of the car.

Today, conjecture as to the causes takes new turns. *Babs* was buried in the sands of Pendine; then, years later, the Ministry of Defence moved in, built an experimental rocket range on the beach, and erected a police hut right above *Babs*, presumably without exact knowledge of the car's whereabouts. As time passed, it was all but forgotten, although local villagers who cherished the memory of popular Parry Thomas continued to put flowers on a nearby cairn. Then Owen Wyn Owen, a lecturer from Bangor University experienced in restoring old cars, thought of exhuming *Babs*, and after much wrangling with the authorities and local interests, obtained permission.

Thus, after 42 years, the remains of the car were dug out and taken away on a lorry to be restored as a historic vehicle, and a detailed examination revealed some interesting things even after so long a passage of time. The radius arm, a suspected cause of the accident, was found to be bent but intact, while from straightening the streamlined fairing it seems that the chain did not, in fact, penetrate this, and may not after all have inflicted Thomas's terrible head injuries. It appears rather that he may have sustained them as the car overturned at over 170 m.p.h.

Whatever the cause, Parry Thomas's death cost Britain a driver of immense skill, immensely admired. He was the first driver fatality in land speed record-breaking in 29 years.

The fatal end: the car after the crash in which Thomas lost his life.

Babs was buried in the sands of Pendine, but forty-two years later Owen Wyn Owen of Bangor arranged for the car to be exhumed for restoration. Apart from salt corrosion of aluminium parts, the car was in remarkably good condition.

8

The age of monsters

'Never before had the attainment of such a high speed been aimed at. Never before had such power been put in a car chassis, and never before had it been necessary to break away from orthodox car construction to such an extent, yet the fact remains that this car [the 1,000 h.p. Sunbeam] was submitted to fewer alterations in design than any other car I know of.'

Sir Henry Segrave in THE LURE OF SPEED

Monsieur Louis Coatalen, that shrewd Breton from Concarneau, chief engineer and racing team manager for the Sunbeam-Talbot-Darracq combine, was nothing if not adaptable. In Sunbeam's Grand Prix days, should their own cars be proved slower than their rivals, he never wasted time trying to catch up but either copied their design or acquired their best designer. He was no mere plagiarist, however, but a clever engineer with his feet on the ground and a board of directors to keep happy.

The 4-litre V12 Sunbeam with which Henry Segrave surprised the world by taking the *LSR* in 1926 at 152·33 m.p.h. was an indication of Coatalen's adaptive genius, but having proved the ability of a small-engined, super-efficient car to take the record from one aero-engined monster, only to lose it to another, he reasoned that, if it had to be power, then power he would use – more than any other.

So he, too, made a monster, the most ingenious monster of its decade and yet, always with the directorate in mind, a remarkably inexpensive one. Within five years the record had risen from just over 130 m.p.h. to just under 175 m.p.h. A Sunbeam had been the first to break 150 m.p.h.; could they now break 200 m.p.h.?

(*Opposite*) In chassis form, the twin-engined 1,000 h.p. Sunbeam was bolted to a running rig and subjected to eight hours of high-speed testing.

Striking frontal appearance of the 1,000 h.p. Sunbeam, the first land speed record with full-width bodywork enveloping the wheels.

That, in fact, was Segrave's question to Coatalen, and one which sparked off the *Patron*'s interest. 200 m.p.h. was a magnificent goal, especially as Campbell had yet to realize his avowed 180 m.p.h. . . .

But the source of power? For Sunbeam to use anything but a Sunbeam engine was unthinkable, yet the biggest aero-engine they ever made during World War I could not equal the Liberty in litreage nor the Napier Lion engine for output. Coatalen's answer was to use not one but two engines. Redundant Sunbeam World War I units were still lying around at Wolverhampton, so he settled for a pair of 22½-litre V12 four-camshaft 48-valve Matabele engines which had actually been used in a racing boat and put out about 435 b.h.p. each at 2,000 r.p.m., then got down to the problem of fitting them into one highly streamlined car.

Like pioneers such as Mors, Baker and Stanley, he visualized a kind of upturned boat for the body, but fully enveloping to enclose the wheels. Within it the engines, each with its own cooling system, would be disposed one at the front and one at the back between the rear wheels, with the driver sitting between. The drive for each engine went to a separate three-speed gearbox ahead of the driver, and then by a shaft and bevels to a cross-shaft and sidechains with armourplate guards.

Having worked out the principle of the car, Coatalen passed the job of design development to Captain J.S.(Jack) Irving, while Dunlops got down to the formidable task of designing and building special tyres, and the driver, Henry Segrave, tackled the complicated arrangements for the record venue. For publicity purposes, the impressive name of the '1,000 h.p. Sunbeam' was agreed upon, even if its total power was somewhat less. It was estimated that the car, weighing 3 tons 16 cwt. with vital fluids aboard, would need a course nine miles long to attain its target speed, and that ruled out any beaches in Europe. Pendine, Southport, Saltburn and Fanöe were all too short and unpredictable, and Segrave decided that the famous Ormond–Daytona beach in Florida, U.S.A., was the only suitable place.

The quest for a course

His backers, who included Castrol, K.L.G., Dunlop, B.P., David Moseley and T.B.André, were less convinced; they preferred the attempt to take place on British soil somewhere. But so convinced was Segrave that Daytona was the only suitable course that he agreed to take the car there at his own expense, even to paying the mechanics who came over with him. Segrave also had the herculean task of persuading the A.A.A., the American premier motoring body, to join the A.I.A.C.R. in order that the latter would recognize any records he might establish on U.S. soil – a thing they had declined to do in the past when de Palma, Milton and Haugdahl made claims for the record.

Then the A.I.A.C.R. demanded full particulars of the A.A.A.'s electrical timing apparatus, plus two independent certificates of accuracy, yet all this was accomplished by the full exercise of Segrave's noted charm and diplomacy. When the 1,000 h.p. Sunbeam chassis and engines were married up, they were mounted in a

(*Opposite, above*) The remarkable 1,000 h.p. Sunbeam, powered by two 22½-litre, 12-cylinder Matabele aero-engines, with which Henry Segrave raised the record to 203·792 m.p.h. in March 1927, bettering Campbell's seven-week-old figure by over 28 m.p.h.

(*Opposite, below*) 1,000 h.p. Sunbeam
Location of engines and transmission.

vast test cradle for a theoretical 210 m.p.h. speed test. The system of starting was ingenious. The rear engine, primed with fuel, was started first by compressed air from bottles, and when it was running a hand clutch transmitted the drive to the front engine and started it up in turn. Once the pair were running in unison they were connected by a positive dog clutch worked by the same hand clutch, and were then controlled as one unit by the accelerator pedal.

Watching the test, Segrave was awed. 'I shall never forget my sensations when I first heard its engines running all out,' he wrote later. 'No words can describe the unimaginable output of power which the 1,000 h.p. machinery seemed to catapult into the building. It was one continuous deafening roar. . . . The wheels were spinning round like semi-invisible discs at 210 m.p.h. Even then we knew that the engines behind them were not putting forth all they were capable of. . . .' The complete chassis was run for eight hours at varying speeds, and as the calculated road speed at 2,000 r.p.m., excluding wheelspin, was 212·5 m.p.h., Coatalen and Irving were confident that the car could do the job. At a total cost of about £5,400 including labour, it should prove a good investment. . . .

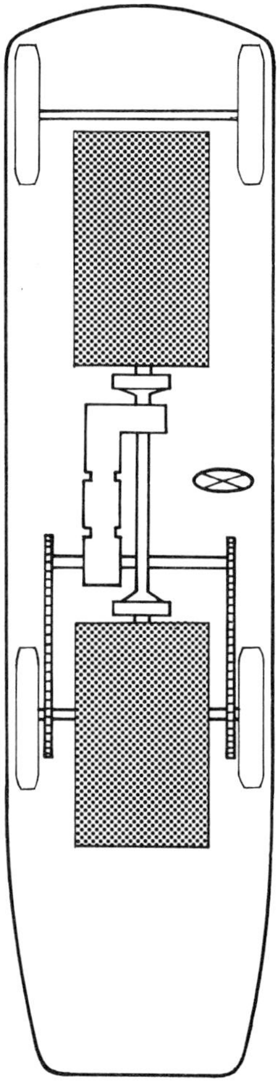

Segrave was less blithe. Relaxing temporarily during the voyage on the *Berengaria* with the Sunbeam secure under covers on the after deck, his peace of mind was broken by the awful news of Parry Thomas's death – due, as it was then believed, to a broken chain. The Sunbeam had chains too. . . . No doubt Coatalen would have preferred a more sophisticated and elegant shaft drive system, but with both time and cost to consider it was expedient to use sidechains; they were well boxed in, at any rate, and from the aesthetic point of view and that of a discerning public who might deplore the use of so primitive a form of transmission by a marque of quality, they were well hidden within the streamlined body. But Segrave remembered how they nearly became red hot during the maximum speed tests at the works, and he and the mechanics took a good long look at them as a precaution.

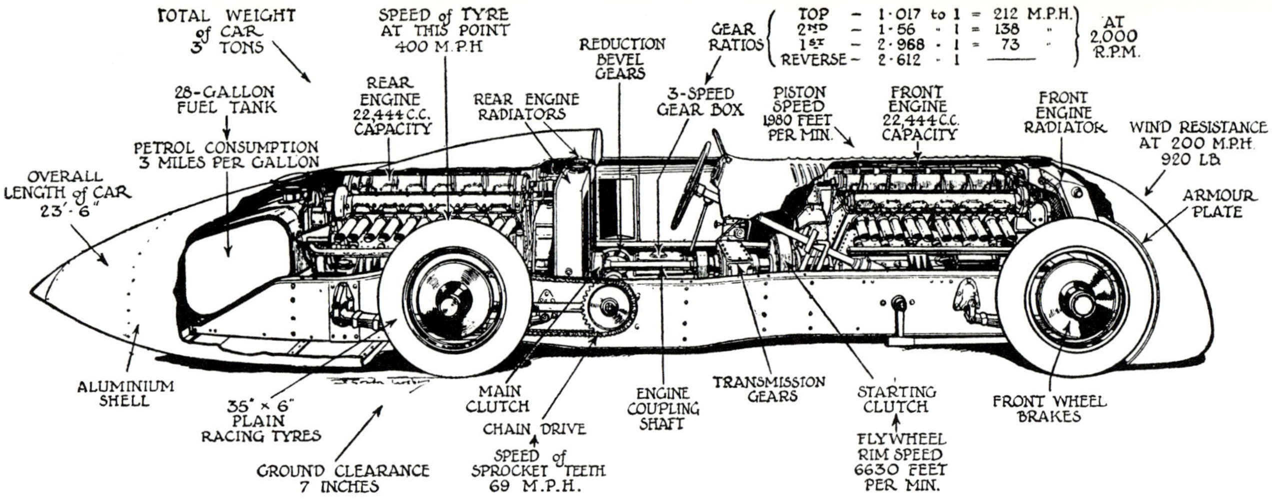

A cutaway drawing showing the disposition of engines and components on the 1,000 h.p. Sunbeam.

The car had scarcely run 300 yards on its own wheels so far, so when they reached Daytona via New York and several heart-warming, hectic receptions, there was much to do. Steering, overheating, wind pressure, gear-change and braking problems manifested themselves and were cured one by one, as was the time-keeping mystery whereby Segrave recorded over thirty different times for one run, thanks to the public treading on the timing wires!

Great day

On Tuesday, 29 March 1927, Segrave and the Sunbeam were ready. The Daytona scene was very different from wet, windy Pendine or Southport; warm sun, a dry, smooth beach, and masses of spectators, some 30,000 of them, in the dunes bordering the course. Land speed record-breaking by foreign cars and drivers was a spectacle new to Americans and they weren't going to miss it, even though it required patience. Many had camped overnight or slept in their cars, and although the course was closed and ready, with marshals in their places by 8.00 a.m., Segrave by arrangement did not start until nearly 10.00 a.m.

The roar, at last, of the two Matabele engines, and the sight of the 1,000 h.p. Sunbeam accelerating away like a bullet made up for all the waiting. A cross-gust

The great Sunbeam flashing over the sands at Daytona. Segrave was the first European to use the famous Florida beach for a land speed record attempt.

caught the squat red car as Segrave aimed it for the measured distance, and it took long, sickening seconds for him to straighten it up; then he was through the kilometre, the mile and the 5 kilometres; again the car swerved, sliced three four-inch-square marker poles off almost flush with the ground like a razor, and skidded a further 400 yards before it was under control again! Then the brakes wouldn't slow the car sufficiently, so Segrave deliberately steered for the shallow sea, hitting it at about 55 m.p.h. and sending up great spouts of water. The spectators were certainly getting good value!

Plus 28 m.p.h.!

His hectic first run finished, Segrave stopped for the Dunlop men to change all tyres. Then a rising roar brought an excited 'Here he comes' from countless throats. Fighting swerves most of the way, Segrave blasted through, trailing a great curtain of flying sand, then wheeled round and rumbled gently back to the A.A.A. timing stand. The silence was tense, then came the announcement that he had succeeded. He had covered the flying kilometre at a mean speed of 202·988 m.p.h., the mile at 203·792 m.p.h. and the 5 kilometres at 202·675 m.p.h.!

Segrave and Sunbeam had bettered Campbell's hard-won record by over 28 m.p.h. – the biggest margin of increase ever – and Segrave was the first man to exceed 200 m.p.h. on land. The news spread over the world by wireless and cable and telephone, while at Daytona the fêting began.

Among the hundreds of cables received by Segrave was one which read 'Damn good show – Campbell'. The sender lost no time in planning to get his record back. *Bluebird* was extensively and again expensively rebuilt, with a new high-boost Napier Lion engine prepared for the Schneider Trophy air race and giving 875 b.h.p. at 3,300 r.p.m. The same chassis and suspension was used, but carrying a completely new and wind-tunnel-tested body designed by Vickers and built by Barker & Co; this had a blunt, closed-off nose, two rear-mounted surface radiators evolved by the Fairey Aviation Co, one mounted each side of the long tail, which embodied a vertical stabilizing fin – the first time such a device featured on a record car. The cockpit, though well faired in now, was still unavoidably high owing to retention of the big F.B.M. epicyclic gearbox; the wheels now wore discs and rear fairings to help reduce drag.

Like Segrave, Malcolm Campbell decided that Daytona with its comforting ten miles of sand (a pier interrupts the full 23-mile stretch) was the best place to attempt a new record now that it was over the 200 m.p.h. mark. However, *Bluebird*'s rebuild took up most of 1927, and he was not ready for action until the beginning of 1928.

Meantime the *LSR* was becoming more and more international. The mysterious French *Djelmo* (see Chapter 19) which had been under construction since 1924 at last put in an appearance in late November of 1927. It had a 10-litre, straight-eight engine and in general resembled an oversize road-racing car rather than a record-

The French 10-litre, straight-eight *Djelmo*, projected in 1924, appeared at last in 1927, when Giulio Foresti made an abortive attempt on the British national record at Pendine. The car slewed at speed and overturned, flinging Foresti (driving bareheaded) out on to the soft sand.

breaker. Fate decreed that it would never be the latter, for trouble assailed it month after month until at last, realizing that it could never approach Segrave's shattering 203·972 m.p.h., its driver Giulio Foresti decided instead to try for the British national speed record, which stood to Campbell at 174·883 m.p.h.

He chose Pendine sands for the attempt, although as usual they were waterlogged and Foresti was hard put to it to top 150 m.p.h. He had no proper, well-equipped organization behind him, and worked alone in a corrugated iron shed off the beach. Although the *Djelmo* seemed very prone to slide off course at a tangent, the dauntless Foresti, casually clad without any headgear, kept trying for a higher speed until suddenly *Djelmo* executed a worse than usual broadside, probably after hitting a soft patch of sand, and rolled over, casting her master out.

This was fortunate, as he could have suffered severe injuries in the cockpit; as it was, he hit the soft sand head first, scraping his unprotected scalp and losing some hair, and dislocating a shoulder. That was the final appearance of *Djelmo* and the last time Pendine figured in an outright land speed record attempt, although Barry Bowles ran his rocket dragster *Blonde Bombshell* there in 1978 (see Chapter 23).

Campbell tries again

By February 1928 the international element had expanded to include American contenders. The fact that Segrave had broken the record in the United States, and had his figures duly ratified by the A.I.A.C.R., encouraged new home-based challengers in the *Black Hawk* Stutz and the White Triplex. Moreover, with Daytona now up to its quarter-century of speed attempts, the Chamber of Commerce hit on the idea of a 25th Aniversary 'Speed Meet', with Campbell's *Bluebird*, the Stutz and the Triplex as the star performers, and a series of class sprints for lesser American cars.

Campbell was due to arrive in Daytona on 12th February, so the 'Meet' began the following day for an unspecified period, drawing numerous spectators who gathered day after day to watch the record-makers. Daytona beach, unfortunately, was in disappointing condition for Campbell's first attempt there, largely due to a strong, prevalent offshore wind which whipped the waves into white horses and left the beach ridged and bumpy.

The impatient Campbell contained himself for four days, then could bear it no longer, and when the weather showed some slight improvement he took *Bluebird* out on test. He soon had her moving fast, and had reached about 180 m.p.h. when he hit a terrific bump which sent the car leaping into the air for thirty feet or more. When it landed, the propeller shaft hit the seat, shooting Campbell into the air, all the shock absorber brackets broke off, and the undershield hit the sand and was ripped away.

So it was back to the workshop for a further three days for repairs, then out came Campbell again for a fast test run, on Sunday 19th February. The wind was still strong and in the wrong quarter, and the beach bumpy; but the crowds were there

1928 saw the first of several metamorphoses of Malcolm Campbell's famous record car. With boosted Napier Lion power unit and improved streamlining, it bettered Segrave's 1927 record by just over 3 m.p.h., setting the new figure at 206·956 m.p.h.

Record breaking was a major public attraction at Daytona beach, as this busy 1927 scene indicates.

in their thousands just in case. The special temporary stands were packed to capacity, marshals and police were everywhere, the banners and flags marking the measured distances flapped in the wind, and at one end the thrilling growl of an ultra-powerful engine began to unleash. Test run? Not Campbell! He decided then and there to try for the record.

Bluebird flashed into view, looking very fast indeed as it took the kilometre, then the mile, but just after crossing the final wire it hit a bad bump. Campbell was thrown half out of his seat into the airstream, which forced his goggles off his eyes and jerked his foot off the accelerator. The sudden lifting off threw the car into an enormous skid in the soft sand on the dunes side, but Campbell let it have its

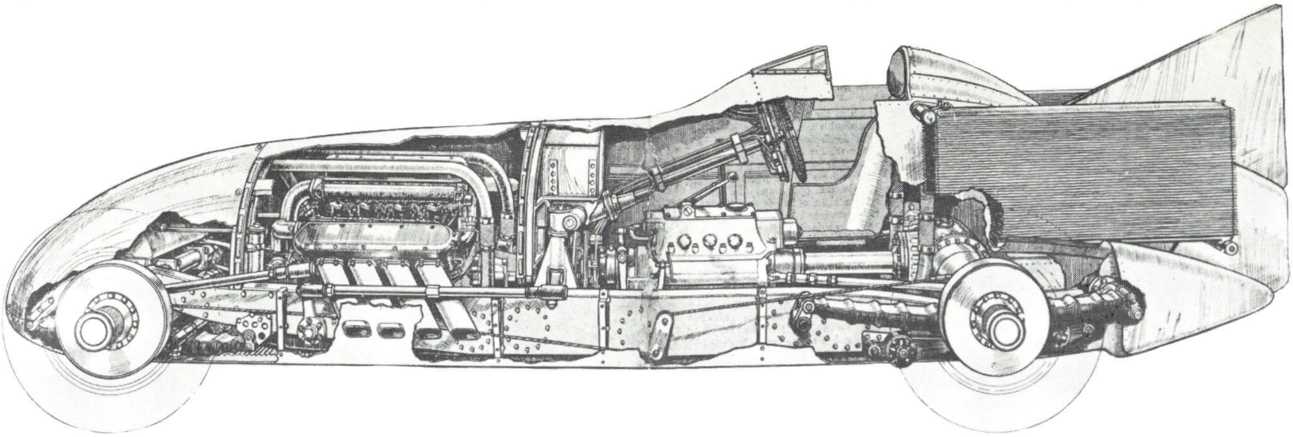

head until the speed dropped, straightened up, wheeled round and promptly started back!

He knew from his rev. counter that he had made a very fast run (a shattering 214·7 m.p.h. in fact!) and by arrangement with the Dunlop technicians he should have stopped to change tyres. Either he decided to risk it, or forgot in the long drawn out tension of that terrifying slide. Mercifully he missed the infamous bump on the return run into the wind, which was so strong that his speed was 'only' 199·9 m.p.h.; mercifully, too, his tyres held. The mean of his speeds none the less meant that he had regained the record from Segrave at 206·956 m.p.h., a comfort to Campbell, who was so utterly exhausted that he could scarcely climb from the high cockpit to receive his well-deserved plaudits.

A cutaway drawing of the Napier-Campbell *Bluebird* in its 1928 form, with sealed-off nose, two rear-mounted aircraft-type surface radiators, and a vertical tail fin. The latter was not fitted during Campbell's record attempts.

Captain Malcolm Campbell, indefatigable record hunter, looks pleased at bettering Segrave's time.

9

America and Britain fight it out

'I reiterate that a car to maintain a speed of more than 200 m.p.h. should not only have an abundance of power, but also an abundance of weight, and the longer the wheelbase the better.'

J.M. White, constructor of the White Triplex Special, 1928.

One post-World War I, 24-litre Lion engine had beaten two World War I Matabeles totalling 44·9 litres. Now two far greater extremes in capacity came out to challenge *Bluebird*. The day after Campbell set his record, ironically, was fine; the wind had changed, the sands smoothed out, and the Stutz and the Triplex made their first tentative runs. Malcolm Campbell, only part-pleased as ever with his new record and knowing his car had more in reserve, wanted to go out too, but the others had to have their turn and when, at last, his chance came round, the incoming tide spoiled it.

No two record cars could have differed more markedly than Frank Lockhart's Stutz and Ray Keech's Triplex Special; they were as different as chalk from cheese, the one the work of an artist taking the high-efficiency scientific approach, the other a barbaric example of brute force and crudity. The Stutz (see Chapter 21 for further details) was a small, exquisitely engineered, superbly streamlined machine with a supercharged 16-cylinder engine of a mere 3 litres, but giving a calculated 385 h.p. in a car weighing only 25 cwt. Frank Lockhart, its designer/driver, was only 25 but was already an Indianapolis 500 winner and had set an epic

Frank Lockhart's exquisite 3-litre, 16-cylinder Stutz *Black Hawk* which failed so dramatically at Daytona.

J.M. White's 81-litre, 36-cylinder three-engined *Triplex*–also known by some as the *Spirit of Elkdom!* – with which Ray Keech took the land speed record from Campbell at a speed of 207·55 m.p.h. on Daytona Beach in April 1928. Keech is standing by the driving seat.

world $1\frac{1}{2}$-litre mile record in 1927 at a fantastic 164·009 m.p.h. with a '91' Miller.

The White Triplex Special was the other extreme, a fearsome, primitive beast sponsored by a Philadelphia wire manufacturer named J.M. White, and using a truck chassis, steering and front axle (inverted). Most of the vehicle was occupied by engines – *three* 12-cylinder, 27-litre Liberty aircraft units, giving a total capacity of 81 litres! Two were disposed side by side behind the driver, with separate propeller shafts driving the solid rear axle by straight bevels, while the third engine was ahead of the driver, with its propeller shaft passing between the others to a third set of bevels on the solid, unsprung rear axle.

The intrepid Ray Keech demonstrates the fearsome Triplex Special's new-found ability to reverse to A.A.A. officials. The auxiliary axle can clearly be seen ahead of the rear wheels.

There was no gearbox and no clutch, the engines driving direct so that only throttle and brakes (on rear wheels only) controlled the car. The intrepid driver sat amidst this turmoil of power with precious little protection apart from a slanting, framed windscreen; the nose was pointed and 'windcutting' in the pioneer sense, and there was no tail, the massive engines and transmission being exposed as on a Formula One Grand Prix car of the late 1960s/early 1970s.

The A.A.A. officials, appalled at this creation, were probably relieved at finding a reason to prevent it running – lack of a reverse gear. But White and his men weren't that easily put off, and devised one as ludicrous as the rule itself, mounting a complete auxiliary axle with two wheels and tyres above the ground, ahead of the rear axle. By working a lever the axle was lowered to the ground and driven through a 500:1 worm gear by one of the engines at a maximum speed of under 1 m.p.h.!

Beauty and the beast

These, then, were the two machines which took to the sands of Daytona in February 1928. Lockhart, lean and light like his car, took first turn. Unluckily supercharger trouble delayed his runs until only two hours of his allotted time remained, and a soft, warm rain had been falling for some time, limiting visibility when at last he made a fast run. He accelerated like a bullet to about 200 m.p.h. when, partly because he couldn't see the course clearly, and partly, alas, because the Stutz was not so stable as it should have been, it veered suddenly to the left, then to the right, went completely out of control, double-somersaulted, and dashed into the sea to a welter of spray. Like a stone in a game of 'ducks and drakes' it skittered over the surface, then finished up on its wheels in about four feet of water, Lockhart still in the cockpit.

There was a rush of people into the sea, while a breakdown truck tore up and unsuccessfully tried to reach the stricken Stutz. In the end a human chain of

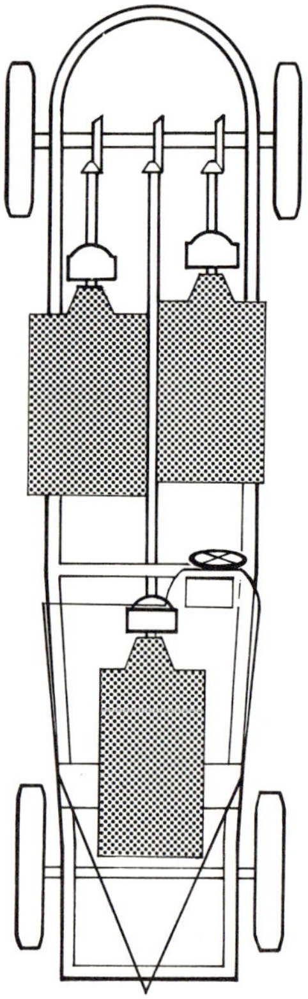

White Triplex
Location of triple engines and transmission

helpers dragged the car out bodily and rescued the trapped Lockhart. Amazingly, apart from a badly cut wrist and shock, he was little hurt, and from a hospital bed was soon planning another attempt when the car was repaired.

Next day out came Keech, massively built like his car. The triple-engined Triplex set up an animal roar as it was pushed into motion by a lorry, and soon was pulsating up and down the course as Keech limbered up for his first serious attempt at the record. When he made it, and the 4-ton monster charged down the course, a water hose in the front engine burst and badly scalded the driver's thighs so he, too, visited hospital, and with this double disappointment the 1928 Daytona 'Speed Meet' was declared closed.

Campbell returned home a record-holder again, while the Americans retired to lick their wounds. Two months later they hit back. The redoubtable Ray Keech returned to Daytona, the Triplex now fitted with a bulkhead between cockpit and engines. And for all its design crudity, the car performed well; better, indeed, than the time-keeping apparatus which clocked him against the wind at 203·97 m.p.h., then failed on the faster return run. Nor could the incensed Keech use that first time in a re-run as the statutory thirty minutes allowed between runs had elapsed before the timing gear was repaired.

There was nothing for it but to make two new runs. Keech did so, recording 201·56 m.p.h. into a very strong wind and, despite a 50 ft. flight when the *Triplex* hit a super-bump and an engine back-fire which burnt his arm, 213·9 m.p.h. with the wind. His mean speed for the flying mile was 207·552 m.p.h., beating Campbell by under 1 m.p.h. but beating him nevertheless. A very brave man had brought the *LSR* honours back to the U.S.A. for the first time, officially, since Marriott and the Stanley Steamer did their 121·57 m.p.h. in 1906. America, if not Malcolm Campbell, was overjoyed.

Eighty-one litres and 36 cylinders having made their impact, three days later Frank Lockhart with 3 litres and 16 cylinders made his bid to beat them with the repaired *Black Hawk* Stutz. The beach was in a bad state; with 'washboard' ridges left by the sea, but Lockhart would not wait for an improvement, and after a working-up run each way, he achieved 203·45 m.p.h., a tremendous velocity on only three litres, but not yet enough.

He went even faster on his return run – 225 m.p.h. was his avowed aim – but then a rear tyre burst when the Stutz was moving at perhaps 220 m.p.h. That was the end; Lockhart's lovely little white car slewed wildly and somersaulted three times, flinging its luckless creator out to almost instant death. It was a bitter end for an American genius after the most courageous David-and-Goliath struggle in *LSR* history.

Britain fights back

To have lost his hard-won record after a mere two months was naturally displeasing to Malcolm Campbell. He resolved to try again, excusing his love for 'having another go' to himself with the patriotic motives which also drove him on. The sobriquet *La Jamais Contente*, applied to old Jenatzy's electric car, epitomized Campbell too; he was never satisfied, which for Britain's sake in those days was as well. He knew *Bluebird*'s shortcomings. The chassis was over-heavy, the streamlining inadequate, and the steering troublesome, while something would have to be done about sealing the cockpit, for he had endured not only noxious engine fumes during his run but an uncomfortable sand-blasting as well from stinging sand particles which somehow found ingress. All these things would have to be put right.

Then came more dramatic news, exciting to the motoring world, worrying to Campbell. Segrave, it was announced, was to take up the challenge to Britain with an all-new car designed by J.S. Irving. Both had left Sunbeams by then, but Segrave had found wealthy sponsorship, and the car would be ready by the spring of 1929. Campbell resolved to speed up his efforts and find a new venue. Daytona was horribly expensive, even by his standards and those of 1928, and its condition too subject to the whim of wind and wave.

Campbell sought somewhere inland. He sought a long time. He considered venues in England, Wales, Ireland, Spain, Syria, Algeria, the Sahara and finally South Africa. There, 450 miles north of Cape Town, was an immense dried-up lake called Verneuk Pan. He made the fullest inquiries concerning this place, which was 37 miles long and certainly seemed the most promising so far. With encouragement from the South African Government and other local interests he decided to try for the record there early in 1929.

Meanwhile, Major Segrave's new project was progressing nicely. It was called the Irving-Napier, or popularly the *Golden Arrow*, and was a very professional

(*Below, left*) Malcolm Campbell's Napier-Campbell *Bluebird* was remodelled yet again for an attempt on the record at Verneuk Pan, South Africa in 1929. This time a new body was made at the Arrol-Aster works in Scotland.

(*Below, right*) A close-up of Bluebird's remodelled body under construction.

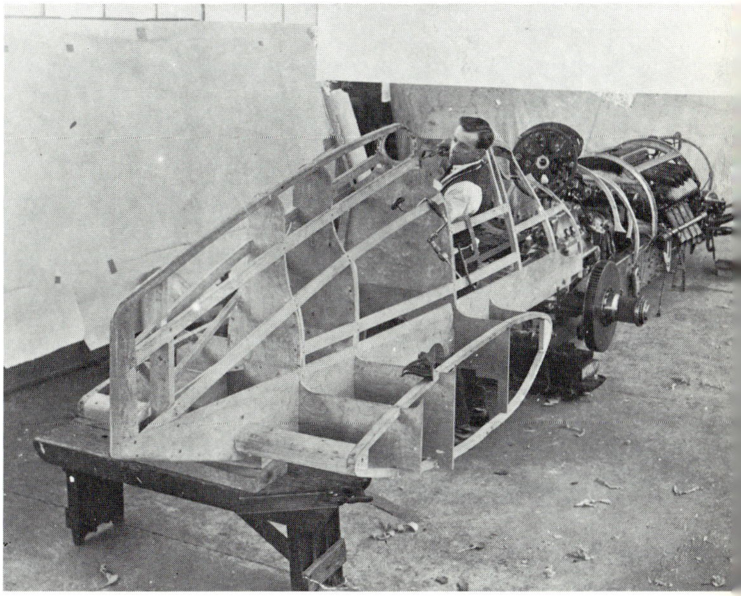

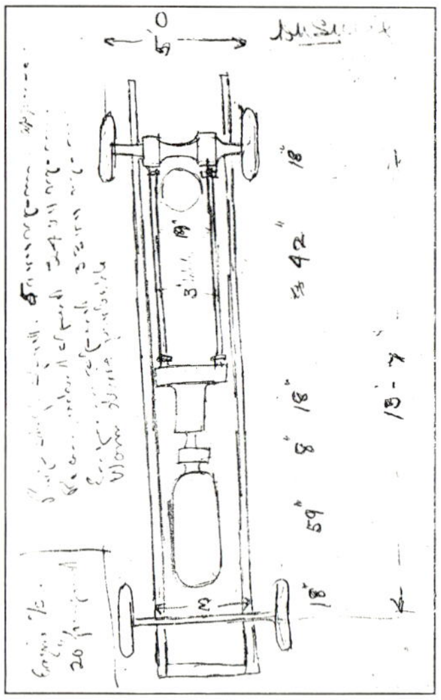

A page from *Golden Arrow* designer Captain J.S. Irving's sketchbook, showing projected twin propeller shaft transmission.

Golden Arrow
Location of engine and transmission

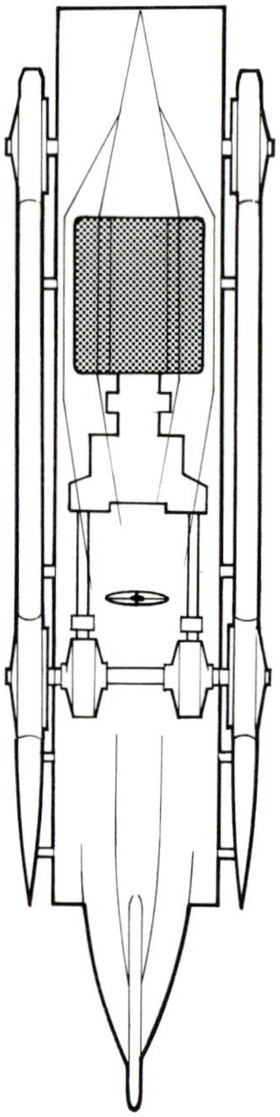

piece of work indeed. Following Campbell's example, Segrave and Irving went to Napiers to hire an engine, a Schneider Trophy unsupercharged racing unit as used in one of the winning Supermarine seaplanes. It gave 925 b.h.p. at 3,300 r.p.m., or slightly more than the 1927 '1,000 h.p.' Sunbeam; and Irving, using his experience with that car as a yardstick, reasoned that to attain an ideal 240 m.p.h. a reduction in frontal area of almost 40 per cent would be required.

So instead of a full-width, wheel-enveloping body he prescribed a car with separately faired wheels, full-depth inter-axle sponsons housing aircraft-type surface radiators, and a bonnet fitting tightly around the three cylinder banks of the engine, as on the 1927 Supermarine S5 aircraft it was borrowed from. A wind-tunnel model helped to develop the final shape, which included a long driver's head-fairing and a vertical tail fin for directional stability. As a precaution, since they were using an untried cooling system, Irving arranged supplementary ice-cooling as used by Frank Lockhart in his Stutz, but thermostatically controlled.

When news of the car circulated, Irving was offered the use, free of charge, of a 1,250 h.p. aero-engine from a foreign manufacturer (no name was ever disclosed but it would most probably have been Fiat). However the all-British nature of the project and their sponsorship commitments already completed meant they had reluctantly to refuse.

Like other distinguished record cars before her, *Golden Arrow* was built at K.L.G.'s Robin Hood works at Putney Vale. Irving designed a special multi-plate clutch with servo assistance (an example subsequently adopted by private car makers), a very compact three-speed gearbox was used, with double drive to twin Hardy-Spicer propeller shafts, and twin bevel final drives without differentials. The object of this duplication was to seat the driver lower between the propeller shafts, which were contra-rotating to obtain a balanced torque effect.

A beam-type tubular front axle made in three parts was employed, with free-sliding semi-elliptic springs, the axle being located by a radius arm linked with a cross-tube. These springs were neatly contained within the flanges of an extremely strong channel-section chassis, while the rear springs were, in fact, two quarter-elliptics clamped lengthwise together by a central casing which also retained the rear axle tube. Special tyres with $\frac{1}{16}$ in. of smooth rubber tread were developed for the car by Dunlops, these being inflated to 125 lb. p.s.i. The body was built by Thrupp & Maberly in aluminium sheeting, the entire car being finished in beautiful gold.

Showing them how

The Irving-Napier was a striking example of professional design and construction, and the actual record operation in 1929 was to similar standards of efficiency. Indeed, few record-breaking ventures can have gone through so slickly and free of snags, giving the U.S.A. a wonderful lesson from 'decadent old England' in professional ability. After a two-way practice run when he attained about 180

The Irving-Napier *Golden Arrow*, one of the most striking record cars of all time, was powered by a 925 h.p. Napier Lion engine. This engine drove the rear wheels from a position set low between the twin propeller shafts, which were located on either side of the driver's seat.

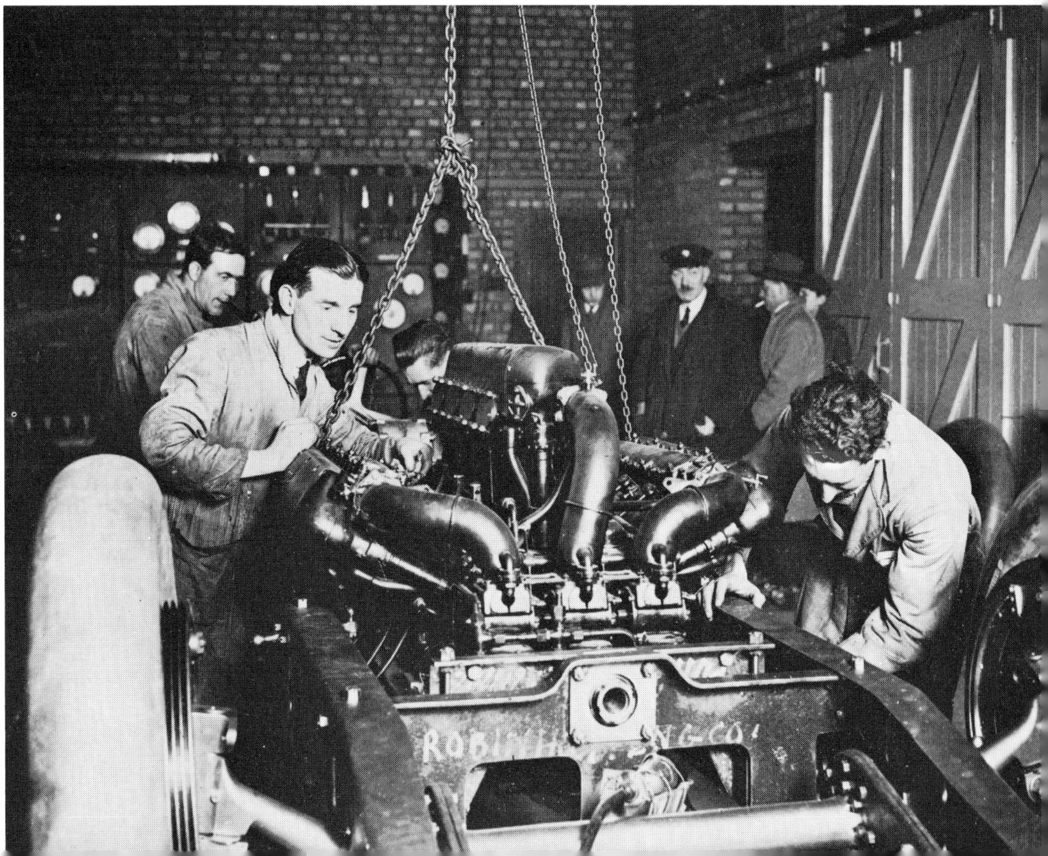

Chassis view of the *Golden Arrow* at the Robin Hood Works of K.L.G. at Putney Vale shows the massive frame construction.

Major Henry Segrave setting the new land speed record at 231·446 m.p.h. in the Irving-Napier *Golden Arrow* at Daytona in March 1929. Segrave was knighted for his achievement.

m.p.h. without finding any serious troubles, Segrave was obliged to wait for a fourteen-day spell of bad weather to blow itself out before he could attempt the record.

The crowd which turned out to watch 'the mad Major' was colossal, being reckoned at between 100,000 and 120,000, and if the figures were American exaggeration it was a vast concourse at even half the number. The marking of the course was this time assisted by powerful red arc lights slung centrally above, between great 50-ft. high trestles at each end of the mile. The beach was not at its best after so much rough sea, with many bumps and ripples, and a faint sea mist lurked in the background. To Segrave, waiting to start, all this was of vital importance, but to the expectant crowd in the dunes and the temporary stands, only the spectacle of the great car in action mattered.

The announcement 'He's started' ended their vigil. There came the deep drone, as of a fighter aircraft diving, as *Golden Arrow* sped into view, a blast of sound and a welter of sand and spray, the car leaping as it hit a bump, then Segrave was through the mile in 15·55 sec. and out of sight. The bump caused an aircock in the cooling system to break away, releasing a thin spray of near-boiling water over the screen, so Segrave switched the coolant temporarily through the reserve ice tanks which Irving had installed, and the broken cock was swiftly plugged during his stop for tyres.

In six minutes he was off again and aiming for the all-important measured mile. There came the car, bulleting past, the shattering exhaust roar in vain pursuit, the sting and patter of falling sand, the whiff of the special B.P. 'dope' fuel, the sound falling away, and everyone impatiently awaited the times. At last came the news of '15·57 seconds', slightly slower than his first run, but quick enough to take America's record away from her comfortably. The A.A.A. were nothing if not thorough. When they announced Segrave's mean speed they gave it to five places of decimals – 231·36246 m.p.h., they said, almost 24 m.p.h. faster than Keech's Triplex. Then they had to rethink and altered it to 231·446 m.p.h., rubbing slightly more salt into the wound.

Next day the Triplex itself came out to try to retrieve the honours. The driver was not Ray Keech this time; he had declined to drive the 81-litre monster any more. Instead a plucky 'outlaw' racing-driver named Lee Bible, who also worked for Jim White as a mechanic on the car, was at the wheel. He clocked an opening run at 183 m.p.h., then speeded up to 202 m.p.h. on the return leg. Unhappily he lifted off too suddenly beyond the mile, and the retarding effect of those three great Liberty motors was like a savage brake, throwing the car off-line into a huge ground loop. The Triplex skidded, ran down a cinematograph operator named Charles Traub, then rolled madly over and over, pitching Lee Bible out and shedding its wheels one by one. When the frantic crowd reached them, both Bible and Traub were dead. Ironically, had Traub not run from his camera he would have survived. The behemoth had headed straight for his tripod, but swerved away at the very last moment, striking him as he fled.

Brave garage mechanic cum 'outlaw' racer Lee Bible stands alongside the Triplex Special, shortly before the accident in which he and cinematograph operator Charles Traub were to lose their lives.

10

The indefatigable Campbell

'We should consider ourselves to be very lucky in that the present-day racing aero-engine is so admirably shaped for fitting into a motor-car.'

Reid A. Railton in THE MOTOR, *1 August 1933.*

Down at Verneuk Pan, South Africa, Malcolm Campbell was having a dreadful time. The car and fifty-six cases of spares, the mechanics, a Dunlop technician, two time-keepers and official R.A.C. time-keeping equipment had all arrived in South Africa. The proposed course, remote from civilization, was far from 'the ideal track' some advisers had told him it was. The mud surface was full of sharp particles of shell which would cut a racing-tyre to ribbons, and there were doubts about the effects of its altitude – some 2,500 feet above sea level – on engine efficiency.

Campbell secured the services of a road-making expert who advised removing the entire top-surface of the Pan for a strip of about twelve miles and relaying it with clay – a prodigious undertaking which required capital and labour. Somehow Campbell found both; the South African Government and the cities of Cape Town and Johannesburg all contributed money, another town sent him a steamroller free, while he managed to hire local labour. Had Campbell known Dutch, the meaning of the word *Verneuk* might have had more significance for him. It means 'cheat', 'deception' or 'fraud', and probably applied to the mirages with which the Pan lured travellers on.

Malcolm Campbell in *Bluebird* raises the dust during his unsuccessful attempt on the *LSR* at Verneuk Pan, May 1929.

During the next few weeks he was involved in an air crash while surveying the course, badly cutting his nose and mouth, and wrecking the plane. The camp in the Pan was flooded out by the first rain in five years, food and water had to be rationed, and the labourers refused to work because they believed there was a hoodoo on the place. It seemed they were right. Next Campbell got the news that Segrave had raised the record to 231·446 m.p.h., and had been knighted for the deed. Then the South African press began campaigning against 'this expensive farce' and 'mad scheme', but Campbell was too deeply committed and pressed on.

His wife returned to England and wired the depressing news that frost had burst all the pipes in their Surrey house and ruined the boilers, doing hundreds of pounds worth of damage, and next Campbell had problems getting *Bluebird* up from Cape Town, as the transport firm concerned grew tired of waiting and sold the special six-wheeled Thornycroft lorry they had agreed to hire him.

The car itself had been modified once again, this time by the Arrol-Aster concern of Dumfries. The surface radiators had been replaced by a normal nose radiator with a pointed, pencil-like grille, and the streamlining was improved, practically if not aesthetically, by a more enclosed cockpit, lower bonnet and deeper tail. When at last the course was ready, and the car brought up on a hastily improvized lorry, action began with the first tests. Alas, *Bluebird*'s 3-ton weight quickly broke through the laboriously laid clay top-surface on to the sharp shale, and they began using up tyres at an alarming rate.

Campbell therefore lost no time in making his actual record attempt, though he must have known his chances of beating Segrave's new speed were slim. The unsupercharged Lion engine was an estimated 11 per cent down on power at that altitude, and so far 215 m.p.h. was the best speed he had reached. In compensation he planned to attack the 5-mile and 5-kilometre records (which worried the Dunlop engineer considerably in view of the tyre situation) and the British mile (South Africa then being in the Empire).

He set 21st April for the attempt, and one local optimist sent up 80,000 bottles of beer to cope with the thirst of the anticipated crowd. But Verneuk Pan was too far from anywhere and only a few hundred hardy spectators turned up. Then the weather turned sour. A strong side wind, dust storms and heavy rain showers delayed things for three days and Campbell, wondering what else that devilish Pan could offer, went clearly mad with frustration. Things cleared on 24th April and he was out at the crack of dawn, the time-keepers took up their posts, *Bluebird* was started up, and the attempt was on.

Malcolm Campbell gave the car its full head all the way through the five miles, trailing a heavy plume of dust and then, to the alarm and despondency of the Dunlop man, plunged straight back on to the return run without changing tyres. But *Bluebird* just had no more performance in reserve. Its mean speed through the kilometre was 217·6 m.p.h., through the mile 217·52 m.p.h., through the 5 kilometres just over 217 m.p.h. and through the 5 miles just over 212 m.p.h. At the end the rear tyres were down to the inner cords but they never burst.

At a personal cost of about £7,000 for the attempt alone, and much discomfort, Campbell had gained three unimportant records – the British mile and the world's 5-kilometre and 5-mile, but he hadn't broken the land speed record, the only one he really wanted. Verneuk Pan, truly a lake of deception, could only be written off as an expensive failure.

The big flop

Still they came, the new contenders for the title of 'world's fastest'. Sir Henry Segrave had renounced cars for boats and land for water, but now Louis Coatalen, creator of the 4-litre and 1,000 h.p. Sunbeams, came forward with an obvious retort to the *Golden Arrow* in the *Silver Bullet*. This was an astonishing machine of an alleged 4,000 h.p., having two 12-cylinder supercharged engines coupled in tandem in a vast car weighing over 4½ tons (see Chapter 19 for further details).

It was to be driven by Brooklands expert Kaye Don, who was destined to have a miserable and frustrating trip to Daytona in March 1930. For all its publicity, its 'specially designed' engines and its Sunbeam pedigree, the *Silver Bullet* just wouldn't perform properly, largely owing to engine troubles centred on the supercharging and induction system, and faulty weight distribution.

With a recalcitrant machine and a very bumpy beach, the highest timed speed Don reached was 186·046 m.p.h., way below the current record. A thoroughly unpleasant sojourn in Florida, with acrimony within the team and outside, ended in car, driver and crew returning unhonoured and unsung to England, with the *Silver Bullet* going down in *LSR* history, not only as one of the biggest record cars, but also as one of its biggest 'lemons'.

The plight of Sunbeam's much publicized record car was, naturally, meat and drink to the hyper-patriotic Campbell, happy to have the extra justification of 'saving Britain's face' in taking yet another crack at the record himself. Once again *Bluebird* was stripped to her component parts, and this time Campbell secured the services of Reid A. Railton, a young engineer at Thomson & Taylor of Brooklands, who had worked with Parry Thomas in his later days.

Campbell's aim was to exceed 250 m.p.h., so the first thing Railton prescribed was more power. Napier were agreeable to hiring out one of their 1929 supercharged Napier Lion racing engines, which put out an impressive 1,450 b.h.p. at 3,600 r.p.m., so the next thing Railton did was to throw out the big F.B.M. epicyclic gearbox which governed the height of Campbell's seating position. He replaced it with a K.L.G.-built 3-speed box, offset to one side by gears, with the driver seated beside it; the propeller shaft and final drive were also offset 7 inches and thus the whole design was lowered.

The old chassis, suspension and steering were retained, but the high, ugly body was discarded for a very shapely new one, built in thirty-six days by Gurney, Nutting & Co. on a framework of steel tubes. The radiator was outrigged on the nose in an isolated housing, its outlet ducts discharging hot air ahead of the engine cover in

Malcolm Campbell's *Bluebird* in its sleek 1931 form, redesigned by Reid Railton and bodied by Gurney, Nutting & Co. Changes included a Schneider Trophy-type Napier Lion engine giving 1,450 b.h.p., offset transmission, and an isolated radiator.

modern Formula I fashion, and the new tail embodied a high stabilizing fin.

The front wheels were still exposed but fitted with after-fairings, and the rear wheels were shrouded both sides. So low was the car now that the steering column was horizontal. A special Triplex glass windshield, steeply inclined and with side pieces, plus a form of cockpit ventilation, made things a lot more comfortable for Malcolm Campbell. Once again Dunlop produced the special tyres, new disc wheels were designed and made, and Ace wheel discs set off this most handsome of *Bluebirds*.

During its construction at Thomson & Taylor at Brooklands, the grim news came that Sir Henry Segrave had lost his life while attacking the world water speed record on Lake Windermere.

Malcolm Campbell's 1931 visit to Daytona was very much a repetition of Segrave's masterly 1929 operation for sheer slickness. Apart from two practice frights, one when a group of spectators somehow got on to the course, the other when the car jumped out of top gear and sent the rev. counter panicking round to its maximum, it was a model performance.

Four miles a minute – and a knighthood

On Thursday, 5 February 1931 the course was bumpy, wet and misty when Campbell brought *Bluebird* out for his attempt to better the *Golden Arrow*'s

231·446 m.p.h. He had his full Daytona quota of bumps and slews, but he clocked a determined 246·575 m.p.h. on the run out, and an equally determined 244·897 m.p.h. on the return mile – a mean of 246·09 m.p.h., and the first time four miles per minute had been exceeded on land. Campbell did not stop for tyres between runs, and the whole mission was accomplished in under five minutes! Malcolm Campbell, long accustomed to adversity, could scarcely believe it.

When he got back to England he was greeted at Southampton by a flight of aircraft which dipped their wings in salute. On landing he was informed that His Majesty the King had graciously consented to Campbell being knighted for his achievements on behalf of Britain, and he was taken to London in a special train, the '*Bluebird* Special', for a Government reception at Westminster Hall. Campbell's cup of bliss was full. He was then 46 and had broken the *LSR* five times; had he decided then to hang up his helmet none could have blamed him, but once again this remarkable man was not satisfied. 245·7 m.p.h. was so close to 250, and *Bluebird* could do it easily. Already he was thinking ahead to 1932. . . .

Around that time came news of a new, unexpected but welcome challenger from 'down under'. An Australian endurance driver, Norman 'Wizard' Smith, planned to take a new Napier Lion-engined car called the *Fred H. Stewart Enterprise* (see Chapter 19 for more details) to Ninety Mile Beach at the top end of New Zealand's North Island to attack world records. Fred Stewart, a Sydney businessman, sponsored the attempt, and Don Harkness, a Sydney engineer, designed the car,

Campbell raised the record to 246·09 m.p.h. in the remodelled *Bluebird* at Daytona, February 1931. The feat earned him a knighthood.

A cutaway drawing of the 1931 Napier Lion-engined *Bluebird*.

which was very similar to the Irving-Napier *Golden Arrow* of 1929, apart from twin tail-fins also serving as rear-wheel fairings, and cooling differences.

The unfortunate Smith met almost as much trouble as Kaye Don in 1930, though he managed to set up a world 10-mile record at 164·084 m.p.h. early in 1932. As a venue Ninety Mile Beach (which was actually about 40 miles long) proved far from ideal, the sand containing countless tiny but destructive shells, while heavy seas soaked the course for weeks on end. Wizard Smith's great aim was the mile – *the* record – but conditions never improved sufficiently and he had to give up.

Apart from that, and some light relief from France in the shape of an incredible machine called the Stapp, which had three Bristol Jupiter radial aircraft engines and four-wheel drive (see Chapter 20 for more details), the years 1931 to 1935 were very much a Campbell benefit, for although reports of new challengers from the United States were bruited around, times were not auspicious for expensive new record-breaking machines and nothing came of any of them, (see Chapter 20).

The year 1932 was comparatively restful for the Campbell *équipe*, but the 250 m.p.h.-plus lure was strong and he went out to Daytona with *Bluebird* just mildly modified. It had a new nose of Grand Prix handsomeness (indeed, it anticipated the

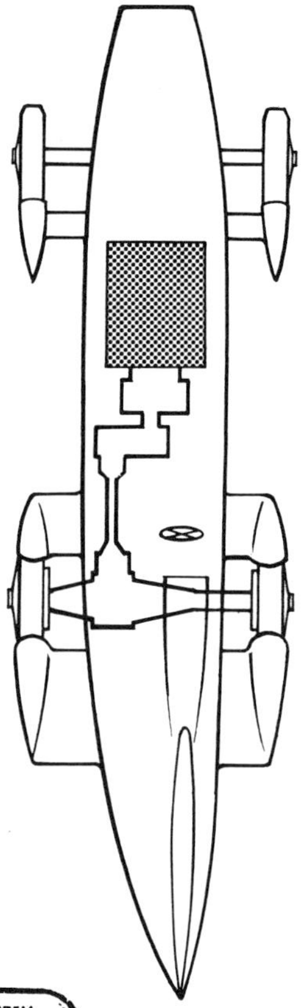

(*Above*)
Bluebird (1931)
Location of engine and transmission

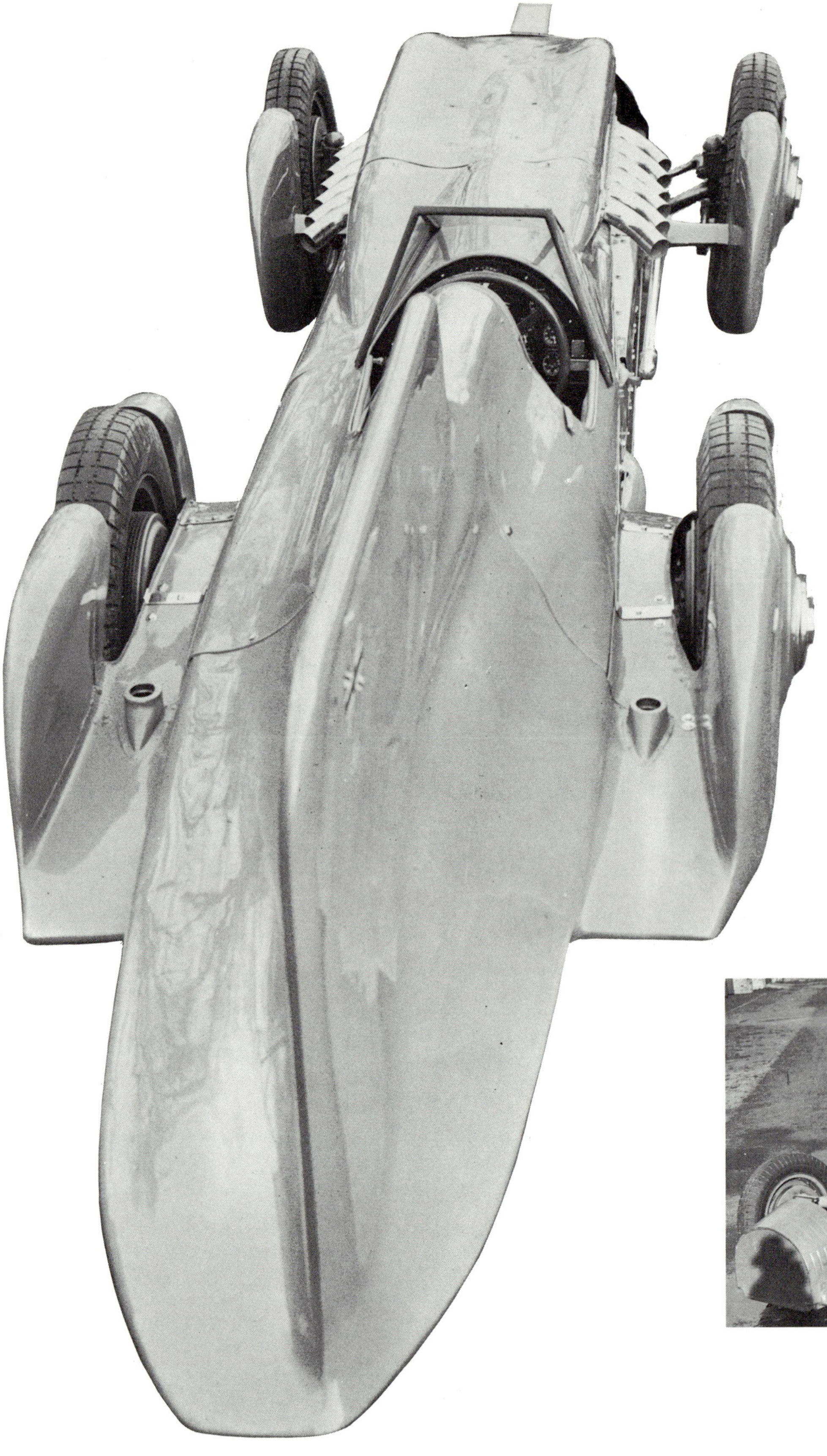

This rear view of the 1933 Rolls-Royce-engined *Bluebird* shows the twelve stub exhausts and the offset bodywork. Sir Malcolm Campbell improved his own record to 272·108 m.p.h. in February of that year. (*Below*) For 1933 Campbell's *Bluebird* had its Napier engine replaced by a 36½-litre Rolls-Royce R-type racing unit.

shape of the later 'thirties) and some small gearbox improvements, sufficient in all for Sir Malcolm to raise the mile by almost 8 m.p.h. to 253·97 m.p.h., with new 5-mile, 5-kilometre and 10-kilometre records thrown in for good measure.

In a *Bluebird* only slightly modified, Sir Malcolm Campbell bettered his own record to 253·97 m.p.h. in February 1932.

A new engine for 'Bluebird'

1933 was more serious, with the faithful Napier Lion at last ousted in favour of a 36½-litre, 2,300 b.h.p. Rolls-Royce V12 R-type supercharged engine, as used to win the 1931 Schneider Trophy air race. Reid Railton of Thomson & Taylor did a superb job of adapting this powerful unit to the existing chassis; a new clutch was fitted, and the body modified to provide a new ram-jet nose intake for the engine, and to accommodate its diverse bulges.

With speeds ever rising, Daytona's effective distance was getting shorter, and the much increased power in *Bluebird* would give greater acceleration in a shorter distance. There were the usual Daytona problems when the Campbell *équipe* made their annual trek – bumps, soft patches and mist; but Campbell, master of his craft as ever, broke his own mile record at a mean of 272·46 m.p.h., the kilometre at 271·636 m.p.h., and the 5-kilometre at 257·295 m.p.h.

Need one add that Sir Malcolm was disappointed? Interviewed on a popular Saturday night wireless programme on his return, he explained that he had strained his wrist while changing gear in practice, and had considerable wheel-spin during the record run, ripping up his tyres – 'though Dunlops did a wonderful job'. Was he worried about other countries taking his record? No, he didn't think so. In fact, he wouldn't mind if they did – it would give him something extra to go for! Was he not considering giving up record-breaking now that he had the record so firmly? No, he wanted Britain to keep the record, and if any foreign car took it away he'd have a crack at getting it back. How far did he think the record could go beyond the 272·46 m.p.h. he had just reached at Daytona? There was no telling, but he personally would get great satisfaction if he could raise it to over 300. . . .

11

From sand to salt

'We were alone in the world; the immensity and the solitude were overpowering; the velocity of the car was fantastic; ahead of us was the horizon, and when we reached it we would topple off into nothingness.'

William D. Rishel, describing a run across the Bonneville salt flats in 1909 at 50 m.p.h.

In 1934 even Sir Malcolm Campbell took a holiday from land speed record-breaking, giving Reid Railton a chance to plan another extensive rebuild of *Bluebird* in comfortable time for 1935. 300 m.p.h. was the target, of course, and this time a very clean, full-width, wheel-enveloping body was designed; the sides were vertical, the new nose broad and flat, and the slot-shaped radiator intake could be blanked off for maximum velocity in the actual measured mile. Underneath this sleek new envelope the greatest innovation was the use, for the first time on a record car, of twin rear wheels, mounted on a novel divided axle with two bevel final drives without differentials.

Idealist Railton also reluctantly resorted to weighting the rear of the frame with lead, further to decrease the demon wheel-spin. The car now scaled 5 tons. The chassis was stiffened up, a new front axle located by radius arms was fitted, and a pair of ingenious airbrakes installed, lying flush in the fairing just behind the rear wheels and servo-operated through the brake pedal. A revised, simpler steering system was fitted, the cockpit was equipped with aircraft-type safety harness, and in all this was a very competent revision of what could be called classic, almost retrograde *LSR* design.

(*Opposite*) In 1935 Sir Malcolm Campbell's famous record car, *Bluebird*, was rebuilt yet again, being fitted with full-width bodywork and twin rear wheels.

(*Below*) In 1984 this interesting wind-tunnel model of the 1935 *Bluebird* surfaced, indicating that Railton had more than one idea for the nose shape.

The fitting of airbrakes in the body surfaces of *Bluebird* behind the rear wheels was an innovation. They are shown here both *in situ* and raised. The offset body meant the flaps were of unequal width.

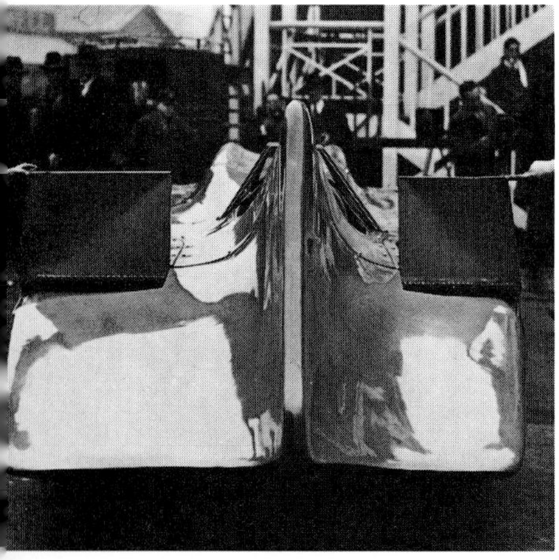

Since Campbell met most of the cost of these rebuilds himself, he could not be blamed for retaining the old frame and suspension, although undoubtedly these were limiting factors in *Bluebird*'s performance. The semi-elliptic springs gave scarcely more than one inch of movement up and down, so that one wonders whether Railton considered dispensing with them altogether and running on solid unsprung axles, as did J. M. White's Triplex at the rear.

It was unfortunate that German engineers, flushed with the success of the all-independently-sprung Mercedes-Benz and Auto Union Grand Prix cars at that time, should criticize *Bluebird*'s antiquated design beneath that superb 1935 body shell as an instance of British technical shortcomings. They never realized (or perhaps they never wanted to realize?) that it was a private venture, paid for largely out of private pockets. Fortunately Reid Railton was soon to give them a very satisfactory answer.

He once again accompanied Sir Malcolm and *Bluebird* to Florida in January of 1935, with 300 m.p.h. the great object of the exercise. Alas, Daytona's sands were capricious again, and Campbell had to wait eight long weeks before a run was

possible. On 7th March a favourable tide left the beach in just passable condition and the almost desperate Campbell went out to essay the record. The course was very bumpy and soft in patches, and repeated wheel-spin dissipated a valuable proportion of *Bluebird*'s 2,350 b.h.p. – and most of the $\frac{1}{16}$ in. of rubber on the Dunlop tyres.

By the end of his first run, at 272·727 m.p.h., Campbell's tyres were virtually devoid of tread. He was faster on the return leg despite hitting a boggy patch which sent *Bluebird* slewing sideways, and incessant bumps which had the car airborne for much of the (almost literally) flying mile. His speed was 281·03 m.p.h., giving a mean of 276·816 m.p.h. after a highly uncomfortable drive.

A miserable 4 m.p.h. increase after all that waiting would have disappointed anyone, let alone Campbell. He stayed on a further fortnight in hopes of better conditions, but in vain. Daytona, it was clear, was now finished as a land speed record venue, and Campbell, more determined than ever to get that 300 m.p.h. before retiring, looked north-west of Florida towards the State of Utah for his final motoring endeavour.

Campbell taking the land speed record for the eighth time, in the Rolls-Royce-engined *Bluebird* at Daytona in 1935. His speed on a bumpy course was 276·816 m.p.h

The great salt waste

In the vast patchwork that makes up the United States between the Atlantic and the Pacific Oceans, boxed in by Nevada, Idaho, Wyoming, Colorado, Arizona and New Mexico, lies Utah, the Mormon State. Through the centre, like a backbone, are the Wasatch mountains, and west of them, in the north of Utah, is the Great Salt Lake. This is the surviving part of what was once a far larger stretch of water measuring some 300 miles by 150, called Lake Bonneville, but with the passing of time this lake dried up completely, leaving an immense desert of salt. They call it the Bonneville salt flats.

The flats, seemingly limitless and with a grim mountain background like a moonscape, were first traversed mechanically by railway in 1909. To ensure a water supply for the locomotives they ran a pipe-line some 35 miles from the mountains to a point on the western edge of the salt near the Nevada border, and there a settlement called Wendover grew around the pipe. Then the Lincoln motor highway was built, linking Salt Lake City with Wendover and, far to the west, San Francisco.

So immense are the Bonneville flats that the curvature of the earth is clearly apparent. In summer they are parched, intensely hot, glaringly white, and were lethal in earlier days to foot travellers lured on by tempting mirages and the desperate need for water never found. In the winter when it rains, however, the water sits on top of the salt, never drains, and takes days to evaporate. A desolate, uncharitable place, Bonneville, but ideal (apart from its height of 4,218 ft. above sea level, its climatic whims, and the treacherous mush areas surrounding the hard core) for at least one thing – setting up car speed records.

Only its remoteness prevented its earlier use. The first record-breaking ever essayed there was in 1914 and involved our old friend the *Blitzen* Benz, driven by a noted leadfoot of the day named 'Terrible' Teddy Tetzlaff. His aim was to break Bob Burman's notorious flying mile American record of 141·37 m.p.h., set up in the same Benz at Daytona, and by stop-watch Tetzlaff did the distance in 25·4 sec., $\frac{1}{5}$ sec. faster than Burman, at 141·73 m.p.h. Stop-watch times only? The A.A.A. didn't want to know, while it is doubtful if the distant A.I.A.C.R. ever even heard about it.

Then Ab Jenkins, noted Mormon driver, began attacking long-distance records on a big circular course he laid out on the salt in 1932, and the fame of the flats became international when John Cobb took out his 23-litre Napier-Railton, built for Brooklands track work, in July 1935, and set up numerous long-distance class records. It needed little persuasion for two other 'record regulars' in Sir Malcolm Campbell and Captain George Eyston to visit Bonneville a month later, and Campbell was entranced, not by the desolation and limitless space, but the chance of breaking the 300 m.p.h. barrier at last.

Campbell's last great ride

Examining the flats carefully, Sir Malcolm was worried at first by the rough appearance of the salt, but Cobb and others assured him that it was not so destructive to tyres as he imagined. So he had *Bluebird*, unaltered since her Daytona frustrations, brought to Wendover, and lost no time in preparing for his attempt at 300 m.p.h. A 12-mile straight stretch of salt was scraped smooth, and a thick black guide-line of oil was laid down the centre. On his first high speed try-out Campbell easily attained 240 m.p.h. and was delighted. There were none of Daytona's appalling bumps, tide ripples or soft patches to worry about; although on the other hand, he had to admit, there was none of the civilization of Florida within easy reach either.

On 3 September 1935, early in the morning before the summer sun was too powerful, he made his attack. At 100 m.p.h. he changed into second gear, at 200 m.p.h. into top, and as he entered the measured mile he closed the radiator inlet. The screen almost instantly filmed with oil, and choking fumes entered the cockpit, but dauntlessly he forced on through the mile. Dizzy from fumes, he momentarily lost the guide-line, swerved, found it again, and then a front tyre burst. Despite a wrist still strapped up after Daytona he held the car, braked hard and stopped, the tyre ablaze. His speed through the mile was 304·311 m.p.h.

Captain Eyston's chief mechanic and co-driver Bert Denly, who was present as a helper, played an extinguisher on the fire while the Dunlop crew changed the other five tyres. They had to wait for the sixth wheel to cool before removing it, but at last Sir Malcolm was ready to go again – when news came of a broken timing wire. Campbell fretted in the baking cockpit, but at last, with five minutes to go before time ran out (at his request the A.I.A.C.R. had increased inter-run servicing time to one hour), he was given the O.K.

He did not use the radiator shutter this time, but he had his foot hard down right through the mile. Anxious about the braking distance to the railway embankment ahead, he braked too suddenly, putting *Bluebird* into a broadside, catching it, and stopping. His rev. counter told him he had just broken the 300 m.p.h. mark on the run back, and thus his mean speed as given by the A.A.A. time-keepers was an intense disappointment – 299·87 m.p.h.

He resolved immediately to try again the following morning, but two hours later was told by the A.A.A.'s chief official that there had been an error in their calculations. They had assessed his time for the second mile as 12·18 sec. whereas it was actually 12·08 sec. His two speeds were 304·311 m.p.h. and 297·947 m.p.h., and thus his average *was* over 300 m.p.h. – 301·129, in fact. Instead of being delighted, Campbell was furious, for the thrill of the accomplishment had become mere anticlimax.

None the less, his goal was achieved. Interviewed by the British magazine *The Motor* in 1933, Campbell had said, 'For my own part I shall never be happy until I have reached the 300 m.p.h. mark, and if I am lucky enough to do this, I shall then retire from the arena.' Now he had done it. It was his ninth and final *LSR*, and thereafter this incredible 50-year-old man devoted his energies to the water speed record. He was still doing so at 63 in 1948, the year he died.

Enter a 'Thunderbolt'

Captain George Eyston was a close friend of Ernest Eldridge, *LSR* holder in 1924 and, like him, a professional records man, a fine engineer, and an exceedingly level-headed driver. He knew all about long-distance class figures, he knew Montlhéry track, outside Paris, even better than Brooklands – the French called him *Le Recordman* – and he garnered literally hundreds of class records with all manner of cars such as Rileys, Bugattis, M.G.s, a Chrysler, a Hotchkiss and a Panhard-Levassor.

In 1935, the year Sir Malcolm Campbell retired, Eyston graduated to a larger record car, specially constructed and called *Speed of the Wind*. He largely designed it himself; it had a single Rolls-Royce Kestrel aero-engine driving the front wheels, and was not fast enough for the land speed record. He had not built it with that in mind; his aim was long-distance Class A (over 8 litres) figures, and with a big reserve of power the car was wonderfully reliable, bringing him much success, first at Montlhéry, later at Bonneville.

It was inevitable that Eyston's thoughts would eventually turn to the land speed record – *the* record in the eyes of the public, and one worth having for its financial rewards, let alone the satisfaction of being 'fastest on earth'. The ambition was there, and some shrewd ideas for the right sort of car to do it too, so when offers of sponsorship came early in 1937 Eyston speedily turned paper plans into metal.

Almost as much at home in France as in England, he had talked over his ideal layout with an engineer from the Peugeot works, had the body design completed by the French coach-builder and aerodynamicist Jean Andreau, and got construction of the car under way at the Bean works at Tipton, Staffs, all in the space of weeks. There was no gentle mulling over the design of *Thunderbolt*, as Eyston's record car came to be called; once sub-contracted, components began coming in; it was a rush job, assembled in six weeks, an incredible feat for such a complex machine.

Although *Thunderbolt* was the largest petrol-engined record car of all, with two supercharged Rolls-Royce Schneider Trophy racing engines having a combined displacement of 73 litres and an output of about 4,700 h.p., eight wheels and a weight of close on 7 tons, it was no crude monster. Given more time for design and construction it could have looked better than it did, but its specification was certainly enterprising, and a refreshing change from the by then monotonous *LSR* formula of one large engine in a lorry-like chassis, well streamlined but only nominally suspended.

Within its whale-like exterior were all sorts of technical surprises. Of the eight wheels, four were at the front, all steering as on a modern 'twin-steer' lorry, and

Colour Plates

THE RECORD BREAKERS

Sunbeam 350 h.p., May 1922

Delage, July 1924

Fiat, July 1924

Sunbeam, 1924 and 1925

Sunbeam, March 1926

Babs, April 1927

Napier-Campbell *Bluebird*, February 1927

Sunbeam 1,000 h.p., March 1927

Napier-Campbell *Bluebird*, February 1928

White Triplex, April 1928

Irving-Napier *Golden Arrow*, March 1929

Bluebird, February 1931

Bluebird, February 1933

Bluebird, March and September 1935

Thunderbolt, November 1937 and August 1938

Thunderbolt, September 1938

Railton, September 1938, August 1939 and September 1947

Spirit of America, August 1963 and October 1964

Bluebird-Proteus, July 1964

Wingfoot Express, October 1964

Green Monster, October 1964 and November 1965

Goldenrod, November 1965

Spirit of America-Sonic 1, November 1965

The Blue Flame, October 1970

Budweiser Rocket, December 1979

Thrust 2, October 1983

THE UNRECOGNISED AND THE UNLUCKY

Mercedes *Flying Dutchman*, January 1905

Packard, February 1919

SUNBEAM 350 H.P.
May 1922, 133·75 m.p.h. (215·25 k.p.h.)
Driven by Kenelm Lee Guinness
V12, single o.h.c., 18·3-litre, 350 b.h.p engine; four-speed gearbox; shaft final drive.

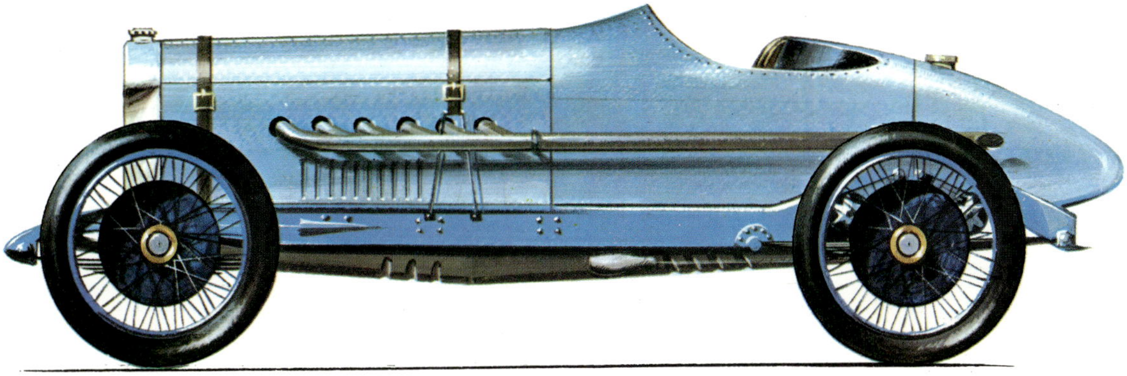

DÉLAGE
July 1924, 143·31 m.p.h. (230·634 k.p.h.)
Driven by René Thomas
V12, o.h.v., 10·6-litre, 280 b.h.p engine; four-speed gearbox; shaft final drive.

FIAT

July 1924, 146·01 m.p.h. (234·986 k.p.h.)

Driven by Ernest Eldridge

6-cylinder, single o.h.c., 21·7-litre, 300 b.h.p engine; four-speed gearbox; chain final drive.

SUNBEAM

1924 and 1925, 146·16 m.p.h. (235·217 k.p.h.), 150·766 m.p.h. (242·80 k.p.h.)

Driven by Malcolm Campbell

V12, single o.h.c., 18·3-litre, 350 b.h.p engine; four-speed gearbox; shaft final drive.

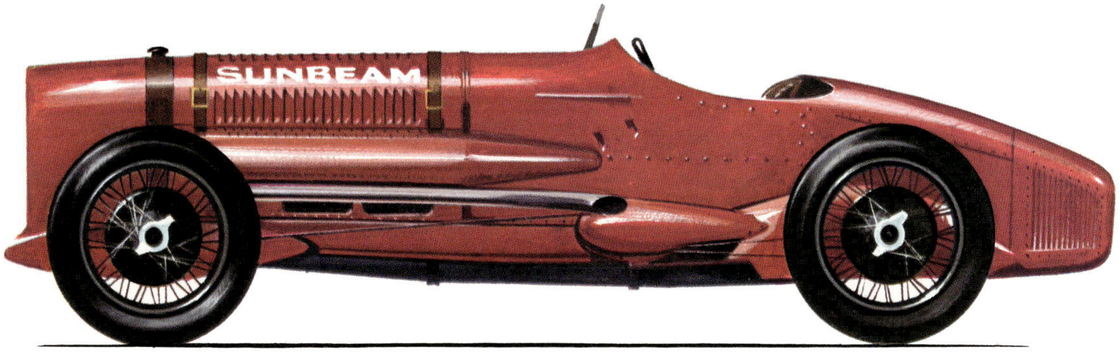

SUNBEAM
March 1926, 152·33 m.p.h. (245·149 k.p.h.)
Driven by Maj. Henry Segrave
V12, twin o.h.c., 4-litre, 306 b.h.p. supercharged engine; four-speed gearbox; shaft final drive

Babs
April 1927, 169·30 m.p.h. (272·458 k.p.h.), 171·01 m.p.h. (275·229 k.p.h.)
Driven by J. G. Parry Thomas
V12, o.h.c., 26·9-litre, 400 b.h.p. 'Liberty' engine; four-speed gearbox; chain final drive.

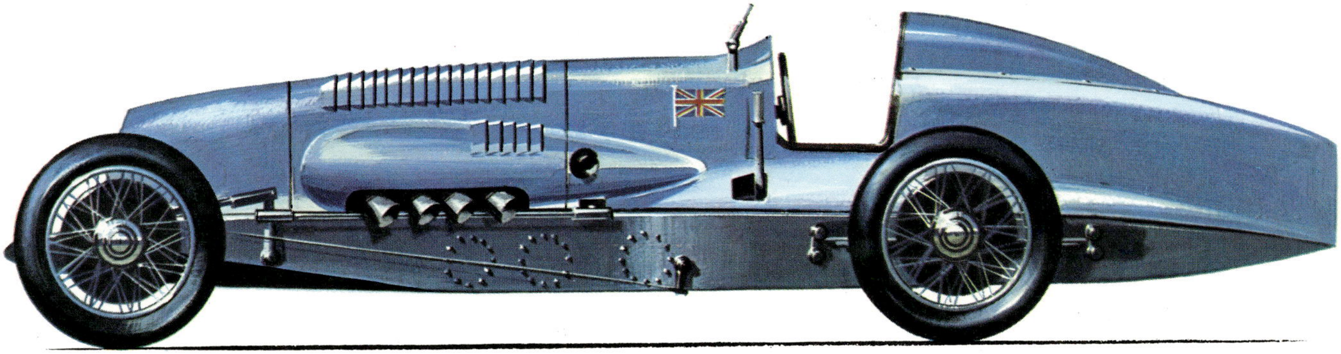

NAPIER–CAMPBELL *Bluebird*

February 1927, 174·883 m.p.h. (281·447 k.p.h.)

Driven by Malcolm Campbell

12-cylinder, o.h.c., 'broad arrow' 22·3-litre, 450 b.h.p Napier 'Lion' engine; F.B.M. three-speed epicyclic gearbox; shaft final drive.

SUNBEAM 1,000 H.P.

March 1927, 203·792 m.p.h. (327·981 k.p.h.)

Driven by Maj. Henry Segrave

Two V12, twin o.h.c., 22·5-litre, 435 b.h.p. engines; two three-speed gearboxes; chain final drive

NAPIER-CAMPBELL *Bluebird*

February 1928, 206·956 m.p.h. (333·062 k.p.h.)

Driven by Malcolm Campbell

12-cylinder o.h.c. 'broad arrow', 22·3-litre, 450 b.h.p. Napier 'Lion' engine; F.B.M. three-speed epicyclic gearbox; shaft final drive.

WHITE TRIPLEX

April 1928, 207·552 m.p.h. (334·022 k.p.h.)

Driven by Ray Keech

Three V12, o.h.c., 26·9-litre, 400 b.h.p 'Liberty' engines; no gearboxes; three shaft final drives to rear axle.

IRVING–NAPIER *Golden Arrow*

March 1929, 231·446 m.p.h. (372·340 k.p.h.)

Driven by Maj. Henry Segrave

12-cylinder, o.h.c. 'broad arrow' 26·9-litre, 925 b.h.p. Napier 'Lion' engine; three-speed gearbox; twin final shaft drives; aircraft-type surface radiators.

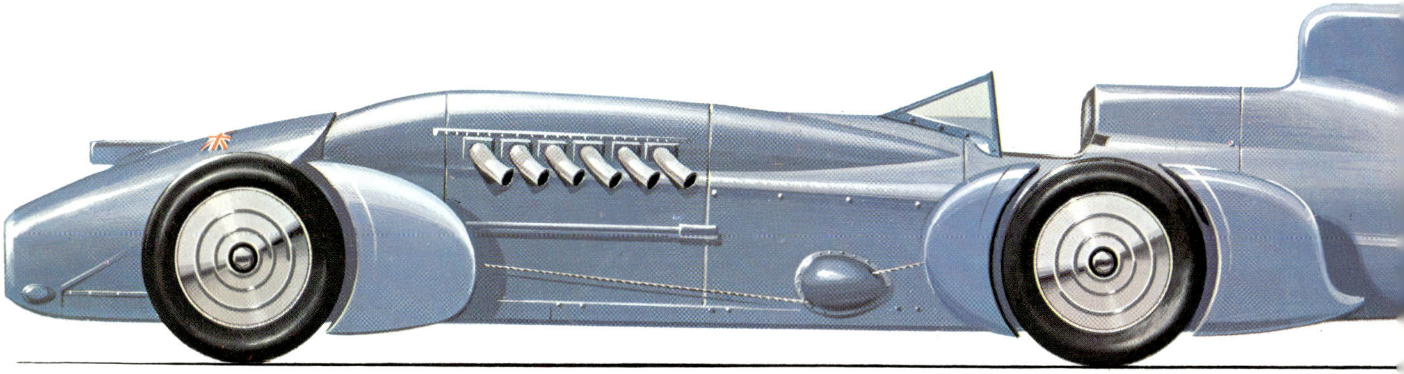

Bluebird

February 1931, 246·09 m.p.h. (395·469 k.p.h.)

Driven by Malcolm Campbell

12-cylinder, o.h.c. 'broad arrow' 26·9-litre, 1,450 b.h.p supercharged Napier 'Lion' engine; three-speed gearbox; offset shaft final drive.

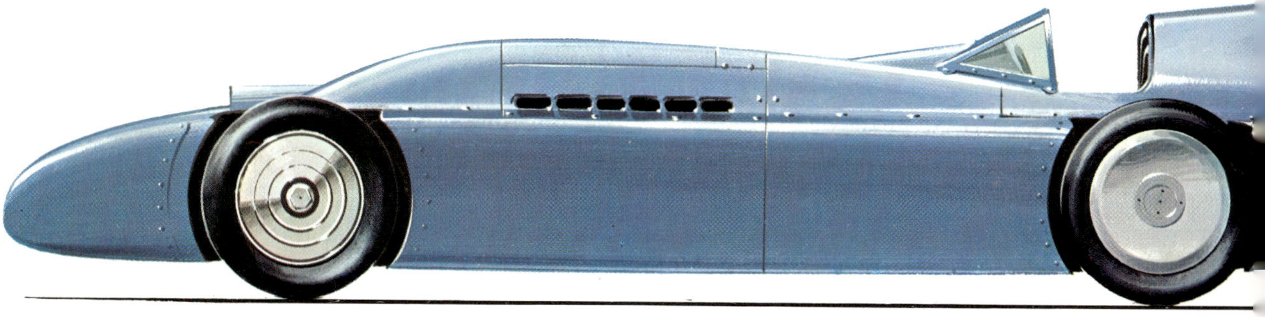

Bluebird

February 1933, 272·46 m.p.h. (438·123 k.p.h.)

Driven by Sir Malcolm Campbell

V12, o.h.c. 36·5-litre, 2,300 b.h.p. supercharged Rolls-Royce 'R' engine; three-speed gearbox; offset shaft final drive.

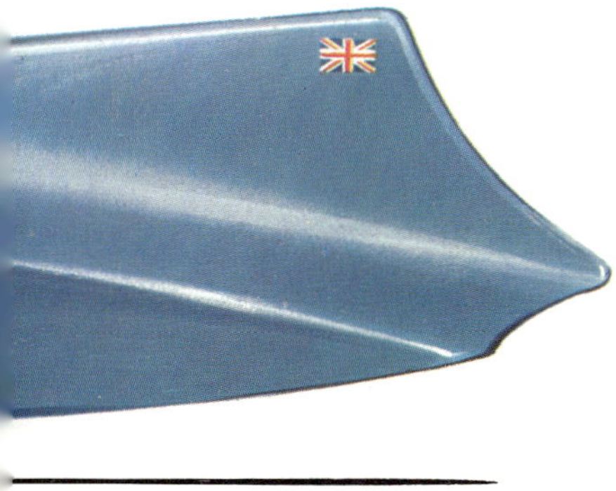

Bluebird

March and September 1935, 276·82 m.p.h. (445·703 k.p.h.), 301·129 m.p.h. (484·818 k.p.h.)

Driven by Sir Malcolm Campbell

V12, o.h.c., 36.5-litre, 2,300 b.h.p. supercharged Rolls-Royce 'R' engine; three-speed gearbox; offset shaft final drive to twin rear wheels.

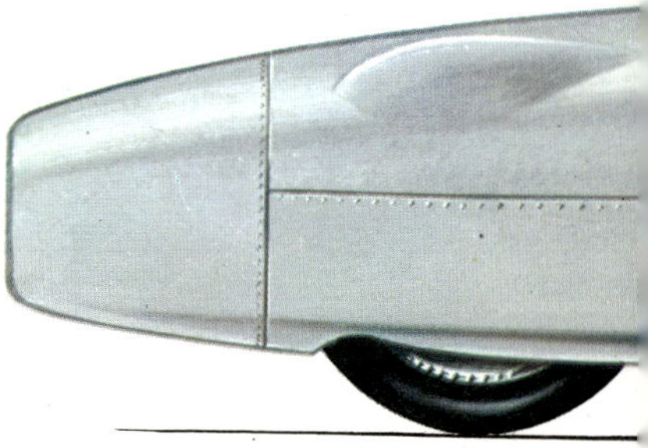

Thunderbolt

November 1937 and August 1938, 312·00 m.p.h. (501·374 k.p.h.), 345·50 m.p.h. (555·93 k.p.h.)

Driven by Capt. George Eyston

Two V12, o.h.c., 36·5-litre, 2,350 b.h.p. supercharged Rolls-Royce 'R' engines; three-speed gearbox; gear final drive to twin rear wheels. Four front wheels in pairs, all steering; independent suspension all round; inboard front disc brakes; rear transmission disc brake.

RAILTON

September 1938, August 1939, and September 1947, 350·20 m.p.h. (563·471 k.p.h.), 369·74 m.p.h. (593·56 k.p.h.), 394·20 m.p.h. (634·267 k.p.h.)

Driven by John Cobb

Two 12-cylinder, o.h.c., 'broad arrow', 26·9-litre, 1,250 b.h.p. supercharged Napier 'Lion' engines; ice cooling; twin three-speed gearboxes; four-wheel drive. Water-cooled transmission brakes; coil spring independent suspension all round. One-piece removable body shell.

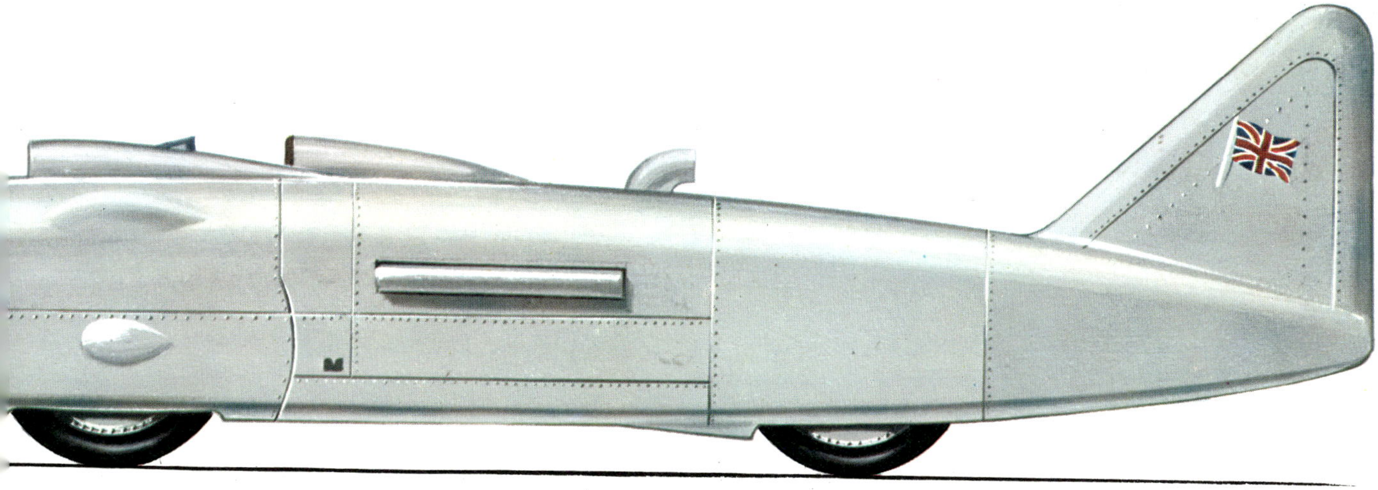

Thunderbolt

September 1938, 357·50 m.p.h. (575·217 k.p.h.)

Driven by Capt. George Eyston

Two V12, o.h.c., 36·5-litre, 2,350 b.h.p supercharged Rolls-Royce 'R' engines; three-speed gearbox; gear final drive to twin rear wheels. Four front wheels in pairs, all steering; independent suspension all round; inboard front disc brakes; rear transmission disc brakes.

Spirit of America

August 1963 and October 1964, 407·45 m.p.h. (655·696 k.p.h.), 468·72 m.p.h. (754.296 k.p.h.), 526·28 m.p.h. (846·926 k.p.h.)

Driven by Craig Breedlove

General Electric J47 5,200 lb. thrust jet power unit; single suspended front wheel; unsprung rear axle carrying two wheels.

Bluebird-PROTEUS (*Wheel-driven*)

July 1964, 403·10 m.p.h. (648·728 k.p.h.)

Driven by Donald Campbell

Bristol-Siddeley 'Proteus' 4,100 s.h.p. gas turbine power unit; two single-speed gearboxes; four-wheel drive. Independent suspension all round by wishbones and oleo-pneumatic struts; air-operated disc brakes. Integral chassis/body structure of Araldite-sealed light alloy with stressed outer skin.

Green Monster

October 1964 and November 1965, 434·02 m.p.h. (698·455 k.p.h.), 536·71 m.p.h. (863·710 k.p.h.), 576·553 m.p.h. (927·829 k.p.h.)

Driven by Art Arfons

General Electric J79 15,000 lb. thrust jet power unit; oleo-pneumatic front suspension; unsprung rear axle.

Goldenrod (*Wheel-driven*)

November 1965, 409·277 m.p.h. (658·636 k.p.h.)

Driven by Bob Summers

Four o.h.v., 6·9-litre, 608 b.h.p. Chrysler engines with fuel injection; two four-speed gearboxes driving to all four wheels.

Wingfoot Express
October 1964, 413·2 m.p.h. (664·95 k.p.h.)
Driven by Tom Green
Westinghouse J46 6,200 lb. triple-jet power unit; oleo-pneumatic suspension to all four wheels.

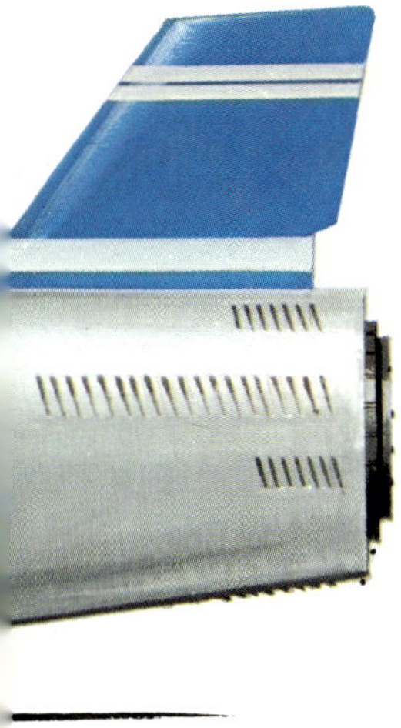

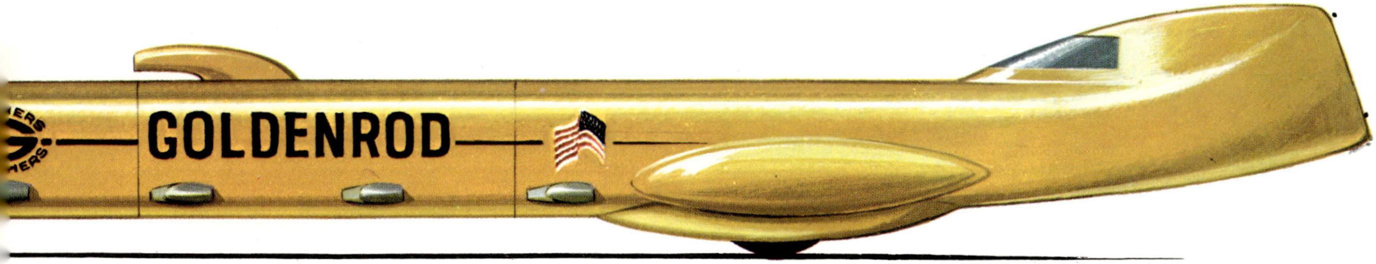

Spirit of America – Sonic I

November 1965, 555·483 m.p.h. (893·921 k.p.h.), 600·601 m.p.h. (966·528 k.p.h.)

Driven by Craig Breedlove

General Electric J79 15,000 lb. thrust jet power unit. Non-independent front suspension by torsion bars; independent rear suspension by torsion bars; disc brakes all round.

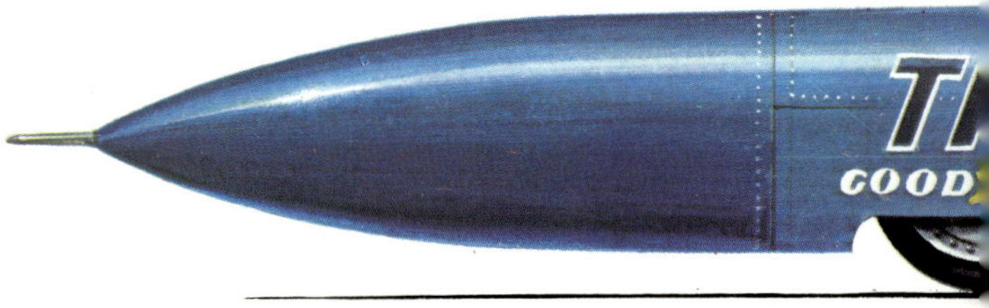

The Blue Flame

October 1970, 630·388 m.p.h. (1,014·496 k.p.h.)

Driven by Gary Gabelich

Reaction Dynamics liquid fuel rocket, 13,000 lb. thrust (35,000 b.h.p.) power unit; coil spring/damper front suspension to closely-paired wheels; solid, unsprung rear axle.

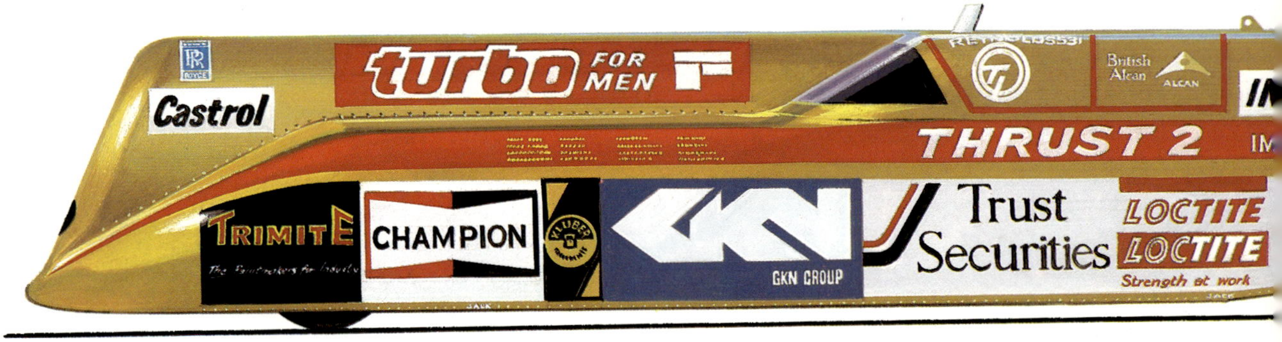

Budweiser Rocket

December 1979, 'Top speed' run 739·666 m.p.h. (1,190·123 k.p.h.) [One Way]

Driven by Stanton Barrett

Romatec V4 solid fuel rocket 24,000 lb. thrust with Sidewinder missile 4–6,000 lb. thrust power unit. Single front wheel.

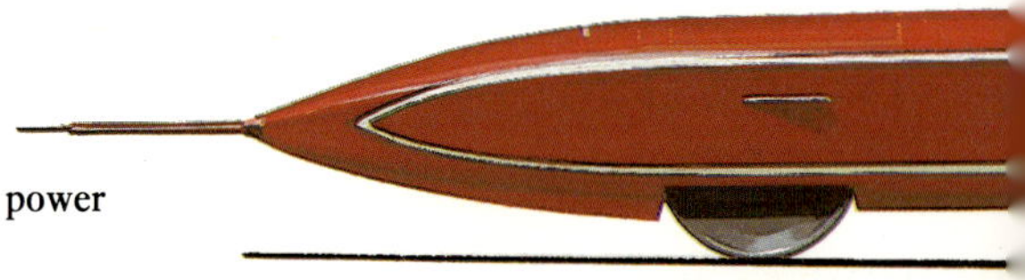

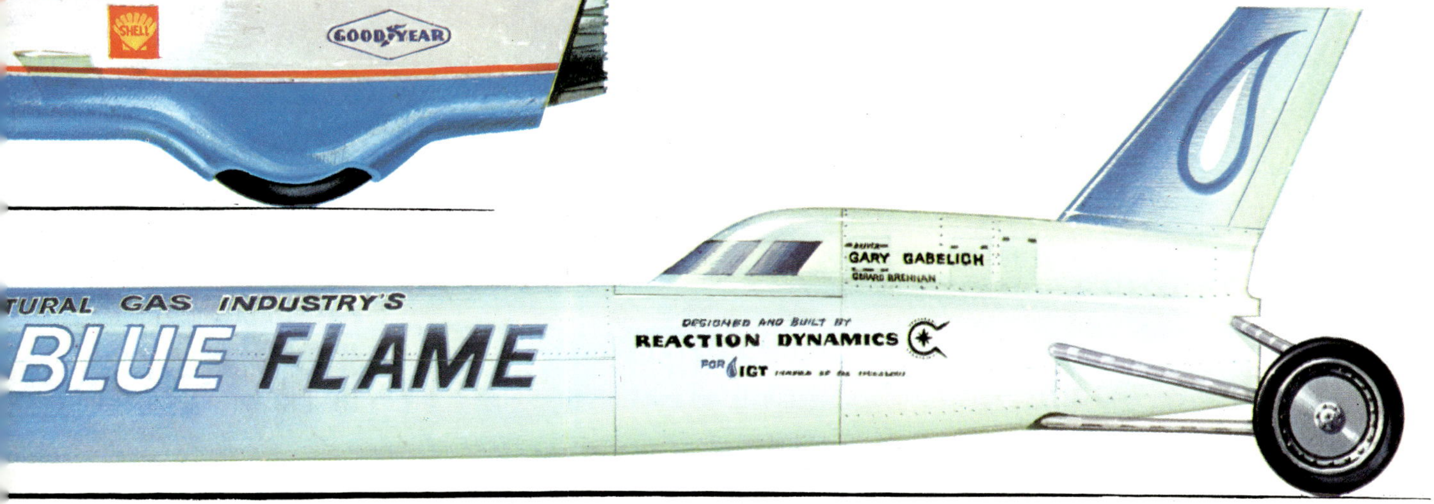

Thrust 2

October 1983, 633·468 m.p.h. (1,019 k.p.h.)

Driven by Richard Noble

Rolls-Royce Avon Mark 302 17,000 lb. thrust jet power unit. All round independent suspension; disc brakes all round.

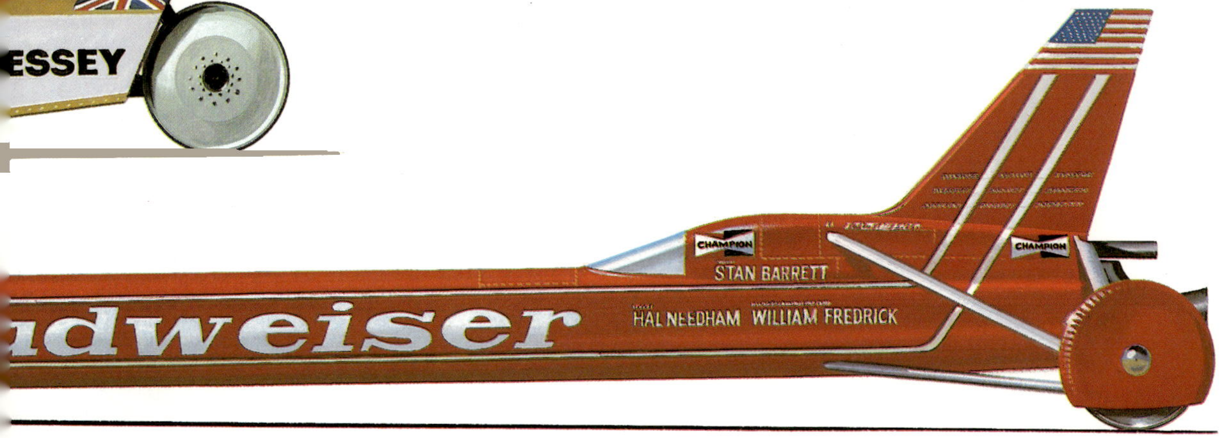

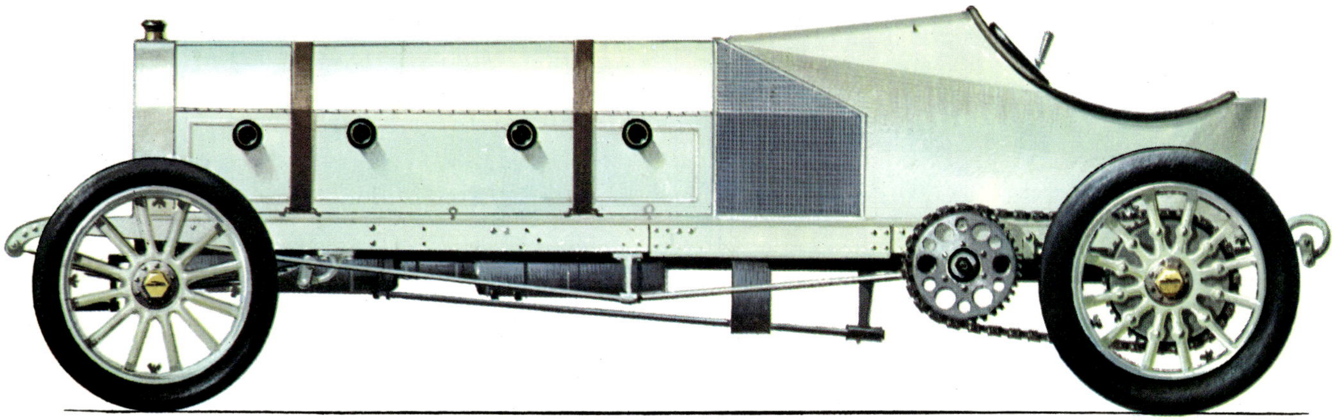

MERCEDES *Flying Dutchman*

January 1905, 109·75 m.p.h.(176·61 k.p.h.)

Driven by Herbert Bowden

Two 4-cylinder, 9·2-litre, 60 b.h.p Mercedes engines in line, coupled together; no geearbox; chain final drive.

PACKARD

February 1919, 149·87 m.p.h. (241·189 k.p.h.)

Driven by Ralph de Palma

V12, o.h.c., 9·9-litre, 240 b.h.p. engine; three-speed gearbox and shaft final drive; semi-elliptic suspension all round.

Captain George Eyston's great twin Rolls-Royce-engined *Thunderbolt* under construction at the Bean works at Tipton, Staffs.

Thunderbolt was push-started at Bonneville by a car with fortified front bumper. The surface of the salt flats was far from even, and the actual course had been scraped smooth.

four at the back on one driven axle with twin tyres each side, the object being to spread the weight and get that mighty power to the track. The two Rolls-Royce engines were mounted side by side between the front and rear wheels, and drove the rear set through separate clutches and a gear train to a massive three-speed gearbox and bevel and crown wheel final drive without a differential.

All the wheels were independently suspended by big transverse leaf springs and sturdy tubular wishbones, and another advanced feature was the use of disc brakes, jointly developed by the Borg & Beck and Lockheed companies. They were of the 'clutch' type in which one face is forced against another, and at the front were mounted inboard of the middle pair of wheels, being connected by extension shafts as on many modern Grand Prix cars, the object being to reduce unsprung weight. The rear disc brake was mounted on the transmission, and further braking was provided by hydraulically operated air flaps, hinged flush in the sides of the tail.

Another departure from tradition was the location of the cockpit, the driver being seated ahead of the engines, behind the second pair of front wheels. To permit a tapering nose, the forward pair of front wheels were of considerably narrower track than their rearward fellows, and the complex steering gear was made for Eyston by the Wolseley concern. The streamlined bodywork completely enclosed everything, and was made by a South Coast boat-building firm from non-corrosive Birmabright aluminium. Air intakes for the engine and exhaust stubs protruded at the top, and a large and ugly 'mouth' in the nose fed air to the radiator. Even more unsightly, but considered necessary, was the huge vertical tail fin to provide directional stability.

This was the aluminium monster at which the Americans understandably gaped astonished when it was uncrated at Wendover early in October 1937.

Thunderbolt completed, showing the huge tail fin.

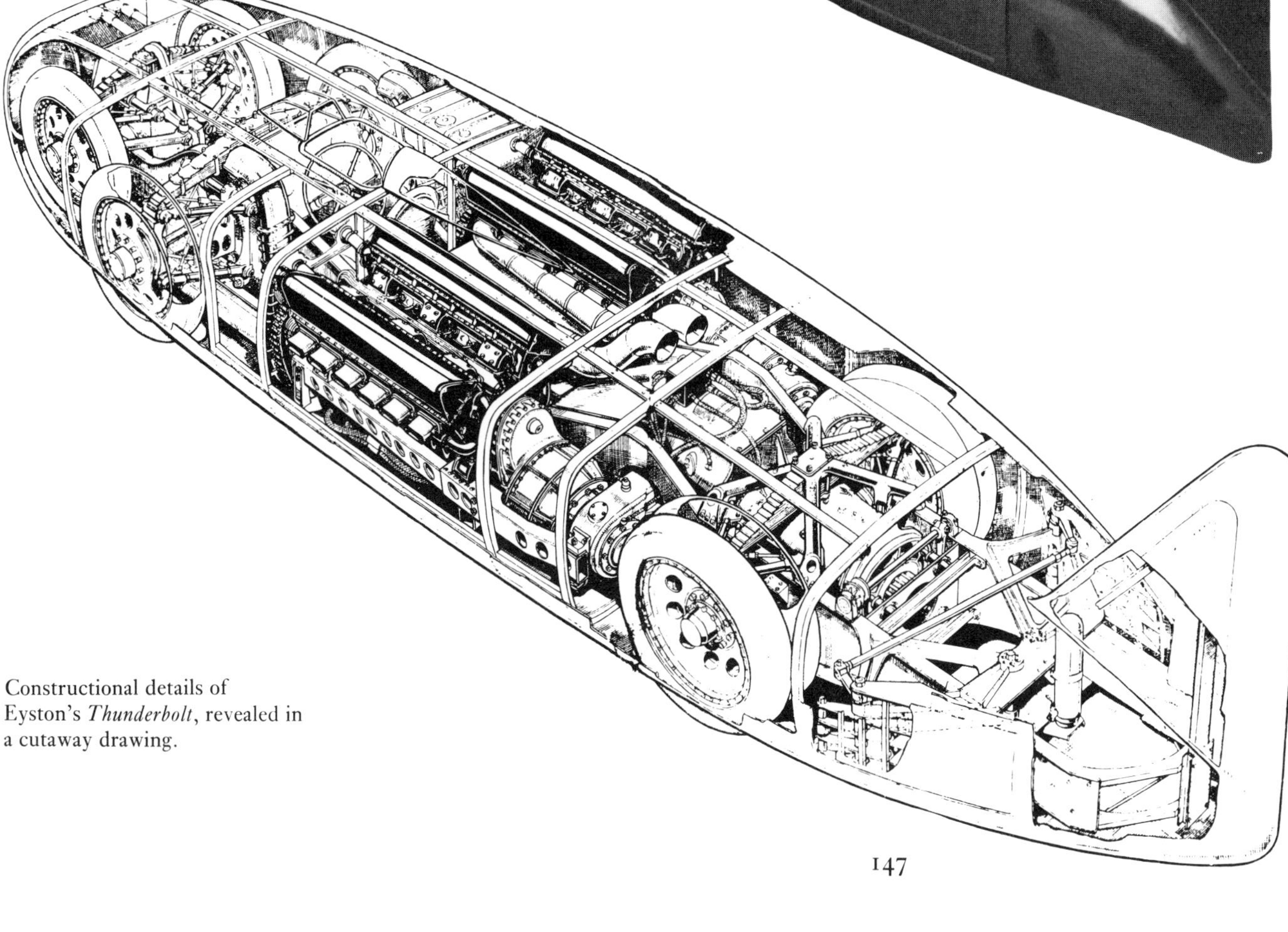

Constructional details of Eyston's *Thunderbolt*, revealed in a cutaway drawing.

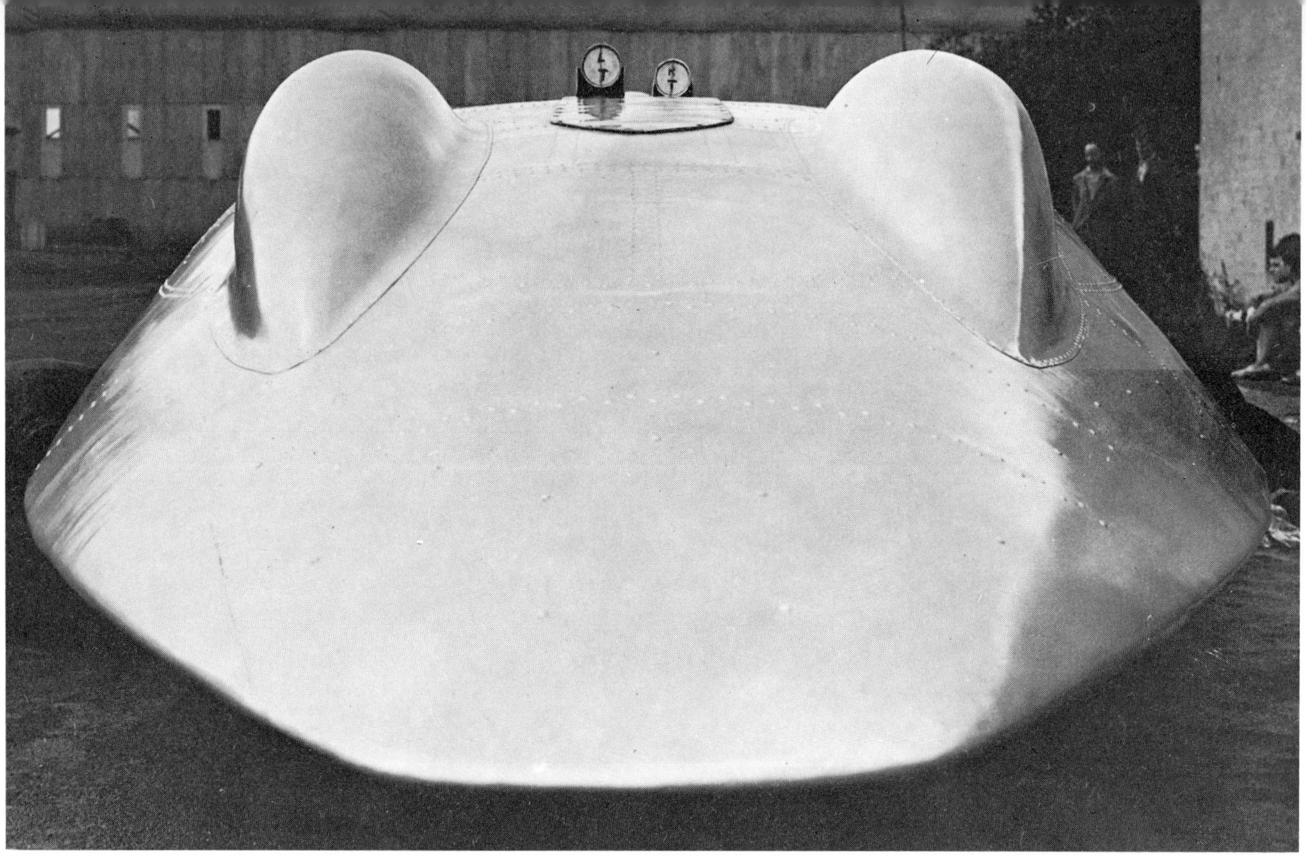

12

The Eyston-Cobb duel

'Two huge metal monsters of marvellous science, guided by intrepid pilots on an arena of blinding salt. It was fantastic; it was a last rare English gesture before the blackness of war fell upon the world.'

L'AUTO, 1939.

Although completely untested when it arrived at the Bonneville salt flats in October 1937, *Thunderbolt*'s engines started up at once and ran without a falter. As soon as Captain Eyston tried to drive off, however, clutch problems denied him a gear and the eagerly anticipated test run had to be postponed. Heavy rain, a flooded course, and design modifications to the clutch absorbed a fortnight, but then, at last, Eyston got moving. He did a steady 230 m.p.h. run or two, and on 28th October managed a timed run one way over the 10-mile course at 309·6 m.p.h.

A similar speed the other way would have broken Campbell's two-year-old record, but instead the dog clutches coupling the two engines failed. In another trial a week later, *Thunderbolt* getting a push start from a car to save the transmission, he recorded a speed of 310·68 m.p.h. in one direction, but again the clutches broke. Two racing engineers in Los Angeles agreed to make up new clutch parts to Eyston's design, and these arrived on 17th November.

At dawn on 19th November with bad weather ominously threatening, Eyston was ready to go. His first flying kilometre was at 305·59 m.p.h. – good, but not intoxicating. But after all wheels were changed and the car refuelled in sixteen minutes, the

(*Opposite, above*) Tail view of John Cobb's beautiful Railton record car of 1938. (*Below*) The two Napier Lion engines were angled one each side of the cranked backbone chassis. The rear track was narrower than the front, to fit inside the body.

Reid A. Railton, creator of Cobb's twin Napier-engined Railton record car; he was previously with Parry Thomas, and designed Campbell's *Bluebirds* from 1931 to 1935.

run back was much faster at 319·11 m.p.h. Visibility was bad, and the great silver car seemed almost to merge with the white salt all around as, with a giant drumming of exhausts, it blasted past. And that was that; two new names on the list of *LSR* holders – Captain G. E. T. Eyston and *Thunderbolt*, mean speed for the kilometre 312·00 m.p.h. and for the mile 311·42 m.p.h.

Half an hour later the weather broke, and Utah's first winter rain and snow began to fall. Knowing that the potential of his mighty car had hardly been extended yet, Eyston, like the famous American general, departed with the vow 'I shall return' firmly on his lips.

'Carte blanche' for an idealist

And now a brilliant new contender came forth.

Reid Railton, B.Sc., A.M.I.A.E., who had so skilfully re-modelled Campbell's *Bluebird* that it could achieve its master's ambition of topping 300 m.p.h., had long wanted *carte blanche* to produce a land speed record car from scratch. His chance came in late 1936 when John R. Cobb, a big, imperturbable man who liked big, imperturbable cars such as the Napier-Railton with which he held the Brooklands lap record, decided to try for the absolute record, and commissioned Thomson & Taylor to design and build a car for him.

Power, as ever, was the top priority, but the primitive use of excess weight to keep the wheels down and get power to the road grated with Railton. He aimed to do it efficiently by designing proper suspension, keeping unsprung weight to a minimum, and driving all four wheels. The trouble was that power inevitably meant big aircraft-type engines, and two at least, requiring a lot of room which Railton begrudged. Accordingly he evolved an ingenious cranked box-section backbone, to which he hung the engines at an angle, one driving the rear wheels, the other the front, each through its own three-speed gearbox. He packed the remaining spaces with ice reservoirs for cooling fuel and oil tanks, etc., and put the driver up in the nose of the car, ahead of the front wheels.

The engines themselves were ten-year-old supercharged Napier Lions, of the type used so successfully in the *Golden Arrow* and the earlier *Bluebirds*. Despite their age (they were designed during World War I) these engines gave a reliable 1,250 b.h.p. at 3,600 r.p.m., and although some 11 per cent of that would be lost at Bonneville altitudes, Railton considered it was adequate in a car intended to weigh just over 3 tons compared with *Thunderbolt*'s 7 tons.

Weight-saving on the engines included elimination of flywheels and clutches. Instead the car was push-started by a truck, and a freewheel mechanism in each gearbox enabled gears to be changed. There was no radiator, ice-cooling from a 75-gallon tank sufficing with thermostat control. Transmission brakes only were used, saving much unsprung weight, and these brakes were cooled by water from the ice-cooling system, after which it was ejected on to the track.

The front suspension was independent by wishbones and traction coil springs,

For easier maintenance at Bonneville, the body of the Railton was made in one piece, quickly removable from the chassis.

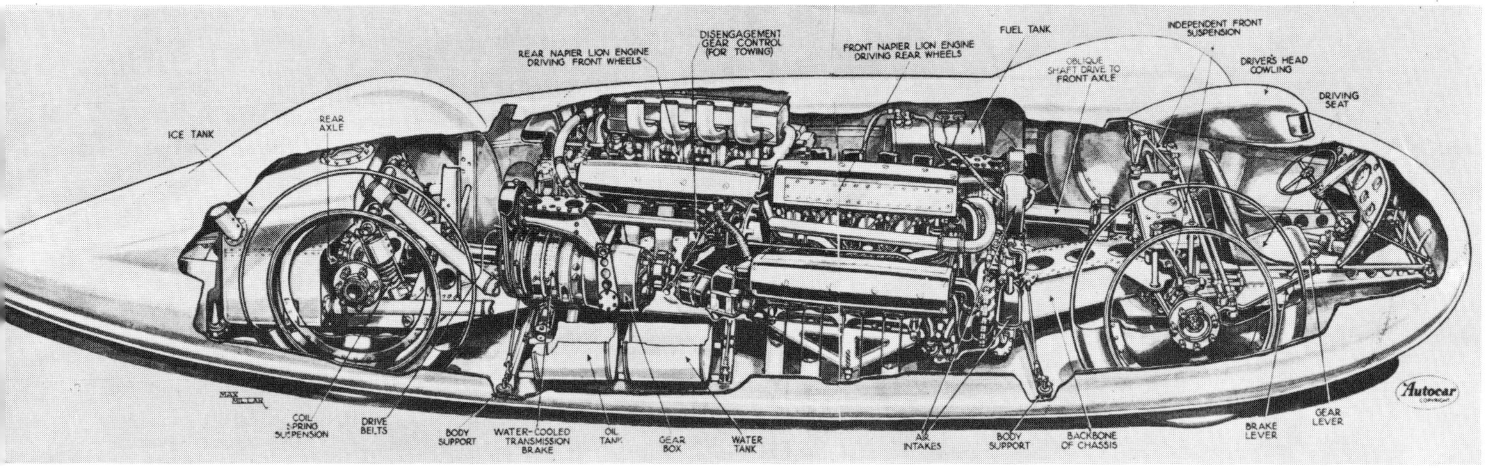

A cutaway drawing showing how two engines, two gearboxes and four-wheel drive were accommodated in the Railton.

the front drive being taken through exposed half-shafts and double universal joints. The rear axle, very 'crab-tracked' (i.e. narrower than the front) was of coil-sprung live type; all coil springs embodied inbuilt rubber damping, anticipating the modern coaxial coil spring-cum-damper suspension unit. The tyres, as ever, were a vital governing factor, both of the car's design and its speed, and once again Dunlop came up trumps with a cover having a tread thickness of only 1/50 in., and designed to withstand a speed of 380 m.p.h.

The bodywork was outstandingly beautiful, exquisitely contoured with a rounded front incorporating the driver's 'conning tower', tapering away to a long, flat, ichthyoid tail with only the wheel humps obtruding. It was designed as a completely detachable shell, attaching to the chassis at eight points and registering neatly with a fixed, full-length undershield. It was made of 18 s.w.g. aluminium by the Northern Aluminium Company, weighed 4 cwt., and was easily lifted off the car for pit work by six men, leaving the mechanicals completely accessible for working on. Unlike *Thunderbolt* the Railton – for that was its simple name – had no stabilizing fin to mar its striking lines, Reid Railton not considering such a fitment necessary, despite having specified such things on Campbell's *Bluebirds* since 1931.

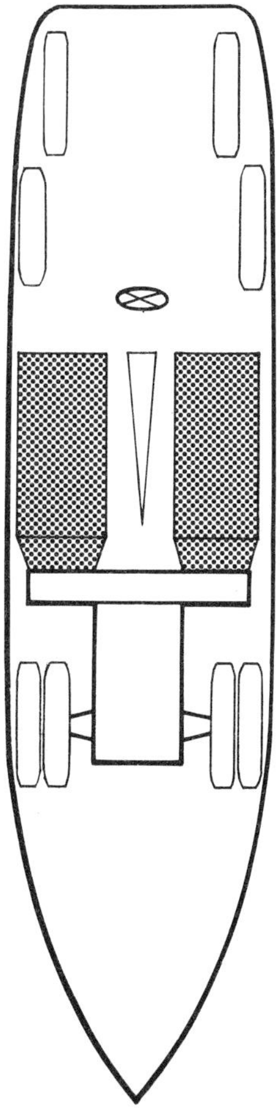

Thunderbolt
Location of engines and transmission

The giants meet

The two British cars *Thunderbolt* and the Railton, so enterprisingly different, made a unique meeting at Bonneville in the summer of 1938. While Eyston and his behemoth were now seasoned runners, the Cobb *équipe* were newcomers to *LSR* spheres, though not to the Bonneville salt, on which Cobb had set many records with his smaller, single-engined Napier-Railton. Eyston arrived first in July with *Thunderbolt*, which had been improved externally by a new front cowling with smaller aperture, a fully enclosed cockpit with a respirator for the driver, a longer tail, adjustable slats on the bonnet top to emit radiator air, and larger air scoops for the centrifugal superchargers of the two Rolls-Royce engines. Within, coil springs replaced the heavy transverse leaf springs in the suspension, saving valuable weight, and the brake actuation was improved with Lockheed servo motors.

Bad weather dogged Eyston until August 24th, a day which was to provide a splendid example of his character. His first run yielded 347·155 m.p.h., way over his record. Hard-nosed time-keeping doyen Art Pillsbury was blunt and to the point about the return, counselling him: 'Get it done and make it good'. Eyston did exactly that, but as *Thunderbolt* slowed Pillsbury realized with horror no mark had registered on the timing tape. Sick with remorse, he could only cry as Eyston bounded up, flushed with pleasure at doing what Art had advised. When he learned the reason for Pillsbury's tears, Eyston simply put his arm round him, told him to pull himself together, and calmly informed the expectant press the run had been nothing more than a practice sortie. There was no harshness or recrimination, then or in the future, such was the big man's generosity.

Unlike Campbell, Eyston never did get ruffled and three days later was back

For his second attempt on the record Eyston had *Thunderbolt*'s bodywork modified. A smaller nose intake, enclosed cockpit, and a longer tail assisted him to a new record in August 1938 at 345·49 m.p.h.

for another shot. At Pillsbury's suggestion the sides of the big car were painted matt black with a yellow disc and arrow so it registered with the 'eye' this time, Art believing the bright sunshine, the car's silver paint and the dazzling whiteness of the salt were to blame for the earlier failure. This time there were no snags. Despite a course shortened because of poor surfaces at either end, Eyston did the kilometre at a mean of 345·21 m.p.h. and the mile at 345·49, slower than he might have achieved on the aborted runs, but still a sensational 33 m.p.h. increase on his own record.

Cobb the imperturbable now came out for the first tentative trials with his elegant car. He put in several runs while the attendant Reid Railton ironed out carburation faults and lesser teething troubles inevitable with a complex new design. By 12 September 1938 both driver and engineer felt ready for sterner work, and Cobb speeded up, averaging 342·5 m.p.h. through the mile; not good enough to beat Eyston, but getting near.

Three days later the Railton was out again, and this time, in a model run, he managed 353·3 m.p.h. one way and 347·2 m.p.h. the other. 'John's got it,' were Eyston's words as the sleek, fish-like Railton slashed by – and indeed he had, at a mean of 350·20 m.p.h. for the mile. Another milestone of speed, 350 m.p.h., had been passed.

The last throw

Well knowing Railton's brilliance and Cobb's tenacity, George Eyston was prepared to have to regain his record, and had already put some improvements to the car in hand. It says much for his ingenuity that he could then and there devise a conversion from radiator to tank cooling for the *Thunderbolt*, although he hadn't the time to fix up an ice tank; the main object was to improve aerodynamics by removing the radiator and covering over the nose completely. This modification, plus removal of the unsightly tail fin, greatly enhanced the looks of Eyston's monster car, and stability was not adversely affected by the fin's absence.

Eyston was out on the flats the morning after Cobb had set his 350·2 m.p.h. figure, and with the briefest of preliminaries departed at speed. The result, after four minutes of ultra-high-speed motoring, was one run at 356·4 m.p.h. for the mile, which he covered in only 10·10 sec., and the return at 358·6 m.p.h. (10·04 sec)! – a mean of 357·50 m.p.h., making John Cobb's Railton record redundant after just one day. Thus Eyston and *Thunderbolt* had the last word in 1938, but it is doubtful if the great car, despite its 73 litres of more modern engines, could approach the 400 m.p.h. for which Cobb was aiming.

In 1939, of course, the world had blacker things on its mind than land speed records, but Cobb, Railton and company were back at Bonneville in August, perilously close to the outbreak of war. Trouble dogged the first attempt on 22nd August, but Cobb tried again the following day. This time, with the course in perfect condition and only a cross-wind and some gear-changing difficulty to worry him, John Cobb blasted away purposefully to clock an electrifying 9·76 sec. for the

In a *Thunderbolt* still further modified with tank cooling, completely closed nose, and minus tail fin, George Eyston broke Cobb's new record one day after it was set, at a speed of 357·50 m.p.h. This figure stood for almost twelve months, when Cobb retook it at 369·70 m.p.h., nine days before the outbreak of World War II.

mile, a speed of 370·75 m.p.h. He stopped at the depot, the body was deftly removed by the mechanics, all tyres were changed, more fuel put in and ice tanks checked, then he was off again.

All eyes watched the horizon; a dot became the sleek silver Railton with black side flash to catch the 'eye'. The car was strangely silent as it rocketed past, trailing a plume of salt and its own harsh exhaust note, outstripped by the car itself. 9·81 sec. through the mile – 366·97 m.p.h. – but his kilometre speeds were faster at 367·92 and 371 m.p.h., giving a mean of 369·74 m.p.h. – a new record. By 6 00 a.m. on 23 August 1939 it was all over – and remained so until World War II had come and gone, and speed records could be thought about again.

The jet threat

The war taught many things, not all of them evil, under pressure. When it started, aircraft were propelled by engines little different fundamentally from those in Captain Eyston's *Thunderbolt*, but turning an airscrew instead of wheels. When it finished, 'reaction' or jet propulsion – whereby a blast of heated gas emitted from a body propels that body along by sheer reaction – had been fully developed. It was infinitely simpler than an internal combustion engine with all its valves, pistons, rockers and cylinders, much less fussy if more voracious about its diet of fuel, and infinitely faster.

Its fiery breath precluded its use in normal road cars, but inevitably as development continued apace in post-war years the jet engine and its brother the gas turbine (in which the burning gases impinge on a turbine wheel and turn a shaft) became available for experiment in fast cars and boats.

As it happened, it was Sir Malcolm Campbell who first proposed using a jet unit, a de Havilland 'Goblin', in the water speed record *Bluebird* boat in 1947. This was not successful for various reasons, among them Sir Malcolm's rapidly failing health, and the jet- and turbine-powered car was yet some years away. When it did come, Sir Malcolm's son Donald was to play a big part in its introduction.

The piston engine's last LSR

Meantime, in the early post-war years, the piston engine was to have its last fling. Most intriguingly, amongst 1945 discoveries in Germany was a somewhat war-battered record car which never ran – an enormous Daimler-Benz with six wheels and a 44-litre DB 603 inverted 12-cylinder aero-engine, (see Chapter 23 for further details). This astonishing car, the work of Dr Porsche, was to have been driven by Hans Stuck, and was destined to run for the record but for the intrusion of war. It could certainly have added rich interest to land speed history.

Fate decreed that this Porsche-Mercedes would never be seen in action, but its most obvious rival, John Cobb's Railton, was brought out of retirement in 1947. Cobb had a long delayed appointment with Bonneville to see what could be done

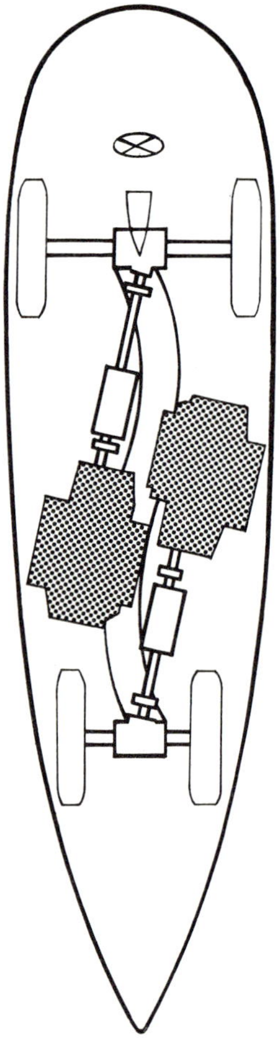

Railton
Location of engines
and transmission

about that 400 m.p.h. target, and the car, looking as lovely as ever, was checked over meticulously at Thomson & Taylor. Reid Railton devised an ingenious auxiliary drive to prevent the engine stalling during gear-changes on freewheel, as was its wont before the war owing to the absence of clutches and flywheels on the engines.

The top gear ratios were slightly raised, and new Dunlop tyres, stronger yet lighter than pre-war, were developed with a full 400 m.p.h. in view. Substantial backing for the venture was provided this time by the Mobil Oil Company in return for publicity, including a change of car name to the Railton-Mobil Special; this was the beginning of a more frank sponsorship in Britain by manufacturers of products used on the car, and is now accepted practice in most branches of motor racing, as it was already in the U.S.A. before the war.

The salt flats, when they reached them in August 1947, were in poor shape, with deep holes pocking the normally smooth salt top surface. They were assiduously filled in and rolled, but a bad section remained on entry to the measured mile which made itself much felt at over 300 m.p.h. Then the Railton's old carburation trouble returned, while new camshafts had to be made in Britain and sent out. A substantial quantity of Dunlop tyres had been brought to Bonneville, but repeated trial runs made serious inroads into these.

By 14th September an attempt on the record became possible at last, and Cobb got in one run at 375·32 m.p.h., well up on his 1939 figure of 369·70 m.p.h. Alas, the bumpy course started a body split which needed curing, and Cobb could not make a return run. Two days later he tried again, and although he encountered much wheel-spin on the bumps his first run was at 385·645 m.p.h. – a winner if he could repeat it. He did much better on the run back, wheels still spinning and the Railton still accelerating as he entered the mile, and travelling at 415 m.p.h. as he left it.

His speed was a rousing 403·135 m.p.h., and the mean was 394·196 m.p.h. – a new *LSR* for Britain. On a smoother course than the Bonneville salt flats in 1947, John Cobb could undoubtedly have taken the record beyond 400 m.p.h. It was not only a tyre shortage which prevented him from trying again; by the following day heavy rain was pounding down, the salt rapidly became waterlogged, and the Bonneville season was well and truly over.

In September 1947 Cobb returned to the famous salt flats with the Railton, now the Railton-Mobil Special, and raised his own record to 394·196 m.p.h. with a one-way run at over 400 m.p.h.

13

Exit the piston engine

'A jet-propelled vehicle would not be a motor-car; it would be a sort of aeroplane dragging its wheels along the course.'

John Cobb

John Cobb's 1947 record with the Railton stood for no less than sixteen years, by far the longest tenure of the *LSR* by one man and one car. Doubtless European preoccupation with post-war recovery and American preoccupation with Korea and other global problems contributed to the apparent indifference to maximum speed honours in the late 'forties and 'fifties. Certainly there were plenty of ultra-powerful ex-service aircraft engines available, but the world did not bite, and the Railton record reigned on.

There were other significant developments, however. In his book *Speed on Salt* published in 1936, Captain George Eyston wrote of the Bonneville salt flats: 'There appears to be no reason why speed tournaments should not be held on fixed dates; record attempts by cars conforming to the various international class limitations; records run by standard cars, by which definition America means cars selected at random from dealers' stocks; a 24-hour race for stock cars; straightaway runs over distances from one kilometre to ten miles . . . .'

Apart from the international classes and the 24-hour race, this shrewd piece of prophecy became fact thirteen years later, when in 1949 the first Bonneville National

(*Opposite*) In 1960 Donald Campbell, son of the illustrious Sir Malcolm, entered the land speed record sphere with a new turbine-propelled car bearing the famous name *Bluebird*.

Speed Trials took place. These meetings, and others on dry lake beds and air-strips, provided fine opportunities for young Americans anxious to try the speed of their 'hotted up' cars against time. The cult of the 'hot rod' began, taking several forms, from ridiculous devices with ancient Model T Ford radiators and bodies, rarely genuine and bulging with potent tuned Ford or Mercury V8 engines, to modern sedans, veritable wolves in sheeps' clothing, possessed of fantastic straight line performance.

Other branches of the sport developed 'drop tank' Specials, using the conveniently shaped wing-tip fuel tanks from World War II combat aircraft as bodies. There were also extremely sophisticated record machines with *svelte* streamlined bodywork inspired by famous record cars such as Gardner's M.G. or the pre-war Mercedes-Benz and Auto Union *stromlinienwagen*, and possessed of truly remarkable performances.

The ugly, uncouth, but electrifying accelerative dragsters, using hotly 'souped' stock V8 engines, also came along, and all this sprint activity taught the Americans a vast amount about extracting maximum power from an engine, getting that power to the road, and attaining fantastic speeds in fantastically small distances. 200 m.p.h., 225 m.p.h., 250 m.p.h., became commonplace, German class records began to fall one by one, and only the ultimate, the absolute world land speed record remained seemingly inviolable.

But it did not want for aspirants. Foremost among them were Mickey Thompson, the Arfons brothers Walt and Art, Athol Graham and Dr Nathan Ostich. Their machinery was richly varied, and as they raced and learned and improved it, their speeds went up and up, beyond the 300 m.p.h. mark, so that when news came of a formidable new British challenger for the *LSR*, several of these Americans felt ready to face it. The great confrontation took place on the Bonneville salt flats in the summer of 1960.

A Campbell and a 'Bluebird' again

The British newcomer was *Bluebird*, Donald Campbell's all-new car with gas turbine power unit. In 1955 Sir Malcolm's only son had made a big impression on the Americans by becoming the first to break 200 m.p.h. on water, at Ullswater, Westmorland, and then by breaking his own record by 14 m.p.h. on Lake Mead, Nevada, U.S.A., one month after his boat sank in the same lake. Perhaps the proximity of Lake Mead to Bonneville, where twenty years earlier his father first topped 300 m.p.h., helped to kindle his interest. Donald Campbell left Nevada with *two* ambitions – a 250 m.p.h. water record, and an over-400 m.p.h. land record.

He discussed the idea with the Norris brothers of Burgess Hill, Sussex, builders of his successful boat; and early in 1956 the basic design specification for the Campbell-Norris or CN7 record car became known. It sounded very formidable. It was to be driven by one Bristol-Siddeley 'Proteus' aircraft type gas turbine unit, as used in the Bristol Britannia airliner. This gave approximately 4,100 shaft h.p.

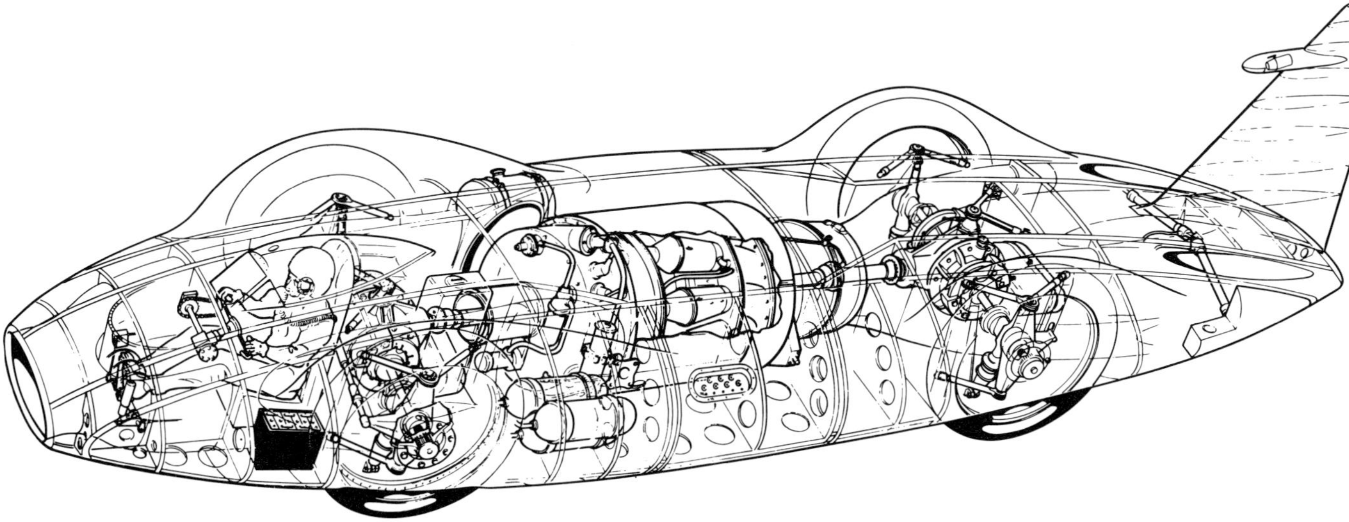

at 11,000 r.p.m., which was distributed to all four wheels by two David Brown single-speed gearboxes with differentials, no clutches or gears being necessary with such torque available. The front gearbox embodied a freewheel to over-run the drive, and Birfield constant velocity couplings were used all round.

Many techniques learned since the war were employed in the car's construction. It had no chassis as such, but a sort of 'egg box' structure of fore-and-aft and cross-members formed by sandwiching $\frac{3}{4}$ in.-thick corrugated alloy foil between two sheets of non-corrosive light alloy, the whole being sealed under pressure with Araldite. Over this frame and formers, a stressed-skin outer shell was built. Four-wheel independent suspension was by wishbones and Girling oleo-pneumatic spring/damper units, and the brakes were of disc type, operated by compressed air and augmented by air brakes in the tail surfaces.

Air for the turbine was admitted through the nose and ducted round the driver, who sat well forward as on the Railton; indeed *Bluebird*'s profile resembled that outstanding car in its purity of line, while its wheelbase was identical. No tail fin was fitted initially, but the symmetry was somewhat spoiled by the vast wheels and specially developed Dunlop 700 × 41 tyres (with 1/50 in. treads) giving an overall

(*Top*) The long, low nose and tall tail-fin (added in 1961) are characteristics of the superbly engineered *Bluebird*-Proteus.

(*Above*) Donald Campbell's *Bluebird*-Proteus turbine-powered record car in detail.

diameter of 4 ft. 4 in. and designed for 475 m.p.h. Special 'Indianapolis'-type automatic lifting jacks were fitted for rapid tyre-changing.

The engine exhausted through two vast ports set flush in the top tail surfaces, where their vast but incidental thrust could assist forward movement. The car was fitted with a 'black box' containing much electronic equipment for recording vital information such as acceleration, speed, suspension movement, roll, and power, for subsequent study. Ready to run, *Bluebird* weighed 9,600 lb. and burned B.P. aviation turbine kerosene at about 1½ m.p.g. at full speed, the fuel being carried in two 12½-gallon tanks.

Here was a land speed record car built for maximum performance without any compromise in specification, irrespective of cost. It became a communal constructional effort between about seventy British firms manufacturing components, and the B.P. Company provided substantial financial backing. Dunlop spent £125,000 on building an underground test plant for the tyres alone; Bristol-Siddeley specially modified the power unit for use in a car; and Motor Panels Ltd, a member of the Rubery-Owen engineering group which built and raced B.R.M. Grand Prix cars, constructed most of the car including the whole body. It was estimated to have cost close to £1 million to build *Bluebird* and another million to mount the entire operation.

The great confrontation

In four years Donald Campbell had broken his own water record four more times, before the Proteus *Bluebird* was complete and running. In August 1960 it arrived at Bonneville with an entourage of over eighty personnel, several auxiliary vehicles, and masses of spares and equipment which set the Americans gasping. When Campbell beheld the opposition lined up against him he, in turn, gasped.

Four great American monsters of fascinating mechanical diversity were fielded against *Bluebird* at this unique gathering. They were Athol Graham's Allison piston aero-engined car of about 3,000 b.h.p.; Art Arfons's *Green Monster*, a similarly engined but more powerful car of about 3,800 b.h.p.; Dr Nathan Ostich's *Flying Caduceus*, a pure jet-engined machine of about 7,000 lb. thrust, and Mickey Thompson's *Challenger 1* with four supercharged Pontiac car engines of about 2,800 b.h.p.

One after another these devices went out on to the famous salt flats, launching the most concerted attack on ultimate speed in *LSR* history. One, Ostich's *Caduceus*, was ineligible by regulations of the F.I.A. (successors to the A.I.A.C.R.) to take the record as it lacked driven wheels, but the doctor was not the first American, nor the last, to cock a snook at European rules. He was much favoured to return the highest speed of all during what would amount to over a month's activity on the salt.

The first to try was Athol Graham of Salt Lake City. His *City of Salt Lake* was a simple, cheaply built car with a U.S.A.F. surplus supercharged V12 Allison aero-engine mounted at the rear and driving the rear wheels. Its chassis was made of

12-in. deep aluminium channel, the axles were unsprung, sundry Cadillac parts featured, and the bodywork owed its origin to an aircraft drop tank, cut into sections to provide the nose, tail and centre sections, with aluminium panelling filling in the gaps.

The unfortunate Mormon preacher Athol Graham (sixth from left) with his unpainted *City of Salt Lake* at Bonneville on the occasion of his 344.761 m.p.h. clocking in December 1959.

The idea of breaking the *LSR* had come to Graham in a vivid dream which the Mormon regarded as a divine revelation. In 1959, flouting the predictions of critical experts unimpressed by his standards of mechanical preparation (more than one described the car as 'a clunker'), he clocked a surprisingly easy 344·761 m.p.h. at Bonneville despite running in December, later than anyone had used the salt. That solidly backed tests of 277, 305 and 308 and was as near as damn it equal to Thompson's 345·33 m.p.h. American record. Everyone began to take interest in the rugged idealist and his unpainted streamliner and on December 27th he hit 303 then 344 m.p.h. again before damaging the torque converter he used as *City*'s transmission. He returned home to make repairs, but was back at Bonneville the following July, *City* sporting a new red paint job and the salt's first STP backing. On August 1st, aided by wife Zeldine and a teenage kid called Otto Anzjon, and under the watchful eyes of Campbell, Arfons, Ostich and Thompson, he took aim at the 400 m.p.h. mark. Worried about many aspects of Graham's engineering and a high crosswind, Thompson counselled caution, but Graham let it be known he had nothing left to learn about speeds below 350.

Using the full power of the Allison – which came from industrialist Bill Boeing's *Miss Wahoo* unlimited hydroplane – he accelerated swiftly despite only two-wheel drive and was travelling well over 300 when the streamliner yawed off course and snapped into a sideways tumble. The tail flew off, and *City* spiralled into the air and landed upside down before pitching over and over. Little hope could be held for Graham. He hadn't worn seat belts, and though the rollover bar withstood the impacts the firewall had intruded into the cockpit and broken his spine. Athol Graham was dead by the time he reached Tooele Hospital 110 miles away.

As Graham prepares for a run, crew-cut young Otto Anzjon (on left-hand side of Graham in cockpit) helps push *City of Salt Lake* to the line. Later Anzjon would repair and drive it after Graham's fatal 1960 accident.

Most experts declared he'd simply accelerated too hard and gone far enough

Dr Nathan Ostich was the first man to use pure jet propulsion in a land speed record attempt, in his cigar-shaped *Flying Caduceus*.

sideways for the crosswind to trip him over *City*'s own wall of air. Later, close inspection suggested the left rear wheel hub had sheared under the load of the massive torque transmitted during Graham's dragster start.

The first jet

This was a sombre start. Five days later, 52-year-old Los Angeles physician Dr Nathan Ostich brought out his weird *Flying Caduceus*, named for the medic's symbol. It was the world's first pure jet record car, but Ostich himself was no stranger to the salt, having run 189·98 m.p.h. in a modified sedan during his 10-year speed career.

Caduceus' 7,000 lb. thrust General Electric J47 turbojet came from a Convair B36 bomber and formed the bulk of the 6,985 lb. car like a great cylinder. The driver was located ahead of the front wheels, in a multi-windowed proboscis. Suspension was derived from Chevrolet truck parts and comprised A-arms and torsion bars; the wheels were outrigged and unstreamlined, shod with Firestone tyres inflated to 200 p.s.i. *Hot Rod Magazine* publisher Ray Brock designed and engineered the car along with hot rod doyen Ak Miller, and the red cigar was wind-tunnelled at California Poly Tech. When it was unveiled in early 1960 Brock and Ostich announced a goal of 500 m.p.h.

Ostich encountered several problems when he took to the salt on August 5th, the worst being a porous fuel pump. On the 10th he did a loafing run at 228 m.p.h. Then, when two civilian experts from Ogden's Hill Air Force Base gave the J47 a static test, the intake ducts, not packed out as normal by ram air, collapsed. After a heroic all-nighter they were repaired and next day Ostich managed 300 m.p.h. on 90 per cent power before they failed again. Severe vibrations also worried Brock and the Doc and they withdrew to LA for a rethink.

They were back by September 5th, but *Caduceus* began sliding sideways around 250, Ostich saving it only by deploying his braking parachute. He blamed the sort of crosswind Graham had encountered, but after another scare at 330 m.p.h. a grabbing brake disc was discovered. After a run at almost full power on the 6th revealed further bugs in the steering, the team withdrew again.

By then Mickey Thompson had got in several runs, including one at 354·33 m.p.h. in the National Speed Trials. His car, the blue-painted *Challenger 1*, was the most complicated of that illustrious 1960 gathering, with its long bonnetful of rebuilt scrap Pontiac engines – four of them disposed in two pairs alongside each other, with four three-speed transmissions and four final drives to front and rear axles, and four centrifugal blowers for cramming the mixture into all the thirty-two greedy inlet tracts (see Chapter 21 for further details of this car).

Over 400 m.p.h.!

The driver was set, slingshot fashion, behind the rear wheels, and with no springs to his axles and Bonneville particularly bumpy that year, he had a rough ride. He had his share of troubles too, mainly with front wheel adhesion which he cured by ballast and an aerofoil above the nose. Then rain washed away the black guide-line and the oil lorry re-laying it became bogged in mudflats. An old hand at the salt, Thompson chanced it without the line, getting in a run at 372 m.p.h. Cheered at this, he followed up with a real scorcher at 406·60 m.p.h. – faster than Cobb's fastest (403·135 m.p.h.) which really set the British visitors talking.

If Thompson could get in a return run as good, America had the *LSR* in her lap – with what was virtually a backyard special. Shades of Ray Keech and the Triplex of 1928! – except that Thompson's car was devilishly ingenious and not merely saurian. Alas, all he got on his run back was the anti-climax of a broken drive shaft. He tried again later, but the salt was in a bad state by then. Next a blower chain broke, and finally he gave up, resting content with his one-way at over 400 m.p.h. – one of the most remarkable efforts in the story of the record.

Art Arfons's appearance with his Allison rear-engined car, the first *Green Monster*, was regrettably brief. He was away smartly, got a 'probe' run at 249·57 m.p.h. with lots obviously still there, but on his return run a bearing went in the final drive. He released his drag 'chute to stop and the nylon line promptly snapped. Realizing that his car was not in the *LSR* class Art Arfons withdrew; but his day was yet to come.

So to Donald Campbell's first attempt at the record which his father broke nine times. He made several gentle runs, working up his speed stage by stage – 120 m.p.h., 170, 175, 240. He had the steering gear ratio reduced but was not too happy with it, then in his fifth run he accelerated much harder from the start and was up to about 345 m.p.h. when, in an accident uncomfortably like Athol Graham's in *City of Salt Lake*, the great blue car went progressively further off the black-lined course and spun sideways. It rolled, leapt into the air, hit the ground again, then bounced four or five times before it skidded on its underside to a stop, strewing bits and pieces, including two wheels, in its wake.

Donald Campbell, held in by his safety harness, was extremely fortunate to emerge from such a horrifying accident with a cracked skull, a pierced eardrum, and diverse cuts and bruises. He himself believed that the oxygen supply he was using had made him light-headed and indifferent when the car began to stray inward from the guide line. As the telemetering device beside the track showed that a speed of 360 m.p.h. had been reached – although possibly somewhat less owing to wheel-spin – it was felt by some that, like the unfortunate Athol Graham, Campbell had tried going too fast too soon.

Thus the first *Bluebird*-Proteus episode ended in ghastly anti-climax. Campbell was hospitalized, and the £1 million car was virtually a write-off. However, almost the first question Donald Campbell asked on recovering consciousness was how soon *Bluebird* could be repaired for another attempt, and on hearing of this, industrialist and Owen Organization chief Sir Alfred Owen, impressed by Campbell's courage, undertook to build another car.

(*Above, top*) The remains of *Bluebird* after spinning off-course at around 345 m.p.h. and rolling and bouncing to a standstill. Safety harness saved Donald Campbell from worse injuries than those he suffered. (*Below*) One of the Dunlop-shod wheels of *Bluebird*, torn off in Campbell's horrifying crash.

ANELS
CONSTRUCTED BY
MOTOR PANELS
COVENTRY
ENGLAND
7

14

Heartbreak corner

'I should never have come to this bloody place [Lake Eyre, 1964]. Never. It was a total error of judgment from the very beginning. Nothing, not one blind, bloody thing has gone right since I first saw the place four years ago.'

Donald Campbell from BLUEBIRD AND THE DEAD LAKE
by John Pearson

Once he had recovered from his chastening accident in *Bluebird* at Bonneville in 1960, Donald Campbell thought seriously about the venue for his next attempt on the record. He decided against using the famous Utah salt flats; the course was not long enough, he felt, while its condition in recent years had certainly deteriorated. Instead B.P., his main sponsors, sought a new course, and after considering sundry other sites they sent a reconnaissance party to Australia to examine a vast dried lake bed which Campbell had been told about. It was called Lake Eyre, and was about 450 miles inland from Adelaide, in South Australia. By ironic coincidence, when Donald Campbell's father was seeking a new course thirty-four years earlier, he was told of that equally 'promising' dried up lake bed, Verneuk Pan, in South Africa, also 450 miles inland, from Cape Town.

Reports to Donald Campbell were encouraging. The salt bed was very hard and flat, and offered boundless run-in distance, but was marred by many islands of salt crystals which would have to be removed somehow. The chance of rain was felt to be remote, none having fallen for many years, but a big snag was the remoteness of the place. The nearest point to the proposed course was Muloorina, a sheep and cattle station some 30 miles away. A road would need to be laid to transport supplies, and a causeway was essential to get down to the lake bed.

With encouragement from Sir Alfred Owen, whose companies constructed the car, a new *Bluebird* was built for Donald Campbell to try again. Here it is contrasted with the 1½-litre, V8 1962–3 Grand Prix B.R.M. also built and raced by the Owen Organisation.

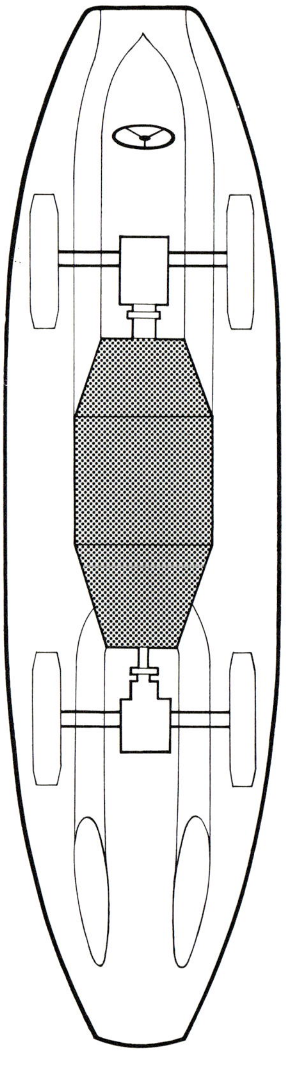

Bluebird-Proteus
Location of gas turbine unit

The decision was taken. Campbell would try for the record at Lake Eyre. The South Australian Government agreed to grade 65 miles of road from the railhead at Marree to Muloorina, and from there to the lake, and to build a 400-yard causeway on to the lake itself. The new *Bluebird*, less beautiful than the old with a huge tail fin deemed essential for stability, was to be shipped out to Australia early in 1962, and the attempt would be made as soon as possible.

This was just the beginning of an ordeal of frustration and discomfort which made Donald Campbell's father's experiences at Verneuk Pan in 1929 seem like a picnic. If Verneuk meant deception, Lake Eyre meant disaster. No rain had fallen there for seven years, but the elements soon atoned for that. Just as the expedition was gearing up, a report came from B.P. Australia that heavy rain had fallen on Lake Eyre, and the trip was postponed. The rain was so heavy that it would not drain off for months; and indeed, over a year passed before *Bluebird* was shipped to Adelaide and the whole vast entourage of men and equipment moved to the 'outback' in the spring of 1963.

In the public's opinion it was high time too. Ambitions too long proclaimed lose their lustre, yet the publicity drum has continually to be beaten in ventures of this kind. *Bluebird*, it was felt, had now been around too long without doing anything, and an impatient world needed action. Campbell and his backers were only too well aware of this, but when *LSR* attempts were so utterly dependent on a long, dead smooth course, and the elements seemed so bent on sabotaging things, they could only grin and bear it.

The grin grew hollower as time passed. Heavy rain again fell, and when the main party had moved in the skies redoubled their efforts and flooded the new course so laboriously and expensively prepared. They sought an alternative, and having probed the salt to ensure sufficient depth for *Bluebird*'s 4-ton weight, and plotted a new 12-mile stretch, it was a case of all hands to the pump in a race against time and the weather. The salt islands were milled away with a rotary cutter towed by a tractor, and by mid-May Donald Campbell was making his first tentative runs, though the salt was soft and wet.

A terrific storm assailed Lake Eyre that night, threatening to inundate *Bluebird* under her canvas covers. Campbell drove her out at dead of night in a howling gale on to the mainland, and next day they found the new course ruined and boxes of spares and miscellaneous gear floating about. Lake Eyre was a drain for thousands of square miles of South Australia around it, and obviously would be useless for months. The party broke up. In the black mood of so much frustration, tempers long tried gave way and bitter words were said.

The press were scornful of the failure, and the public, unaware of the rigours and difficulties encountered, grew more restive still. So did some of Campbell's sponsors, especially when woefully ill-timed news came that an American named Craig Breedlove had exceeded 400 m.p.h. without apparent difficulty on the despised Bonneville salt flats in a jet-powered three-wheeler. Useless for Campbell and his supporters to stress that such a machine could not officially take the land speed record. Someone with an ex-fighter aircraft jet on wheels had done 407 m.p.h. – why couldn't Campbell do better with all *Bluebird*'s sophisticated equipment?

Donald Campbell suffered that particular comparison which any son of a famous father has to endure. The 'old man' had broken the record nine times, and now Fate maliciously conspired to prevent his son breaking it even once. A new record would clear the air, show the world that Campbell and *Bluebird could* do it. Instead critics pointed out that 'the boy' had never gone motor-racing like his father, knew nothing about high-speed motoring, and had never yet exceeded 300 m.p.h. (though defenders emphasized his magnificent performances on water and his six absolute water records). It was all highly unpleasant, and savoured of the time when Kaye Don, too, was pilloried by the ignorant because he could not break the record with *Silver Bullet* in 1930.

Zeldine tries again

Meanwhile, *City of Salt Lake*'s tragic story hadn't ended with Athol Graham's death. Salt Lakers had pressured widow Zeldine's insurance company into paying up when it baulked because of the nature of Graham's death, and they had a collection which raised some $3,000. Thus many were appalled when it became known Zeldine Graham intended to use the money for another crack at the record after 17-year-old Anzjon had persuaded her to let him rebuild the shattered car.

Despite ill-concealed hostility, the duo was back on the salt for the 1962 Speed Week and the youngster did a fine job to turn 254 m.p.h. in one direction. Zeldine lost no time applying to official Joe Petrali for a record run sanction. Worried by the car's history, Petrali advised Anzjon on several design factors he wanted altered – in particular that overstressed rear axle – but though Otto listened politely he hadn't put any of Joe's recommendations into effect by the time the car was ready to go. Realizing there was little he could do based on *City*'s past speed, Petrali compromised with Graham, who agreed to Anzjon rigging up a device to measure loads on the axle.

In his first all-out attempt, Anzjon was over 200 m.p.h. and accelerating when the overloaded left rear Firestone let go, and for the second time in its career *City* travelled the wrong way up across the salt flats *en route* to destruction. This time its driver walked away. Poor Anzjon, however, had little time left. In the winter of 1962, in the Salt Lake City Hospital in which Zeldine Graham worked, he died of leukaemia, never realizing until the last days that he had the disease. His parents, who had kept the news from him, had been instrumental in persuading the Grahams to let their car-crazy son work on the streamliner in the first place.

Mrs Graham talked of pursuing her husband's vision despite the fresh tragedy, and with Harry Muhlbach at the wheel a further rebuilt *City of Salt Lake* once more headed for Bonneville.

In October 1963 the flame red car ran again, but was dogged by problems with the new parachute braking system. On the 11th Muhlbach ran 10 miles down the course without realizing the 'chute had deployed itself, later commenting that he had nearly lost control twice because of the problem. Then, on his first run on the 12th, *City* yet again veered out of control and slid upside down for 1,000 ft. Like Anzjon, Muhlbach lived to tell his tale, venturing the opinion he'd been travelling 'around 395' at the time. Joe Petrali, now well used to *City*'s antics, offered 240 m.p.h. was nearer the mark – 'and sideways, at that'.

Shaken by yet another crash, Zeldine pondered until November before announcing yet another try for 1964. Firestone, however, wasn't interested in having its reputation sullied by inadequate engineering and was in any case closer involved with Art Arfons. Nobody else was interested in helping out financially with the car's third rebuild in as many years. There was also a fair degree of opposition as Salt Lakers feared another fatality in the ill-starred racer.

When the insurance companies also frowned, Zeldine Graham was finally forced to accept financial if not spiritual defeat and as jetsters Breedlove and Arfons prepared to kick the big record into the 500s her late husband's dream at last slipped beyond her determined grasp.

Ostich gets serious

(*Below and opposite*) Lacking a fourth wheel, Craig Breedlove's jet-powered *Spirit of America* was not technically a car in the eyes of the F.I.A., but it became fastest on land none the less in August 1963 at 407·45 m.p.h. Front and rear views here show the clean, purposeful form.

Dr Nathan Ostich revealed similar determination to Mrs Graham. After the disappointments in 1960 he had planned to return again to Bonneville in November of that year, only to be thwarted by the weather. He sat out 1961 too, unhappy with the salt's condition. By August 1962, however, he was back at Bonneville ready for some serious full-power runs. After a 206 m.p.h. warm-up he pushed into the 300s by the 9th. However, as *Caduceus* entered the third of the course's 12 miles he sensed trouble. He was up to 330 by mile seven when he yawed into a spectacular slide. He got the car slowed, but under the strain the left front suspension failed and its wheel ripped away. Ostich popped his 'chute and the crippled three-wheeler ground to a halt on its belly. It had been the Doc's thirteenth run on the salt. . . .

Still dissatisfied with directional stability he was moved to comment: 'It's impossible to control *Flying Caduceus* with wheels. The handling is perfect between 319 and 324, but after that even a small yaw is sufficient to push it permanently off-line. There's no holding it. The only way to control it at speed is with a rudder.'

By September 1963 the long red speed tube was back for a third and final try, but plenty of things were different. There was a new tail fin, which acted as a steerable rudder to improve the car's response; there was a smaller fin mounted beneath the jetpipe so the rear fin area would equal that of the nose, making sure wind force would act equally front and rear; there was a new steering ratio and a damper to kill the shimmying problem; the suspension was revised, the truck components giving way to Heim joints; there were new Firestones. Just under 10 inches wide, they were an inch narrower than the previous rubber, reducing frontal area.

And finally, there was Craig Breedlove's 407·45 m.p.h. clocking to contend with. A lot of other Americans were talking of jetcars (see Chapter 22) and for Ostich

(Below) Spirit of America
Location of jet power unit

(*Right*) A partly cutaway view of the three-wheeled *Spirit of America*, showing rear location of the General Electric J47 aircraft jet power unit.

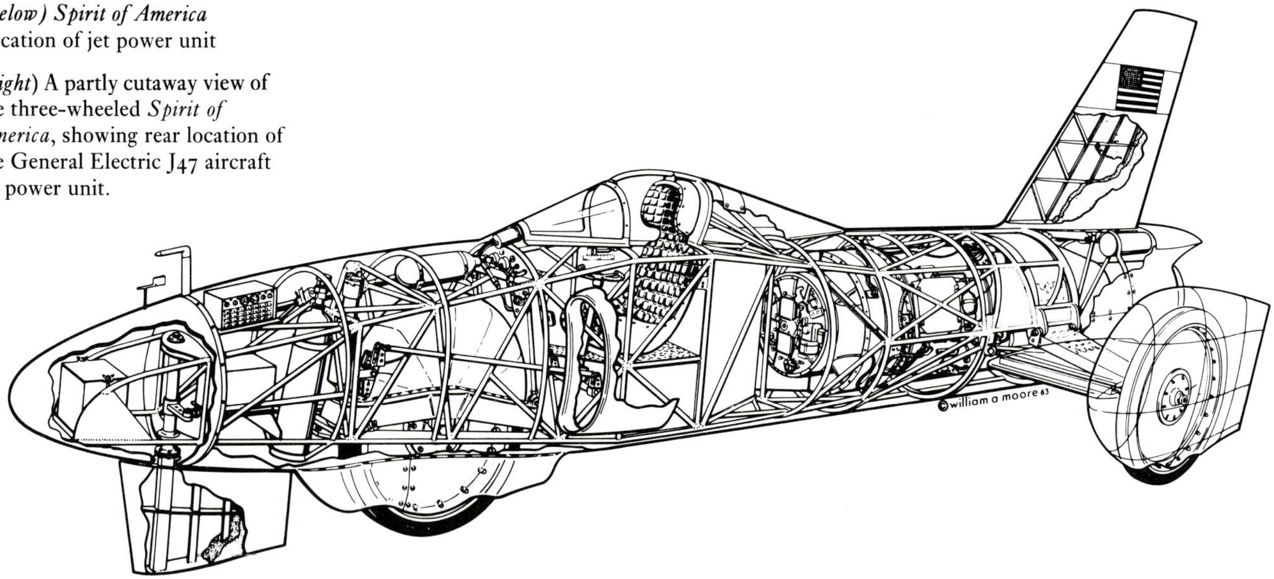

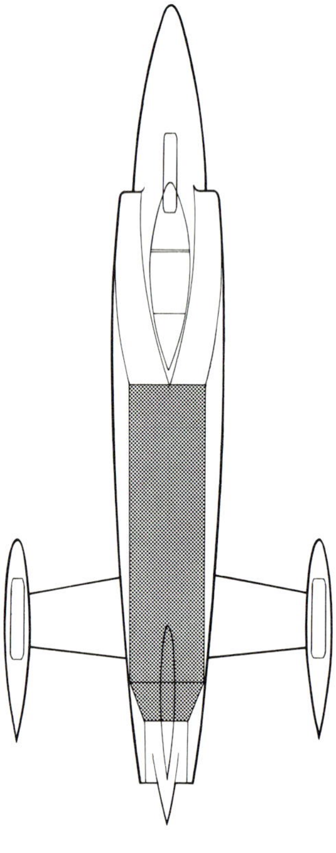

and his four-year-old concept it was now or never.

On Thursday, September 19th salt conditions were good, but when Ostich and his crew checked in on the Sunday a rain storm left a quarter of an inch of water over much of the course. By Monday, however, Ostich ran, and by Thursday afternoon he'd clocked eight runs over the nine-mile course. His first run at 253 m.p.h. was 100 more than planned, as the car felt so stable, but near disaster came at the end of the second as he hit 323 then slowed to 75. *Caduceus*' wheels locked on soggy salt and the more Ostich applied pedal pressure the more he felt the brakes had failed. He was headed directly for a large flood when the car veered right on to the soft salt with half a mile to spare, finally spinning to a halt and damaging only Ostich's ego. The next six runs netted 314, 350, 359, 354, 351 and 355, the last four made at full throttle. Something was amiss.

While *Caduceus* was now handling beautifully, the engine just wouldn't register more than 94 per cent of its maximum revs, which effectively put it a vital 25 per cent down on thrust. Since the J47 had never given trouble before, an engine expert hadn't been considered a necessity, so Project Engineer Brock and Chief Mechanic Allen Bradshaw tried vainly to trace the problem, centring attention on the fuel system. Then a civilian expert was flown in from Salt Lake City, but was also unable to pinpoint a reason for the J47's sluggishness. Held by wooden chocks and chained to two trucks whose brakes were firmly applied, the jetcar underwent static test after static test, without success. Despite everything, the 28 ft. streamliner just couldn't summon that extra muscle to crack the 400 and Ostich reluctantly headed home to LA, a rumoured $100,000 poorer.

He made noises about returning as and when his crew could tickle 100 per cent from the powerplant, but never did. Whenever asked about his valiant efforts, and those of rival Breedlove, he would say: 'I get sick every time I think about it.'

The dragster man

Who was this Craig Breedlove who had added fuel to the fires of controversy? He was a typical Californian dragster specialist who devoted all his spare time to the pursuit of speed, and did so well at it that his cars became his full-time occupation. His ambition to break the *LSR* came early and he pursued it doggedly, with the example of Mickey Thompson's valiant effort in 1960 before him.

Like Dr Nathan Ostich, he chose jet power rather than a piston engine, a surplus General Electric J47 aircraft unit costing no more than a junk V12 Allison. He met two aerodynamics experts, and between them they thrashed out a design. A scale model was wind-tunnel tested, altered, altered again, and finalized, then Breedlove started building his car, which he called *Spirit of America*, in his backyard garage.

Soon he ran out of money and looked for sponsorship. His sincerity, expert knowledge and enthusiasm won over Shell and Goodyear, both of whom agreed to support him. Nobody seemed worried that the *Spirit* was a pure jet-driven three-wheeler and thus would not comply with the F.I.A.'s stipulation that a successful *LSR* machine must have at least four wheels, two of them driven, to get official recognition, yet the great aim was to beat John Cobb's 394·20 m.p.h. record set up in 1947.

Tests began in August 1962, just before Glenn Leasher's ill-fated *Infinity* (see Chapter 22) was due on the salt. Breedlove reached 300 m.p.h., 349 and 365, but encountered steering troubles due to problems with the controllable canard fin mounted under the nose, whose purpose was to control changes in direction in conjunction with braking one or other of the rear wheels. The front wheel was non-steerable at this stage, but even though it was later discovered the fin hadn't had sufficient movement, Breedlove elected to give the front wheel about 4 degrees of movement and added a 6 ft. tail fin for extra stability.

In its new form the unique 3-ton three-wheeler resembled nothing more than a grounded jet fighter with its tricycle undercarriage down and its wings removed. The single front wheel was partly recessed in the nose; the intakes for the J47 were on each side, and the driver sat in an enclosed cockpit above them. The rear wheels, outrigged on a faired dead axle, were fully streamlined; the profile was very clean and effective, and the engineering and finish of the car were highly professional. It looked anything but the backyard venture it started as when 26-year-old Craig Breedlove brought it out on to the course at Bonneville at dawn on 5 August 1963.

There had been some late trouble with the automatic drag parachute release, and Breedlove decided to use his manual release. The 8-mile-long, 100 ft.-wide course had been extended by dragging an extra 2 miles clean, giving him $4\frac{1}{2}$ miles for acceleration, 1 mile for the record, and $4\frac{1}{2}$ miles to slow up. At 6.30 a.m. the 'course clear' signal came, T-shirted mechanics and helpers moved back, and Breedlove took up the engine to a screaming 90 per cent of its maximum 4,000 lb. thrust, straining against the chocks. At his signal these were removed; he held the car on the rear wheel brakes, then released them.

Spirit of America moved slowly forward, then suddenly shrieked away as the hot gases bit. The salt was bumpy but she was through the mile in under 9 sec. Breedlove cut his motor, the two drag 'chutes flew out, he braked progressively, and the world's fastest tricycle stopped. More Shell fuel was put in and the 'chutes repacked, but no tyres had to be changed – a marked difference from former *LSR* attempts. Jet cars do not wear out tyres like driven wheels, and amazingly the 4 ft. diameter, 8 × 39 in. special Goodyear covers he was using had served throughout the previous week of trial runs as well as the actual record attempt! While he was waiting, Breedlove got the U.S.A.C. time-keepers' report – 388·47 m.p.h.

For the return burst, Breedlove took the J47 up to 95 per cent, let go the brakes and whooshed away beyond the horizon. In the timing stand were officials of the Fédération Internationale Motocycliste (F.I.M., the European body which governs two- and three-wheeled competitions and records, and which was perfectly prepared to accept a three-wheeled jet record), officials of the United States Automobile Club (U.S.A.C., also ready to recognize a jet-powered vehicle), and Goodyear and Shell representatives. All of them watched the blue-and-white projectile hurtling across the salt and passing beyond vision. There was a tense silence, then Joe Petrali, one-time famous American racing motor-cyclist and U.S.A.C. steward, said quietly, 'Gentlemen, we have a new land speed record.'

Craig Breedlove's speed through the return mile was a shattering 428·37 m.p.h., and his mean speed was 407·45 m.p.h., beating both Cobb's and Thompson's best speeds. He may not have broken the record in the eyes of the F.I.A. but he had unquestionably driven faster on land than anyone else. Knowing he had performance left, Breedlove was eager to go out and improve on his record there and then, but his sponsors restrained him. They advised him to rest content.

Craig Breedlove.

Per ardua ad 403.1 m.p.h.

It was with something akin to despair that Donald Campbell returned to Muloorina in April 1964 to try once again for the *LSR*. This time it had to be done on a stricter budget, for B.P. had withdrawn their backing and finances were tighter, making an early success all the more imperative. Alas, in defiance of Lake Eyre's weather records, rain had again fallen abundantly in the weeks before, and when *Bluebird* was being towed on a trailer across the lake the crust collapsed and trailer and car tilted alarmingly. They were righted, tilted again 100 yards further on, but eventually the car was in her tent.

Corrosion from the salt had badly affected her exterior and also the electrical connections, and the Proteus proved very difficult to start. On 1st May it rained again, leaving the carefully prepared strip in four inches of water. The hunt began for yet another new course. A reasonably firm stretch of salt was found, but it was two vital miles shorter and only forty yards wide. Some frantic work with Land

Rovers towing girders scraped it clean, and on 5th May Campbell began tests again.

The salt had also got at the new parachute-stabilizing device, but chief mechanic Leo Villa made it work, and despite *Bluebird* making deep ruts in the soggy salt Campbell worked up to 300 m.p.h., only to encounter severe vibration. Ken Norris eventually traced this to salt clinging to the wheels, emulsifying under heat from the brakes while the car was halted, running to the bottom of the wheels and upsetting their balance. On 28th May *Bluebird* did 352 m.p.h. on 70 per cent power from the Proteus and all looked set for a try at the record when strong side winds sprang up, the car being blown 18 feet off-course at just over 300 m.p.h. Days passed before they eased off, and by then the course was so bumpy, soft and rutted that the unlucky Campbell had to give up for several further weeks.

In July 1964 the *Bluebird* party returned to Lake Eyre – 'Heartbreak Corner' – for another attempt. The course had been filled and graded and Campbell, aware that Craig Breedlove was preparing for another run at Bonneville, decided to dispense with test runs and go for the record as soon as possible. Yet again, almost unbelievably, it rained and one end of the strip became waterlogged! He had lost two precious miles for accelerating and braking, but with the Proteus 'tweaked' to give full power, he did a very bumpy 320 m.p.h. try-out on 14th July.

All was ready on the 16th, but this time a gusty side wind blew all day and yet again Donald Campbell had to contain himself for another twenty-four hours. Things were better next morning, however, and without more ado Campbell went for the record, not forgetting to take his famous mascot, 'Mr Whoppit' the bear. Despite wheel-spin much of the way and a rut which almost threw her out of control, *Bluebird* clocked 403·10 m.p.h. for the down mile. Leo Villa and helpers changed the tyres, and refuelled and recharged the air cylinders for the brakes and driver's air supply, while Campbell said very little.

Then he was off again for the return run, and amazingly the speed was identical – 403·10 m.p.h.! His tyres had taken terrible punishment, the offside rear cover being through to the fabric, while the course was littered with chunks of rubber. But they'd done it; they'd really got the official record for wheel-driven cars at last!

Campbell was asked if he had enjoyed the run. 'No, it was awful,' he replied. 'The car was all over the place.' If he had burst into tears from sheer reaction on learning that he had broken the record after so much bitter struggle, it would have been understandable. 'Instead I felt a wave of resentment that it all had to be so difficult, and relief that I'd got the bastard at last,' he later told the author in an interview.

So, after seventeen years and two months, John Cobb's land speed record of 394·196 m.p.h. had been broken by another wheel-driven car. It was vindication at last for Donald Campbell, although he knew that, given the good conditions he had expected from the treacherous Lake Eyre, he could add 40 m.p.h. to his speed. Very wisely he made no more attempts, but went in quest of his sixth water speed record instead. He got it, too, at Lake Dumbleyung, on the last day of 1964.

By then his hard-won car record had been eclipsed four times by American jet-powered cars, and the absolute record was 130 m.p.h. higher!

Although eclipsed by Breedlove's *Spirit of America*, Donald Campbell at last succeeded in breaking Cobb's 1947 land speed record in July 1964 at Lake Eyre, Australia, where he achieved a desperate 403·10 m.p.h.

WINGFOOT EXPRESS
GOODYEAR
GOODYEAR
Mobil

15

The great jet battle

'A land vehicle propelled by its own means, running on at least four wheels not in line with each other, which must always be in contact with the ground; the steering must be assured by at least two of the wheels, and the propulsion by at least two of the wheels.'

Definition of an automobile, from F.I.A. regulations.

In the eyes of Craig Breedlove and many other Americans, poor Donald Campbell's record did not exist at all. 'Who the hell are the F.I.A.? If they don't like our car they can do the other thing – we *got* the record,' said Breedlove, and to show their indifference to European efforts at control, he and his sponsors prepared the *Spirit of America* tricycle for an attempt to better their own figure of 407·45 m.p.h. Before they were quite ready, however, two new challengers came somewhat unexpectedly upon the scene.

One was *Wingfoot Express*, built by Walt Arfons of Akron; the other was *Green Monster*, built by Art Arfons, his younger brother, also of Akron. Both were entirely independent operations, for the two brothers rarely spoke to each other and went their own ways. The *Wingfoot* had a 6,200 lb. thrust Westinghouse J46 triple-jet engine, four wheels and little else, apart from an enclosed cockpit for the driver, a streamlined, partly transparent tapering nose for him to see through, and a tail-fin high above the great maw of the business end of the jet unit.

Twenty-four feet long and weighing 42¾ cwt., it was a compact car with oleo-pneumatically sprung axles and small diameter wheels mounting Goodyear tyres.

On 2 October 1964, engineer/driver Tom Green of Elmhurst, Illinois, added his name to the illustrious list of land speed record-holders with this Westinghouse J46 jet-powered, four-wheeler built by Walt Arfons, and called *Wingfoot Express*. Green averaged 413·2 m.p.h. through the flying mile at Bonneville.

Walt Arfons did not believe the huge wheels on Campbell's *Bluebird* were necessary. 'You need a small car for the land speed record,' he said. 'We had an arrow in mind – weight and fin feathers in the rear, tapering almost to a point in front.' The *Wingfoot Express*, so named after the place where Goodyear lighter-than-air blimps are made (Goodyear were sponsoring the car), was jointly built by 47-year-old Walt Arfons and an engineer named Tom Green from Elmhurst, Illinois.

It was ready for tests on the salt by the spring of 1963. There followed the usual chapter of incidents and drama that add up to 'know-how', but by the end of the year the car had topped 315 m.p.h., and 1964 looked hopeful. Walt Arfons could no longer drive following a heart attack, so engineer Green gallantly took the job on. After endless tests they booked the salt flats for one week to attempt the *LSR* in late September–early October 1964, but the *Wingfoot* had performed indifferently for so long that Walt and Tom were dismissed as 'shoestring boys' who would never make the big grade.

Most of their week was a mixture as before; seven times up and seven times back Green had swept over the flats, and 313 m.p.h. was his highest speed. On the fourth day they fitted a new J46 engine, a quicker job than it sounds; on the fifth day cross-winds howled all day over the course; on the sixth fuel pump trouble spoiled their morning, and in the afternoon Arfons made more adjustments to the power unit, told Green not to forget to use the after-burner, and waved him off.

It was 4.00 p.m. with the sun blazing down on the glaring white flats as Green moved up, and bored U.S.A.C. time-keepers prepared to clock yet another run. He was off with the soughing of the J46 changing to a scream, and suddenly the timers stiffened. 'Hey, the *Wingfoot* just did the mile at 406·5 m.p.h.!' But Tom Green was worried about the engine. Arfons made a quick check and found that a piece of metal, perhaps a bolt, had got into the turbine, damaging four blades before disappearing.

There was nothing they could do about it within the time limit, so Green hopefully set off on the return leg. Three times he used the after-burner, and in three huge spurts the car had blasted through the mile at 420·07 m.p.h. – new record at 413·2 m.p.h. mean! Two more new names had joined the long list of land speed record-holders.

Art replies

What followed cannot have made the Arfons brothers any more ready to speak to each other. Three days after the *Wingfoot*'s surprise success, on Monday 5th October, 38-year-old Art Arfons brought out *his* jet car, the *Green Monster* with General Electric 15,000 lb. thrust J79 engine as used in the Hustler bomber. It was a truly crude and massive device, a veritable blowpipe on wheels, wheels smaller, even, than those on the *Wingfoot* and wearing specially designed tyres by Firestone, major sponsors of the *Monster*, which was painted green, red and white.

The front end was one vast intake with a central supersonic probe like the stamen

Art Arfons's massive 17,500 h.p. J79 jet-powered *Green Monster*, with which he shattered Tom Green's record at 434·02 m.p.h.

of some strange orchid. The tail was one vast outlet, with above it a stabilizing fin; while on the nearside the driver sat in an outrigged cockpit merged into the wheel fairings as if by an afterthought. There was no rear suspension at all – just a 2-ton Ford truck solid axle – but at the front a 1937 Lincoln beam axle with Dodge truck stub axles was sprung by aircraft-type hydro-pneumatic legs and steered by Dodge truck mechanism. A large aerofoil was situated above the nose to keep it down.

This apparently unsophisticated brute was often compared to the *Triplex Special* of 1928, but in reality was a tribute to Arfons' sheer mechanical aptitude. When he was searching for a J79 power unit, all he could find was a junk unit with serious compressor blade damage. General Electric refused to supply any handbooks and believed it had stymied Art; when it discovered the 'junkyard genius of the jetset' had not only managed to rebuild the engine, but had it working like new, it made strenuous – and totally fruitless – efforts to buy it back! All told, *Green Monster* cost Arfons little more than £6,000, compared with *Bluebird*'s near million, yet with an engine of almost double the output of its rivals it had enormous potential. Its first run on Bonneville on 5th October was a mere 396·3 m.p.h., but Arfons showed what lay in reserve by clocking a sizzling 479 m.p.h. on the run back – an average of 434·02 m.p.h. and an easy new record, just loafing along on 60 per cent power.

Then out came Craig Breedlove on 13th October to do something about these interlopers on *Spirit of America*'s territory. His car had been checked and refined in detail and fitted with a newly rebuilt surplus J47 engine giving up to 500 lb. more thrust over the 5,200 lb. of his 1963 unit. The streamlining had also been improved and braking pressure increased. For sheer ease of accomplishment Breedlove out-Arfonsed Arfons, just blasting out, blasting back, and there was another new record at 468·72 m.p.h. But even more was to come.

Brakeless at over 500 m.p.h.

Two days later Breedlove and the *Spirit* went out and did it all over again, this time at a sensational 526·28 m.p.h.! This awesome performance ended in an even more awesome one when, just after leaving the measured mile, Breedlove released his drag parachute, which promptly broke away from its anchorage. At 500 m.p.h.-plus it was asking too much of the Goodyear single disc brakes on the rear wheels to stop the car, designed as they were to work from 150 m.p.h. down after the 'chute had done its stuff. The brakes burned out and *Spirit of America* careered remorselessly off the end of the cleared course, zipped through a row of telephone poles, felling one at the base like a matchstick, flew about 150 feet through the air, and finished up in a lake of brine, 5 miles off course. There it was all but submerged, only its tail projecting. Breedlove, narrowly escaping drowning, managed to get out of the cockpit and swam for dry land, the first driver to break the 500 m.p.h. barrier. Climbing out, he quipped bravely 'For my next act I'll set myself afire!'

Still that stupendous '64 season was not over. Twelve days after Breedlove's dramatic performance, Art Arfons was back with the mighty *Green Monster*. Taking a run-in of only 2 miles and using his afterburners for acceleration, his first mile was a bumpy 515·98 m.p.h. On learning how 'slow' he'd been he simply stepped up the power of his J79 and rocketed back over the bumps at 559·18 m.p.h. . . . a new record, 536·71 m.p.h.! Were it not so staggering it would have been monotonous. John Cobb's record of 394·20 m.p.h. stood for sixteen years, and now, within one month, the *LSR* had fallen *five* times and been raised by a further 142½ m.p.h.!

The F.I.A. clarifies things

There was a further momentous happening during that unique month. At their October meeting the F.I.A. agreed to recognize land speed records established by cars without driven wheels; or, to quote the International Sporting Code, '. . .vehicles which, contrary to the definition of an automobile, are propelled

Eight days after Art Arfons took Green's record, Breedlove took Arfons's record at 468·72 m.p.h. Two days later he broke his own record at 526·28 m.p.h., only to lose his braking when the drag parachute tore away on his second run. *Spirit of America* charged off-course, hit a telephone pole, leapt into the air and finished up in a brine lake. Pictures show (*top*) the *Spirit* braking safely on its parachute after the first run; (*centre*) its three tracks in the salt through the telephone poles; (*below*) the car in the lake and Breedlove among the onlookers after swimming ashore.

otherwise than through their wheels; cars equipped with jet engines and ground effect vehicles (hovercraft). This category shall be known as International Records for Special Vehicles.'

Thus *LSR* cars with driven wheels rated as 'Automobiles' and jets etc., as 'Specials', creating two classes of *LSR* holder in future. The first new record thus to be recognized officially was Art Arfons's 536·71 m.p.h., and he became the first American officially to hold the *LSR* since Ray Keech's valiant 207·55 m.p.h. at Daytona in 1928 with the Triplex Special. Said Arfons: 'I am elated beyond words at the F.I.A.'s approval. This is the jet age, and I'm glad they are going to recognize it.'

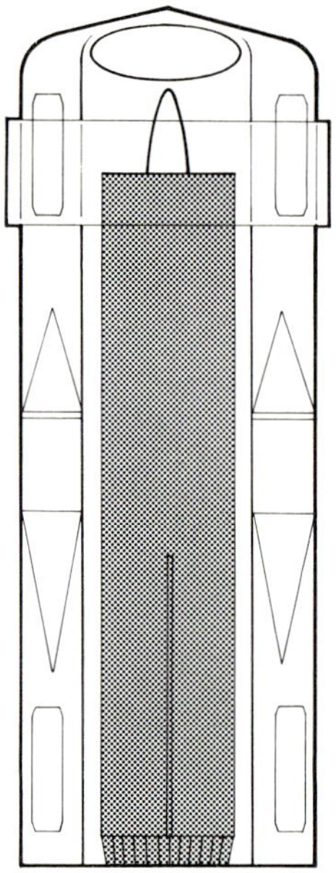

Green Monster
Location of jet power unit

The dizzy round

1965 proved scarcely less eventful. Three *LSR* contenders turned out to add enormous interest to the annual Bonneville 'Nationals' held between August and November. First to appear was a wild innovation in record cars – a rocket-powered, delta-shaped machine built by the ever-enterprising Walt Arfons, sponsored by Goodyear, and bearing the same *Wingfoot Express* name tag as his 1964 jet car. It used multi-J.A.T.O. (jet-assisted take-off) rockets which imparted tremendous acceleration but were of insufficient duration to make the distance. The fastest speed Arfons's driver Bobby Tatroe attained during several trouble-fraught sessions on the salt was 476·6 m.p.h. for the kilometre, after which Arfons withdrew

Twelve days after Breedlove's dramatic accident, Arfons and his *Green Monster* raised the record yet again to 536·71 m.p.h. – the fifth new land speed record within a month!

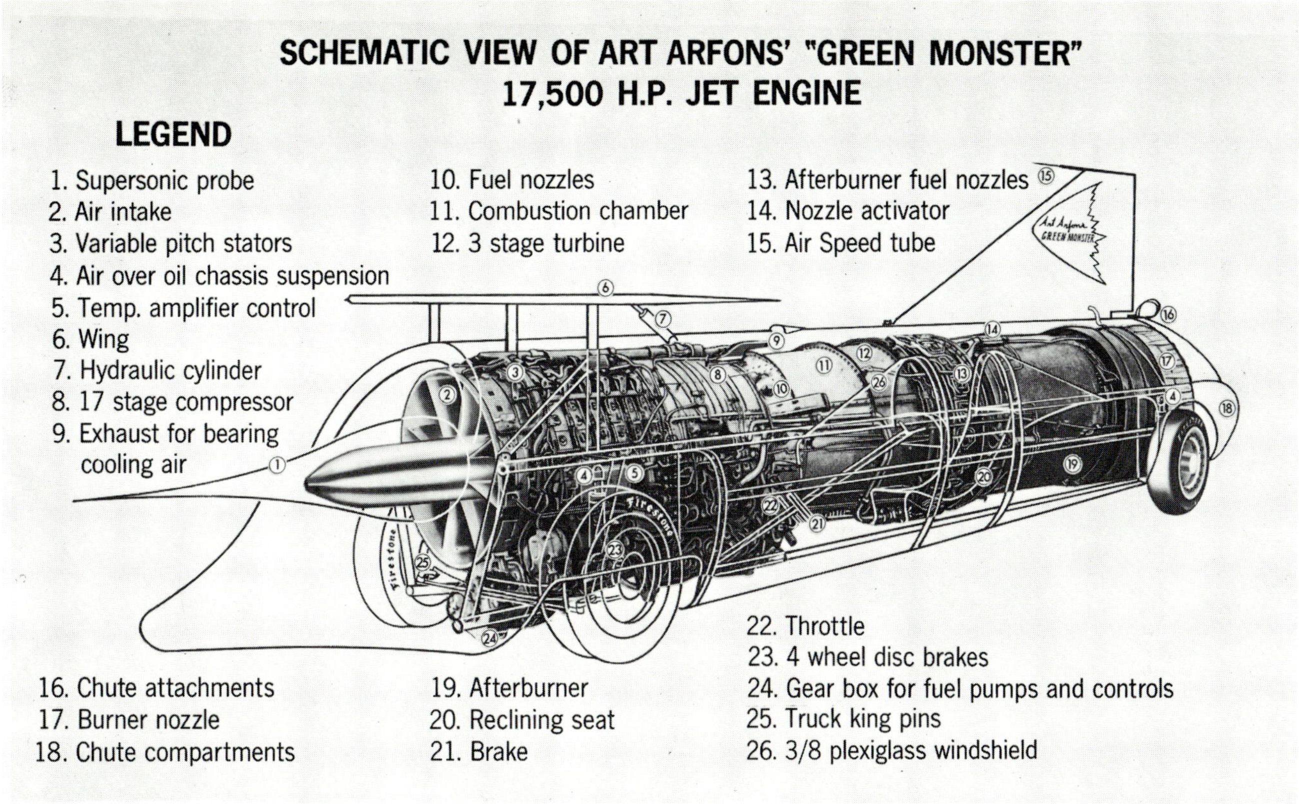

(*Above*) Cutaway drawing of the *Green Monster* – virtually an immense blowlamp on wheels.

the car to think again (see Chapter 17 for further details).

Goodyear probably put more hope into the new car they sponsored for Craig Breedlove the same year. Originally, he considered building a J79-powered version of the existing *Spirit*, but ultimately opted for an all-new shape. It had four wheels this time (the F.I.A. climbed down on jet-power units but would not give way on three-wheelers), and a General Electric J79 turbojet unit similar to that in Art Arfons's *Green Monster*. It gave 15,000-lb. thrust and a speed potential of over 800 m.p.h., and was designed by Breedlove himself. Although infinitely better-looking than the *Monster*, the tenet 'If it looks right it *is* right' could not justly apply to this machine.

It had a vaguely rectangular body form, very smoothly clad in fibreglass and aluminium panels, slightly waisted and merging into two wheel-covers almost entirely shrouding the wheels. These were only 25 in. in diameter at the front and 39 in. in diameter at the rear, with special Goodyear low-profile tyres designed to withstand 850 m.p.h. stresses. The front axle was a tubular beam with torsion bar springing, while the rear suspension was independent, also by torsion bars. This car retained the name *Spirit of America*, but was sub-titled *Sonic 1*.

Its nose tapered to a needle-sharp point, and Breedlove's cockpit with narrow slot window and pistol-grip steering control instead of a wheel was just ahead of the front wheels, with the great intake for the jet motor above it. The body was topped with the usual high tail-fin, and braking was by a Hemis-Flo drag parachute

(*Below*) *Spirit of America-Sonic I* Location of jet power unit

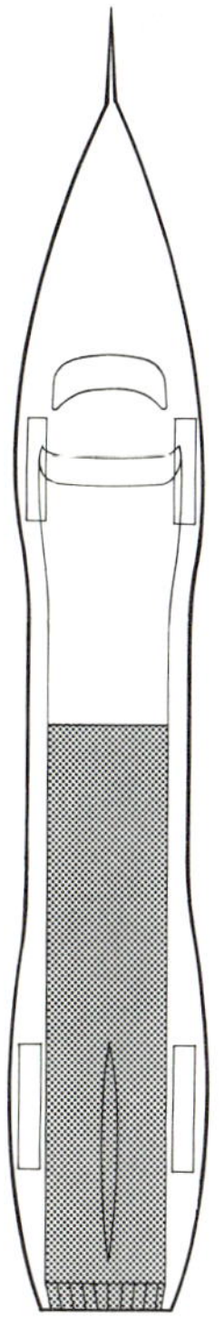

1965 brought forth Craig Breedlove's second *Spirit of America*, the *Sonic I*. It had four wheels to satisfy the F.I.A. and a General Electric J79 jet engine as in Arfons's *Green Monster*. In November it retook his record at 555·483 m.p.h. Front and rear views show Breedlove's efforts to minimize drag around the wheels.

GOODYEAR

developed by Goodyear, plus single disc brakes of aircraft type on all four wheels, designed to operate from 200 m.p.h. The car's waisted centre earned it the nickname 'the Coca-Cola bottle', but it was superbly engineered and finished.

Sonic 1 was built with considerable secrecy to surprise Art Arfons, and appeared about twelve months after he created his 536·71 m.p.h. record. The old *Spirit of America* tricycle, repaired after its brine bath at Bonneville, went on permanent exhibition at the Chicago Science Museum as America's first successful jet-propelled record car, and all attention focused on the new *Spirit*. As ever, there were early snags. High-speed test-runs indicated that the frame needed strengthening; the nose caved in and the side panels were pulling loose under pressure, an air intake duct cracked, and the front end tended to lift.

Cures for these ailments included body reinforcements and the cutting of louvres to relieve internal pressures. Even so, *Sonic 1* went out of control at 600 m.p.h. when the nose lifted, shot 1,000 feet off-course when the drag 'chute failed, and ended up uncomfortably close to the scene of Breedlove's 1964 brine bath. Larger nose fins were fitted and re-angled to keep the front wheels on the ground, and on 2 November 1965 *Sonic 1* went for the record.

Five days after Breedlove's new car took its first land speed record, Art Arfons in *Green Monster* retook the record at 576·553 m.p.h. On his second run, however, the offside rear tyre burst, tearing away a drag parachute and sending the car off-course at 550 m.p.h. The front end was badly damaged against an iron marker post before Arfons regained control and stopped the car. (*Right*) the crippled *Monster*.

It was a straightforward operation once again, and although Breedlove did not fully extend his new machine he took Arfons's record very comfortably, clocking 555·483 m.p.h. through the kilometre, and 555·127 m.p.h. through the mile. Then he stood back to see what *Green Monster* could do in retaliation.

Art Arfons had his fiery behemoth waiting in the wings ready to counter Breedlove's latest blow. He let his rival enjoy his new record for five days, then on 7th November moved out on to the salt. Without any preliminaries he took a 2-mile run-in (which he later said was too long!) and was through the timing traps and back again at 576·553 m.p.h. for the mile and 572·545 m.p.h. for the kilometre. But record-breaking is no sinecure; just past the mile on his return run the offside rear tyre, of 1964-type built for 600 m.p.h. maximum, burst at just over that velocity.

The flying rubber ripped away the right-hand parachute and the combined 'chute electrical firing gear, and Art Arfons's cockpit over on the nearside filled with smoke. He veered off-course and struck an iron marker post, smashing the fibre-glass front of the car and ripping the right front tyre. Arfons broke the glass in the cockpit to get some vision and moved back on course, all at over 550 m.p.h., then released his second parachute manually and pulled up about $3\frac{1}{2}$ miles away.

999B

16

Over 600 m.p.h.

'The world land speed record has meaning. . . . It's an international thing. The rich Englishmen used to hold all the records, but now I hold them. I'm patriotic. That's why I named my car the *Spirit of America*.'

Craig Breedlove, interviewed in CAR LIFE.

With the weather deteriorating as the 1965 Bonneville season ran out, a quick retort by Craig Breedlove to Art Arfons's slick 576·553 m.p.h. performance was expected. Instead the tense to-and-fro dance between the giant jets was interrupted by a comely and interesting newcomer to the international records stage. The Summers brothers, Bill and Bob, of Ontario, California, had been around the Bonneville flats a long time, hot-rodding Chrysler products with notable success, and in 1964, with the F.I.A.'s introduction of separate record categories for 'Specials' and wheel-driven cars, they set out to challenge Donald Campbell's 403·1 m.p.h. in the 'automobile' class.

Like Mickey Thompson they chose four basically stock American V8s – 6·9-litre Chrysler 'hemi-head' pushrod o.h.v.s with fuel injection, each putting out 608 b.h.p. on a ferocious fuel diet. Unlike Thompson, however, they put their engines in a row, and coupled all four together to drive front and rear wheels through two four-speed gearboxes. The front suspension was independent, the rear axle was crab-tracked, the frame embodied four separate engine bays, and the frontal area must have reached an all-time 'low' for a 2,400 b.h.p. car.

(*Opposite*) The beautiful lines of *Goldenrod* as seen from a helicopter during the 1965 Bonneville speed meeting.

(*Overleaf*) *Goldenrod*, the car with which Bob Summers beat Donald Campbell's wheel-driven land speed record at 409·277 m.p.h. in November 1965.

GOLDENROD
SUMMERS
BROTHERS

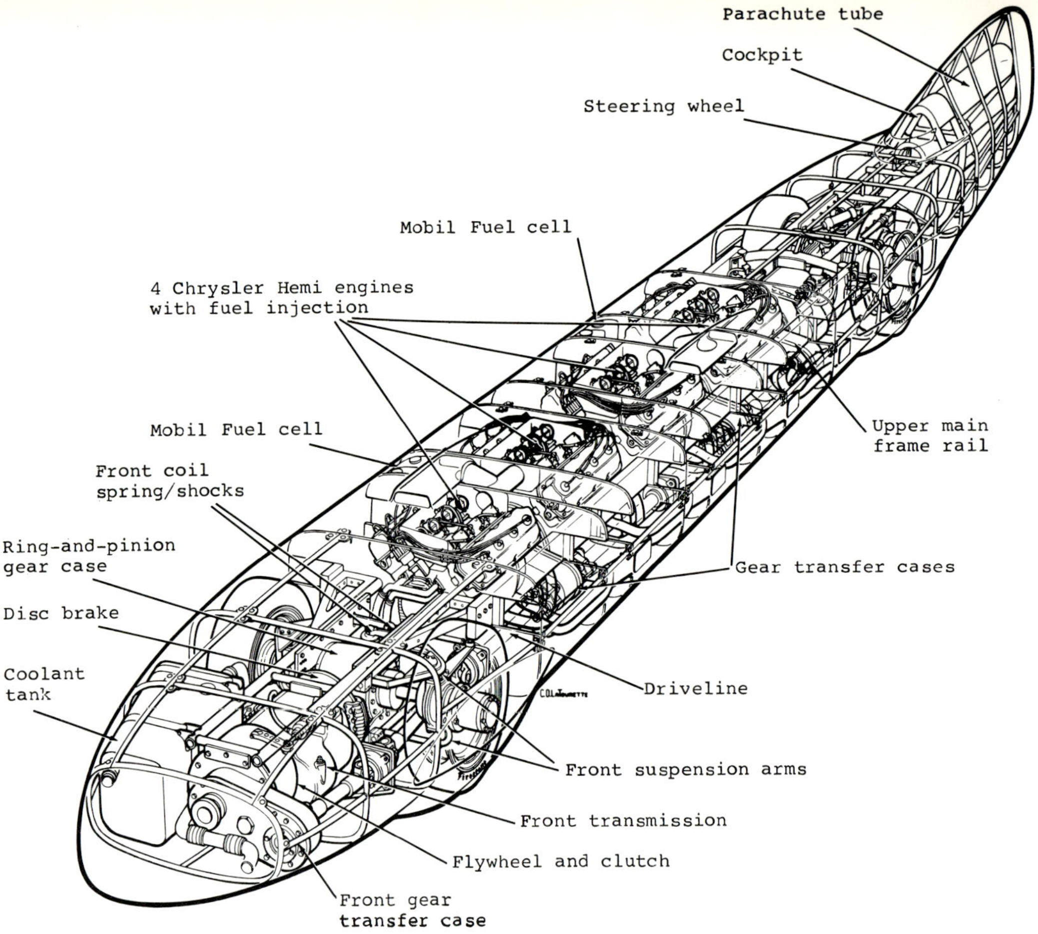

Goldenrod's four Chrysler 6·9-litre, 'hemi-head' V8 engines were disposed in one row.

The body contained the minimum of humps – four for the wheels, four smaller ones for slight engine protrusions, and two intakes on the top, while the driver, 28-year-old Bob Summers, sat dragster-fashion behind the rear wheels in a very neat enclosed cockpit combined with a stabilizing fin. Despite its great length of bonnet the car was compact, measuring 32 ft. overall, and was certainly one of the most attractive record contenders to appear at Bonneville since the days of Cobb's Railton. It was painted gold and called *Goldenrod.*

Inevitably four highly boosted internal combustion engines were more temperamental to maintain than one vast turbojet, and the Summers brothers had their quota of trouble before getting *Goldenrod* to record pitch. Breaking up of rubber couplings in the drive train, one recalcitrant engine, front wheel-bearing failure, and transfer gear breakage between two engines were among their problems, as

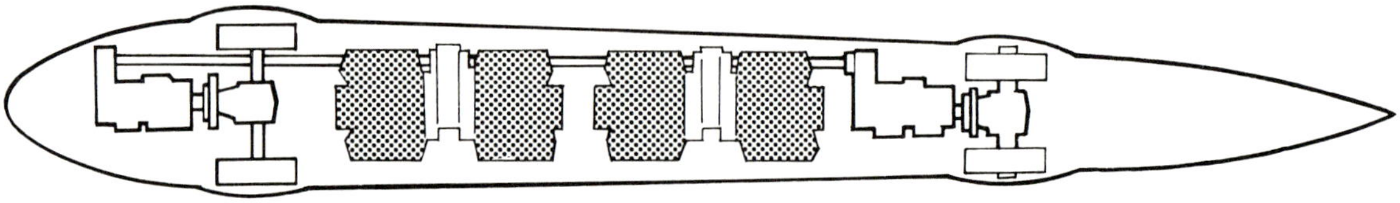

well as a dose of Bonneville rain. But they persevered, working up to 373·51 m.p.h. and then a one-way 405·09 m.p.h. in third gear, in between rush trips to their workshop for modifications, with time getting worryingly short.

The astonishingly low build of Bob Summer's *Goldenrod*.

Then Firestone, one of their sponsors, offered to share the week of 7th–14th November on the flats with Art Arfons, and when Art did his salt-quaking 576-plus m.p.h. with its dramatic aftermath on the 7th, the Summers had the place almost to themselves. They needed most of the time getting *Goldenrod* sweet, but on 11th November Bob Summers did 404·66 m.p.h. one way through the kilometre, only to have both rear wheel bearings fail. With two days left and the weather threatening they worked all night, had the car ready next day, and with light rain falling, *Goldenrod* went for the record.

Summers never got out of third gear, but he took the wheel-driven *LSR* with two superb runs, attaining 417 m.p.h. at the end of his first mile, and averaging 409·277 m.p.h. Now Donald Campbell hadn't even a record to show for all his sufferings in Australia, and the United States had the double.

Last word by Breedlove

Now everyone waited to see what Craig Breedlove would do. Showing remarkable trust in his wife Lee's driving ability, he had handed *Sonic 1* over to her on 4th

November, two days after his 555·127 m.p.h. effort, and after careful instructions and coaching let her loose on the salt. Plucky Mrs Breedlove put in four runs and emerged as the world's fastest women driver at a mean speed of 308·56 m.p.h. Then Arfons did his 576 m.p.h. and Breedlove got down to business.

It took him eight days of limbering the car up, but by using the afterburner he was confident of putting *Green Monster* in its place and becoming the first to top 600 m.p.h. On 15th November he accomplished this ambition very neatly with 593·178 m.p.h. one way for the mile, and 608·201 m.p.h. the other way. That made his average speed a resounding 600·601 m.p.h., though *Sonic 1* took some holding to do it, her nose still trying to lift and the car buffeting fiercely, while he could feel the frame flexing under him. But the record was his and one more barrier – 600 m.p.h. – had been crossed. Then the weather closed in and Bonneville 1965 was over.

Art Arfons improved his *Green Monster* during 1966, fitting new hydro-pneumatic independent rear suspension to replace the Ford 2-ton truck axle. He

Eight days after Art Arfons set the record at 576·553 m.p.h., Craig Breedlove in *Spirit of America – Sonic I* deprived him of it by clocking a mean through the flying mile of 600·601 m.p.h., with one run at 608·201 m.p.h., This record stood for five years, until broken by Gary Gabelich in the *Blue Flame*, the rocket-powered car which achieved a speed of 622·407 m.p.h. for the same distance.

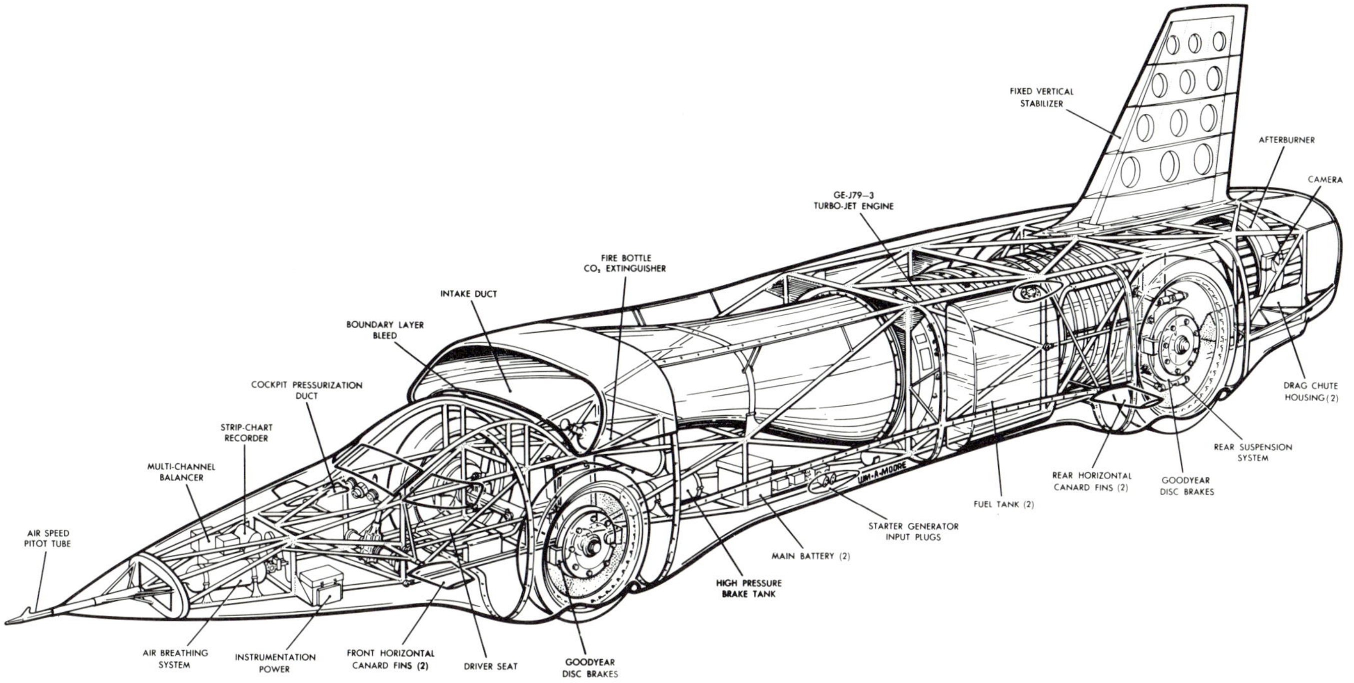

A cutaway view of the J79 turbojet-powered *Spirit of America – Sonic I.*

also lengthened the nose and enlarged the supersonic probe, altered the air intake shape at the bottom to discourage lift, and made other minor modifications to the body. The result was a weight increase all up from 6,500 lb. to 7,000 lb., but with an afterburning 15,000 lb. thrust J79 at hand, Arfons was not over-worried at that.

Alas, luck was not with him this time. On 17 November 1966 he set out on his first run to try and beat Breedlove's 600 m.p.h. when a bearing in the offside front wheel broke up at around 610 m.p.h. The car gave an immense lurch, snatched itself out of Arfons's control, cartwheeled end over end, then rolled over and over for a mile, scattering wreckage all over the salt, some of it $4\frac{1}{2}$ miles from where *Green Monster* ended up, pounded into junk.

Fantastically, 40 year-old Arfons survived the world's fastest motor accident, and emerged with only a severely cut face, largely caused by flying salt. Once recovered from his spectacular 610 m.p.h. accident, the gallant Arfons planned a new and improved *Green Monster* which was completed in 1968 and in which he hoped to top 700 m.p.h. and break the sound barrier. We conclude this chapter with a series of questions put to Art Arfons in 1968 and his very interesting replies.

Questions and answers on Arfons's world land speed record

Q. What does it feel like to go 500 miles per hour?
A. When you are only travelling $\frac{3}{4}$ in. off the ground, the sensation of speed is tremendous. The land markers go by awfully fast. It only took me two miles to accelerate to over 550 so the pull on my body was tremendous.
Q. What is the speed potential of your *Green Monster?*
A. Without any major changes I think it will exceed 650. When I made my 571

The curious frontal aspect of *Sonic I*, with Breedlove's wide, tinted screen below the huge intake for the turbojet unit.

m.p.h. run I still had 5,000 horsepower left. My major concern right now is the sound barrier, which is about 683 at Bonneville. I think the J79 engine could go 1,000 m.p.h. if it was in a car designed to break the sound barrier. The sound barrier will create a lot of problems, however.

Q. What will happen when a land vehicle breaks the sound barrier at Bonneville?

A. No one knows at this point. The big problem is counteracting the shock waves. A lot of research in correct design will have to be done before this can be accomplished. If you didn't have the right body design and you broke the sound barrier on land the shock waves could disintegrate your car.

Q. What possesses men to risk their lives in attempting these near supersonic speeds on land?

A. Well, to me, breaking the land speed record was my ultimate goal. I'm a drag racer by profession and I think this is the ultimate goal in drag racing. Most people want to reach the top in their chosen field. This was the top for me.

Q. What does the public gain from a world land speed record?

A. Basically, I think there's a certain pioneering aspect to these runs. A hundred years from now the future generation may be travelling this fast on special highways or other transportation systems. We find out many things when we're travelling this fast about how to build better bearings, wheels, brakes, tyres and streamline body designs.

Firestone has learned a lot about tyres at ultra-high speeds in these runs. I think the aircraft industry will benefit in the future from this also in building better bearings, brakes, tyres and wheels for fast jet take-offs and landings.

Q. Could you drive the *Green Monster* to the grocery store?

A. It wouldn't run like the family wagon, but I could drive it on the open highway. We built this car to steer and drive easily. The engine is so powerful, however, that you couldn't run it at speeds much less than 80 m.p.h., which would be too fast for the public highway.

Q. What kind of fuel consumption do you get?

A. I wouldn't win any economy runs. The car drinks about 68 gallons of kerosene a minute.

Q. Do these high-speed runs frighten you?

A. I've spent many a sleepless night before I run, but once I get in the car and fire it up I lose my butterflies. I think most race drivers feel the same way.

Q. How long did it take you to build the *Green Monster?*

A. My associate, Ed Snyder, and I worked for twelve months on this car. We had the part-time assistance of a couple of other men and we figure that we have got over 5,000 man-hours in the construction time. We worked fourteen to sixteen hours a day the last three months on the project.

Q. Most land speed attempts have required from $250,000 to $6 million. How much did you spend on the *Green Monster?*

A. Well, this is a hard question to answer. Ed Snyder and I hand-made the body and just about every other piece of equipment in the car. This saved us thousands of dollars. The engine we used cost the government over $200,000 new but we picked it up at a surplus store for about $5,000. Ed and I only have about $10,000 cash in the car. Firestone built the special tyres and wheels for it which was a major expense. The cost was over $50,000 for these tyres and wheels. By the time everything was paid for, the runs, including all the miscellaneous costs and the cost of timing by the United States Auto Club, I would say that about $100,000 was tied up in the entire project.

Art Arfons, three times holder of the land speed record.

GOODYEAR
WINGFOOT EXPRESS
Walt Arfons
GOODYEAR

17

The rocket age dawns

'It is, basically, a long piece of pipe . . . .'

Gary Gabelich in SPORTS ILLUSTRATED

The idea of propelling a car by rockets could hardly be new. Many a boy (and his father) watching a 'sky-rocket' shoot upward with a thrilling 'whoosh' must have pondered the effect were the firework mounted on wheels and fired horizontally. Pyrotechnically-powered vehicles were a 'natural' for early motoring cartoonists, and although very probably there were earlier experiments, the intrepid pioneer who first put theory into practice and actually tried rocket propulsion of a car seems to have been the German, Fritz von Opel of the famous Russelsheim motor manufacturing concern.

In 1927 von Opel and engineers Valier and Sander built an experimental vehicle, *Rak 1*, using an Opel chassis, a battery of twelve solid fuel rockets, and the world's first 'spoilers' or aerofoils, aimed to provide downward thrust and stabilize the car, and mounted behind the front wheels. The car worked, with limitations, so *Rak 2*, with a lower, improved chassis, twenty-four electrically-fired rockets, and bigger aerofoils, followed in May 1928, when von Opel attained a speed of 195 k.p.h. (121·2 m.p.h.) in a short, violent run on the Avus track in Berlin's Grunewald.

(*Opposite*) The first land speed record attempt at Bonneville employing rocket propulsion was made by the redoubtable Walt Arfons's *Wingfoot Express II*. In the first version, seen here, fifteen 1,000 lb. thrust J.A.T.O. (jet-assisted take-off) solid fuel rockets were installed. By the time the driver, Bobby Tatroe, had reached 406 m.p.h. all fifteen had burnt out.

Rocket propulsion was by no means a feature new to racing cars – Fritz von Opel of the famous German motor manufacturing concern sponsored two cars, *Rak 1* and *Rak 2*, in 1928. Both were designed by Max Valier, and used powder rockets. Demonstrating *Rak 2* at the Avus track in Berlin, von Opel exceeded 125 m.p.h.

With the land speed record then standing at 207·552 m.p.h. to Ray Keech's Triplex Special, clearly rocket propulsion was no challenger yet. Another German, Heylandt, experimented in the 'thirties with a rocket car running on liquid oxygen, but his interests were in developing a new motive power for normal road cars and not in breaking speed records, and over thirty years were to elapse before a serious attempt on the *LSR* was contemplated with rocket power.

J.A.T.O. experiments

It was in 1964 that Walt Arfons, ever the experimenter, Tom Green of *Wingfoot Express* fame, and John Wolf saw potential in the Aerojet J.A.T.O. (jet-assisted take-off) solid fuel rockets used to help laden aircraft into the sky. With Goodyear encouragement they built a special delta-shaped car called *Wingfoot Express II* with tail installation for a battery of J.A.T.O. 1,000 lb. thrust units. The car had a narrow 18-in. front track, very wide 12-ft. rear track, and a slender aluminium body with a long fibreglass nose. The Arfons team experimented with firing all the rockets at once, and in series to obtain progressive acceleration; with fifteen rockets installed the *Wingfoot* delta did a standing mile on the Bonneville salt at 247·59

m.p.h. with a terminal speed of 406·4 m.p.h. This gives an idea of rocket acceleration, marred only by its poor duration – about 14 sec.

They then installed twenty-five J.A.T.O.'s, fifteen in the tail and five on each side, and driver Bobby Tatroe had a frightening experience when trying for the flying mile in October 1965. As he tore away with a spectacular play of flame at his tail, two of the rockets fell out, shorting the wiring and causing others to fire the wrong way. Sudden fierce retardation resulted, and a baffled Tatroe stopped to find the *Wingfoot's* bodywork and undercarriage much damaged by obvious explosions.

Only three days later, on 22nd October, Tatroe in the repaired car achieved 476·6 m.p.h. one way through the flying kilometre by firing the rockets in sequence. Trying for the flying mile, the car was up around 580 m.p.h. when it ran out of thrust again. By that time Walt Arfons's brother Art, and Craig Breedlove, were already battling for 600 m.p.h. with their jets, and so, realizing the limitations of solid fuel rocketry with ready-made firing-pieces, Walt Arfons and company abandoned their experimental pyrotechnics. This action, incidentally, deprived Bonneville of a highly stirring spectacle!

Against a typical Bonneville skyline, Walt Arfon's outrageous *Wingfoot Express II* cuts an almost surreal outline. When the final version had its fifteen J.A.T.O. rockets in the tail supplemented by five more in each side of the car, Tatroe approached 580 m.p.h. but again ran out of thrust halfway through the official mile.

Cold science moves in

At about the same time that Walt Arfons was scheming out his *Wingfoot Express II* a former employee of the American Institute of Gas Technology (I.G.T.) named Dick Keller and a friend, Ray Dausman, conceived a highly ambitious plan to build a liquid-fuel rocket-powered car capable of attacking the land speed record. Compared with a solid-fuel rocket, which is simply fired and blasts off under full power until it has expended its energy, the liquid fuel rocket can be controlled by throttling like an internal combustion engine, and is altogether less restrictive. First used in World War II on the German V2 'revenge weapon', liquid fuel propulsion has since figured extensively in space applications, and in the lunar module which first put men on the Moon from Apollo II.

Its uses in a high-speed car in simpler form were obviously tempting, and Keller and Dausman believed that Breedlove's 600·601 m.p.h. record could easily be surpassed. The first stage of their project was to make a small-scale rocket motor and establish its working principle. Stage two was to build a rocket-powered dragster and convince influential quarters that their scheme merited support; and stage three was the construction of an actual car to go for the *LSR*. Such was their drive and tenacity of purpose that all three objectives were accomplished within six years.

It was in the autumn of 1964 that Keller and Dausman completed their prototype rocket engine, giving 25 lb. thrust, and successfully fired it. The working principle of the unit, as used in many liquid-fuel rocket applications, exploits the obliging characteristics of hydrogen peroxide (H_2O_2), a water-like liquid well known for its antiseptic properties and for turning brunettes into blondes, but which also, when broken down into its components, water and oxygen, can become a violent producer of energy. A catalyst is required to effect this breakdown or decomposition, and research has proved a 'mat' of silver and nickel wire to be highly effective, the hydrogen peroxide decomposing almost instantaneously (in 2 milli-seconds).

Great heat (1,370° F.) is thereby generated, turning the water into superheated steam which, together with separated oxygen in gaseous form, passes through the rocket nozzle with tremendous velocity, providing the necessary reaction to give forward movement. Control of the rocket unit remains simple; cut off the fuel and the motor stops; no ignition is required, and fire risk is non-existent. Add the further advantage that its emissions are infinitely less toxic than those of an internal combustion petrol engine, and the future potential of such power for driving a turbine in an ordinary road car becomes significant.

Proving a principle

Having established that their small-scale engine worked, the partners moved on to stage two – building a rocket dragster. For this they were joined by Peter Farnsworth, a dragster expert and technician, and in 1965 the trio formed Reaction

Thirty-nine years after the Opel rocket-powered racing car came Reaction Dynamics' X-1 dragster, which set dragstrip records throughout the U.S.A.

Dynamics Inc. at Milwaukee, Wisconsin, with Farnsworth as president, Keller as secretary/treasurer, and Dausman as vice-president. The dragster's engine was an enlarged edition of the 25 lb. thrust prototype, putting out 2,500 lb. thrust, equivalent to 2,800 b.h.p. at full throttle – a formidable output for a compact unit weighing only 56 lb. and measuring 2 ft. in length by 12 in. in diameter.

The engine fitted comfortably at the rear of a beautifully engineered little vehicle called the X-1 or *Rislone Rocket*, resembling a slightly elongated Formula 1 car with covered-in cockpit rather than the ugly, ill-balanced freak that customarily represents the *genus* dragster. In the nose were two stainless steel spherical tanks, containing inert nitrogen (N_2) gas used to pressurize the fuel into the rocket chamber at 425 lb. p.s.i. The hydrogen peroxide was contained in a cylindrical 13-gal. tank mounted vertically behind the driver. A tubular space frame, all-independent suspension and four-wheel disc brakes plus three drag parachutes featured, and the car scaled a mere $7\frac{1}{4}$ cwt. empty, and just over $10\frac{1}{4}$ cwt. with fuel and driver.

One day in August 1967, drag expert Chuck Suba and the handsome little X-1 appeared at U.S. 30 drag strip at Crown Point, Illinois, and put up a remarkable performance, covering a standing $\frac{1}{4}$-mile in 5·41 sec., accelerating in the first 1,000 feet, then shutting off and coasting the remaining 320 feet! Thereafter, throughout 1967 X-1 repeatedly defeated its turbojet dragster rivals.

Now Reaction Dynamics got down to stage three of their project, construction of the actual land speed record car. For this they sought a sponsor, and a 265 m.p.h. demonstration run by the X-1 dragster helped persuade the Institute of Gas Technology (I.G.T.) to back the car, which would run on their liquified natural gas product known as LNG, in combination with hydrogen peroxide. Support was forthcoming from many members of the American natural gas industry and numerous components manufacturers, and the car was to be called the *Blue Flame*. Many specialists from the Illinois Institute of Technology joined the project alongside the Reaction Dynamics team, and over seventy lucky students were able to join in on the design side of the work.

The engine was jointly designed by Reaction Dynamics and James McCormick of the Engineering Design Services Co. of Buffalo, New York. It followed the basic principle of the smaller prototype units, but the LNG. (liquified by cooling to minus 258° F.) passed from a helium-pressurized aluminium tank into the rocket motor: 75 per cent through a central intake, and 25 per cent through a peripheral duct into a finned heat exchanger; while the hydrogen peroxide passed from a compressed air-pressurized stainless steel tank, through the outer jacket of the motor, to decompose on the catalyst pack.

The resultant superheated steam and oxygen flowed over the heat exchanger, converting the 25 per cent of LNG. into gas which ignited as it joined the hot oxygen stream. This raised the temperature to the point where the other 75 per cent of LNG., injected as a liquid, reacted with the remaining oxygen and ignited. The resultant thrust from the approximately 17 in.-diameter annulus could attain

Reaction Dynamics' *Blue Flame* with driver, Gary Gabelich.

a maximum of 22,000 lb., or an equivalent 58,000 b.h.p. in a 'burn' lasting 20 sec., but for the first, sub-sonic record attempt it was decided to keep the engine throttled to give only 13,000 lb. thrust. This was still equivalent to an awe-inspiring 35,000 h.p., making the internal combustion, petrol-burning engine look very out of date. The unit, designated the RD HP-LNG.-22,000-V, contributed only $6\frac{7}{8}$ cwt. to the *Blue Flame*'s total weight of 2 tons 19 cwt.

Reaction Dynamics built the car at their Milwaukee plant. It measured 38 ft. 2·6 in. overall inclusive of the pilot tube in the nose, making *Blue Flame* the longest record car so far built, over 1 ft. longer than Breedlove's *Sonic 1*. The shape, evolved after extensive wind-tunnel tests on a model, was broadly that of a missile, with the long, slender fuselage and covered-in cockpit merging into a high tail-fin. The two front wheels were close together, giving a 9 in. track, whereas the rear wheels were well apart (7 ft. track) with a wheelbase of 25·5 ft. The chassis comprised a 20 ft. semi-monocoque centre span in aluminium with welded steel tube nose and rear sections, all clad in riveted aluminium sheeting.

The front wheels had a ball-joint linkage with coaxial coil spring-cum-damper units, and steering was at the ratio of 91:1, only slight wheel movement being desirable with the delta arrangement. *Blue Flame* thus had a turning radius of $\frac{1}{4}$-mile! The rear axle was solid and unsprung, and although provision was made for fairings over the wheels, it was found that the handling, if not the appearance, was better without them. Braking was by Kelsey-Hayes 15 in. diameter discs on the rear wheels, plus two drag parachutes – one 7.3 ft. in diameter for below 650 m.p.h., and the other 16 ft. in diameter for below 250 m.p.h. There was also a second reserve parachute system installed in the car; each system could be operated as the primary system and was completely independent of the other in all ways.

The tyres, similar to those on Breedlove's *Sonic 1*, were hand-made 8 × 25 in. Goodyears of bias-belted construction, with paper-thin smooth treads, and inflated with compressed dry air to 350 lb. p.s.i.

It had been hoped to complete *Blue Flame* in 1969, but the strikes sweeping the American car industry, plus technical problems, delayed things, and it was not until July 1970 that the car was ready for static tests and then taken to Utah in September. The famous Bonneville salt flats have seen many remarkable vehicles since the day that Teddy Tetzlaff took the *Blitzen* Benz there in 1914, but surely none of such scientific interest as the *Blue Flame*. Petrol, turbine and jet power seemed crude before the cold, ruthless, almost mystic power of the long, silver-blue cylinder on wheels, and its attendants resembled scientists and doctors rather than the oil-smeared motor mechanics of earlier days.

A fatal accident in a dragster had tragically deprived Reaction Dynamics of their number one driver for the *Blue Flame*, Chuck Suba, so the honour went to a 30-year-old Californian named Gary Gabelich. Of Jugoslav origin, Gabelich was born at San Pedro, California, in 1940, and quickly made a name in his youth as a successful hot-rod and dragster pilot. He drove a turbine-powered car at Bonneville at 349.8 m.p.h. in 1962, and also raced motor-cyles and drag-boats. He worked

(*Opposite*) The *Blue Flame* and Gary Gabelich getting under way to a trail of smoke and vapour.

with North American Aviation, undergoing long environment tests in space capsules under simulated zero gravity conditions and making protracted parachute jumps. All of this richly qualified him to drive *Blue Flame* and fined him to a peak of physical condition for the job ahead.

It was 14 September 1970 when the car reached Bonneville from Milwaukee. Three days of preparation elapsed, then began a long series of trial-and-error test runs. There were teething troubles, of course. A mixture impurity caused excessive heat which damaged the fuel injectors; the catalyst 'mat' became defective; the motor's fiery tail burned the drag 'chute cords, so that *Blue Flame* ran over 12 miles before stopping – and a seal in the hydrogen peroxide circuit failed. But gradually the snags were overcome, and Gabelich's speeds rose: 397·7 m.p.h., 515·76 m.p.h., 590·26 m.p.h., and then, on 18th October, an intoxicating 621·53 m.p.h. one way. Alas, before the return run that seal failed again and made it impossible to pressurize the H_2O_2 for the return run.

Time, weather and fuel were now running short. To avert the loss of precious 'seconds' of fuel used on take-off, it was decided to push the car from standstill to about 35 m.p.h. with a pick-up truck, and this tiny saving brought success. On 23 October 1970, just before noon, Gary Gabelich climbed into the cockpit and was strapped in by his mechanics, who then snapped the canopy shut on him. The truck went into action, and with *Blue Flame* rolling smartly Gabelich touched off the rocket engine and blasted away on the southward run, leaving a trail of whitish smoke and vapour.

Over 1,000 k.p.h.

(*Opposite below, left*) Ray Dausman of Reaction Dynamics compares the tiny 25 lb. thrust prototype rocket unit with the 22,000 lb. maximum thrust engine of the *Blue Flame*. (*Right*) A section of the Reaction Dynamics' LNG-fuelled rocket motor of the *Blue Flame*. Hydrogen peroxide enters the outer jacket to decompose on the catalyst pack into water and oxygen, which subsequently become superheated steam and gaseous oxygen. LNG passes through the centre duct and becomes hot gas which ignites when meeting the hot oxygen stream. The resultant 13,000 lb. thrust on the 1970 version of this motor produced a new record speed at over 630 m.p.h. through the flying kilometre.

It didn't take very long to make this particular piece of speed history – but it seemed long enough to Dick Keller, Pete Farnsworth, the Reaction Dynamics crew, and numerous Institute of Gas Technology personnel, waiting on the salt for the U.S.A.C. time-keepers' verdict. It came: 3·543 sec. (631·367 m.p.h.) for the kilometre, 5·829 sec. (617·602 m.p.h.) for the mile.

Forty-eight and one-half tense, interminable minutes passed while the LNG and hydrogen peroxide tanks were recharged. Then the rocket blast thundered over the vast flats, and the *Blue Flame* was on its return run, through the kilometre, the mile, and away to the north end. Silence ensued.

'It's all right this time . . .' came a voice over the intercom. Gabelich's return times and speeds were 3·554 sec. (629·412 m.p.h.) through the kilometre, 5·739 sec. (627·287 m.p.h.) for the mile. This was *it;* Gabelich, Reaction Dynamics and the Institute of Gas Technology had wrested the record from the jets and inaugurated the rocket era on the historic Bonneville salt flats. Back at Wendover for the last five weeks much champagne had been kept on ice, waiting for something to celebrate; that day the corks flew happily.

The official figure issued by the F.I.A./U.S.A.C. were 630·388 m.p.h. for the flying kilometre – the new absolute land speed record – and 622·407 m.p.h. for the

THE BLUE FLAME
REACTION DYNAMICS
GOODYEAR

REACTION DYNAMICS

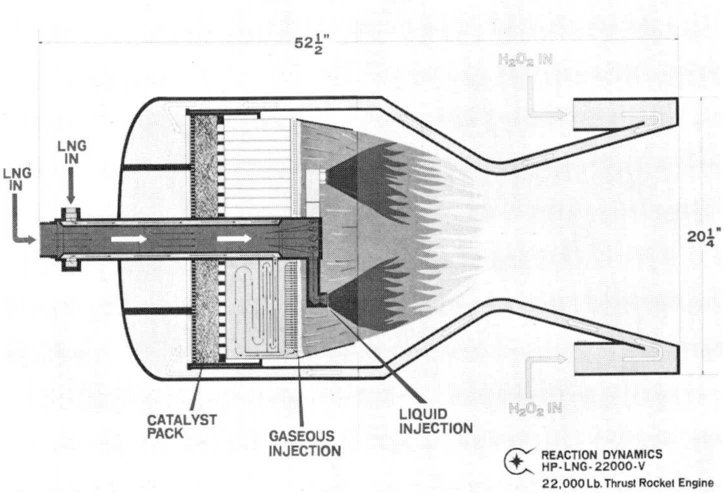
52½"
H_2O_2 IN
LNG IN
LNG IN
20¼"
H_2O_2 IN
CATALYST PACK
GASEOUS INJECTION
LIQUID INJECTION
REACTION DYNAMICS
HP-LNG-22000-V
22,000 Lb. Thrust Rocket Engine

Pictured just after setting the record, the men who mattered in the *Blue Flame* project: from *left* to *right*, Pete Farnsworth and Dick Keller of Reaction Dynamics, driver Gary Gabelich, and Dean Dietrich of the American natural gas industry.

(*Opposite*) A striking view of the *Blue Flame* bogged in soft salt after burning its parachute lines and coasting 3 miles beyond the 10-mile course at Bonneville.

flying mile. These figures, apparently in slight conflict with the calculated means of the speeds, were reached by computing the mean *times*. Because the Americans use the British mile as a standard measure rather than the metric kilometre, news releases gave the new record at the lower speed of 622·407 m.p.h., whereas the *Blue Flame* had genuinely topped *Sonic 1*'s figure by over 30 m.p.h. Unofficially the car peaked at over 650 m.p.h. in the measured mile, which beat (again unofficially) the claimed fastest manned vehicle on earth of any kind, Lt.-Col. J. P. Stapp's rocket-propelled sled which achieved 632 m.p.h. on steel rails.

Colour Plates

THE UNRECOGNISED AND THE UNLUCKY (CONTD)

Duesenberg, April 1920

Black Hawk Stutz, 1928

Challenger, September 1960

THE UNCONFIRMED AND THE UNSUCCESSFUL

Baker Electric *Torpedo*, May 1902

Fiat 300 h.p., December 1913

Wisconsin Special, 1922

Djelmo, November 1927

Napier-Campbell *Bluebird*, April 1929

Fred H. Stewart Enterprise, May 1932

Wingfoot Express II, October 1965

THE UNTRIED AND THE PAPER PROJECTS

Stapp-Jupiter, 1932

Daimler-Benz T80, 1939

Dixon *Dart*, 1936

Schmid-Orpheus, 1959

DUESENBERG

April 1920, 156·03 m.p.h. (251·094 k.p.h.)

Driven by Tommy Milton

Two single o.h.c. straight-eight, 5-litre, 92 b.h.p. engines, mounted side by side; no gearboxes; twin propellor shaft final drive; semi-elliptic suspension all round.

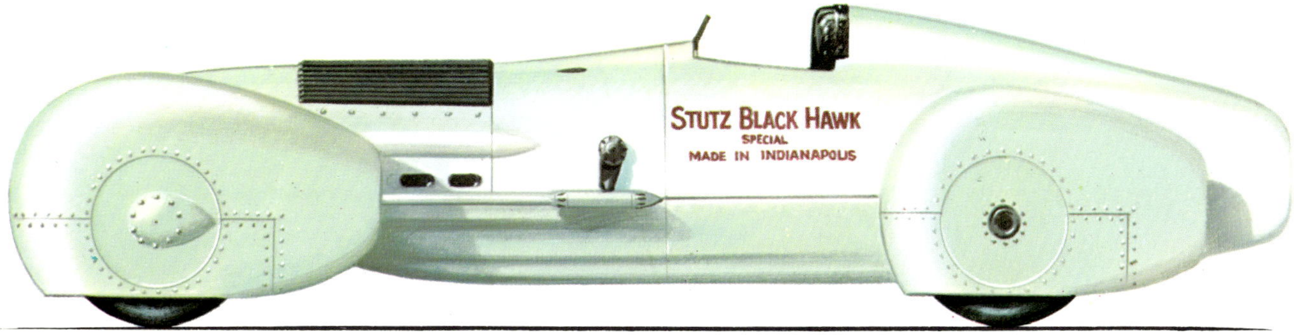

Black Hawk Stutz

1928, 203·45 m.p.h. (327·40 k.p.h.)

Driven by Frank Lockhart

16-cylinder, four o.h.c., 3-litre, twin-supercharged ice-cooled engine; three-speed gearbox; quarter-elliptic suspension all round; four-wheel hycraulic brakes; shaft final drive.

Challenger

September 1960, 406·60 m.p.h. (654·329 k.p.h.) [One way]

Driven by Mickey Thompson

Four V8, o.h.v., 6·7-litre, 700 b.h.p. Pontiac engines with four General Motors Rootes-type superchargers and fuel injection, mounted in pairs, side by side, driving front and rear wheels through three-speed gearboxes. No suspension; wheel and parachute braking.

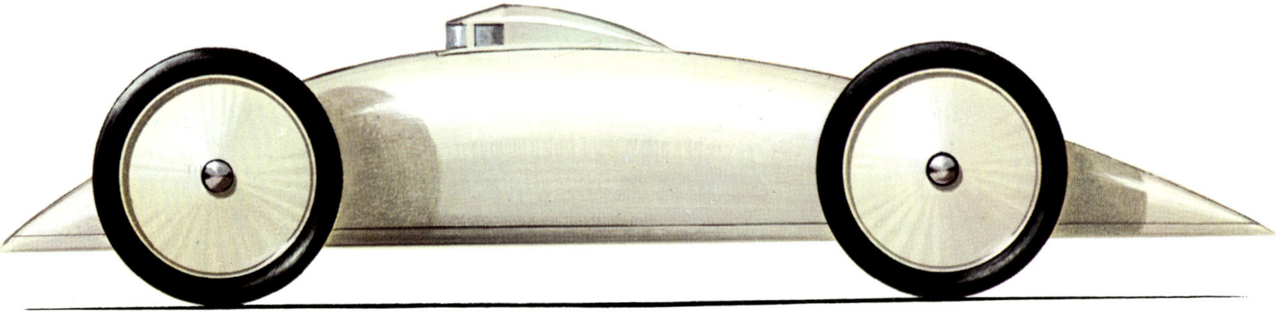

BAKER ELECTRIC *Torpedo*

May 1902, 78·00 m.p.h. approx. (127·00 k.p.h.) [Unofficial]

Driven by Walter C. Baker

Mid-located electric motor; no gearbox; chain final drive to rear wheels. Inboard rear band brakes; enclosed, streamlined bodywork of wood, with driver and mechanic installed in tandem.

FIAT 300 H.P.

December 1913, 132·37 m.p.h. (213·01 k.p.h.) [One way]

Driven by Arthur Duray

4-cylinder, single o.h.c., 28·3-litre, 290 b.h.p. engine; four-speed gearbox; chain final drive. Semi-elliptic suspension all round.

Wisconsin Special

1922, 180 m.p.h. approx. (290·00 k.p.h.) [Unofficial]

Driven by Sig Haugdahl

6-cylinder, single o.h.c., 12·5-litre Wisconsin engine; three-speed gearbox; shaft final drive. Semi-elliptic suspension all round.

Djelmo

November 1927, 155 m.p.h. approx. (248·00 k.p.h.) [Unofficial]

Driven by Giulio Foresti

Straight-eight, twin o.h.c., 10-litre engine; two-speed gearbox; shaft final drive. Semi-elliptic suspension all round.

Silver Bullet

March 1930, 186·046 m.p.h. (297·6 k.p.h.) [Unofficial]

Driven by Kaye Don

Two V12, twin o.h.c., 24-litre, supercharged, ice-cooled engines in tandem; three-speed gearbox and twin propellor shaft final drive. Semi-elliptic springs all round; hydraulic operation of clutch and four-wheel brakes; twin tail fins incorporating air-brake.

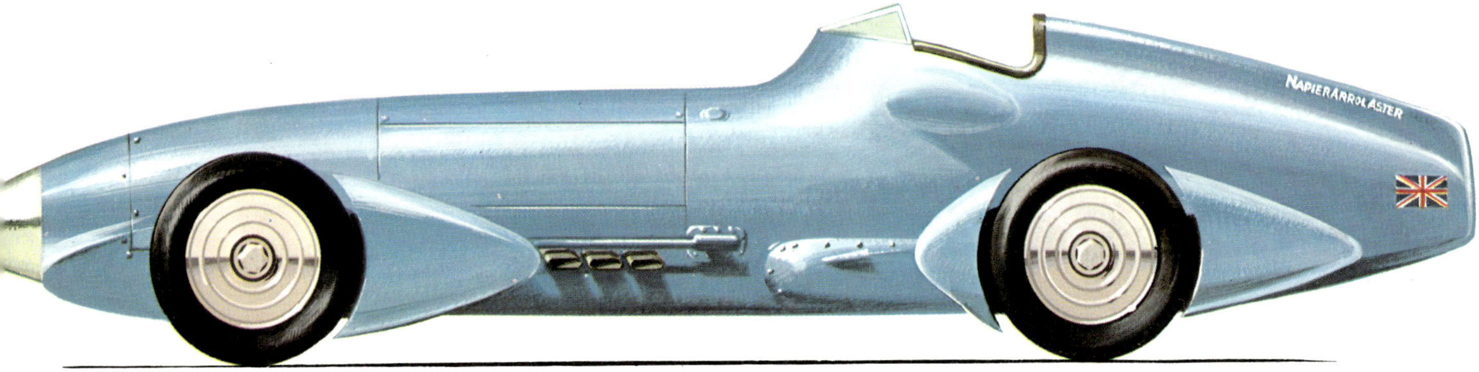

NAPIER-CAMPBELL *Bluebird*
April 1929, 217·6 m.p.h. (350·17 k.p.h.)
Driven by Malcolm Campbell
12-cylinder, o.h.c. 'broad arrow', 22·3-litre, 450 b.h.p. Napier 'Lion' engine; F.B.M. three-speed epicyclic gearbox; shaft final drive.

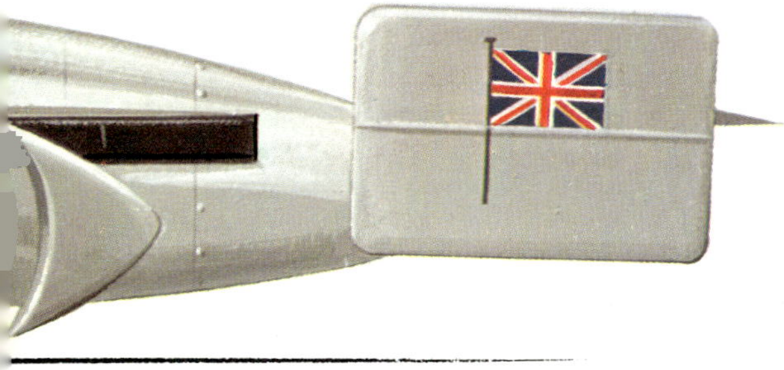

FRED H. STEWART *Enterprise*
May 1932, 180 m.p.h. approx. (288·00 k.p.h.)
Driven by 'Wizard' Smith
12-cylinder, o.h.c. 'broad arrow', 22·3-litre, 1,450 b.h.p Napier 'Lion' engine; three-speed gearbox. Twin propellor shaft final drive.

Wingfoot Express II
October 1965, 476·6 m.p.h. (766·97 k.p.h.) [One way]
Driven by Bobby Tatroe
Twenty-five 1,000 lb. thrust Aerojet solid fuel rockets. Closely-paired front wheels; ultra-wide rear track.

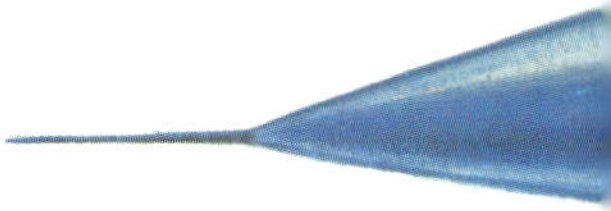

STAPP–JUPITER
1932
Three 800 h.p. Bristol-Jupiter, air-cooled radial engines converted to turbines; four-wheel drive.

DAIMLER–BENZ T80

1939

One inverted V12, 44·5-litre, 1,750 b.h.p. DB 603 Daimler-Benz engine with fuel injection and supercharging driving the two rear pairs of wheels. Independent suspension all round; twin aerofoils on bodysides.

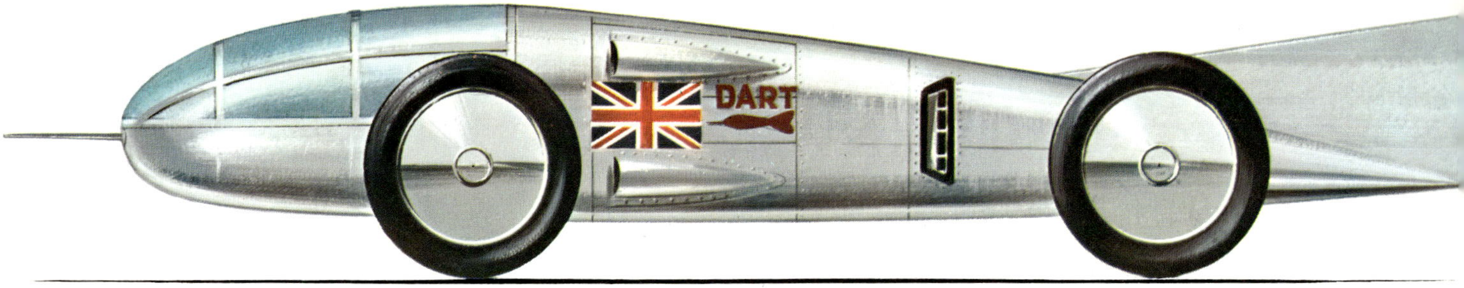

DIXON *Dart*

1937

Approximately 10-litre, supercharged, two-stroke swashplate engine driving all four wheels; backbone chassis; transmission brakes.

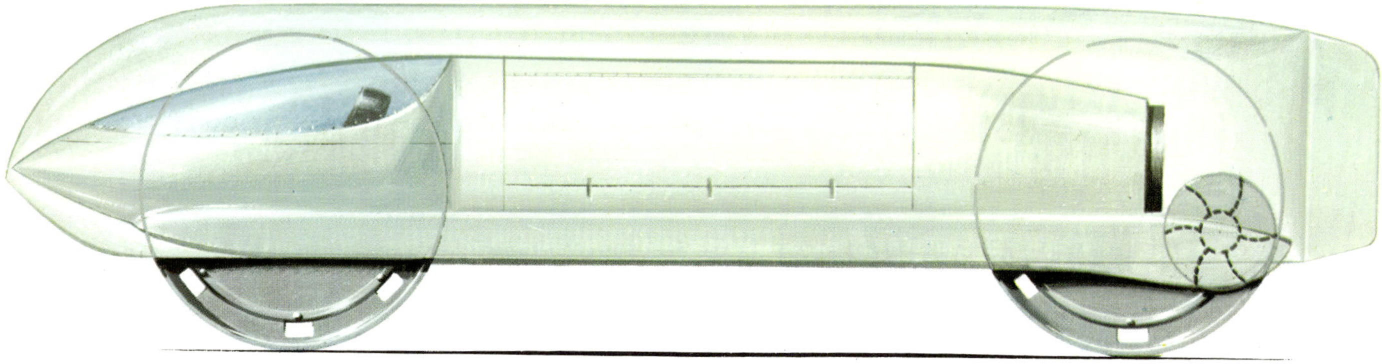

SCHMID-ORPHEUS

1959

Bristol-Orpheus gas turbine power unit, 60 per cent free drive, 40 per cent drive through 'paddle' geared to rear wheels. Tyreless 'tread ring' wheels with sprung hubs; rigid axles; disc and air brakes.

18

The greatest stunt

'I sure hope people don't compare this to Evel Knievel trying to jump a dump truck. This is a scientific and engineering achievement.'

Hal Needham, owner of *Budweiser Rocket*

Bill Fredrick – or William von Fredrick as he was occasionally styled – first moved into land speed record circles with his *Valkyrie 1* jet car in 1962 (see Chapter 22). That project didn't reap success, but subsequently the former butcher from Woodland Hills, California, *would* leave his mark on the land speed record story, as the centrepin of its most controversial of all projects: The *Budweiser Rocket*.

In publicity material, Fredrick described how he dreamed of breaking the Sound Barrier (750 m.p.h.) on land even when the record was Cobb's 394 m.p.h. By 1969 he was involved as a consultant on the successful *Blue Flame* project and two years later débuted his own rocket car, a tricycle called *Courage of Australia*.

This 27 ft. vehicle was intended as a 45 per cent scale model of a second version, to be capable of 1,000 m.p.h. 28-year-old Australian Vic Wilson would pilot the full-size car through the Sound Barrier on the infamous Lake Eyre in his homeland, Fredrick calculating Mach One at Eyre's altitude as 759 m.p.h. *Courage* would accelerate to 300 m.p.h. in 3 seconds, 600 in 12·5 and the speed of sound in 18.

With the smaller model, sponsored by Wynn's, Wilson turned the quarter mile in 5·107 sec. at 311·41 m.p.h. at California's Orange County International Raceway

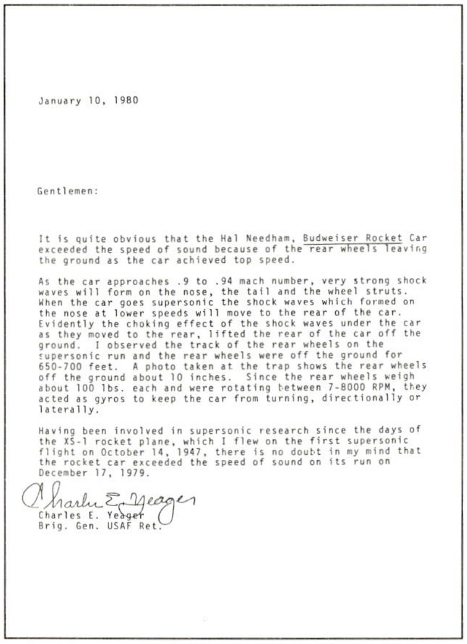

January 10, 1980

Gentlemen:

It is quite obvious that the Hal Needham, Budweiser Rocket Car exceeded the speed of sound because of the rear wheels leaving the ground as the car achieved top speed.

As the car approaches .9 to .94 mach number, very strong shock waves will form on the nose, the tail and the wheel struts. When the car goes supersonic the shock waves which formed on the nose at lower speeds will move to the rear of the car. Evidently the choking effect of the shock waves under the car as they moved to the rear, lifted the rear of the car off the ground. I observed the track of the rear wheels on the supersonic run and the rear wheels were off the ground for 650-700 feet. A photo taken at the trap shows the rear wheels off the ground about 10 inches. Since the rear wheels weigh about 100 lbs. each and were rotating between 7-8000 RPM, they acted as gyros to keep the car from turning, directionally or laterally.

Having been involved in supersonic research since the days of the XS-1 rocket plane, which I flew on the first supersonic flight on October 14, 1947, there is no doubt in my mind that the rocket car exceeded the speed of sound on its run on December 17, 1979.

Charles E. Yeager
Charles E. Yeager
Brig. Gen. USAF Ret.

As the final stroke to persuade the world the *Budweiser Rocket* had broken the Sound Barrier on land, Project S.O.S. solicited this testimony from Brigadier General Chuck Yeager, the man who first exceeded the speed of sound in flight.

in Irvine on November 11th. The little racer weighed only 1,100 lb. wet and used only 75 per cent of the 6,100 lb. of thrust from its hydrogen peroxide rocket motor. After the Irvine record it was shipped to Australia for the Ampol series and though weather and track conditions down under conspired against superfast runs, Wilson broke all Australian records with a 5·9 sec. pass through the quarter on the Queensland drag strip, passing the timing lights at 265 m.p.h.

Satisfied, Fredrick began the serious work on the larger version for 1972. Length was now down to 44 ft., but the larger *Courage* would also be a chrome molybdenum semi-monococque tricycle. Its engine would weigh a mere 341 lb. but would be five times more potent than *Courage I*'s, with a maximum thrust of 35,000 lb.

Reigning speedking Gary Gabelich was to be the pilot of what would basically be a slimmer *Blue Flame*. Indeed, Fredrick planned to boost power by injecting liquefied natural gas, as had Reaction Dynamics. Ironically, though, in view of the Natural Gas Association's backing for *Blue Flame*, the LNG wasn't actually used during Gabelich's record runs. . . .

On April 7, 1972, Gary had been badly hurt when his four-wheel-drive Funny Car crashed and burst into flames at Orange County. The left-handed speedster had his left hand virtually torn off, and his left leg was shattered. Only after many operations and two scares when it seemed that gangrene would force surgeons to amputate the leg, did he stage an incredible recovery. Indeed, when this author met him again at Black Rock Desert in 1983 the man who once had less than 50 per cent use of his left hand proved the master in a game of doubles pool against Messrs Tremayne and heir apparent Richard Noble. . . .

By 1975 Fredrick's dream was running out of steam, Gabelich unable to interest backers in paying for him to break his own record. Then Fredrick was approached by drag racer Billy Meyer, whose uncle offered to bankroll the proposed rocket car under the name of his company's product. Thus *Courage of Australia* came temporarily to be known as the *Aquaslide 'n' Dive Special* and construction finally got under way.

The match races

As part of the ballyhoo surrounding the project even at an early stage, there was plentiful talk of a great speed joust, a side by side match race at Bonneville. Initially when it seemed Gabelich would be at the controls, it was the Californian versus former speedking Craig Breedlove, in his *Spirit of America Sonic 2*. When Meyer stepped in, the match was rewritten and the youngster would instead face veteran Art Arfons in *Green Monster*. Eventually, production difficulties slowed things down figuratively and literally and Top Rank, which was to have promoted the great contest, lost interest. Most sane observers, aware of the difficulty of getting one car to run fast, straight and reliably in safety, breathed sighs of relief that nobody would, after all, be crazy enough to try running *two* within a quarter mile of one another.

Meanwhile, Meyer's father Paul purchased an interest in the project, and as owner of the Success and Motivation Institute of Waco, Texas, persuaded Fredrick the car should be rechristened the *SMI Motivator*. By 1976 the machine was completed, now measuring 42 ft. and weighing 2,990 lb. dry. Predictably, Fredrick hadn't messed about. He had sought assistance and advice only from the most highly qualified and prestigious sources. Ray Van Aiken of the US Ordnance Test Station at China Lake Rocket Sled Research Center supplied ground effects data relating to supersonic velocity, and this dictated the *Blue Flame*-like upturned triangle cross-section of the fuselage. Joe Sargent, an ex-Northrop Corporation man who ran NASA's computers during Neil Armstrong's moonwalk, designed and produced a computer system in which telemetering devices in the car's nosecone monitored 17 discrete functions – such as front wheel loading and pitch attitude – and relayed data to a remotely located computer, where it was logged for subsequent study.

The rocket engine, designed and built by Fredrick like the rest of the sleek vehicle, was rated at a maximum 24,000 lb. of thrust and eventually put only 320 lb. on the scales. Theoretical top speed had fallen to a more conservative 850 m.p.h., with zero to 400 a mere three seconds' travel.

One of the most intriguing aspects of the car – and there were many – was the use of solid metal wheels manufactured from spun aluminium alloy. Each was 32 in. in diameter and weighed 120 lb. Distinctive centre keels were used to provide lateral stability, but otherwise the tread area was bald. Fredrick was pioneering uncharted territory, and would subsequently achieve a highly significant breakthrough. From now on, other contenders would no longer have to worry about interesting the major tyre manufacturers in spending millions developing ultra-high speed rubber; now anyone could draw on the *Motivator*'s data and run their own metal wheels, with the crucially important advantage that punctures would be a thing of the past.

Early in 1976 came hints of the controversial nature of the project, as Meyer was no longer the pilot. Hollywood stuntman Hal Needham, veteran of '25 years and 45 broken bones' and later to achieve greater fame as the writer and director of the Burt Reynolds *Smokey and the Bandit* films, succeeded him as driver. There was also a plan to have a female pilot in the car, to smash Lee Breedlove's long-standing but quite unofficial 'ladies' record'. The choice here was brilliant: 28-year-old part-Irish, half-Cherokee Indian Kitty Linn O'Neil. Born in Corpus Christi, Texas, O'Neil had a background of water-speed skiing and Junior Olympic platform diving, and had established herself as a fearless stuntwoman. Deaf since birth, she attributed her extraordinary success to her ability to concentrate wholly on the task in hand, without having to listen to distracting sounds.

Fredrick opened talks with US Air Force officials at Edwards Air Force Base, landing site for early attempts on the Sound Barrier in flight and formerly famous as Muroc Dry Lake and then Rogers Dry Lake. Meanwhile, Mud Lake, Tonopah, was examined as a possible venue. First, however, the *Motivator* was taken to El Mirage (near Edwards) and then Bonneville. It was then tried on Alvord Desert, Oregon. For some reason, Black Rock Desert, later to become famous through

(*Above*) Young Billy Meyer proudly shows off an artist's impression of the *Aquaslide 'n' Dive Special*, later to become the *SMI Motivator*. (*Below*) The *Motivator* broke fresh grounds by making successful use of solid aluminium wheels. These proved every bit as suitable as highly inflated rubber tyres on normal rims, and obviated the risk of punctures.

Slimmed-down *Blue Flame* shape is more than evident in this shot of the *SMI Motivator* lance during trials on Bonneville's salt.

Richard Noble's efforts, was not considered, despite very similar make-up to Alvord.

On September 26th O'Neil averaged 358·10 m.p.h. at El Mirage, but publicity refused to claim this as a new ladies' mark as the run was uni-directional. Later, on December 5th, Kitty hit a 'top speed' of 524·017 m.p.h. in her second of two runs through a kilometre trap at Alvord. The next day she managed a run at 514·120 m.p.h., her peak speed variously declared as 591 and 618. On her second run she was slightly slower, but her two-way average was 512·710 m.p.h. On 60 per cent of the *Motivator*'s power, she had set a new ladies' land speed 'record'.

That was when the problems began in earnest. O'Neil wanted a shot at Gabelich's record. On December 7th, the Marvin Glass toy company of Chicago, which was backing the Alvord runs, found itself in an embarrassing position. It was all geared to manufacture 'Hal Needham, Hollywood Stunt Man' dolls as and when he broke the record. The idea of O'Neil doing that – and she showed every ability to do so – didn't go down so well, as there weren't any O'Neil dolls in the pipeline. Marvin Glass then announced it didn't feel land speed record breaking was a ladylike activity and put a male chauvinist spanner in the works by threatening to file an injunction if she made further runs.

Needham had already achieved a declared 619·99 m.p.h. at Bonneville on October 14, damaging the *Motivator* and shaking himself up when he ran overcourse on to rough salt, and wasn't in a fit state to take over from O'Neil. Thus Frederick called it a day, and acquiesced to Glass' threats by naming first Teresa Gillette and then airline stewardess Simone Boisseree as O'Neil's replacements. Behind the scenes, however, O'Neil's stuntman husband Duffy Hambleton tried unsuccessfully for an injunction to prevent the *Motivator* running without his wife at the helm, but did manage to stop any other woman climbing aboard.

Thus 1977 saw Fredrick and Needham at Mud Lake for further trials, but now some of their movie background seemed to rub off on to the project. Deliberate sabotage was suspected when water was found in the fuel of support aircraft, and acid was poured over the *Motivator*'s braking 'chutes. The atmosphere was curdled as fingers of suspicion were pointed at Hambleton, and was heightened by the sui-

cide of the Needham doll inventor as he faced four murder charges. Needham, nevertheless, put in three test runs, but ran off course on the third, clocked at 548·9 m.p.h., after 'chute failure. He ran into sage brush and rough ground and took off for 164 ft. before crashing back on to the crumbly surface. Fredrick wanted to haul back to base to X-ray the chassis, and his decision was endorsed by other events. The Bureau of Land Management was in favour of him using Mud Lake, but part of the eight-mile course was on Nellis Air Force Base, where officials rather sat on the fence when trying to decide whether Fredrick and co. were welcome. Initially they allowed them to run without actually granting permission, fearful of setting an unwanted precedent, but after the accident, the rumoured sabotage and the general hoo-ha they decided against further runs. For Fredrick 1977 was another wrap and for the *SMI Motivator* it was literally the end of the road. But Frederick would be back, and so would Needham. They would have a new car, sponsor and driver.

Bill Fredrick (ninth from left) poses with the *Motivator* and some of its crew at Bonneville. Standing right by the tail fin is Jim Deist, pioneer of the parachute as a means of slowing high-speed projectiles.

The Budweiser Rocket

Just as he did with the *Motivator*, Fredrick began the *Rocket*'s design with the dimensions of the human body. Thus the cockpit was no wider than 20 in. In fact, it was so confined, the pilot was barely able to draw a full breath. 39 ft. 2 in. long, the *Rocket* measured 8 ft. 10 in. to the top of its tail fin, 39 in. to the top of the rear-mounted cockpit, and only 24 in. to the top of its pencil-slim fuselage. The single front wheel was of 32 in. diameter, the rears 30. Rear track was 10 ft. For the car's first runs at Bonneville, the Romatec V4 rocket engine was rated at 13,000 lb. of thrust.

The backer for the new lance was Anheuser-Busch, famous for its Budweiser beer, while Stanton Barrett was the nominated pilot. The son of a Baptist minister and himself a devout Christian, Barrett was a quiet man who shunned the star lifestyle. At 15 he was undefeated lightweight Golden Gloves champion in his native St Louis, Missouri, and after graduation from high school enrolled as a medical

Stan Barrett poses with the controversial *Budweiser Rocket* at Edwards Air Force Base in 1979. A devout Christian, this quiet man from Bishop, California, made an immense contribution to Frederick's project.

technician with the Air Force. There was a spell of testing aerospace escape systems, followed by plans to attend pre-med school at the University of Oregon prior to a return to the Air Force as a flight surgeon. However, a chance meeting saw him land a bit part in the Jimmy Stewart movie *Shenandoah*, being filmed near the campus. On the set he first met Needham, who eventually persuaded him to forget acting and concentrate on stunt work. Since then the karate black belt has performed all the major stunts in Reynolds' film *Hooper* and has others such as *Airport '77* and *When Time Ran Out* with Paul Newman to his credit. He gave up stunts in 1978, when Needham asked him to drive the planned rocket car, turning instead to a punishing training schedule at his ranch in Bishop, California. There he would run 10 miles a day, do 500 sit-ups a day and bounce a medicine ball on his stomach to ready himself for the rigours of the task ahead. A dedicated family man, he and his wife prayed for success, and Barrett was never afraid to admit his fear. 'Fear can be healthy unless it hampers your ability to peform,' he once remarked, adding: 'I don't think a man is brave unless he's frightened.'

Thus the stage was set for Fredrick and Needham to return to the Bonneville Salt Flats in September 1979, but the day before Barrett's scheduled first run on the 9th it was revealed by *Los Angeles Times* reporter Shav Glick that the project wasn't going to play by existing land speed record rules. Instead, Fredrick planned to move into a new dimension in an attempt to smash the Sound Barrier. A cleverly devised plan was evolved, neatly to bypass the inconvenient rules of the game that stated a record would be the result of computing the average time for two passes, one in either direction, through a measured mile or kilometre, within one hour of each other. And each run, of course, would itself be an average of the vehicle's speed and time through the measured distance.

Instead, Fredrick and Needham decided to use their 'top speed' concept, meaning they would simply record their peak speed and take that as a new mark. There would be no measured mile or kilo. Instead there would be the standard drag strip 132 ft. speed trap and the National Hot Rod Association (NHRA), a member of the US committee which represents all major sanction bodies in the FIA, would 'sanction' the trap and provide respected official Bernie Partridge to ensure the trap and timing clocks were accurate for each run. The American Motorcycle Association would be asked to sanction the three-wheeler's runs and apply to the FIM for recognition.

To facilitate the new concept, Budweiser's publicity machine slipped into reheat with a highly successful campaign to persuade the media this was the New Way. Nevertheless, scepticism remained rife and two clear camps became established: Bud fans and non-Bud fans.

On September 10th Barrett reached a one-way peak speed of 638·637 m.p.h. on the salt and the publicity machine lost no time boasting it was not only faster than Gabelich's two-way record, but also beat his one-way best of 631·367 m.p.h. American land speed record expert Deke Houlgate wrote this author: 'Old Joe Petrali did a spin in his grave. He was always dead set against revealing one-way run speeds and never really forgave Mickey Thompson for ballyhooing his own one-way run.'

On his run, Barrett had run off the end of the course on to rough salt, and again a Fredrick missile suffered pounding. Conditions that year were far from perfect, and Project SOS (Speed of Sound) eventually declared the flats unsafe for Sound Barrier attempts.

Now a rumour began to circulate in news circles that Needham had a million dollar deal with Budweiser, and would collect $300,000 when the record fell; the rest would come with the Sound Barrier. CBS had taken the footage it required for television and duly showed it, but critiques of the runs were said to have forfeited Needham that first instalment. Shav Glick led a wave of criticism and investigative journalism, and discovered the 132 ft. trap was not, after all, used. Instead a 52·8 ft. (1/100th of a mile) zone was employed. This upset the non-Buds even more.

Gary Gabelich: 'How can they say he broke my one-way record? I don't hold any one-way record in the first place because there is no such thing. The only land speed record is a two-way run and the two runs cannot be separated.'

Art Arfons: 'It's made a joke out of people who laid their lives on the line, some of whom lost their lives trying to break the record legitimately.'

Craig Breedlove: 'I don't like the public relations campaign to adjust the format to fit the effort. If Barrett breaks the Sound Barrier one way and someone then goes and does it both ways, Barrett's run will always overshadow the other one. I don't like that.'

The Buds responded quickly.

Hal Needham: 'It's not an official record? What's official? We did it, out in front of God and everybody, for everyone to see. If that's not official, what is? It's good enough for us. We know we did it.'

Mickey Thompson defended the one-way run and opined: 'Perhaps its time to change the rules for the simple reason there is no place long enough to do it.'

Ironically, Breedlove was not resistant to change when he ran his non-wheel driven *Spirit of America* through the rulebook in 1962, whereas Thompson, still hopeful with *Challenger*, was adamant pure thrust cars shouldn't be allowed in just because 400 m.p.h. was proving a tough nut for wheel driven cars to crack!

Before God or not, Needham began to realize, despite the dramatic CBS portrayal on television, that it wasn't enough. In the weeks following the 'record' run much speculation surrounded the reason why it took so long to calculate Barrett's speed after he'd stopped that reporters had had time to return to Wendover before it was announced. There were strong suggestions Budweiser was refusing to pay for a record.

Meanwhile, another problem was becoming apparent. The *Blue Flame* had had to be push started to help eke out its fuel supply and rumour suggested that the faster *Budweiser* went, the less chance it had of completing a significant measured distance, hence the short trap idea. Hydrogen peroxide-fuelled rocket cars are fuel voracious and the chemical's low specific impulse (see Chapter 23) creates a vicious circle that runs as follows: more fuel is needed to last through the measured distance, which means the car has to be larger and heavier, which in turn requires more power to maintain performance, which in turn consumes more fuel. Moreover, catching Barrett's peak speed had proved as difficult as downing a B52 with a pop gun. It was suggested he would hit 650 m.p.h. then hit the trap at 575. Even when his run-up position was backed up he would coast through the same trap. It was proving just too elusive to be effective. And that little problem finally set up what became in the eyes of many the master stroke, which it was hoped would satisfy Anheuser-Busch and the media when the Sound Barrier attempt was made. NHRA disappeared quietly to be replaced by the lesser-known International Hot Rod Association (IHRA), and Earl Flanders would look after three sets of traps set 52·8 ft. apart with special sensors accurate to a millionth of a second. However, there was one more idea. When the media arrived *en masse* at Edwards Air Force Base on December 17th the speed trap was duly set up, but largely ignored. Instead, the US Air Force itself would participate in the run by bouncing radar signals off a satellite, and by gridding the entire record run course so that the vehicle could be monitored as it passed from zone to zone, on the US taxpayers' most sophisticated computers. The scheme was designed to lend credibility to Needham's claims and to prove his assertion that the old system was a dinosaur in the age of moonshots.

Earlier in the month, on the 3rd, the brave Barrett had clocked 643·086 m.p.h., as ever, one-way. He backed that with 677·328 on the 11th and 692·774 two days before the scheduled Sound Barrier assault. Military radar had in fact clocked the rocket at 698·86 m.p.h. on the 11th.

Fredrick calculated it had taken 90 per cent of the *Budweiser*'s power to go 677, adding: 'We barely used 13,000 lb. of thrust to go 638 at Bonneville, but we'll need more than twice that to go another 100.'

Accordingly, he had arranged to extract more from the Romatec V4. For the Edwards runs it used polybutadiene as a bi-propellant, this solid fuel taking the form of doughnut rings within the engine. As the hydrogen peroxide became superheated steam and oxygen when passed over the silver catalyst pack in the normal way, the polybutadiene became gaseous and ignited, boosting thrust to some 24,000 lb. The difficulty replacing the solid fuel rings was yet one more reason why the old rules, requiring no more than an hour between runs, had to be bypassed. And if there wasn't quite enough power, Fredrick had added a Sidewinder missile to the car, capable of providing an extra 4–6,000 lb. of thrust. With full power, the *Budweiser Rocket* was said to be capable of 6G acceleration, with zero to 140 m.p.h. in one second.

In the chill dawn on December 17th, Barrett finally made The Run. Pummelled and battered as the tricycle skipped over the surface, he punched in the Sidewinder 12 sec. into the run at 640 m.p.h., encountered tremendous buffeting and then a smoothing out – 'A quiet period', Barrett remembered. At maximum speed he uttered one word: 'Wow!' There was no sonic boom.

The run took scant seconds; calculating the speed took seven hours. At first there was near panic when the first reading was 30 m.p.h. after a water truck had

been picked up by the radar. As the media grew more impatient – the run took place at 7.26 a.m. – came the news that Barrett's 'top speed' was 739·666 m.p.h. – Mach 1·0106.

According to Houlgate the satellite system was intended only as an early warning against invasion and few missed the way Air Force Flight Test Center Vice Commander Colonel Pete Knight hedged in his mailgram to verify the speeds. He said:

'In cooperation with Speed of Sound engineering personnel, the Air Force has performed a review of the limited accelerometer, photographic, air speed and radar data taken during the Speed of Sound land speed attempts on Rogers Dry Lake at Edwards Air Force Base in November–December 1979.

'Within the accuracy of the speed measuring devices used, it is our judgement that the overall objective of attaining Mach One (the speed of sound) with a land vehicle was achieved at 7.26am on December 17, 1979.'

The publicity machine felt moved to try one more ploy. It was time to pull in a big gun, time for a drop of the Right Stuff. A letter dated January 10th, 1980, and signed by Brig. General Charles E. Yeager – the fabled Chuck Yeager who in 1947 had broken the Sound Barrier in flight over Edwards in the Bell X-1 – was circulated (see page 222), as if to provide the definitive endorsement. Thus ended the most controversial and least official record attempt in history. In terms of absolutes, the *Budweiser Rocket* was clocked going faster than any other land vehicle, yet all other land vehicles had been built to comply with specific rules, so comparisons become redundant. Experts remain split; some regard the *Budweiser* as the world's fastest, others ignore it as a scam. Needham has become a leading movie director. Fredrick, who built beautifully made racers of striking elegance and who could surely have designed a 'street legal' rocket car had he wished, is still one of the top riggers of film stunts with his rocketry.

Stan Barrett tried his hand at NASCAR racing (as team-mate to Harry Gant in Needham's Skoal Bandit team) without real success, but was happy to use his achievement as a platform to communicate his basically Biblical message to the young. Asked once if he was disappointed he couldn't run the rocket on one occasion because of a malfunction, he responded: 'Heck, no. It means I've got another day to live.' He wasn't joking. The SOS project owed much to the bravery of this quiet, pleasant American idealist.

But whatever Bill Fredrick and his *Budweiser Rocket* did achieve – and opinions are sharply divided as to precisely what it was – it certainly *wasn't* the world Land Speed Record. And by the standards to which most other contenders have adhered throughout history, it most certainly wasn't official.

(*Above*) December 17, 1979, and Barrett begins the most controversial run in *LSR* history. He reported severe buffeting followed by a smoothing out period, but nobody heard the expected sonic boom.

(*Opposite page*) A man, a dream, and a record. The job finally done, after nine years of unending struggle, Briton Richard Noble celebrates his achievement with *Thrust 2* in the evening stillness of Nevada's Black Rock Desert, October 4 1983.

PLESSEY
PLESSEY
British Alcan
ALCAN
SERVICES
THR
2
IMI Norgren Enots
PLESSEY
LOCTITE
LOCTITE
Strength at work
FOR MEN
Castrol
GKN
GKN GROUP
CHAMPION

19

A noble thrust

'. . . there comes a time when you think am I going to do anything . . . or shall I let it go?'

Richard Noble, interviewed in *MOTORING NEWS, 1980*

The notion that crumbling old Britain could still be a force in the high-speed game, let alone the possibility that anyone was actually prepared to follow in Donald Campbell's fading wheeltracks, was frequently met with scepticism – and sometimes open derision – in many British and foreign quarters during the 1970s. Hadn't Campbell's accident in 1967 closed the nation's book once and for all?

Among those who very definitely thought otherwise was a Twickenham businessman called Richard Noble. As a 6-year-old he had gazed in awe as John Cobb's sleek silver and red jet hydroplane *Crusader* floated by the pier on Loch Ness in September 1952, and from that moment the child became hooked on anything to do with speed and speed records. By 10 he had assimilated Eric Burgess' book *Rocket Propulsion*, and begun amassing all he could on record-breaking cars. The seeds of a dream to become the fastest man on earth had been sown.

By 1974, his taste for adventure only partly sated by two overland expeditions (one to Cape Town, the other via India and Pakistan), he began planning the first steps of his campaign, while working as a consultant for Management Centre Europe. A beloved Triumph TR6 was sold, an aged but very sound Rolls-Royce Derwent jet engine acquired, and slowly Britain's first pure thrust car was put together. Noble designed it himself and did the majority of the building. In later

Britain's first pure-jet car was *Thrust 1*. Later dubbed a 'cathedral on wheels' by Noble himself, it nevertheless served its purpose admirably and set Project Thrust rolling before its accident in 1977.

years he would describe it as a cathedral on wheels, but initially he was content to christen it *Thrust I*.

The rationale was simple. *Thrust I* would be the starter vehicle, to gain experience operating and driving a jet car, and to generate valuable publicity and credibility. *Thrust 2* would be much more powerful and complex and would serve as a high-speed demonstrator/exhibition vehicle to attract backers for *Thrust 3*, the record car.

In March 1977, Noble and his fledgling team were at R.A.F. Fairford in Gloucester for some serious high-speed runs. *Thrust 1* was travelling around 200 m.p.h. when a wheel bearing seized and pitched the ungainly machine into a series of airborne rolls before it slewed to a halt upside down. Noble, having the presence of mind to switch off the fuel supply in mid-air, walked away unscathed. And as the disconsolate team trudged home, the remains of the wreck were sold to a scrapyard. They raised £175.

Some might have called it a day, but Noble wasn't prepared to. That left two options. Build another *Thrust 1* or somehow move on to *Thrust 2*. The latter course was chosen.

Realizing the importance of credibility and publicity, Noble first addressed senior R.A.F. personnel at the Ministry of Defence, obtaining a surplus Rolls-Royce Avon 210 jet engine with full reheat. That then became the central feature of an unusual display stand at the Earls Court Motorfair Show that October, attracting thousands of visitors and convincing T.I. Reynolds to build the spaceframe chassis.

The latter, like the rest of *Thrust 2*, had been designed by a quiet engineer named John Ackroyd. He first learned of the project when sitting on a beach as a deckchair attendant, reading a magazine feature describing how Noble had issued a press release seeking a designer for a 650 m.p.h. car. With a background that among other things encompassed spells with British Hovercraft Corporation, Porsche, Messerschmitt and running the Enfield electric car project, Ackroyd was clearly the man for the job. Initially, as Noble strove to raise the money, he worked part-time, becoming full-time on May 1, 1978. Working for months in solitude in the kitchen of a derelict house on the Isle of Wight, he took Noble's original *Green Monster*-like concept and refined it. As a mark of his ability, no significant changes had to be incorporated in *Thrust 2*'s life, and it would establish itself as the most stable car in *LSR* history. As an interesting aside, prior to building his original *Spirit of America*, Craig Breedlove considered the *Green Monster*/*Thrust* concept of driver sitting alongside engine, but was persuaded against it by a meeting with William Turner and Fred Williams – mathematician and aerodynamicist respectively at Hughes Aircraft. They believed the layout inherently *un*stable and counselled Breedlove to adopt their tricycle layout. . . .

Through 1978 and 1979 Noble worked tirelessly to interest British industry in his venture, and Project Thrust gradually began to realize some of its immediate goals. Along the way he had to fight prejudice against the record, a hangover from the delays the hapless Campbell had had to endure awaiting suitable weather condi-

Thrust 2 was a very different proposition, thanks to John Ackroyd's unbridled design genius. Here the gold, red and white streamliner is the focus of attention at Bonneville during the troubled 1981 campaign. In the background, in shorts, is the ubiquitous Ron Benton, later to achieve fame on the Black Rock Desert with his own speed record (see text) . . . .

tions on Lake Eyre. Slowly, the 27 ft. streamliner progressed. In May 1980 the engine was given a static test in full reheat at R.A.F. Coningsby, prior to the first driving trials at Leconfield. They brought the first problems, for Noble had trouble reaching any sort of meaningful speed and only later did he and Ackroyd realize how unsuitable the bumpy surface had been. All that was put behind the team on September 24th and 25th, however, when Noble and the bodyless jetcar set six new British land speed records at R.A.F. Greenham Common. Among them, Barry Bowles' 218·71 m.p.h. flying quarter-mile mark was shattered at 259·74, but the most significant was a new 248·87 m.p.h. figure for the flying mile.

Even better news was to come, for later in the year wind tunnel tests conducted by British Aerospace at Filton revealed *Thrust 2* to have a speed potential of 650 m.p.h. From that moment *Thrust 3* was forgotten. *Thrust 2* would be the record attempt car.

Steadily, the credibility was built up, along with a list of sponsors and contributors that would swell to 211 by October 1983. By the time the fully completed *Thrust 2* was unveiled to the press at a function in Birmingham in June 1981, a more powerful Avon Mark 302 engine had been installed, boosting power from 15,000 to 17,000 lb. of thrust. By September the gold, white and red machine had been shipped out to Bonneville, where it would run for the first time on its solid metal wheels.

Rude shock

Like Slick Gardner, Noble and his team were in for a rude shock. Initial tests were conducted without reheat and at 270 m.p.h. Noble found the car that had been so stable on Lightning wheels shod with Dunlop rubber on British airfields, developed a mind of its own on the salt flats. Time and again it would veer to the right, and as speeds progressed into the 300s the same thing happened, Noble avoiding trouble only by allowing *Thrust* to veer into rough salt off the intended course. Morale began to flag and the inevitable doubts were raised over his ability to do the job. Slowly, however, attention to ride heights and suspension settings – particularly the car's toe-in – brought an improvement. The British had years of experience to make up on the Americans, who had been running pure jets since 1960, and as 400 m.p.h. came in sight the mood picked up. Then, on October 10th, came a turning point. On his first run Noble hit only 392 m.p.h., no better than the previous day. During a shambolic turnround which saw among other things the fuel truck break down, Noble became furious. For the first time, he used full reheat on his return run. The ploy yielded two things: vastly improved stability at low speed, and a speed of 447·029 m.p.h. through the kilometre, despite a loose battery connection which cut the fuel supply partway through the measured distance. The average speed was 418·118 m.p.h., a long way from Gabelich's record but the fastest speed ever achieved by a British car or driver. But for the battery problem, *Thrust 2* would have peaked over 500 m.p.h. From that run onward, the car would always be driven with full reheat during a run, in direct contrast to Arfons and Breedlove, who tended to use their afterburners intermittently.

That night, as team members celebrated some real progress at last, it began raining. By the following day the salt lay four inches under water. It was Donald Campbell and the accursed Lake Eyre all over again. There was nothing to do but return home to plan another shot for 1982.

With improvements made in the light of the Bonneville experience, the most significant of which was a change from four- to six-inch-wide front wheels, *Thrust 2* was taken to Greenham Common for final tests before the 1982 attempt. On June 17th it had just been declared fit by Ackroyd when Noble tried one more run, with parachute specialist Mike Barrett as passenger in the second cockpit designed into the car for publicity purposes. It was to be a disaster. Noble kept the power on a fraction too long on the perilously short runway, ran out of braking distance and had to take to the grass at 180 m.p.h., destroying the front of the car. Worse still, the only Avon 302 that had been available to the team ingested stones and debris and was feared a write-off. Bonneville was off, at least temporarily.

Miraculously, Noble and Barrett held a bitterly disappointed team together and in 12 work-packed weeks *Thrust 2* was repaired, one of the most telling contributions coming from R.A.F. Binbrook, where the team's engine specialist John Watkins was stationed. Personnel at the airbase thoroughly rebuilt the engine, alleviating the trickiest problem. There was still no spare available, and Rolls-Royce's bill for repairs would have amounted to a budget-wrecking five-figure sum. . . .

Thanks to Don Vesco's generosity, the Thrust team was to be allowed to share his salt time in September, but when the vanguard arrived on the 27th it was obvious the course was through for another year. Freak weather conditions had again flooded the flats and even in Salt Lake City some 120 miles distant, occupants were fleeing their homes to escape the floods. Such was the weather cycle that the Nationals were cancelled again in 1983, and only ran on a short course in 1984.

Incredibly, in one of the most outstanding feats in record history, Noble and his team found a new site and relocated in six short days. To have returned home without even turning a wheel was unthinkable, and a desperate search of Utah, Oregon and Nevada was initiated. It yielded the Black Rock Desert, an alkali playa 120 miles north of the gambling town of Reno, Nevada. Once part of prehistoric Lake Lahontan and a dried mud lake, rather than a salt flat, it was smooth, spacious and accessible. Noble and his team moved into the nearest town, Gerlach. And then more problems arose. Before *Thrust 2* could run on the desert, Noble needed a permit from the B.L.M., which has responsibility for protecting most of the Nevada environment. Some protestors objected to the jetcar, but with the enthusiastic help of the townsfolk of Gerlach and nearby Empire, Noble won through, and on October 4th *Thrust 2* made its first tentative run – towed at 30 m.p.h. behind the team's Range Rover. The 1982 attempt had started at last, and Ken Norris, drafted in as team manager after the organizational problems of 1981 at Bonneville, opined the desert was the best record course he had ever seen.

Over the following days the team fought myriad problems. Noble made one run with his foot resting lightly on the brake pedal, cooking the Lucas-Girling discs. Then he released his parachutes too soon on runs that yielded a best speed average of 468.972 m.p.h., which broke his own 'record'. Then the engine had to be given a static test at nearby Fallon Airbase after it seemed to lack power. Then Noble hit a shallow depression on the course and the front suspension had to be rebuilt. All the time winter was approaching, but the speeds began to build up, and on October 23rd, the 12th anniversary of Gabelich's record, an unofficial average over 500 m.p.h. was achieved. Then it rained.

It was November 3rd before the gold car turned a wheel again in anger, and despite some shambolic organization during the turnround, Noble upped his British car and driver mark to 575·652 m.p.h. The record was coming into sight. Allied to the weather problems, though, was the pressure exerted by the team's unrelenting schedule. Key team members had been under continuous pressure since the Greenham accident, and it was beginning to take its toll. November 4th was to be the make or break day. Since *Thrust 2* was always run under full power, its speed through the measured distances being determined by the length of run-up, Norris and Ackroyd 'pulled the elastic' back as far as possible, the course being shortened as the south end refused to dry after the rain. There were delays as the U.S.A.C. timekeepers had to relocate their timing lights and the measured distances to equate the run-up and deceleration zones. This time the team had its act together, but the shortened course and a lack of power kept Noble's average down to 590·551 m.p.h. It broke his own record and *Thrust 2* actually peaked at 615 m.p.h. on the faster run, but that didn't disguise the need for an extra 40 m.p.h.

That night in Bruno's Country Club, the project's HQ, the team was divided. Some were in favour of another try the following day. Others, ground down by the punishing toll of events, were in favour of another postponement. The latter faction won through. The team would return home, refettle the car, and plan a final throw of the dice for 1983.

And it would be final, for Noble's sponsors were prepared to tolerate just one

(*Above*) At the end of each run at Bonneville, salt would cling to *Thrust 2*'s solid aluminium wheels as the car slowed, necessitating laborious scraping before further runs. Once the vehicle reached high speed, centrifugal force would throw off the sticky white compound. (*Below*) Noble prepares for the breakthrough run on October 10, 1981, when Thrust 2 ran with complete stability and full reheat for the first time on its solid wheels.

more go. When the team returned to Gerlach in September 1983 there was a fresh sense of purpose. *Thrust 2* boasted more power after Rolls-Royce had reset the engine, the underside of the chassis had been tidied to reduce drag and a new fuel system was incorporated to cope with the extra power.

'For Britain and for the hell of it . . .'

In his first run, using only a three-quarter-mile run-up, Noble hit 394·477 m.p.h., enthusing about the car's performance. Then he had to stand down for three days when high winds prevailed, but this year morale was so high the team indulged in humour by making a film of oldest member Ron Benton setting a new land speed record of 57·070 m.p.h. on a portable toilet!

By September 20th things were back to normal, and Noble hit 488·465 m.p.h. with double his previous run-up, and backed that with 582·712 on his return run. The next day problems getting the reheat to establish delayed proceedings, but Noble upped his 'record' to 606.469 m.p.h., faster than Breedlove's jetcar record but a fraction beneath the one per cent improvement required to make it official. The one run made on the 22nd, under the watchful eyes of Gary Gabelich, saw a speed of 607·903 m.p.h., a meagre improvement and the first sign of the trouble that ensured Noble did not win his record easily. During the run the engine flamed out, and fears grew that it had surged – ingested so much air that it had been unable to cope and had vomited it back out through the intake, to the detriment of the compressor blades. If that *was* the case the engine would be wrecked. It even seemed possible it was the end of the road for *Thrust*.

Eventually, John Watkins was able to join the team in America, having been kept back in Britain by recent promotion, and he joined with Rolls-Royce's representative George Webb to establish that the engine *hadn't* surged but *had* been severely overheated. A static test at Reno Airport proved successful, but now the pressure was really on, for once again winter was approaching, and sponsorship agreements stretched only to the end of September. On the 29th, the anniversary of Noble's childhood idol's death on Loch Ness, *Thrust 2* achieved its fastest speed to date: 622·837 m.p.h. It was faster than Gabelich's record by a tiny fraction, but the onboard monitoring equipment revealed the peak speed to be very little better than the average, indication that the car had reached its maximum. Worse, air-lock problems in the fuel system – later solved – prevented a return run being made within the allotted hour.

One solution was to find a longer course on the desert, to allow the elastic to be stretched further, but a detailed search yielded nothing any better than the existing track, which was again damp at one end and therefore shorter than had been hoped. *Thrust 2* was run briefly on the 30th to test the original 4 in. wide Bonneville front wheels, in the hope of reducing frontal area and surface drag, but the test was negative. Now Ackroyd knew the remaining avenues that were open. It was clear transonic drag – the transitional point between subsonic and supersonic –

was building up so much that below certain temperatures *Thrust 2* did not have sufficient power to better 623 m.p.h., so Ackroyd decided future runs would be made not in the early morning, as had been the case up till then, but at the hottest part of the day. The speed of sound (Mach 1) increases with temperature and he reasoned that for a given Mach number speed will increase with temperature. Given the 43 degree temperature in which the 623 m.p.h. run had been made, he calculated *Thrust 2*'s Mach number as ·834, indicating that by running in a temperature 30 degrees higher the 623 m.p.h. speed could rise to 643, enough to break the record. As added insurance, small shockwave deflectors were fitted ahead of the front wheels, the underside was polished to mirror finish by panel specialist Brian Ball and the rake of the car was very subtly altered to take some loading off the front wheels, to ensure that they would plane over the crumbly surface rather than plough through it and increase rolling drag.

Regular telephone communication with the sponsors was successful in persuading the 'Magnificent Seven' – Castrol, Champion, GKN, Initial Services, Loctite, Plessey and Trimite – to contribute sufficient for *one more week* and on October 4th Noble finally got his chance. In a 75-degree temperature his first run was at 624·241 m.p.h. for the mile, 626·240 for the kilometre. He had started at the crumblier north end, and the return run, which started on a better surface, was expected to be quicker. It was. Noble achieved 642·971 m.p.h. for the mile, 642·051 for the kilometre, officially peaking at *Thrust 2*'s 650 m.p.h. design speed. His average for the mile, 633·468 m.p.h., finally brought his dream to reality, and the land speed record back to Britain.

Although the kilometre average of 634·051 m.p.h. was better than Gabelich's 630·388 figure, it did not meet F.I.S.A.'s one per cent requirement, so a third run was made in a vain attempt to add that record to the tally. It yielded only 620·555 m.p.h., but it didn't really matter. Noble had done enough. The team had found the 'window in the weather' in the nick of time, for the following day, though hotter, brought high winds which lasted the remainder of the week, and would have prevented further runs. . . .

When the dust had barely settled, the new fastest man on earth revealed he had done it 'For Britain and for the hell of it. . . .'

Moments after its record breaking performance, the Isle of Wight-built jetcar rests under a dying sun on the beautiful Black Rock Desert, whose mud polygon make-up is nicely illustrated in this shot.

(*Above, left*) Bad day at Black Rock. On the day it was feared *Thrust*'s engine had surged, Norris, Noble, Gabelich, Tom Palm and Ackroyd (fifth, sixth, eighth, ninth and tenth from left respectively) gloomily discuss the car's sluggish performance. Far left is Benton, while chief engineer Gordon Flux stands between Noble and Gabelich. (*Right*) The static engine test at Reno Airport that proved such fears groundless. As Norris stands by the left rear wheel (*Thrust 2* was ferried round on its 'normal' wheels and rubber tyres) Rolls-Royce engineer George Webb, in cap, stands in front of Ackroyd.

The sound barrier at last?

Though Noble's improvement over Gabelich's record seems small on paper, it does amount to a signficant, 33 m.p.h., improvement over Breedlove's old jetcar record, and is an indication of just how difficult and expensive it will be to break the much-vaunted sound barrier on land. Depending on altitude and temperature, it could be as low as 730 m.p.h. and the signs are that several challengers (see Chapter 23 for more details) are likely to appear in the next few years.

Already, Craig Breedlove is building his rocket-powered *Spirit of America, Sonic 2*, other rocket ventures including Sammy Miller's project, Bill Gaynor's *City of Sterling* and Col. Joe Kittinger's plans with High Velocity Inc. Then Art Arfons' plans to surprise everyone with a 5,000 lb. thrust super small jetcar.

When discussing such contenders, Richard Noble expresses delight. 'I desperately hope somebody breaks our record quickly. It would be a terrible shame if it were to stand as long as Gabelich's. The sooner it gets broken, the sooner we can get started on *Thrust 3* and have another go.'

Noble has promised he will not be the driver in a subsequent Thrust programme, and already John Ackroyd has begun making design studies for a jet-powered supersonic vehicle.

With the likelihood of renewed activity on the wheel-driven front, and serious challenges for the outright mark, land speed record breaking is on the crest of a new wave. Indeed, Noble foresees the possibility of the record being contested along the lines of the old Schneider Trophy air races.

Despite the *Budweiser Rocket* controversy, nobody really knows what will happen when a car breaks through the sound barrier, but one thing remains certain – brave men will continue to step forward in a bid to find out.

20

Wheel-driven revival?

'Each time I think of Richard Noble and Project Thrust I marvel at what he accomplished as far as getting sponsors. I guess we are just going to continue knocking on companies' doors.'

Tom Palm, founder of V.P. Research

The wheel-driven land speed record was under 'attack' by the Americans some time before the great 1960 assault, but the sad truth is most of the contenders given the '400 m.p.h.' tag by over-enthusiastic owners were not really up to the task. Several of the machines ostensibly designed to smash Cobb's record had trouble getting even three-quarters of the way there, but if you had a Bonneville streamliner in the early 50s, it seemed mandatory that it had 'outright record potential'.

Typical of the *genre* was Glenn Pengry's *Le Blanc Special*, which closely echoed the *Railton Special*'s shape and pre-dated Campbell's *Bluebird CN7*. When it first appeared at the Bonneville Nationals in 1953 the technical committee kicked it out on several technical counts, including a chassis that flexed in the middle whenever the car was jacked up. Pengry rebuilt it satisfactorily for 1954 and '55 but at the latter's Nationals was severely injured when the four-wheel-drive, twin-Chrysler-engined machine spun and flipped.

Another anxious to leave his mark was Californian Ermie Immerso. In 1959 his twin Chrysler-powered *Kraft Auto Special* reached only 289 m.p.h. Re-engined with a single 7·3-litre Lincoln V8 and rechristened the *Dean Van Lines Special*,

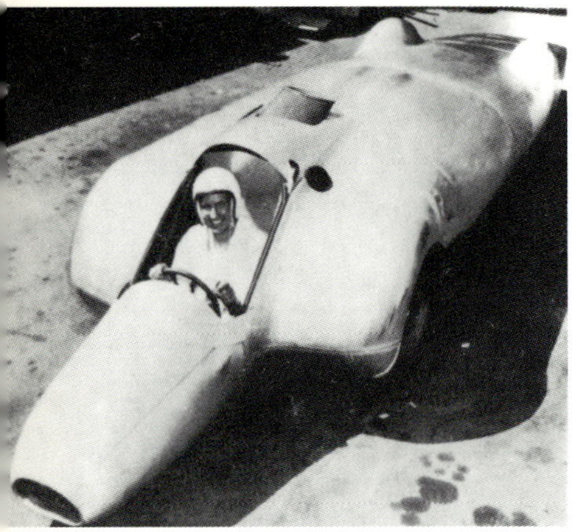

(*Above*) Art Arfons still remains convinced his curious *Anteater* has 400 m.p.h. plus potential as a wheel-driven contender. (*Below*) Bob Funk demonstrates the beautifully clean lines of his sadly stillborn *Special*.

the Rod Schapel-designed machine again disappointed in 1961. By the following year Ermie had crammed *four* Ford V8s into its frame to run 283, boosting that to a more respectable 302 in 1963, the first year in which he named one of his vehicles *Thunderbird*. He went better still in '64, hitting 352 m.p.h.

Although more famous for his jetcars, Art Arfons ran his Allison V12-engined four-wheel-drive *Green Monster No. 12* at Bonneville in 1960 and 1961 before switching to No. 14, *Cyclops*. The *Anteater*, as the car was dubbed, hit 249 m.p.h. first time out but ran into clutch trouble and Arfons left the stage to Ostich, Graham, Campbell and Thompson. The following August he improved to 313·78 m.p.h. before transferring to Daytona's oval racetrack in an intriguing and little-known attempt to win the $10,000 prize put up by circuit owner Bill France for the first 180 m.p.h. lap.

Used to Bonneville's wide open space, Art couldn't get to grips with the closeness of Daytona's walls, nor its 31-degree banked turns, and managed only 118. British racing driver Brian Naylor was also present, testing his own car, and jumped at the opportunity to try *Anteater*. In an amazing display he worked quickly up to 134 when a water hose burst and badly scalded him. France kept his money and Arfon's began thinking about jets, though still convinced of *Anteater*'s potential.

While success eluded many, the contenders still kept coming. Bob Funk, of Upland, California, believed streamlining to be more important than sheer power. Accordingly, his quadruple 6·5-litre Chevrolet-powered *Bob Funk Special* boasted ultra-slippery lines. It was designed to be 20 ft. 4 in. long and only 4½ ft. wide and 29 in. high, and with a frontal area of only 9·6 ft. and a drag coefficient of a mere 0·12 (by comparison normal road cars are around 0·34) it certainly had potential. Funk's project motto was 'Positive ideas produce positive results', but sadly no sponsors took positive views.

Also highly interesting was the 1963 *Stormy Mangham Chevy*. Breedlove's *Spirit of America* was classified as a motorcycle and sidecar, but the *Stormy Mangham*, also christened *Big John*, really *was* a motorcycle. Just after the Nationals, Stormy Mangham and driver Johnny Allen tested their twin-wheeled creation and though timed only by handheld stopwatches, Allen reached 310 m.p.h. with 'plenty to spare'. When Walt Arfons decided not to run the *Wingfoot Express* in late September the duo moved in under threatening skies. A defective O-ring stopped the driving wheel's Firestone holding pressure initially but once that was rectified Allen got away, quickly retracting the bike's side-mounted stabilizers. That was a mistake, for when the engine cut out *Big John* tumbled on its side, fortunately without serious damage. On October 1st Allen managed 196 m.p.h., but had a rough ride on bad salt at the course's southern end. On the run back he achieved only 164, but accelerated to 240 on the smooth salt outside the measured mile. On a shorter but smoother course he then managed 267·08 m.p.h., but parachute failure and smoke and fumes from the overworked front brake spoiled the day. Then came another 267 before clutch failure. With conditions so unfavourable it prompted the team to withdraw and, despite Allen's conviction, *Big John* never did crack the 400.

(*Above, left*) Craig Breedlove shows off his *American Spirit*, later converted into a rocket dragster when AMC pulled out of racing. (*Above, right*) Ron Henderson's *Conquest*-Duesenberg got to initial construction stage, but was never finished.

Another never to realize its potential was Ron Henderson's Duesenberg-powered *Conquest* of 1965. This was to have used a 1930 Model J 7·3-litre Duesie engine mated via a Scheifer Dual Drive clutch to a two-speed Cadillac transmission. Weight was to have been between 2,400 and 2,800 lb. and the driver sat high in the tail in dragster fashion. The tubular spaceframe chassis was built, but the streamliner never ran, unlike Craig Breedlove's *American Spirit*. After his 1965 unlimited record, Craig interested American Motors in backing a wheel-driven car, which featured two close-paired front wheels with the rears outrigged, giving the appearance of a mini *Blue Flame*. Breedlove ran at Bonneville in November 1968, but torrential rains and subsequent flooding in his Torrance base literally drowned the project and *American Spirit* was later converted into the rocket-powered *English Leather Special* as part of the campaign for backing for the new unlimited car. Later, in 1972, Breedlove obtained Tonia Campbell's consent to use her late husband's *Bluebird CN7* for a wheel-driven attempt. Breedlove planned to relocate the cockpit to the rear in the interest of giving the driver a better chance of detecting yaw, but the *Bluebird America* project foundered when backers stayed away.

Meanwhile, Bonneville's salt was pounded by another challenger, B&N Automotive's *Motion 1*.

(*Above*) Johnny Allen prepares for a 267 m.p.h. run on Stormy Mangham's intriguing motorcycle, *Big John*.

Another tragedy

This streamliner was powered by two blown 7·4-litre Chrysler V8s, each producing over 1,000 b.h.p., and was designed for 450 m.p.h. When it first appeared at the Bonneville Nationals in 1969 it was quickly nicknamed 'Rhinosaurus' due to its unusual appearance. The driver sat aft, behind the rear engine, while the front was mounted right in the nose, necessitating an unsightly cowling bulge akin to a rhino's horn. Because of the drive system *Motion 1* required push-starting up to 80 m.p.h. and initially the engines refused to clean out thereafter. However, by the end of the meet, driver Noel Black and partner Bert Petersen saw their creation set the fastest speed, at 335·820 m.p.h.

In September 1970 the 3,700 lb., 29½ ft. car was back on the salt for the Nationals, each day of which was sponsored by a different company. On *Champion* Monday, Black coaxed *Motion 1* to another fastest time of meet, this time hitting a promising 352 m.p.h. average, only two miles an hour away from Mickey Thompson's old record set with *Challenger 1*.

(*Right*) B&N Automotive's distinctive Motion 1 was christened 'Rhinosaurus' on account of its front engine cowling. It ran well at Bonneville in 1969, but driver Noel Black crashed fatally in 1970.

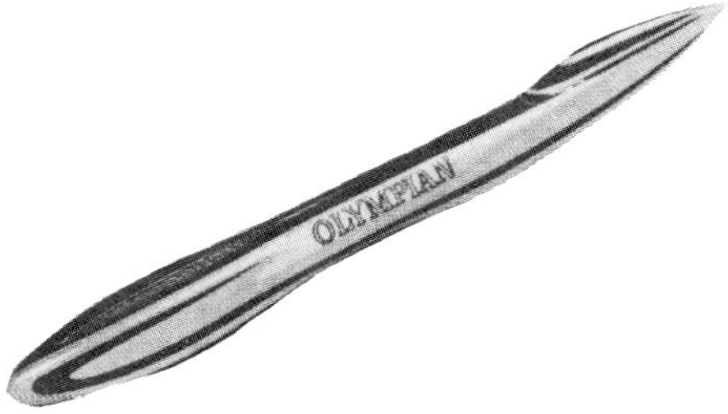

(*Above*) The Lufkin/McGrath/Hielscher *Olympian* promised much with beautiful, clean shape, while Dean Moon's *Moonliner* (*below*) was to have been run by Gary Gabelich.

Kawasaki Tuesday was spoiled by rain, which left mile four slick for *STP* Wednesday. There were three accidents in three hours. Mel Chastain went end for end at 280 in Bill Burke's *Rapid Transit* into which, against Burke's counsel, he had installed Bob Herda's blown 4·9-litre Chrysler. He suffered a broken arm and concussion. Then Melvin Hoy walked away after his belly tank lakester spun into a barrel roll and landed back on its wheels after axle failure at 240.

Then came Noel Black. He had the Firestone-shod machine up to 330 m.p.h. between miles four and five when suddenly it snapped sideways and rolled. Fragments exploded in all directions and Black was thrown from the wreckage. He succumbed to his injuries five hours later in Salt Lake City Hospital.

Many theories were advanced to explain *Motion 1*'s accident; the most likely was loss of the four-wheel-drive vehicle's traction on the slippery surface.

Simultaneously, 'Bonneville' Bob McGrath was pressing on with his plans for *Olympian*. It was 33 ft. long but only 34 in. wide, and featured twin turbocharged Chevrolet powerplants mated to three-speed automatic transmissions and ran on Firestones. It was a product of liaison between Bonneville Nationals regular McGrath and long-time partner Jack Lufkin, and drag racer Bill Hielscher, who was originally to have driven it. *Olympian* was stated to have a design speed in excess of 500 m.p.h. and certainly looked the part, being every bit as sleek as the Summers Brothers' *Goldenrod* and some 14 in. narrower. McGrath intended to make his record try in October 1970, around the same time Goodyear had the salt booked for Gary Gabelich, and as well as the wheel-driven record announced he would try for 23 lesser marks within the following two years. Ultimately, though, *Olympian* never turned a wheel in anger.

The same could be said of Dean Moon's 1975 *Moonliner*, another 450 m.p.h. contender built by the man famous for his 'Mooneye' custom and racing accessories. The *Moonliner* was to have been powered by an Allison V12 aero-engine rated at 2,440 b.h.p. and was the brainchild of Robert Johnson and Bob Kelly. Had it run, Gary Gabelich was the nominated pilot. . . .

In England, meanwhile, Malcolm Olley experimented with a Rolls-Royce Derwent turbojet installed in his *Pink Panther* dragster as part of a programme to build a wheel-driven contender. Olley hoped to crack 400 m.p.h. in Britain with the jetcar to raise the backing for the wheel-driven version, but met with little financial success. As he was planning construction of *Pink Panther*, Ermie Immerso was again active on the hallowed salt of Bonneville. A new *Thunderbird* appeared, this time in the hands of his son Marvin. Sitting astern of two Avco Lycoming T53-L turbines mounted side by side, he endured disappointment after disappointment as speeds progressed slowly to a new National Turbine record of 264·903 m.p.h.

by November 1978 before an accident destroyed the car.

Undaunted, however, father and son began preparing an all-new *Thunderbird* turbine for 1985, aiming confidently at the 500 mark and spearheading a revival of interest in the wheel-driven record.

Thunderbird II utilizes four-wheel drive and the Lycoming engines from its predecessor. Again they are mounted side by side, the left driving the front wheels, the right the rears via a synchronized differential. All-up weight of this highly attractive car is 5,000 lb. and the wheels are shod with Mickey Thompson's own make of tyres, designed specially by the former record breaker himself.

And by an ironic twist, Mickey is also likely to make one last attempt to rid himself of the wheel-driven record bug. His exploits with *Challenger I* are outlined in Chapter 21; after that venture he injured his back driving a limited class speedboat in 1961 and settled into building up his business interests. By 1968, though, he had interested the Ford Motor Company in backing an all-new contender known as the *Autolite Special*. Naturally, it used Ford engines, a supercharged 7-litre producing 1,260 b.h.p behind the driver, a normally aspirated 810 b.h.p version in front. The 5,400 lb. racer measured 30 ft. in length, 34 in. in width and was only 27 in. high at the sleek nose. Ford boffins believed the aerodynamics to be good for 500 m.p.h. and the *Autolite Special* certainly showed promise when Thompson gave it initial trials at Bonneville in late October 1968. On the 30th he reached 303 m.p.h. after two miles but skidded violently, eventually missing the U.S.A.C. time-keepers' hut by 75 yards. Thompson believed he would have reached 435 had he stayed on course. Twice more the car ran in 1969. On the first occasion it hit 360, its onboard telemetry system checking out exactly with the time-keepers' figures according to its driver. He managed 411 one-way and on another occasion stated he saw 442·625 m.p.h. on the car's instruments. However, he slid wildly again on that run and veered far enough off course not to cut the timing light. The car was returned to Los Angeles for a checkover, but when Ford pulled out

After years of piston engine heartache, Ermie Immerso put two Lycoming turbines in his handsome *Thunderbird*, and son Marvin broke the National turbine record in November 1978.

(*Above*) Now the Immersos plan a fresh attempt with this sleek challenger, using the same engines from the previous *Thunderbird*.

(*Below*) Mickey Thompson, seen here at Bonneville in 1968 in the attractive *Autolite Special*, has plans for a new attempt with the same vehicle, although power source is as yet unknown.

(*Opposite page*) Rick and Nolan White took their single-engined *Spirit of Autopower* for trials on Black Rock Desert in September 1983, but were unimpressed with its crumbly surface.

of racing Thompson was forced to give up. Four years later, in 1973, he sold the car to Don Alderson, who intended to use his own Milodon-built Chrysler engines and have Kelly Brown do the driving. The car was renamed *Conquest 1*, echoing Ron Henderson's earlier project. Then in 1983 Thompson repurchased the vehicle and is planning an attempt with either himself or son Danny at the wheel.

At one stage rumour connected the Summers with a new turbine car with which to defend their record, but Bob denied this, explaining he and Bill were committed to their thriving business. However, Immerso and Thompson will not be short of competition. Bonneville regulars Rick and Nolan White tried their 7·4-litre blown Chevrolet-powered *Spirit of Autopower* on the Black Rock Desert during Richard Noble's successful 1983 campaign, and despite very limited power are confident their single-engined, four-wheel-drive car can muster sufficient speed. Motorcycle maestro Don Vesco is readying his latest creation, the Bel-Ray Kawasaki *Sky Tracker* for a fresh attempt, having been washed out in 1980 and 1981 at Bonneville and then, after sportingly offering to share his salt time with the delayed Thrust team in 1982, had it happen a third time. This incredible four-wheeled streamliner packs twin Kawasaki Z1300 6-cylinder turbocharged engines and runs on solid aluminium wheels. To enhance traction, the resourceful holder of the motorcycle land speed record at 318·598 m.p.h. trusts to special epoxy and abrasive paint mix and machined grooves in the wheels' contact surfaces.

Also hoping to horn in on the wheel-driven act is brother Rick, who survived

131
SPIRIT of AUTOPOWER

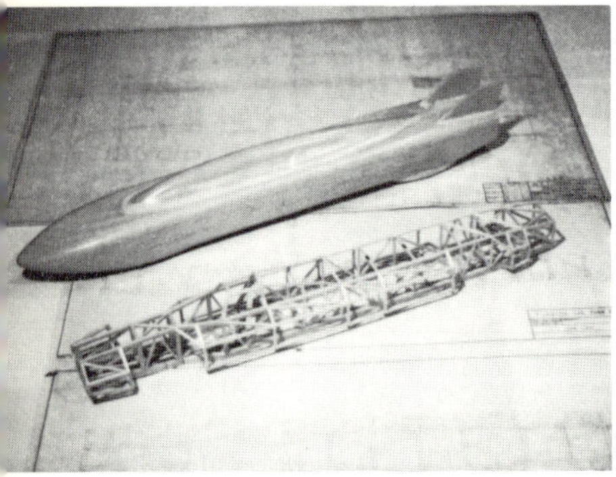

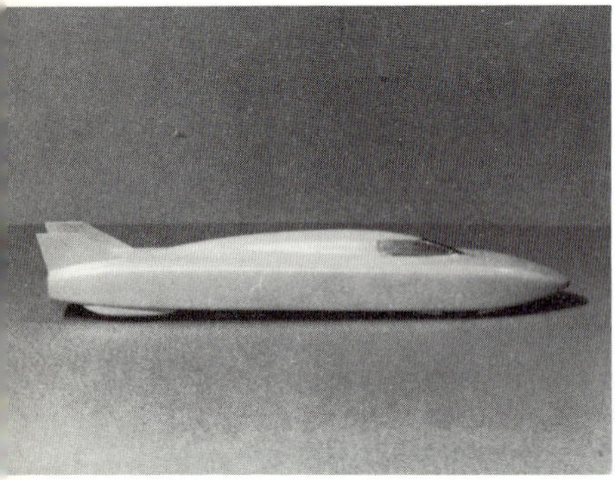

Prime contender for the Summers' record is V. P. Research's *Minnesota*, seen top and bottom in chassis and wind tunnel model form, and centre as a fullsize mock-up. It boasts a 0.53:1 power to weight ratio, compared to *Goldenrod's* 0.30:1 figure.

invertion at 325 m.p.h. at Bonneville in 1981 and plans a twin 5·7-litre Chevrolet-powered racer whose key to performance will be aerodynamic excellence. The vehicle will be two-wheel drive, the rears being mounted in tandem as in the Summers brothers' successful pre-*Goldenrod* '*Pollywog*' streamliner of 1962.

Meanwhile, in Indianapolis, veteran drag racing chassis man Mike Spitzer plans the *Indy Challenger*. This will use four aluminium smallblock Chevrolet V8s, the front pair being normally aspirated, the rears supercharged. By 1984 Spitzer had completed the spaceframe and claimed the body shape was good for 600 m.p.h.

Finally, in Minneapolis, V.P. Research is putting together the *Minnesota* turbine-engined challenger. Run by former Project Thrust team member Tom Palm and partner Paul Vickroy, who'll drive, V.P.R. aims to break the wheel-driven record as the initial stage in a programme to build a supersonic jetcar (see Chapter 23). Power for the wheel-driven car will be provided by a 1,750 s.h.p. G.E. T-58 turbine mated to an SCS reverse reduction gearbox and Ford differential, only the rear wheels being driven. Overall length is 23 ft. 8 in. and maximum width 38 in., while frontal area is only 8·2 sq. ft. In its initial wind tunnel tests Palm's concept performed very impressively, the model indicating a drag coefficient of only 0·112 compared with *Goldenrod*'s 0·117. Work began in March 1985.

Boost for Bonneville

Where will new wheel-driven attempts take place? The Whites were unimpressed with the Black Rock Desert's crumbly surface, which is better suited to pure-thrust vehicles, but it seems Bonneville has been granted a reprieve by the weather gods. According to Palm in April 1985, the long period the flats have spent under water has been highly beneficial, but the real key has been the cutting of special drainage channels beneath Interstate 80, which bisects the salt. The channels were cut to relieve pressure from the Kaiser Aluminum plant side and resulted in a superhigh concentration of pure salt water flooding back on to the flats, whose own surface-bonding potash content has for so long been extracted by local industries.

Palm reported: 'The prospects are unreal. The salt is *three* to *four* inches thick (in 1981 *Thrust 2* had fractions of an inch) and old hands are saying the flats have never been in such good condition since racing started there in the 1940s'.

Spitzer originally considered running on the treacherous Lake Eyre, but like others is certain to see the 'new' Bonneville as the wheel-driven racer's salvation.

There is another certainty. Had they been allowed, the Summers could have boosted their own record. On November 14, 1965, the day after the 409 run, Bob beat his new mark easily. Against his better judgement he'd earlier allowed himself to be persuaded to fit larger air scoops to feed the Chrysler engines. After much begging he was allowed a final day's running with the smaller original scoops just to prove his point. He ran 425 m.p.h. comfortably one-way, before sponsors stepped in to prevent a return on the grounds that their publicity machines were already geared around the previous day's 409 m.p.h. record. . . .

21

The unrecognised and the unlucky

'All that Tommy Milton ever got for pushing the land speed record to 156.046 m.p.h. in 1920 was a sterling silver tea service from the Goodyear Tire and Rubber Company.'

Griff Borgeson in
THE GOLDEN AGE OF THE AMERICAN RACING CAR

There are numerous anachronisms in *LSR* records, particularly in the earlier years. Refusal by the A.C.F. or the A.I.A.C.R. to accept figures timed by apparatus or methods of which they did not approve deprived more than one worthy non-French contender of official land speed record honours. Similarly, American refusal to meet A.I.A.C.R. regulations stipulating the mean of two runs in opposite directions as the only fair figure, meant the confusion of two sets of world records, with some spectacular American speeds, attained under the most favourable circumstances, dimming the feats of European contemporaries.

Thus Oldfield's 131·275 m.p.h. with the *Blitzen* Benz, and Burman's dubious 141·37 m.p.h. with the same car a year later, completely eclipsed Hornsted's modest but official 124·10 m.p.h. of 1914, the first two-way record to be recognized. Guinness's 1922 speed of 133·75 m.p.h. pales before the 149·875 m.p.h. of de Palma's Packard in 1919 and Milton's Duesenberg speed of 156·03 m.p.h. in 1920, and even if one were to deduct 15 m.p.h. for favourable winds, those two fine American cars would still have been faster than the Sunbeam.

Other cars were ruled out, not by regulations, but by sheer bad luck. 'Ifs' and 'might haves' feature just as much in record-breaking as in motor-racing, and such is fate that a venture fully deserving of success is cheated by chance, whereas less worthy rivals enjoy success. Outstanding examples are Frank Lockhart's *Black Hawk* Stutz of 1928 and Mickey Thompson's *Challenger* of 1960. In this chapter, then, are described those cars denied the record by legal foible or ill fortune.

1905 Mercedes 'Flying Dutchman' (Herbert Bowden)

Only restrictive regulations seem to have denied this enterprising 'Special' the land speed record honours which it earned on Daytona Beach during the 1905 Florida Speed Week. After raising Arthur Macdonald's brand new flying mile record with the Napier by a humiliating 5 m.p.h. from 104·65 m.p.h. to 109·75 m.p.h., owner/driver Herbert Bowden of Boston was disqualified on grounds that the *Flying Dutchman* exceeded the maximum weight limit of 1,000 kg. (2,204 lb.) which applied to all races and sprints at the meeting. Inexplicably, this seems to have disqualified the car from *LSR* honours too, although it was electrically timed by six chronometers which agreed to within $\frac{1}{10}$th sec. under A.A.A. supervision.

The 120 h.p. 'straight-eight' power unit of the car was actually two Mercedes '60' engines, one taken from a car, the other from a launch, and installed in tandem in a lengthened Mercedes chassis, on which the driver sat right over the rear axle, anticipating the modern dragster layout. Although it typified the *LSR* 'freak' as a vehicle in which sheer power for straight-line velocity took priority over roadholding, steering, flexibility and other more subtle car qualities, the *Flying Dutchman* was no crude monster but a neat and expertly engineered machine, estimated to have cost Bowden over $50,000.

The crankshaft taking the power from the two four-cylinder 'halves' was machined from two nickel steel billets, interconnected and carrying a single large flywheel at the rear. There was no gearbox, sheer torque getting the car swiftly on the move, and final drive was through side chains. Total weight of over 23½ cwt. was some 450 lb. over the Speed Week limit, a factor of which Bowden, if not the organizers, must surely have been aware.

1919 Packard V12 (Ralph de Palma)

At a time when the A.I.A.C.R.-recognized land speed record stood at 124·10 m.p.h. to L. G. Hornsted's 200 h.p. Benz, there can be very little doubt that Ralph de Palma's 12-cylinder Packard '905' was truly the world's fastest car in 1919–20. On 12 February 1919 at Daytona beach, Florida, it was timed through the flying mile in 24·02 sec., a speed of 149·875 m.p.h., and this was accepted by the A.A.A. as a new land speed figure.

By then the Americans were fully aware of A.I.A.C.R. requirements that speed records should be timed in opposite directions, the actual record figure being the mean of two runs, and it seems curious that de Palma apparently did not make a timed return run, just to ensure world-wide recognition, rather than American only, for what was a remarkable achievement.

The Packard '905', first built in 1916 with a smaller 5-litre engine, was fitted for the record attempt with a larger 904·4 cu. in. (14·8-litre) V12 cylinder aircraft-type unit, the forerunner of the Liberty engine which went into quantity production during the latter part of World War I (and which also powered Parry Thomas's record car *Babs* and the Triplex Special). The Packard experimental unit gave about 240 b.h.p. at 2,400 r.p.m., the chassis was of stock 'Twin Six' touring type modified to take the larger engine, and the car weighed about $30\frac{1}{4}$ cwt.

An ordinary production pattern three-speed Packard gearbox was used, and de Palma even had the luxury of an electric starter and full floorboarding. The single-seater body carried a faired head-rest on top of its very graceful tail, the front dumb-irons were faired in, and aluminium discs fitted to the wire wheels. That this Packard was no mere sprinter de Palma demonstrated by setting further U.S. records from 2 to 20 miles at Daytona, while he subsequently drove it through the streets of Denver City on a demonstration run at 120 m.p.h.

Driven by Ralph de Palma, this 14·8 litre, V12-engined Packard '905' attained 149·875 m.p.h. through a mile at Daytona in February 1919. Timed one way only, the figure was not recognized by the A.I.A.C.R. in Europe, though accepted as an American land speed record.

1920 Twin-engined Duesenberg (Tommy Milton)

In 1919 the Duesenberg Company, operated by Fred and August Duesenberg, built one of the world's first overhead camshaft straight-eight racing engines for the Indianapolis 500 Miles Race. The engines measured 296·9 cu. in. (5 litres) and gave a modest 92 b.h.p. at 3,800 r.p.m. When the capacity limit for racing was reduced in 1920 to 183 cu. in. (3 litres) the Duesenbergs were left with three of the now redundant 5-litre engines on their hands.

It was Duesenberg's principal driver Tommy Milton who, while lying in hospital recovering from bad burns sustained in a 1919 race crash, hit on the idea of using two of these engines in a special car to attack de Palma's American record of 149·875 m.p.h. He consulted the Duesenbergs, offering to meet costs of building the car himself, and they agreed to work with him on the project.

The two units were installed side by side, driving a solid rear axle by separate propeller shafts and final drives; there were no gearboxes. Milton himself did much of the design and construction, and the car had a specially made chassis carrying well-streamlined single-seat bodywork with a steeply inclined nose and high tail with head fairing for the driver. As both the engines were identical, their exhausts discharging on the offside, the nearside engine's exhaust manifold was in between the two units under the bonnet, making things pretty hot and uncomfortable for Milton.

The 'Double Duesey', as it was nicknamed, was first tested by up-and-coming Jimmy Murphy, who unofficially exceeded 151 m.p.h., much to Milton's wrath. He tried to exceed this figure, but running on sand at high speed is notably debilitating to performance and the car went slower and slower. In the end Milton stripped both engines right down in a windproof tent, rebuilt them, and tried

The ingenious 10-litre, twin-engined Duesenberg with which Tommy Milton broke de Palma's record at 156·03 m.p.h. in 1920, again at Daytona. Again the A.I.A.C.R. declined to accept the figure.

again. This time he was successful, setting a new mile record at 156·03 m.p.h.

Reports conflict on details of subsequent happenings. One account has it that Milton drove on, aiming to break records up to 5 miles, when the car caught fire in the third mile. Another report, supported by Milton's own recollection of things later in his life, states that he was making a return run when the car caught fire during the first mile, and that the 156·03 m.p.h. was his mean speed for the two runs. (If so, it was never accepted by the A.I.A.C.R.).

Whatever the truth, Milton found the heat from the two engines, together with fumes coming up the steering tube, highly unpleasant, and when these increased he realized there was an under-bonnet fire, probably of petrol and oil in the undertray. He completed the mile even so, then stopped and extinguished the blaze with sand.

The Milton record was only recognized in its own country.

The frontal aspect of the Duesenberg looks commendably slim considering it bears two engines side by side.

1928 'Black Hawk' Stutz (Frank Lockhart)

This is one of the saddest yet at the same time most inspiring *LSR* stories of all. Frank Lockhart was a genius at designing, preparing and driving racing and record cars. His first Indianapolis '500' race was in 1926 – and he won it. The following year he set an astonishing 1-mile record with a razor-tuned $1\frac{1}{2}$-litre single-seater Miller at a mean speed of 160·01 m.p.h., and a best at 171 m.p.h., on the dry bed of Lake Muroc, California.

From this remarkable 91 cu. in. Miller sprang his land speed record car. At the time Lockhart was working in the experimental department of the Stutz Motor Company at Black Hawk, Indianapolis, and they agreed to help him in the construction of an *LSR* machine. As a result, it was called the *Black Hawk* Stutz, but it was very much a Lockhart design, adapting many Miller parts and some by Stutz. He took two '91' twin overhead camshaft blocks and crankshafts and combined them at 30 degrees to each other to produce a 3-litre 16-cylinder engine.

The crankshafts were geared together, and two centrifugal superchargers, each with its own Zenith down-draught carburettor, and running at three-and-a-half times engine speed, were driven off the rear of each block. Power output of this impressive engine was an estimated 385 b.h.p. at 7,500 r.p.m., passed through a three-speed gearbox and a worm-drive rear axle which helped to lower car height by about six inches.

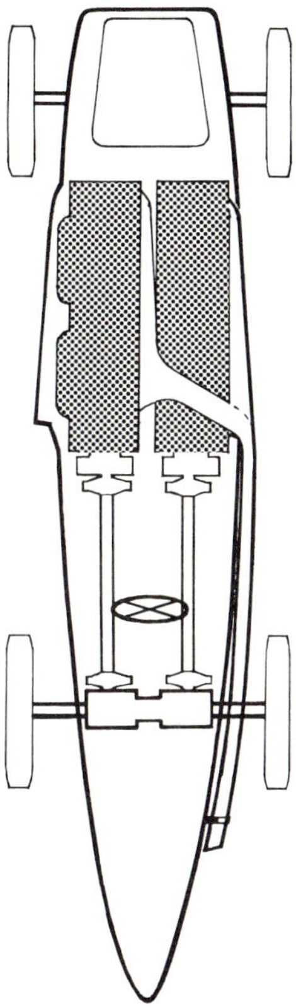

Twin-engined Duesenberg. Location of engines and transmission

The chassis was very narrow and light, and tapered in at the rear to the contours of the tail. Front suspension was by two pairs of quarter-elliptics, placed only 11 in. apart, and machined from solid, inclusive of the front end mountings which formed the centrepiece of the axle. The rear suspension was similar, and large-diameter shock absorbers were fitted all round. Objectives of the springing system, evolved for Lockhart by Zenas Weisel, were to keep the suspension within the narrow body and out of drag areas, and to keep axle movement absolutely parallel with the frame so that steering was unaffected. Since spring movement was only $\frac{3}{4}$ in. one wonders why the designers did not dispense with the complication of such limited springing and specify rigid axles.

Another advanced feature was the fitting of hydraulically-operated brakes to all four wheels, the first on any record car; they were of Lockheed type with 16 in. × 3 in. drums. Externally the car was a masterpiece of trim, efficient streamlining. Nothing was allowed to obtrude needlessly into the airflow. The front axle was faired, the wheels were covered by light alloy spats, those at the front turning with the wheels, and the nose was closed over. There was no radiator; instead, engine cooling was by 75 lb. of ice in a tank through which the engine coolant flowed. This was good for five miles at full throttle before the temperature exceeded 180° F., and was a system later adopted on other *LSR* machines.

The entire engine compartment was sealed off, and a carefully designed under-shield ran from nose to tail. Mounted above the engine, flush with the bonnet, were two cast aluminium aircraft-type manifold intercoolers to reduce the air/fuel mixture temperature. The two carburettors breathed through holes in the scuttle top, and the exhaust stubs were flush with the bonnet sides. The entire body was reminiscent of the Mercedes-Benz Grand Prix cars of ten years later, and was surely unequalled in its time for aesthetic beauty.

As was so often the case with such enterprises, financial problems reared their ugly head. In order to balance percentage costs for the car totalling about $35,000, met by Stutz and other sponsors, Lockhart used most of his own capital, earned in racing. He also committed himself by accepting cash payments from various component makers, including $20,000 from the Mason Tire Company. He used their tyres in preference to Firestones because of the financial offer and because he simply couldn't afford to have Firestone build special tyres anyway. With his heavy financial burden, Lockhart just had to go for the record as soon as possible.

After maddening troubles at Daytona, first with clutch slip, then with power deficits, it was found that laminar flow across the carburettor intakes was restricting

(*Above*) Frank Lockhart in his Stutz *Black Hawk* with 16-cylinder, 3-litre engine comprising two $1\frac{1}{2}$-litre Miller racing units. (*Below*) The Stutz proved hard to hold at high speed, and at Daytona in February 1928 the car skidded and pitched into the sea. In a subsequent attempt, a tyre burst at well over 200 m.p.h.: the car was smashed to pieces and Lockhart killed.

air intake. Scoops were fitted on the bonnet top and running improved, so in February 1928, while Campbell and Keech were also at Daytona, Lockhart essayed a high speed run. The story is told in more detail in Chapter 9, but in a squall of rain it seems that Lockhart deviated from the course into some soft sand. This threw the Stutz into a skid which ended in a roll and an alarming submersion in the sea, from which car and driver were rescued by speedy helpers and a long rope.

The car went back to Stutz for repairs while Lockhart recovered in hospital, and by April both were back at the beach for another try. On 25 April 1928 Lockhart put in two warming-up runs, one at 198·29 m.p.h. which rated as an American 2–3-litre class record. Then he went for the record which by then stood at 207·552

In 1958–59 the enterprising Mickey Thompson built this car around four 6·7-litre Pontiac V8 engines, one pair driving the front wheels, the other the rear. In 1960 he supercharged the engines and on 9th September covered a flying mile one way at 406·60 m.p.h., beating John Cobb's record by over 12 m.p.h. On the return run a drive shaft broke, robbing Thompson and *Challenger* of land speed record honours. (*Below*) Location of engines and transmission.

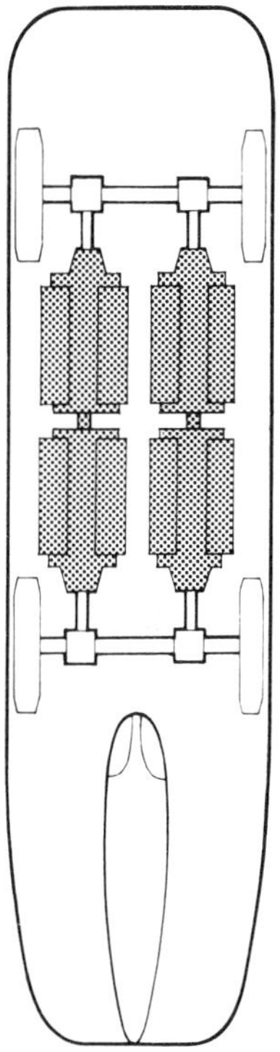

m.p.h. to Ray Keech's Triplex. Lockhart's first run – on 3 litres, remember! – was at 203·45 m.p.h.; his second was fatal.

The lovely little white car was entering the measured mile at an estimated 220 m.p.h. when the right rear tyre collapsed. Later inquiry revealed that it had been cut by a clam shell when Lockhart braked hard after his previous run. Malcolm Campbell had counselled him to change tyres between runs, but with only 20 minutes' grace Lockhart elected not to, mindful of the amount of time needed to remove and replace the wheel spats. When the Stutz had finished smashing, bouncing and pounding its way over the sand – and miraculously hurdling a clutch of spectators – it was a wreck, and poor Frank Lockhart, thrown out near the end of its mad contortions, was near death. He died in hospital.

Some engineers suggest it was the worm-drive, a necessary hangover from Stutz's road cars, that really caused Lockhart's death, believing that on the overrun the gearset was sufficiently inefficient to lock the rear wheels, a fatal occurrence on such a light, swift vehicle.

1960 'Challenger' I (Mickey Thompson)

In the momentous gathering of record-essaying machinery at the Bonneville salt flats in 1960, the most creditable and ingenious was Mickey Thompson's *Challenger 1*. Creditable because, unlike his rivals, Thompson stuck to car-type engines, ingenious because of the way in which he harnessed four of them to get the kind of power needed for *LSR* work. There was a marked parallel between the two Californians Frank Lockhart and Mickey Thompson. Both pursued their aims despite often precarious cash reserves; both were fervently and wholly dedicated to their cause; and both applied an outstanding degree of enterprise and perfectionism to it.

In 1958 Thompson, an inveterate record-maker in numerous categories on numerous dragstrips and Bonneville, decided to build a car for the *LSR*. By mid-

Thompson's *Challenger* was a tribute to his design genius, as the sleek lines of the 1959 version reveal. Few *LSR* contenders got quite such a raw deal from Fate.

1959 the car was completed, just in time for an important press preview arranged by Goodyear, who were sponsoring the car. It had four Pontiac 6·7-litre, V8-pushrod o.h.v. engines bought from a scrap-yard, arranged in two pairs back-to-back in a tubular chassis, also made from scrap material. Each engine had its own clutch and pre-war La Salle three-speed gearbox, each its own overdrive and final drive. The front engines drove the front wheels, the rear engines and the rear wheels.

The axles were completely unsprung, which was no worse than many of the unsympathetic suspensions used on other record cars. The magnesium alloy wheels, made by Halibrand, were of small diameter, and wore Goodyear tubeless tyres made to Thompson's specification. The engines had been stripped, rebuilt by engine-wizard Fritz Voight, and equipped with Hilborn-Travers fuel injection. Collective clutch control and gear-changing were through one pedal and gear lever, while to assist wheel-braking Thompson introduced the first parachute brake used on an *LSR* machine.

Rear track was 7 in. narrower than the front and the rear wheels were enclosed within the body, while the driver's seat, beneath a hinged glass canopy, was behind the rear wheels, sling-shot style. The whole car was much smaller than the average monster, measuring only 19 ft. 7 in. overall, with a wheelbase of 9 ft. 1 in., but those four big American iron engines and transmissions were heavy, and the car scaled 6,000 lb. which rose to 7,000 by 1960.

Challenger 1 first ran in tests at Edwards Air Force Base, which stands where the famous Muroc dry lake bed course used to be, in August 1959. The selector rods broke, leaving the car in second gear, but Thompson worked up to about 200 m.p.h. when the car struck a 3-inch bump at an intersection. It aviated for over twenty yards, landed slightly askew, and went into an enormous spin. Emerging shaken but unscratched from this, Thompson took *Challenger 1* to Bonneville for the National Speed Trials, where he clocked 332 m.p.h. When the parachute brake was released, however, it threw the car into a see-saw motion which ended in a vast slide. Next time he fitted two 'chutes and lengthened the lines to 75 ft., putting in a 362 m.p.h. run without trouble.

He tried for the *LSR* in September 1959, but after much delay through rain, a broken underpan, sticking gears and other snags, his quickest speed was a disappointing 367·83 m.p.h. one way, though he broke four world records for 5 kilometres, 5 miles, 10 kilometres and 10 miles by way of compensation. Using a more potent 40 per cent nitromethane fuel mix he tried again, only to have his oxygen supply fail when a tube detached itself, and he breathed in toxic fumes of oil, fuel and exhaust. He managed to brake and was in a coma when they lifted him out.

For 1960 Mickey Thompson supercharged the Pontiac engines with four General Motors' diesel Roots-type blowers, which raised the output from 2,000 to almost 3,000 h.p. He also refined the streamlining where possible, and booked the Bonneville salt for early in September, before Donald Campbell was due to try his luck with *Bluebird*. Further details of Thompson's 1960 effort appear in Chapter 13; he suffered the usual troubles and frustrations attendant to *LSR* bids, got one run in at 372·67 m.p.h., then ballasted the front of the car to eradicate nose-lift and fitted new clutches to improve pick-up.

After further runs he adjusted the ballast, only to run out of time on the salt. Campbell sportingly let him encroach on *Bluebird*'s allowance, and on 9th September Thompson tried again. This time everything worked well, and he did the mile in an epic 406·60 m.p.h., over 12 m.p.h. faster than Cobb's Railton, which held the record. On the return run, accelerating with all the power the engines could give, Thompson's luck, and a drive shaft, broke, and *Challenger*'s moment of glory was over.

Replacing the shaft would take longer than the permitted hour, so Thompson pulled out, content at least with topping 400 m.p.h. one way. He tried again two years later with *Challenger* but a bumpy course, and the pain of a back injured in a speedboat accident, denied him success. By 1968 he was back with the *Autolite Special* for a new try and by 1984 he was considering a third crack at the elusive record (see Chapter 20), which is still a mere 3 m.p.h. faster than the 406 he achieved with *Challenger*.

Mickey Thompson getting into *Challenger 1* before setting off on his American national record run. Car is in 1959 form, without superchargers.

22

The unconfirmed and the unsuccessful

'All the experience gained in the construction of the first Sunbeam record-breaker, and all the lessons learned in succeeding British and American trials on Daytona Beach, have been embodied in the new venture. . . . In design and construction [the Sunbeam *Silver Bullet*] worthily upholds the high standard set by the two earlier British machines.'

THE AUTOCAR, *15 November 1929*

Some cars just didn't make the grade; the 300 h.p. Fiat, the *Djelmo*, the *Silver Bullet*, are instances. Over-optimism or miscalculation by the designers, or some technical or other mishap denied them success. Other cars 'made the grade' according to their drivers or sponsors, but not according to official records; the intriguing *Wisconsin Special* of Sig Haugdahl is an example. Such cars are described in this chapter.

(*Opposite*) Due to its supercharging arrangements the Sunbeam *Silver Bullet* proved very prone to catch fire. After Sunbeam abandoned their efforts with it, the car was acquired by Lancashire driver, Jack Field, who tried unsuccessfully to reach competitive speeds with it on Southport beach in 1934. Here he and helpers grapple with yet another conflagration.

1902 Baker Electric 'Torpedo' (Walter C. Baker)

Although the first land speed records were established by electric cars, these were soon outpaced by steam and petrol, and the 1902 Baker *Torpedo* constituted a 'last kick' by electricity. It was an amazing design for the period, with very advanced streamlining in which, for the first time, driver and mechanic were kept out of the airflow. General shape and layout anticipated the modern racing car, and the big wheels are suggestive of Donald Campbell's *Bluebird* of sixty years later.

Walter C. Baker, successful Cleveland, Ohio manufacturer of electric touring cars

The 1902 Baker *Torpedo* was electricity's last kick against the advancing petrol engine. Though of flimsy construction the heavy batteries it required meant a weight of $18\frac{3}{4}$ cwt. After attaining an unofficial 78 m.p.h. it crashed at Staten Island in May 1902 when braking to avoid encroaching spectators, killing two of them.

('the aristocrats of motordom'), decided in 1901 to build a really fast car. He analysed the needs (maximum of power, minimum of friction and wind resistance, and low centre of gravity) and set out to balance them against the one unavoidable handicap with an electric car – the heavy weight when sufficient batteries are carried. The resultant *Torpedo* had a nominally 12 h.p. Elwell Parker motor and forty Gould batteries to drive it. It had a frame of angle-iron, transverse-leaf front suspension and longitudinal leaf springs at the rear, all completely enclosed within the 'inverted boat'-type body.

This body was made of white pine and basswood framing, with oil cloth neatly stretched over and pinned, and finished originally in black and later in white enamel. The wood-rimmed wire wheels, also covered with oil cloth 'discs', measured no less than $56\frac{1}{2}$ in. in diameter with very thin-section Goodrich tyres fitted, these being inflated to 125 lb. p.s.i. The wheels and many other running parts ran on ball bearings, and like a modern Formula I car the motor was mounted ahead of the rear wheels. Final drive was by two chains, one each end of the armature shaft, to sprockets each side of a differential on the rear axle. Inboard band brakes worked on the final drive sprockets, and steering was of 'marine' type by steel wire cables. Total weight was about 3,100 lb., much of that being batteries.

Boldest expedient of all was the accommodation for the driver, W.C. Baker himself, and his mechanic or 'electrician', C.E. Denzer, seated in tandem within that shapely but claustrophobic body-shell. Fitted into the top of the hull was a padded, streamlined 'coaming' with curved mica window, and Baker's seating was arranged so that his head fitted comfortably inside this 'fixed crash helmet'. The unfortunate Denzer, seated behind Baker, saw less of what was going on but got enough light to watch the voltameter and tachometer, and both he and the driver were held in place by heavy webbing cross-braces – surely the world's first safety belts?

Before this car could display its full potential it was involved in a most unfortunate accident. For its début Baker entered it for a speed trial meeting organized by the Automobile Club of America on the Staten Island boulevard, New York, in May 1902. The course was second-rate, steeply cambered and with a tram-track crossing it in the last quarter. An enormous number of spectators turned out, and crowd control was poor. Baker had covered a mile at an unofficial 78 m.p.h. (3 m.p.h. faster than Serpollet's record) during practice, but in the actual sprint the crowd encroached dangerously on the road at the far end of the mile.

Rushing towards them, his warning horn hooting loudly, Baker swerved and braked hard, locking the rear wheels. The car skittered on, hit the tram tracks at an angle, and the right-hand rear wheel collapsed. The *Torpedo* leapt skywards, then ploughed into the massed spectators, killing two and injuring nine others. Baker and Denzer, both uninjured thanks to their safety harness, were arrested on a homicide charge pending inquiry, but were eventually exonerated. The press of the day, however, made much of the accident, blaming it on the inadequate wheel strength and faulty steering of the Baker.

The car was later rebuilt into the shorter wheelbased *Torpedo Kid*, and raced at Daytona where, in 1904, it was said to have reached an unofficial 104 m.p.h.; while at Cleveland, its home town, it was reported to have clocked a less than credible 120 m.p.h. for 10 miles. . . .

1910 300 h.p. Fiat (P. Bordino and A. Duray)

Coming from makers renowned for the symmetry and balance of their racing-car designs, the monstrous 300 h.p. Fiat rates as something of an aesthetic lapse on their part, although undeniably impressive. The objective, clearly, was the usual one in a record car – abundant power – so they took one of their immense S76 overhead camshaft airship engines, a lofty 4-cylinder measuring 190 × 250 mm. – over 7 litres per cylinder! – giving a displacement of 28,353 c.c. and an output of 290 b.h.p. at 1,900 r.p.m.

This bulky power pack was installed in a slender but well cross-braced frame, semi-elliptically sprung all round; transmission was by a Hele-Shaw multi-plate clutch, four-speed gearbox and chain final drive. The driver sat right over the rear axle, and the 300 h.p. Fiat wore a very shapely tail for its period. Despite much preliminary testing and development in Italy by Nazzaro, Scales, Fagnano and other Fiat works drivers, this car never fulfilled expectations. It was brought to Brooklands in 1911 and driven by Pietro Bordino, who, according to Fiat information, broke the 1-mile record in 31 sec., averaging 195 k.p.h. or 121·17 m.p.h. Neither contemporary records nor William Boddy in his Brooklands history bears this out. Bordino also took the Fiat to Saltburn sands, but they were in poor condition, and the hapless Italian could not achieve any respectable speeds. The 39 cwt. car eventually sank in the boggy sand and had to be hauled out.

Fiat also claim that the 300 h.p. car was taken to Long Island, New York, in April 1912, where 'it improved its former record by covering a mile in 20·2 sec., reaching the fantastic speed of 290 k.p.h.'. That means 180·206 m.p.h. – certainly a

The 300 h.p. Fiat, with towering 28·35-litre airship engine, was built in an effort to break the *Blitzen* Benz hold on the land speed record. It never succeeded, although Arthur Duray clocked 132·37 m.p.h. one way at Ostend in 1913.

record claim unsubstantiated elsewhere! In 1913 the car was acquired by the Russian Prince Boris Soukhanoff, who took it to Moscow, but found that driving the huge Fiat was a job for a professional. He hired the Belgian Arthur Duray, who after an abortive attempt at Brooklands took the Fiat to his favourite road at Ostend on 8 December 1913 in an effort to break the *Blitzen* Benz hold on the *LSR*. In bad weather he attained 132·37 m.p.h. through the kilometre, beating Barney Oldfield's 131·275 m.p.h. of 1910. Unfortunately, the car broke down on the return run, thereby forfeiting recognition under the new A.I.A.C.R. two-way rule. For this attempt the car was fitted with a radiator cowl closing the intake to a narrow vertical slot. Duray stated that he could never utilize the full power of the machine, and that getting into fourth gear was an adventure, owing to the short braking area beyond the kilometre at Ostend.

1922 'Wisconsin Special' (Sig Haugdahl)

Following in the footsteps of Ralph de Palma and Tommy Milton, both of whom he had watched closely during their record attempts at Daytona, the American 'outlaw' driver Sigmund ('Sig') Haugdahl constructed a land speed contender around a big 5 in. × 6½ in. World War I, 250 h.p. Wisconsin all-aluminium 6-cylinder aero-engine. Using a stock chassis boxed and strengthened, he built a narrow, low-drag, single-seater body with steeply angled screen, driver's head fairing, and a somewhat ornamental radiator cowling following the style of the contemporary Frontenac as raced so successfully at Indianapolis.

The streamlining was excellent, the cowling connecting below with a full-length undershield and merging with the base of the tail in one clean flow. Six short exhaust stubs protruded from the bonnet, and the rear wire wheels carried flush

The Fiat at full speed on test in Italy.

Few accurate details are available of Sig Haugdahl's aero-engined *Wisconsin Special* or of the speeds it achieved. 180 m.p.h. was claimed for it at Daytona in 1922, but it was also credited with speeds of 170·7 m.p.h. and 162 m.p.h., none being recognized, even by the American authorities.

discs both inside and out. Much uncertain information surrounds this car, and it is not known whether Haugdahl used these discs or not on his record attempt. Although no official speed seems ever to have been announced by the A.A.A. or any other U.S. authority, the car was claimed to reach a speed of 180 m.p.h. on Daytona beach in 1922 – an impressive increase, if accurate, on Milton's 156·03 m.p.h. of two years earlier. In later photographs of the car it bears the legend 'Sig Haugdahl's 3-Mile-a-Minute *Wisconsin Special*', although that does not, of course, give the claim any official status.

Early in 1923 it was announced in *The Autocar* that Haugdahl, credited with having attained a speed of 170·7 m.p.h., was expected to bring his car to Brooklands, and in another account he was credited with a flying kilometre in 13·8 sec., a speed of 162 m.p.h., though this, too, went unrecorded officially. While his record achievements remain obscure, Sig Haugdahl gave valuable publicity to the need for careful wheel-balancing on high-speed cars. Although not the pioneer of the practice, he found during runs at Daytona that wheel patter developed into a tremendous and dangerous vibration at 150 m.p.h. After careful investigation he experimented with balance weights on the wheels, getting a marked improvement in handling at high speeds, 'running up to 180 m.p.h.'

1924–7 'Djelmo' (G. Foresti)

This sophisticated and expensive machine ranks as one of the 'mystery' cars of record-breaking. The project was financed by Prince Djelalledin, an Egyptian living in Paris, and designed by the Paris-based Italian engineer Edmond Moglia, earlier associated with Sunbeam-Talbot-Darracq. The name *Djelmo* is a combination of the foreparts of their two names, and the car was built in Paris, many parts being sub-contracted.

Its specification suggests an oversize Grand Prix racing car rather than a records 'Special', and it was, it seems, based on a design produced by Louis Coatalen and Vincenzo Bertarione of Sunbeam in reply to the 10½-litre V12 Delage. They never built the car, and sold the design to Prince Djelalledin for £6,000. The engine was a

The *Djelmo's* record-breaking efforts came to a hapless end in November 1927 when the treacherously soft sands of Pendine beach in Wales deflected it from its course; it overturned, flinging the unhelmeted driver, Giulio Foresti (*above* with his wife before the attempt) out on to his head. Miraculously, he escaped little hurt.

big 10-litre, twin-overhead-camshaft straight-eight with cylinders in two blocks of four, and four valves per cylinder. Bore and stroke were 107 × 140 mm., and output with four Claudel Hobson carburettors was claimed to be 355 b.h.p. at 3,000 r.p.m. There were reports of supercharging the engine, but this was never carried out.

The very substantial engine-bearers were bolted direct to the chassis, giving it valuable bracing, and a 2-speed-plus reverse gearbox in unit with the engine was used. The eight exhausts discharged into one large pipe emerging from the undershield midway between front and rear wheels. The chassis embodied an elaborate aluminium casting encasing the front dumb-irons, springs and base of radiator; the front springs passed centrally through the forged front axle in the manner employed on Fiat and Bugatti cars. The rear wheels were notably crab-tracked ($37\frac{1}{2}$ in. compared with 56 in. at the front), no differential was fitted, the rear semi-elliptic springs were underslung, and the rear axle was enclosed.

Bodywork of the *Djelmo* was clean and impressive, particularly from the frontal aspect. The driver was Giulio Foresti, who raced Schmid and Bugatti cars at that time. Plans were to take the car to the U.S.A. for an attempt on the record in 1925, either on a dry lake such as Muroc in the Mojave desert of California, or at Daytona beach, but the car was persistently down on performance. Despite tests at Arpajon and Miramas it never made an attempt on the *LSR* until 1927.

Then Foresti brought it to Pendine Sands in Wales in August of that year, only to encounter persistent engine trouble. Eventually he managed some fast runs, but the record which stood at 133·75 m.p.h. when *Djelmo* was first laid down had risen to 203·79 m.p.h. by the time it was ready. A rather hopeless attempt on the British record, which stood to Campbell at 174·883 m.p.h., ended in November 1927, when Pendine's treacherously soft sand caught Foresti out at about 150 m.p.h. *Djelmo* swerved, rolled over, and was severely damaged, although Foresti, whose cheerful habit it was to drive without a protective helmet, emerged comparatively unscathed

apart from a scraped scalp and a shaking.

At one stage Moglia gave serious thought to an ultra-low-slung *Djelmo II*, to be powered by two of the straight-eight engines with the driver mounted amidships, but in all probability Prince Djelalledin tired of spending his money on such distractions, for nothing more was heard of the project.

1930 Sunbeam 'Silver Bullet' (Kaye Don)

At a time when Grand Prix racing was in a decline there was a kind of dramatic aura about massive-engined land speed record cars. Thomas's *Babs*, Segrave's 1,000 h.p. Sunbeam, Campbell's *Bluebird*, Segrave's *Golden Arrow* and its saurian American rival, the Triplex Special, had followed each other into the front-page news, and when, ten months after the *Golden Arrow* did its epic 231·446 m.p.h., an all-new monster called the Sunbeam *Silver Bullet* was announced, the world looked to it to perform in an equally spectacular manner.

Everything pointed to success: the car had the pedigree behind it of a marque which had built three successful record-breakers already, and unlike the 1927 Sunbeam 1,000 h.p., it was not a 'compromise' using available parts but an all-fresh design by Louis Coatalen. It certainly looked impressive, with its enormously long bonnet closely housing two great Sunbeam-Coatalen V12 engines of a combined output given in Coatalen's typically generous style as '4,000 h.p.' Its silver body was long and sleek, its shapely nose was completely blanked off, the wheels had after-fairings, and on each side of the tail were rectangular stabilizing fins with a horizontal hinged air brake in between.

Although at the time it was claimed the 12-cylinder engines were specially designed and built for the car, one suspects they were evolved from, or were the advance experimental units for, one of Coatalen's aero-engine designs. They were cast in aluminium with Nitralloy steel cylinder liners measuring 140 × 130 mm.; the cylinder blocks were angled at 50 degrees, the four valves per cylinder were not inclined as in a pent-proof head but parallel, and were operated by twin overhead camshafts. Capacity was 24 litres but no specific power output was ever volunteered. The 'hush-hush' aspect seized upon by the press well suited Coatalen's publicity-conscious mind.

The crankshaft and big ends ran in roller bearings, and supercharging was by a huge centrifugal blower, located behind the two engines and turning at 17,000 r.p.m., drawing its mixture from two big Amal carburettors, and pumping it at perhaps 7 lb. p.s.i. to the engines through large diameter induction manifolds. To keep head resistance down, cooling was by an ice chest and water tank installed where the radiator would have been, an idea used by Lockhart in 1928 and Irving in 1929.

The engines were coupled, not by direct shafting but by drop gears and a secondary shaft. A three-speed gearbox gave theoretical speeds of 125, 166 and 248 m.p.h. at 2,400 r.p.m., and took the drive through twin propeller shafts in the same

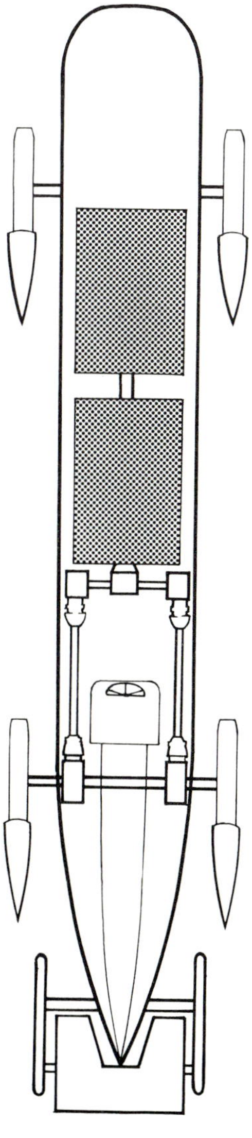

Sunbeam *Silver Bullet*
Location of engines and transmission

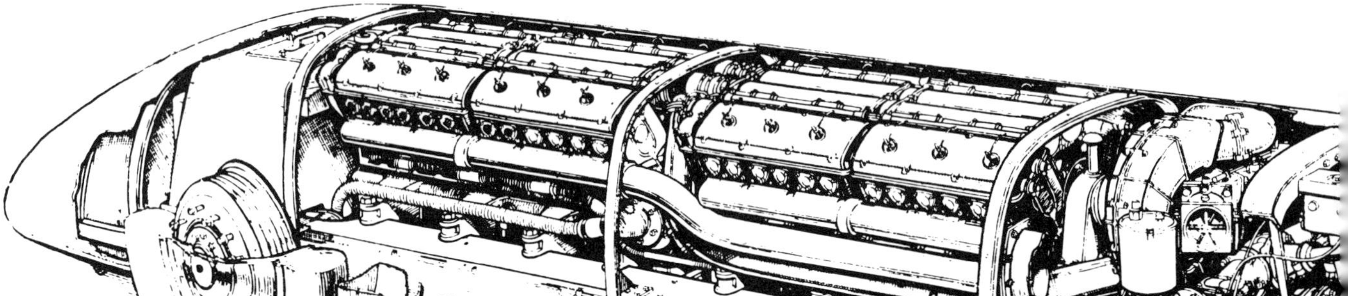

A cutaway drawing showing the *Silver Bullet*'s two huge engines mounted in line, with centrifugal supercharger behind them, and twin propeller shafts copied from Irving's *Golden Arrow*. The twin stabilizing fins and horizontal air brake on the tail were novel.

The unfortunate Sunbeam *Silver Bullet* with which Kaye Don was to attack the land speed record at Daytona in 1930. Despite a proclaimed output of 4,000 h.p. from its two special Sunbeam 12-cylinder engines, it could not approach within 45 m.p.h. of Segrave's 231·446 m.p.h. record with *Golden Arrow*.

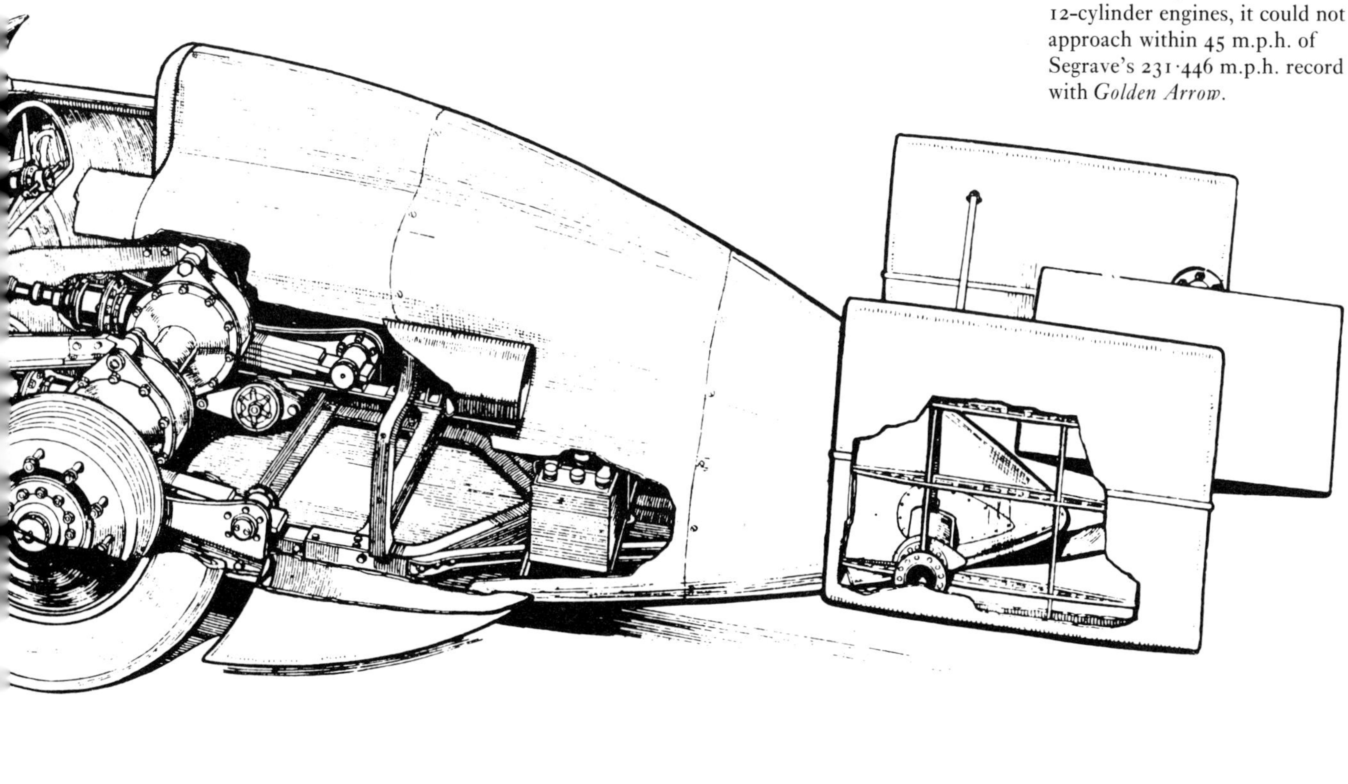

way as in *Golden Arrow* to keep the driver low in the car. The four wheel-brakes were hydraulically operated and water-cooled (for the first time on an *LSR* machine). The frame, which owed much to Irving's *Golden Arrow*, was immensely strong, measuring 13½ in. at its deepest point, and the suspension was by the usual stiff semi-elliptics with about 1¼ in. up-and-down movement. Both front and rear axles were located by massive arms, and throughout the design no effort was made to keep weight low, it being accepted at that time that plenty of weight was essential to keep the vehicle on the ground. Overall it scaled slightly over 4½ tons. The streamlining was thorough, to the extent of recessing the rectangular exhaust pipes flush into the body sides.

The driver of *Silver Bullet* was Kaye Don, Brooklands star on Sunbeam cars, and the team sailed early in 1930 for Daytona. Despite the Sunbeam *cachet*, and the usual magnanimous press releases, it soon became clear that something was gravely wrong with the project. The specially constructed engines, never tested beforehand, started their teething troubles at Daytona instead of on the test bed at Wolverhampton. Moreover, the supercharging arrangements were very suspect; the close proximity of the exhaust manifolds to the long inlet galleries meant that the latter grew far too hot, and incoming gas was exploded before ever reaching the cylinders, the resultant impact running back to the blower and repeatedly shattering its blades and causing fires.

The unfortunate Kaye Don had little chance of success. The Daytona beach in March 1930 was in a very bumpy state and the long chassis'd *Silver Bullet* bumped abominably with only approximate control. Don's highest timed speed was 186·046 m.p.h., way below the current record; beyond that the engines persistently misfired. Moreover, the lack of success undermined morale in the team, there was friction between Coatalen and Don, whom the wilder American newspaper columnists accused of being scared of the car, whereas, in fact, the car just would not run cleanly or quickly.

In the end the whole entourage returned to England with, as one U.S. paper said, 'their bulldog tails between their legs', and the avowed intention of modifying the car and coming back to Daytona for a fresh attempt. This never came to anything, and although subsequently both Jack Field and Freddy Dixon tried to make the recalcitrant *Bullet* work, neither succeeded.

1931 'Fred H. Stewart Enterprise' ('*Wizard*' *Smith*)

Adding to the world-wide interest in the *LSR* came this Australian venture of the early 'thirties. Imitation being the sincerest form of flattery, Captain Jack Irving must have felt complimented, for the car followed his 1929 *Golden Arrow* design closely. Fred H. Stewart, prominent Sydney businessman, sponsored it, desiring his car to be entirely British- and Empire-made. Don J. Harkness, a Sydney engineer, designed it around one of the latest 1,450 b.h.p. Napier Lion racing engines, then still on the Government secret list. On the *Enterprise* it drove through

The *Fred H. Stewart Enterprise* with which the Australian driver Norman 'Wizard' Smith aspired to take the land speed record on Ninety Mile Beach, North Island, New Zealand, in 1931–32. The huge, unsightly radiator was fitted after early cooling troubles. Problems with the course and the car denied Smith the record, though he set a world 10-mile record at 164·084 m.p.h.

a three-speed gearbox and twin propeller shafts and final drives.

Harkness took considerable interest in aerodynamics (his firm later produced the Harkness and Hillier racing aircraft), and although the car's lines were inspired by *Golden Arrow* they also embodied some interesting original features. Instead of the full-length inter-wheel sponsons which on Irving's car housed the surface radiators, Harkness used ice cooling and fitted rear-wheel fairings which extended to form twin stabilizing fins.

The *Enterprise* was taken late in 1931 to Ninety Mile Beach in North Island, New Zealand. Preparing the course and installations was a pioneering job reminiscent of Campbell's Verneuk Pan expedition of 1929, and the New Zealand course was almost as troublesome. The main problems were that the beach was often excessively wet with heavy ocean tides, while the sand contained many razor-sharp toheroa shells which menaced Smith's stock of tyres. The car itself gave problems, mainly with the experimental cooling, and in the end this was replaced by a huge and unsightly nose radiator enclosed in a crude box which ruined the 'Irving line' of the car and, one suspects, the aerodynamics.

Smith found it best to use a course close to the sea; and to combat the problem of spray flying back from the front wheels on to his windshield, two of his engineers jury-rigged a special rotating device attached to the screen which, like a naval 'clear-view' screen, dispelled all spray. Unfortunately the all too abundant water also worried his engine, and during a bid for the record on 1 May 1932, he had reached about 180 m.p.h. on a very soggy beach when a magneto shorted out; misfiring set in, a carburettor fire started, and the run ended prematurely.

Thus the very patient official time-keepers provided by the Auckland Automobile Association never had a land speed record to time, but 'Wizard' Smith did set one world record earlier on – the 10-mile at 164·084 m.p.h., well below the 300 m.p.h. target they had hoped to approach.

One of the record's forgotten victims was Glenn Leasher, in Romeo Palamides' jet-powered *Infinity*. The bold drag racer from San Mateo paid the price for recklessness, and for years *Infinity*'s tattered shards were left to guard the entrance to the hallowed salt.

1962 'Infinity' (Glenn Leasher)

Whether the F.I.A. approved of jetcars or not, by 1962 America was full of record-contending vehicles which pursued the example set by Dr Nathan Ostich, Westinghouse's J46 or General Electric's J47 turbojets being the most popular powerplants.

From an early age, 26-year-old Glenn Leasher of San Mateo dreamed of being the fastest man on earth. And as a crestfallen Craig Breedlove quit the salt in early September 1962, *Spirit of America* still full of teething bugs, he prepared for his own attempt on Cobb's long-standing mark. Leasher had befriended Oakland hot-rodder Romeo Palamides in an 11-year drag-racing career established on the strips of California, and persuaded him to design *Infinity*, a streamlined shell constructed around an afterburning J47. Breedlove dismissed *Infinity* as 'a hot rod with a jet engine', but some of its features were interesting. The long proboscis housing the driver was part of the jet intake, to help smooth out the airflow. Sadly, it placed the driver in a position where he had neither the chance to assess yaw accurately nor sufficient protection against accident.

Infinity missed the National Speed Trials from August 19th through 25th as it only arrived on the final day, when only pre-qualified vehicles could run. It reportedly made a slowish run after the trials, but was shipped back to base for attention to a chassis problem which arose.

By September 9th, however, Leasher was back on the salt and made three fast runs, his best speed an encouraging 330 m.p.h. The 'hot rod' might have sat on a Ford front axle, but at least it steered, where *Spirit of America* wouldn't. Leasher was ready for business. On the 10th he calmly smoked a cigarette and listened as time-keeper Joe Petrali counselled him to try a few more slow-speed runs. Leasher agreed, only to remark to his crew chief as Petrali moved out of earshot: 'This time I'm gonna go for broke.' As Marion Dunn, Sports Writer for the *Salt Lake Tribune* put it: 'apparently, sitting alone in the cockpit, he changed his mind and death climbed in as co-pilot.'

On that run, Leasher used a drag-racing technique new to the salt. He knew the variable area jetpipe on the J47 would increase thrust if closed down to its smallest setting with the afterburner on, a ploy used during 'combat emergency' and dutifully logged by service pilots on landing. Holding *Infinity* stationary with his left foot on the brakes he built up thrust before blasting down the long black line. Watched by a vast television audience, he'd gone $1\frac{1}{8}$ miles down the course when *Infinity* yawed violently at an estimated 250 m.p.h.-plus. The silver jetcar danced on its nose, crushing Leasher, then launched into a series of rolls that scattered its remains over two miles. Leasher died instantly.

What went wrong? Why didn't Leasher deploy his parachute when he sensed trouble? Nobody knew for sure. It was suggested his starting technique had over-temperatured the elderly J47, causing it to fail at speed. Some thought he had either tried to drive through the yaw, or been sitting too far forward to sense it in time. The experts' view was that the lack of a tail fin, allied to the rotational effect of the J47's compressor blades, destabilized *Infinity*. Whatever, sitting right in that vulnerable proboscis, Leasher never stood a chance once the critical angle of yaw had been exceeded.

1962 Green Monster No. 14 'Cyclops' (Art Arfons)

The Leasher tragedy exacerbated a problem jetcar owners and drivers were having with insurance companies. At the Nationals the insuring company rejected the jet-cars on a disagreement concerning cover against property damage and public liability. Art Arfons had only been able to run his *Green Monster Cyclops* by paying a rumoured $190 premium every time it was prepared for action.

After *Anteater*, Arfons turned his ideas to jets, as brother Walt had. He constructed a sturdy spaceframe into which he installed an afterburning J47, and called it *Green Monster Cyclops* because of its single headlight. That enabled the machine to be run at night drag races, and it was typical of its *genre*, with minimal bodywork and largely exposed engine. *Cyclops* proved quick on the strips and Arfons took it to the 1962 Nationals to assess its maximum speed. In qualifying he hit 338·91 m.p.h., averaging 330·013 for a new record in the Jet class. The car drew much comment, particularly because of its aerofoil just behind the cockpit, designed to kill front-end lift. But for insufficient fuel tankage, which prevented him using the afterburner as much as he wished on each run, Art felt he could have been faster still, even with such an unstreamlined shape. He then turned his thoughts to a J79-powered vehicle, the *Green Monster* in which he would achieve worldwide fame. In 1967 he mounted *Cyclops*, front wheels and all, on a pair of pontoons and announced he would use it to attack the water speed record. Initial flotation tests were carried out, but the attempt never went ahead. . . .

1962 'Valkyrie 1' (Chuck Hatcher and Gary Gabelich)

Bill Fredrick's *Valkyrie 1* was regarded by many experts at Bonneville in 1962 as 'the jetcar most likely to succeed' and drew high praise for its detail construction work. Working with partner Fred Hartman, the 21-year-old former butcher from Woodland Hills, California, fashioned a strong spaceframe from 1¾ in. 4130 chrome moly steel, the wheelbase measuring 130 in. and the overall length 23 ft. Weight,

Art Arfons moved into the jet league with *Green Monster No 14 'Cyclops'*, which showed immense potential at Bonneville in 1962 despite its lack of streamlining. That potential was never realised once Art got his hands on a General Electric J79 power unit. . . .

Bill Fredrick's first *LSR* vehicle was the slippery *Valkyrie 1*, which should have run at Bonneville in 1962. Most experts felt it was the best of the new breed of jets, but insurance problems prevented it running anywhere but the drag strips, where Gary Gabelich usually handled the driving duties.

too, was modest in comparison with rivals, the Westinghouse J46 streamliner tipping the scales at a mere 2,960 lb.

Valkyrie bristled with new ideas. Initially, Fredrick intended to run solid wheels comprising magnesium centres with steel rims. Subsequently, however, this revolutionary idea was mothballed, to appear again in the seventies. Instead, Fredrick turned to Halibrand for 18 in. mag wheels shod with Firestone tyres. Also changed after initial tests was the means of feeding the jet air. To begin with air entered directly into a plenum chamber between intake and driver, but later small slots were cut in the sleek aluminium shell to allow more direct flow. Beam axles were employed and, like *Flying Caduceus*, *Valkyrie* was suspended by torsion bars.

Fredrick and his crew were on the salt for the August 1962 Nationals, but the insurance problem prevented any serious runs by nominated driver Chuck Hatcher. He did fire it in the practice area, however, and like Leasher made one short dash. The Leasher accident kept the insurance companies sour, but at the Winternationals Show at the end of the year the car won the Ford Motor Company top award in the Experimental category.

The Bonneville problem decided Fredrick on running *Valkyrie* on drag strips instead, and late in 1962 the first jetcar duel was organized at Famosa, north of Bakersfield, California. Driving *Valkyrie* was a young trainee astronaut already making a name for himself in drag racing – Gary Gabelich. His opposition came from Bob Smith, driving Romeo Palamides' 31 ft. J47-powered *The Untouchable*, which resembled the ill-starred *Infinity* without its streamlined shell.

Smith took the first of three heats, but Gabelich won the second and third to take the overall victory, describing Fredrick's car as 'riding as smooth as a big Caddie'. Subsequently, the car was sold to Mickey Thompson, who had Gabelich drive it when the latter wasn't also sampling *The Untouchable*.

If *Valkyrie* was denied its chance to attack the record, both Fredrick and Gabelich at least got *their* chances later on. . . .

1976 'Blonde Bombshell' (Barry Bowles)

Like many to be bitten by the speed bug, Briton Barry Bowles was quick to realize major projects don't happen overnight, so approached his goal of the land speed record in stages. The first was to construct Britain's first rocket-powered dragster, the *Blonde Bombshell*. The 31-year-old company secretary obtained one of the last Bristol-Siddeley Gamma 201 hydrogen peroxide-fuelled motors that had been part of Britain's abortive Black Knight missile programme – and a much more powerful Stentor motor. The former was installed in a spaceframe dragster chassis; the latter was intended for the outright record car.

In November 1976 the *Bombshell* made its first tentative runs at Santa Pod Raceway, construction having been undertaken by respected drag racers John Harrison and the late Allan Herridge of H&H Racecraft. Through 1977 Bowles sorted problems with the fuel pressurizing system and after wrangles with the RAC over the safety aspect of rocket-powered vehicles, took the *Bombshell* to Elvington airfield in Yorkshire in October, having been banned from running in public. There he hit 231 m.p.h. one-way and averaged 218·71 to establish a new British flying quarter-mile record.

Further modified, the *Bombshell* was taken to Pendine Sands, scene of earlier outright record attempts, in April 1978, Bowles determined to make the first 400 m.p.h. run on British soil. After the usual frustrations, he made his attempt on the 24th. Behind the scenes, he had received word from Goodyear that the tyre giant disapproved vehemently of him using its particular type of 250 m.p.h. rubber for such a high-speed attempt. Bowles' spokesman countered that Goodyear's warning applied only to the front tyres, which had been replaced with a different manufacturer's products.

Whatever, as Bowles approached 280 m.p.h. the left rear tyre exploded, and the *Bombshell* yawed right, then left, then right again before launching into a spectacular flip captured by television crews. The brave Bowles emerged with only minor cuts and bruises from the tangled wreckage, and though *Bombshell* was subsequently rebuilt, the bad publicity he received from what some saw as foolhardy valour effectively killed his outright record project.

1978 Andersen's 'Pea Soup Monster' (Slick Gardner)

Slick Gardner of Santa Ines Valley, California, was the first man to drive a jetcar on solid (forged aluminium) wheels. In 1978 he purchased Art Arfons' rebuilt *Green Monster*, had it equipped with Cragar wheels and obtained backing from the Andersen company, hence the car's colourful name Andersen's *Pea Soup Monster*.

After initial trials at El Mirage, Slick took the *Monster* to Bonneville in November 1978 with hopes of erasing Gary Gabelich's 622·407 m.p.h. record. He came home chastened after a series of frightening lurches around 300 sapped his confidence. Cragar took another look at its wheels and deleted the spiked treads, and with smoother wheels, similar to those of the *SMI Motivator* and the *Budweiser Rocket*, the car was carted back to the salt in December the following year, with Arfons himself along as counsellor. What little thunder it could muster was stolen by *Budweiser*'s antics at Edwards AFB, but in any case Gardner was in trouble.

'The acceleration was too much for him', Arfons recalls. 'We turned her down so much she'd barely hold an afterburner flame.' Added to that the *Monster* kept breaking through the patchy salt and though, according to Art, Slick hit 552 m.p.h. before a big off-course moment, he decided enough was enough. The *Monster* still rests outside Gardner's home, looking decidedly dishevelled.

As this book went to press two Australians, Coleman and McGahnius, were considering using the *Monster* for an attempt on Donald Campbell's 403·1 m.p.h. mark, which still stands as Australia's official land speed record, Lake Eyre being the venue. At the same time, they were also considering construction of a new vehicle specifically for the attempt, to be know as *Aussie Invader*.

23

The untried and the paper projects

'In the motor world, as in the boxing ring, a sensational contender may look like a champion, with speed, power, style – everything except the winning punch. Around such a machine hangs the aura of that intriguing world of "if".'

Fred Horsley, WORLD'S FASTEST CARS

Some cars just had no chance and never turned a serious wheel. Ineffective design, a world war, lack of money – the causes are varied. Some never went beyond the drawing board, or their inventor's mind. In this chapter some of the interesting ones are described.

1932 Stapp-Jupiter (Réné Stapp)

Possessing an outline vaguely suggestive of Art Arfons's *Green Monster* of thirty-two years later, the Stapp of 1932 was far wilder in concept and infinitely less successful. M. Réné Stapp of Chatou, a Paris suburb, had his own peculiar ideas about streamline and motive power, and the wherewithal to practise them in the metal. He took three 800 h.p. Bristol Jupiter radial aircraft engines, mounted them at the rear of an old Voisin chassis, and built a vast cylindrical body around them.

The original Voisin engine was retained in its normal place 'for starting purposes', and the three Jupiters were converted into 'internal combustion turbines', although the inventor did not divulge his method in detail apart from stating that the pistons

(*Opposite, above*) The Daimler-Benz T80, in the foreground, with DB 603 aero-engine driving four rear wheels. It was with this car, designed by Dr Porsche, that Germany intended to wrest the land speed record from Britain. The attempt was only foiled by Hitler's attack on Poland and the resultant outbreak of World War II in 1939. (*Below*) Structural details of the T80: *left* how the inverted V12 engine was mounted in the middle of the tubular chassis, with the driver seated ahead of it; *right* how the body framework was built up. The interesting aerofoils on the body sides were added afterwards.

The incredible Stapp 'record car' of 1932 with three Bristol-Jupiter radial aero-engines modified to function as turbines, and driving all four wheels. It caught fire on La Baule sands and was destroyed.

were removed. The conversion could account for the 'discharge' tubes alongside the tail and the 'pepper-pot' stern which contained twenty-two large outlets. M. Stapp had two claims to fame, one for building the first 'turbine-powered' record contender, the other for being the first to prescribe four-wheel drive, the engines, he claimed, driving all four wheels by 'electric transmission'.

It is uncertain whether this extraordinary vehicle was a hoax or sheer optimism. Certainly the streamlining came into the latter category, with the car's huge frontal area, a tail-fin some 6 in. thick with unfaired trailing edge, and the curious accommodation for driver and mechanic. They seemingly had to stand amidships like a railway engine driver and fireman on the footplate, with the driver peering out of a hatch rather than through a protective window.

The Stapp was destined to attack the *LSR* at Daytona, but after a demonstration run in the streets of Paris (!), running, we suspect, on the Voisin engine alone, it was taken to the sands of La Baule, Brittany, for further tests. There it quickly burst into flames and, mercifully, destroyed itself, giving time, however, for the inventor and his mechanic to jump clear.

Daimler-Benz T80
Location of engine and transmission.

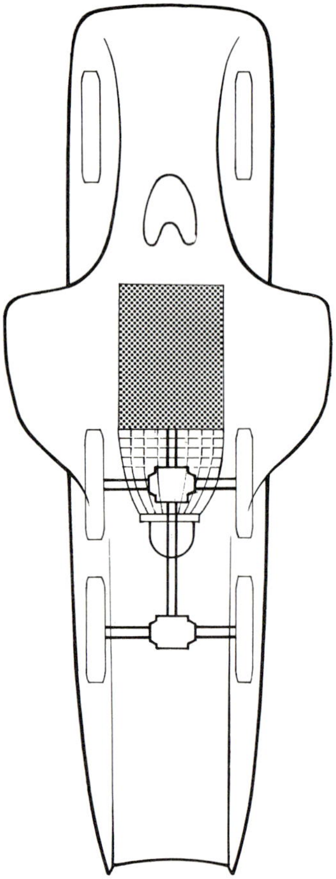

1939 Daimler-Benz T80

This was a very much more serious project, and one which could have altered *LSR* history but for the coming of World War II. The remarkable Daimler-Benz T80 was very much on the secret list when being built in 1939, and its existence was first revealed to the late Laurence Pomeroy, the noted technical author, in 1945 when he was visiting the site of the factory at Stuttgart. Designed by Dr Ferdinand Porsche, this remote descendant of the famous *Blitzen Benz rekordwagen* of before World War I was built around a $44\frac{1}{2}$-litre supercharged Daimler-Benz DB 603 V12 inverted aircraft engine with Bosch direct fuel injection.

The chassis, made of deep oval-section steel tubing, had six large diameter wire wheels and Continental tyres; the engine was located amidships with the driver ahead of it, and drive was to the four rear wheels through an early form of hydraulic torque convertor dispensing with gear-changing. The track was remarkably narrow at 4 ft. 4 in. front and 3 ft. 10 in. rear, and the all-enveloping bodywork amounted virtually to two huge longitudinal fins enclosing the wheels, with very shallow, low-drag panelling in between. The driver's cockpit was enclosed; the radiator was in the nose.

A highly interesting feature was the use of twin aerofoils on the body sides. The

Burly Bob Knapp reclines in the chassis frame of his mammoth *Bob Knapp Special*, which was to have used *two* J47s. The car was never finished, but Bob later had success in Class C with Bob Herda, who achieved 298.359 m.p.h. in November 1967 in the *Herda-Knapp Streamliner*.

upper foils were angled to increase loading on the driven rear wheels, while the lower foils were horizontal. Later the lower foils were deleted, and the uppers angled at five degrees. Even more significant was a device in the transmission to override throttle control and automatically reduce power output to counter wheelspin.

The DB 603 engine was rated in 1939 at 1,750 b.h.p. at 2,700 r.p.m., but probably 3,000 b.h.p. could have been made available at higher r.p.m. and boost, when a speed of over 450 m.p.h. might have been expected from a car weighing between 2 and $2\frac{1}{4}$ tons. The record at the time stood to John Cobb (Railton) at 369·70 m.p.h. The driver was to have been Hans Stuck, the famous Auto Union Grand Prix and hillclimb champion. While this would almost undoubtedly have created considerable friction with regular Mercedes-Benz drivers Rudolf Caracciola, Hermann Lang and Manfred von Brauchitsch, it should be borne in mind that the entire project was Stuck's idea in the first place. The Austrian wanted to be the fastest man on land (and water) and took his concept to Porsche, who refined it to the point where they sold Daimler-Benz on the idea of building the T80.

Stuck wanted to run at Bonneville, but because the Air Ministry had had the final say before the project got the green light, he had to concede to its order that an attempt be made on German soil. Accordingly, plans were laid to construct a seven-mile long, 100 ft. wide addition to the autobahn at Dessau. Such a dictate was reminiscent of the folly that saw Auto Union insist on Bernd Rosemeyer's fatal class record attempt on a public road in 1938.

Prior to World War II the T80 was delayed as Daimler-Benz continually improved the engine, while tests with the intended continental tyres were far from promising. Eventually the silver streamliner missed the boat, but remains today, slightly battered and minus its engine, at the Daimler-Benz Museum at Stuttgart-Unterturkheim, Germany.

1962 'Bob Knapp Special' (Bob Knapp)

Probably the most leviathan record contender since the 1928 *White Triplex* was the Special dreamed up by burly Bob Knapp, head of Knapp Automotive and Dyno Tuning of Palo Alto, California.

In 1961 he managed to shoehorn a Chevrolet Corvette V8 into a hapless Austin Healey Sprite, and his 1962 project was a behemoth to be powered by *two* J47s. By September a spaceframe strong enough to house the powerplants had been constructed. Broad, long and massive, it was fully triangulated, safety features including the wise precaution of an automatic kill switch that would be activated if one engine flamed out, and gauges on each wheel to assess load. Solid axles were planned, with braking by discs and triple parachutes.

With over 11,000 lb. thrust and an all-up weight of $5\frac{1}{2}$ tons, the *Bob Knapp Special* would have been a fearsome device in every sense, but sadly it never made it to the salt.

1970 'MacDonald-O'Hare Special'

In November 1970 commercial airline pilot and drag race enthusiast Jack MacDonald and businessman Terry O'Hare revealed a three-wheeled jetcar with which they intended to set a new Australian land speed record in September the following year. In its initial tests it was equipped with a Rolls-Royce turbojet of unspecified type, but it was intended the 4,000 lb. car would use two jets when it attacked Donald Campbell's 403·1 m.p.h. mark set on Lake Eyre in 1964. No attempt was made.

CHADI 9 undergoes a static engine test in 1972, yet another of the years in which a Russian challenge on the *LSR* was mooted.

1972 'Chadi-9'

(*Above*) Breedlove's original mock-up for *Spirit of America – Sonic 2* was a fullsize sales tool which incorporated the planned four rocket engines in its tail. The later version uses only one.

Like the boy who cried wolf, the rumour machine has continually suggested that the Russians plan to attempt the land speed record. Over the years various sketches or photographs of interesting-looking vehicles from behind the Iron Curtain have been released, emanating from the Institute of Higher Learning in Kharkov, where Vladimir Nikitin works.

A jetcar named CHADI-9 (the ninth model in a series of designs from Charkowskom Awtomobilno-Doroschnom Institut, to give Nikitin's department its full name) was developed around a 5,000 lb. thrust turbojet and was originally to have been ready for trials in 1971, but these were delayed until 1972.

Since then further photographs of cars purported to have supersonic potential have been circulated, but so far nothing concrete has emerged.

In March 1966, in response to a fresh bout of rumours of a Russian onslaught, STP Oil Treatment president Andy Granatelli patriotically promised to build a new American contender should Craig Breedlove's 600·601 m.p.h. record fall. In 1978 the rumours began again as, predictably, they did when Richard Noble broke the record in 1983.

Only time will tell if the Soviets really are interested in making a serious challenge to what has predominantly been an Anglo-American benefit.

1984 'Spirit of America, Sonic 2' (Craig Breedlove)

Following the Torrance floods which killed the *American Spirit* programme (see Chapter 20), Craig Breedlove converted the engineless vehicle into a rocket dragster. He'd been invited initially to drive *Blue Flame*, but disagreed with many of Dick Keller's design viewpoints; the renamed *English Leather Special* was effectively a scale version of the full-size rocket car Breedlove hoped to build to break Gabelich's record and in 1973 he hit 377 m.p.h. over the quarter mile at Bonneville, although the N.H.R.A. later slapped a ban on rocket cars for a while.

At various stages, Breedlove talked of a water speed attempt, running *Bluebird CN7*, toyed with another dragster and sold real estate, but on December 1, 1982, he began work on a full-size mock-up of *Spirit of America, Sonic 2*. This débuted at the Long Beach Show accompanying the Grand Prix in March 1983, shortly

(*Below*) Breedlove, now like Arfons, Palm, Gaynor and Miller, a member of the new World Speed Record Association which aims to raise a huge prize fund for future record contenders, and again drags up the talk of side by side runs, is confident the new *Spirit* at present under construction will punch through the Sound Barrier on land.

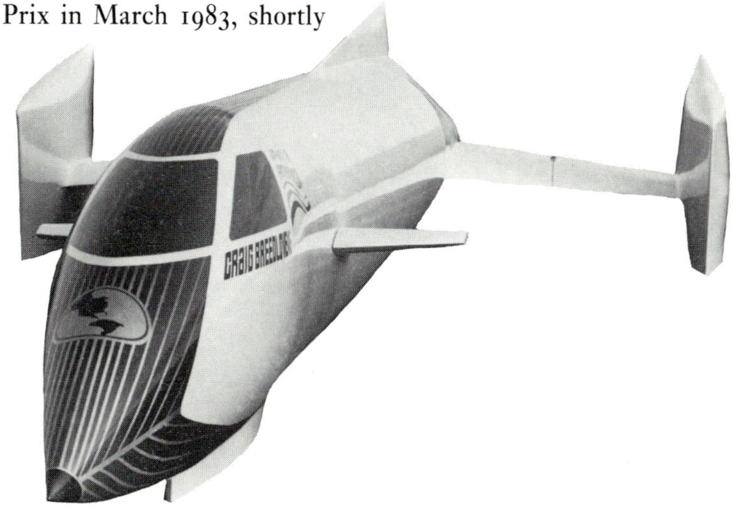

after his 46th birthday. Based on the original 44 ft. design shown in the early 70s, the model measured 39 ft. 2 in. and had *four* 7,500 lb. thrust rocket engines in the tail. Instead of the originally intended mix of unsymmetrical dimenthyl hydrazene and nitrogen tetraoxide, the 1983 version would use hydrogen peroxide and be constructed of advanced composites with a new filament winding process pioneered by the Grumman aircraft company. Such was the envisaged thirst of the design, an automobile engine would be installed simply to act as a fuel pump!

The mock-up was really a giant sales tool, and having visited the Black Rock Desert to assess Noble's efforts in September 1983 Breedlove continued his search for serious backing. In 1984 he found it. Through an association with Hollywood movie financers, Bruce Friedman & Associates, he obtained sufficient budget to initiate the build programme in December 1984, although this was not expected to be fully under way until the early months of 1985.

By this point, the basic, pencil-slim fuselage with pilot sitting right in the nose, was unchanged. The power unit was very different, however. Hydrogen peroxide is difficult to obtain in America, and in any case has a low specific impulse. That means the unit force per unit weight of the fuel (measured in seconds) is low. Hydrogen peroxide's specific impulse is 170 seconds; cordite, for example, is 308, while the Space Shuttle's oxygen and hydrogen mix is 495!

Thus the four 'thrusters' were scrapped, Breedlove intending to test with a single, 10,000 lb. thrust motor and then use a single, 30,000 lb. thrust unit for his record attempt. Both engines – built by Ron Gardner at TRW – will burn monomethyl hydrazene and superleaded gasoline, which has a much better specific impulse.

Breedlove was very impressed with the Black Rock Desert as a course, having considered White Sands in New Mexico and Edwards AFB, commenting: 'I thought it was great. It was a bit soft in 1983, but it's smooth and has plenty of distance.'

With composite solid wheels, *Spirit of America, Sonic 2* would be well suited

Bill Gaynor of Atwood, Colorado, poses alongside his mammoth *City of Sterling* as it slowly takes shape in his workshops. He speaks of a maximum power output in excess of 63,000 lb. thrust and a top speed well over 1,000 m.p.h. for his four-wheeled rocket monster.

to the surface and he intends to make his first test runs there in mid-1986, assuming everything goes to plan and permission is granted by the B.L.M. Now a hardened veteran of land speed attempts, Breedlove won't be drawn into giving a speed prediction for his new car, offering: 'We'll just see how well it goes before I open my mouth.'

1984 'City of Sterling'

One of the most outlandish yet sincere projects is Bill Gaynor's *City of Sterling*, which at 42 ft. in length is also likely to be one of the longest *LSR* cars.

Forty-three-year-old Gaynor from Atwood, Colorado, holds a degree in aeronautical engineering and has lectured in advanced maths, subsonic aerodynamics and wind tunnel test practice. He began planning Project 1000 in the 1970s, envisaging using *seven* rocket powerplants, each producing 6,500 lb. thrust on 70 per cent strength hydrogen peroxide, Eventually, his plan calls for 90 per cent strength fuel to be used, boosting thrust from 45,500 lb. to a scarcely credible 63,000.

Project 1000 aims to better the existing record, then break the sound barrier before finally topping 1,000 m.p.h. And if that isn't enough, Gaynor estimates *City*'s maximum speed as 1,450 m.p.h.!

The project's declared financial details also make interesting reading. Gaynor's board of directors has overall responsibility for settling the distribution of the team's gross income along charitable lines. To help establish a foundation ministering to the needs of handicapped children will go 50 per cent; to establish a foundation for the families of terminally ill children under 21 and to assist families enduring hardships in local Logan county will go 20 per cent; to establish a foundation to provide educational assistance to local and area students will go 15 per cent; and the same amount will also go to locally needy cases at the board's discretion. No details of the manner in which income will be generated have been disclosed.

The giant car was partway completed at Gaynor's Atwood base in late 1984, although photographs indicate it still has a long way to go. The bulky fuselage houses the vast supplies of fuel required, while all four wheels are outrigged and enclosed in large spats. The driver, who has yet to be nominated, will sit right in the nose. It will be interesting to see how *City of Sterling* escapes the vicious circle of hydrogen peroxide's low specific impulse, if indeed it does. Gaynor, naturally, is full of optimism and anticipates an attempt on the Black Rock Desert sometime in 1986.

1984 'Vanishing Point' (Sammy Miller)

Drag racing regulars at Britain's Santa Pod Raceway need no introduction to colourful New Jerseyman Sammy Miller, renowned for his exploits with the *Oxygen* and *Vanishing Point* rocket-powered dragsters. Since the late 1970s he has specialized in sub 4 sec. runs over the quarter mile, with terminal velocities over 300 m.p.h.!

Veteran drag racer Sammy Miller is no stranger to rockets. Since the late seventies he has thrilled race fans throughout Europe with his mind boggling acceleration runs in Santa Pod's *Vanishing Point* and *Oxygen* dragsters. Now he is planning to run this rocket-powered tricycle through the Sound Barrier, partly because he sees the record as his, partly 'to prove to Mr Needham that his car didn't do it'.

Having missed a land speed record opportunity with Tony Fox's *Proud American* when that project was shelved, Miller has long dreamed of becoming the first man to break the sound barrier on land and is one of many adamant that the *Budweiser Rocket* did *not* achieve that feat.

Working with George Garboden of G.G. Industries, Miller is confident his hydrogen peroxide rocket engine is the most efficient of its type. On ordinary peroxide it has been tested to 12,000 lb. thrust and with a bi-propellant (probably kerosene) believes it will produce 16,500 lb. thrust. In addition, he plans if necessary to use two solid fuel booster rockets each capable of producing 7,000 lb. thrust, giving this vehicle a 30,500 lb. thrust potential.

Initially, Miller began work on his own chassis, a complex and expensive confection of triangular bulkheads and large-diameter stressed tubing acting as the fuel tankage. However, the car he now has ready for a record attempt is believed to be that built for Kitty O'Neil in 1981 by Ky Michaelson of Space Age Racing, Bloomington, Minneapolis. A computer analysis of the *Budweiser Rocket*-like projectile indicates a speed potential of 800 m.p.h. and the man who once openly challenged Hal Needham to a private acceleration race to settle which has the faster car, would like nothing more than to set the first *official* sound barrier record. 'I think the Budweiser team Mickey Moused its programme; there wasn't even a sonic boom. I aim to do it within the two-way rules, so it's fully legal. *Then* I'll apologize to Mr Needham if there isn't a sonic boom.'

Miller's partner, Rory Calhoun, had booked the Black Rock Desert from October 16, 1983, when Project Thrust's B.L.M. permit expired, but at the last minute a sponsorship deal is believed to have turned sour. Now Miller is seeking a backer prepared to make it worth his while before he makes his official attempt.

1984 'Green Monster' (Art Arfons)

Legendary racer Art Arfons simply doesn't seem able to kick the speed habit, just like one-time Bonneville arch-rival Craig Breedlove.

'I have an engine and wheels laid out here in Pickle Road,' he said in October 1984, 'and I'm about ready to start a build programme on the chassis. Problem is, I don't get sponsors, so I have to pay for everything from my own pocket.'

The man who survived the world's fastest land accident in 1966 is candid about his new attempt. 'I just want the 700. I'd just as soon let someone else find out what happens when the sound barrier is broken.'

His new car will use forged aluminium wheels and Arfons, like Breedlove, is impressed with the Black Rock Desert, on which such equipment functions well. His new car, however, will be a major departure from the *Green Monster*, which won him worldwide acclaim and three records in the mid-1960s. Arfons promises something really radical, adding: 'I'll only have 5,000 lb. of thrust. My new car will be so light and small I won't require all that power I had before . . ..'

It took Gabelich 13,000 lb. thrust to hit 622 m.p.h., Noble 17,000 to reach 633. 700 m.p.h. on 5,000 lb. thrust? If it was anyone but Arfons making the suggestion it would be ridiculed, but with the 'junkyard genius of the jetset' somehow you can never be sure. Arfons hopes to make his attempt in the spring of 1986, but only time will tell if his latest theories are correct.

In the meantime, he can expect yet more competition from a fellow countryman. Colonel Joe Kittinger, who hit world headlines in 1984 by ballooning across the Atlantic ocean, is reportedly interested in making a land speed record attempt and is currently working with Dick Keller and Arvil Porter of *Blue Flame* fame, under their High Velocity Inc. banner. Kittinger has a reputation as a doer and a strong background in fund raising, which should make what amounts to a continuation of the late Gary Gabelich's *The American Way* project a very strong contender.

Another project which never went beyond the model stage – the twin-engined, four-wheel drive *Yankee Doodle* of 1936, which Lou Fengler was to have driven.

On paper only . . .

During the course of over seventy years of record breaking, many ambitious cars were inevitably mooted on paper, but never became reality. Finance was the usual stumbling block, for man, though rarely short of new ideas, is all too often short of money. Sponsors for *LSR* machines are rare people, motivated either by sheer enthusiasm, by patriotic reasons, or by the advertising benefits accruing to success – but always rare.

In the 'thirties, when 'getting the record' was rated a highly important national accomplishment, several interesting new cars were projected, but the shaky economy of the time killed their chances. The Americans, in particular, smarted under the continual hold Britain had over the record, and a number of ambitious projects were announced.

J.M. White, the Philadelphia manufacturer who sponsored the Triplex Special of 1928, was one who announced in 1930 that he was planning a new four-wheel-drive car with which he would raise the record to 500 m.p.h.! Then in 1931 Harlan Fengler of the Cragar Corporation mocked up two rare Miller W24 marine engines, for which he claimed a total 3,000 b.h.p., as the power source for a new American contender to be called *America 1*. As part of his scheme to raise the $75,000 budget he launched a campaign whereby every dollar contribution was matched with a small metal replica of the car. Famed American racer Pete de Paolo would be the driver. There were few takers and the project foundered. In May the following year Miller engines again featured in an American concept. Veteran racer Barney Oldfield wanted his 1910 record back and persuaded legendary race car builder-designer Harry A. Miller to pen the four-wheel-drive *Miller-Oldfield*. This time one of Miller's V24 marine engines was selected. With Roots supercharging it boasted 3,000 b.h.p., and de Dion suspension fore and aft, with twin quarter elliptic springing, was also part of the ambitious package. The wheels barely protruded from a sleek shell not dissimilar to a bloated race car shape, and Oldfield would have been enclosed by a glass cockpit canopy. Again, there were no takers.

Barney Oldfield, land speed record holder in 1910, with a model of the projected Miller-Oldfield record car of 1932; it was to have had a 3,000 h.p., 24-cylinder engine and four-wheel drive.

Another project, the *Yankee Doodle*, closely resembled Sir Malcolm Campbell's *Bluebird* in 1935 form, though it was painted in America's colours of blue and white. It was to have had two horizontally opposed 12-cylinder engines, one in front and one behind, with the driver in between, as on the 1,000 h.p. Sunbeam of 1927 but driving all four wheels. The weight would have been about 4 tons, ground clearance $7\frac{1}{2}$ in., and estimated speed 350 m.p.h. The driver was to have been Lou Fengler.

1920 Austin V12

Between 1910 and 1912, Herbert Austin's V12 engine was installed in a succession of water speed record boats, culminating in the twin-engined *Maple Leaf IV* setting a new water speed record and winning the British International Trophy – the famous Harmsworth Trophy – in 1912.

For its time, the original 1910 engine was highly advanced. The 12 cast-iron cylinders were fitted in an aluminium crankcase, the crank itself running in seven main bearings. Twin overhead camshafts were chain-driven and the twin carburettored, twin magneto'd unit produced 300 b.h.p. By 1911 this had risen to a most impressive 380.

In 1920 Austin and fellow countryman Arthur Waite began thinking of a land speed record car to be powered by the V12, basing their concept on the chassis of the Austin 3-ton truck. This featured an unusually lowline spaceframe and a very interesting transmission. The layshaft ran alongside the input and output shafts, making the four-speed unit very flat. The casing also housed the differential and two output shafts were employed, running independently along the chassis siderails to bevel gears enclosed in each rear wheel hub.

If ever a transmission was suited to a land speed car, it was this one, for it would allow the driver to sit far lower than contemporary designs, with consequent benefit to aerodynamic efficiency.

Campbell achieved 150·76 m.p.h. with the semi-streamlined 350 h.p. Sunbeam in 1925; with his bespoke 450 b.h.p. Campbell-Napier *Bluebird* in 1927 he achieved 174·883 m.p.h., the latter vehicle providing an interesting comparison with the proposed Austin design as the shape of Joseph Maina's gearbox obliged the driver to sit far higher than was desirable.

In 1920, the official record stood to Hornsted's Benz at 124·10 m.p.h. Previous Austin racing cars had boasted smooth shapes, so taking into account the lowline transmission it is probabl the car would have been more slippery than its contemporaries. What would it have achieved that year with 380 b.h.p., 180 more than the Benz? Sadly, historians can only speculate, for this interesting project went no further.

Fred. W. Dixon, a famous figure in British racing in the 'thirties who projected a highly unconventional record car called the *Dart*, with backbone chassis, 2-stroke swash-plate engine and four-wheel drive.

1936 Dixon '*Dart*'

Nothing came of these projects, and in Britain other exciting plans were also stillborn, in particular from the nimble mind of F. W. (Freddy) Dixon, one of Britain's most talented tuner/drivers of the 'thirties. It was around 1936 that he first ventilated his hopes and ideas for a truly revolutionary *LSR* machine which, from its potential shape, he called the *Dart*. As a lifelong enemy of surplus weight, Dixon cringed at the average record car with its deliberately massive chassis and vast engines. He actually bought (for £10!) the ill-fated 1930 Sunbeam *Silver Bullet*, with ideas of scrapping its trouble-fraught induction system and supercharger, and fitting multi-carburettors. After brief ownership, however, he dismissed it as 'brute force and bloody ignorance' and took a clean sheet of paper.

It was a pity the *Dart* went no further than that. When Dixon had finalized it, it was ultra-small, ultra-light and ultra-streamlined. It had a wide front track and narrow rear track, the driver sat out in front in the extreme nose, and the chassis was a single hollow backbone through which the drive passed to all four independently sprung wheels. Most remarkable of all was the engine, which was to be a supercharged two-stroke of 10 to 12 litres, working on the swash-plate principle; i.e. with a central 'wobble plate' instead of a crankshaft, actuated by the radially disposed pistons and connecting rods; the whole unit measuring only 23 in. in diameter but putting an estimated 250 b.h.p. through each of the four wheels.

Limited slip differentials were to feature, and braking was on the transmission line only and not on the wheels. The entire car would taper from the driver's rounded cockpit in the nose to a feathered (finned) tail, hence the name *Dart*. Such a specification sounds pretty fantastic, but when conceived by a man of Dixon's ability it had to be taken seriously. Such a car could have diverted *LSR* minds from their eternal 'vast engine in vast car' formula. Development of that swash-plate engine alone would have expended considerable time and money, however, and lack of finance killed it.

1936 Seaman project

Another British racing-driver, Richard J.B. Seaman, also entertained ideas of a land speed record car. After 1935 when *LSR* contenders left the bumpy Daytona beach for the broad salt flats of Bonneville in Utah, the Daytona Board of Commerce, missing the extra influx of visitors which a record attempt always brought to Ormond–Daytona, offered a £20,000 bonus to the next successful contender on their beach.

Although he was a very skilled professional road-racing driver with a dislike for track-racing, Seaman was attracted by this prize, and was presumably prepared to tolerate Daytona's notorious caprices if he could get the record there. His plan was to use two Napier Dagger 24-cylinder aircraft engines, unusual for the 'H' formation of their cylinders and their twin crankshafts, installed in an all-independently-suspended, four-wheel-drive chassis. He was in negotiation with Napiers over the loan of two such engines, but Seaman became a progressively busier man from 1937 onwards when he joined the Mercedes-Benz Grand Prix team, and nothing came of the venture.

In 1955 legendary Bonneville class and long-distance record breaker Abner Jenkins gave consideration to a gas turbine-engined *Mormon Meteor IV* for a crack at the 400 m.p.h. mark, but did not proceed, and by the end of the decade the ready availability of turbine power units broadened the imagination of designers, although departing somewhat from the basic concept of an automobile. The design projected by German engineer Leopold F. Schmid typified the bold solution a modern technical mind could produce for age-old problems.

1960/1962 Schmid-Orpheus

Ing. Leopold Schmid worked with Porsche at Zuffenhausen for many years, and bringing a fresh approach saw tyres as the limiting factor as speeds rose nearer the sound barrier. He designed a revolutionary tyreless wheel comprising an outside 'tread ring' of light alloy whose outer surface was grooved to provide traction on the salt at Bonneville, the chosen venue.

The tread ring was T-shaped, the T's supporting leg registering in a slot in the middle of the two-piece wheel. Its padded inner end met a rubber ring acting as the suspension around the hub of the wheel. An outer wheel disc surrounded the rubber element and acted as a damper. Each wheel thus contained its own suspension and, apart from swivel pins for the front pair, the axles were rigidly attached to the chassis.

Schmid chose a Bristol Siddeley (later Rolls-Royce) Orpheus turbojet engine (similar to that used by Donald Campbell in his last water speed record attempt) for propulsion, but to meet the F.I.A.'s ruling that to be classified as an automobile a car should have two or more driven wheels he introduced an ingenious device. This comprised a paddle wheel geared to the rear axle and placed in the jet stream. Thus 60 per cent of the Orpheus' 4,500 lb. thrust went in pure reaction, the other 40 driving the paddle to give 'drive' to the rear wheels.

Initially, the Schmid's bodywork comprised two full-length vertical sponsons enclosing the four huge-diameter wheels, the turbojet being mounted on a flat, horizontal centre section, aft of the driver. All-up weight would be around 4,300 lb. Rather than employ parachutes, braking would be by discs on all four wheels in conjunction with air brakes in the sponsons.

By 1959 plans for Abarth of Turin to build the chassis and Pininfarina the bodywork were well advanced and in contrast to most other conventional projects, some of the hardware – the wheels in particular – was actually built and tested. German Rainer Gunzler was nominated as driver.

After two years of further research, the shape of the Schmid was altered quite dramatically. The flat centre section was cut away so only fairings over the axles actually connected sponsons and engine frame and in a further attempt to kill worrying front-end lift seen in the wind tunnel an aerofoil was added above the engine air intake. The cockpit metamorphosed into a pointed proboscis and Schmid's own drawings were stamped 'Final shape. Not to be revealed until arrival at Bonneville.'

Schmid made concerted efforts to find a German sponsor for his exciting and technically liberated project, without success, and was finally obliged to throw in the towel when Bristol-Siddeley refused him the use of an engine on the grounds

(*Above*) The original wind tunnel model of the *Schmid-Orpheus* had a full-length horizontal platform and vertical pontoons, but further detailed work on its aerodynamics resulted in a revised shape (*below*). The latter was then drawn to full scale, the plans stamped 'Final shape. Not to be revealed until arrival at Bonneville. Sadly, the project went only a small way past the drawing board stage when Bristol Siddeley refused to release an Orpheus engine to the Germans.

Porsche engineer Leopold Schmid evolved this remarkable record machine around a Bristol-Orpheus gas turbine engine in the late 'fifties. To comply with the F.I.A. regulations for wheel-driven cars, the thrust from the exhaust impinges partially on a paddle-type drive wheel geared to the rear wheels. Tyreless wheels with sprung hubs are another revolutionary feature. So far no sponsor has come forward to build a full-size Schmid-Orpheus.

that it did not want to jeopardize British land speed record attempts.

Less sensible a project was well-known British pilot Dizzy Addicott's plan to remove the wings from a jet aircraft and use the fuselage as the basis for a record attempt car in the mid-1960s. Predictably, he didn't proceed with his idea.

1965/1973 Campbell-MacKnight-Norris 'Bluebird Mach 1·1 then CMN-8' (Donald Campbell/Nigel MacKnight)

When he died on Coniston Water on January 4, 1967, Donald Campbell was attempting to establish his *eighth* water speed record, at over 300 m.p.h., in an effort to interest backers in his latest project – a rocket-powered car to crack the sound barrier.

A mock-up had been built in 1965, to a design by Ken Norris. It was a needle-nosed concept in which Campbell would sit right up front, ahead of the single front wheel, the fuel tanks and engines, and the rear wheels were outrigged on aerofoil-section arms and enclosed in large spats which also acted as vertical stabilizers. The full-scale mock-up was put on show at Campbell's house, *Roundwood*, along with the *Bluebird CN7* wheel-driven car and the successful but ill-fated *K7* hydroplane, but Campbell was very disappointed at the lukewarm reaction his latest venture received.

The Mach 1·1 (*CMN-8*), as the new *Bluebird* was to be known, was 22 ft. long, had a track of 11 ft. and a height of 3 ft. and sat on a 12 ft. wheelbase. Its weight would be around the 4,000 lb. mark and it would be propelled by two Bristol-Siddeley BS 605 rocket-assisted take-off (RATO) engines mounted one above the other in the tail. The units, similar to that used in Barry Bowles' *Blonde Bombshell*, were rated around 4,200 lb. thrust each. Four were acquired. The projectile would run on solid metal wheels and one of the most interesting aspects of the project was that the Jamaican government at one stage expressed interest in constructing a 12- to 14-mile track on which Campbell could realize his car's 840 m.p.h. design potential. On the same track he also intended to aim for 450 m.p.h. with the *CN7*. With the rocket car attracting little interest, he also thought of trying for the standing start record with *CN7*, but Dunlop was not keen. Then, in June 1966, Campbell's friend Peter Bolton severely damaged *CN7* in a demonstration run at Debden, Essex.

With Campbell's death, it seemed the rocket car project had also died, but in late 1973 19-year-old Briton Nigel MacKnight took up the challenge with Leo Villa's blessing, taking over the role of 'kingpin' and driver. Norris would remain a design consultant, with Greville Dawson doing the detail work at Ken's recommendation, the latter having tried to get things on the road between 1968 and 1971. Several significant British companies indicated positive support, among them Accles and Pollock, which would supply tubing for structural components, Triplex, Smiths Industries, Rubery Owen, Automotive Products, Ciba-Geigy, which would supply aluminium honeycomb and adhesives, Ferodo and Girling. And, interestingly, Jaguar Cars agreed to supply a suitably modified XJ12 on which Vickers metal wheels would be mounted prior to extensive tests scheduled for Pendine Sands. . . .

Ultimately, MacKnight was unable to raise the sponsorship for the project, but believes to this day: 'The countless meetings I had with the supporting companies and potential sponsors kept the idea of a British *LSR* car firmly "on the map" as far as many influential people were concerned. Many of them, I believe, eventually supported Richard Noble's efforts.'

With the rocket project apparently stillborn, MacKnight refused to give up, and turned his attention to reviving the *CN7*, partly to provide some degree of continuity between Campbell's project and his own. *Bluebird* required major surgery after its Debden injuries, but apart from the aforementioned companies, which were keen, David Brown Gear Industries agreed to refurbish the spiral-bevel gearboxes and Rolls-Royce, Bristol Division, to overhaul the Proteus gas turbine. This project looked distinctly promising, until it became clear that the participation of one vital company – Dunlop – could not be obtained. The tyre giant's 500 m.p.h. test equipment had been converted for other uses and without a supply of new tyres the project fizzled out.

Over the years the *CN7* has been the subject of sporadic interest from would-be wheeldriven challengers, among them Tony Densham and Craig Breedlove. As late as 1982, Richard Noble made noises about trying to run the big blue car when things looked bleak for *Thrust 2* on the Black Rock Desert, but it was more a case of musing aloud than seriously considering a change of tack. Ultimately, the same tyre supply problem stymied each contender.

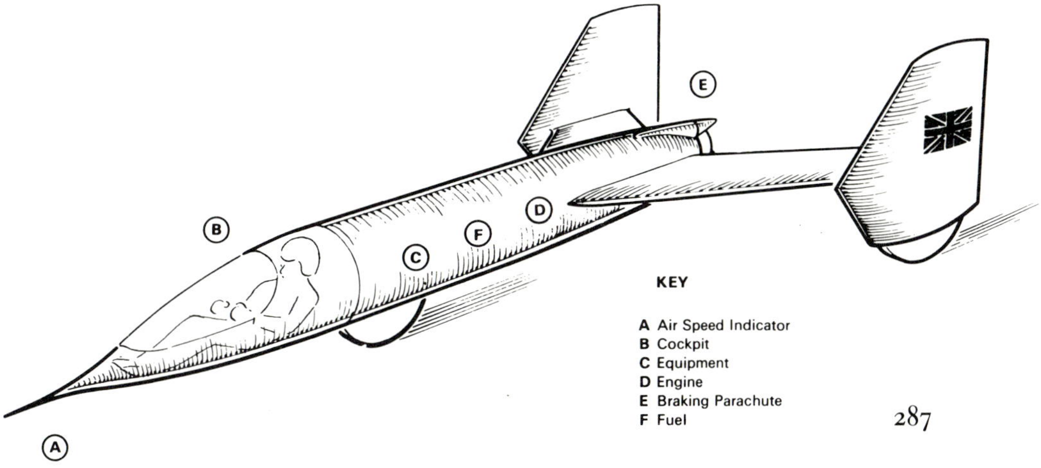

Ken Norris' original artwork of Donald Campbell's proposed *Bluebird Mach 1.1* reveals driver sitting right in the nose, and rear wheels set well apart in shrouded fins acting as vertical stabilisers. For details of the final shape for the Campbell-MacKnight-Norris *CMN-8*, see back cover.

1966 'Wingfoot Express III'

After the débâcle of the rocket-powered *Wingfoot Express II* in 1965, semi-retired Walt Arfons began experimenting with steam power. On its first outing, his steam-powered dragster flipped at 200 m.p.h. with Bob Tatroe at the controls, but the Grand Rapids, Michigan, driver was full of enthusiasm for its sheer acceleration.

Arfons began envisaging a new machine with a glass-fibre nose attached to a stainless steel tank 30 in. in diameter. 'By having a tank ready with water pre-heated to 470 degrees Fahrenheit, we can shave turnaround time to under 20 minutes,' he explained. A hydraulically operated throttle valve would comprise the rocket engine's only moving component and the system would basically consist of the special tank, the throttle and a special heating unit.

Seven thousand pounds of the *Wingfoot*'s 10,000 lb. starting weight would be its energy-giving steam, all of which would be released in the first 30 or 40 seconds of a run.

Despite the idea's promise, Walt stayed retired and steam never did get its big chance for a comeback.

1970 'Gyronaut X-2 and X-3'

One of the most prolific aerodynamicists and vehicle designers around Bonneville in the 1960s and early 1970s was Alex Tremulis, who was very closely involved with Walt Arfons on the design of the *Wingfoot Express II*. Responsible for the design of a two-wheeled *automobile* for Ford – the Ford Gyron – his eccentric flair found little favour with the Detroit giant's executives and he turned his mind to record-breaking motorcycles. Teaming up with motorcycle racer Bob Leppan he produced the Gyronaut X-1 streamliner with which Leppan set a new record of 245·667 m.p.h. at Bonneville on August 25, 1965.

Predictably, Tremulis began thinking of two-wheeled vehicles to break the wheel-driven and outright land speed records. The X-2 would be powered by a 7-litre Chrysler with fuel injection and supercharging, and be capable of 500 m.p.h. The X-3 would be powered by a 9,000 lb. thrust rocket engine and have a speed potential of 1,000 m.p.h.

Neither vehicle was built, but Tremulis' place in land speed record history was assured by his suggestion to Goodyear executives that the most fitting end for the *Wingfoot Express II* would be to launch it vertically and let it rest forever wherever it nosed down. . . .

1973 'Mach 1' (Johnny Conway)

One of the least believable paper projects emerged in 1973, when Australian Johnny Conway announced his plans to break the wheel-driven and sound barrier marks with a 36-engined, 16-wheeler to be know as *Mach 1*.

The result of a 'clean sheet' approach, *Mach 1* would be 34 ft. long, 3 ft. wide and 19 in. high, and Conway, an experienced pilot and intended driver of the still-born Sky-bike project, would be unable to see out from his prone position beneath the 2 ft. tail fin. Instead of watching his course in the normal manner, he would monitor his and *Mach 1*'s high-speed progress via a television screen!

Power source for the car was equally unlikely: 32 separate rotary engines, possibly Sarichs, with four power strokes per revolution. Conveniently, full details were regarded as confidential, but each engine would be of 2·5-litre capacity and capable of producing 410 b.h.p. at 14,000 r.p.m. The engines would be coupled in eight blocks of four, with an 18 in. diameter, 4 in. wide light alloy wheel attached to the end of each unit. There would be no transmission, clutch or wheel brakes, and *Mach 1* would require push-starting to 50 m.p.h. With direct drive to the wheels, drive for items such as superchargers would be handled by another *four* engines, a pair at each end of the car, and their speed would be dictated by that of the vehicle.

To comply with F.I.A. regulations on steering, the foremost engine/wheel units would turn through a nominal two degrees, fins and two thrust-jet engines in the nose taking care of real directional changes.

To slow the vehicle, a reverse-thrust jet motor, a parachute and servo-actuated air brakes would be employed.

Backing for this incredible venture was to come from a small company called Sanron Enterprises, the project being wholly Australian. The sound barrier car would be similar to the wheel-driven version but would utilize engines similar to the Sky-bike, in which Conway at one stage proposed to vault Ayers Rock, Sydney Heads and the entrance of Port Phillip Bay, Melbourne. He described them as '10,000 lb. thrust rocket motors that drive rotary engines *inside* the wheels', but did not elect to elucidate.

Just as ludicrous as the mechanical details were the proposed venues. Lake Eyre was originally the chosen site, on which 450 m.p.h. was thought to be a reasonable wheel-driven target, but for the sound barrier attempt it was planned to build a special rubberized track. This would be a whopping 18 miles long but only 30 ft. wide, with a ½ in. layer of rubber compound atop the base hardcore. Even in 1973 a cost of 600,000 Australian dollars was envisaged just for the track.

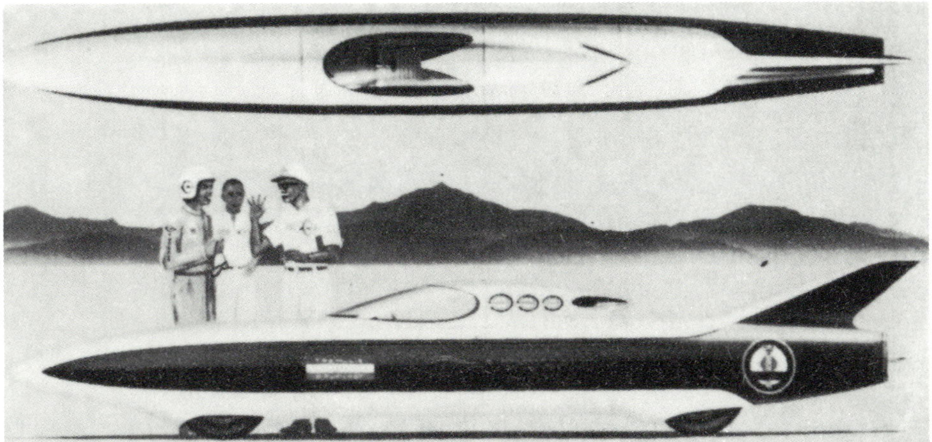

Alex Tremulis (on right in artwork) was confident his *Gyronaut X-2* concept, with a frontal area of only 5 sq. ft. and a Cd of 0.10, would be capable of 500 m.p.h. on 7 litres, while a rocket-powered version might double that. To back such claims, he had only to point to Bob Leppan's 245.667 m.p.h. motorcycle record with the X-1.

Four and a half years after his first announcement Conway had made little headway, although he claimed to have sold the television rights for the Sky-bike jumps for £1·75 million and planned a motorcycle record attempt just for good measure to limber up for and finance the car records.

He was last heard of planning to make his land speed attempts on the salty wastes of Australia's Lake Lefroy. . . .

1974 Project Blue Star (Tony Densham, David Purley)

David Gossling was a senior design engineer in Hawker Siddeley's space division, and when the Blue Streak missile project was cancelled was one of several talented personnel to feel a sense of loss. Then it occurred to him that two Rolls-Royce turbine-driven fuel pumps from the project might just provide sufficient horsepower to boost a car to a new wheel-driven land speed record.

Thus was born *Project Blue Star*, which was designed to carry on the tradition of *Bluebird*. Initially, Gossling envisaged a four-wheeled vehicle of tricycle configuration, the front wheels mounted in tandem. Each Rolls fuel pump would produce 3,200 b.h.p. on a mixture of oxygen and kerosene, more than enough to drive the rear wheels. As an added bonus, the exhaust gases would produce a degree of thrust once they had passed through the turbines. It was intended that *Blue Star* have full suspension via equal-length wishbones and coil/air spring units at

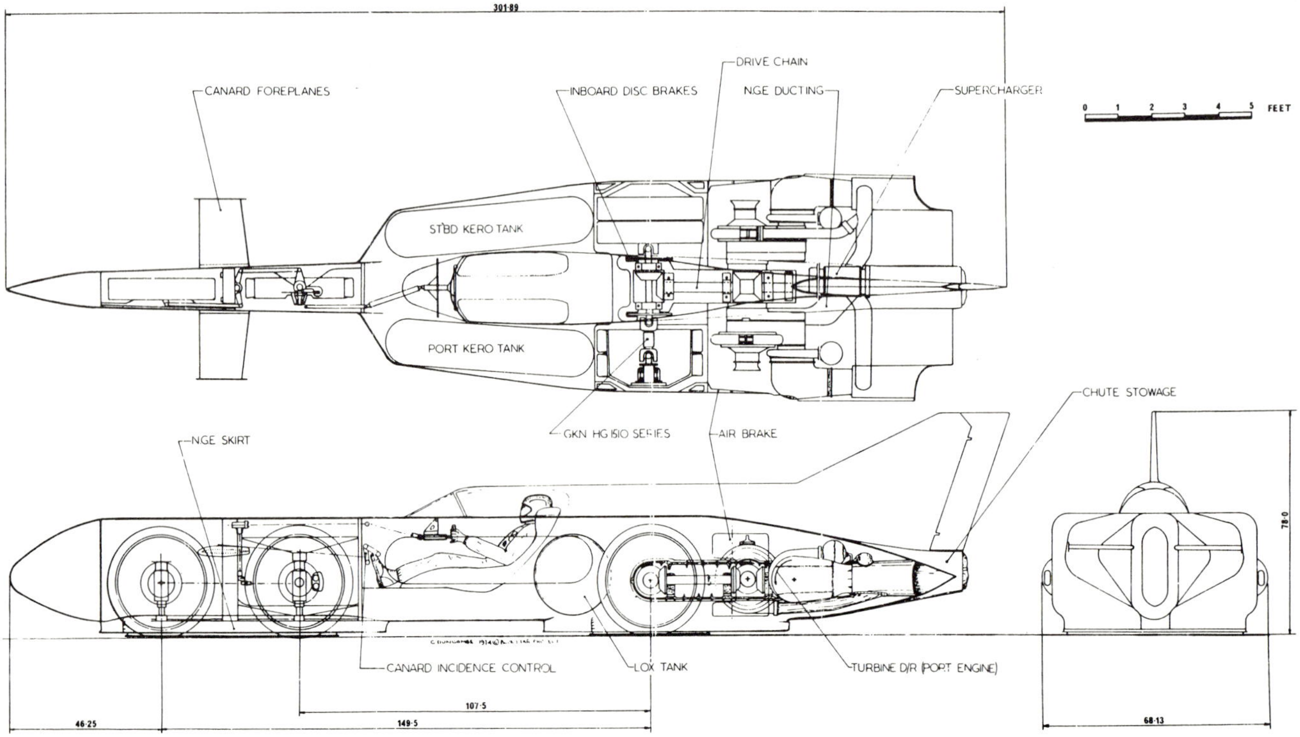

One of David Gossling's original design concepts for *Project Blue Star* featured a needle-slim nose flaring out to a wide, ground effect section housing cockpit and power plants. This later evolved into a far slimmer vehicle, but sadly promising progress was negated when Gossling perished in a motorcycle accident in the summer of 1977.

the rear, and a sliding pillar system with integral spring/damper units at the front, steering lock being a mere six degrees. Like the 1970 Chaparral 2J CanAm racer, *Blue Star* would create a low-pressure area round the rear wheelboxes, so that ground effect would enhance traction and stability.

Working with some very well-qualified individuals, such as Professor E.R. Ellis, head of automotive studies at the Cranfield Institute of Technology (which adopted the project), and Professor John Stollery, head of aerodynamics who did design work on *Bluebird CN7* and *Bluebird K7*, Gossling reached agreement for British drag racer Tony Densham to handle the driving chores and a target maximum of 550 m.p.h. was revealed. Densham had actually attempted to borrow the *CN7* from Beaulieu for a wheeldriven attempt in 1973, and was at the time regarded as the country's top drag racing exponent.

Over the following two years the design concept was altered progressively, although the Rolls-Royce RZ2 fuel pumps remained the intended power source. The Mk 1 was a crude, chisel-nosed device, but the tricycle Mk 2 showed promise. Mk 3 was very different, being much slimmer and longer and mounting the pilot well aft. Mk 4 was shorter and wider, with the pilot amidships and, like Mk 3, the front wheels side by side. The Mk 5 was a departure, with the smallest possible frontal area uppermost in the list of design considerations. With less than 10 ft. frontal area and 6,400 b.h.p. Mk 5 was believed by Gossling to have outright record potential, given the right weather conditions at Bonneville. Mk 6 was the final concept, differing only from Mk 5 insofar as the use of a hybrid rocket motor capable of producing between 12,000 and 15,000 lb. thrust was envisaged, 'easily enough to break the sound barrier' according to Gossling.

Work commenced on a glass-fibre mock-up which was displayed throughout the final months of 1976, and on the driver front courageous British racing driver, the late David Purley was called in to replace Densham. At the same time model Valli, who raced boyfriend Chris Meek's MG Midget, was mentioned as possible lady pilot.

Gossling was still fighting hard to raise the minimum £250,000 he believed his solid-wheeled contender needed when he suffered a motorcycle accident in the summer of 1977. Sadly, he succumbed to his injuries and his dreams of a new British record for the 38 ft. long, 24 in. wide *Blue Star* streamliner died with him.

1974 'Proud American'

In the early 1970s Minneapolis businessman Tony Fox built up an enviable reputation for his 'Tony Team' and its rocket dragster *Pollution Packer*. With Dick Keller (of *Blue Flame* fame) as designer, Ky Michaelson as crew chief and occasional driver, and Dave Anderson as regular pilot the Tony Team amassed a whole series of acceleration records in addition to converting Reaction Dynamics' X-1 rocket dragster into *Sonic Challenger*, a rocket-powered snowmobile!

It was thus somewhat inevitable that millionaire Fox should turn his mind to a supersonic record car. Anderson, sadly, died in an accident in 1974 and his regular

Tony Fox went to the trouble of having this mock-up of his proposed *Proud American* rocket car built, but when the 'Tony Team' failed to attract backing he switched his concentration to aircraft production instead.

replacement was a young New Jerseyman called Sammy Miller. A mock-up of the new contender, patriotically to be dubbed *Proud American*, was built and displayed. It measured 45 ft. in length and its intended power output from the hydrogen peroxide rocket was 35,000 lb. of thrust.

The project hung fire for some time, even though Fox's industries should have been able to raise the necessary finance. Then in 1977 Fox took the decision to shelve it, preferring to concentrate his energies developing the new Foxjet ST/600 aeroplane. Miller, denied an opportunity to attack the sound barrier, subsequently achieved fame in Britain through his exploits with Santa Pod Raceway's *Vanishing Point* and *Oxygen* rocket dragsters and is still planning his own record attempt.

1981–5 'Minnesota' (Paul Vickroy)

When Project Thrust was at Bonneville in 1981 a young U.S. Air Force engineering student strapped his ten-speed racer on the back of his primer-grey Ford and drove from Minneapolis to Wendover to watch. His name was Thomas Palm and he became a team member. The 22-year-old had his own land speed record design, a twin-jet car to be called *Minnesota*. Two Pratt & Whitney J57s, as used in the F8 Crusader, would provide 34,000 lb. of thrust for the 50 ft. vehicle, which would be the longest ever to run on the salt. The 40 in. front wheels would be mounted close together forward of the cockpit, with the rears outrigged slightly either side of the engines.

By 1982 a Missile Crew Chief, Palm was back to help Thrust, with a modified design to reveal. This time the concept was single-engined, with a triangular cross-section apexed towards the bottom to ward off sonic shockwaves. Length was down to 40 ft. and with outrigged rear wheels the vehicle was much slimmer. Subsequently, a third concept has been promoted and this J57-powered vehicle is the one Palm hopes to raise finance for by breaking the wheel-driven record with a turbine-engined machine (see Chapter 20).

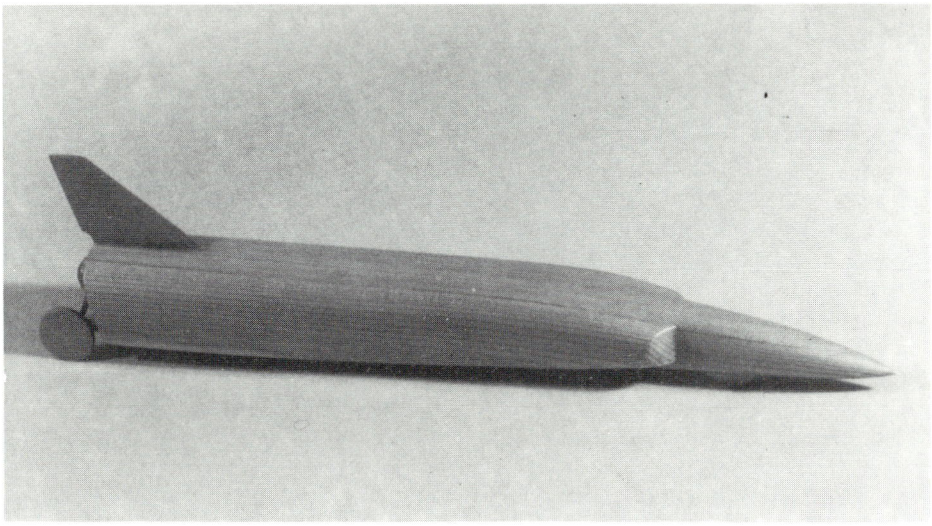

Tom Palm's third-generation design for the *Minesota* supersonic jetcar clearly shows John Ackroyd's influences. Palm intends to break the wheel-driven record as the first step in his long-term Sound Barrier programme, V. P. Research partner Paul Vickroy doing the driving.

His partner in V.P. Research, Paul Vickroy, will be the driver, while Palm will handle liaison with sponsors, operations and fund raising, saying: 'I feel the driver should only have to worry about driving, nothing else. With the high speeds we'll be encountering he will have enough psychological and physical problems to worry about.'

1981 'The American Way' (Gary Gabelich)

Even as Gary Gabelich set his 622·407 m.p.h. record in October 1970, the Reaction Dynamics crew knew its design was outdated, and work started soon after on a Mk 2 version. The near strike amongst crew members, quelled by Gabelich himself, and the fact that the *Blue Flame* did not use liquefied natural gas on its record run, as stipulated in the contract with the Natural Gas Association, meant ownership of the original car passed from Reaction Dynamics' hands.

Undeterred, Dick Keller evolved a slimmer version of the *Flame* which used a similar power unit that boasted 21,000 lb. of thrust, 8,000 more. By 1981 this had ceased to be known as *Blue Flame Mk 2* and was officially *The American Way*, but two years later, when the author met Gabelich in Long Beach, the latter announced he had lost interest in trying to get people to back him to break his own record. Then, of course, *Thrust 2* set a new mark and the former king regained his enthusiasm, visiting the British team on the Black Rock Desert and revealing his latest Keller design, which featured aerofoil sections similar to those on Lee Taylor's rocket boat *US Discovery II* to mount the wheels to the fuselage. There was also talk of an even more powerful engine from TRW, capable of nearly 35,000 lb. of thrust.

Then in January 1984, motorcycling in Los Angeles, he collided with a truck. Gary wasn't wearing a crash helmet, and died instantly.

Where are they now?

Several land speed record-breaking cars still survive; this list details their whereabouts.

Camille Jenatzy's 1899 *La Jamais Contente*: Musée Nationale de la Voiture et du Tourisme, Chateau de Compiègne, Oise, France.

Henry Ford's 1904 Ford '999' (sister car to the *Arrow*): Henry Ford Museum, Dearborn, Michigan, U.S.A.

Fred Marriott's 1906 Stanley *Rocket*: remains of car and a working replica in Birthplace of Speed Museum, Highway 1, Daytona, Florida, U.S.A., although this museum is currently closed to the public; engine remains in the Museum of History and Technology, Smithsonian Institution, Washington D.C., U.S.A.

1909–11 *Blitzen Benz*: one example in the Daimler-Benz Museum, Stuttgart-Unterturkheim, Germany; another believed to be in the U.S.A.

Kenelm Lee Guinness' 1922, 350 h.p. Sunbeam (also, of course, used by Capt. Malcolm Campbell): National Motor Museum, Beaulieu, Hants, England.

Sig Haugdahl's 1922 *Wisconsin Special*: Museum of Antique Autos, Princeton, Mass., U.S.A.

René Thomas' 1923, $10\frac{1}{2}$-litre V12 Delage: jointly owned by Cecil Clutton and Jonty Williamson and still appearing in British vintage events.

Ernest Eldridge's 1924, 300 h.p. Fiat: Fiat Centro Storico, Turin, Italy.

Henry Segrave's 1926, 4-litre V12 Sunbeam: rebuilt in 1932 by Sir Malcolm Campbell; currently owned and raced in British vintage events by Neil Corner. A second car, fitted with a Napier Lion engine, appears as the Sunbeam-Napier. First car in Midland Motor Museum, Bridgnorth, Salop.

J.G. Parry Thomas' 1927 *Babs*: exhumed from Pendine Sands in 1969 by Owen Wyn Owen of Capel Curig, Wales. Now virtually fully restored and in full working order.

Henry Segrave's 1927, 1,000 h.p. Sunbeam: National Motor Museum, Beaulieu, Hants, England.

Henry Segrave's 1929 *Golden Arrow*: Now back in National Motor Museum, Beaulieu, Hants, England, after extensive 1984 tour of Australia.

Malcolm Campbell's 1935 *Bluebird*: in the Hall of Fame, Alabama Motor Speedway, Talladega, Alabama, U.S.A. Currently the subject of a project instigated by Ian Robinson, former Project Thrust team member and now with the Patrick Collection, to repurchase car for Britain and have it fully restored to working order.

John Cobb's 1938–47 Railton-Mobil Special: Museum of Science and Industry, Birmingham, England.

1939 Mercedes-Benz T80: Daimler-Benz Museum, Stuttgart-Unterturkheim, Germany.

Dr Nathan Ostich's 1960 *Flying Caduceus*: currently in Harrah's, Reno, Nevada, U.S.A.

Donald Campbell's 1960–64 *Bluebird CN7*: National Motor Museum, Beaulieu, Hants, England.

Craig Breedlove's 1962–64 *Spirit of America*: Museum of Science and Industry, Jackson Park, Chicago, Illinois, U.S.A.

Art Arfons' 1964–66 *Green Monster*: rebuilt after 1966 accident, now owned by Slick Gardner of Santa Ines Valley, California, U.S.A.

Bob and Bill Summers' 1965 *Goldenrod*: Museum of Speed, Wendover, Utah, U.S.A.

Craig Breedlove's 1965 *Spirit of America, Sonic 1*: Cleveland Auto Historical Society, Cleveland, Ohio, U.S.A.

Reaction Dynamics' 1970 *Blue Flame*: Auto und Technik Museum, Sinsheim, West Germany.

1975 Dean Moon *Moonliner*: still owned by Dean in Santa Fe Springs, California, U.S.A.

1979 *Budweiser Rocket*: Museum of History and Technology, Smithsonian Institution, Washington D.C., U.S.A.

Richard Noble's 1981–83 *Thrust 2*: owned by Thrust Cars Ltd., still currently touring auto shows/exhibitions.

Walt Arfons' *Wingfoot Expresses* (jet and rocket) were both broken up by their creator.

Sir Malcolm Campbell's 1935 *Bluebird* rests in this tatty state in the Hall of Fame at Alabama Motor Speedway, but former Project Thrust team member Ian Robinson is spearheading a project to buy back the famous charger for Britain. The long-term aim is to restore the vehicle to full running order.

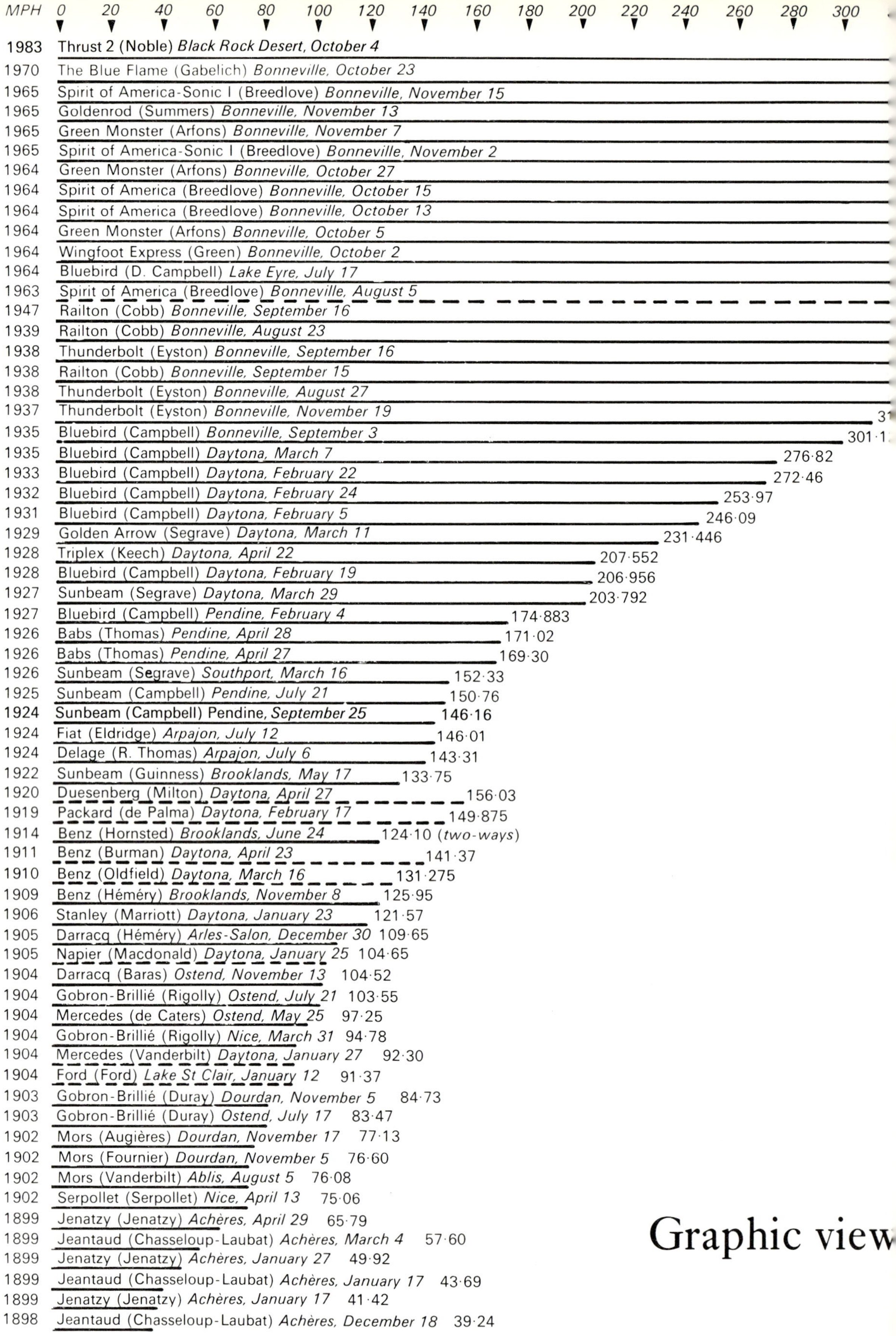
MPH 0 20 40 60 80 100 120 140 160 180 200 220 240 260 280 300
1983 Thrust 2 (Noble) Black Rock Desert, October 4
1970 The Blue Flame (Gabelich) Bonneville, October 23
1965 Spirit of America-Sonic I (Breedlove) Bonneville, November 15
1965 Goldenrod (Summers) Bonneville, November 13
1965 Green Monster (Arfons) Bonneville, November 7
1965 Spirit of America-Sonic I (Breedlove) Bonneville, November 2
1964 Green Monster (Arfons) Bonneville, October 27
1964 Spirit of America (Breedlove) Bonneville, October 15
1964 Spirit of America (Breedlove) Bonneville, October 13
1964 Green Monster (Arfons) Bonneville, October 5
1964 Wingfoot Express (Green) Bonneville, October 2
1964 Bluebird (D. Campbell) Lake Eyre, July 17
1963 Spirit of America (Breedlove) Bonneville, August 5
1947 Railton (Cobb) Bonneville, September 16
1939 Railton (Cobb) Bonneville, August 23
1938 Thunderbolt (Eyston) Bonneville, September 16
1938 Railton (Cobb) Bonneville, September 15
1938 Thunderbolt (Eyston) Bonneville, August 27
1937 Thunderbolt (Eyston) Bonneville, November 19
1935 Bluebird (Campbell) Bonneville, September 3 301·1
1935 Bluebird (Campbell) Daytona, March 7 276·82
1933 Bluebird (Campbell) Daytona, February 22 272·46
1932 Bluebird (Campbell) Daytona, February 24 253·97
1931 Bluebird (Campbell) Daytona, February 5 246·09
1929 Golden Arrow (Segrave) Daytona, March 11 231·446
1928 Triplex (Keech) Daytona, April 22 207·552
1928 Bluebird (Campbell) Daytona, February 19 206·956
1927 Sunbeam (Segrave) Daytona, March 29 203·792
1927 Bluebird (Campbell) Pendine, February 4 174·883
1926 Babs (Thomas) Pendine, April 28 171·02
1926 Babs (Thomas) Pendine, April 27 169·30
1926 Sunbeam (Segrave) Southport, March 16 152·33
1925 Sunbeam (Campbell) Pendine, July 21 150·76
1924 Sunbeam (Campbell) Pendine, September 25 146·16
1924 Fiat (Eldridge) Arpajon, July 12 146·01
1924 Delage (R. Thomas) Arpajon, July 6 143·31
1922 Sunbeam (Guinness) Brooklands, May 17 133·75
1920 Duesenberg (Milton) Daytona, April 27 156·03
1919 Packard (de Palma) Daytona, February 17 149·875
1914 Benz (Hornsted) Brooklands, June 24 124·10 (two-ways)
1911 Benz (Burman) Daytona, April 23 141·37
1910 Benz (Oldfield) Daytona, March 16 131·275
1909 Benz (Héméry) Brooklands, November 8 125·95
1906 Stanley (Marriott) Daytona, January 23 121·57
1905 Darracq (Héméry) Arles-Salon, December 30 109·65
1905 Napier (Macdonald) Daytona, January 25 104·65
1904 Darracq (Baras) Ostend, November 13 104·52
1904 Gobron-Brillié (Rigolly) Ostend, July 21 103·55
1904 Mercedes (de Caters) Ostend, May 25 97·25
1904 Gobron-Brillié (Rigolly) Nice, March 31 94·78
1904 Mercedes (Vanderbilt) Daytona, January 27 92·30
1904 Ford (Ford) Lake St Clair, January 12 91·37
1903 Gobron-Brillié (Duray) Dourdan, November 5 84·73
1903 Gobron-Brillié (Duray) Ostend, July 17 83·47
1902 Mors (Augières) Dourdan, November 17 77·13
1902 Mors (Fournier) Dourdan, November 5 76·60
1902 Mors (Vanderbilt) Ablis, August 5 76·08
1902 Serpollet (Serpollet) Nice, April 13 75·06
1899 Jenatzy (Jenatzy) Achères, April 29 65·79
1899 Jeantaud (Chasseloup-Laubat) Achères, March 4 57·60
1899 Jenatzy (Jenatzy) Achères, January 27 49·92
1899 Jeantaud (Chasseloup-Laubat) Achères, January 17 43·69
1899 Jenatzy (Jenatzy) Achères, January 17 41·42
1898 Jeantaud (Chasseloup-Laubat) Achères, December 18 39·24

Graphic view

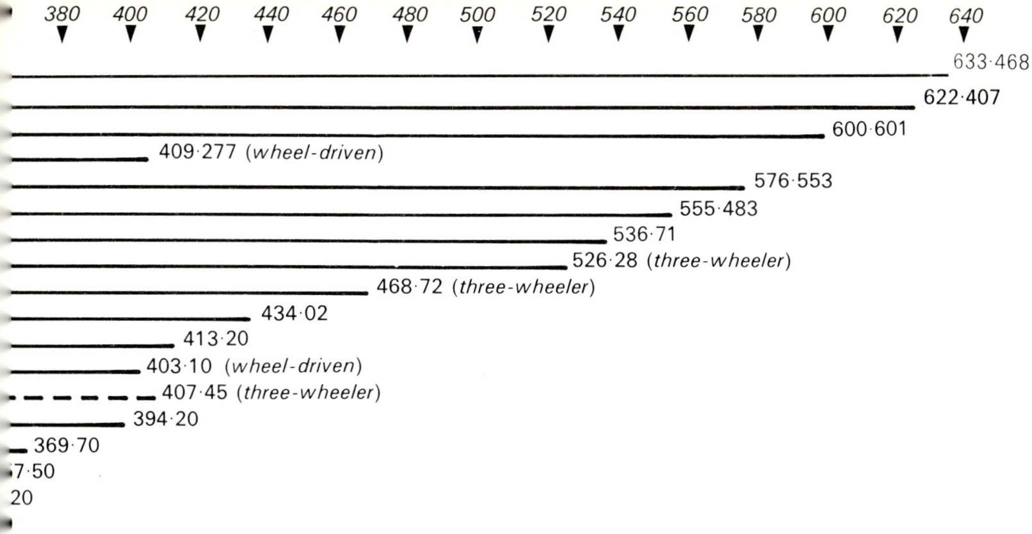

rise in record-breaking speeds, 1898–1983

------- *Not recognised by European authority*

Contrasts in specifications and costs

Car and date	*Engine capacity (litres)*	*Approx. output (b.h.p.)*	*Overall length*	*Wheelbase*	*Approx. weight (cwts.)*	*Approx. price*	*Speed attained (m.p.h.)*
La Jamais Contente, 1899	Electric	40 *b.h.p.*	11*ft.* 9½*in.*	6*ft.*	29	—	65·79
Gobron–Brillié, 1904	13·6	110 *b.h.p.*	13*ft.* 2½*in.*	9*ft.* 10½*in.*	19·5	—	103·55
Darracq V8, 1905	22·5	200 *b.h.p.*	—	8*ft.* 6*in.*	19·25	—	109·65
Stanley *Rocket*, 1906	Steam	120 *b.h.p.*	—	8*ft.* 4*in.*	14·5	—	121·57
Blitzen Benz, 1909–11	21·5	200 *b.h.p.*	—	9*ft.* 4*in.*	23·6	—	131·275
Sunbeam 350 h.p., 1922–5	18·3	350 *b.h.p.*	—	—	31·25	—	150·76
Fiat *Mephistopheles*, 1924	21·7	300 *b.h.p.*	17*ft.* 6*in.*	—	35·75	£225	146·01
Sunbeam V12, 1926	4·0	306 *b.h.p.*	—	—	18·3	—	152·33
Babs, 1926–7	27·0	400 *b.h.p.*	20*ft.* 3*in.*	11*ft.* 6*in.*	39	£780	171·02
Napier–Campbell *Bluebird*, 1927	23·9	502 *b.h.p.*	—	12*ft.* 1½*in.*	58	£9,700	174·883
1,000 h.p. Sunbeam, 1927	44·8	900 *b.h.p.*	20*ft.*	—	75	£5,400	203·792
White *Triplex*, 1928	81·2	1,400 *b.h.p.*	—	14*ft.* 7½*in.*	72	£725	207·552
Golden Arrow, 1929	23·9	930 *b.h.p.*	—	14*ft.*	69·75	£10,060	231·446
Bluebird, 1935	36·6	2,350 *b.h.p.*	28*ft.* 3*in.*	13*ft.* 8*in.*	100	£16,000	301·129
Thunderbolt, 1937–8	73·2	4,700 *b.h.p.*	36*ft.*	—	140	—	357·50
Railton, 1938–47	47·9	2,500 *b.h.p.*	28*ft.* 3*in.*	13*ft.* 6*in.*	65	£8,000	394·20
Spirit of America, 1962–4	Turbo-jet	5,200 *lbt.*	37*ft.*	—	60	—	526·28
Bluebird–Proteus	Turbine	4,100 *s.h.p.*	30*ft.*	13*ft.* 6*in.*	85·75	£900,000	403·1
Green Monster, 1964–5	Turbo-jet	15,000 *lbt.*	21*ft.*	14*ft.* 2*in.*	58	£6,250	576·553
Spirit of America–Sonic I, 1965	Turbo-jet	15,000 *lbt.*	34*ft.* 7*in.*	16*ft.* 10*in.*	71·5	—	600·601
Blue Flame, 1970	Rocket	13,000 *lbt.*	38*ft.* 2½*in.*	25*ft.* 5*in.*	62·5	—	630·388
Thrust 2, 1981–3	Turbo-jet	17,000 *lbt.*	27*ft.*	20*ft.* 10*in.*	80	£1·75M	633·468

Abbreviations used in the text

A.A.A.	American Automobile Association, the governing body of motor sport in the U.S.A.
A.C.F.	Automobile Club de France, the original international racing and record-governing body, based in Paris.
A.C.G.B.I.	Automobile Club of Great Britain and Ireland, forerunners of the Royal Automobile Club (R.A.C.).
A.F.B.	Air Force Base, or American military aerodrome.
A.I.A.C.R.	Association International des Automobiles Clubs Reconnus, the Paris-based international body which governed racing and record-breaking in succession to the A.C.F., from 1909 to 1939, when it was succeeded by the F.I.A.
A.M.C.	American Motors Corporation.
B.L.M.	Bureau of Land Management
F.B.M.	Foster-Brown-Maina, a gearbox manufactured by Beard & Fitch Ltd.
F.I.A.	Fédération Internationale de l'Automobile, the world governing body for motor sport and record-breaking since World War II.
F.I.M.	Fédération Internationale Motocycliste, the European body which governs two- and three-wheeled competitions.
F.I.S.A.	Federation Internationale du Sport Automobile
I.G.T.	American Institute of Gas Technology, sponsors of the 1970 record-holding *Blue Flame*.
J.A.T.O.	Jet-assisted take-off.
M.C.F.	Moto Club de France.
R.A.C.	Royal Automobile Club, England.
U.S.A.C.	United States Automobile Club.

Index

(Page numbers in italics refer to illustration captions)